Computational Methods
for Optimizing Distributed Systems

This is Volume 173 in
MATHEMATICS IN SCIENCE AND ENGINEERING
A Series of Monographs and Textbooks
Edited by RICHARD BELLMAN, *University of Southern California*

The complete listing of books in this series is available from the Publisher upon request.

Computational Methods for Optimizing Distributed Systems

K. L. TEO

School of Mathematics
University of New South Wales
Sydney, Australia
and
Department of Industrial and Systems Engineering
National University of Singapore

Z. S. WU

Department of Mathematics
Zhongshan University
China

1984

ACADEMIC PRESS, INC.
(Harcourt Brace Jovanovich, Publishers)
Orlando San Diego San Francisco New York London
Toronto Montreal Sydney Tokyo São Paulo

ACADEMIC PRESS, INC.
Orlando, Florida 32887

United Kingdom Edition published by
ACADEMIC PRESS, INC. (LONDON) LTD.
24/28 Oval Road, London NW1 7DX

Library of Congress Cataloging in Publication Data

Teo, K. L.
Computational methods for optimizing distributed systems.

(Mathematics in science and engineering)
Includes bibliographies and index.
1. Differential equations, Parabolic–Numerical solutions. 2. Boundary value problems--Numerical solutions. 3. Distributed parameter systems.
I. Wu, Z. S. II. Title. III. Series.
QA377.T43 1984 515.3'53 83-15737
ISBN 0-12-685480-7 (alk. paper)

PRINTED IN THE UNITED STATES OF AMERICA

84 85 86 87 9 8 7 6 5 4 3 2 1

In Memory of

My grandmother, Tey Tan

To

My parents

My wife,

Lyanne (Lye-Hen)

My children,

James, Thomas, and Cheryl

KLT

My father

My mother

My wife,

Zhan Hui

My son,

Zi Jian

ZSW

Contents

III. *Optimal Control of First Boundary Problems: Strong Variation Techniques*

IV. *Optimal Policy of First Boundary Problems: Gradient Techniques*

V. *Relaxed Controls and the Convergence of Optimal Control Algorithms*

VI. *Optimal Control Problems Involving Second Boundary-Value Problems*

Preface

Optimal control theory of distributed parameter systems has been a very active field in recent years; however, very few books have been devoted to the study of computational algorithms for solving optimal control problems. For this reason we decided to write this book. Because the area is so broad, we confined ourselves to optimal control problems involving first and second boundary-value problems of a linear second-order parabolic partial differential equation. However, the techniques used are by no means restricted to these problems. They can be and in some cases already have been applied to problems involving other types of distributed parameter systems. Our aim is to devise computational algorithms for solving optimal control problems with particular emphasis on the mathematical theory underlying the algorithms. These algorithms are obtained by using a first-order strong variational method or gradient-type methods.

The book is divided into six chapters. Chapter I presents certain basic mathematical theory needed to follow the rest of the book. Chapter II is devoted to a review of the basic theory of first and second boundary-value problems of a linear second-order parabolic partial differential equation.

Chapter III deals with an optimal control problem involving first boundary-value problems of a linear second-order parabolic partial differential equation. Our aim is to produce a computational algorithm for solving this optimal control problem by using a first-order strong variational technique. Numerical considerations of the strong variational algorithm are also included in this chapter.

In Chapter IV a class of optimization problems similar to that of Chapter III is considered. The main difference is that both controls and parameter vectors, rather than just controls as in the previous chapter, are assumed to act on the coefficients of the differential operator.

The purpose of Chapter V is to present and illustrate a more natural convergence theory for the algorithm of Chapter III (respectively Chapter IV).

Finally, Chapter VI deals with optimal control problems involving second boundary problems of a linear second-order parabolic partial differential equation.

The prerequisites for this book are elements of measure theory and functional analysis, usually covered in senior undergraduate mathematics courses. However, all the mathematical concepts and facts needed are summarized in Chapter I, where most of the facts are stated without proofs. Engineers and applied scientists interested in the field should be able to follow the book with the aid of Chapter I. The discussion sections in Chapters III–VI are devoted to related research topics. These include (i) crucial points for the success of the techniques; (ii) origins of the methods; (iii) discussion and comparison of the relevant results in the literature; and (iv) discussion of possible extensions of the methods.

The treatment of the topics presented here is deep, but the coverage is by no means encyclopedic. In fact, the material is based, in the main, on the research carried out by the authors, their associates, and the past and present graduate students of the first author, especially Dr. D. W. Reid, during the last several years. We hope that this book will be useful to those who wish to enter the field of optimal control theory involving distributed parameter systems with special emphasis on computational algorithms.

The first author wishes to acknowledge Professor N. U. Ahmed, who introduced him to the field of modern optimal control theory involving distributed parameter systems, for his constant encouragement and collaboration. He also wishes to thank Professor A. T. Bharucha-Reid, L. Cesari, M. N. Oguztoreli, B. D. O. Anderson, and B. S. Goh for their constant support and encouragement. The second author is very grateful to the late Professor Zheng Zeng-Tong for guiding him in his earlier research in mathematics.

A sizable part of the first author's contribution was done during the period (from November 1982 to May 1983) when he was on study leave as a senior teaching fellow in the Department of Mathematics at the National University of Singapore. He wishes to acknowledge the University of New South Wales for granting him this leave and the National University of Singapore for making his stay there a thoroughly enjoyable and exciting experience.

The second author's contribution was carried out in the Department of Mathematics and the Advanced Research Centre at Zhongshan University, China. He wishes to thank the department and the centre, their staffs, and the university for their assistance and support.

Our special thanks go to Dr. K. G. Choo who read and criticized the entire manuscript in great detail, and helped with the proofreading of the manuscript. Our thanks also go to Drs. D. W. Reid, D. J. Clements, and R. P. Agarwal for many helpful discussions and advice. We would also like to thank Mrs. H. Langley, Mrs. Chye Lee-Lang, and Mrs. L. Dooley for typing the manuscript and to express our appreciation to Professor R. Bellman and the staff of Academic Press for their expert cooperation. Last but not least, we wish to thank our families, especially our wives, for their support and understanding.

K. L. Teo
Z. S. Wu

CHAPTER I

Mathematical Background

I.1. Introduction†

For the convenience of the reader, this chapter is devoted to a brief review of some basic results in measure theory and functional analysis that will be needed in the later chapters. However, most of their proofs are omitted.

I.2. Some Basic Concepts in Functional Analysis

I.2.1. TOPOLOGICAL SPACES

Let X be a nonempty set. A topology $\mathscr{T}$ on X is a family of subsets of X such that X itself and the empty set $\varnothing$ belong to $\mathscr{T}$ and that $\mathscr{T}$ is closed under

† Chapters are labeled by Roman numerals, I, II, III, ... Numbered Sections are labeled by chapter and section number, i.e., Section 3 of Chapter II is labeled "II.3." Within the same chapter, the third Section is called "Section 3," but outside that chapter, Section 3 of Chapter V is referred to as "Section V.3."

finite intersections and arbitrary unions. The set X together with the topology $\mathcal{T}$ is called a topological space and denoted by $(X, \mathcal{T})$. Members of $\mathcal{T}$ are called *open sets*. A set A is called a *neighborhood* of $x \in X$ if there exists an element $U \in \mathcal{T}$ such that $x \in U \subset A$. A point $x \in X$ is called an *accumulation point* of the set $B \subset X$ if every neighborhood of x contains points of B other than x. A set is a *closed set* if it contains all its accumulation points. Thus a set $B \subset X$ is closed if and only if its complement $X \backslash B$ is open.

A set B together with its accumulation points is called the *closure* of B and denoted by $\bar{B}$. The *interior* $\operatorname{int}(A)$ of a set A is the set of all those (interior) points that have neighborhoods contained in A. On the one hand, if $A \subset X$ and $\bar{A} = X$, then A is said to be *dense* in X. On the other hand, if $A \subset X$ and $\operatorname{int}(A) = \varnothing$, then A is said to be *nowhere dense*. If X contains a countable subset that is dense in X, it is called *separable*. The *boundary* ∂A of a set A is the set of all accumulation points of both A and $X \backslash A$. Thus $\partial A = \bar{A} \cap (\overline{X \backslash A})$. If A is open, then ∂A consists only of those accumulation points of A.

A sequence $\{x^n\} \subset X$ is said to converge to a point $x \in X$, denoted by $x^n \xrightarrow{\mathcal{T}} x$, if each neighborhood of x contains all but a finite number of elements of the sequence.

A topological space is called *Hausdorff* if it satisfies the *separation axiom*: for any $x, y \in X$ such that $x \neq y$, x and y have disjoint neighborhoods.

Let $(X, \mathcal{T})$ and $(Y, \mathcal{U})$ be topological spaces and $f: X \to Y$ be a mapping (function). Then f is said to be continuous at $x^0 \in X$ if, for every neighborhood U of $f(x^0)$, $f^{-1}(U) \equiv \{x \in X : f(x) \in U\}$ is a neighborhood of x^0. We say that f is continuous if it is continuous at every $x \in X$. Thus f is continuous if and only if for every open (resp. closed) set $A \subset Y$, $f^{-1}(A)$ is open (resp. closed) in X. If h is a one-to-one mapping of X onto Y and if both h and h^{-1} are continuous, then h is called a *homeomorphic mapping*, or a *homeomorphism*. The two topological spaces $(X, \mathcal{T})$ and $(Y, \mathcal{U})$ are *homeomorphic* if there exists a homeomorphism between X and Y.

Let $\mathcal{T}_1$ and $\mathcal{T}_2$ be two topologies on X. We say that $\mathcal{T}_1$ is *stronger* than $\mathcal{T}_2$ or, equivalently, $\mathcal{T}_2$ is *weaker* than $\mathcal{T}_1$ if $\mathcal{T}_1 \supset \mathcal{T}_2$.

Let $(X, \mathcal{T})$ be a topological space and A be a nonempty subset of X. The family $\mathcal{T}_A \equiv \{A \cap B : B \in \mathcal{T}\}$ is a topology on A and is called the *relative topology* on A induced by the topology $\mathcal{T}$ on X.

A family $\mathcal{B}$ of subsets of X is a *base* for a topology $\mathcal{T}$ on X if $\mathcal{B}$ is a subfamily of $\mathcal{T}$ and, for each $x \in X$ and each neighborhood U of x, there is a member V of $\mathcal{B}$ such that $x \in V \subset U$. A family $\mathcal{S}$ of subsets of X is a *subbase* for a topology $\mathcal{T}$ on X if the family of finite intersections of members of $\mathcal{S}$ is a base for $\mathcal{T}$.

Let $(X, \mathcal{T})$ be a topological space, $A \subset X$, and $\mathcal{G} = \{G_i\}$ be a subfamily of $\mathcal{T}$ such that $A \subset \bigcup G_i$. Then $\mathcal{G}$ is called an (*open*) *covering* of A. If every open covering of A contains a finite subfamily that covers A, then A is *compact*. If every sequence in A contains a subsequence that converges to a point in A, then A is *sequentially compact*. If every sequence in A contains a subsequence that converges to a point in X, then A is *conditionally sequentially compact*. A compact subset of a Hausdorff (topological) space is closed.

A function $d: X \times X \to R^1$ is called a *metric function*, or simply a *metric*, if it satisfies: (i) $d(x, y) \geq 0$, and $d(x, y) = 0$ if and only if $x = y$; (ii) $d(x, y) = d(y, x)$; and (iii) $d(x, y) \leq d(x, z) + d(z, y)$. The metric topology $\mathscr{T}_d$ on X is generated by the base $D(x, \varepsilon) \equiv \{y \in X : d(x, y) < \varepsilon\}$, for $x \in X$ and $\varepsilon > 0$. The set X together with the metric topology $\mathscr{T}_d$ is called a *metric space* and is denoted by (X, d). This topology separates points in X [i.e., (X, d) is a Hausdorff space] and, moreover, it separates disjoint closed sets in X [i.e., (X, d) is also a *normal space*]. A sequence $\{x^n\}$ in a metric space is called a *Cauchy sequence* if $d(x^n, x^m) \to 0$ as $n, m \to \infty$. A metric space is said to be *complete* if every Cauchy sequence converges to an element of the space. A metric space X is called *totally bounded* if, for every $\varepsilon > 0$, there is a finite collection of open balls of radius ε that covers X. Thus a metric space is compact if and only if it is both complete and totally bounded. A compact metric space is separable (i.e., it has countable base). In a metric space, compactness and sequentially compactness are equivalent.

Consider two metric spaces (X_1, d_1) and (X_2, d_2). A function f from X_1 to X_2 is said to be *uniformly continuous* if, for any $\varepsilon > 0$, there exists a $\delta > 0$ such that

$$d_2(f(x), f(y)) < \varepsilon$$

whenever $x, y \in X_1$ and $d_1(x, y) < \delta$.

Let (X_i, d_i), $i = 1, \ldots, n$, be metric spaces and $X \equiv \prod_{i=1}^n X_i \equiv X_1 \times \cdots \times X_n$. The *product topology* on X is the metric topology induced by the metric function

$$d(x, y) \equiv \sum_{i=1}^{n} d_i(x_i, y_i),$$

where $x \equiv (x_1, \ldots, x_n)$, $y \equiv (y_1, \ldots, y_n)$, and $x_i, y_i \in X_i$, $i = 1, \ldots, n$. If each (X_i, d_i) is complete (resp. separable, resp. compact), then (X, d) is complete (resp. separable, resp. compact).

Let (X_1, d_1) and (X_2, d_2) be, respectively, compact and complete metric spaces. Let $C(X_1, X_2)$ be the set of all continuous functions from X_1 to X_2. A subset $H \subset C(X_1, X_2)$ is said to be *equicontinuous* if, for each $x \in X_1$ and any $\varepsilon > 0$, there is a neighborhood U of x such that $d_2(f(x), f(y)) < \varepsilon$ for all $y \in U$ and $f \in H$.

The function $\tilde{d}$: $C(X_1, X_2) \times C(X_1, X_2) \to R^1$ defined by

$$\tilde{d}(f, g) \equiv \sup\{d_2(f(x), g(x)) : x \in X_1\}$$

is a metric on $C(X_1, X_2)$. The set $C(X_1, X_2)$ together with the metric $\tilde{d}$ is a complete metric space and is denoted by $(C(X_1, X_2), \tilde{d})$.

THEOREM 2.1. Ascoli–Arzela *Let* (X_1, d_1) *and* (X_2, d_2) *be, respectively, compact and complete metric spaces. Then* $H \subset C(X_1, X_2)$ *is conditionally sequentially compact in* $(C(X_1, X_2), \tilde{d})$ *if and only if* H *is equicontinuous and, for each* $x \in X_1$, $H(x) \equiv \{f(x): f \in H\}$ *is conditionally sequentially compact in* (X_2, d_2).

Consider a metric space (X, d). A real valued function f defined on X is said to be *upper (resp. lower) semicontinuous* at $x_0 \in X$ if, for any $\varepsilon > 0$, there exists a $\delta > 0$ such that $f(x_0) \geq f(x) - \varepsilon$ (resp. $f(x_0) \leq f(x) + \varepsilon$) for all $x \in E \equiv \{x \in X : d(x, x_0) < \delta\}$. Thus it follows that f is continuous at x_0 if and only if it is both upper semicontinuous and lower semicontinuous at x_0. We say that f is upper (resp. lower) semicontinuous if it is upper (resp. lower) semicontinuous at every $x \in X$.

I.2.2. LINEAR TOPOLOGICAL SPACES

Let X be both a (real) linear space and a topological space. It is called a *linear topological space* if the mappings

(i) $(x, y) \to x + y$ of $X \times X$ into X, and
(ii) $(\alpha, x) \to \alpha x$ of $R^1 \times X$ into X

are continuous. Since the translate of X by a fixed element of X is a homeomorphism of X onto itself, the topology is completely determined by a neighborhood base of the zero element.

A set K in X is said to be *convex* if $\alpha x + (1 - \alpha)y \in K$ for any $x, y \in K$ and $0 \leq \alpha \leq 1$. A linear topological space is called a *locally convex linear topological space* if every neighborhood of the zero element of X contains a convex neighborhood of zero.

A (real) linear space X is a (real) *normed linear space*, or simply (real) *normed space*, if with each $x \in X$ there corresponds a real number $\|x\|$, called the *norm* of x, with the properties: (i) $\|x\| \geq 0$ and $\|x\| = 0$ if and only if $x = 0$; (ii) $\|\alpha x\| = |\alpha| \|x\|$ for any $\alpha \in R^1$, $x \in X$; and (iii) $\|x + y\| \leq \|x\| + \|y\|$ for any $x, y \in X$. Since a topology can be induced by the metric $d(x, y) \equiv \|x - y\|$, it is easy to see that a normed linear space is also a locally convex linear topological space. A complete normed linear space is called a *Banach space*.

A (real) *inner product* on a (real) linear space X is a function $\langle \cdot, \cdot \rangle$ from $X \times X$ into R^1 such that (i) $\langle x, x \rangle \geq 0$ and $\langle x, x \rangle = 0$ if and only if $x = 0$; (ii) $\langle x, y \rangle = \langle y, x \rangle$; and (iii) $\langle \lambda x + \mu y, z \rangle = \lambda \langle x, z \rangle + \mu \langle y, z \rangle$ for any $\lambda, \mu \in R^1$ and $x, y, z \in X$. If we let $\|x\| \equiv (\langle x, x \rangle)^{1/2}$, then X becomes a normed linear space. A *Hilbert space* is a complete normed linear space, where the norm is induced by the inner product.

I.2.3. LINEAR FUNCTIONALS AND DUAL SPACES

Let $X \equiv (X, \|\cdot\|_X)$ and $Y \equiv (Y, \|\cdot\|_Y)$ be normed linear spaces and $f: X \to Y$ be a linear mapping. If there exists a constant M such that $\|f(x)\|_Y \leq M\|x\|_X$ for all $x \in X$, then f is said to be *bounded*, and $\|f\| \equiv \sup\{\|f(x)\|_Y : \|x\|_X \leq 1\}$ is called the *norm*, or the *uniform norm*, of f. If and only if f is bounded, it is continuous. Let $\mathscr{L}(X, Y)$ be the set of all continuous linear mappings from X to Y. Then with the uniform norm, $\mathscr{L}(X, Y)$ is a normed linear space. If Y is a Banach space, then $\mathscr{L}(X, Y)$ is also a Banach space.

In particular, let X be a normed linear space, and let $Y = R^1$. Then the set of all continuous mappings from X to Y becomes the set of all continuous linear functionals on X. This space $\mathscr{L}(X, R^1)$, which is denoted by X^*, is called the *dual space* of X. The set X' of all linear functionals (not necessarily continuous) on X is called the *algebraic dual* of X. Clearly $X^* \subset X'$. The dual of X^*, also known as the *second dual* of X, is denoted by X^{**}.

An element $x^* \in X^*$ defines a continuous linear functional with values $\langle x^*, x\rangle \equiv x^*(x)$ at $x \in X$. For a fixed $x \in X$, it is clear that the bilinear form also defines a continuous linear functional on X^*, and we can write it as $x^*(x) \equiv J_x(x^*)$. The correspondence $x \to J_x$ from X to X^{**} is called the *canonical mapping*. Define

$$X_0^{**} \equiv \{x^{**} \in X^{**} : x^{**} = J_x, x \in X\}.$$

Clearly X_0^{**} is a linear manifold of X^{**}. The canonical mapping $x \to J_x$ from X onto X_0^{**} is one-to-one and norm preserving. Thus $x \to J_x$ is an isometric isomorphism of X onto X_0^{**}. On this basis, we may regard X as a subset of X^{**}. If, under the canonical mapping $X = X^{**}$, then X is called *reflexive*. If X is reflexive, then so is X^*. If X is a Hilbert space, then, for each $x^* \in X^*$, there exists a $y \in X$ such that $x^*(x) = \langle y, x\rangle$ for all $x \in X$ and that $\|x^*\| = \|y\|_X$. Thus X^* is isometrically isomorphic to X, and hence a Hilbert space is a reflexive Banach space.

Let X be a Banach space and X^* be its dual. The norm topology is called the *strong topology*. Apart from this topology, elements of X^* can also be used to generate another topology called the *weak topology* (i.e., the weakest topology on X under which all the elements of X^* are still continuous). A base for the weak topology consists of all neighborhoods of the form

$$N(x_0, F^*, \varepsilon) \equiv \{y \in X : |x^*(y - x_0)| < \varepsilon, x^* \in F^*\},$$

where $x_0 \in X$, F^* is any finite subset of X^* and $\varepsilon > 0$.

Since a strongly convergent sequence is weakly convergent, a weakly closed set is strongly closed. However, the converse is not necessarily true. But, we have the following theorem.

THEOREM 2.2. Mazur *A convex subset of a normed linear space X is weakly closed if and only if it is strongly closed.*

THEOREM 2.3. Banach–Saks–Mazur *Let X be a normed linear space and $\{x^n\}$ be a sequence in X converging weakly to $\bar{x}$. Then there exists a sequence of finite convex combinations of $\{x^n\}$ that converges strongly to $\bar{x}$.*

THEOREM 2.4. Eberlein–Šmulian *A subset of a Banach space X is weakly compact if and only if it is weakly sequentially compact.*

For any Banach space X we have already introduced two topologies on its dual space X^*: (i) the strong (norm) topology; and (ii) the weak topology (i.e., the topology induced by X^{**}). Since, under the canonical mapping, $X \subset X^{**}$, the topology induced by X on X^* is weaker than the weak topology. This topology is called the *weak* (w^*) topology*. A base for the weak* topology is a family that consists of all sets of the form

$$N(x_0^*, F, \varepsilon) \equiv \{x^* \in X^* : |x^*(x) - x_0^*(x)| < \varepsilon, x \in F\},$$

where $x_0^* \in X^*$, F is a finite subset of X and $\varepsilon > 0$. If X is reflexive, then the weak and weak* topology are equivalent.

THEOREM 2.5. Alaoglu *The closed unit ball in X^* is w^* compact* (*i.e., compact in the weak* topology*).

THEOREM 2.6. *A subset of X^* is w^* compact if and only if it is* (*strongly*) *bounded and w^* closed.*

I.3. Some Basic Concepts in Measure Theory

I.3.1. MEASURABLE SPACES

Let X be a set. A class $\mathscr{D}$ of subsets of X is called a *ring* if it is closed under finite unions and set differences. If $\mathscr{D}$ also contains X, then it is called an *algebra*. If an algebra is closed under countable unions, then it is called a *σ algebra*. The set X together with a σ algebra $\mathscr{S}$ is called a *measurable space* and is denoted by $(X, \mathscr{S})$. Elements of $\mathscr{S}$ are called *measurable sets*.

A function $f: X \to R^1 \cup \{\pm\infty\}$ is said to be *measurable* if for any open interval U of $R^1 \cup \{\pm\infty\}$ we have $f^{-1}(U) \in \mathscr{S}$. Also, f is called a *simple function* if there is a finite, disjoint class $\{A_1, \ldots, A_n\}$ of measurable sets and a finite set $\{a_1, \ldots, a_n\}$ of real numbers such that $f(x) = \sum_{i=1}^n a_i \chi_{A_i}(x)$, where χ_{A_i} is the *characteristic* (*indicator*) *function* of A_i (equal to 1 on A_i and 0 on $X \backslash A_i$). Every nonnegative measurable function is the limit of a monotonically increasing sequence of nonnegative simple functions.

Let X and Y be measurable spaces and $f: X \to Y$ be a mapping. We call the mapping f measurable if, for every measurable set U in Y, $f^{-1}(U)$ is measurable in X.

I.3.2. MEASURE SPACES

Let $(X, \mathscr{S})$ be a measurable space. A *measure* on the σ algebra $\mathscr{S}$ is a mapping $\mu: \mathscr{S} \to R^+ \cup \{+\infty\}$, where $R^+ \equiv \{x \in R^1 : x \geq 0\}$, such that

(i) $\mu(\varnothing) = 0$; and
(ii) if $S_1, S_2, \ldots \in \mathscr{S}$ is a sequence of disjoint sets, then

$$\mu\left(\bigcup_{i=1}^{\infty} S_i\right) = \sum_{i=1}^{\infty} \mu(S_i).$$

The triple $(X, \mathscr{S}, \mu)$ is called a *measure space*. The measure μ is said to be finite if $\mu(X) < \infty$.

Let us give an outline of the procedure for constructing measures. Often μ is defined only on a ring $\mathscr{E}$ on X. Then μ is extended to all subsets of X by its *outer measure*

$$\mu^*(A) \equiv \inf\left\{\sum_{i=1}^{\infty} \mu(E_i) : E_1, E_2, \ldots \in \mathscr{E}, A \subset \bigcup_{i=1}^{\infty} E_i\right\}.$$

The basic properties of μ^* are that it is increasing, countably subadditive (i.e., $\mu^*(\bigcup_{i=1}^{\infty} A_i) \leq \sum_{i=1}^{\infty} \mu^*(A_i)$), and extends μ. A set E is called μ^* *measurable* if

$$\mu^*(A) = \mu^*(A \cap E) + \mu^*(A \cap (X \setminus E)), \qquad \text{for all } A \subset X.$$

The μ^* measurable sets form a σ algebra including $\mathscr{E}$, and μ^* restricted to this σ-algebra is a measure extending μ.

As an example, let $\mathscr{E}$ consist of all the subsets of R^1 that are of the form $\bigcup_{i=1}^{n} E_i$, where $E_i \equiv [a_i, b_i)$, $i = 1, 2, \ldots$ are disjoint half open intervals. Then $\mathscr{E}$ is a ring. Define a mapping μ on $\mathscr{E}$ such that

$$\mu\left(\bigcup_{i=1}^{n} E_i\right) = \sum_{i=1}^{n} (b_i - a_i).$$

Then μ is a measure on $\mathscr{E}$. By the procedure just described, μ can be extended to a σ algebra $\tilde{\mathscr{B}}$ containing $\mathscr{E}$. This measure on $\tilde{\mathscr{B}}$ is called *Lebesgue measure*, and the elements of $\tilde{\mathscr{B}}$ are called *Lebesgue measurable sets*. Let $\mathscr{B}$ be the smallest σ algebra generated by $\mathscr{E}$. Clearly, $\mathscr{B}$ is also the smallest σ algebra generated by all open (or closed) sets in R^1. Elements of $\mathscr{B}$ are called *Borel sets*, and μ restricted on $\mathscr{B}$ is called *Borel measure*.

I.3.3. INTEGRALS

Let $\phi \equiv \sum_i a_i \chi_{A_i}$ be a simple function on a measure space $(X, \mathscr{S}, \mu)$. The integral of ϕ with respect to the measure μ is defined by

$$\int_X \phi(x)\mu(dx) = \sum_i a_i \mu(A_i).$$

Let f be a nonnegative measurable function. We say that f is *integrable* if $\int_X f(x)\mu(dx) < \infty$, where

$$\int_X f(x)\mu(dx) \equiv \sup\left\{\int_X \phi(x)\mu(dx) : \phi \text{ is a simple function and } 0 \le \phi \le f\right\}.$$

For any measurable function $f\colon X \to R^1 \cup \{\pm\infty\}$ we can write $f = f^+ - f^-$, where $f^+ = \max\{f, 0\}$ and $f^- = \max\{-f, 0\}$. The function f is *integrable* if $\int_X f^+(x)\mu(dx) < \infty$ and $\int_X f^-(x)\mu(dx) < \infty$. The integral of f is

$$\int_X f(x)\mu(dx) = \int_X f^+(x)\mu(dx) - \int_X f^-(x)\mu(dx).$$

The following convergence results are well known.

THE FATOU LEMMA. *If $\{f^n\}$ is a sequence of nonnegative measurable functions on X, then*

$$\int_X \varliminf_{n\to\infty} f^n(x)\mu(dx) \le \varliminf_{n\to\infty} \int_X f^n(x)\mu(dx).$$

THE MONOTONE CONVERGENCE THEOREM. *If $\{f^n\}$ is an increasing sequence of nonnegative measurable functions on X such that $f^n \to f$ pointwise in X, then f is measurable and*

$$\int_X f(x)\mu(dx) = \lim_{n\to\infty} \int_X f^n(x)\mu(dx).$$

THE LEBESGUE DOMINATED CONVERGENCE THEOREM. *If $\{f^n\}$ is a sequence of measurable functions on X, $f^n \to f$ a.e. (almost everywhere), and there exists an integrable function g on X such that $|f^n| \le g$ a.e., then $\int_X f(x)\mu(dx) = \lim_{n\to\infty} \int_X f^n(x)\mu(dx)$.*

Let T be a measurable function from a measure space $(X, \mathscr{S}, \mu)$ into a measurable space $(Y, \mathscr{F})$. Then T assigns a measure ν on $\mathscr{F}$, where ν is defined by

$$\nu(F) = \mu(T^{-1}(F)), \qquad \text{for all} \quad F \in \mathscr{F}.$$

It is convenient and natural to write $\nu = \mu T^{-1}$.

THEOREM 3.1. H.1, Theorem C, p. 163 *Let T be a measurable function from a measure space $(X, \mathcal{S}, \mu)$ into a measurable space $(Y, \mathcal{F})$ and g be a measurable function on Y. Then*

$$\int_Y g(y)(\mu T^{-1})(dy) = \int_X (g)T(x)\mu(dx),$$

provided any one of the integrals exists.

I.3.4. FUBINI'S THEOREM

Let $(X_1, \mathcal{S}_1, \mu_1)$ and $(X_2, \mathcal{S}_2, \mu_2)$ be measure spaces, and $\mathcal{S}_1 \times \mathcal{S}_2$ denotes the σ algebra generated by $\{A \times B : A \in \mathcal{S}_1, B \in \mathcal{S}_2\}$. Then, there exists a unique measure on $\mathcal{S}_1 \times \mathcal{S}_2$, denoted by $\mu_1 \times \mu_2$, such that

$$(\mu_1 \times \mu_2)(A \times B) = \mu_1(A)\mu_2(B).$$

This measure is called the *product measure*.

Fubini's theorem states that if $f: X_1 \times X_2 \to R^1 \cup \{\pm\infty\}$ is $\mu_1 \times \mu_2$ integrable, then

$$\begin{aligned}\iint_{X_1 \times X_2} f(x_1, x_2)(\mu_1 \times \mu_2)(d(x_1, x_2)) &= \int_{X_1}\left\{\int_{X_2} f(x_1, x_2)\mu_2(dx_2)\right\}\mu_1(dx_1) \\ &= \int_{X_2}\left\{\int_{X_1} f(x_1, x_2)\mu_1(dx_1)\right\}\mu_2(dx_2).\end{aligned} \tag{3.1}$$

If the spaces are σ finite (i.e., each of them is the countable union of measurable sets of finite measure), and if one of the iterated integrals in (3.1) exists, then the function f is $\mu_1 \times \mu_2$ integrable; hence the second iterated integral also exists and (3.1) holds.

Let $(X_i, \mathcal{S}_i, \mu_i)$, $i = 1, \ldots, n$ be measure spaces. We can define, similar to the case of $n = 2$, the product measure space of these measure spaces. It is denoted by $(\prod_{i=1}^n X_i, \prod_{i=1}^n \mathcal{S}_i, \prod_{i=1}^n \mu_i)$. For each $i = 1, \ldots, n$, if $X_i = R^1$ and μ_i is the corresponding Lebesgue measure, then the completion of the product measure obtained in R^n (i.e., an extension of the product measure such that all the subsets of sets of zero measure are measurable) is called the *n dimensional Lebesgue measure.*

I.3.5. THE L_p SPACES

Let $(X, \mathcal{S}, \mu)$ be a measure space and $p \in [1, \infty)$. Define

$$L_p(X, \mathcal{S}, \mu) \equiv \{f: X \to R^1 \cup \{\pm\infty\} : |f|^p \text{ is integrable on } X\}.$$

This space is also denoted by $L_p(X)$ whenever there is no ambiguity. In particular, if $A \subset R^n$ is a Lebesgue measurable set, $L_p(A)$ always means the L_p space on A that endows with the Lebesgue measure.

Also, $L_p(X)$ equipped with the norm $\|f\|_{p,X} \equiv (\int_X |f(x)|^p \mu(dx))^{1/p}$ is a Banach space (here we identify all those elements of $L_p(X)$ that are equal a.e.).

The triangle inequality is called the *Minkowski inequality*. Besides, if $f \in L_p(X)$ and $g \in L_q(X)$, where $1 < p,\ q < \infty$ and $1/p + 1/q = 1$, then $fg \in L_1(X)$ and $|\int_X f(x)g(x)\mu(dx)| \leq \|f\|_{p,X}\|g\|_{q,X}$ (Hölder's inequality). It is well known that the dual space $L_p^*(X)$ of $L_p(X)$, $1 \leq p < \infty$, is $L_q(X)$, where $1/p + 1/q = 1$. In fact, the mapping $\phi\colon L_q(X) \to L_p^*(X)$ given by

$$\phi(g)(f) = \int_X g(x)f(x)\mu(dx), \qquad f \in L_p(X)$$

is an isometric isomorphism. In particular, for the Hilbert space $L_2(X)$, the dual space $L_2^*(X)$ of $L_2(X)$ is $L_2(X)$.

For $p = \infty$, we define

$$L_\infty(X) \equiv \{f\colon X \to R^1 \cup \{\pm\infty\} : |f| \leq M \text{ a.e. for some } M > 0\},$$

and

$$\|f\|_{\infty,X} \equiv \operatorname*{ess\,sup}_{x \in X} |f(x)|.$$

$L_\infty(X)$ equipped with the norm $\|\cdot\|_{\infty,X}$ is a Banach space. Furthermore, we have $L_1^*(X) = L_\infty(X)$, but only $L_\infty^*(X) \supset L_1(X)$.

If μ is a Lebesgue measure, then $\mu(dx)$ is written as dx. This convention is used throughout the rest of this text.

THEOREM 3.2. A.1, p. 26 *Suppose $\mu(X) < \infty$. If $f \in L_p(X)$ for $1 \leq p < \infty$, and if there is a constant K such that $\|f\|_p \leq K$ for all such p, then $f \in L_\infty(X)$ and $\|f\|_\infty \leq K$.*

The next two theorems will be needed in Section 6. The first is the well-known Luzin's theorem.

THEOREM 3.3. *Let A be a measurable subset of R^n with finite measure. If f is a measurable function on A, then, for any $\varepsilon > 0$, there exists a closed set $A_\varepsilon \subset A$ such that $\mu(A \backslash A_\varepsilon) < \varepsilon$ and the function f is continuous on A_ε.*

THEOREM 3.4. *Let Ω be an open bounded subset of R^n and U be a compact subset of R^r. If f is a Carathéodory function on $\Omega \times U$ (i.e., $f(x, \cdot)$ is continuous on U for almost all $x \in \Omega$, and $f(\cdot, u)$ is measurable on Ω for each $u \in U$), then, for any $\varepsilon > 0$, there exists a closed set $\Omega_\varepsilon \subset \Omega$ such that $\mu(\Omega \backslash \Omega_\varepsilon) < \varepsilon$ and the function f is continuous on $\Omega_\varepsilon \times U$.*

The proof of this theorem is similar to that of Lemma 3.2 of [Kr. 1, pp. 37–38].

I.3.6. SIGNED MEASURES

Let $(X, \mathscr{S})$ be a measurable space. A *signed measure* is a mapping $\nu: \mathscr{S} \to R^1 \cup \{\pm\infty\}$ such that (i) ν assumes at most one of the values $\pm\infty$; (ii) $\nu(\varnothing) = 0$; and (iii) if $A_1, A_2, \ldots \in \mathscr{S}$ are disjoint, then $\nu(\bigcup_i A_i) = \sum_i \nu(A_i)$. The measurable space $(X, \mathscr{S})$, together with a signed measure ν, is called *signed measure space* and denoted by $(X, \mathscr{S}, \nu)$.

The *Jordan–Hahn decomposition theorem* states that if ν is a signed measure, we can write $\nu = \nu^+ - \nu^-$, where ν^+ and ν^- are positive measures on $\mathscr{S}$, and are disjoint (i.e., there are sets $A, B \in \mathscr{S}$ such that $X = A \cup B$, $A \cap B = \varnothing$, $\nu^+(A) = 0$ and $\nu^-(B) = 0$). The positive measure $|\nu| \equiv \nu^+ + \nu^-$ is called the *total variation* of ν, or the *absolute value* fo ν.

I.4. Some Function Spaces

This section is devoted to the discussion of various function spaces that will be needed in the later chapters.

Let Ω be a bounded open connected set (i.e., bounded domain) in R^n with boundary $\partial\Omega$ and closure $\overline{\Omega}$. Let $I \equiv (0, T)$ and $Q \equiv \Omega \times I$.

I.4.1. SOME SPACES OF CONTINUOUS FUNCTIONS

Let N denote the set of all nonnegative integers and N^n be the n copies of N. If $\beta \equiv (\beta_1, \ldots, \beta_n) \in N^n$, we call β a multiindex and let $|\beta| \equiv \sum_{i=1}^n \beta_i$. The notation D^β represents the partial derivative $(\partial^{\beta_1 + \cdots + \beta_n})/(\partial x_1^{\beta_1} \cdots \partial x_n^{\beta_n})$. For functions ϕ defined on $Q = \Omega \times I$, $D_t^\alpha D_x^\beta \phi$ represents the partial derivatives of ϕ, in which D_x^β, $\beta \in N^n$, stands for D^β with respect to x in Ω, and D_t^α, $\alpha \in N$, stands for D^α with respect to t in I.

Let m be a given nonnegative integer. Define

$$C^m(\Omega) \equiv \{\phi : D_x^\beta \phi, |\beta| \le m, \text{ are continuous functions on } \Omega\},$$

$C^0(\Omega) \equiv C(\Omega)$, the space of all continuous functions on Ω, and $C^\infty(\Omega) \equiv \bigcap_{j=0}^\infty C^j(\Omega)$. Let $C_0^m(\Omega)$ (resp. $C_0^\infty(\Omega)$) denote all those elements in $C^m(\Omega)$ (resp. $C^\infty(\Omega)$) that have compact supports in Ω.

Since Ω is open, functions in $C^m(\Omega)$ are not necessarily bounded on Ω. However, if $\phi \in C^m(\Omega)$ is bounded and uniformly continuous on Ω, then it has a unique, bounded continuous extension to $\overline{\Omega}$.

Let $C^m(\overline{\Omega})$ be the set of all those functions ϕ in $C^m(\Omega)$ for which $D_x^\beta \phi$, for all $\beta \in N^n$ such that $|\beta| \le m$, are bounded and uniformly continuous on Ω. Also, $C^m(\overline{\Omega})$ is a Banach space with the norm

$$\|\phi\|_{C^m(\overline{\Omega})} \equiv \sum_{|\beta| \le m} \sup_{x \in \Omega} |D_x^\beta \phi(x)|.$$

Let $C^{2m,m}(\overline{Q})$ denote the set of all those functions ϕ that are bounded and uniformly continuous on Q together with the derivatives $D_t^\alpha D_x^\beta \phi$ for all $\alpha \in N$ and $\beta \in N^n$ such that $|\beta| + 2\alpha \le 2m$. When $m = 0$, $C^{2m,m}(\overline{Q})$ will mean $C^{0,0}(\overline{Q}) \equiv C(\overline{Q})$. The set $C^{2m,m}(\overline{Q})$, where the integer $m \ge 0$, is a Banach space with the norm

$$\|\phi\|_{C^{2m,m}(\overline{Q})} \equiv \sup_{|\beta|+2\alpha\le 2m} \left\{ \sup_{(x,t)\in Q} |D_t^\alpha D_x^\beta \phi(x,t)| \right\}.$$

Let $\alpha \in (0, 1)$ and j be a nonnegative integer. Define

$$\langle \phi \rangle_{\overline{\Omega}}^{(\alpha)} \equiv \sup_{x,x'\in\Omega} \left\{ \frac{|\phi(x) - \phi(x')|}{|x - x'|^\alpha} \right\},$$

and

$$\langle \phi \rangle_{\overline{\Omega}}^{(j)} \equiv \sum_{|\beta|=j} \left\{ \sup_{x\in\Omega} |D_x^\beta \phi(x)| \right\}.$$

Let λ be a given positive noninteger and $\mathscr{H}^\lambda(\overline{\Omega})$ be the linear space of all those elements ϕ in $C^{[\lambda]}(\overline{\Omega})$ for which the norm $|\phi|_{\overline{\Omega}}^{(\lambda)}$ is finite, where $[\lambda]$ denotes the largest integer less than λ and

$$|\phi|_{\overline{\Omega}}^{(\lambda)} \equiv \sum_{|\beta|=[\lambda]} \langle D_x^\beta \phi \rangle_{\overline{\Omega}}^{(\lambda-[\lambda])} + \sum_{j=0}^{[\lambda]} \langle \phi \rangle_{\overline{\Omega}}^{(j)},$$

and $\mathscr{H}^\lambda(\overline{\Omega})$ is a Banach space and is called a *Hölder space*.

For functions ϕ on $Q \equiv \Omega \times I$, we can define a similar Hölder space $\mathscr{H}^{\lambda,\lambda/2}(\overline{Q})$ with the norm

$$|\phi|_{\overline{Q}}^{(\lambda,\lambda/2)} \equiv \sum_{2\alpha+|\beta|=[\lambda]} \|D_t^\alpha D_x^\beta \phi\|_{x,\overline{Q}}^{(\gamma_1)} + \sum_{0<\lambda-2\alpha-|\beta|<2} \|D_t^\alpha D_x^\beta \phi\|_{t,\overline{Q}}^{(\gamma_2)} + \sum_{j=0}^{[\lambda]} \|\phi\|_{\overline{Q}}^{(j)},$$

where $\gamma_1 \equiv \lambda - [\lambda]$, $\gamma_2 \equiv (\lambda - 2\alpha - |\beta|)/2$,

$$\|\psi\|_{x,\overline{Q}}^{(\gamma_1)} \equiv \sup_{(x,t),(x',t)\in Q} \left\{ \frac{|\psi(x,t) - \psi(x',t)|}{|x - x'|^{\gamma_1}} \right\},$$

$$\|\psi\|_{t,\overline{Q}}^{(\gamma_2)} \equiv \sup_{(x,t),(x,t')\in Q} \left\{ \frac{|\psi(x,t) - \psi(x,t')|}{|t - t'|^{\gamma_2}} \right\},$$

and

$$\|\psi\|_{\overline{Q}}^{(j)} \equiv \sum_{2\alpha+|\beta|=j} \sup_{(x,t)\in Q} \{|D_t^\alpha D_x^\beta \psi(x,t)|\}.$$

Again, $\mathscr{H}^{\lambda,\lambda/2}(\overline{Q})$ is a Banach space.

Next, we shall consider some function spaces in which the elements are defined on the boundary $\partial\Omega$ of the bounded domain Ω. To proceed further we need to introduce some definitions concerning the boundaries. A bounded domain Ω is said to have a *piecewise smooth* boundary if its closure $\bar{\Omega}$ can be represented in the form $\bar{\Omega} = \bigcup_{k=1}^{N} \bar{\Omega}_k$, where $Q_k \cap \Omega_l = \varnothing$ for $k \neq l$; and each part $\bar{\Omega}_k$ can be homeomorphically mapped onto the n dimensional unit ball or cube by means of a function $Z^k \equiv (Z_1^k, \ldots, Z_n^k)$, $Z_i^k \in C^1(\bar{\Omega}_k)$, $i = 1, \ldots, n$, having Jacobian $|\text{grad } Z^k|$ greater than some positive number δ. *This condition is assumed throughout the rest of the text without further mention.*

Let $x^0 \equiv (x_1^0, \ldots, x_n^0)$ be any point on the boundary $\partial\Omega$. We shall call $(y_1, \ldots, y_n)$ a local (Cartesian) coordinate system with origin at x^0 if y and x are connected by the equations $y_i = \sum_{k=1}^{n} a_{ik}(x_k - x_k^0)$, $i = 1, 2, \ldots, n$, where a_{ik} form an orthogonal numerical matrix and the y_n axis has the direction of the outward (with respect to Ω) normal to $\partial\Omega$ at x_0.

Let m_1 be a positive integer and $l_1 > 1$ be a noninteger. The boundary $\partial\Omega$ of the bounded domain Ω is said to belong to the class C^{m_1} (resp. $\mathscr{H}^{l_1}$) if there exists a number $\rho > 0$ such that the intersection S of $\partial\Omega$ with a ball $K_{x^0,\rho}$ of radius ρ with center at an arbitrary point $x^0 \in \partial\Omega$ is a connected surface, the equation of which in the local coordinate system $(y_1, \ldots, y_n)$ with origin at x^0 has the form $y_n = \omega(y_1, \ldots, y_{n-1})$, where $y' \equiv (y_1, \ldots, y_{n-1}) \in D$, $\omega(y') \in C^{m_1}(\bar{D})$ (resp. $\mathscr{H}^{l_1}(\bar{D})$), and the domain D is the projection of S onto the plane $y_n = 0$.

Since $\partial\Omega$ is bounded and closed, a finite subcovering may be chosen from the covering $\{K_{x,\rho} : x \in \partial\Omega\}$ of $\partial\Omega$. The collection of finite pieces $S_1, \ldots, S_N$ corresponding to such a finite covering will be called *the covering of the boundary by pieces of the class* C^{m_1} *(resp.* $\mathscr{H}^{l_1}$*)*.

Suppose a function $\phi(x)$ is given on the boundary $\partial\Omega$ that is of the class C^{m_1} (resp. $\mathscr{H}^{l_1}$). Since $\partial\Omega$ is of the class C^{m_1} (resp. $\mathscr{H}^{l_1}$), there is a finite covering S_k, $k = 1, \ldots, N$, of the class C^{m_1} (resp. $\mathscr{H}^{l_1}$) for $\partial\Omega$, and each S_k, in a certain local coordinate system $(y_1^{(k)}, \ldots, y_n^{(k)})$, is described by the equation $y_n^{(k)} = \omega^{(k)}(y_1^{(k)}, \ldots, y_{n-1}^{(k)})$, where $(y_1^{(k)}, \ldots, y_{n-1}^{(k)}) \in D_k$, $\omega^{(k)} \in C^{m_1}(\bar{D}_k)$ (resp. $\mathscr{H}^{l_1}(\bar{D}_k)$), and the domain D_k is the projection of S_k onto the plane $y_n^{(k)} = 0$. Let $\phi^{(k)}(y)$, $y \in D_k$ be the function into which the function $\phi(x)$, $x \in S_k$ goes under the mapping of S_k onto D_k.

Let $C^m(\partial\Omega)$, where $\partial\Omega$ is in the class C^{m_1} and the integer $m \in [1, m_1]$, be the set of all functions ϕ with the finite norm

$$\|\phi\|_{C^m(\partial\Omega)} \equiv \sup_{1 \leq k \leq N} \|\phi^{(k)}\|_{C^m(\bar{D}_k)}.$$

Let $\mathscr{H}^l(\partial\Omega)$, where $\partial\Omega$ is in the class $\mathscr{H}^{l_1}$ and the noninteger $l \in (1, l_1]$, be the set of all functions ϕ for which the norm

$$|\phi|_{\partial\Omega}^{(l)} \equiv \sup_{1 \leq k \leq N} |\phi^{(k)}|_{\bar{D}_k}^{(l)}$$

is finite.

Note that under different coverings of $\partial\Omega$ the corresponding norms in $C^m(\partial\Omega)$ (resp. $\mathscr{H}^l(\partial\Omega)$) turn out to be equivalent.

REMARK 4.1. Let Ω be a bounded domain with boundary $\partial\Omega$ belonging to the class C^1. If ϕ is a function defined on Ω, the values of ϕ on $\partial\Omega$ cannot, in general, be determined uniquely. However, if ϕ is in $C(\overline{\Omega})$, then there exists a unique continuous function $\tilde{\phi}$ on $\overline{\Omega}$ such that $\phi(x) = \tilde{\phi}(x)$ for all $x \in \Omega$. The restriction of $\tilde{\phi}$ to $\partial\Omega$ is called the *trace* of the function $\phi \in C(\overline{Q})$ on $\partial\Omega$ and is denoted by $\phi|_{\partial\Omega}$. Furthermore, if $\partial\Omega$ is of the class C^{m_1} (resp. $\mathscr{H}^{l_1}$) and ϕ is a function in $C^m(\overline{\Omega})$ (resp. $\mathscr{H}^l(\overline{\Omega})$), then $\phi|_{\partial\Omega}$ belongs to $C^m(\partial\Omega)$ (resp. $\mathscr{H}^l(\partial\Omega)$).

Next, we wish to consider smooth functions given on the curvilinear surface $\Gamma \equiv \partial\Omega \times [0, T]$. As before, m_1 is a positive integer and $l_1 > 1$ a noninteger. Suppose $\partial\Omega$ is of the class C^{m_1} (resp. $\mathscr{H}^{l_1}$). Let $\partial\Omega$ be covered by sets $S_1, \ldots, S_N$ in the manner just described in the definition of the space $C^m(\partial\Omega)$ (resp. $\mathscr{H}^l(\partial\Omega)$). Let $\phi^{(k)}(y, t)$, $y \in D_k$, be the function into which the function $\phi(x, t)$, $x \in S_k$, goes under the mapping of S_k onto D_k, and let $\sigma_k \equiv D_k \times [0, T]$. The space $C^{2m,m}(\Gamma)$ (resp. $\mathscr{H}^{l,l/2}(\Gamma)$) can be defined in a similar way as in the case of $C^m(\partial\Omega)$ (resp. $\mathscr{H}^l(\partial\Omega)$). Let $C^{2m,m}(\Gamma)$, where $\partial\Omega$ is in the class C^{m_1} and m an integer such that $2m \in [0, m_1]$, be the set of all those functions ϕ for which the norm

$$\|\phi\|_{C^{2m,m}(\Gamma)} \equiv \sup_{1 \le k \le N} \|\phi^{(k)}\|_{C^{2m,m}(\bar{\sigma}_k)}$$

is finite. Here the space $C^{2m,m}(\Gamma)$ will mean the space $C^{0,0}(\Gamma) \equiv C(\Gamma)$ when $m = 0$. We denote by $\mathscr{H}^{l,l/2}(\Gamma)$, where $\partial\Omega$ is in the class $\mathscr{H}^{l_1}$ and l a non-integer such that $l \in (1, l_1]$, the set of all functions ϕ with the norm

$$|\phi|_\Gamma^{(l,l/2)} \equiv \sup_{1 \le k \le N} |\phi^{(k)}|_{\bar{\sigma}_k}^{(l,l/2)}.$$

As in the case of $C^m(\partial\Omega)$ (resp. $\mathscr{H}^l(\partial\Omega)$), we note that under different coverings of $\partial\Omega$ the corresponding norms in $C^{2m,m}(\Gamma)$ (resp. $\mathscr{H}^{l,l/2}(\Gamma)$) turn out to be equivalent.

REMARK 4.2. The result presented in Remark 4.1 carries over in a natural way to the case involving the curvilinear surface Γ.

Our next aim is to define measurability and integrability of functions given on the boundary $\partial\Omega$, together with other related concepts.

To begin, let $\partial\Omega$ be of the class C^1. Then there is a finite covering S_k, $k = 1, \ldots, N$ of $\partial\Omega$ such that every S_k is, in a certain local coordinate system $(y_1^{(k)}, \ldots, y_n^{(k)})$, described by the equation $y_n^{(k)} = \omega^{(k)}(y_1^{(k)}, \ldots, y_{n-1}^{(k)})$,

$(y_1^{(k)}, \ldots, y_{n-1}^{(k)}) \in D_k$, $\omega^{(k)} \in C^{m_1}(\bar{D}_k)$. Suppose that the set F is contained in S_k for some k, $k = 1, \ldots, N$. Let

$$\mathscr{E} \equiv \{(y_1^{(k)}, \ldots, y_{n-1}^{(k)}) \in D_k : (y_1^{(k)}, \ldots, y_{n-1}^{(k)}, \omega^{(k)}(y_1^{(k)}, \ldots, y_{n-1}^{(k)})) \in F\}.$$

We say that F is a set of surface measure zero if $\mathscr{E}$ is a set of measure zero in R^{n-1}. A set E on $\partial\Omega$ is called a set of surface measure zero if each of the sets $E \cap S_k$, $k = 1, \ldots, N$ is a set of surface measure zero. Note that the set $E \subset \partial\Omega$ being a set of surface measure zero is independent of the choice of the covering $S_1, \ldots, S_N$ of $\partial\Omega$. On the basis of this concept, definitions of a.e. convergence on $\partial\Omega$ and the space $L_\infty(\partial\Omega)$ can be understood similarly as those of their counterparts in the case in which $\partial\Omega$ is replaced by Ω.

Let ϕ be a function defined on $\partial\Omega$, and $\phi^{(k)}(y)$, $y \in D_k$, be the function into which the function $\phi(x)$, $x \in S_k$, goes under the mapping of S_k onto D_k. We say that the function ϕ is *measurable* (resp. *integrable*) if each of the functions $\phi^{(k)}$, $k = 1, \ldots, N$ is measurable (resp. integrable) in D_k, $k = 1, \ldots, N$. It is known that

$$\int_{\partial\Omega} \phi \, ds = \sum_{k=1}^{N} \int_{D'_k} \phi^{(k)} \sqrt{1 + |\text{grad}\, \omega^{(k)}|^2} \, dy_1^{(k)} \cdots dy_{n-1}^{(k)},$$

where $D'_1 = D_1$ and D'_k, $k > 1$ is the pojection of $S_k \setminus \bigcup_{i=1}^{k-1} \bar{S}_i$ onto the plane $y_n^{(k)} = 0$.[†]

REMARK 4.3. Let $\partial\Omega$ be in the class C^1 and S_k, $k = 1, \ldots, N$, be a finite covering of $\partial\Omega$. Define $\Gamma \equiv \partial\Omega \times [0, T]$ and $\sigma_k \equiv D_k \times [0, T]$. Then all that we have said concerning functions given on the boundary $\partial\Omega$ carry over in a natural way to curvilinear surface Γ. In particular, the corresponding version of the formula (4.1) is

$$\int_{\Gamma} \phi \, ds \, dt = \sum_{k=1}^{N} \int_{\sigma'_k} \phi^{(k)} \sqrt{1 + |\text{grad}\, \omega^{(k)}|^2} \, dy_1^{(k)} \cdots dy_{n-1}^{(k)} \, dt, \tag{4.2}$$

where $\sigma'_k \equiv D'_k \times I$, $D'_1 = D_1$ and D'_k, for $k > 1$, is the projection of $S_k \setminus \bigcup_{i=1}^{k-1} \bar{S}_i$ onto the plane $y_n^{(k)} = 0$.

REMARK 4.4. The L_p space on $\partial\Omega$, denoted by $L_p(\partial\Omega)$, can be understood as the space of all those functions on $\partial\Omega$ for which the norm $\|\cdot\|_{p,\partial\Omega}$ is finite,

[†] Numbered equations are labeled by section and equation number, i.e., the seventh equation in Section 3 is called Eq. (3.7). Outside its own chapter, the chapter number is given as well, e.g., Eq. (II.3.7) is equation number 7 in Section 3 of Chapter II.

The same convention is used for Theorems (resp. Lemmas, resp. Remarks, resp. Figures, resp. Tables) also, except that Theorem (resp. Lemmas, resp. Remarks, resp. Figures, resp. Tables) numbers are not enclosed in parentheses. Theorem (resp. Lemma, resp. Remark, resp. Figure, resp. Table) III.3.1 is located in Section 3 of Chapter III and is the first Theorem (resp. Lemma, resp. Remark, resp. Figure, resp. Table) within that Section.

where $\|\cdot\|_{p,\partial\Omega}$ is defined similarly to the norm $\|\cdot\|_{p,\Omega}$ in the space $L_p(\Omega)$, but with Ω and dx being replaced by $\partial\Omega$ and ds, respectively, also $L_p(\partial\Omega)$ is a Banach space. Furthermore, it also possesses properties similar to those satisfied by $L_p(\Omega)$.

I.4.2. SOME SOBOLEV SPACES

We first describe the concept of *generalized (weak) partial derivative.* Let Ω be a bounded domain in R^n, $f \in L_1(\Omega)$ and $\beta \in N^n$. The function $g \in L_1(\Omega)$ is said to be a *βth generalized (weak) partial derivative* of the function f if, for each $\psi \in C_0^{|\beta|}(\Omega)$,

$$\int_\Omega f(x) D^\beta \psi(x)\, dx = (-1)^{|\beta|} \int_\Omega g(x)\psi(x)\, dx.$$

This generalized partial derivative is denoted by $D^\beta f$.

If f is sufficiently smooth so that it has a continuously partial derivative $D^\alpha f$ in the classical sense, then $D^\alpha f$ is also the generalized partial derivative of f. Of course, $D^\alpha f$ may exist in the generalized sense without existing in the classical sense. For example, a continuous function f on R^1, which has a bounded derivative f' except at finitely many points, has a derivative in the weak sense.

Next, we shall briefly discuss the relationship between the generalized derivatives and their integral averages. Let ρ be a real-valued function belonging to $C_0^\infty(R^n)$ and having the following properties:

(i) $\rho(x) \geq 0$ for all $x \in R^n$,
(ii) $\rho(x) = 0$ for all $|x| \geq 1$, and
(iii) $\int_{R^n} \rho(x)\, dx = 1$.

As an example, we may take

$$\rho(x) = \begin{cases} K \exp\{-1/(1-|x|^2)\} & \text{if } \ |x| < 1, \\ 0 & \text{if } \ |x| \geq 1, \end{cases}$$

where the positive constant K is chosen so that the condition (iii) is satisfied. For $\varepsilon > 0$, the function $\rho_\varepsilon(x) \equiv \varepsilon^{-n}\rho(x/\varepsilon)$ belongs to $C_0^\infty(R^n)$ and satisfies: (i) $\rho_\varepsilon(x) \geq 0$ for all $x \in R^n$; (ii) $\rho_\varepsilon(x) = 0$ for all $|x| \geq \varepsilon$; and (iii) $\int_{R^n} \rho_\varepsilon(x)\, dx = 1$.

For $\varepsilon > 0$ and $\phi \in L_1^{\mathrm{loc}}(R^n) \equiv \{\phi : \phi \in L_1(A)$ for any measurable set $A \subset R^n$ such that $\bar{A}$ is compact$\}$, define

$$\phi_\varepsilon(x) \equiv \int_{R^n} \rho_\varepsilon(x-y)\phi(y)\, dy. \tag{4.3}$$

Then ϕ_ε belongs to $C^\infty(R^n)$ and is called the *integral average of ϕ.*

THEOREM 4.1. A.1, Lemma 2.18, pp. 29–30 *Let ϕ be a function that is defined on R^n and equal to zero identically outside the domain Ω. Then the following statements are valid.*

(i) *If $\phi \in L_1(\Omega)$, then $\phi_\varepsilon \in C^\infty(R^n)$.*

(ii) *Suppose that $\phi \in L_1(\Omega)$ and has compact support $A \subset \Omega$. Then for $\varepsilon > 0$ but smaller than the distance between A and $\partial\Omega$, $\phi_\varepsilon \in C_0^\infty(\Omega)$.*

(iii) *If $\phi \in L_p(\Omega)$, where $1 \le p < \infty$, then $\phi_\varepsilon \in L_p(\Omega)$, $\|\phi_\varepsilon\|_{p,\Omega} \le \|\phi\|_{p,\Omega}$ and $\lim_{\varepsilon \downarrow 0} \|\phi_\varepsilon - \phi\|_{p,\Omega} = 0$.*

(iv) *If $\phi \in C(\Omega)$ and G is a subdomain of Ω such that $\bar{G}$ is compact and contained in Ω, then $\lim_{\varepsilon \downarrow 0} \phi_\varepsilon(x) = \phi(x)$ uniformly on G.*

(v) *If $\phi \in C(\bar{\Omega})$, then $\lim_{\varepsilon \downarrow 0} \phi_\varepsilon(x) = \phi(x)$ uniformly on Ω.*

Note that $C_0(\Omega)$ is dense in $L_p(\Omega)$ for $p \in [1, \infty)$. Thus in view of Theorem 4.1, $C_0^\infty(\Omega)$ is also dense in $L_p(\Omega)$ for $p \in [1, \infty)$.

THEOREM 4.2. So.1, pp. 35–36 *Let ϕ and ϕ_ε be as in Theorem 4.1 and suppose that ϕ, $D^\beta\phi \in L_1(\Omega)$, where $D^\beta\phi$ denotes the βth generalized partial derivative of ϕ. Then the following two statements are valid.*

(i) *$D^\beta\phi_\varepsilon = [D^\beta\phi]_\varepsilon$ in Ω_ε, where $[\psi]_\varepsilon$ denotes the integral average of ψ, and Ω_ε is a subdomain of Ω such that the distance between Ω_ε and $\partial\Omega$ is greater than ε.*

(ii) *If $D^\beta\phi \in L_p(\Omega)$, then $D^\beta\phi_\varepsilon \to D^\beta\phi$ in $L_p(\Omega)$.*

We now introduce *Sobolev spaces* of integer order. These spaces are defined on the bounded domain Ω in R^n.

For a nonnegative integer m and $p \in [1, \infty]$, let

$$W_p^m(\Omega) \equiv \{\phi \in L_p(\Omega) : D^\beta\phi \in L_p(\Omega), |\beta| \le m\}.$$

$W_p^m(\Omega)$ is a Banach space with the norm

$$\|\phi\|_{p,\Omega}^{(m)} \equiv \sum_{|\beta| \le m} \|D^\beta\phi\|_{p,\Omega}.$$

Note that $W_p^m(\Omega)$ is separable for $p \in [1, \infty)$ and reflexive if $p \in (1, \infty)$. In particular, $W_2^m(\Omega)$ is a separable Hilbert space with inner product

$$\langle\phi, \psi\rangle_\Omega^{(m)} \equiv \sum_{|\alpha| \le m} \langle D^\alpha\phi, D^\alpha\psi\rangle,$$

where $\langle\phi, \psi\rangle \equiv \int_\Omega \phi(x)\psi(x)\,dx$ is the inner product in $L_2(\Omega)$. It is clear that $W_p^0(\Omega) = L_p(\Omega)$. If $\partial\Omega$ is of the class C^m, then it is known that $C^\infty(\bar{\Omega})$ (and hence $C^m(\bar{\Omega})$) is dense in $W_p^m(\Omega)$, where $p \in [1, \infty)$ and the integer $m \ge 0$.

THEOREM 4.3. LSU.1, Theorem 2.1, p. 61 *Let Ω be a bounded domain with boundary $\partial\Omega$ belonging to the class C^m, where the integer $m \geq 1$. Then for any $\phi \in W_p^m(\Omega)$, $1 \leq p < \infty$, it is true that*

$$\|\phi\|_{q,\partial\Omega} \leq K_1 \|\phi\|_{p,\Omega}^{(m)}, \tag{4.4a}$$

$$\|\phi\|_{q,\Omega} \leq K_2 \|\phi\|_{p,\Omega}^{(m)}, \tag{4.4b}$$

and

$$|\phi|_{\Omega}^{(\alpha)} \leq K_3 \|\phi\|_{p,\Omega}^{(m)}. \tag{4.4c}$$

The first (resp. second) holds for $q \in [1, p(n-1)/(n-pm)]$ (resp. $q \in [1, pn/(n-pm)]$) if $n > pm$ and $q \in [1, \infty)$ if $n = pm$. The third is valid for $n < pm$ with $\alpha \leq (pm-n)/p$, $\alpha < 1$. The constants K_1, K_2, and K_3 depend at most on n, p, m, q, Ω, and $\partial\Omega$. Here the dimension n of the x space is assumed to be two or greater.

REMARK 4.5. If $n < pm$, then it follows from the inequality (4.4c) that the trace $\phi|_{\partial\Omega}$ of the function $\phi \in W_p^m(\Omega)$ on $\partial\Omega$ can be viewed as indicated in Remark 4.1. When $n \geq pm$, more care is necessary in interpreting the trace $\phi|_{\partial\Omega}$ of the corresponding function $\phi \in W_p^m(\Omega)$ on $\partial\Omega$. To explain this concept we note that $C^m(\bar{\Omega})$ is dense in $W_p^m(\Omega)$. Thus there exists a sequence $\{\phi_k\} \subset C^m(\bar{\Omega})$ such that $\|\phi^k - \phi\|_{p,\Omega}^{(m)} \to 0$ as $k \to \infty$. Clearly, the function ϕ^k have traces $\phi^k|_{\partial\Omega}$ on $\partial\Omega$. Then inequality (4.4a) signifies that these traces converge in $L_q(\partial\Omega)$ to a function $\hat{\phi}$ such that

$$\|\hat{\phi}\|_{q,\partial\Omega} \leq K_1 \|\phi\|_{p,\Omega}^{(m)},$$

where $\hat{\phi}$ is called the *trace* of the function $\phi \in W_p^m(\Omega)$ on $\partial\Omega$ and denoted by $\phi|_{\partial\Omega}$. Note that the preceding inequality with $\|\hat{\phi}\|_{q,\partial\Omega}$ (i.e., $\|\phi|_{\partial\Omega}\|_{q,\partial\Omega}$) written as $\|\phi\|_{q,\partial\Omega}$ is inequality (4.4a). Note also that $\phi|_{\partial\Omega}$ is independent of the choice of the sequence $\{\phi^k\}$ that approximates ϕ.

REMARK 4.6. If $n = m = 1$ and $p = 2$, it can be easily shown that the following inequality is valid.

$$\sup_{x\in\Omega} |\phi(x)| \leq K \|\phi\|_{2,\Omega}^{(1)}$$

for any $\phi \in W_2^1(\Omega)$, where the constant K is independent of $\phi \in W_2^1(\Omega)$.

From inequalities (4.4b), (4.4c), and the inequality appeared in Remark 4.6, it is easy to obtain the following inequalities, which are known as Sobolev inequalities.

$$\|\phi\|_{q,\Omega} \leq K_4(\|\phi_x\|_{2,\Omega} + \|\phi\|_{2,\Omega}) \tag{4.5a}$$

and

$$\sup_{x \in \Omega} |\phi(x)| \leq K_5(\|\phi_x\|_{2,\Omega} + \|\phi\|_{2,\Omega}), \tag{4.5b}$$

where

$$\|\phi_x\|_{2,\Omega} \equiv \left(\int_\Omega \left\{ \sum_{i=1}^n [\phi_{x_i}(x)]^2 \right\} dx \right)^{1/2}.$$

The first inequality holds for $q \in [1, 2n/(n-2)]$ if $n > 2$ and $q \in [1, \infty)$ if $n = 2$. The second inequality is valid for $n = 1$. The constants K_4 and K_5 are independent of $\phi \in W_2^1(Q)$.

Remark 4.7. If $\phi \in C(\overline{\Omega}) \cap W_p^m(\Omega)$, then it is known that its trace as the trace of a function in $C(\overline{\Omega})$ and that of a function in $W_p^m(\Omega)$ coincide.

Let $\mathring{W}_p^m(\Omega)$, $1 \leq p < \infty$, denote the closure of $C_0^\infty(\Omega)$ in the norm of $W_p^m(\Omega)$, $1 \leq p < \infty$. Clearly, $\mathring{W}_p^0(\Omega) = L_p(\Omega)$ for $p \in [1, \infty)$. Furthermore, since the boundary $\partial\Omega$ of the domain Ω is assumed to be piecewise smooth, it is known that

$$\mathring{W}_p^1(\Omega) = \{\phi \in W_p^1(\Omega) : \phi|_{\partial\Omega} = 0\}.$$

THEOREM 4.4. LSU.1, Theorem 2.2, pp. 62–63 *Let Ω be a bounded domain, $p \geq 1$, $\phi \in \mathring{W}_p^1(\Omega)$ and $m \geq 1$. Define*

$$\|\phi_x\|_{p,\Omega} \equiv \left(\int_\Omega \left\{ \sum_{i=1}^n [\phi_{x_i}(x)]^2 \right\}^{p/2} dx \right)^{1/p},$$

and

$$\alpha \equiv \left(\frac{1}{m} - \frac{1}{q} \right) \left(\frac{1}{n} - \frac{1}{p} + \frac{1}{m} \right)^{-1}.$$

Then

$$\|\phi\|_{q,\Omega} \leq \beta(\|\phi_x\|_{p,\Omega})^\alpha (\|\phi\|_{m,\Omega})^{1-\alpha},$$

where

(i) $q \in [m, \infty]$ *and* $\beta = (1 + (p-1)m/p)^\alpha$ *if* $p \geq n = 1$;
(ii) $q \in [m, np/(n-p)]$ *and* $\beta = ((n-1)p/(n-p))^\alpha$ *if* $n > 1$, $p < n$, *and* $m \leq np/(n-p)$;
(iii) $q \in [np/(n-p), m]$ *and* $\beta = ((n-1)p/(n-p))^\alpha$ *if* $n > 1$, $p < n$, *and* $m \geq np/(n-p)$; *and*
(iv) $q \in [m, \infty)$ *and* $\beta = \max\{(q(n-1)/n)^\alpha, (1 + (p-1)m/p)^\alpha\}$ *if* $p \geq n - 1$.

I.4.3. CERTAIN SOBOLEV SPACES ON Q

The aim of this subsection is to introduce the Sobolev spaces $W_p^{2,1}(Q)$, $W_2^{1,0}(Q)$, $V_2(Q)$ and $V_2^{1,0}(Q)$, where $Q \equiv \Omega \times I$. Furthermore, some of the important properties of these spaces will also be stated.

To begin, let $L_{p,r}(Q)$, $1 \leq p,\ r \leq \infty$, denote the Banach space of all measurable real-valued functions ϕ on Q with the norm $\|\phi\|_{p,r,Q}$ defined by

$$\|\phi\|_{p,r,Q} \equiv \left\{ \int_I \left[\int_\Omega |\phi(x,t)|^p\, dx \right]^{r/p} dt \right\}^{1/r} \qquad \text{for} \quad 1 \leq p, \quad r < \infty;$$

$$\|\phi\|_{p,\infty,Q} \equiv \operatorname*{ess\,sup}_{t \in I} \{ \|\phi(\cdot, t)\|_{p,\Omega} \} \qquad \text{for} \quad 1 \leq p < \infty, \quad r = \infty;$$

$$\|\phi\|_{\infty,r,Q} \equiv \left\{ \int_I (\|\phi(\cdot, t)\|_{\infty,\Omega})^r\, dt \right\}^{1/r} \qquad \text{for} \quad p = \infty, \quad 1 \leq r < \infty;$$

and

$$\|\phi\|_{\infty,\infty,Q} \equiv \operatorname*{ess\,sup}_{(x,t) \in Q} |\phi(x,t)| \qquad \text{for} \quad p = \infty, \quad r = \infty.$$

Recall that $\|\cdot\|_{p,\Omega}$ and $\|\cdot\|_{\infty,\Omega}$ are, respectively, the norms in the Banach spaces $L_p(\Omega)$ and $L_\infty(\Omega)$. For simplicity, we denote $L_{p,p}(Q)$ and $\|\cdot\|_{p,p,Q}$ by $L_p(Q)$ and $\|\cdot\|_{p,Q}$, respectively.

Remark 4.8. Under the situation of Remark 4.3, $L_{p,r}(\Gamma)$, where $1 \leq p$, $r \leq \infty$, can be undestood as the space of all those functions on Γ for which the norm $\|\cdot\|_{p,r,\Gamma}$ is finite, and where $\|\cdot\|_{p,r,\Gamma}$ is defined similarly to the norm $\|\cdot\|_{p,r,Q}$ in the space $L_{p,r}(Q)$, but with Q, Ω, and dx being replaced by Γ, $\partial\Omega$, and ds, respectively. Also $L_{p,r}(\Gamma)$ is a Banach space. Furthermore, it also possesses properties similar to those satisfied by $L_{p,r}(Q)$.

Let $W_p^{2,1}(Q)$, $p \geq 1$, denote the Banach space of all those functions ϕ in $L_p(Q)$ for which the norm

$$\|\phi\|_{p,Q}^{(2,1)} \equiv \|\phi\|_{p,Q} + \|\phi_t\|_{p,Q} + \sum_{i=1}^{n} \|\phi_{x_i}\|_{p,Q} + \sum_{i,j=1}^{n} \|\phi_{x_i x_j}\|_{p,Q}$$

is finite, where $\phi_t \equiv \partial\phi/\partial t$, $\phi_{x_i} \equiv \partial\phi/\partial x_i$, and $\phi_{x_i x_j} \equiv \partial^2\phi/\partial x_i\, \partial x_j$.

Note that $W_2^{1,0}(Q)$ is the Hilbert space of all those real-valued measurable functions defined on Q with the inner product

$$\langle \phi, \psi \rangle_{W_2^{1,0}(Q)} \equiv \iint_Q \left\{ \phi(x,t)\psi(x,t) + \sum_{i=1}^{n} \phi_{x_i}(x,t)\psi_{x_i}(x,t) \right\} dx\, dt.$$

Also, $W_2^{1,1}(Q)$ is the Hilbert space of all those real-valued measurable functions defined on Q with the inner product

$$\langle \phi, \psi \rangle_{W_2^{1,1}(Q)} \equiv \iint_Q \left\{ \phi(x,t)\psi(x,t) + \sum_{i=1}^{n} \phi_{x_i}(x,t)\psi_{x_i}(x,t) + \phi_t(x,t)\psi_t(x,t) \right\} dx\, dt;$$

$V_2(Q)$ the Banach space of all those functions ϕ in $W_2^{1,0}(Q)$ for which the norm

$$|\phi|_Q \equiv \|\phi\|_{2,\infty,Q} + \|\phi_x\|_{2,Q}$$

is finite, where

$$\|\phi_x\|_{2,Q} = \left(\iint_Q \left\{\sum_{i=1}^{n} (\phi_{x_i}(x,t))^2\right\} dx\,dt\right)^{1/2};$$

and $V_2^{1,0}(Q)$ the Banach space of all those functions ϕ in $V_2(Q)$ that are continuous in t (with respect to the norm in $L_2(\Omega)$). The norm in $V_2^{1,0}(Q)$ is

$$\|\phi\|_Q \equiv \sup_{t\in I}\{\|\phi(\cdot,t)\|_{2,\Omega}\} + \|\phi_x\|_{2,Q}.$$

Note that a function ϕ is said to be continuous in t with respect to the norm in $L_2(\Omega)$ if $\|\phi(\cdot, t+\Delta t) - \phi(\cdot,t)\|_{2,\Omega} \to 0$ as $\Delta t \to 0$. Note also that $V_2^{1,0}(Q)$ is the completion of $W_2^{1,1}(Q)$ in the norm $\|\cdot\|_Q$.

The symbol $\circ$ over $W_p^{2,1}(Q)$, $W_2^{1,0}(Q)$, $W_2^{1,1}(Q)$, $V_2(Q)$, or $V_2^{1,0}(Q)$ indicates restriction to those elements of the respective spaces that vanish on $\Gamma \equiv \partial\Omega \times [0,T]$. All these spaces are complete.

THEOREM 4.5. LSU.1, pp. 74–75 *Let Ω be a bounded domain and q, r be arbitrary parameters satisfying:*

$$(1/r) + (n/2q) = n/4,$$

where

$$r \in [2,\infty], \quad q \in [2, 2n/(n-2)] \quad \text{for} \quad n > 2;$$

$$r \in [2,\infty], \quad q \in [2,\infty) \quad \text{for} \quad n = 2;$$

$$r \in [4,\infty], \quad q \in [2,\infty] \quad \text{for} \quad n = 1.$$

Then the following statements are valid:

(i) *If $\phi \in \mathring{V}_2(Q)$, then*

$$\|\phi\|_{q,r,Q} \le \beta_1 |\phi|_Q.$$

where the constant β_1 depends only on n, q as indicated in Theorem 4.4.

(ii) *If $\phi \in V_2(Q)$, then*

$$\|\phi\|_{q,r,Q} \le \beta_2 |\phi|_Q,$$

where the constant β_2 depends on β_1, T, and the Lebesgue measure of Ω.

For $\phi \in L_{q,r}(Q)$ with $q, r > 1$, the averagings of ϕ in t are defined by

$$\phi_h(x,t) \equiv (1/h)\int_t^{t+h} \phi(x,\tau)\,d\tau, \qquad h > 0.$$

It is known that $\phi_h \to \phi$ in the norm of $L_{q,r}(\Omega \times (0, T-\delta))$, where $\delta \in (0,T)$. This result can be found in [LSU.1, pp. 84–85].

THEOREM 4.6. *Let* $\phi \in V_2^{1,0}(Q)$. *Then*

(i) $\phi_h \in W_2^{1,1}(\Omega \times (0, T-\delta))$, *for* $0 < h < \delta$.

(ii) $\lim_{h\downarrow 0} \|\phi_h - \phi\|_{\Omega\times(0,T-\delta)} = 0$.

(iii) $\lim_{h\downarrow 0} \|\phi_h - \phi\|_{q,r,\Omega\times(0,T-\delta)} = 0$ *with* q, r *subject to restriction as given in Theorem* 4.5.

The first conclusion of the theorem is obvious, and a proof of the second conclusion can be found in [LSU.1, pp. 86–87]. The last conclusion follows from (ii) and Theorem 4.5(ii).

THEOREM 4.7. LSU.1, Lemma 4.12, p. 89 *Let* Ω *be a bounded domain. Suppose that* $\{\psi^k\}$ *is a dense subset of* $\mathring{W}_2^1(\Omega)$ *(resp.* $W_2^1(\Omega)$*) and that* d_k *are arbitrarily continuously differentiable functions equal to zero for* $t = T$. *Then the class of functions of the form* $\sum_{k=1}^N d_k(t)\psi^k(x)$ *is dense in* $\mathring{\tilde{W}}_2^{1,1}(Q)$ *(resp.* $\tilde{W}_2^{1,1}(Q)$*). Here*

$$\mathring{\tilde{W}}_2^{1,1}(Q) \equiv \{\phi \in \mathring{W}_2^{1,1}(Q) : \phi(x, T) = 0 \textit{ for all } x \in \Omega\}$$

and

$$\tilde{W}_2^{1,1}(Q) \equiv \{\phi \in W_2^{1,1}(Q) : \phi(x, T) = 0 \textit{ for all } x \in \Omega\}.$$

REMARK 4.9. (i) Let $\Omega \subset R^n$ be a bounded domain with boundary $\partial\Omega$ belonging to the class C^m, $n \geq 2$, and ϕ be a function in $W_2^{1,0}(Q)$. It is known that $C^m(\bar{Q})$ is dense in $W_2^{1,0}(Q)$. Thus there exists a sequence $\{\phi^k\} \subset C^m(\bar{Q})$ such that $\|\phi^k - \phi\|_{2,Q}^{(1,0)} \equiv \langle \phi^k - \phi, \phi^k - \phi \rangle_{W_2^{1,0}(Q)} \to 0$ as $k \to \infty$. Clearly, these functions ϕ^k have traces $\phi^k|_\Gamma$ on Γ. Furthermore, for each $t \in [0, T]$ and any integers k, $l \geq 1$, $\phi^k(\cdot, t) - \phi^l(\cdot, t)$ is in $C^m(\bar{\Omega})$. Thus by virtue of inequality (4.4a) we have

$$(\|\phi^k(\cdot, t) - \phi^l(\cdot, t)\|_{2,\partial\Omega})^2 \leq (K_1)^2(\|\phi^k(\cdot, t) - \phi^l(\cdot, t)\|_{2,\Omega}^{(1)})^2, \tag{4.6}$$

where the constant K_1 is independent of $t \in [0, T]$ and integers $k, l \geq 1$. Integration of (4.6) with respect to $t \in (0, T)$ yields the inequalities

$$\|\phi^k - \phi^l\|_{2,\Gamma} \leq K_1 \|\phi^k - \phi^l\|_{2,Q}^{(1,0)}, \qquad k, l = 1, 2, \ldots . \tag{4.7}$$

Since $\|\phi^k - \phi^l\|_{2,Q}^{(1,0)} \to 0$ as k, $l \to \infty$, it follows that $\|\phi^k - \phi^l\|_{2,\Gamma} \to 0$ as k, $l \to \infty$. This implies that $\{\phi^k|_\Gamma\}$ is a Cauchy sequence in $L_2(\Gamma)$. Accordingly there is a function $\hat{\phi} \in L_2(\Gamma)$ such that $\phi^k|_\Gamma$ converge in $L_2(\Gamma)$ to $\hat{\phi}$ and that

$$\|\hat{\phi}\|_{2,\Gamma} \leq K_1 \|\phi\|_{2,Q}^{(1,0)}. \tag{4.8}$$

The function $\hat{\phi}$, which is independent of the choice of the sequence $\{\phi^k\}$ to approximate $\hat{\phi}$, is called the *trace* of the function $\phi \in W_2^{1,0}(Q)$ on Γ and denoted by $\phi|_\Gamma$. Conventionally inequality (4.8) is written as

$$\|\phi\|_{2,\Gamma} \leq K_1 \|\phi\|_{2,Q}^{(1,0)},$$

where $\|\phi\|_{2,\Gamma}$ is used to denote $\|\phi|_\Gamma\|_{2,\Gamma}$.

(ii) Consider the case of $n = 1$. Let (without loss of generality) $\Omega \equiv (a, b)$ and ϕ be a function in $W_2^{1,0}(Q)$. Clearly, for almost every $t \in [0, T]$, $\phi(\cdot, t) \in W_2^1(\Omega)$. Thus from Remark 4.6 (rather than inequality (4.4a) as in the previous case), it follows that, for almost every $t \in [0, T]$, $\phi(\cdot, t)$ has the trace on $\partial\Omega \equiv \{a, b\}$ and satisfies

$$|\phi(a, t)|^2 \leq (K)^2(\|\phi(\cdot, t)\|_{2,\Omega}^{(1)})^2, \tag{4.9a}$$

$$|\phi(b, t)|^2 \leq (K)^2(\|\phi(\cdot, t)\|_{2,\Omega}^{(1)})^2, \tag{4.9b}$$

for almost all $t \in [0, T]$. These inequalities, in turn, imply that

$$\|\phi(a, \cdot)\|_{2,I} + \|\phi(b, \cdot)\|_{2,I} \leq \tilde{K}\|\phi\|_{2,Q}^{(1,0)},$$

where $\tilde{K} \equiv 2K$ and $\phi(a, \cdot)$ together with $\phi(b, \cdot)$ is called the *trace* of the function $\phi \in W_2^{1,0}(Q)$ on $\partial\Omega \equiv \{a, b\}$.

The next theorem can be found in [LSU.1, p. 78].

THEOREM 4.8. *Let Ω be a bounded domain with boundary $\partial\Omega$ belonging to the class C^1 and q, r be arbitrary parameters satisfying the relation*:

$$1/r + (n-1)/2q = n/4,$$

where

$$r \in [2, \infty], \qquad q \in [2(n-1)/n, 2(n-1)/(n-2)] \qquad \text{for} \quad n \geq 3;$$

$$r \in (2, \infty], \qquad q \in [1, \infty) \qquad \text{for} \quad n = 2;$$

$$r = q = 4 \qquad \text{for} \quad n = 1.$$

Then for any $\phi \in V_2(Q)$

$$\|\phi\|_{q,r,\Gamma} \leq \beta_3|\phi|_Q, \tag{4.10}$$

where the constant β_3 depends only on n, q, T, and the Lebesgue measure of Ω.

To clarify the meaning of Theorem 4.8, we note that $V_2(Q) \subset W_2^{1,0}(Q)$. Thus the trace $\phi|_\Gamma$ on Γ of ϕ considered as a function in $V_2(Q)$ is that of the same ϕ considered as a function in $W_2^{1,0}(Q)$. However, since ϕ is in $V_2(Q)$, it follows from Theorem 4.8 that its trace $\phi|_\Gamma$ on Γ satisfies also the inequality (4.10).

I.4.4. SEVERAL CONVERGENCE THEOREMS

This subsection contains a list of several useful convergence theorems. The first is

THEOREM 4.9. NT.4, Lemma 4.2, p. 592 *Let Ω be a bounded measurable subset of R^n. Suppose that $\{\phi^k\}$ and $\{\psi^k\}$ are two sequences of real-valued* *measurable functions defined on Ω such that the following assumptions are satisfied:*

(i) $\phi^k \to \phi$ *a.e. on* Ω *and there exists a constant* $M_1 > 0$ *such that*

$$\sup_k |\phi^k(x)| \leq M_1 \qquad \text{a.e.} \quad \text{on } \Omega.$$

(ii) $\psi^k \xrightarrow{w} \psi$ *in* $L_2(\Omega)$ *and there exists a constant* $M_2 > 0$ *such that*

$$\sup_k \|\psi^k\|_{2,\Omega} \leq M_2.$$

Then, $\phi^k\psi^k \xrightarrow{w} \phi\psi$ *in* $L_2(\Omega)$.

THEOREM 4.10. NT.4, Lemma 4.3, p. 593 *Let* $Q \equiv \Omega \times I$ *be a bounded measurable subset of* R^{n+1} *and* $\{\phi^k\}$ *be a bounded sequence in* $L_{2,r}(Q)$, *where* $r \in (1, 2]$. *If* $\phi^k \to \phi$ *a.e. on* Q, *then there exists a subsequence* $\{\phi^{k(l)}\}$ *of the sequence* $\{\phi^k\}$ *such that* $\phi^{k(l)} \xrightarrow{w} \phi$ *in* $L_{2,r}(Q)$.

THEOREM 4.11. NT.4, Lemma 4.4, p. 594 *Let* $Q \equiv \Omega \times I$ *be a bounded measurable subset of* R^{n+1} *and* $\{\phi^k\}$ *be a sequence of functions in* $V_2^{1,0}(Q)$. *If* $\phi^k \xrightarrow{s} \phi$ *in* $V_2^{1,0}(Q)$, *then* $\phi^k \xrightarrow{w} \phi$ *in* $L_{2,p}(Q)$ *where* $p \geq 1$.

THEOREM 4.12. Aro.1, Lemma 3, p. 633 *Let* $Q \equiv \Omega \times I$ *be a bounded measurable subset of* R^{n+1} *and* $\{\phi^k\}$ *be a sequence of functions in* $L_2(Q)$ *such that* $\phi^k \xrightarrow{w} \phi$ *in* $L_2(Q)$. *If* $\|\phi^k\|_{2,\infty,Q} \leq K$ *independently of* k, *then* $\|\phi\|_{2,\infty,Q} \leq K$.

THEOREM 4.13. *Let* $Q \equiv \Omega \times I$ *be a bounded measurable subsets in* R^{n+1} *and* $\{\phi^k\}$ *be a sequence in* $L_2(Q) \cap L_{q,r}(Q)$, $1 \leq q, r \leq \infty$. *Suppose, as* $k \to \infty$,

$$\iint_Q \phi^k \eta \, dx\, dt \to \iint_Q \phi\eta \, dx\, dt \tag{4.11}$$

for any $\eta \in L_2(Q)$, *where* $\phi \in L_2(Q)$; *and*

$$\iint_Q \phi^k \eta \, dx\, dt \to \iint_Q \tilde{\phi}\eta \, dx\, dt \tag{4.12}$$

for any $\eta \in L_{\bar{q},\bar{r}}(Q)$, *where* $\tilde{\phi} \in L_{q,r}(Q)$, $(1/q) + (1/\bar{q}) = 1$ *and* $(1/r) + (1/\bar{r}) = 1$. *Then* $\phi(x, t) = \tilde{\phi}(x, t)$ *a.e. in* Q.

Proof. There are four cases to be considered. In all these cases the assumption on the boundedness of the set Q plays an important role in their proofs and hence is used without further mention.

(i) $q, r \geq 2$. Then $\bar{q}, \bar{r} \leq 2$. Clearly, $L_2(Q) \subset L_{\bar{q},\bar{r}}(Q)$, and hence (4.12) is valid for any $\eta \in L_2(Q)$. This together with (4.11) implies the conclusion.

(ii) $q, r \leq 2$. Then $\bar{q}, \bar{r} \geq 2$. Thus $L_{\bar{q},\bar{r}}(Q) \subset L_2(Q)$, and hence (4.11) is valid for any $\eta \in L_{\bar{q},\bar{r}}(Q)$. This together with (4.12) gives rise to the conclusion.

(iii) $q \geq 2$, $r \leq 2$. Then $\bar{q} \leq 2$, $\bar{r} \geq 2$. Clearly, $L_{\bar{r}}(Q) \subset L_{\bar{q},\bar{r}}(Q) \cap L_2(Q)$, and hence both (4.11) and (4.12) are valid for any $\eta \in L_{\bar{r}}(Q)$. Thus the conclusion follows readily.

(iv) $q \leq 2$, $r \geq 2$. Then $\bar{q} \geq 2$, $\bar{r} \leq 2$. Clearly, $L_{\bar{q}}(Q) \subset L_{\bar{q},\bar{r}}(Q) \cap L_2(Q)$, and hence both (4.11) and (4.12) hold for any $\eta \in L_{\bar{q}}(Q)$. Thus we obtain the conclusion. ■

THEOREM 4.14. *Let Q be as defined in Theorem 4.13 and $\{\phi^k\}$ be a bounded sequence in $L_{q,r}(Q)$, $1 \leq q, r \leq \infty$. Suppose $\{\phi^k\}$ is also contained in $L_2(Q)$ and is such that*

$$\iint_Q \phi^k \eta \, dx \, dt \to \iint_Q \phi \eta \, dx \, dt \tag{4.13}$$

for any $\eta \in L_2(Q)$, where $\phi \in L_2(Q)$. Then $\phi \in L_{q,r}(Q)$ and, as $k \to \infty$,

$$\iint_Q \phi^k \eta \, dx \, dt \to \iint_Q \phi \eta \, dx \, dt \tag{4.14}$$

for any $\eta \in L_{\bar{q},\bar{r}}(Q)$, where $(1/q) + (1/\bar{q}) = 1$ and $(1/r) + (1/\bar{r}) = 1$.

Proof. Since $\{\phi^k\}$ is a bounded sequence in $L_{q,r}(Q)$, there exists a subsequence $\{\phi^{k(l)}\}$ and a function $\tilde{\phi} \in L_{q,r}(Q)$ such that, as $l \to \infty$,

$$\iint_Q \phi^{k(l)} \eta \, dx \, dt \to \iint_Q \tilde{\phi} \eta \, dx \, dt$$

for any $\eta \in L_{\bar{q},\bar{r}}(Q)$. Thus by virtue of this together with (4.13) and Theorem 4.13, we deduce that $\phi \in L_{q,r}(Q)$ and, as $l \to \infty$,

$$\iint_Q \phi^{k(l)} \eta \, dx \, dt \to \iint_Q \phi \eta \, dx \, dt$$

for any $\eta \in L_{\bar{q},\bar{r}}(Q)$.

Clearly, it can be shown that for any subsequence of the sequence $\{\phi^k\}$ there exists a further subsequence such that the above conclusion is valid. Thus the conclusion is also valid with respect to the whole sequence, and hence the proof is complete. ■

The next theorem contains a well-known result on lower semicontinuity of certain functions.

THEOREM 4.15. *Let $\Omega_1 \subset R^r$ and $\Omega_2 \subset R^s$ be such that Ω_1 is open with compact closure and Ω_2 is compact and convex. Let ϕ be a continuous function defined on $\Omega_1 \times \Omega_2$, $\phi(x, \cdot)$ be convex on Ω_2 for each $x \in \Omega_1$, and $\{y^k\}$ be a* *sequence of measurable functions defined on* Ω_1 *with values in* Ω_2. *If* $y^k \overset{w^*}{\to} y^0$ *in* $L_\infty(\Omega_1, R^s) \equiv \{y \equiv (y_1, \ldots, y_s) : y_i \in L_\infty(\Omega_1), i = 1, \ldots, s\}$, *then*

$$\int_{\Omega_1} \{\phi(x, y^0(x))\}\, dx \leq \underline{\lim}_{k \to \infty} \int_{\Omega_1} \{\phi(x, y^k(x))\}\, dx.$$

The following well-known result is useful in deriving pointwise necessary conditions for optimality from its integral version (cf. Theorem 3.2.8 of [AT.5]).

THEOREM 4.16. *Let* Ω *be a measurable subset of* R^n, $\phi \in L_p(\Omega, R^s) \equiv \{\phi \equiv (\phi_1, \ldots, \phi_s) \colon \phi_i \in L_p(\Omega),\ i = 1, \ldots, s\}$, $1 \leq p < \infty$, $x \in \Omega$ *be a regular point of* ϕ, *and* $\{\Omega_k\}$ *be a decreasing sequence of measurable subsets of* Ω *such that* $x \in \Omega_k$ *for all* k *and* $\lim_{k\to\infty} |\Omega_k| = 0$, *where* $|\Omega_k|$ *denotes the Lebesgue measure of* Ω_k. *Then*

$$\lim_{k \to \infty} \frac{1}{|\Omega_k|} \int_{\Omega_k} \phi(\theta)\, d\theta = \phi(x).$$

I.5. Relaxed Controls

The aim of this section is to discuss some results concerning relaxed controls.

Let G be a bounded open set in R^n and U be a compact set in R^m. Let $L_\infty(G, U)$ be the class of all m vector valued functions f: $G \to U$ with each component in $L_\infty(G)$.

For the optimal control problems to be considered later, the admissible controls are usually taken from the space $L_\infty(G, U)$. Unfortunately, $L_\infty(G, U)$ is not sequentially compact with respect to the L_∞ norm. Thus the limit points of sequences of admissible controls are not guaranteed to exist. This weakness will affect the convergent results to be designed in searching for optimal controls. The goal, then, is to embed $L_\infty(G, U)$ into some larger topological space in which the closure of $L_\infty(G, U)$ is sequentially compact. The main problem is to find a concrete representation of this larger space and of the closure of $L_\infty(G, U)$. The closure of $L_\infty(G, U)$ will be called *the class of relaxed controls.*

First, let us introduce some notation. Let Σ_U denote the Borel σ algebra on U (i.e., the smallest σ algebra containing all open sets of U), $fm(U)$ be the set of all finite (signed) measures on the measurable space (U, Σ_U), $fm^+(U)$ be the set of all nonnegative measures in $fm(U)$, $pm(U)$ be the set of all probability measures in $fm^+(U)$, $|\nu|$ be the variation of the measure $\nu \in fm(U)$, $C(U)$ be the set of all real-valued continuous functions on U, $L_1(G, C(U))$

be the set of all mappings $\phi\colon G \to C(U)$ such that $\int_G \sup_{u\in U} |\phi(x, u)|\, dx < \infty$, where the integration is with respect to the Lebesgue measure on G, and $L_1(G, C(U))^*$ be the dual space of $L_1(G, C(U))$.

We now embed $L_\infty(G, U)$ in the topological dual $L_1(G, C(U))^*$ of $L_1(G, C(U))$, by identifying each $u \in L_\infty(G, U)$ with the element $l_u \in L_1(G, C(U))^*$, given by

$$l_u(\phi) = \int_G \phi(x, u(x))\, dx$$

for all $\phi \in L_1(G, C(U))$.

To construct an alternative representation of $L_1(G, G(U))^*$ that "naturally" extends $L_\infty(G, U)$, we consider the set $\mathcal{N}$ of all the mappings $v\colon G \to fm(U)$ satisfying (i) ess $\sup_{x\in G} |v(x)|(U) < \infty$; and (ii) for each $\phi \in L_1(G, C(U))$, $\int_U \phi(x, u)v(x)(du)$ is measurable in G. By a version of the Dunford–Pettis theorem, we see that $\mathcal{N}$ is algebraically isomorphic to $L_1(G, C(U))^*$ such that each $v \in \mathcal{N}$ corresponds to a $l_v \in L_1(G, C(U))^*$, where $l_v(\phi) = \int_G [\int_U \phi(x, u)v(x)(du)]\, dx$, for $\phi \in L_1(G, C(U))$. Then we can topologize $\mathcal{N}$ with the weak* topology of $L_1(G, C(U))^*$. Moreover, it follows from the isomorphism between $\mathcal{N}$ and $L_1(G, C(U))^*$ that the unit ball $\{l\colon \|l\| \le 1\}$ in $L_1(G, C(U))^*$ coincides with the set $\mathcal{M} \equiv \{v \in \mathcal{N}\colon \text{ess}\sup_{x\in G} |v(x)|(U) \le 1\}$ in $\mathcal{N}$. It follows from an application of the Alaoglu theorem that the unit ball in $L_1(G, C(U))^*$ is sequentially compact in the weak* topology, and consequently the set $\mathcal{M}$ is also sequentially compact.

A (measurable) relaxed control is defined to be an element v of $\mathcal{N}$ for which $v(x) \in pm(U)$ for almost all $x \in G$. Let $\mathcal{V}$ be the set of all such relaxed controls. Since $\mathcal{V}$ is a closed subset of $\mathcal{M}$, $\mathcal{V}$ is also sequentially compact. Clearly, the set $L_\infty(G, U)$ of all admissible controls can be embedded in $\mathcal{V}$ by identifying each element $u \in L_\infty(G, U)$ with the Dirac measure $\delta_u \in \mathcal{V}$ (i.e., for each $x \in G$, $\delta_{u(x)}$ is a unit, positive measure in $pm(U)$ concentrated at the point $u(x)$). It can be shown that with the topology in $\mathcal{N}$, the set $\mathcal{V}$ is the closure of $L_\infty(G, U)$.

Let $\{v^k\}$ be a sequence of relaxed controls in $\mathcal{V}$ and $v \in \mathcal{V}$. If v^k converges to v in $\mathcal{N}$, then we say that v^k converges to v *in the sense of control measure* (*iscm*). For future references, the next theorem presents a formal statement on the sequential compactness of the set $\mathcal{V}$ of relaxed controls.

THEOREM 5.1. *Suppose that $\{v^k\} \subset \mathcal{V}$. Then there exists a subsequence $\{v^{k(l)}\}$ and an element $v \in \mathcal{V}$ such that $v^{k(l)} \xrightarrow{\text{iscm}} v$, as $l \to \infty$.*

For any $v \in \mathcal{V}$ and for any $\phi \in L_1(G, C(U))$, $\phi[v]$ *is a real-valued integrable* function on G defined by

$$\phi[v](x) \equiv \int_U \phi(x, u)v(x)(du).$$

Since the set $L_\infty(G, U)$ of admissible controls is contained in $\mathscr{V}$, $\phi[v]$ is clearly defined for each $u \in L_\infty(G, U)$, in which case $\phi[v](x) = \phi(x, u(x))$, for all $x \in G$, where $v = \delta_u$.

THEOREM 5.2. TCWC.1, Lemma 3.2 *Suppose that* $\{v^k\} \subset \mathscr{V}$ *and* $v \in \mathscr{V}$. *Then the following statements are equivalent:*

(a) $v^k \xrightarrow{\text{iscm}} v$.
(b) *For each* $\phi \in L_1(G, C(U))$,

$$\int_G \phi[v^k](x)\, dx \to \int_G \phi[v](x)\, dx.$$

(c) *For each* $\phi \in C(G \times U)$,

$$\int_G \phi[v^k](x)\, dx \to \int_G \phi[v](x)\, dx,$$

(d) *For each* $\phi \in C(G \times U)$ *and for each Lebesgue measurable set* $E \subset G$,

$$\int_E \phi[v^k](x)\, dx \to \int_E \phi[v](x)\, dx.$$

Proof. It follows from the definition of the iscm convergence that (a) and (b) are equivalent.

(b) $\Rightarrow$ (d) For each $\phi \in C(G \times U)$ and for each Lebesgue measurable set $E \subset G$, $\chi_E \phi \in L_1(G, C(U))$, where $\chi_E(x)$ is the characteristic function of E.

(d) $\Rightarrow$ (c) Set E equal to G.
(c) $\Rightarrow$ (b) It follows from the fact that $C(G \times U)$ is dense in $L_1(G, C(U))$. ■

The next theorem is the heart of a number of convergence results in Chapter V.

THEOREM 5.3. TCWC.1, Lemma 3.3 *Let* $\{v^k\} \subset \mathscr{V}$, $v \in \mathscr{V}$ *and* $v^k \xrightarrow{\text{iscm}} v$. *Suppose* $\{\phi^k\} \subset L_1(G, C(U))$, $\phi \in L_1(G, C(U))$ *and* $\phi^k \xrightarrow{s} \phi$ *in* $L_1(G, C(U))$, *i.e.*,

$$\int_G \sup_{u \in U} |\phi(x, u) - \phi^k(x, u)|\, dx \to 0.$$

Then

$$\int_G \phi^k[v^k](x)\, dx \to \int_G \phi[v](x)\, dx.$$

Proof. For each k

$$\left|\int_G \phi[v^k](x)\,dx - \int_G \phi^k[v^k](x)\,dx\right|$$

$$\leq \int_G \left|\int_U (\phi(x,u) - \phi^k(x,u))v^k(x)(du)\right| dx$$

$$\leq \int_G \left\{\int_U \sup_{v\in U} |\phi(x,v) - \phi^k(x,v)|\,v^k(x)(du)\right\} dx$$

$$= \int_G \sup_{v\in U} |\phi(x,v) - \phi^k(x,v)|\,dx = \|\phi - \phi^k\|_{L_1(G,C(U))},$$

where $\|\cdot\|_{L_1(G,C(U))}$ is the norm in $L_1(G, C(U))$. Hence

$$\left|\int_G \phi[v](x)\,dx - \int_G \phi^k[v^k](x)\,dx\right|$$

$$\leq \left|\int_G \phi[v](x)\,dx - \int_G \phi[v^k](x)\,dx\right| + \|\phi - \phi^k\|_{L_1(G,C(U))}.$$

The result then follows from Theorem 5.2 ■

REMARK 5.1. Convergence in $L_1(G, C(U))$ includes convergence in each of $L_\infty(G)$, $L_1(G)$ and $C(G \times U)$ in the sense that if ϕ^k converges to ϕ in any of $L_\infty(G)$, $L_1(G)$ or $C(G \times U)$, then ϕ^k converges to ϕ in $L_1(G, C(U))$.

I.6. Multivalued Functions

Multivalued functions, also called set-valued functions, play an important role in control theory. The aim of this section is to present a selection theorem that is essential in proving the existence of measurable controls. However, we only treat a very special case that is directly useful for our purpose.

Let $\mathscr{K}$ be the set of all nonempty compact subsets of R^m. For $y \in R^m$, $A \in \mathscr{K}$, the distance $\rho(y, A)$ of y from A is defined by

$$\rho(y, A) = \inf\{|y - a| : a \in A\}.$$

We now define, for $A, B \in \mathscr{K}$,

$$d(A, B) = \frac{1}{2}\left\{\sup_{a\in A} \rho(a, B) + \sup_{b\in B} \rho(b, A)\right\};$$

d is a metric on $\mathscr{K}$ and is called the *Hausdorff metric* on $\mathscr{K}$.

Let Ω be a bounded open set in R^n. A mapping $F: \Omega \to \mathscr{K}$ is called a compact multivalued function. The mapping F is said to be continuous if it is continuous with respect to the Hausdorff metric on $\mathscr{K}$. F is said to be measurable if, for any closed set $D \subset R^m$, the set $\{x \in \Omega: F(x) \cap D \neq \emptyset\}$ is (Lebesgue) measurable.

THEOREM 6.1. Filippov *Let Ω be a bounded open subset in R^n, U be a compact subset in R^m, $g: \Omega \times U \to R^1$ be such that, for each $u \in U$, $g(\cdot, u)$ is measurable on Ω, and, for each $x \in \Omega$, $g(x, \cdot)$ is continuous on U. Let $F(\cdot)$ be a continuous multivalued function defined on Ω such that for each $x \in \Omega$, $F(x)$ is a nonempty compact subset of U. Define*

$$g(x, F(x)) = \{g(x, u): u \in F(x)\}.$$

If $\gamma(x)$ is a measurable function on Ω with value $\gamma(x) \in g(x, F(x))$, then there exists a measurable function $u(x)$ with values in $F(x)$ such that $\gamma(x) = g(x, u(x))$ almost everywhere in Ω.

Proof. For given $x \in \Omega$ and $\gamma(x) \in g(x, F(x))$, we choose $u \in F(x)$ with smallest first component and satisfying $\gamma(x) = g(x, u)$. If there is more than one, we take that with the smallest second component, and so on. The smallest values exist since g is continuous in U and $F(x)$ is compact, hence $\{u \in F(x): g(x, u) = \gamma(x)\}$ is compact.

We shall show by induction that the function $u(x) = (u_1(x), u_2(x), \ldots, u_m(x))$ so chosen are measurable. Suppose $u_1(x), \ldots, u_{s-1}(x)$ are measurable (if $s = 1$ there is nothing to assume). We are now going to show that $u_s(x)$ is measurable. By Theorem 3.3 and Theorem 3.4 it follows that, for any $\varepsilon > 0$, there exists a closed set $\Omega_\varepsilon \subset \Omega$ of measure greater than $\mu(\Omega) - \varepsilon$ (where μ is the Lebesgue measure on R^n) such that $\gamma(x), u_1(x), \ldots, u_{s-1}(x)$ are continuous on Ω_ε, and $g(x, u)$ is continuous on $\Omega_\varepsilon \times U$. We shall show that for any number a the set $\{x \in \Omega_\varepsilon : u_s(x) \leq a\}$ is closed.

Suppose this were false. Then there exists a sequence $\{x^k\}$ in Ω_ε such that

$$x^k \to x' \in \Omega_\varepsilon, \qquad u_s(x^k) \leq u_s(x') - \varepsilon_1, \quad \varepsilon_1 > 0. \tag{6.1}$$

Since $|u_i(x)|$ is bounded by a constant for all i and x, a subsequence of the sequence $\{x^k\}$ can be chosen, which is again denoted by $\{x^k\}$, so that $u_i(x^k) \to u_i'$ for $i = 1, \ldots, m$. Since $u(x^k) \in F(x^k)$ and F is continuous on Ω and $F(x')$ is closed, $u' = (u_1', \ldots, u_m') \in F(x')$. From (6.1) and the continuity of the functions $u_i(x)$, $i = 1, 2, \ldots, s - 1$ on Ω_ε, it follows that

$$\begin{aligned} u_i' &= u_i(x') \qquad \text{for} \quad i = 1, \ldots, s-1, \\ u_s' &\leq u_s(x') - \varepsilon_1. \end{aligned} \tag{6.2}$$

Taking limit in the identity $g(x^k, u_1(x^k), \ldots, u_m(x^k)) = \gamma(x^k)$. From this and (6.2) we see that $u_s(x')$ is not the smallest value of u_s satisfying the equation

$$g(x', u_1(x'), \ldots, u_{s-1}(x'), u_s, \ldots, u_m) = \gamma(x').$$

This contradicts the definition of $u_s(x)$. Thus the set $\{x \in \Omega_\varepsilon : u_s(x) \leq a\}$ must be closed. This means that u_s is measurable on Ω_ε. This, in turn, implies that u_s is measurable on $\Omega_{1/k}$ for each positive integer k, and hence is measurable on $\bigcup_{k=1}^{\infty} \Omega_{1/k}$. Since $\mu(\Omega \setminus \bigcup_{k=1}^{\infty} \Omega_{1/k}) = 0$, u_s is measurable on Ω. The proof is complete. ■

Note that the proof of this theorem is adapted from that of Lemma 8.2 of [HL.1, p.31]. For more information on multivalued functions we refer the reader to [HJV.1, Io.1, W.1].

The next theorem is well known.

THEOREM 6.2. *Let Q be an open subset in R^n with compact closure, U be a nonempty compact convex subset in R^m, and $\mathcal{U}$ be the class of all those measurable functions from Q into U. Then, $\mathcal{U}$ is a weak* compact subset in $L_\infty(Q, R^m)$.*

I.7. Bibliographical Remarks

To close this chapter we wish to indicate the main references. The basic references for Section 1.2 are [DS.1], [HL.1], [L.1] and [Cho.1]. In Section 1.3, most of the results can be found in [H.1]. For Section 1.4, the main references are [H.1], [LSU.1], [Mik.1], and [AT.5]. For more information about the concept of trace, we refer the interested reader to [KJF.1]. Results in Section 1.5 are taken from [War.1] and [TCWC.1]. A special case of multivalued functions treated in Section 1.6 is adapted from that presented in [HL.1]. Additional information can be found in [HJV.1].

CHAPTER II

Boundary Value Problems of Parabolic Type

II.1. Introduction

In this chapter our aim is to study first and second boundary-value problems for a linear second-order parabolic partial differential equation, in both general and divergence forms. The main reference of this chapter is [LSU.1]. Thus all the definitions and assumptions† are drawn from that source. Our presentation is, however, influenced by that of [AT.5], [Aro.1], [Mik.1], and [IKO.1].

Note that the results included in this chapter are not necessarily in their sharpest or most general form, they are simply tailored to a form suitable for application in the later chapters.

† Within the same chapter, the third assumption, is called Assumption (A.3). Outside its own chapter, the third assumption in Chapter II is referred to as Assumption (II.A.3).

II.2. Boundary-Value Problems—Basic Definitions and Assumptions

Let Ω be a bounded domain in R^n with its boundary and closure denoted by $\partial\Omega$ and $\bar{\Omega}$, respectively. *Unless otherwise stated it is assumed throughout this chapter that the boundary $\partial\Omega$ belongs to the class C^3.* Let T be a fixed positive constant. In $R^{n+1} \equiv R^n \times \{-\infty < t < \infty\}$, we consider a bounded cylinder.

$$Q \equiv \{(x, t) : x \in \Omega, t \in (0, T)\},$$

of height T. Let Γ and $\bar{Q}$ denote, respectively, the lateral surface

$$\Gamma \equiv \{(x, t) : x \in \partial\Omega, t \in [0, T]\}$$

and the closure

$$\bar{Q} = \{(x, t) : x \in \bar{Q}, t \in [0, T]\}$$

of this cylinder. For $\tau \in [0, T]$ let Ω_τ be the set

$$\Omega_\tau \equiv \{(x, t) : x \in \Omega, t = \tau\};$$

in particular, the sets

$$\Omega_0 \equiv \{(x, t) : x \in \Omega, t = 0\},$$

and

$$\Omega_T \equiv \{(x, t) : x \in \Omega, t = T\}$$

are, respectively, the base and the top of the cylinder Q.

In cylinder Q we consider a class of linear second-order parabolic partial differential equations in divergence form:

$$L\phi \equiv \phi_t - \sum_{i=1}^{n} \left\{ \left[\sum_{j=1}^{n} a_{ij}(x, t)\phi_{x_j} + a_i(x, t)\phi \right]_{x_i} + b_i(x, t)\phi_{x_i} \right\} - c(x, t)\phi$$
$$= \sum_{i=1}^{n} (F_i)_{x_i}(x, t) - f(x, t). \tag{2.1}$$

The assumptions on the coefficients and forcing terms of this equation are to be specified later.

If $\phi \in C^{2,1}(Q) \cap C(Q \cup \Gamma \cup \bar{\Omega}_0)$ and it satisfies Eq. (2.1) everywhere in Q, the initial condition

$$\phi|_{t=0} = \phi_0 \tag{2.2}$$

everywhere in Ω_0, and the boundary condition

$$\phi|_\Gamma = 0 \tag{2.3}$$

everywhere in Γ, then ϕ is called a classical solution of the first boundary-value problem for Eq. (2.1).

For convenience the first boundary-value problem for Eq. (2.1) will be referred to as the first boundary-value problem [(2.1), (2.2), and (2.3)].

If $\phi \in C^{2,1}(Q) \cap C(Q \cup \Gamma \cup \overline{\Omega}_0) \cap C^{1,0}(Q \cup \Gamma)$ and it satisfies Eq. (2.1) everywhere in Q, the initial condition (2.2) everywhere in Ω_0, and the boundary condition

$$\left(\frac{\partial \phi}{\partial \mathcal{N}} + \sigma(s, t)\phi\right)\Big|_\Gamma = \Psi, \tag{2.4}$$

everywhere in Γ, then ϕ is called a classical solution of the second boundary-value problem for Eq. (2.1). In boundary condition (2.4)

$$\frac{\partial \phi}{\partial \mathcal{N}} \equiv \sum_{i=1}^{n} \left[\sum_{j=1}^{n} a_{ij}(x, t)\phi_{x_j} + a_i(x, t)\phi\right] \cos \theta_i,$$

and, for each $i = 1, \ldots, n$, θ_i is the angle formed by the outward normal to $\partial\Omega$ with the x_i axis.

Similarly, the second boundary-value problem for Eq. (2.1) will be referred to as the second boundary-value problem [(2.1), (2.2), and (2.4)].

If functions a_{ij}, a_i, and F_i, $i, j = 1, \ldots, n$, are nondifferentiable with respect to x, then neither the first boundary-value problem nor the second boundary-value problem can have a classical solution. Thus under this situation we need to consider solutions in some weaker sense. To start with, we assume, for the time being, that

(i) ϕ is a classical solution of the second boundary-value problem; and
(ii) all the other functions involved in (2.1), (2.2), and (2.4) are sufficiently smooth.

Under the preceding conditions we multiply Eq. (2.1) by $\eta \in \tilde{W}_2^{1,1}(Q)$, where

$$\tilde{W}_2^{1,1}(Q) \equiv \{\eta \in W_2^{1,1}(Q) : \eta(x, T) = 0 \text{ for } x \in \Omega\},$$

and integrate the resulting relation over the cylinder Q. Then by performing integration by parts and using initial condition (2.2) and boundary condition (2.4) we obtain

$$-\iint_Q \phi\eta_t \, dx \, dt + \int_0^T \{\mathcal{L}_1(\phi, \eta)(t) + \mathcal{L}_2(\phi, \eta)(t) + \mathcal{L}_3(\hat{f}, \eta)(t)\} \, dt$$

$$= \int_\Omega \phi_0(x)\eta(x, 0) \, dx, \tag{2.5}$$

where

$$\mathscr{L}_1(\phi, \eta)(t) \equiv \int_\Omega \left\{ \sum_{i=1}^n \left(\sum_{j=1}^n a_{ij}(x, t)\phi_{x_j} + a_i(x, t)\phi \right)\eta_{x_i} - \left(\sum_{i=1}^n b_i(x, t)\phi_{x_i} + c(x, t)\phi \right)\eta \right\} dx, \tag{2.6}$$

$$\mathscr{L}_2(\phi, \eta)(t) \equiv \int_{\partial\Omega} \{(\sigma(s, t)\phi - \Psi(s, t)\}\eta\} \, ds, \tag{2.7}$$

and

$$\mathscr{L}_3(\hat{f}, \eta)(t) \equiv \int_\Omega \left\{ \sum_{i=1}^n F_i(x, t)\eta_{x_i} + f(x, t)\eta \right\} dx. \tag{2.8}$$

We now consider the first boundary-value problem and assume, additionally, that

$$\eta|_\Gamma = 0. \tag{2.9}$$

Then it can be easily verified that the corresponding version of the integral identity (2.5) is

$$-\iint_Q \phi\eta_t \, dx \, dt + \int_0^T \{\mathscr{L}_1(\phi, \eta)(t) + \mathscr{L}_3(\hat{f}, \eta)(t)\} \, dt = \int_\Omega \phi_0(x)\eta(x, 0) \, dx, \tag{2.10}$$

for any $\eta \in \tilde{\mathring{W}}_2^{1,1}(Q)$, where

$$\tilde{\mathring{W}}_2^{1,1}(Q) \equiv \{\eta \in \mathring{W}_2^{1,1}(Q) : \eta(x, T) = 0 \text{ for } x \in \Omega\}.$$

Integral identity (2.5) is equivalent to the second boundary-value problem if all the functions are sufficiently smooth. Otherwise, integral identity (2.5) makes sense for appropriate functions ϕ and η, whereas the second boundary-value problem as such does not. A similar conclusion is also valid for the first boundary-value problem.

Let us now introduce the notion of weak solutions of the first and second boundary-valued problems.

DEFINITION 2.1. *A function $\phi: Q \to R^1$ is called a weak solution from the space $V_2(Q)$ (resp. $V_2^{1,0}(Q)$) of the first boundary-value problem* [(2.1), (2.2), *and* (2.3)] *if $\phi \in \mathring{V}_2(Q)$ (resp. $\mathring{V}_2^{1,0}(Q)$) and satisfies integral identity* (2.10) *for all $\eta \in \tilde{\mathring{W}}_2^{1,1}(Q)$.*

DEFINITION 2.2. *A function $\phi: Q \to R^1$ is called a weak solution from the space $V_2(Q)$ (resp. $V_2^{1,0}(Q)$) of the second boundary-value problem* [(2.1), (2.2), *and* (2.4)] *if $\phi \in V_2(Q)$ (resp. $V_2^{1,0}(Q)$) and satisfies integral identity* (2.5) *for all $\eta \in \tilde{W}_2^{1,1}(Q)$.*

The following conditions are assumed, unless otherwise stated, throughout this chapter.

(A.1) For each $i, j = 1, \ldots, n$, $a_{ij}: Q \to R^1$ is measurable and bounded.

(A.2) There exist positive constants α_l and α_u such that

$$\alpha_l |\xi|^2 \leq \sum_{i,j=1}^{n} a_{ij}(x, t)\xi_i \xi_j \leq \alpha_u |\xi|^2,$$

for all $\xi \equiv (\xi_1, \ldots, \xi_n) \in R^n$, uniformly with respect to all $(x, t) \in \bar{Q}$, where $|\xi| \equiv [\sum_{i=1}^{n} (\xi_i)^2]^{1/2}$.

(A.3) $a_i: Q \to R^1, b_i: Q \to R^1, i = 1, \ldots, n$, and $c: Q \to R^1$ are measurable and satisfy, respectively, the inequalities

$$\left\| \sum_{i=1}^{n} (a_i)^2 \right\|_{q_1, r_1, Q} \leq M_1, \qquad \left\| \sum_{i=1}^{n} (b_i)^2 \right\|_{q_1, r_1, Q} \leq M_1, \qquad \|c\|_{q_1, r_1, Q} \leq M_1,$$

where $M_1 \equiv M_1(q_1, r_1)$ is a positive constant and q_1 and r_1 any pair of constants subject to the restriction:

$$1/r_1 + n/2q_1 = 1,$$

$$q_1 \in \left(\frac{n}{2}, \infty\right], \quad r_1 \in [1, \infty) \qquad \text{for} \quad n \geq 2, \tag{2.11}$$

$$q_1 \in [1, \infty], \quad r_1 \in [1, 2] \qquad \text{for} \quad n = 1.$$

(A.4) $F_i: Q \to R^1$, $i = 1, \ldots, n$ are measurable and satisfy the inequality

$$\|F\|_{2,Q} \leq \tilde{M}_2,$$

where $\|F\|_{2,Q} \equiv \|\{\sum_{i=1}^{n} (F_i)^2\}^{1/2}\|_{2,Q}$ and $\tilde{M}_2$ is a positive constant.

(A.5) $f: Q \to R^1$ is measurable and satisfies the inequality

$$\|f\|_{q_2, r_2} \leq M_2,$$

where $M_2 \equiv M_2(q_2, r_2)$ is a positive constant and q_2 and r_2 any pair of constants subject to the restriction:

$$1/r_2 + n/2q_2 = 1 + \frac{n}{4},$$

$$q_2 \in \left[\frac{2n}{n+2}, 2\right], \quad r_2 \in [1, 2] \qquad \text{for} \quad n \geq 3, \tag{2.12}$$

$$q_2 \in (1, 2], \quad r_2 \in [1, 2) \qquad \text{for} \quad n = 2,$$

$$q_2 \in [1, 2], \quad r_2 \in [1, \tfrac{4}{3}] \qquad \text{for} \quad n = 1.$$

(A.6) $\phi_0 \in L_2(\Omega)$.

(A.7) $\sigma: \Gamma \to R^1$ is measurable and satisfies the inequality

$$\|\sigma\|_{q_3, r_3, \Gamma} \leq M_3,$$

where $M_3 \equiv M_3(q_3, r_3)$ is a positive constant and q_3 and r_3 are any pair of constants subject to the restriction:

$$\begin{aligned} &1/r_3 + (n-1)/2q_3 = \tfrac{1}{2}, \\ &\qquad q_3 \in (2n-1, \infty], \quad r_3 \in [2, \infty) \qquad \text{for} \quad n > 2, \\ &\qquad q_3 \in (1, \infty), \quad r_3 \in (2, \infty) \qquad \text{for} \quad n = 2, \\ &\qquad q_3 = 2, \quad r_3 = 2 \qquad \text{for} \quad n = 1. \end{aligned} \tag{2.13}$$

(A.8) $\Psi: \Gamma \to R^1$ is measurable and satisfies the inequality

$$\|\Psi\|_{q_4, r_4, \Gamma} \leq M_4,$$

where $M_4 \equiv M_4(q_4, r_4)$ is a positive constant and q_4 and r_4 any pair of constants subject to the restriction:

$$\begin{aligned} &1/r_4 + (n-1)/2q_4 = n/4 + \tfrac{1}{2}, \\ &\qquad q_4 \in [(2n-1)/n, (2n-2)/(n-2)], \\ &\qquad r_4 \in [1, 2] \qquad \text{for} \quad n > 2, \\ &\qquad q_4 \in (1, \infty], \quad r_4 \in [1, 2) \qquad \text{for} \quad n = 2, \\ &\qquad q_4 = \tfrac{4}{3}, \quad r_4 = \tfrac{4}{3} \qquad \text{for} \quad n = 1. \end{aligned} \tag{2.14}$$

REMARK 2.1. With $\{q_k, r_k\}$, $k = 1, 3$, subject to conditions (2.11) and (2.13), respectively, we define

$$\lambda_k = 2q_k/(q_k - 1), \qquad \mu_k = 2r_k/(r_k - 1), \qquad k = 1, 3.$$

Then it can be easily verified that $\{\lambda_k, \mu_k\}$, $k = 1, 3$, satisfy, respectively, the conditions given in Theorem I.4.5 and Theorem I.4.8.

REMARK 2.2. Similarly, with $\{q_k, r_k\}$, $k = 2, 4$, subject to conditions (2.12) and (2.14), respectively, we can easily verify that $\bar{q}_k, \bar{r}_k, k = 2, 4$, defined by

$$\bar{q}_k = q_k/(q_k - 1), \qquad \bar{r}_k = r_k/(r_k - 1),$$

satisfy, respectively, the conditions given in Theorem I.4.5 and Theorem I.4.8.

II.3. Three Elementary Lemmas

This section is devoted to three elementary lemmas.

LEMMA 3.1. *For any $\phi \in V_2(Q)$, the following conditions are satisfied:*

(i) $\sum_{j=1}^{n} a_{ij}\phi_{x_j} \in L_2(Q)$, $i = 1, \ldots, n$;
(ii) $a_i\phi \in L_2(Q)$, $i = 1, \ldots, n$;
(iii) $c\phi \in L_{\lambda_1, \mu_1}(Q)$;
(iv) $\sum_{i=1}^{n} b_i\phi_{x_i} \in L_{\lambda_1, \mu_1}(Q)$;
(v) $F_i \in L_2(Q)$, $i = 1, \ldots, n$;
(vi) $f \in L_{q_2, r_2}(Q)$;
(vii) $\sigma\phi \in L_{\lambda_3, \mu_3}(\Gamma)$;
(viii) $\Psi \in L_{q_4, r_4}(\Gamma)$.

Proof. The conclusions of (v), (vi), and (viii) are just the restatements of assumptions (A.4), (A.5), and (A.8), respectively.

For the proofs of the remaining parts of the lemma, the hypothesis $\phi \in V_2(Q)$ will be used throughout without further mention.

For (i) From the Cauchy–Schwartz inequality and assumption (A.1), we have

$$\left\| \sum_{j=1}^{n} a_{ij}\phi_{x_j} \right\|_{2,Q} \le N\sqrt{n}\,\|\phi_x\|_{2,Q} < \infty, \quad i = 1, \ldots, n, \tag{3.1}$$

where

$$N \equiv \max_{i,j=1,\ldots,n} \|a_{ij}\|_{\infty,Q}$$

and

$$\|\phi_x\|_{2,Q} \equiv \left\| \left[\sum_{i=1}^{n} (\phi_{x_i})^2 \right]^{1/2} \right\|_{2,Q}.$$

For (ii) From Hölder's inequality, assumption (A.3), and Theorem I.4.5, it follows that

$$\left\| \left(\sum_{i=1}^{n} (a_i\phi)^2 \right)^{1/2} \right\|_{2,Q} \le (M_1)^{1/2}\beta_2 |\phi|_Q < \infty, \tag{3.2}$$

where the constant β_2 is as defined in Theorem I.4.5.

For (iii) From the Cauchy–Schwartz inequality, Hölder's inequality, and assumption (A.3), we obtain

$$\left\| \sum_{i=1}^{n} b_i\phi_{x_i} \right\|_{\lambda_1, \mu_1, Q} \le (M_1)^{1/2} \|\phi_x\|_{2,Q} < \infty. \tag{3.3}$$

For (iv) From Hölder's inequality, assumption (A.3), and Theorem I.4.5, we deduce that

$$\|c\phi\|_{\lambda_1,\mu_1,Q} \leq \beta_2 M_1 |\phi|_Q < \infty. \tag{3.4}$$

For (vii) From Hölder's inequality, assumption (A.7), and Theorem I.4.8, it follows that

$$\|\sigma\phi\|_{\lambda_3,\mu_3,\Gamma} \leq \beta_3 M_2 |\phi|_Q < \infty, \tag{3.5}$$

where the constant β_3 is as defined in Theorem I.4.8. This completes the proof of the lemma. ■

In view of integral identities (2.5) and (2.10), we observe that they make sense only if all the integrals involved are finite for some $\phi \in V_2(Q)$ and for any $\eta \in W_2^{1,1}(Q)$. Thus we need

LEMMA 3.2. *All the integrals involved in integral identity* (2.5) *are finite, for any $\phi \in V_2(Q)$ and for any $\eta \in W_2^{1,1}(Q)$.*

Proof. By hypotheses, $\phi \in V_2(Q)$ and $\eta \in W_2^{1,1}(Q)$. These two facts will be used throughout the proof without further mention.

For the first integral The conclusion follows readily from Hölder's inequality.

For the second integral From the Cauchy–Schwartz inequality, Cauchy's inequality, and inequality (3.1), we obtain

$$\left\| \sum_{i,j=1}^{n} a_{ij}\phi_{x_j}\eta_{x_i} \right\|_{1,Q} \leq N\sqrt{n}\,\|\phi_x\|_{2,Q}\|\eta_x\|_{2,Q} < \infty. \tag{3.6}$$

For the third integral From the Cauchy–Schwartz inequality, Cauchy's inequality, and inequality (3.2) we deduce that

$$\left\| \sum_{i=1}^{n} a_i\phi\eta_{x_i} \right\|_{1,Q} \leq (M_1)^{1/2}\beta_2 |\phi|_Q \|\eta_x\|_{2,Q} < \infty. \tag{3.7}$$

For the fourth integral From Hölder's inequality, inequality (3.3), and Theorem I.4.5 it follows that

$$\left\| \sum_{i=1}^{n} b_i\phi_{x_i}\eta \right\|_{1,Q} \leq \beta_2 (M_1)^{1/2} \|\phi_x\|_{2,Q} |\eta|_Q < \infty. \tag{3.8}$$

For the fifth integral From Hölder's inequality, inequality (3.4), and Theorem I.4.5 we obtain

$$\|c\phi\eta\|_{1,Q} \leq (\beta_2)^2 M_1 |\phi|_Q |\eta|_Q < \infty. \tag{3.9}$$

For the sixth integral From Hölder's inequality, inequality (3.5) and Theorem I.4.8 it follows that

$$\|\sigma\phi\eta\|_{1,\Gamma} \leq (\beta_3)^2 M_3 |\phi|_Q |\eta|_Q < \infty. \tag{3.10}$$

For the seventh integral From Hölder's inequality, assumption (A.8), and Theorem I.4.8 we deduce that

$$\|\Psi\eta\|_{1,\Gamma} \leq \beta_3 \|\Psi\|_{q_4, r_4, \Gamma} |\eta|_Q < \infty. \tag{3.11}$$

For the eighth integral From the Cauchy–Schwartz inequality, Cauchy's inequality, and assumption (A.4) we obtain

$$\left\| \sum_{i=1}^{n} F_i \eta_{x_i} \right\| \leq \tilde{M}_2 \|\eta_x\|_{2,Q} < \infty. \tag{3.12}$$

For the ninth integral From Hölder's inequality, assumption (A.5), and Theorem I.4.5 it follows that

$$\|f\eta\|_{1,Q} \leq \beta_2 M_2 |\eta|_Q < \infty. \tag{3.13}$$

For the integral on the right-hand side Since $W_2^{1,1}(Q) \subset V_2^{1,0}(Q)$ we deduce from the Cauchy–Schwartz inequality and assumption (A.6) that

$$\|\phi_0 \eta(\cdot, 0)\|_{1,Q} \leq \|\phi_0\|_{2,\Omega} \|\eta(\cdot, 0)\|_{2,\Omega} < \infty. \tag{3.14}$$

The proof is now complete. ■

REMARK 3.1. Since $V_2^{1,0}(Q)$ and $\overset{\circ}{V}{}_2^{1,0}(Q)$ are subspaces of $V_2(Q)$, it is obvious that the conclusions of Lemmas 3.1 and 3.2 are valid for the case when $\phi \in V_2^{1,0}(Q)$ or $\phi \in \overset{\circ}{V}{}_2^{1,0}(Q)$.

The next lemma will be needed in Chapter VI.

LEMMA 3.3. *Consider the second boundary-value problem* [(2.1), (2.2), *and* (2.4)]. *Let* $\phi \in V_2(Q)$. *Then* ϕ *is a weak solution of the second boundary-value problem if and only if it satisfies, for almost all* $\tau \in [0, T]$, *the following integral identity*:

$$\int_\Omega \phi(x, \tau)\eta(x, \tau)\, dx - \int_0^\tau \int_\Omega \phi(x, t)\eta_t(x, t)\, dx\, dt$$
$$+ \int_0^\tau \{\mathscr{L}_1(\phi, \eta)(t) + \mathscr{L}_2(\phi, \eta)(t) + \mathscr{L}_3(\hat{f}, \eta)(t)\}\, dt = \int_\Omega \phi_0(x)\eta(x, 0)\, dx, \tag{3.15}$$

for any $\eta \in W_2^{1,1}(Q)$.

Proof. First we show that condition (3.15) implies that (2.5) holds for any $\eta \in \tilde{W}_2^{1,1}(Q)$. Take $\eta \in W_2^{1,1}(Q)$ such that $\eta(x, t) = 0$ for all $(x, t) \in \Omega \times [T - \varepsilon, T)$. Then by taking $\tau > T - \varepsilon$ in (3.15), (2.5) holds for such η and hence for all $\eta \in \tilde{W}_2^{1,1}(Q)$. Conversely, suppose that (2.5) holds for all

$\eta \in \tilde{W}_2^{1,1}(Q)$. We shall show that condition (3.15) is true. For this, let $\varepsilon > 0$ be a small number and let μ_ε be the function defined by

$$\mu_\varepsilon(t, \tau) = \begin{cases} 1, & t \in [0, \tau - \varepsilon], \\ (\tau - t)/\varepsilon, & t \in [\tau - \varepsilon, \tau], \\ 0, & t \in [\tau, T]. \end{cases}$$

Let $\hat{\eta}$ be an arbitrary element of $W_2^{1,1}(Q)$. Then it is clear that $\eta_\varepsilon(\cdot, \cdot) \equiv \mu_\varepsilon(\cdot, \tau)\hat{\eta}(\cdot, \cdot) \in W_2^{1,1}(Q)$ and equal to zero for $t \geq \tau$. Thus by substituting this η_ε into (2.5), we have

$$\begin{aligned} &-\iint_Q \{\phi(x, t)[\mu_\varepsilon(t, \tau)\hat{\eta}_t(x, t) + (\mu_\varepsilon)_t(t, \tau)\hat{\eta}(x, t)]\}\, dx\, dt \\ &\quad + \int_0^\tau \{\mathscr{L}_1(\phi, \eta_\varepsilon)(t) + \mathscr{L}_2(\phi, \eta_\varepsilon)(t) + \mathscr{L}_3(\hat{f}, \eta_\varepsilon)(t)\}\, dt \\ &= \int_\Omega \{\phi_0(x)\mu_\varepsilon(0, \tau)\hat{\eta}(x, 0)\}\, dx. \end{aligned} \tag{3.16}$$

From the definition of μ_ε it is clear that

(i) the right-hand side of the preceding equality is

$$\int_\Omega \{\phi_0(x)\mu_\varepsilon(0, \tau)\hat{\eta}(x, 0)\}\, dx = \int_\Omega \phi_0(x)\hat{\eta}(x, 0)\, dx,$$

(ii) the first integral on the left-hand side of the equality is

$$\begin{aligned} &-\iint_Q \{\phi(x, t)[\mu_\varepsilon(t, \tau)\hat{\eta}_t(x, t) + (\mu_\varepsilon)_t(t, \tau)\hat{\eta}(x, t)]\}\, dx\, dt \\ &\quad = -\int_0^\tau \int_\Omega \{\phi(x, t)\mu_\varepsilon(t, \tau)\hat{\eta}_t(x, t)\}\, dx\, dt \\ &\quad\quad + \frac{1}{\varepsilon}\int_{\tau-\varepsilon}^\tau \int_\Omega \phi(x, t)\hat{\eta}(x, t)\, dx\, dt. \end{aligned} \tag{3.17}$$

Note that the function $\Psi(\cdot) \equiv \int_\Omega \phi(x, \cdot)\hat{\eta}(x, \cdot)\, dx$ is integrable on $[0, T]$. Thus

$$\lim_{\varepsilon \downarrow 0} \frac{1}{\varepsilon}\int_{\tau-\varepsilon}^\tau \int_\Omega \{\phi(x, t)\hat{\eta}(x, t)\}\, dx\, dt = \int_\Omega \phi(x, \tau)\hat{\eta}(x, \tau)\, dx \tag{3.18}$$

for almost all $\tau \in [0, T]$.

For the first integral on the right-hand side of (3.17) it follows from Lebesgue's dominated convergence theorem that

$$\lim_{\varepsilon \downarrow 0} \int_0^\tau \int_\Omega \{\phi(x, t)\mu_\varepsilon(t, \tau)\hat{\eta}_t(x, t)\}\, dx\, dt = \int_0^\tau \int_\Omega \{\phi(x, t)\hat{\eta}_t(x, t)\}\, dx\, dt. \tag{3.19}$$

Letting $\varepsilon \to 0$ in (3.17), we obtain from (3.18) and (3.19) the first two integrals on the left-hand side of (3.15).

It remains to show that the second integral on the left-hand side of (3.16) tends to the third integral on the left-hand side of (3.15) as $\varepsilon \downarrow 0$. Actually, this conclusion follows easily from the definition of the function η_ε and the hypotheses of the lemma. Thus the proof is complete. ∎

II.4. A Priori Estimates

To derive a priori estimates for solutions from the space $V_2^{1,0}(Q)$ of the boundary-value problems under discussion we need

LEMMA 4.1. *Let $\phi \in V_2(Q)$ be such that*

$$\tfrac{1}{2}\|\phi(\cdot, t)\|_{2,\Omega}^2\Big|_{t=t_1}^{t=t_2} + \int_{t_1}^{t_2} \{\mathscr{L}_1(\phi, \phi)(t) + \mathscr{L}_2(\phi, \phi)(t) + \mathscr{L}_3(\hat{f}, \phi)(t)\}\, dt \le 0 \tag{4.1}$$

for almost all $t_1, t_2 \in [0, T]$, including $t_1 = 0$. Then ϕ satisfies

$$|\phi|_Q \le K_1\{\|\phi(\cdot, 0)\|_{2,\Omega} + \|F\|_{2,Q} + \|f\|_{q_2,r_2,Q} + \|\Psi\|_{q_4,r_4,\Gamma}\}, \tag{4.2}$$

where the positive constant K_1 depends only on $n, \alpha_l, M_1, q_k, r_k, k = 2, 4$; and $q_k, r_k, k = 2, 4$, are subject to the restrictions (2.12) *and* (2.14), *respectively.*

Proof. Throughout the proof t_1 and t_2 are to be understood as being chosen so that inequality (4.1) is satisfied. Bearing this convention in mind, we now break the proof up into a series of steps.

Step 1 From Cauchy's inequality

$$ab \le \frac{\varepsilon}{2} a^2 + \frac{1}{2\varepsilon} b^2, \qquad \varepsilon > 0, \qquad a, b \in R^1, \tag{4.3}$$

with $\varepsilon = \alpha_l/2$, we obtain

$$a_i \phi \phi_{x_i} \le \frac{\alpha_l}{4}(\phi_{x_i})^2 + \frac{1}{\alpha_l}(a_i \phi)^2,$$

and

$$b_i \phi_{x_i} \phi \le \frac{\alpha_l}{4}(\phi_{x_i})^2 + \frac{1}{\alpha_l}(b_i \phi)^2.$$

Thus

$$\left\|\sum_{i=1}^n \{a_i \phi \phi_{x_i} + b_i \phi_{x_i} \phi\} + c\phi^2\right\|_{1, Q(t_1, t_2)} \le \frac{\alpha_l}{2}\|\phi_x\|_{2, Q(t_1, t_2)}^2 + \|G\phi^2\|_{1, Q(t_1, t_2)}, \tag{4.4}$$

where

$$Q(t_1, t_2) \equiv \Omega \times (t_1, t_2), \tag{4.5}$$

and

$$G \equiv \frac{1}{\alpha_l} \sum_{i=1}^{n} \{(a_i)^2 + (b_i)^2\} + c. \tag{4.6}$$

From the Cauchy–Schwartz inequality we have

$$\left| \sum_{i=1}^{n} F_i \phi_{x_i} \right| \leq \left[\sum_{i=1}^{n} (F_i)^2 \right]^{1/2} \left[\sum_{i=1}^{n} (\phi_{x_i})^2 \right]^{1/2}. \tag{4.7}$$

By virtue of inequality (4.1) it follows from assumption (A.2) and inequalities (4.4) and (4.7) that

$$\begin{aligned} \tfrac{1}{2} \|\phi(\cdot, t)\|_{2,\Omega}^2 \Big|_{t=t_1}^{t=t_2} &+ \frac{\alpha_l}{2} \|\phi_x\|_{2, Q(t_1, t_2)}^2 \\ \leq \|G\phi^2\|_{1, Q(t_1, t_2)} &+ \left\| \left[\sum_{i=1}^{n} (F_i)^2 \right]^{1/2} \left[\sum_{i=1}^{n} (\phi_{x_i})^2 \right]^{1/2} \right\|_{1, Q(t_1, t_2)} \\ &+ \|f\phi\|_{1, Q(t_1, t_2)} + \|\sigma\phi^2\|_{1, \Gamma(t_1, t_2)} + \|\Psi\phi\|_{1, \Gamma(t_1, t_2)}, \end{aligned} \tag{4.8}$$

where

$$\Gamma(t_1, t_2) \equiv \partial\Omega \times (t_1, t_2). \tag{4.9}$$

Step 2 From Hölder's inequality we obtain

$$\|G\phi^2\|_{1, Q(t_1, t_2)} \leq \|G\|_{q_1, r_1, Q(t_1, t_2)} \|\phi\|_{\lambda_1, \mu_1, Q(t_1, t_2)}^2; \tag{4.10}$$

$$\left\| \left[\sum_{i=1}^{n} (F_i)^2 \right]^{1/2} \left[\sum_{i=1}^{n} (\phi_{x_i})^2 \right]^{1/2} \right\|_{1, Q(t_1, t_2)} \leq \|F\|_{2, Q(t_1, t_2)} \|\phi_x\|_{2, Q(t_1, t_2)}; \tag{4.11}$$

$$\|f\phi\|_{1, Q(t_1, t_2)} \leq \|f\|_{q_2, r_2, Q(t_1, t_2)} \|\phi\|_{\bar{q}_2, \bar{r}_2, Q(t_1, t_2)}; \tag{4.12}$$

$$\|\sigma\phi^2\|_{1, \Gamma(t_1, t_2)} \leq \|\sigma\|_{q_3, r_3, \Gamma(t_1, t_2)} \|\phi\|_{\lambda_3, \mu_3, \Gamma(t_1, t_2)}^2; \tag{4.13}$$

and

$$\|\Psi\phi\|_{1, \Gamma(t_1, t_2)} \leq \|\Psi\|_{q_4, r_4, \Gamma(t_1, t_2)} \|\phi\|_{\bar{q}_4, \bar{r}_4, \Gamma(t_1, t_2)}, \tag{4.14}$$

where λ_k, μ_k, $k = 1, 3$, are defined in Remark 2.1; and $\bar{q}_k$, $\bar{r}_k$, $k = 2, 4$, are defined in Remark 2.2.

Using inequalities (4.10)–(4.14), Theorems I.4.5, and Theorem I.4.8 it can be easily verified from inequality (4.8) that

$$\begin{aligned}\|\phi(\cdot, t_2)\|_{2,\Omega}^2 &+ \alpha_l \|\phi_x\|_{2,Q(t_1,t_2)}^2 \\ &\leq \|\phi(\cdot, t_1)\|_{2,\Omega}^2 + H_1(t_1, t_2)|\phi|_{Q(t_1,t_2)}^2 + I_1(t_1, t_2)|\phi|_{Q(t_1,t_2)} \\ &\quad + H_2(t_1, t_2)|\phi|_{Q(t_1,t_2)}^2 + I_2(t_1, t_2)|\phi|_{Q(t_1,t_2)} \equiv J(t_1, t_2), \end{aligned} \tag{4.15}$$

where

$$H_1(t_1, t_2) \equiv 2(\beta_2)^2 \|G\|_{q_1, r_1, Q(t_1,t_2)}, \tag{4.16}$$

$$I_1(t_1, t_2) \equiv 2\beta_2 \|f\|_{q_2, r_2, Q(t_1,t_2)}, \tag{4.17}$$

$$H_2(t_1, t_2) \equiv 2(\beta_3)^2 \|\sigma\|_{q_3, r_3, \Gamma(t_1,t_2)}, \tag{4.18}$$

and

$$I_2(t_1, t_2) \equiv 2\beta_3 \|\Psi\|_{q_4, r_4, \Gamma(t_1,t_2)}. \tag{4.19}$$

By virtue of the definitions of $Q(t_1, t_2)$, $H_k(t_1, t_2)$, and $I_k(t_1, t_2)$, $k = 1, 2$, it follows readily from inequality (4.15) that

$$\|\phi(\cdot, t)\|_{2,\Omega}^2 + \alpha_l \|\phi_x\|_{2,Q(t_1,t_2)}^2 \leq J(t_1, t_2), \tag{4.20}$$

for almost all $t \in [t_1, t_2]$. Letting $\alpha_1 \equiv \min\{1, \alpha_l\}$ we obtain

$$\alpha_1\{\|\phi(\cdot, t)\|_{2,\Omega}^2 + \|\phi_x\|_{2,Q(t_1,t_2)}^2\} \leq J(t_1, t_2),$$

for almost all $t \in [t_1, t_2]$. This, in turn, implies the following two inequalities:

$$\|\phi(\cdot, t)\|_{2,\Omega} \leq \left[\frac{1}{\alpha_1} J(t_1, t_2)\right]^{1/2},$$

for almost all $t \in [t_1, t_2]$, and

$$\|\phi_x\|_{2,Q(t_1,t_2)} \leq \left[\frac{1}{\alpha_1} J(t_1, t_2)\right]^{1/2}.$$

From these two inequalities it follows that

$$|\phi|_{Q(t_1,t_2)} \leq 2\left[\frac{1}{\alpha_1} J(t_1, t_2)\right]^{1/2}.$$

Consequently, we have

$$|\phi|_{Q(t_1,t_2)}^2 \leq \frac{4}{\alpha_1} J(t_1, t_2). \tag{4.21}$$

Step 3 Note that inequality (4.21) is valid for all those $t_1, t_2 \in [0, T]$ as long as they can be used, respectively, as upper and lower limits of integration as required in inequality (4.1). Clearly, almost any pair of elements from $[0, T]$ can be chosen as such t_1 and t_2. Let $\varepsilon \in (0, T)$ be arbitrary and let T_1 be a point in $(T - \varepsilon, T]$ such that it can be used as upper limit. We now divide the interval $[0, T_1]$ into a finite number of subintervals, namely,

$$[t_0 = 0, t_1], [t_1, t_2], \ldots, [t_{s-1}, t_s = T_1].$$

Here, $\{t_k\}_{k=1}^s$ are chosen in such a way that they can be used as limits.

Define

$$H(t_{k-1}, t_k) = H_1(t_{k-1}, t_k) + H_2(t_{k-1}, t_k), \tag{4.22}$$

where H_1 and H_2 are as defined by (4.16) and (4.18), respectively. If

$$H(0, T_1) \le \alpha_1/8, \tag{4.23}$$

then the interval $[0, T_1]$ does not need to be subdivided, that is, $s = 1$. Otherwise, the partitions are to be such that

$$\alpha_1/16 \le H(t_{k-1}, t_k) \le \alpha_1/8, \tag{4.24}$$

for all $k = 1, \ldots, s$. The first part of this inequality is to ensure that the number s is finite. Indeed, from conditions (2.11) and (2.13) we observe readily that $r_1 < \infty$ and $r_3 < \infty$. Thus either $r_1 \ge r_3$ or $r_3 > r_1$. However, since both cases can be handled in the same way, we shall consider the case when $r_1 \ge r_3$. In this situation we have

$$\begin{aligned}
\sum_{k=1}^{s} [H(t_{k-1}, t_k)]^{r_1} &\le 2^{r_1}\left\{\sum_{k=1}^{s} [H_1(t_{k-1}, t_k)]^{r_1} + \sum_{k=1}^{s} [(H_2(t_{k-1}, t_k))^{r_3}]^{r_1/r_3}\right\} \\
&\le 2^{r_1}\left\{\sum_{k=1}^{s} [H_1(t_{k-1}, t_k)]^{r_1} + \left[\sum_{k=1}^{s} (H_2(t_{k-1}, t_k))^{r_3}\right]^{r_1/r_3}\right\} \\
&\le 2^{r_1}\{2^{r_1}(\beta_2)^{2r_1}\|G\|_{q_1, r_1, Q}^{r_1} + [2^{r_3}(\beta_3)^{2r_3}\|\sigma\|_{q_3, r_3, \Gamma}^{r_3}]^{r_1/r_3}\} \\
&\equiv N < \infty.
\end{aligned}$$

Thus it follows from the first part of inequality (4.24) that

$$s(\alpha_1/16)^{r_1} \le N.$$

Hence the number s is finite.

Step 4 Define

$$I(t_{k-1}, t_k) = I_1(t_{k-1}, t_k) + I_2(t_{k-1}, t_k), \tag{4.25}$$

where I_1 and I_2 are as defined by (4.17) and (4.19), respectively. Let $J(t_{k-1}, t_k)$ be as defined in (4.15). Then applying inequality (4.21) to each of the subintervals $\{[t_{k-1}, t_k]\}_{k=1}^{s}$, we obtain

$$|\phi|^2_{Q(t_{k-1},t_k)} \le \frac{4}{\alpha_1}\{\|\phi(\cdot, t_{k-1})\|^2_{2,\Omega} + H(t_{k-1}, t_k)|\phi|^2_{Q(t_{k-1},t_k)} + I(t_{k-1}, t_k)|\phi|_{Q(t_{k-1},t_k)}\}, \tag{4.26}$$

where H and I are defined by (4.22) and (4.25), respectively. Since $H(t_{k-1}, t_k) \le \alpha_1/8$, by (4.24), it follows immediately from (4.26) that

$$|\phi|^2_{Q(t_{k-1},t_k)} \le \frac{8}{\alpha_1}\{\|\phi(\cdot, t_{k-1})\|^2_{2,\Omega} + I(t_{k-1}, t_k)|\phi|_{Q(t_{k-1},t_k)}\}. \tag{4.27}$$

By Cauchy's inequality (4.3) with $\varepsilon = \alpha_1/8$, we have

$$I(t_{k-1}, t_k)|\phi|_{Q(t_{k-1},t_k)} \le (4/\alpha_1)[I(t_{k-1}, t_k)]^2 + (\alpha_1/16)|\phi|^2_{Q(t_{k-1},t_k)}.$$

Thus inequality (4.27) is reduced to

$$\begin{aligned} |\phi|^2_{Q(t_{k-1},t_k)} &\le \frac{16}{\alpha_1}\|\phi(\cdot, t_{k-1})\|^2_{2,\Omega} + \frac{64}{(\alpha_1)^2}[I(t_{k-1}, t_k)]^2 \\ &\le (\alpha_2)^2\{\|\phi(\cdot, t_{k-1})\|_{2,\Omega} + I(t_{k-1}, t_k)\}^2, \end{aligned} \tag{4.28}$$

for all $k = 1, \ldots, s$, where

$$(\alpha_2)^2 \equiv \max\{16/\alpha_1, 64/(\alpha_1)^2\}.$$

This, in turn, implies the following two inequalities:

$$\|\phi\|_{2,\infty,Q(t_{k-1},t_k)} \le \alpha_2\{\|\phi(\cdot, t_{k-1})\|_{2,\Omega} + I(0, T_1)\}, \tag{4.29}$$

and

$$\|\phi_x\|_{2,Q(t_{k-1},t_k)} \le \alpha_2\{\|\phi(\cdot, t_{k-1})\|_{2,\Omega} + I(0, T_1)\}. \tag{4.30}$$

From inequality (4.28), we can readily verify that

$$\|\phi(\cdot, t_k)\|_{2,\Omega} \le (\alpha_2)^k\|\phi(\cdot, 0)\|_{2,\Omega} + \sum_{l=1}^{k}(\alpha_2)^l I(0, T_1). \tag{4.31}$$

Thus inequality (4.29) is reduced to

$$\|\phi\|_{2,\infty,Q(t_{k-1},t_k)} \le (\alpha_2)^k\|\phi(\cdot, 0)\|_{2,\Omega} + \sum_{l=1}^{k}(\alpha_2)^l I(0, T_1), \tag{4.32}$$

and hence

$$\|\phi\|_{2,\infty,Q(0,T_1)} \le \alpha_3\{\|\phi(\cdot, 0)\|_{2,\Omega} + I(0, T_1)\}, \tag{4.33}$$

where

$$\alpha_3 \equiv \sum_{k=1}^{s}(\alpha_2)^k + \sum_{k=1}^{s}\sum_{l=1}^{k}(\alpha_2)^l.$$

Similarly, by applying inequality (4.31) to inequality (4.30), we obtain

$$\|\phi_x\|_{2,Q(0,T_1)} \leq \alpha_3\{\|\phi(\cdot, 0)\|_{2,\Omega} + I(0, T_1)\}. \tag{4.34}$$

Combining the two inequalities (4.33) and (4.34), it follows that

$$|\phi|_{Q(0,T_1)} \leq 2\alpha_3\{\|\phi(\cdot, 0)\|_{2,\Omega} + I(0, T_1)\}. \tag{4.35}$$

Since $T_1 \in (T - \varepsilon, T]$ and $\varepsilon > 0$ is arbitrary, the conclusion of the lemma follows readily from inequality (4.35).

This completes the proof. ■

For the first boundary-value problem, we have the following lemma.

LEMMA 4.2. *Let $\phi \in V_2(Q)$ be such that*

$$\tfrac{1}{2}\|\phi(\cdot, t)\|_{2,\Omega}^2\Big|_{t=t_1}^{t=t_2} + \int_{t_1}^{t_2} \{\mathscr{L}_1(\phi, \phi)(t) + \mathscr{L}_3(\hat{f}, \phi)(t)\}\, dt \leq 0, \tag{4.36}$$

for almost all $t_1, t_2 \in [0, T]$, including $t_1 = 0$. Then ϕ satisfies

$$|\phi|_Q \leq K_2\{\|\phi(\cdot, 0)\|_{2,\Omega} + \|F\|_{2,\Omega} + \|f\|_{q_2,r_2,Q}\}, \tag{4.37}$$

where the constant K_2 depends only on n, α_l, M_1, q_2, and r_2; q_2 and r_2 are subject to restriction (2.12).

Proof. The proof is similar to that given for Lemma 4.1. ■

With $\rho \in (0, T)$, let $\eta \in W_2^{1,1}(Q(-\rho, T))$ be an element that is equal to zero for $t \geq T - \rho$ and for $t \leq 0$. Consider the function

$$\eta_{\bar{\rho}}(x, t) \equiv \frac{1}{\rho}\int_{t-\rho}^{t} \eta(x, \tau)\, d\tau. \tag{4.38}$$

Then it can be easily verified that

$$\eta_{\bar{\rho}t} = \eta_{t\bar{\rho}}. \tag{4.39}$$

REMARK 4.1. It can be easily verified that the averaging operation in t, $(\ )_{\bar{\rho}}$, commutes with differentiation with respect to x.

Let g and h be any functions in $L_2([-\rho, T])$, and assume that at least one of them is equal to zero on the intervals $[-\rho, 0]$ and $[T - \rho, T]$. Consider the functions

$$g_\rho(t) = \frac{1}{\rho}\int_{t}^{t+\rho} g(\tau)\, d\tau, \tag{4.40}$$

and

$$h_{\bar{\rho}}(t) = \frac{1}{\rho}\int_{t-\rho}^{t} h(\tau)\, d\tau. \tag{4.41}$$

Then by interchanging the order of integration with respect to t and τ, we obtain

$$\int_0^T gh_{\bar{\rho}}\, dt = \int_0^{T-\rho} g_\rho h\, dt. \tag{4.42}$$

Let $\eta \in V_2^{1,0}(Q(-\rho, T))$. Since $W_2^{1,1}(Q(-\rho, T))$ is dense in $V_2^{1,0}(Q(-\rho, T))$, it follows that there exists a sequence of elements $\{\eta_m\}_{m=1}^{\infty}$ in $W_2^{1,1}(Q(-\rho, T))$ such that

$$\eta_m \xrightarrow{s} \eta, \tag{4.43}$$

(strongly) in $V_2^{1,0}(Q(-\rho, T))$.

For a fixed t_1, with $0 < t_1 \leq T - \rho$, we can find the integer $k \geq 1$, such that $t_1 - (1/k) > 1/k$. For each of such integers $k \geq 1$ we consider the piecewise linear function e_k defined by

$$e_k(t) \equiv \begin{cases} 0 & \text{for} \quad t \leq 0, \\ kt & \text{for} \quad 0 \leq t \leq 1/k, \\ 1 & \text{for} \quad (1/k) \leq t \leq t_1 - (1/k), \\ k(t_1 - t) & \text{for} \quad t_1 - (1/k) \leq t \leq t_1, \\ 0 & \text{for} \quad t \geq t_1. \end{cases} \tag{4.44}$$

Define

$$\eta_{m,k} = n_m e_k. \tag{4.45}$$

Then the following two properties of the function $\eta_{m,k}$ can be easily verified:

(i) $\eta_{m,k} \in W_2^{1,1}(Q(-\rho, T))$ and $\eta_{m,k}$ are equal to zero for $t \leq 0$ and for $t \geq t_1$; and

(ii) $\eta_{m,k} \xrightarrow{s} \eta$ in $V_2^{1,0}(Q(0, t_1))$, as $m, k \to \infty$, independent of the order of taking limits.

From Theorem I.4.5 and Theorem I.4.8, it follows, respectively, that

$$\|\eta_{m,k}\|_{\lambda_1, \mu_1, Q(0,t_1)} \leq \beta_2 |\eta_{m,k}|_{Q(0,t_1)}, \tag{4.46}$$

and

$$\|\eta_{m,k}\|_{\lambda_3, \mu_3, \Gamma(0,t_1)} \leq \beta_3 |\eta_{m,k}|_{Q(0,t_1)}, \tag{4.47}$$

where $\lambda_k, \mu_k, k = 1, 3$, are defined in Remark 2.1.

Using the two inequalities (4.46) and (4.47), we easily deduce from property (ii) of the functions $\eta_{m,k}$ that

$$\eta_{m,k} \xrightarrow{s} \eta \tag{4.48a}$$

and

$$\eta_{m,k}|_{\Gamma(0,t_1)} \xrightarrow{s} \eta|_{\Gamma(0,t_1)}, \tag{4.48b}$$

in $V_2^{1,0}(Q(0, t_1)) \cap L_{\lambda_1, \mu_1}(Q(0, t_1))$ and $L_{\lambda_3, \mu_3}(\Gamma(0, t_1))$, respectively, as $m, k \to \infty$, independent of the order with respect to m and k.

Let $\phi \in V_2^{1,0}(Q)$. Then the functions ϕ_ρ, $\rho > 0$, as defined by (4.40), are also in $V_2^{1,0}(Q)$. Furthermore, it follows from Lemma 3.1 that

$$\begin{aligned}
&\text{(i)} && \left(\sum_{j=1}^{n} a_{ij}\phi_{x_j} + a_i\phi\right)_\rho \in L_2(Q), \qquad i = 1, \ldots, n, \\
&\text{(ii)} && (c\phi)_\rho \in L_{\lambda_1, \mu_1}(Q); \\
&\text{(iii)} && \left(\sum_{i=1}^{n} b_i\phi_{x_i}\right)_\rho \in L_{\lambda_1, \mu_1}(Q); \\
&\text{(iv)} && (F_i)_\rho \in L_2(Q), \qquad i = 1, \ldots, n; \\
&\text{(v)} && f_\rho \in L_{q_2, r_2}(Q); \\
&\text{(vi)} && (\sigma\phi)_\rho \in L_{\lambda_3, \mu_3}(\Gamma); \\
&\text{(vii)} && \Psi_\rho \in L_{q_4, r_4}(\Gamma).
\end{aligned} \tag{4.49}$$

REMARK 4.2. For any $q, r \in [1, \infty)$, let g be an element in $L_{q,r}(Q)$. Consider the functions g_ρ, $\rho > 0$, defined by (4.40). Then it follows that

$$g_\rho \xrightarrow{s} g, \tag{4.50}$$

in $L_{q,r}(Q(0, T - \delta))$, as $\rho \to 0$, where δ, $0 < \delta < T$, is arbitrary. However, if g is, instead, an element in $V_2^{1,0}(Q)$, then it is clear from Theorem I.4.6 that

$$g_\rho \xrightarrow{s} g, \tag{4.51}$$

in $V_2^{1,0}(Q(0, T - \delta))$ as $\rho \to 0$. Hence, by virtue of Theorems I.4.5 and I.4.8 we have

$$g_\rho \xrightarrow{s} g, \tag{4.52a}$$

in $L_{q,r}(Q(0, T - \delta))$, as $\rho \to 0$, and

$$g_\rho|_{\Gamma(0, T-\delta)} \xrightarrow{s} g|_{\Gamma(0, T-\delta)} \tag{4.52b}$$

in $L_{\tilde{q}, \tilde{r}}(\Gamma(0, T - \delta))$ as $\rho \to 0$, where $\{q, r\}$ and $\{\tilde{q}, \tilde{r}\}$ are subject to the restrictions given in Theorems I.4.5 and I.4.8, respectively. In particular,

$$g_\rho \xrightarrow{s} g \tag{4.53a}$$

in $L_{\lambda_1, \mu_1}(Q(0, T - \delta))$ as $\rho \to 0$, and

$$g_\rho|_{\Gamma(0, T-\delta)} \xrightarrow{s} g|_{\Gamma(0, T-\delta)} \tag{4.53b}$$

in $L_{\lambda_3, \mu_3}(\Gamma(0, T - \delta))$ as $\rho \to 0$, where λ_k and μ_k, $k = 1, 3$, are defined in Remark 2.1.

REMARK 4.3. Consider the second (resp. first) boundary-value problem [(2.1), (2.2), and (2.4)] (resp. [(2.1), (2.2), and (2.3)]). Suppose that ϕ is a weak solution from the space $V_2^{1,0}(Q)$. Then it is easily verified that all the functions involved in the boundary-value problem under discussion can be extended before hand onto $Q(0, T+\delta)$ with all the properties of these functions preserved, where δ, $0 < \delta < T$, is arbitrary but fixed.

LEMMA 4.3. *Consider the second boundary-value problem* [(2.1), (2.2), *and* (2.4)]. *If ϕ is a weak solution from the space $V_2^{1,0}(Q)$, then it satisfies:*

$$\tfrac{1}{2}\|\phi(\cdot,t)\|_{2,\Omega}^2\Big|_{t=0}^{t=t_1} + \int_0^{t_1}\{\mathscr{L}_1(\phi,\phi)(t) + \mathscr{L}_2(\phi,\phi)(t) + \mathscr{L}_3(\hat{f},\phi)(t)\}\,dt = 0, \tag{4.54}$$

for all $t_1 \in [0, T]$.

Proof. We break the proof up into a series of steps.

Step 1 With $\rho \in (0, T)$, let $\hat{\eta}$ be an element in $W_2^{1,1}(Q(-\rho, T))$ that is equal to zero for $t \geq T - \rho$ and for $t \leq 0$. Then the function $\hat{\eta}_{\bar{\rho}}$, as defined by (4.38), is in $W_2^{1,1}(Q)$ and is equal to zero for $t = 0$ and for $t = T$. Thus it follows that

$$-\iint_Q \phi\hat{\eta}_{\bar{\rho}t}\,dx\,dt + \int_0^T\{\mathscr{L}_1(\phi,\hat{\eta}_{\bar{\rho}})(t) + \mathscr{L}_2(\phi,\hat{\eta}_{\bar{\rho}})(t) + \mathscr{L}_3(\hat{f},\hat{\eta}_{\bar{\rho}})(t)\}\,dt = 0, \tag{4.55}$$

because ϕ is, by hypothesis, a weak solution of the second boundary-value problem.

From equalities (4.39) and (4.42), we obtain

$$\begin{aligned}
-\iint_Q \phi\hat{\eta}_{\bar{\rho}t}\,dx\,dt &= -\iint_Q \phi\hat{\eta}_{t\bar{\rho}}\,dx\,dt \\
&= -\iint_{Q(0,T-\rho)} \phi_\rho\hat{\eta}_t\,dx\,dt \\
&= \iint_{Q(0,T-\rho)} \phi_{\rho t}\hat{\eta}\,dx\,dt,
\end{aligned} \tag{4.56}$$

where the last equality follows from applying integration by parts.

By virtue of Remark 4.1 and equality (4.42), it can be easily verified that

$$\begin{aligned}
&\int_0^T\{\mathscr{L}_1(\phi,\hat{\eta}_{\bar{\rho}})(t) + \mathscr{L}_2(\phi,\hat{\eta}_{\bar{\rho}})(t) + \mathscr{L}_3(\hat{f},\hat{\eta}_{\bar{\rho}})(t)\}\,dt \\
&\quad = \iint_{Q(0,T-\rho)}\Bigg\{\sum_{i=1}^n\Bigg(\sum_{j=1}^n a_{ij}\phi_{x_j} + a_i\phi + F_i\Bigg)_\rho \hat{\eta}_{x_i} \\
&\qquad + \Bigg(\sum_{i=1}^n b_i\phi_{x_i} + c\phi + f\Bigg)_\rho \hat{\eta}\Bigg\}\,dx\,dt + \iint_{\Gamma(0,T-\rho)}(\sigma\phi - \Psi)_\rho\hat{\eta}\,ds\,dt.
\end{aligned} \tag{4.57}$$

From equalities (4.55)–(4.57) we obtain

$$\iint_{Q(0,T-\rho)} \phi_{\rho t}\hat{\eta}\, dx\, dt + \iint_{Q(0,T-\rho)} \left\{ \sum_{i=1}^{n} \left(\sum_{j=1}^{n} a_{ij}\phi_{x_j} + a_i\phi + F_i \right)_\rho \hat{\eta}_{x_i} + \left(\sum_{i=1}^{n} b_i\phi_{x_i} + c\phi + f \right)_\rho \hat{\eta} \right\} dx\, dt + \iint_{\Gamma(0,T-\rho)} (\sigma\phi - \Psi)_\rho \hat{\eta}\, ds\, dt = 0. \tag{4.58}$$

Step 2 Let $\eta \in V_2^{1,0}(Q(-\rho, T))$. With $t_1 \in (0, T-\rho)$, let us construct a sequence of functions $\{\eta_{m,k}\}$ from η according to formula (4.45). Then by virtue of property (i) of the functions $\eta_{m,k}$, it is clear from equality (4.58) that

$$\iint_{Q(0,t_1)} \left\{ \phi_{\rho t}\eta_{m,k} + \sum_{i=1}^{n} \left(\sum_{j=1}^{n} a_{ij}\phi_{x_j} + a_i\phi + F_i \right)_\rho (\eta_{m,k})_{x_i} + \left(\sum_{i=1}^{n} b_i\phi_{x_i} + c\phi + f \right)_\rho \eta_{m,k} \right\} dx\, dt + \iint_{\Gamma(0,t_1)} (\sigma\phi - \Psi)_\rho \eta_{m,k}\, ds\, dt = 0, \tag{4.59}$$

for any positive integers m and k. Thus from relation (4.48) and properties (4.49), it can be easily verified that equality (4.59), in the limit with respect to m, k (independent of order), reduces to

$$\iint_{Q(0,t_1)} \left\{ \phi_{\rho t}\eta + \sum_{i=1}^{n} \left[\sum_{j=1}^{n} a_{ij}\phi_{x_j} + a_i\phi + F_i \right]_\rho \eta_{x_i} + \left(\sum_{i=1}^{n} b_i\phi_{x_i} + c\phi + f \right)_\rho \eta \right\} dx\, dt + \iint_{\Gamma(0,t_1)} (\sigma\phi - \psi)_\rho \eta\, ds\, dt = 0. \tag{4.60}$$

Since ϕ_ρ, $\rho > 0$, is always in $V_2^{1,0}(Q)$, Eq. (4.60) is, in particular, true for $\eta = \phi_\rho$, that is,

$$\iint_{Q(0,t_1)} \left\{ \phi_{\rho t}\phi_\rho + \sum_{i=1}^{n} \left[\sum_{j=1}^{n} a_{ij}\phi_{x_j} + a_i\phi + F_i \right]_\rho (\phi_\rho)_{x_i} + \left(\sum_{i=1}^{n} b_i\phi_{x_i} + c\phi + f \right)_\rho \phi_\rho \right\} dx\, dt + \iint_{\Gamma(0,t_1)} (\sigma\phi - \Psi)_\rho \phi_\rho\, ds\, dt = 0. \tag{4.61}$$

Step 3 Since ϕ is in $V_2^{1,0}(Q)$, it depends continuously on t strongly in $L_2(\Omega)$. Thus we have

$$\lim_{\rho \to 0} \|\phi_\rho(\cdot, t)\|_{2,\Omega}^2 = \|\phi(\cdot, t)\|_{2,\Omega}^2,$$

for all $t \in [0, T]$. Hence, it follows from the first term of equality (4.61) that

$$\lim_{\rho \to 0} \iint_{Q(0,t_1)} \phi_{\rho t}\phi_\rho\, dx\, dt = \tfrac{1}{2}\|\phi(\cdot, t)\|_{2,\Omega}^2 \Big|_{t=0}^{t=t_1}. \tag{4.62}$$

For the remaining terms of equality (4.61) we can verify from Remark 4.1 the hypothesis that $\phi \in V_2^{1,0}(Q)$, Lemma 3.1, and Remark 4.2 that

$$\lim_{\rho \to 0} \left[\iint_{Q(0,t_1)} \left\{ \sum_{i=1}^{n} \left(\sum_{j=1}^{n} a_{ij}\phi_{x_j} + a_i\phi + F_i \right)_\rho (\phi_\rho)_{x_i} + \left(\sum_{i=1}^{n} b_i\phi_{x_i} + c\phi + f \right)_\rho \phi_\rho \right\} dx\, dt + \iint_{\Gamma(0,t_1)} (\sigma\phi - \Psi)_\rho \phi_\rho \, ds\, dt \right]$$

$$= \iint_{Q(0,t_1)} \left\{ \sum_{i=1}^{n} \left(\sum_{j=1}^{n} a_{ij}\phi_{x_j} + a_i\phi + F_i \right) \phi_{x_i} + \left(\sum_{i=1}^{n} b_i\phi_{x_i} + c\phi + f \right) \phi \right\} dx\, dt + \iint_{\Gamma(0,t_1)} (\sigma\phi - \Psi)\phi \, ds\, dt, \tag{4.63}$$

for any $t_1 \leq T - \delta$, where δ, $0 < \delta < T$, is arbitrary.

Using (4.61) and combining (4.62) and (4.63), we obtain

$$\tfrac{1}{2}\|\phi(\cdot, t)\|_{2,\Omega}^2 \Big|_{t=0}^{t=t_1} + \int_0^{t_1} \{\mathscr{L}_1(\phi, \phi)(t) + \mathscr{L}_2(\phi, \phi)(t) + \mathscr{L}_3(\hat{f}, \phi)(t)\}\, dt = 0, \tag{4.64}$$

for all $t_1 \leq T - \delta$. Thus by virtue of Remark 4.3 the proof is complete. ■

For the first boundary-value problem [(2.1), (2.2), and (2.3)], we have the following.

LEMMA 4.4. *Consider the first boundary-value problem* [(2.1), (2.2), *and* (2.3)]. *If ϕ is a weak solution from the space $V_2^{1,0}(Q)$, then it satisfies:*

$$\tfrac{1}{2}\|\phi(\cdot, t)\|_{2,\Omega}^2 \Big|_{t=0}^{t=t_1} + \int_0^{t_1} \{\mathscr{L}_1(\phi, \phi)(t) + \mathscr{L}_3(\hat{f}, \phi)(t)\}\, dt = 0, \tag{4.65}$$

for all $t_1 \in [0, T]$.

The proof of Lemma 4.3 carries over almost word for word to the proof of the present lemma. The only major modification is to replace the space $V_2^{1,0}(Q)$ by the space $\overset{\circ}{V}{}_2^{1,0}(Q)$. The reason for this modification is because of boundary condition (2.3).

From Lemmas 4.3 and 4.1 we obtain the following.

THEOREM 4.1. *Consider the second boundary-value problem* [(2.1), (2.2), *and* (2.4)]. *If ϕ is a weak solution from the space $V_2^{1,0}(Q)$, then it satisfies:*

$$\|\phi\|_Q \leq K_1\{\|\phi_0\|_{2,\Omega} + \|F\|_{2,Q} + \|f\|_{q_2,r_2,Q} + \|\Psi\|_{q_4,r_4,\Gamma}\}, \tag{4.66}$$

where the constant K_1 *depends only on* n, α_l, M_1, q_k, *and* r_k, $k = 2, 4$; *and* q_k *and* r_k, $k = 2, 4$, *are subject to restrictions* (2.12) *and* (2.14), *respectively.*

For the first boundary-value problem it follows from Lemmas 4.4 and 4.2 that we have the following theorem.

THEOREM 4.2. *Consider the first boundary-value problem* [(2.1), (2.2), *and* (2.3)]. *If* ϕ *is a weak solution from the space* $V_2^{1,0}(Q)$, *then it satisfies*

$$\|\phi\|_Q \leq K_2\{\|\phi_0\|_{2,\Omega} + \|F\|_{2,Q} + \|f\|_{q_2,r_2,Q}\}, \tag{4.67}$$

where the constant K_2 *depends only on* n, α_l, M_1, q_2, *and* r_2; *and* q_2 *and* r_2 *are subject to restrictions* (2.12).

REMARK 4.4. Consider the second boundary-value problem with f and Ψ replaced by $\sum_{i=1}^{n_2} f_i$ and $\sum_{i=1}^{n_4} \Psi_i$, respectively. Suppose that

$$\|f_i\|_{q_{2,i},r_{2,i},Q} \leq M_{2,i}, \qquad i = 1, \ldots, n_2, \tag{4.68}$$

and

$$\|\Psi_i\|_{q_{4,i},r_{4,i},\Gamma} \leq M_{4,i}, \qquad i = 1, \ldots, n_4, \tag{4.69}$$

where $M_{2,i} \equiv M_{2,i}(q_{2,i}, r_{2,i})$, $i = 1, \ldots, n_2$, and $M_{4,i} \equiv M_{4,i}(q_{4,i}, r_{4,i})$, $i = 1, \ldots, n_4$; and $\{q_{2,i}, r_{2,i}\}$, $i = 1, \ldots, n_2$, and $\{q_{4,i}, r_{4,i}\}$, $i = 1, \ldots, n_4$, are subject to restrictions (2.12) and (2.14), respectively. Then by following arguments similar to those given for Lemmas 4.1 and 4.3 and Theorem 4.1, we observe that the corresponding conclusions are valid. However, the terms $\|f\|_{q_2,r_2,Q}$ and $\|\Psi\|_{q_4,r_4,\Gamma}$ in Lemma 4.1 and Theorem 4.1 are to be replaced by

$$\sum_{i=1}^{n_2} \|f_i\|_{q_{2,i},r_{2,i},Q}, \qquad \text{and} \qquad \sum_{i=1}^{n_4} \|\Psi_i\|_{q_{4,i},r_{4,i},\Gamma},$$

respectively.

REMARK 4.5. Similar to Remark 4.4 the corresponding conclusions of Lemmas 4.2 and 4.4 and Theorem 4.2 are valid for the first boundary-value problem with f replaced by $\sum_{i=1}^{n_2} f_i$, where f_i, $i = 1, \ldots, n_2$, are assumed to satisfy inequalities (4.68). However, in the present situation, only the term $\|f\|_{q_2,r_2,Q}$ is to be replaced by

$$\sum_{i=1}^{n_2} \|f_i\|_{q_{2,i},r_{2,i},Q},$$

because the first boundary-value problem does not involve Ψ and hence $\sum_{i=1}^{n_4} \Psi_i$.

II.5. Existence and Uniqueness of Solutions

In this section our aim is to prove that the second (resp. first) boundary-value problem has a unique weak solution from the space $V_2^{1,0}(Q)$. Let us first of all show that any weak solution from the space $V_2(Q)$ of the second (resp. first) boundary-value problem is in $V_2^{1,0}(Q)$ (resp. $\mathring{V}_2^{1,0}(Q)$). More precisely, for the second boundary-value problem, we have the following theorem.

THEOREM 5.1. *Consider the second boundary-value problem* [(2.1), (2.2), *and* (2.4)]. *If* ϕ *is a weak solution from the space* $V_2(Q)$, *then* $\phi \in V_2^{1,0}(Q)$.

Proof. We break the proof up into a series of steps.

Step 1 Since, by hypothesis, ϕ is a weak solution from the space $V_2(Q)$, we have

$$-\iint_Q \phi\eta_t \, dx\, dt + \int_0^T \{\mathscr{L}_1(\phi, \eta)(t) + \mathscr{L}_2(\phi, \eta)(t) + \mathscr{L}_3(\hat{f}, \eta)(t)\}\, dt$$
$$= \int_\Omega \phi_0(x)\eta(x, 0)\, dx, \tag{5.1}$$

for any $\eta \in \tilde{W}_2^{1,1}(Q)$. Define

$$G_i = \sum_{j=1}^n a_{ij}\phi_{x_j} + a_i\phi + F_i, \qquad i = 1, \ldots, n, \tag{5.2}$$

$$g = \sum_{i=1}^n b_i\phi_{x_i} + c\phi, \tag{5.3}$$

and

$$h = \sigma\phi. \tag{5.4}$$

In view of Lemma 3.1 we see that $G_i \in L_2(Q)$, $i = 1, \ldots, n$, $g \in L_{\lambda_1, \mu_1}(Q)$, and $h \in L_{\lambda_3, \mu_3}(\Gamma)$, where λ_k, μ_k, $k = 1, 3$, are defined in Remark 2.1.

Using (5.2)–(5.4), equality (5.1) can be written as

$$\iint_Q \phi\eta_t\, dx\, dt + \int_\Omega \phi_0(x)\eta(x, 0)\, dx = \iint_Q \left\{\sum_{i=1}^n G_i\eta_{x_i} + (g + f)\eta\right\} dx\, dt$$
$$+ \iint_\Gamma (h - \Psi)\eta\, ds\, dt. \tag{5.5}$$

Step 2 Let $\phi^*(x, t)$ be defined on $Q(-\infty, \infty)$ by

$$\phi^*(x, t) = \begin{cases} \phi(x, t), & (x, t) \in Q[0, T], \\ \phi(x, -t), & (x, t) \in Q[-T, 0], \\ 0, & |t| > T. \end{cases} \tag{5.6}$$

The functions G_i^*, $i = 1, \ldots, n$, g^*, f^*, h^*, and Ψ^* are defined similarly. From the definitions of these functions it follows that the corresponding version of equality (5.5) is

$$\iint_{Q(-\infty,\infty)} \phi^* \eta_t \, dx \, dt = \iint_{Q(-\infty,\infty)} \left\{ \sum_{i=1}^{n} G_i^* \eta_{x_i} + (g^* + f^*)\eta \right\} dx \, dt + \iint_{\Gamma(-\infty,\infty)} (h^* - \Psi^*)\eta \, ds \, dt, \tag{5.7}$$

where η is any element in $W_2^{1,1}(Q(-\infty, \infty))$ that is equal to zero for $|t| > T$.

Let w be an element in $C^1((-\infty, \infty))$ such that the following properties are satisfied:

(i) w is an even function;

(ii) $w(t) = 1$ for all $t \in [-T + \delta, T - \delta]$, where δ is some positive number; and

(iii) $w(t) = 0$ for all $|t| \geq T$.

Let $\hat{\eta} \in W_2^{1,1}(Q(-\infty, \infty))$. Then we consider the function

$$\eta(x, t) \equiv w(t)\hat{\eta}(x, t).$$

With such a η, equality (5.7) takes the form

$$\iint_{Q(-\infty,\infty)} \phi^* w \hat{\eta}_t \, dx \, dt = \iint_{Q(-\infty,\infty)} \left\{ \sum_{i=1}^{n} G_i^* w \hat{\eta}_{x_i} + (g^* w + f^* w - \phi^* w_t)\hat{\eta} \right\} dx \, dt + \iint_{\Gamma(-\infty,\infty)} (h^* - \Psi^*) w \hat{\eta} \, ds \, dt.$$

Now, let $\tilde{\phi}^* \equiv \phi^* w$ and let $\tilde{G}_i^*$, $i = 1, \ldots, n$, $\tilde{g}^*$, $\tilde{f}^*$, $\tilde{h}^*$, and $\tilde{\Psi}^*$ be defined similarly. Then the preceding equality is reduced to

$$\iint_{Q(-\infty,\infty)} \tilde{\phi}^* \hat{\eta}_t \, dx \, dt = \iint_{Q(-\infty,\infty)} \left\{ \sum_{i=1}^{n} \tilde{G}^* \hat{\eta}_{x_i} + (\tilde{g}^* + \tilde{f}^* - \phi^* w_t)\hat{\eta} \right\} dx \, dt + \iint_{\Gamma(-\infty,\infty)} (\tilde{h}^* - \tilde{\Psi}^*)\hat{\eta} \, ds \, dt. \tag{5.8}$$

Step 3 Let $\bar{\eta} \in V_2^{1,0}(Q(-\infty, \infty))$ and $\bar{\eta}_{\bar{\rho}}$ be as defined by (4.38). Then it is clear that $\bar{\eta}_{\bar{\rho}} \in W_2^{1,1}(Q(-\infty, \infty))$ and hence $\bar{\eta}_{\bar{\rho}}$ can be used as $\hat{\eta}$ in equality (5.8). Replacing $\hat{\eta}$ in (5.8) by $\bar{\eta}_{\bar{\rho}}$ and applying relation (4.39) and Remark 4.1, we obtain

$$\iint_{Q(-\infty,\infty)} \tilde{\phi}^* \bar{\eta}_{t\bar{\rho}}\, dx\, dt$$
$$= \iint_{Q(-\infty,\infty)} \left\{ \sum_{i=1}^n \tilde{G}_i^* (\bar{\eta}_{x_i})_{\bar{\rho}} + (\tilde{g}^* + \tilde{f}^* - \phi^* w_t) \bar{\eta}_{\bar{\rho}} \right\} dx\, dt$$
$$+ \iint_{\Gamma(-\infty,\infty)} (\tilde{h}^* - \tilde{\Psi}^*) \bar{\eta}_{\bar{\rho}}\, ds\, dt. \tag{5.9}$$

Using relation (4.42), equality (5.9) becomes

$$\iint_{Q(-\infty,\infty)} (\tilde{\phi}^*)_\rho \bar{\eta}_t\, dx\, dt$$
$$= \iint_{Q(-\infty,\infty)} \left\{ \sum_{i=1}^n (\tilde{G}_i^*)_\rho \bar{\eta}_{x_i} + (\tilde{g}^* + \tilde{f}^* - \phi^* w_t)_\rho \bar{\eta} \right\} dx\, dt$$
$$+ \iint_{\Gamma(-\infty,\infty)} (\tilde{h}^* - \tilde{\Psi}^*)_\rho \bar{\eta}\, ds\, dt. \tag{5.10}$$

Step 4 Let $\alpha \in W_2^1(\Omega)$ (for definition, see Section I.4.2) and $\beta \in C_0^1((-\infty, \infty))$. Consider the function

$$\bar{\eta}(x, t) \equiv \alpha(x)\beta(t).$$

Then $\bar{\eta} \in V_2^{1,0}(Q(-\infty, \infty))$, so by substituting such an $\bar{\eta}$ into equality (5.10), we obtain

$$\int_{-\infty}^{\infty} \beta_t(t) \left[\int_\Omega (\tilde{\phi}^*)_\rho(x, t) \alpha(x)\, dx \right] dt$$
$$= \int_{-\infty}^{\infty} \beta(t) \left\{ \int_\Omega \left[\sum_{i=1}^n (\tilde{G}_i^*)_\rho(x, t) \alpha_{x_i}(x) + [\tilde{g}^*(x, t) + \tilde{f}^*(x, t) \right.\right.$$
$$\left. - \phi^*(x, t) w_t(t)]_\rho \alpha(x) \right] dx$$
$$\left. + \int_{\partial\Omega} [\tilde{h}^*(s, t) - \tilde{\Psi}^*(s, t)]_\rho \alpha(s)\, ds \right\} dt. \tag{5.11}$$

Thus from the definition of the generalized derivative (d/dt) we have

$$-(d/dt)\int_{\Omega}(\tilde{\phi}^*)_\rho(x,t)\alpha(x)\,dx$$
$$=\int_{\Omega}\left[\sum_{i=1}^{n}(\tilde{G}_i^*)_\rho(x,t)\alpha_{x_i}(x)+(\tilde{g}^*(x,t)+\tilde{f}^*(x,t)-\phi^*(x,t)w_t(t))_\rho\alpha(x)\right]dx$$
$$+\int_{\partial\Omega}(\tilde{h}^*(s,t)-\tilde{\Psi}^*(s,t))_\rho\alpha(s)\,ds, \tag{5.12}$$

for almost all t.

Define

$$C((-\infty,\infty),L_2(\Omega))\equiv\{u:\|u(\cdot,t)\|_{2,\Omega}\text{ is continuous in }t\in(-\infty,\infty)\}.$$

Then we note that, for each $\rho>0$, $(\tilde{\phi}^*)_\rho\in C((-\infty,\infty),L_2(\Omega))$. Furthermore, the generalized derivative $(\tilde{\phi}^*)_{\rho t}$, of $(\tilde{\phi}^*)_\rho$, is in $L_2(Q(-\infty,\infty))$. Thus the function $\int_\Omega(\tilde{\phi}^*)_\rho(x,\cdot)\alpha(x)\,dx$ is continuous in t and satisfies

$$(d/dt)\int_{\Omega}(\tilde{\phi}^*)_\rho(x,t)\alpha(x)\,dx=\int_{\Omega}(\tilde{\phi}^*)_{\rho t}(x,t)\alpha(x)\,dx, \tag{5.13}$$

for almost all t.

Combining equalities (5.12) and (5.13) we obtain

$$-\int_{\Omega}(\tilde{\phi}^*)_{\rho t}(x,t)\alpha(x)\,dx$$
$$=\int_{\Omega}\left\{\sum_{i=1}^{n}(\tilde{G}_i^*)_\rho(x,t)\alpha_{x_i}(x)+(\tilde{g}^*(x,t)+\tilde{f}^*(x,t)-\phi^*(x,t)w_t(t))_\rho\alpha(x)\right\}dx$$
$$+\int_{\partial\Omega}(\tilde{h}^*(s,t)-\tilde{\Psi}^*(s,t))_\rho\alpha(s)\,ds,$$

for almost all t. Therefore, for any pair of ρ_1,ρ_2 we have

$$\int_{\Omega}[(\tilde{\phi}^*)_{\rho_1 t}(x,t)-(\tilde{\phi}^*)_{\rho_2 t}(x,t)]\alpha(x)\,dx$$
$$=\int_{\Omega}\Bigg\{\sum_{i=1}^{n}[(\tilde{G}_i^*)_{\rho_2}(x,t)-(\tilde{G}_i^*)_{\rho_1}(x,t)]\alpha_{x_i}(x)$$
$$+[((\tilde{g}^*)_{\rho_2}(x,t)-(\tilde{g}^*)_{\rho_1}(x,t))+((\tilde{f}^*)_{\rho_2}(x,t)-(\tilde{f}^*)_{\rho_1}(x,t))$$
$$-((\phi^*w_t)_{\rho_2}(x,t)-(\phi^*w_t)_{\rho_1}(x,t))]\alpha(x)\Bigg\}dx$$
$$+\int_{\partial\Omega}[((\tilde{h}^*)_{\rho_2}(s,t)-(\tilde{h}^*)_{\rho_1}(s,t))-((\tilde{\Psi}^*)_{\rho_2}(s,t)-(\tilde{\Psi}^*)_{\rho_1}(s,t))]\alpha(s)\,ds, \tag{5.14}$$

for almost all t.

Since, for any $\rho_1, \rho_2 > 0$, $((\tilde{\phi}^*)_{\rho_1} - (\tilde{\phi}^*)_{\rho_2}) \in W_2^{1,1}(Q(-\infty, \infty))$, it follows readily that, for each $t \in (-\infty, \infty)$, $((\tilde{\phi}^*)_{\rho_1}(\cdot, t) - (\tilde{\phi}^*)_{\rho_2}(\cdot, t)) \in W_2^1(\Omega)$. Thus by substituting $(\tilde{\phi}^*)_{\rho_1} - (\tilde{\phi}^*)_{\rho_2}$ for α in equality (5.14) and then using Remark 4.1, we deduce that

$$\begin{aligned}
&\int_\Omega [(\tilde{\phi}^*)_{\rho_1 t}(x,t) - (\tilde{\phi}^*)_{\rho_2 t}(x,t)][(\tilde{\phi}^*)_{\rho_1}(x,t) - (\tilde{\phi}^*)_{\rho_2}(x,t)]\,dx \\
&\quad = \int_\Omega \Big\{ \sum_{i=1}^n [(\tilde{G}_i^*)_{\rho_2}(x,t) - (\tilde{G}_i^*)_{\rho_1}(x,t)][(\tilde{\phi}_{x_i}^*)_{\rho_1}(x,t) - (\tilde{\phi}_{x_i}^*)_{\rho_2}(x,t)] \\
&\qquad + [((\tilde{g}^*)_{\rho_2}(x,t) - (\tilde{g}^*)_{\rho_1}(x,t)) + ((\tilde{f}^*)_{\rho_2}(x,t) - (\tilde{f}^*)_{\rho_1}(x,t)) \\
&\qquad - ((\phi^* w_t)_{\rho_2}(x,t) - (\phi^* w_t)_{\rho_1}(x,t))][(\tilde{\phi}^*)_{\rho_1}(x,t) - (\tilde{\phi}^*)_{\rho_2}(x,t)] \Big\}\,dx \\
&\quad + \int_{\partial\Omega} \Big\{ [(\tilde{h}^*)_{\rho_2}(s,t) - (\tilde{h}^*)_{\rho_1}(s,t)] - [(\tilde{\Psi}^*)_{\rho_2}(s,t) - (\tilde{\Psi}^*)_{\rho_1}(s,t)] \Big\} \\
&\quad \times [(\tilde{\phi}^*)_{\rho_1}(s,t) - (\tilde{\phi}^*)_{\rho_2}(s,t)]\,ds, \qquad (5.15)
\end{aligned}$$

for almost all t. Denote the right-hand side of equality (5.15) by

$$H_{\rho_1,\rho_2}(t).$$

The left-hand side of equality (5.15) is just

$$\tfrac{1}{2}(d/dt)\|(\tilde{\phi}^*)_{\rho_1}(\cdot,t) - (\tilde{\phi}^*)_{\rho_2}(\cdot,t)\|_{2,\Omega}^2,$$

for almost all t, so we have

$$\tfrac{1}{2}(d/dt)\|(\tilde{\phi}^*)_{\rho_1}(\cdot,t) - (\tilde{\phi}^*)_{\rho_2}(\cdot,t)\|_{2,\Omega}^2 = H_{\rho_1,\rho_2}(t), \qquad (5.16)$$

for almost all t. Therefore, by integrating equality (5.16) over any interval (t_1, t_2), it follows that

$$\tfrac{1}{2}\|(\tilde{\phi}^*)_{\rho_1}(\cdot,t) - (\tilde{\phi}^*)_{\rho_2}(\cdot,t)\|_{2,\Omega}^2 \Big|_{t=t_1}^{t=t_2} = \int_{t_1}^{t_2} H_{\rho_1,\rho_2}(t)\,dt,$$

for all t_1 and t_2. Setting $t_1 = -\infty$ and t_2 arbitrary, we obtain, in particular, that

$$\tfrac{1}{2}\|(\tilde{\phi}^*)_{\rho_1}(\cdot,t_2) - (\tilde{\phi}^*)_{\rho_2}(\cdot,t_2)\|_{2,\Omega}^2 = \int_{-\infty}^{t_2} H_{\rho_1,\rho_2}(t)\,dt. \qquad (5.17)$$

Step 5 Since ϕ^* is an even function that is equal to zero for $|t| > T$ and since $w \in C^1((-\infty, \infty))$, it follows from Theorem I.4.5 that

$$\|\phi^* w_t\|_{\lambda_1,\mu_1,Q(-\infty,\infty)} \leq N|\phi|_Q,$$

where λ_1, μ_1 are defined in Remark 2.1 and $N \equiv 2^{1/\mu_1}M\beta_2$ with $M \equiv \sup_{-T\le t\le T}|w_t(t)|$ and β_2 as defined in Theorem I.4.5. Thus

$$(\phi^* w_t)_\rho \xrightarrow{s} \phi^* w_t \tag{5.18}$$

in $L_{\lambda_1,\mu_1}(Q(-\infty, \infty))$ as $\rho \to 0$.

Next, we note that $\tilde{\phi}^*, \tilde{G}_i^*, i = 1, \ldots, n, \tilde{g}^*, \tilde{f}^*, \tilde{h}^*$, and $\tilde{\Psi}^*$ are even functions of t that are equal to zero for $|t| > T$ and that $\tilde{\phi}^* \in W_2^{1,1}(Q(-\infty, \infty))$. Thus by virtue of Lemma 3.1, Theorem I.4.5, relation (5.18), and Theorem I.4.8, we can readily verify that

$$\begin{aligned}
&\sum_{i=1}^{n} \|(\tilde{G}_i^*)_{\rho_2} - (\tilde{G}_i^*)_{\rho_1}\|_{2,Q(-\infty,\infty)}\|(\tilde{\phi}_x^*)_{\rho_1} - (\tilde{\phi}_x^*)_{\rho_2}\|_{2,Q(-\infty,\infty)} \\
&\quad + \|(\tilde{g}^*)_{\rho_2} - (\tilde{g}^*)_{\rho_1}\|_{q_1,r_1,Q(-\infty,\infty)}\|(\tilde{\phi}^*)_{\rho_1} - (\tilde{\phi}^*)_{\rho_2}\|_{\lambda_1,\mu_1,Q(-\infty,\infty)} \\
&\quad + \|(\tilde{f}^*)_{\rho_2} - (\tilde{f}^*)_{\rho_1}\|_{q_2,r_2,Q(-\infty,\infty)}\|(\tilde{\phi}^*)_{\rho_1} - (\tilde{\phi}^*)_{\rho_2}\|_{\bar{q}_2,\bar{r}_2,Q(-\infty,\infty)} \\
&\quad + \|(\phi^* w_t)_{\rho_2} - (\phi^* w_t)_{\rho_1}\|_{\lambda_1,\mu_1,Q(-\infty,\infty)}\|(\tilde{\phi}^*)_{\rho_1} - (\tilde{\phi}^*)_{\rho_2}\|_{q_1,r_1,Q(-\infty,\infty)} \\
&\quad + \|(\tilde{h}^*)_{\rho_2} - (\tilde{h}^*)_{\rho_1}\|_{q_3,r_3,\Gamma(-\infty,\infty)}\|(\tilde{\phi}^*)_{\rho_1} - (\tilde{\phi}^*)_{\rho_2}\|_{\lambda_3,\mu_3,\Gamma(-\infty,\infty)} \\
&\quad + \|(\tilde{\Psi}^*)_{\rho_2} - (\tilde{\Psi}^*)_{\rho_1}\|_{q_4,r_4,\Gamma(-\infty,\infty)}\|(\tilde{\phi}^*)_{\rho_1} - (\tilde{\phi}^*)_{\rho_2}\|_{\bar{q}_4,\bar{r}_4,\Gamma(-\infty,\infty)} \\
&\quad \to 0,
\end{aligned} \tag{5.19}$$

as $\rho_1, \rho_2 \downarrow 0$, where

$$\|(\tilde{\phi}_x^*)_{\rho_1} - (\tilde{\phi}_x^*)_{\rho_2}\|_{2,Q(-\infty,\infty)} \equiv \left\| \left\{ \sum_{i=1}^{n} [(\tilde{\phi}_{x_i}^*)_{\rho_1} - (\tilde{\phi}_{x_i}^*)_{\rho_2}]^2 \right\}^{1/2} \right\|_{2,Q(-\infty,\infty)},$$

$\lambda_k, \mu_k, k = 1, 3$, are defined in Remark 2.1 and $\bar{q}_k, \bar{r}_k, k = 2, 4$, are defined in Remark 2.2.

By writing out the right-hand side of equality (5.17) explicitly and then applying Hölder's inequality to all the integrals involved, it follows from (5.19) that

$$\|(\tilde{\phi}^*)_{\rho_1}(\cdot, t) - (\tilde{\phi}^*)_{\rho_2}(\cdot, t)\|_{2,\Omega} \to 0,$$

as $\rho_1, \rho_2 \downarrow 0$ uniformly with respect to $t \in (-\infty, \infty)$. Thus $\{(\tilde{\phi}^*)_\rho\}$ is a Cauchy sequence in $L_2(\Omega)$ uniformly with respect to $t \in (-\infty, \infty)$. This, in turn, implies that $(\tilde{\phi}^*)_\rho$ converges strongly in $L_2(\Omega)$ uniformly with respect to $t \in (-\infty, \infty)$. On this basis, it is clear that the limit function $\tilde{\phi}^*$, ($\tilde{\phi}^*(x, t) \equiv \phi^*(x, t)w(t)$), is equivalent in $Q(-\infty, \infty)$ to an element in $C((-\infty, \infty), L_2(\Omega))$. Thus from the definitions of the functions ϕ^* and w, it follows that $\phi \in V_2^{1,0}(Q(0, T - \delta))$, where δ, $0 < \delta < T$, is arbitrary. Therefore, by virtue of Remark 4.3, the proof is complete. ■

For the first boundary-value problem, we have the following.

THEOREM 5.2. *Consider the first boundary-value problem* [(2.1), (2.2), *and* (2.3)]. *If ϕ is a weak solution from the space $V_2(Q)$, then $\phi \in \mathring{V}_2^{1,0}(Q)$.*

The proof of this theorem is almost a word by word reproduction of that given for Theorem 5.1. The only major difference is the replacement of the space $V_2^{1,0}(Q)$ by the space $\overset{\circ}{V}{}_2^{1,0}(Q)$. This is owing to boundary condition (2.3) of the present problem.

To present a result on the existence of solutions from the space $V_2(Q)$ of the second (resp. first) boundary-value problem, we need some more preparation.

Let $\{\gamma^k\}$ be a bounded sequence of elements in $V_2(Q)$ (and hence in $W_2^{1,0}(Q)$) such that γ^k (resp. $(\gamma^k)_{x_i}$, $i = 1, \ldots, n$) converges to γ (resp. γ_{x_i}, $i = 1, \ldots, n$) weakly in $L_2(Q)$, as $k \to \infty$. If $\zeta \in W_2^{1,1}(Q)$, then it is true that

$$\iint_Q \zeta_t \gamma^k \, dx\, dt \to \iint_Q \zeta_t \gamma \, dx\, dt, \tag{5.20}$$

as $k \to \infty$ [since $\zeta_t \in L_2(Q)$];

$$\sum_{i,j=1}^{n} \iint_Q a_{ij} \zeta_{x_j} (\gamma^k)_{x_i} \, dx\, dt \to \sum_{i,j=1}^{n} \iint_Q a_{ij} \zeta_{x_j} \gamma_{x_i} \, dx\, dt, \tag{5.21}$$

as $k \to \infty$ [because of Lemma 3.1(i)];

$$\sum_{i=1}^{n} \iint_Q a_i \zeta (\gamma^k)_{x_i} \, dx\, dt \to \sum_{i=1}^{n} \iint_Q a_i \zeta \gamma_{x_i} \, dx\, dt, \tag{5.22}$$

as $k \to \infty$ [because of Lemma 3.1(ii)]; and

$$\sum_{i=1}^{n} \iint_Q F_i (\gamma^k)_{x_i} \, dx\, dt \to \sum_{i=1}^{n} \iint_Q F_i \gamma_{x_i} \, dx\, dt, \tag{5.23}$$

as $k \to \infty$ [because of Lemma 3.1(v)].

Since $\{q_2, r_2\}$ and $\{q_4, r_4\}$ are subject to restrictions (2.12) and (2.14), respectively, we deduce from Theorems I.4.5 and I.4.8 that

$$\|\gamma^k\|_{\bar{q}_2, \bar{r}_2, Q} \le N_1 |\gamma^k|_Q,$$

and

$$\|\gamma^k\|_{\bar{q}_4, \bar{r}_4, \Gamma} \le N_2 |\gamma^k|_Q,$$

where the constants N_1 and N_2 are independent of the integers k; and $\bar{q}_l, \bar{r}_l$, $l = 2, 4$, are defined in Remark 2.2. Thus by using Lemma 3.1(vi) and Lemma 3.1(viii), respectively, it follows from Theorem I.4.14 that

$$\iint_Q f \gamma^k \, dx\, dt \to \iint_Q f \gamma \, dx\, dt, \tag{5.24}$$

as $k \to \infty$, and

$$\iint_{\Gamma} \Psi \gamma^k \, ds \, dt \to \iint_{\Gamma} \Psi \gamma \, ds \, dt, \tag{5.25}$$

as $k \to \infty$.

From Remark 2.1 and Theorem I.4.5, we obtain

$$\|\gamma^k\|_{\bar{\lambda}_1, \bar{\mu}_1, Q} \leq N_0 |\gamma^k|_Q,$$

where the constant N_0 is independent of integer k; and $\bar{\lambda}_1$, $\bar{\mu}_1$ are such that $(1/\lambda_1) + (1/\bar{\lambda}_1) = 1$ and $(1/\mu_1) + (1/\bar{\mu}_1) = 1$. Then by virtue of Lemma 3.1(iii) and (iv), it follows, respectively, from Theorem I.4.14 that

$$\iint_{Q} c\zeta\gamma^k \, dx \, dt \to \iint_{Q} c\zeta\gamma \, dx \, dt, \tag{5.26}$$

as $k \to \infty$; and

$$\sum_{i=1}^{n} \iint_{Q} b_i \zeta \gamma^k \, dx \, dt \to \sum_{i=1}^{n} \iint_{Q} b_i \zeta \gamma \, dx \, dt, \tag{5.27}$$

as $k \to \infty$.

Similarly, by virtue of Remark 2.1 and Theorem I.4.8, we have

$$\|\gamma^k\|_{\bar{\lambda}_4, \bar{\mu}_4, \Gamma} \leq N_3 |\gamma^k|_Q,$$

where the constant N_3 is independent of integer k; and $\bar{\lambda}_4$, $\bar{\mu}_4$ are such that $(1/\lambda_4) + (1/\bar{\lambda}_4) = 1$ and $(1/\mu_4) + (1/\bar{\mu}_4) = 1$. Thus it follows from Lemma 3.1(vii) and Theorem I.4.14 that

$$\iint_{\Gamma} \sigma\zeta\gamma^k \, ds \, dt \to \iint_{\Gamma} \sigma\zeta\gamma \, ds \, dt, \tag{5.28}$$

as $k \to \infty$.

REMARK 5.1. Suppose that $\zeta \in V_2(Q)$ and that $\{\gamma^k\}$ is a bounded sequence of elements in $W_2^{1,1}(Q)$ such that γ^k (resp. $(\gamma^k)_{x_i}$, $i = 1, \ldots, n$) converges to γ (resp. γ_{x_i}, $i = 1, \ldots, n$) weakly in $L_2(Q)$, as $k \to \infty$. Then by following exactly the same arguments as those given for relations (5.21)–(5.28), we can easily verify that the corresponding versions of these results are also valid.

THEOREM 5.3. *The second boundary-value problem* [(2.1), (2.2), *and* (2.4)] *admits a weak solution* ϕ *from the space* $V_2(Q)$.

Proof. The proof is by Galerkin method and is broken up into a series of steps.

Step 1 Let $\{v_k\}_{k=1}^{\infty}$ be a fundamental system in $W_2^1(\Omega)$. Suppose, in addition, $\{v_k\}_{k=1}^{\infty}$ is orthonormal in $L_2(\Omega)$. For each positive integer m we denote by V_m the finite dimensional subspace of $L_2(\Omega)$ spanned by the elements v_k, $k = 1, \ldots, m$. Then we seek a solution of the problem obtained from the problem [(2.1), (2.2), and (2.4)] by orthogonal projection onto this subspace. More precisely, we look for an element

$$\phi^m(x, t) \equiv \sum_{l=1}^{m} y_l^m(t) v_l(x) \tag{5.29}$$

in V_m, so that the following conditions are satisfied:

$$(d/dt)\langle \phi^m(\cdot, t), v_k \rangle_\Omega + \mathscr{L}_1(\phi^m, v_k)(t) + \mathscr{L}_2(\phi^m, v_k)(t) + \mathscr{L}_3(\hat{f}, v_k)(t) = 0; \tag{5.30}$$

and

$$\langle \phi^m(\cdot, 0), v_k \rangle_\Omega = \langle \phi_0, v_k \rangle_\Omega, \tag{5.31}$$

where $k = 1, \ldots, m$ and $\langle \cdot, \cdot \rangle_\Omega$ denotes the usual inner product in $L_2(\Omega)$.

Since the sequence $\{v_k\}$ is orthonormal in $L_2(\Omega)$, Eq. (5.30) is reduced to

$$\dot{y}_k^m(t) = \sum_{l=1}^{m} A_{kl}(t) y_l^m(t) + B_k(t), \qquad k = 1, \ldots, m, \tag{5.32}$$

where

$$\dot{y}_k^m(t) \equiv (d/dt) y_k^m(t),$$

$$A_{kl}(t) \equiv -\mathscr{L}_1(v_l, v_k)(t) - \mathscr{L}_2(v_l, v_k)(t),$$

and

$$B_k(t) \equiv -\mathscr{L}_3(\hat{f}, v_k)(t).$$

Similarly, conditions (5.31) can be written as

$$y_k^m(0) = \langle \phi_0, v_k \rangle_\Omega, \qquad k = 1, \ldots, m. \tag{5.33}$$

Thus by virtue of Bessel's inequality it follows that

$$\sum_{k=1}^{m} [y_k^m(0)]^2 \leq \|\phi_0\|_{2,\Omega}^2. \tag{5.34}$$

From Lemma 3.1 we can easily verify that the coefficients A_{kl} and B_k of the ordinary differential equation (5.32) are elements in $L_2((0, T))$. Thus for each positive integer m the problem involving the ordinary differential equation (5.32) and initial conditions (5.33) admits a unique solution y_k^m, and hence element ϕ^m is uniquely determined by Eq. (5.29). This gives rise to a sequence of elements $\{\phi^m\}$ in $W_2^{1,1}(Q)$.

According to the Galerkin method, the solution of the second boundary-value problem [(2.1), (2.2), and (2.4)] is approximated by the elements ϕ^m. To substantiate this, we must show that the sequence $\{\phi^m\}$ admits a subsequence, again indexed by m, which converges in some sense to ϕ. Thus we first need to show that the sequence $\{\phi^m\}$ satisfies certain a priori estimates uniformly with respect to m.

Step 2 Multiplying (5.30) by y_k^m and summing over k from 1 to m, and then integrating over $(0, \tau)$, we obtain, by using (5.29), the identity

$$\tfrac{1}{2}\|\phi^m(\cdot, t)\|_{2,\Omega}^2\Big|_{t=0}^{t=\tau} + \int_0^\tau \{\mathscr{L}_1(\phi^m, \phi^m)(t) + \mathscr{L}_2(\phi^m, \phi^m)(t) + \mathscr{L}_3(\hat{f}, \phi^m)(t)\}\, dt = 0. \tag{5.35}$$

Thus by virtue of Lemma 4.1 it follows that

$$|\phi^m|_Q \le K_1\{\|\phi^m(\cdot, 0)\|_{2,\Omega} + \|F\|_{2,Q} + \|f\|_{q_2, r_2, Q} + \|\Psi\|_{q_4, r_4, \Gamma}\}, \tag{5.36}$$

where the constant K_1 is independent of integers m.

From (5.29), we have

$$[\phi^m(x, 0)]^2 = \sum_{k,l=1}^{m} y_k^m(0) y_l^m(0) v_k(x) v_l(x).$$

Since $\{v_k\}$ is orthonormal in $L_2(\Omega)$, it follows that

$$\|\phi^m(\cdot, 0)\|_{2,\Omega}^2 = \sum_{k=1}^{m} [y_k^m(0)]^2. \tag{5.37}$$

Combining (5.37) and (5.34), we obtain

$$\|\phi^m(\cdot, 0)\|_{2,\Omega} \le \|\phi_0\|_{2,\Omega}. \tag{5.38}$$

Hence, inequality (5.36) is reduced to

$$|\phi^m|_Q \le \tilde{K}_1, \tag{5.39}$$

where the constant $\tilde{K}_1$ is independent of integers m. Thus it follows from Hölder's inequality that

$$\|\phi^m\|_{2,Q} \le T^{1/2}\|\phi^m\|_{2,\infty,Q} \le T^{1/2}\tilde{K}_1 \equiv \tilde{K}_2. \tag{5.40}$$

Step 3 From inequalities (5.39) and (5.40) it is clear that the sequence $\{\phi^m\}$ is a bounded subset in $W_2^{1,0}(Q)$. Since $W_2^{1,0}(Q)$ is a reflexive Banach space, every bounded subset of $W_2^{1,0}(Q)$ is weakly conditionally sequentially compact and so $\{\phi^m\}$ is weakly conditionally sequentially compact in

$W_2^{1,0}(Q)$. Thus there exists a subsequence of the sequence $\{\phi^m\}$, again indexed by m, and an element $\phi \in W_2^{1,0}(Q)$ such that

$$\phi^m \xrightarrow{w} \phi, \tag{5.41}$$

in $W_2^{1,0}(Q)$ as $m \to \infty$. Furthermore,

$$\phi^m \xrightarrow{w} \phi, \tag{5.42}$$

in $L_2(Q)$, as $m \to \infty$.

By inequalities (5.39) and (5.40) and relation (5.42), it follows from Theorem I.4.12 that $\phi \in L_{2,\infty}(Q)$. On this basis, we conclude from relation (5.41) that $\phi \in V_2(Q)$.

Step 4 To show that ϕ is a weak solution from the space $V_2(Q)$, it remains to verify that ϕ satisfies integral identity (2.5). For this, let ξ_k be arbitrary elements in $C^1([0, T])$ with $\xi_k(T) = 0$ for each k. With each positive integer $\overline{m} \le m$, we consider the element

$$\eta^{\overline{m}}(x, t) \equiv \sum_{k=1}^{\overline{m}} \xi_k(t) v_k(x). \tag{5.43}$$

Clearly, $\eta^{\overline{m}}$ depends on the choice of ξ_k. Let Ξ denote the class of all such $\eta^{\overline{m}}$. Then by virtue of Theorem I.4.7, we note that Ξ is dense in $\tilde{W}_2^{1,1}(Q)$.

Multiplying (5.30) by ξ_k, summing over k from 1 to $\overline{m}$, integrating the result over $(0, T)$, and then performing the integration by parts to the first term of the obtained equality, and using $\xi_k(T) = 0$ for each k, we obtain

$$\int_0^T \{-\langle \phi^m(\cdot, t), \eta_t^{\overline{m}}(\cdot, t)\rangle_\Omega + \mathscr{L}_1(\phi^m, \eta^{\overline{m}})(t) + \mathscr{L}_2(\phi^m, \eta^{\overline{m}})(t) + \mathscr{L}_3(\hat{f}, \eta^{\overline{m}})(t)\}\, dt$$
$$= \langle \phi^m(\cdot, 0), \eta^{\overline{m}}(\cdot, 0)\rangle_\Omega. \tag{5.44}$$

Note that, for each positive integer $\overline{m} \le m$, $\eta^{\overline{m}}$ is an element in $\tilde{W}_2^{1,1}(Q)$ and hence in $W_2^{1,1}(Q)$. Thus by replacing $\{\phi^m\}$ for $\{\gamma^k\}$ and $\eta^{\overline{m}}$ for ζ in relations (5.20)–(5.28), it follows that equality (5.44), in the limit as $m \to \infty$, is reduced to

$$\int_0^T \{-\langle \phi(\cdot, t), \eta_t^{\overline{m}}(\cdot, t)\rangle_\Omega + \mathscr{L}_1(\phi, \eta^{\overline{m}})(t) + \mathscr{L}_2(\phi, \eta^{\overline{m}})(t) + \mathscr{L}_3(\hat{f}, \eta^{\overline{m}})(t)\}\, dt$$
$$= \lim_{m\to\infty} \langle \phi^m(\cdot, 0), \eta^{\overline{m}}(\cdot, 0)\rangle_\Omega. \tag{5.45}$$

Recall that $\{v_k\}$ is a fundamental system in $W_2^1(\Omega)$, that $\{v_k\}_{k=1}^\infty$ is orthonormal in $L_2(\Omega)$, and that Parseval's equality holds for any element in $L_2(\Omega)$ and hence for ϕ_0. Thus by virtue of (5.33) and (5.34), we have

$$\sum_{k=1}^m [y_k^m(0)]^2 \to \|\phi_0\|_{2,\Omega}^2,$$

as $m \to \infty$. Then by equality (5.37) we deduce from this relation that

$$\phi^m(\cdot, 0) \xrightarrow{s} \phi_0,$$

in $L_2(\Omega)$, as $m \to \infty$. This, in turn, implies that

$$\langle \phi^m(\cdot, 0), \eta^{\bar{m}}(\cdot, 0)\rangle_\Omega \to \langle \phi_0, \eta^{\bar{m}}(\cdot, 0)\rangle_\Omega, \tag{5.46}$$

as $m \to \infty$.

Combining (5.45) and (5.46), we obtain

$$\int_0^T \{-\langle \phi(\cdot, t), \eta_t^{\bar{m}}(\cdot, t)\rangle_\Omega + \mathscr{L}_1(\phi, \eta^{\bar{m}})(t) + \mathscr{L}_2(\phi, \eta^{\bar{m}})(t) + \mathscr{L}_3(\hat{f}, \eta^{\bar{m}})(t)\}\, dt$$
$$= \langle \phi_0, \eta^{\bar{m}}(\cdot, 0)\rangle_\Omega. \tag{5.47}$$

To show that ϕ satisfies integral identity (2.5), we now let $\eta \in \tilde{W}_2^{1,1}(Q)$. Since Ξ is dense in $\tilde{W}_2^{1,1}(Q)$, there exists a sequence $\{\eta^{\bar{m}}\}$ of elements in Ξ such that

$$\eta^{\bar{m}} \xrightarrow{s} \eta,$$

in $W_2^{1,1}(Q)$, as $\bar{m} \to \infty$. Then it follows that

$$\eta_t^{\bar{m}} \xrightarrow{s} \eta_t,$$

in $L_2(Q)$, as $\bar{m} \to \infty$, and so

$$\iint_Q \phi \eta_t^{\bar{m}}\, dx\, dt \to \iint_Q \phi \eta_t\, dx\, dt \tag{5.48}$$

as $\bar{m} \to \infty$.

Choose such a sequence $\{\eta^{\bar{m}}\}$ in equality (5.47). Then by substituting $\{\eta^{\bar{m}}\}$ for $\{\gamma^k\}$ and ϕ for ζ in relations (5.21)–(5.28), it follows from Remark 5.1 that

$$\lim_{\bar{m}\to\infty} \int_0^T \{\mathscr{L}_1(\phi, \eta^{\bar{m}})(t) + \mathscr{L}_2(\phi, \eta^{\bar{m}})(t) + \mathscr{L}_3(\hat{f}, \eta^{\bar{m}})(t)\}\, dt$$
$$= \int_0^T \{\mathscr{L}_1(\phi, \eta)(t) + \mathscr{L}_2(\phi, \eta)(t) + \mathscr{L}_3(\hat{f}, \eta)(t)\}\, dt. \tag{5.49}$$

Using (5.48) and (5.49) it follows from (5.47) that, as $\bar{m} \to \infty$,

$$-\iint_Q \phi \eta_t\, dx\, dt + \int_0^T \{\mathscr{L}_1(\phi, \eta)(t) + \mathscr{L}_2(\phi, \eta)(t) + \mathscr{L}_3(\hat{f}, \eta)(t)\}\, dt$$
$$= \int_\Omega \phi_0(x)\eta(x, 0)\, dx, \tag{5.50}$$

which is just integral identity (2.5). Hence, ϕ is a weak solution from the space $V_2(Q)$.

This completes the proof. ■

For the first boundary-value problem, we have the following theorem.

THEOREM 5.4. *The first boundary-value problem* [(2.1), (2.2), *and* (2.3)] *admits a weak solution ϕ from the space $V_2(Q)$.*

Proof. The proof is similar to that given for Theorem 5.3. The major modifications are listed as follows:

(i) Because of the first boundary condition (2.3), sequence $\{v_k\}$ (in Step 1 of the proof) is to be chosen from $\mathring{W}_2^1(\Omega)$; not just from $W_2^1(\Omega)$.

(ii) Because of the absence of the second boundary condition (2.4), the term $\mathscr{L}_3(\phi, \eta)$ is to be dropped everywhere in the proof.

(iii) Again, because of the first boundary condition (2.3), we need to show (in Step 3 of the proof) that ϕ is in $\mathring{V}_2(Q)$, not just in $V_2(Q)$. Indeed, from (i), $\{v_k\}$ is a sequence of elements in $\mathring{W}_2^1(\Omega)$. Hence, $\{\phi^m\}$ is now a sequence of elements in $\mathring{W}_2^{1,0}(Q)$. Thus by exactly the same arguments, we can show that there exists a subsequence of the sequence $\{\phi^m\}$, again indexed by m, and an element ϕ in $W_2^{1,0}(Q)$ such that $\phi^m \xrightarrow{w} \phi$ in $W_2^{1,0}(Q) \cap L_2(Q)$, as $m \to \infty$. Furthermore, $\phi \in V_2(Q)$. Now, according to the Banach–Saks–Mazur theorem there exists a subsequence $\{\phi^{m(l)}\}$ of the sequence $\{\phi^m\}$ such that the average

$$\hat{\phi}^k \equiv \frac{1}{k} \sum_{l=1}^{k} \phi^{m(l)} \xrightarrow{s} \phi,$$

in $W_2^{1,0}(Q)$, as $k \to \infty$. Since $\{\phi^m\} \subset \mathring{W}_2^{1,0}(Q)$ and $\mathring{W}_2^{1,0}(Q)$ is complete, it follows that $\phi \in \mathring{W}_2^{1,0}(Q)$. Since ϕ is also an element in $V_2(Q)$, we conclude that $\phi \in \mathring{V}_2(Q)$.

This completes the proof. ■

We shall now show, in the next theorem, that the second boundary-value problem has a unique solution from the space $V_2^{1,0}(Q)$.

THEOREM 5.5. *The second boundary-value problem* [(2.1), (2.2), *and* (2.4)] *has a unique weak solution from the space $V_2^{1,0}(Q)$.*

Proof. From Theorems 5.3 and 5.1, we see that the second boundary-value problem [(2.1), (2.2), and (2.4)] has a weak solution ϕ from the space $V_2^{1,0}(Q)$.

It remains to prove the uniqueness. By contrary, we assume that $\tilde{\phi}$ were a distinct weak solution from the space $V_2^{1,0}(Q)$ for the given problem. Then it can be easily verified that the function

$$\Phi \equiv \phi - \tilde{\phi}$$

is a weak solution from the space $V_2^{1,0}(Q)$ of the problem [(2.1), (2.2), and (2.4) with $(F_i)_{x_i} = 0$, $i = 1, \ldots, n$, $f = 0$, $\phi_0 = 0$ and $\Psi = 0$. Thus by virtue of Theorem 4.1 it follows that $\|\Phi\|_Q = 0$. Hence $\Phi = 0$ and so $\phi = \tilde{\phi}$. The proof is complete. ■

For the first boundary-value problem [(2.1), (2.2), and (2.3)], we have this theorem.

THEOREM 5.6. *The first boundary-value problem* [(2.1), (2.2), *and* (2.3)] *has a unique weak solution from the space* $V_2^{1,0}(Q)$.

Proof. The proof is similar to that given for Theorem 5.5. The major differences are the replacement of Theorems 5.3, 5.1, and 4.1 by Theorems 5.4, 5.2, and 4.2, respectively. ■

REMARK 5.2. Following arguments similar to those given for Theorems 5.1 and 5.5, we observe that the corresponding conclusions are valid for the generalized version of the second boundary-value problem stated in Remark 4.4.

REMARK 5.3. Similar to Remark 5.2, the corresponding conclusions of Theorems 5.2 and 5.6 are valid for the generalized version of the first boundary-value problem stated in Remark 4.5.

II.6. A Continuity Property

For each positive integer m, let L^m be a linear second-order parabolic partial differential operator in cylinder Q, defined by

$$L^m\phi \equiv \phi_t - \sum_{i=1}^{n} \left\{ \left[\sum_{j=1}^{n} a_{ij}^m(x,t)\phi_{x_j} + a_i^m(x,t)\phi \right]_{x_i} + b_i^m(x,t)\phi_{x_i} \right\} - c^m(x,t)\phi.$$

For the corresponding second boundary-value problem we refer to the one that consists of the equation

$$L^m\phi = \sum_{i=1}^{n} [F_i^m]_{x_i}(x,t) - f^m(x,t) \tag{6.1}$$

in Q, the initial conditions

$$\phi|_{t=0} = \phi_0^m \tag{6.2}$$

in Ω, and the boundary condition

$$\left(\left[\frac{\partial \phi}{\partial \mathcal{N}} + \sigma^m(s,t)\phi \right] \right|_{\Gamma} = \Psi^m \tag{6.3}$$

in Γ.

Similarly, for the corresponding first boundary-value problem, we refer to the one that consists of Eq. (6.1), initial condition (6.2), and the boundary condition

$$\phi|_\Gamma = 0, \tag{6.4}$$

in Γ.

We now assume, and throughout this section, that a_{ij}^m, $i, j = 1, \ldots, n$; a_i^m, $i = 1, \ldots, n$; b_i^m, $i = 1, \ldots, n$; c^m; F_i^m, $i = 1, \ldots, n$; f^m; ϕ_0^m; σ^m; and Ψ^m satisfy the corresponding parts of assumptions (A.1)–(A.8), in Section II.2, uniformly with respect to m. Then the sequence of the second boundary-value problems [(6.1), (6.2), and (6.3)] generates a *unique* sequence of the weak solutions $\{\phi^m\}$ from the space $V_2^{1,0}(Q)$. Similarly, the sequence of the first boundary-value problems [(6.1), (6.2), and (6.4)] also generates a unique sequence of the weak solutions $\{\phi^m\}$ from the space $V_2^{1,0}(Q)$.

THEOREM 6.1. *Consider the sequence of the second boundary-value problems* [(6.1), (6.2), *and* (6.3)]. *Suppose that a_{ij}^m converge to a_{ij}, almost everywhere in Q, and that a_i^m, b_i^m, c^m, F_i^m, f^m, ϕ_0^m, σ^m, and Ψ^m converge, respectively, to a_i, b_i, c, F_i, f, ϕ_0, σ, and Ψ strongly in the spaces they belong. If these limit functions also satisfy the corresponding parts of assumptions* (A.1)–(A.8), *then*

$$\phi^m \xrightarrow{s} \phi,$$

in $V_2^{1,0}(Q)$, as $m \to \infty$, where ϕ is the weak solution from the space $V_2^{1,0}(Q)$ of the limit problem [(2.1), (2.2), *and* (2.4)].

Proof. Since, for each positive integer m, ϕ^m is the weak solution from the space $V_2^{1,0}(Q)$ of the second boundary-value problem [(6.1), (6.2), and (6.3)], we have

$$-\iint_Q \phi^m \eta_t \, dx\, dt + \int_0^T \{\mathscr{L}_1^m(\phi^m, \eta)(t) + \mathscr{L}_2^m(\phi^m, \eta)(t) + \mathscr{L}_3(\hat{f}^m, \eta)(t)\}\, dt$$
$$= \int_\Omega \phi_0^m(x)\eta(x, 0)\, dx, \tag{6.5}$$

for all $\eta \in \tilde{W}_2^{1,1}(Q)$, where

$$\mathscr{L}_1^m(\phi^m, \eta)(t) \equiv \int_\Omega \left\{\sum_{i=1}^n \left[\sum_{j=1}^n a_{ij}^m(x, t)\phi_{x_j}^m + a_i^m(x, t)\phi^m\right]\eta_{x_i} - \left[\sum_{i=1}^m b_i^m(x, t)\phi_{x_i}^m + c^m(x, t)\phi^m\right]\eta\right\} dx,$$

$$\mathscr{L}_2^m(\phi^m, \eta)(t) \equiv \int_{\partial\Omega} \{[\sigma^m(s, t)\phi^m - \Psi^m(s, t)]\eta\}\, ds,$$

and

$$\mathscr{L}_3(\hat{f}^m, \eta)(t) \equiv \int_\Omega \left\{ \sum_{i=1}^n F_i^m(x, t)\eta_{x_i} + f^m(x, t)\eta \right\} dx.$$

Similarly, for the limit problem [(2.1), (2.2), and (2.4)], we have

$$-\iint_Q \phi\eta_t \, dx \, dt + \int_0^T \{\mathscr{L}_1(\phi, \eta)(t) + \mathscr{L}_2(\phi, \eta)(t) + \mathscr{L}_3(\hat{f}, \eta)(t)\} \, dt$$
$$= \int_\Omega \phi_0(x)\eta(x, 0) \, dx, \tag{6.6}$$

for all $\eta \in \tilde{W}_2^{1,1}(Q)$, where $\mathscr{L}_1$, $\mathscr{L}_2$, and $\mathscr{L}_3$ are given by (2.6), (2.7), and (2.8), respectively.

For each positive integer m, let

$$\psi^m \equiv \phi^m - \phi.$$

Then it is clear that $\psi^m \in V_2^{1,0}(Q)$.

Subtracting (6.6) from (6.5) we obtain

$$-\iint_Q \psi^m\eta_t \, dx \, dt + \int_0^T \{\mathscr{L}_1^m(\psi^m, \eta)(t) + \tilde{\mathscr{L}}_2^m(\psi^m, \eta)(t) + \tilde{\mathscr{L}}_3(\hat{g}^m, \eta)(t)\} \, dt$$
$$= \int_\Omega [\phi_0^m(x) - \phi_0(x)]\eta(x, 0) \, dx, \tag{6.7}$$

for all $\eta \in \tilde{W}_2^{1,1}(Q)$, where

$$\tilde{\mathscr{L}}_2^m(\psi^m, \eta)(t) \equiv \int_{\partial\Omega} \{[\sigma^m(s, t)\psi^m(s, t) - (\bar{\sigma}^m(x, t) + \tilde{\Psi}^m(s, t))]\eta\} \, ds,$$
$$\tilde{\mathscr{L}}_3(\hat{g}^m, \eta)(t) \equiv \int_\Omega \left\{ \sum_{i=1}^n G_i^m(x, t)\eta_{x_i} + [g^m(x, t) + \tilde{f}^m(x, t)]\eta \right\} dx; \tag{6.8}$$

with

$$\bar{\sigma}^m \equiv (\sigma - \sigma^m)\phi, \qquad \tilde{\Psi}^m \equiv \Psi^m - \Psi,$$
$$G_i^m \equiv \sum_{j=1}^n (a_{ij}^m - a_{ij})\phi_{x_j} + (a_i^m - a_i)\phi + (F_i^m - F_i), \qquad i = 1, \ldots, n,$$
$$g^m \equiv -\left[\sum_{i=1}^n (b_i^m - b_i)\phi_{x_i} + (c^m - c)\phi \right], \tag{6.9}$$
$$\tilde{f}^m \equiv f^m - f.$$

From Lemma 3.1 we can easily verify that $\bar{\sigma}^m \in L_{\lambda_3, \mu_3}(Q)$, $\tilde{\Psi}^m \in L_{q_4, r_4}(Q)$, $G_i^m \in L_2(Q)$, $i = 1, \ldots, n$, $g^m \in L_{\lambda_1, \mu_1}(Q)$, and $\tilde{f}^m \in L_{q_2, r_2}(Q)$, where λ_k, μ_k, $k = 1, 3$, are defined in Remark 2.1. Thus by virtue of the generalized version of Theorem 5.5, as specified in Remark 5.2, it follows that, for each positive integer m, ψ^m is the unique weak solution from the space $V_2^{1,0}(Q)$ of the second boundary-value problem [(6.1), (6.2), and (6.3)], with F_i^m, $i = 1, \ldots, n$, f^m, ϕ_0^m, and Ψ^m replaced, respectively, by G_i^m, $i = 1, \ldots, n$, $g^m + \tilde{f}^m$, $\phi_0^m - \phi_0$, and $\bar{\sigma}^m + \tilde{\Psi}^m$. On this basis we deduce from the generalized version of Theorem 4.1, as specified in Remark 4.4, that

$$\|\psi^m\|_Q \leq K\left\{\|\phi_0^m - \phi_0\|_{2,\Omega} + \left\|\left[\sum_{i=1}^{n} (G_i^m)^2\right]^{1/2}\right\|_{2,Q} + \|g^m\|_{\lambda_1, \mu_1, Q} + \|\tilde{f}^m\|_{q_2, r_2, Q} + \|\bar{\sigma}^m\|_{\lambda_3, \mu_3, Q} + \|\tilde{\Psi}^m\|_{q_4, r_4, Q}\right\}. \tag{6.10}$$

Thus by using the convergent properties imposed in the hypotheses, it follows from (6.9) that each term on the right-hand side of (6.10) approaches to zero as $m \to \infty$, therefore $\|\psi^m\|_Q \to 0$ as $m \to \infty$. Hence $\phi^m \xrightarrow{s} \phi$ in $V_2^{1,0}(Q)$, as $m \to \infty$. This completes the proof. ■

Using a similar argument as that given for Theorem 6.1 with some obvious modifications, we can show (in the next theorem) that the corresponding version of the theorem is valid for the first boundary-value problems.

THEOREM 6.2. *Consider the sequence of the first boundary-value problems* [(6.1), (6.2), *and* (6.4)]. *Suppose that a_{ij}^m converge to a_{ij}, almost everywhere in Q, and that a_i^m, b_i^m, c^m, F_i^m, f^m, and ϕ_0^m converge, respectively, to a_i, b_i, c, F_i, f, and ϕ_0 strongly in the spaces they belong. If these limit functions also satisfy the corresponding parts of assumptions* (A.1)–(A.6), *then*

$$\phi^m \xrightarrow{s} \phi,$$

in $V_2^{1,0}(Q)$, as $m \to \infty$, where ϕ is the weak solution from the space $V_2^{1,0}(Q)$ of the limit problem [(2.1), (2.2), *and* (2.3)].

II.7. Certain Properties of Solutions of Equation (2.1)

In this section we shall present a list of results concerning the properties of weak solutions of the parabolic partial differential Eq. (2.1) as such, without involving the initial and boundary conditions. Their proofs are very lengthy. To limit the size of the section, they are omitted.

To begin we need this definition.

DEFINITION 7.1. *A function $\phi: Q \to R^1$ is called a weak solution from the space $V_2^{1,0}(Q)$ of Eq.* (2.1) *if $\phi \in V_2^{1,0}(Q)$ and satisfies the integral identity*

$$-\iint_Q \phi\eta_t \, dx\, dt + \int_0^T \{\mathscr{L}_1(\phi, \eta)(t) + \mathscr{L}_3(\hat{f}, \eta)(t)\}\, dt = 0, \tag{7.1}$$

for any $\eta \in \mathring{\tilde{W}}_2^{1,1}(Q)$ with $\eta|_{t=0} = 0$.

From the preceding definition we note that weak solutions of Eq. (2.1) do not need to satisfy the initial or boundary condition in any sense. In addition, we also note that integral identity (7.1) can be obtained from either integral identity (2.5) or integral identity (2.10) by choosing $\eta \in \mathring{\tilde{W}}_2^{1,1}(Q)$ with $\eta|_{t=0} = 0$.

To present the results, stronger conditions are required to be imposed on the forcing terms and the first- and zero-order coefficients of Eq. (2.1). More precisely, we need

(A.9) $a_i: Q \to R^1$; $b_i: Q \to R^1$, $i = 1, \ldots, n$; $c: Q \to R^1$, $F_i: Q \to R^1$, $i = 1, \ldots, n$; and $f: Q \to R^1$ are measurable and satisfy, respectively, the following inequalities:

$$\left\| \sum_{i=1}^n (a_i)^2 \right\|_{q,r,Q} \le M_5;$$

$$\left\| \sum_{i=1}^n (b_i)^2 \right\|_{q,r,Q} \le M_5;$$

$$\|c\|_{q,r,Q} \le M_5;$$

$$\left\| \sum_{i=1}^n (F_i)^2 \right\|_{q,r,Q} \le M_5;$$

and

$$\|f\|_{q,r,Q} \le M_5,$$

where $M_5 \equiv M_5(q, r)$ is a positive constant; and q and r are any pair of constants subject to the restriction

$1/r + n/2q = 1 - \tau,$

$$q \in \left[\frac{n}{2(1-\tau)}, \infty\right], \qquad r \in \left[\frac{1}{1-\tau}, \infty\right], \qquad 0 < \tau < 1, \qquad \text{for } n \ge 2,$$

$$q \in [1, \infty], \qquad r \in \left[\frac{1}{1-\tau}, \frac{2}{1-2\tau}\right], \qquad 0 < \tau < \tfrac{1}{2}, \qquad \text{for } n = 1. \tag{7.2}$$

Throughout this section we assume that (A.1), (A.2), and (A.9) are satisfied.

THEOREM 7.1. *Let ϕ be a weak solution from the space $V_2^{1,0}(Q)$ of Eq.* (2.1) *and suppose there exists a positive constant M_6 such that*

$$|\phi(x, t)| \leq M_6,$$

for all $(x, t) \in \Gamma_T$, where $\Gamma_T \equiv \Gamma \cup \{(x, t) : x \in \Omega, t = 0\}$. Then

$$\|\phi\|_{\infty, Q} \leq K_3 M_7,$$

where $M_7 \equiv \max\{M_6, 1\}$ and the constant K_3 is determined by n, α_l, M_5, q, and r.

For Hölder's continuity properties of solutions of Eq. (2.1), we have

THEOREM 7.2. *Let ϕ be a weak solution from the space $V_2^{1,0}(Q)$ of Eq.* (2.1). *If there exists a positive constant M_8 such that*

$$\|\phi\|_{\infty, Q} \leq M_8,$$

then $\phi \in \mathscr{H}^{\iota, \iota/2}(\bar{Q})$, with $\iota \in (0, 1)$ determined by n, α_l, α_u, q, and r. In addition, suppose $\hat{Q}$ is a subdomain contained in the domain Q and is separated from the boundary Γ_T of $\bar{Q}$ by a positive distance d. Then

$$|\phi|_{\hat{Q}}^{(\iota, \iota/2)} \leq K_4,$$

where the positive constant K_4 depends only on n, M_8, α_l, α_u, M_5, q, and r.

REMARK 7.1. Comparing Definition 7.1 with Definitions 2.1 and 2.2, it can be easily verified that any weak solution from the space $V_2^{1,0}(Q)$ of either the first or second boundary-value problem must also be a weak solution from the space $V_2^{1,0}(Q)$ of Eq. (2.1). In fact, this conclusion is also true for the case when the domain Q of Eq. (2.1) is replaced by any subdomain $\hat{Q}$ (contained in Q).

II.8. Boundary-Value Problems in General Form

In this section we shall consider first and second boundary value problems for a linear second-order parabolic partial differential equation in *general form.* Results concerning the existence and uniqueness of the solution from the space $W_p^{2,1}(Q)$ of the boundary-value problems under discussion are presented. These results are obtained from more general results reported in [LSU.1]. The proofs of these more general results are very complicated and lengthy. To limit the size of this section they are omitted. We refer the interested reader to [LSU.1]—a celebrated book on the theory of parabolic partial differential equations. What we shall do here is to accept these general results and then use them, among others, to derive stronger conclusions for special cases that we shall encounter in the later chapters on optimal control theory.

In the cylinder Q we consider a class of linear second-order parabolic partial differential equations (in general form) of the form

$$L\phi \equiv \phi_t - \sum_{i,j=1}^{n} a_{ij}(x,t)\phi_{x_i x_j} - \sum_{i=1}^{n} b_i(x,t)\phi_{x_i} - c(x,t)\phi = f(x,t), \quad (8.1)$$

where

$$\phi_t \equiv \frac{\partial \phi}{\partial t}, \qquad \phi_{x_i} \equiv \frac{\partial \phi}{\partial x_i}, \qquad \text{and} \qquad \phi_{x_i x_j} \equiv \frac{\partial^2 \phi}{\partial x_i\, \partial x_j}.$$

Recall Eq. (2.1) and suppose that $a_{ij} \in C^1(\bar{Q})$, $i, j = 1, \ldots, n$; $a_i \equiv 0$; and $F_i \equiv 0$, $i = 1, \ldots, n$. Then the resulting equation can be reduced to the form of Eq. (8.1).

If $\phi \in C^{2,1}(Q) \cap C(Q \cup \Gamma \cup \bar{\Omega}_0)$ and ϕ satisfies Eq. (8.1) everywhere in Q, initial condition (2.2) everywhere in Ω_0, and boundary condition (2.3) everywhere in Γ, then it is called a classical solution of the first boundary-value problem for Eq. (8.1).

As in Section II.2, the first boundary-value problem for Eq. (8.1) will be referred to as the first boundary-value problem [(8.1), (2.2), and (2.3)].

If $\phi \in C^{2,1}(Q) \cap C(Q \cup \Gamma \cup \bar{\Omega}_0) \cap C^{1,0}(Q \cup \Gamma)$ and ϕ satisfies Eq. (8.1) everywhere in Q, initial condition (2.2) everywhere in Ω_0, and boundary condition

$$\left[\sum_{i=1}^{n} \sigma_i(x,t)\phi_{x_i} + \sigma(x,t)\phi\right]\Bigg|_{\Gamma} = \Psi \quad (8.2)$$

everywhere in Γ, then it is called a classical solution of the second boundary-value problem for Eq. (8.1).

Similarly, the second boundary-value problem for Eq. (8.1) will be referred to as the second boundary-value problem [(8.1), (2.2), and (8.2)].

For the existence of classical solutions of the boundary-value problems under discussion, the coefficients, forcing term, and initial and boundary functions are required to be sufficiently smooth. These assumptions cannot be possibly met in the study of optimal control problems involving bounded measurable controls. It is because of this reason alone that we shall also be concerned with solutions from the space $W_p^{2,1}(Q)$, besides classical solutions, of the boundary-value problems under consideration.

DEFINITION 8.1. *A function* $\phi: Q \to R^1$ *is called an almost everywhere solution of the first boundary-value problem* [(8.1), (2.2), *and* (2.3)] *if* $\phi \in W_p^{2,1}(Q)$, $p > 3/2$, *and* ϕ *satisfies Eq.* (8.1) *almost everywhere in* Q, *initial condition* (2.2) *almost everywhere in* Ω_0, *and boundary condition* (2.3) *almost everywhere in* Γ.

DEFINITION 8.2. *A function* $\phi: Q \to R^1$ *is called an almost everywhere solution of the second boundary value problem* [(8.1), (2.2), *and* (8.2)] *if* $\phi \in W_p^{2,1}(Q)$, $p > 3$, *and* ϕ *satisfies Eq.* (8.1) *almost everywhere in* Q, *initial condition* (2.2) *almost everywhere in* Ω_0, *and boundary condition* (8.2) *almost everywhere in* Γ.

In the preceding two definitions all the partial derivatives are to be understood as in the generalized sense. Furthermore, it is the trace of ϕ that is involved in the initial and boundary conditions.

To continue we need to introduce the concept of *compatibility condition.* This condition is used to guarantee that the initial and boundary conditions are properly matched along the boundary of the base Ω_0 of cylinder Q. The order of smoothness of solutions of either the first or second boundary-value problems depends not only on the order of smoothness of the coefficients, forcing term, and data, but also on the order of compatibility condition.

To begin, we introduce the following notation:

$$\psi^{(k)}(x) \equiv \left.\frac{\partial^k \psi(x, t)}{\partial t^k}\right|_{t=0},$$

and

$$\mathscr{A}^{(l)}\left(x, t, \frac{\partial}{\partial x}\right)\psi \equiv \sum_{i,j=1}^{n} \frac{\partial^l a_{ij}(x, t)}{\partial t^l} \frac{\partial^2 \psi}{\partial x_i \partial x_j} + \sum_{i=1}^{n} \frac{\partial^l b_i(x, t)}{\partial t^l} \frac{\partial \psi}{\partial x_i} + \frac{\partial^l c(x, t)}{\partial t^l} \psi.$$

For the boundary-value problems under discussion we note that

$$\phi^{(0)}(x) = \phi_0(x),$$

when $k = 0$, and

$$\phi^{(1)}(x) = \mathscr{A}^{(0)}(x, 0, \partial/\partial x)\phi_0(x) + f^{(0)}(x),$$

when $k = 1$. With $k = 2, 3, \ldots,$ the functions $\phi^{(k)}$ are determined by the following recursion relations:

$$\phi^{(k+1)}(x) = \sum_{l=0}^{k} \binom{k}{l} \mathscr{A}^{(l)}(x, 0, \partial/\partial x)\phi^{(k-l)}(x) + f^{(k)}(x).$$

Recall boundary condition (2.3). We observe that the boundary function is a zero valued function. Thus the first boundary-value problem [(8.1), (2.2), and (2.3)] is said to satisfy the compatibility condition of order $m \geq 0$ if

$$\phi^{(k)}(x)|_{\partial\Omega} = 0, \qquad k = 0, 1, \ldots, m.$$

In particular,

$$\phi_0(x)|_{\partial\Omega} = 0,$$

when $k = 0$, and

$$[\mathscr{A}^{(0)}(x, 0, \partial/\partial x)\phi_0(x) + f^{(0)}(x)]|_{\partial\Omega} = 0,$$

when $k = 1$.

We now consider the second boundary-value problem [(8.1), (2.2), and (8.2)]. This second boundary-value problem is said to satisfy the compatibility condition of order $m \geq 0$ if

$$\sum_{l=0}^{k} \binom{k}{l} \left\{ \sum_{i=1}^{n} \sigma_i^{(k-l)}(x) \frac{\partial \phi^{(l)}(x)}{\partial x_i} + \sigma^{(k-l)}(x)\phi^{(l)}(x) \right\}\Bigg|_{\partial\Omega} = \Psi^{(k)}(x),$$
$$k = 0, 1, \ldots, m.$$

In particular,

$$\left\{ \sum_{i=1}^{n} \sigma_i^{(0)}(x) \frac{\partial \phi^{(0)}(x)}{\partial x_i} + \sigma^{(0)}(x)\phi_0(x) \right\}\Bigg|_{\partial\Omega} = \Psi^{(0)}(x),$$

when $k = 0$.

We are now in a position to present the results on the existence and uniqueness of almost everywhere solutions of the boundary-value problems under discussion. For the first boundary-value problem, we have the following theorem.

THEOREM 8.1. *Consider the first boundary-value problem* [(8.1), (2.2), *and* (2.3)]. *Suppose that the following conditions are fulfilled*

(i) $a_{ij}: \bar{Q} \to R^1$, $i, j = 1, \ldots, n$, *are continuous*;

(ii) *The assumption* (A.2) *is satisfied*;

(iii) $b_i: \bar{Q} \to R^1$, $i = 1, \ldots, n$; $c: \bar{Q} \to R^1$; *and* $f: \bar{Q} \to R^1$ *are measurable and bounded*; *and*

(iv) $\phi_0 \in C_0^2(\Omega)$.

Then the first boundary-value problem has a unique almost everywhere solution ϕ. *Furthermore, if the second-order coefficients* a_{ij} *and the domain* Ω *together with its boundary* $\partial\Omega$ *are assumed, additionally, to be fixed, then* ϕ *satisfies*

$$\|\phi\|_{p,Q}^{(2,1)} \leq K\{\|f\|_{\infty,Q} + \|\phi_0\|_{\infty,\Omega}^{(2)}\}, \tag{8.3}$$

for all $p > \frac{3}{2}$, *including* $p = \infty$, *where the constant* K *depends only on* T *and bounds for* b_i, $i = 1, \ldots, n$, *and* c *on* $\bar{Q}$.

Proof. From condition (iv) we note that the first boundary-value problem satisfies the compatibility condition of order 0. Thus from this together with other hypotheses of the theorem, we can easily verify that all the conditions of Theorem 9.1 of [LSU.1, Chapter IV, pp. 341–342] are satisfied. Hence, it follows that the first boundary-value problem admits a unique almost everywhere solution ϕ. Now, from the same theorem and [LSU.1, Part 1 of Lemma 3.4, Chapter II, p. 82], we obtain

$$\|\phi\|_{p,Q}^{(2,1)} \leq N_0\{\|f\|_{p,Q} + \|\phi_0\|_{p,\Omega}^{(2)}\}, \tag{8.4}$$

for all $p > \frac{3}{2}$, where the constant N_0 depends only on T, and bounds for b_i, $i = 1, \ldots, n$, and c on $\bar{Q}$. However, Q is bounded and fixed. Thus it follows from the assumptions on f and ϕ_0 that

$$\|\phi\|_{p,Q}^{(2,1)} \leq N_1\{\|f\|_{\infty,Q} + \|\phi_0\|_{\infty,\Omega}^{(2)}\},$$

for all $p > \frac{3}{2}$. Since this inequality is true for all $p > \frac{3}{2}$ and the constant N_1 is independent of p, the conclusion of the theorem follows from Theorem I.3.2. ■

From [LSU.1, Lemma 3.3, Chapter II, p. 80], we have this corollary.

COROLLARY 8.1. *Suppose that the conditions of Theorem* 8.1 *are satisfied and that* $p > n + 2$. *Then*

$$|\phi|_{\bar{Q}}^{(1+\mu,(1+\mu)/2)} \leq \hat{K}\|\phi\|_{p,Q}^{(2,1)}, \tag{8.5}$$

where $\mu = 1 - [(n+2)/p]$, $|\cdot|_{\bar{Q}}^{(\lambda,\lambda/2)}$ *denotes the norm in the Hölder space* $\mathscr{H}^{\lambda,\lambda/2}(\bar{Q})$ *(see Section I.4.1.), and the constant* $\hat{K}$ *depends only on* Q *and* p.

We now consider the second boundary-value problem. The result parallel to that of Theorem 8.1 is given in this theorem.

THEOREM 8.2. *Consider the second boundary-value problem* [(8.1), (2.2), *and* (8.2)]. *Suppose that the compatibility condition of order* 0 *is satisfied and that the following conditions are fulfilled*:

(i) $a_{ij}: \bar{Q} \to R^1$, $i, j = 1, \ldots, n$, *are continuous*;

(ii) *Assumption* (A.2) *is satisfied*;

(iii) $b_i: \bar{Q} \to R^1$, $i = 1, \ldots, n$; $c: \bar{Q} \to R^1$; *and* $f: \bar{Q} \to R^1$ *are measurable and bounded*;

(iv) σ_i, $i = 1, \ldots, n$, *and* σ *are in* $C^1(\Gamma)$;

(v) *There exists a positive constant* α_b *such that*

$$\left|\sum_{i=1}^{n} \sigma_i(x,t) n_i(x)\right| \geq \alpha_b$$

for all $(x,t) \in \Gamma$, *where* $n(x) \equiv (n_1(x), \ldots, n_n(x))$ *denotes the outward normal to* $\partial\Omega$ *from the point* $x \in \partial\Omega$;

(vi) *There exists a function* $\hat{\Psi} \in C^2(\bar{Q})$ *such that* $\hat{\Psi}|_\Gamma = \Psi$; *and*

(vii) $\phi_0 \in C^2(\bar{\Omega})$.

Then the second boundary-value problem has a unique almost everywhere solution ϕ. *Furthermore, if the second-order coefficients* a_{ij} *and domain* Ω

together with its boundary $\partial\Omega$ are assumed, additionally, to be fixed, then ϕ satisfies

$$\|\phi\|_{p,Q}^{(2,1)} \leq K\{\|f\|_{\infty,Q} + \|\phi_0\|_{\infty,\Omega}^{(2)} + \|\hat{\Psi}\|_{\infty,Q}^{(2,1)}\}, \tag{8.6}$$

for all $p > 3$, including $p = \infty$. The constant K depends only on T and bounds for b_i, $i = 1, \ldots, n$, and c on $\bar{Q}$.

Proof. From the remark made in [LSU.1, p. 351] we note that an analogous version of Theorem 9.1 of [LSU.1, pp. 341–342] is valid for the second boundary-value problem, but with $p > 3$ (rather than with $p > \frac{3}{2}$ as in the case of the first boundary-value problem). Then by applying [LSU.1, Lemma 3.4, p. 82] to the corresponding version of the a priori estimate (9.3) in Theorem 9.1 of [LSU.1, pp. 341–342], we can show that

$$\|\phi\|_{p,Q}^{(2,1)} \leq N_0\{\|f\|_{p,Q} + \|\phi_0\|_{p,\Omega}^{(2)} + \|\hat{\Psi}\|_{p,Q}^{(2,1)}\}, \tag{8.7}$$

for all $p > 3$, where the constant N_0 depends only on T and bounds for b_i, $i = 1, \ldots, n$, and c on $\bar{Q}$. (Here, we recall that the second-order coefficients a_{ij}, domain Ω, and boundary $\partial\Omega$ are assumed to be fixed.) The rest of the proof is similar to that of Theorem 8.1. ■

In the rest of this section we shall present two theorems on the existence and uniqueness of classical solutions, one for the first boundary-value problem and one for the second boundary-value problem. These two theorems are, respectively, special cases of Theorems 5.2 and 5.3 of [LSU.1, p. 320].

The following theorem is for the first boundary-value problem:

THEOREM 8.3. *Consider the first boundary-value problem* [(8.1), (2.2), *and* (2.3)], *and let $\iota \in (0, 1)$. Suppose that the compatibility condition of order* 1 *is satisfied and that the following conditions are fulfilled*:

(i) *Assumption* (A.2) *is satisfied*;
(ii) a_{ij}, $i, j = 1, \ldots, n$; b_i, $i = 1, \ldots, n$; c *and* f *are in* $\mathscr{H}^{\iota,\iota/2}(\bar{Q})$;
(iii) $\phi_0 \in \mathscr{H}^{\iota+2}(\bar{\Omega})$.

Then the first boundary-value problem has a unique classical solution ϕ which is also in $\mathscr{H}^{\iota+2,(\iota/2)+1}(\bar{Q})$.

For the second boundary-value problem, we have the following theorem.

THEOREM 8.4. *Consider the second boundary-value problem* [(8.1), (2.2), *and* (8.2)], *and let $\iota \in (0, 1)$. Suppose that the compatibility condition of order* 0 *is satisfied and that the following conditions are fulfilled*:

(i) *Conditions* (i)–(iii) *of Theorem* 8.3 *are satisfied*;
(ii) $\sigma_i \in \mathscr{H}^{\iota+1,(\iota+1)/2}(\Gamma)$, $i = 1, \ldots, n$, *and* $\sigma \in \mathscr{H}^{\iota+1,(\iota+1)/2}(\Gamma)$
(iii) $\Psi \in \mathscr{H}^{\iota+1,(\iota+1)/2}(\Gamma)$; *and*
(iv) *Condition* (iv) *of Theorem* 8.2 *is satisfied.*

Then the second boundary-value problem has a unique classical solution ϕ that is also in $\mathscr{H}^{\iota+2,(\iota/2)+1}(\bar{Q})$.

II.9. A Maximum Principle

The aim of this section is to prove a maximum principle for solutions of a class of first boundary-value problems in divergence form.

Consider Eq. (2.1) with $(F_i)_{x_i} = 0$, $i = 1, \ldots, n$, and $f = 0$, that is,

$$L\phi = 0, \qquad (x, t) \in Q. \tag{9.1}$$

Then the corresponding first boundary-value problem will be referred to as the first boundary-value problem [(9.1), (2.2), and (2.3)]. This first boundary-value problem is in the divergence form and admits a unique weak solution from the space $V_2^{1,0}(Q)$.

The following is a well-known theorem on the maximum principle for classical solutions of the first boundary-value problem [(8.1), (2.2), and (2.3)].

THEOREM 9.1. *Consider the first boundary-value problem* [(8.1), (2.2), *and* (2.3)], *and let* ϕ *be a classical solution of the problem. Suppose that*

$$\sum_{i,j=1}^{n} a_{ij}(x, t)\xi_i\xi_j > 0, \tag{9.2}$$

on Q *for any nonzero vector* $\xi \equiv (\xi_1, \ldots, \xi_n) \in R^n$, *and that there exists some constant* M *such that* $c(x, t) < M$ *on* $\bar{Q}$. *Then* $\phi(x, t) \geq 0$ *in* Q *provided* $f(x, t) \geq 0$ *in* Q *and* $\phi_0(x) \geq 0$ *in* $\bar{\Omega}$.

Proof. Consider the case when $M \leq 0$. Then $c(x, t) < 0$ in $\bar{Q}$. Assume that ϕ were negative at some point of Q. Since $\phi_0(x) \geq 0$ in $\bar{\Omega}$ and ϕ is a classical solution, there exists a point $(x^0, t^0) \in Q \cup (\Omega \times \{T\})$ such that ϕ attains its minimum at (x^0, t^0). Thus we have

$$(\partial\phi/\partial x_i)(x^0, t^0) = 0, \qquad i = 1, \ldots, n, \tag{9.3}$$

$$(\partial\phi/\partial t)(x^0, t^0) \leq 0, \tag{9.4}$$

and

$$c(x^0, t^0)\phi(x^0, t^0) > 0. \tag{9.5}$$

Note that the pure second-order partial derivatives with respect to the variables x_i at the minimum point (x^0, t^0) are nonnegative in any direction. In particular,

$$(\partial^2\phi/\partial y_k^2)(x^0, t^0) \geq 0, \tag{9.6}$$

in any direction of

$$y_k \equiv \sum_{l=1}^{n} K_{kl}(x_l - x_l^0),$$

where $K \equiv (K_{kl})$ is a nondegenerate matrix. From (9.2) we see that the matrix $A \equiv (a_{ij})$ is diagonalizable and hence we may choose the matrix K to be such that

$$KAK^T = \operatorname{diag}(\lambda_{11}, \ldots, \lambda_{nn}),$$

where K^T denotes the transpose of K and

$$\lambda_{kk}(x, t) = \sum_{i, j=1}^{n} K_{kj} a_{ij}(x, t) K_{ki}, \qquad k = 1, \ldots, n.$$

Thus it follows from (9.2) that

$$\lambda_{kk}(x, t) > 0, \qquad k = 1, \ldots, n, \tag{9.7}$$

in $\bar{Q}$.

By the change of variables $y_k = \sum_{l=1}^{n} K_{kl}(x_l - x_l^0)$ and the definition of λ_{kk}, we obtain

$$\sum_{i, j=1}^{n} a_{ij} \frac{\partial^2 \phi}{\partial x_i \, \partial x_j} = \sum_{k=1}^{n} \lambda_{kk} \frac{\partial^2 \phi}{\partial y_k^2}.$$

Thus by virtue of inequalities (9.6) and (9.7), we have

$$\sum_{i, j=1}^{n} a_{ij}(x^0, t^0) \frac{\partial^2 \phi}{\partial x_i \, \partial x_j} (x^0, t^0) \geq 0. \tag{9.8}$$

Using (9.3)–(9.5) and (9.8) we readily deduce from Eq. (8.1) that $f(x^0, t^0) < 0$. This is a contradiction and hence the proof is complete for the case when $M \leq 0$.

We now consider the case when $M > 0$. Define

$$\psi(x, t) = \phi(x, t) e^{-\lambda t}, \qquad (x, t) \in Q,$$

where λ is a number to be determined later. Clearly, the function ψ satisfies

$$\psi_t(x, t) - \sum_{i, j=1}^{n} a_{ij}(x, t) \psi_{x_i x_j}(x, t) - \sum_{i=1}^{n} b_i(x, t) \psi_{x_i}(x, t) - (c(x, t) - \lambda) \psi(x, t)$$
$$= f(x, t) e^{\lambda t},$$

for all $(x, t) \in Q$. We may now choose $\lambda > M$. With such a choice we have $c(x, t) - \lambda < 0$. Thus by the result already obtained, it follows that $\psi(x, t) \geq 0$ in $\bar{Q}$ and hence

$$\phi(x, t) = \psi(x, t) e^{\lambda t} \geq 0,$$

in $\bar{Q}$. This completes the proof. ■

Theorem 9.1 will be used later to obtain a maximum principle for weak solutions of the problem [(9.1), (2.2), and (2.3)]. To begin, we assume throughout the rest of this section that the following conditions hold:

(A.10) a_{ij}, $i, j = 1, \ldots, n$, satisfy assumptions (A.1)–(A.2).

(A.11) $a_i: \bar{Q} \to R^1$; $b_i: \bar{Q} \to R^1$, $i = 1, \ldots, n$; $c: \bar{Q} \to R^1$ are measurable and bounded.

(A.12) $\phi_0 \in C(\bar{\Omega})$.

Since T is finite and Ω is bounded, it is clear that $Q \equiv \Omega \times (0, T)$ is also bounded. Thus assumption (A.11) implies assumption (A.3) of Section II.2 and assumption (A.9) of Section II.7. Therefore, all the results reported in Section II.2–II.7, inclusively, are valid under assumptions (A.10)–(A.12).

To obtain a maximum principle for weak solutions of the first boundary-value problem [(9.1), (2.2), and (2.3)], we need to take integral averages [for definition, see formula (I.4.3)] of the coefficients of the operator L. Thus it will be convenient to regard L as being defined throughout the $(n + 1)$-dimensional (x, t) space. More precisely, we adopt the convention that

$$L\psi = \psi_t - \sum_{i,j=1}^{n} \psi_{x_i x_j}, \tag{9.9}$$

for all $(x, y) \in R^{n+1} \backslash Q$.

Similarly, we extend the domain of definition of the initial function ϕ_0 by setting

$$\phi_0 = 0 \tag{9.10}$$

for all $x \in R^n \backslash \Omega$.

For each integer $m \geq 1$, let a_{ij}^m, $i, j = 1, \ldots, n$; a_i^m, $i = 1, \ldots, n$; b_i^m, $i = 1, \ldots, n$; and c^m denote, respectively, the integral averages of a_{ij}, $i, j = 1, \ldots, n$; a_i, $i = 1, \ldots, n$; b_i, $i = 1, \ldots, n$; and c. Define the operators

$$L^m\psi = \psi_t - \sum_{i=1}^{n} \left\{ \left[\sum_{j=1}^{n} a_{ij}^m(x, t)\psi_{x_j} + a_i^m(x, t)\psi \right]_{x_i} + b_i^m(x, t)\psi_{x_i} \right\} - c^m(x, t)\psi. \tag{9.11}$$

From the definition of integral averages it can be easily verified that the coefficients of the operators L^m satisfy the corresponding assumptions (A.10)–(A.12) uniformly with respect to m. For each integer $m \geq 1$, let ϕ_0^m denote the integral average of ϕ_0. Let $\{\Omega^m\}$ be a sequence of open domains such that

$$\bar{\Omega}^m \subset \Omega^{m+1} \subset \bar{\Omega}^{m+1} \subset \Omega,$$

for all $m \geq 0$ and $\lim_{m\to\infty} \Omega^m = \Omega$.

Let $g_m \in C_0^\infty(\Omega)$ be such that $g_m(x) = 1$ in Ω^{m-1} and $0 \leq g_m(x) \leq 1$ elsewhere.

Consider the sequence of first boundary-value problems:

$$L^m\phi = 0, \qquad (x, t) \in Q, \tag{9.12}$$

$$\phi|_{t=0} = g_m\phi_0^m, \qquad x \in \Omega, \tag{9.13}$$

$$\phi|_\Gamma = 0, \qquad (x, t) \in \Gamma. \tag{9.14}$$

From Theorem I.4.1 we note that ϕ_0^m and the coefficients of Eq. (9.12) are all C^∞ functions. Thus by virtue of the properties of the functions g_m, it follows that, for each integer $m \geq 1$, all the hypotheses of Theorem 8.3 are satisfied, including the compatibility condition of order 1. Therefore, for each integer $m \geq 1$, the first boundary-value problem [(9.12), (9.13), and (9.14)] has a unique classical solution ϕ^m from the space $\mathscr{H}^{\iota+2,(\iota/2)+1}(\bar{Q})$. However, by Theorem 5.6, ϕ^m is also the unique weak solution from the space $V_2^{1,0}(Q)$.

THEOREM 9.2. *Let* $\{\phi^m\}$ *be the sequence of classical solutions from* $\mathscr{H}^{\iota+2,(\iota/2)+1}(\bar{Q})$ *of the problems* [(9.12), (9.13), *and* (9.14)] *and* ϕ *the weak solution from the space* $V_2^{1,0}(Q)$ *of the problem* [(9.1), (2.2), *and* (2.3)]. *Then there exists a subsequence* $\{\phi^{m(l)}\}$ *of the sequence* $\{\phi^m\}$ *such that, as* $l \to \infty$,

$$\phi^{m(l)} \xrightarrow{w} \phi,$$

$$\phi_{x_i}^{m(l)} \xrightarrow{w} \phi_{x_i}, \qquad i = 1, \ldots, n,$$

in $L_2(Q)$. *Furthermore, if* $\phi_0(x) \geq 0$ *in* Ω, *then* $\phi(x, t) \geq 0$ *in* Q.

Proof. Recall that, for each integer $m \geq 1$, ϕ^m is also the unique weak solution from the space $V_2^{1,0}(Q)$ of the problem [(9.12), (9.13), and (9.14)], and that the operators L^m have a uniform structure with respect to m that is completely determined by the structure of the operator L. Thus by Theorem 4.2, we have

$$\|\phi^m\|_Q \leq K_2\|g_m\phi_0^m\|_{2,\Omega}, \tag{9.15}$$

where the constant K_2 is independent of m. It is easy to verify that

$$\|g_m\phi_0^m\|_{2,\Omega} \leq \|\phi_0\|_{2,\Omega}.$$

Thus inequality (9.15) is reduced to

$$\|\phi^m\|_Q \leq K_2\|\phi_0\|_{2,\Omega}. \tag{9.16}$$

This, in turn, implies that

$$\|\phi_x^m\|_{2,Q} \leq K_2\|\phi_0\|_{2,\Omega}, \tag{9.17}$$

and

$$\|\phi^m\|_{2,Q} \leq T^{1/2}K_2\|\phi_0\|_{2,\Omega}. \tag{9.18}$$

Thus $\{\phi^m\}$ and $\{\phi_{x_i}^m\}$, $i = 1, \ldots, n$, can be considered as bounded subsets of $L_2(Q)$. Since bounded sets in $L_2(Q)$ are weakly conditionally sequentially compact, it follows that there exists a subsequence $\{\phi^{m(l)}\}$ of the sequence $\{\phi^m\}$ such that, as $l \to \infty$,

$$\phi^{m(l)} \xrightarrow{w} \phi \quad \text{in} \quad L_2(Q), \tag{9.19}$$

and

$$\phi^{m(l)}_{x_i} \xrightarrow{w} \phi_{x_i}, \qquad i = 1, \ldots, n, \qquad \text{in} \quad L_2(Q). \tag{9.20}$$

This, in turn, implies that

$$\phi^{m(l)} \xrightarrow{w} \phi, \tag{9.21}$$

in $W_2^{1,0}(Q)$, as $l \to \infty$.

According to the Banach–Saks–Mazur theorem there exists a further subsequence $\{\phi^{m(l(k))}\}$ such that

$$\hat{\phi}^j \equiv \frac{1}{j} \sum_{k=1}^{j} \phi^{m(l(k))} \xrightarrow{s} \phi, \tag{9.22}$$

in $W_2^{1,0}(Q)$, as $j \to \infty$. Since ϕ^m and hence $\hat{\phi}^j$ are in $\mathring{W}_2^{1,0}(Q)$, it is clear that $\phi \in \mathring{W}_2^{1,2}(Q)$. Thus from the estimates (9.16) and (9.18) and relation (9.19), it follows from Theorem I.4.12 that $\phi \in \mathring{V}_2(Q)$.

Next, we shall show that ϕ is a weak solution from the space $V_2(Q)$ of the problem [(9.1), (2.2), and (2.3)]. For this, let η be an arbitrary element in $\mathring{W}_2^{1,1}(Q)$ that is equal to zero for $t = T$. Since, for each integer $m \geq 1$, ϕ^m is the weak solution from the space $V_2^{1,0}(Q)$ of the problem [(9.12), (9.13), and (9.14)], it follows that

$$-\iint_Q \phi^m \eta_t \, dx \, dt + \int_0^T \mathscr{L}_1^m(\phi^m, \eta)(t) \, dt = \int_\Omega g_m(x)\phi_0^m(x)\eta(x, 0) \, dx, \tag{9.23}$$

where $\mathscr{L}_1^m$ is as defined by (2.6) with the coefficients a_{ij}, $i, j = 1, \ldots, n$; a_i, $i = 1, \ldots, n$; b_i, $i = 1, \ldots, n$; and c replaced by a_{ij}^m, $i, j = 1, \ldots, n$; a_i^m, $i = 1, \ldots, n$; b_i^m, $i = 1, \ldots, n$; and c^m, respectively.

Let α denote any of the coefficients of the operator $\mathscr{L}_1$ defined by (2.6) and α^m the integral averages of α. By assumptions (A.1) and (A.11), it follows from Theorem I.4.1 that α^m converge strongly to α in $L_p(Q)$ for any $p \in [1, \infty)$, as $m \to \infty$. Clearly, $\{\alpha^m\}$ contains a subsequence that, again indexed by m, converges almost everywhere in Q to α, as $m \to \infty$. Thus by using estimates (9.17) and (9.18) and relations (9.19) and (9.20), we deduce from Theorem I.4.14 that the sequence

$$\left\{\int_0^T \mathscr{L}_1^{m(l)}(\phi^{m(l)}, \eta) \, dt\right\}$$

converges (through an appropriate further subsequence, if necessary) to

$$\int_0^T \mathscr{L}_1(\phi, \eta) \, dt,$$

that is,

$$\lim_{l\to\infty}\int_0^T \mathscr{L}_1^{m(l)}(\phi^{m(l)}, \eta)\,dt = \int_0^T \mathscr{L}_1(\phi, \eta)\,dt. \tag{9.24}$$

From the properties of functions g_m, we note that g_m converge to 1 everywhere in Q. Furthermore, we note also that ϕ_0^m converge strongly to ϕ_0 in $L_2(\Omega)$. Thus it follows that

$$g_m\phi_0^m \xrightarrow{s} \phi_0,$$

in $L_2(\Omega)$, as $m \to \infty$; in particular,

$$\lim_{l\to\infty}\int_\Omega g_{m(l)}\phi_0^{m(l)}\eta\,dx = \int_\Omega \phi_0\eta\,dx. \tag{9.25}$$

From relation (9.19) we have

$$\lim_{l\to\infty}\iint_Q \phi^{m(l)}\eta_t\,dx\,dt = \iint_Q \phi\eta_t\,dx\,dt. \tag{9.26}$$

Combining the relations (9.24)–(9.26) we obtain from (9.23) that

$$-\iint_Q \phi\eta_t\,dx\,dt + \int_0^T \mathscr{L}_1(\phi, \eta)\,dt = \int_\Omega \phi_0\eta\,dx. \tag{9.27}$$

Hence, ϕ is a weak solution from the space $V_2(Q)$ of the problem [(9.1), (2.2), and (2.3)]. Thus from Theorems 5.2 and 5.6, it follows that ϕ is the unique weak solution from the space $V_2^{1,0}(Q)$.

It remains to prove the second part of the theorem. For this, we recall that, for each integer $l \geq 1$, $\phi^{m(l)}$ is the classical solution of the problem [(9.12), (9.13), and (9.14)] with m replaced by $m(l)$. Since $\phi_0(x) \geq 0$ in Ω, it is clear that $\phi_0^{m(l)}(x) \geq 0$ in Ω. Thus by the maximum principle reported in Theorem 9.1, we deduce that $\phi^{m(l)}(x, t) \geq 0$ in Q. Let $\hat{Q}$ be a compact subset of Q. Furthermore, by assumption (A.12), it follows from Theorem 7.1 that the sequence $\{\|\phi^{m(l)}\|_{\infty, Q}\}$ is uniformly bounded. Thus from Theorem 7.2 $\{\phi^{m(l)}\}$ is equicontinuous in $\hat{Q}$. Therefore, by virtue of the Ascoli–Arzela theorem, there exists a subsequence of the sequence $\{\phi^{m(l)}\}$, again denoted by $\{\phi^{m(l)}\}$, such that

$$\phi^{m(l)} \xrightarrow{u} \phi,$$

in $\hat{Q}$, as $l \to \infty$. Thus

$$\phi(x, t) \geq 0,$$

for almost all $(x, t) \in \hat{Q}$. Since $\hat{Q}$ is an arbitrary compact subset of Q and by Theorem 7.2, ϕ is continuous in Q, it follows that

$$\phi(x, t) \geq 0,$$

for all $(x, t) \in Q$. This completes the proof. ■

CHAPTER III

Optimal Control of First Boundary Problems: Strong Variation Techniques

III.1. Introduction

In this chapter we shall consider a class of optimal control problems involving first boundary-value problems of a parabolic type. This class of optimal control problems corresponds naturally to a class of stochastic optimal control problems with Markov terminal time. The details may be found in Appendix A.1 as well as references.

The aim of this chapter is to use the strong variational technique to devise a computational algorithm for solving the optimal control problem under discussion. A convergence property of the algorithm is investigated; and the question concerning the discretization of the algorithm is also briefly discussed. Two examples arising in the study of the renewable resource management are solved by using the discretized algorithm.

III.2. System Description

As in Section II.2, Ω is a bounded domain in R^n with its boundary and closure denoted by $\partial\Omega$ and $\overline{\Omega}$, respectively. Again it is assumed throughout this chapter that *the boundary* $\partial\Omega$ *belongs to the class* C^3. Let T be a fixed positive constant, $Q \equiv \Omega \times (0, T)$, $\Gamma \equiv \partial\Omega \times [0, T]$, and $\overline{Q} \equiv \overline{\Omega} \times [0, T]$. Let n_1 be an integer with $0 < n_1 \leq n$. Then for any $x \equiv (x_1, \ldots, x_n) \in R^n$, define

$$\hat{x} \equiv (x_1, \ldots, x_{n_1}) \in R^{n_1}, \qquad \hat{\hat{x}} \equiv (x_{n_1+1}, \ldots, x_n) \in R^{n-n_1};$$

and let

$$\hat{\Omega} \equiv \{\hat{x} \in R^{n_1} : x \in \Omega\}, \qquad \hat{\hat{\Omega}} \equiv \{\hat{\hat{x}} \in R^{n-n_1} : x \in \Omega\}, \qquad \hat{Q} \equiv \hat{\Omega} \times (0, T),$$

$$\Omega_{\hat{x}} \equiv \{\hat{\hat{x}} \in R^{n-n_1} : (\hat{x}, \hat{\hat{x}}) \in \Omega\}, \qquad \Omega_{\hat{\hat{x}}} \equiv \{\hat{x} \in R^{n_1} : (\hat{x}, \hat{\hat{x}}) \in \Omega\}.$$

Let U be a given nonempty compact and convex subset of R^m. A measureable function $u: \hat{Q} \to U$ is called *an admissible control. Let* $\mathcal{U}$ *denote the class of all such admissible controls.*

We consider the first boundary-value problem:

$$L(u)\phi(x, t) = f(x, t, u(\hat{x}, t)), \qquad (x, t) \in Q \tag{2.1a}$$

$$\phi|_{t=0} = \phi_0, \qquad x \in \Omega \tag{2.1b}$$

$$\phi|_{\Gamma} = 0, \qquad (x, t) \in \Gamma, \tag{2.1c}$$

where $u \in \mathcal{U}$ and, for each $u \in \mathcal{U}$, $L(u)$ is a linear second-order parabolic partial differential operator in general form defined by

$$L(u)\psi \equiv \psi_t - \sum_{i,j=1}^{n} a_{ij}(x, t)\psi_{x_i x_j} - \sum_{i=1}^{n} b_i(x, t, u(\hat{x}, t))\psi_{x_i} - c(x, t, u(\hat{x}, t))\psi. \tag{2.2}$$

Since the problem (2.1) is in the form of the one studied in Section II.8, the solution of the problem is to be understood as in the sense defined therein. More precisely, it is to be understood as in the sense of the following.

DEFINITION 2.1. *For each* $u \in \mathcal{U}$, *a function* $\phi(u): Q \to R^1$ *is called an almost everywhere solution of problem* (2.1) *if it belongs to the space* $W_\infty^{2,1}(Q)$ *and satisfies Eq.* (2.1*a*) *almost everywhere in* Q, *initial condition* (2.1*b*) *almost everywhere in* Ω, *and boundary condition* (2.1*c*) *almost everywhere in* Γ.

For the initial and boundary conditions mentioned in the Definition 2.1 $\phi(u)|_{\partial Q}$ is to be understood as the trace of $\phi(u)$, where $\partial Q \equiv \Gamma \cup \Omega_0$ and $\Omega_0 \equiv \Omega \times \{0\}$.

Since Q is bounded, it follows that Definition 2.1 is a generalization of the corresponding classical notion.

We assume throughout this chapter that the following conditions are satisfied.

(A.1) $a_{ij} \in C(\bar{Q})$, $i, j = 1, \ldots, n$.

(A.2) There exists positive constants $\alpha_l, \alpha_u > 0$ such that

$$\alpha_l |\xi|^2 \leq \sum_{i,j=1}^{n} a_{ij}(x, t)\xi_i \xi_j \leq \alpha_u |\xi|^2,$$

for all $\xi \equiv (\xi_1, \ldots, \xi_n) \in R^n$ and for all $(x, t) \in \bar{Q}$, where $|\xi|^2 \equiv \sum_{i=1}^n (\xi_i)^2$.

(A.3) b_i, $i = 1, \ldots, n$, c and f are in $C(\bar{Q} \times U)$.

(A.4) $\phi_0 \in C_0^2(\Omega)$.

Remark 2.1. Let α denote any of the functions appearing in assumption (A.3). Define

$$\alpha(u) \equiv \alpha(\cdot, \cdot, u(\cdot, \cdot)),$$

for all $u \in \mathscr{U}$. Then it is clear that α can be considered as a mapping from $\mathscr{U}$ into $L_\infty(Q)$.

Note that assumptions (A.1)–(A.4) imply the hypotheses of Theorem II.8.1. Thus from the same theorem, it follows that, for each $u \in \mathscr{U}$, problem (2.1) admits a unique almost everywhere solution $\phi(u)$ that satisfies the estimate

$$\|\phi(u)\|_{p,Q}^{(2,1)} \leq K_0\{\|f(u)\|_{\infty,Q} + \|\phi_0\|_{\infty,Q}^{(2)}\},$$

for all $p \in (\frac{3}{2}, \infty]$, where the constant K_0 is independent of $u \in \mathscr{U}$. Thus using (A.3) and (A.4), we can find a constant K_1, independent of $u \in \mathscr{U}$, such that

$$\|\phi(u)\|_{p,Q}^{(2,1)} \leq K_1, \tag{2.3}$$

for all $p \in (\frac{3}{2}, \infty]$.

Next, it follows from Corollary II.8.1 that

$$|\phi(u)|_Q^{(1+\mu, (1+\mu)/2)} \leq K_2 \|\phi(u)\|_{p,Q}^{(2,1)}, \tag{2.4}$$

for all $p > n + 2$, where $\mu = 1 - (n + 2)/p$, $|\cdot|_Q^{(\lambda, \lambda/2)}$ denotes the norm in the Hölder space $\mathscr{H}^{\lambda,\lambda/2}(\bar{Q})$, and the constant K_2 depends only on Q and p. In particular, when $p = 2(n + 2)$ we have

$$|\phi(u)|_Q^{(3/2, 3/4)} \leq K_2 \|\phi(u)\|_{2(n+2),Q}^{(2,1)}. \tag{2.5}$$

Thus by virtue of estimate (2.3) it follows that

$$|\phi(u)|_Q^{(3/2, 3/4)} \leq K_3, \tag{2.6}$$

where $K_3 \equiv K_1 K_2$ and so is again independent of $u \in \mathscr{U}$.

In the rest of the chapter let $\phi(u)$ denote the almost everywhere solution of problem (2.1) corresponding to each $u \in \mathscr{U}$. Clearly, ϕ can be considered as a mapping from $\mathscr{U}$ into $W_{\infty}^{2,1}(Q)$.

Since $U \subset R^m$ is compact, $\mathscr{U}$ is a bounded subset of $L_{\infty}(\hat{Q}, R^m)$. Thus the norm in $\mathscr{U}$ is that induced by the norm in $L_{\infty}(\hat{Q}, R^m)$, that is,

$$\|u\|_{\mathscr{U}} \equiv \operatorname*{ess\,sup}_{(\hat{x},t)\in\hat{Q}} \left\{ \left[\sum_{i=1}^{m} (u_i(\hat{x}, t))^2 \right]^{1/2} \right\}, \qquad u \equiv (u_1, \ldots, u_m) \in \mathscr{U}.$$

REMARK 2.2. Let α be as defined in Remark 2.1. Since $\bar{Q} \times U$ is compact, it is easy to verify that α is a uniformly continuous mapping from $\mathscr{U}$ into $L_{\infty}(Q)$.

THEOREM 2.1. *The mapping $\phi\colon \mathscr{U} \to W_{\infty}^{2,1}(Q)$ is uniformly continuous.*

Proof. Let $u^1, u^2 \in \mathscr{U}$. Then from Theorem A.2.1 (of Appendix II), we obtain

$$\|\phi(u^1) - \phi(u^2)\|_{\infty,Q}^{(2,1)} \leq N \left\{ \sum_{i=1}^{n} \|b_i(u^1) - b_i(u^2)\|_{\infty,Q} + \|c(u^1) - c(u^2)\|_{\infty,Q} \right.$$
$$\left. + \|f(u^1) - f(u^2)\|_{\infty,Q} \right\},$$

where the constant N is independent of $u^1, u^2 \in \mathscr{U}$. Thus by virtue of Remark 2.2 the mapping ϕ is uniformly continuous. ■

III.3. The Optimal Control Problems

Consider the dynamic system (2.1). If we wish to formulate an optimal control problem, we need to specify a functional that gives a measure of the performance of the system corresponding to each $u \in \mathscr{U}$. This functional is called the cost functional.

The class of cost functionals considered in this chapter is

$$J(u) = \int_{\Omega} \gamma(x, \phi(u)(x, T))\, dx, \tag{3.1}$$

where $\phi(u)$ is the almost everywhere solution of problem (2.1) corresponding to the control $u \in \mathscr{U}$, and $\gamma\colon \Omega \to R^1$ is a real-valued function.

We shall assume that γ satisfies the following conditions:

(A.5)

(i) γ is a Carathéodory function defined on $\bar{\Omega} \times R^1$;
(ii) $\gamma(\cdot, \theta) \in L_1(\Omega)$ for *some* $\theta \in R^1$;

(iii) there exists a Carathéodory function $g: \bar{\Omega} \times R^1 \to R^1$ such that

$$\gamma(x, \theta^1) \leq \gamma(x, \theta^2) + g(x, \theta^2)(\theta^1 - \theta^2),$$

for almost all $x \in \Omega$ and for all $\theta^1, \theta^2 \in R^1$;

(iv) $g(\cdot, 0) \in L_\infty(\Omega)$; and

(v) there exists a constant K_4 such that

$$|g(x, \theta^1) - g(x, \theta^2)| \leq K_4 |\theta^1 - \theta^2|,$$

for almost all $x \in \Omega$ and for all $\theta^1, \theta^2 \in R^1$.

Our optimal control problem may now be specified.

Problem (P) Subject to the dynamic system (2.1), find a control $u^* \in \mathscr{U}$ such that

$$J(u^*) \leq J(u),$$

for all $u \in \mathscr{U}$. This control u^* is called an optimal control.

The aim of this chapter is to use the strong variational method to produce a computational algorithm for solving problem (P). For this, we need to introduce a system that is known as the adjoint system because its differential operator $L^*(u)$ is the formal adjoint of the operator $L(u)$. More precisely,

$$L^*(u)\psi \equiv -\psi_t - \sum_{i=1}^{n} \left[\sum_{j=1}^{n} a_{ij}(x, t)\psi_{x_j} + a_i(x, t, u(\hat{x}, t))\psi \right]_{x_i} - c(x, t, u(\hat{x}, t))\psi, \tag{3.2}$$

where

$$a_i(x, t, u(\hat{x}, t)) \equiv \sum_{j=1}^{n} \frac{\partial a_{ij}(x, t)}{\partial x_j} - b_i(x, t, u(\hat{x}, t)), \qquad i = 1, \ldots, n. \tag{3.3}$$

Note that the functions a_i are not necessarily measurable under assumptions (A.1) and (A.3). Thus assumption (A.1) is to be replaced throughout the rest of this chapter by a stronger assumption given subsequently.

(A.1)′ There exists a constant K_5 such that

$$|a_{ij}(x, t) - a_{ij}(x', t')|/(|x - x'| + |t - t'|) \leq K_5,$$

for all $i, j = 1, \ldots, n$ and for all $(x, t), (x', t') \in \bar{Q}$.

Under assumptions (A.1)′ and (A.3), we see that, for each $u \in \mathscr{U}$, the functions $a_i(\cdot, \cdot, u(\cdot, \cdot))$, $i = 1, \ldots, n$, are measurable and bounded on $\bar{Q}$.

The adjoint system is now given as

$$L^*(u)z = 0, \qquad (x, t) \in Q, \tag{3.4a}$$

$$z|_{t=T} = g(x, \phi(u)(x, T)), \qquad x \in \Omega, \tag{3.4b}$$

$$z|_{\Gamma} = 0, \qquad (x, t) \in \Gamma, \tag{3.4c}$$

where g is a function given in assumption (A.5).

Note that the differential operator $L^*(u)$ is in divergence form and that the differentiability assumption on the first-order coefficients b_i is not suitable in the study of optimal control problems involving bounded measurable controls. Thus adjoint problem (3.4) does not admit almost everywhere solutions. For this reason we introduce a weaker sense of solutions in the following.

DEFINITION 3.1. *For each $u \in \mathcal{U}$, a function $z(u): Q \to R^1$ is called a weak solution of adjoint problem* (3.4) *if it belongs to the space $\mathring{V}_2^{1,0}(Q)$ and satisfies the integral identity*:

$$\begin{aligned}\int_{\Omega} g(x, \phi(u)(x, T))\eta(x, T)\,dx &= \iint_Q \Bigg\{ z(u)(x, t)\eta_t(x, t) \\ &\quad + \sum_{i=1}^{n} \left[\sum_{j=1}^{n} a_{ij}(x, t)z(u)_{x_j}(x, t) + a_i(x, t, u(\hat{x}, t))z(u)(x, t) \right] \eta_{x_i}(x, t) \\ &\quad - c(x, t, u(\hat{x}, t))z(u)(x, t)\eta(x, t) \Bigg\}\,dx\,dt, \end{aligned} \tag{3.5}$$

for all $\eta \in \mathring{W}_2^{1,1}(Q)$ that are equal to zero for $t = 0$.

Letting $t = T - t'$ and then setting $\hat{z}(x, t) \equiv z(x, T - t)$, adjoint problem (3.4) is reduced to

$$\hat{L}^*(u)\hat{z} = 0, \qquad (x, t) \in Q \tag{3.6a}$$

$$\hat{z}|_{t=0} = g(x, \phi(u)(x, T)), \qquad x \in \Omega \tag{3.6b}$$

$$\hat{z}|_{\Gamma} = 0, \qquad (x, t) \in \Gamma, \tag{3.6c}$$

where, for each $u \in \mathcal{U}$, the operator $\hat{L}^*(u)$ is defined by

$$\begin{aligned}\hat{L}^*(u)\psi \equiv \psi_t - \sum_{i=1}^{n} \left[\sum_{i,j=1}^{n} a_{ij}(x, T - t)\psi_{x_j} + a_i(x, T - t, u(\hat{x}, T - t))\psi \right]_{x_i} \\ - c(x, T - t, u(\hat{x}, T - t))\psi. \end{aligned} \tag{3.7}$$

Since Q and U are bounded, assumptions (A.1)′, (A.2), (A.3), and (A.4) imply assumptions (II.A.1), (II.A.2), (II.A.3), and (II.A.6). Thus it follows from Theorem II.5.6 that, for each $u \in \mathscr{U}$, problem (3.6) has a unique weak solution $\hat{z}(u)$ from the space $V_2^{1,0}(Q)$ (in the sense of Definition II.2.1). Furthermore, by Theorem II.4.2 there exists a constant K_6, independent of the control $u \in \mathscr{U}$, such that

$$\|\hat{z}(u)\|_Q \leq K_6\{\|g(\cdot, \phi(u)(\cdot, T))\|_{2,\Omega}\}. \tag{3.8}$$

From estimate (2.6), it is clear that $\phi(u)(\cdot, T)$ is bounded on $\bar{\Omega}$ uniformly with respect to $u \in \mathscr{U}$. Thus by virtue of assumption (A.5) (iv) and (v), estimate (3.8) is reduced to

$$\|\hat{z}(u)\|_Q \leq K_7, \tag{3.9}$$

where the constant K_7 is independent of $u \in \mathscr{U}$.

We now return to the adjoint problem (3.4). From the definition of $\hat{z}$, it follows that the adjoint problem admits, for each $u \in \mathscr{U}$, a unique weak solution $z(u)$ that satisfies the estimate

$$\|z(u)\|_Q \leq K_7, \tag{3.10}$$

where K_7 is the same constant as in estimate (3.9).

In the rest of this chapter let $z(u)$ denote the weak solution of the adjoint problem (3.4) corresponding to $u \in \mathscr{U}$. Since Q is bounded, $\mathring{V}_2^{1,0}(Q)$ is continuously embedded in $L_1(Q)$. Thus by virtue of (3.10) there exists a constant K_8, independent of $u \in \mathscr{U}$, such that

$$\|z(u)\|_{1,Q} \leq K_8. \tag{3.11}$$

On this basis z can be considered as a mapping from $\mathscr{U}$ into $L_1(Q)$.

In view of Definitions II.2.1 and II.7.1 we observe that $\hat{z}(u)|_\Gamma = 0$ and that $\hat{z}(u)$ is also a weak solution from the space $V_2^{1,0}(Q)$ of Eq. (3.6a) in the sense of Definition II.7.1. Observe also that the assumption on the boundary $\partial\Omega$ is the same in Chapter II and in this chapter. Furthermore, since Q and U are bounded, assumptions (A.1) and (A.3) imply assumption (II.A.9). Thus all the hypotheses of Theorem II.7.1 are satisfied. Therefore,

$$|\hat{z}(u)(x, t)| \leq K_9, \tag{3.12}$$

for almost all $(x, t) \in Q$, where the constant K_9 is independent of $u \in \mathscr{U}$.

Inequality (3.12) together with the hypotheses of Theorem II.7.1 imply the hypotheses of Theorem II.7.2. Thus it follows that $\hat{z}(u)$ is continuous on Q.

From the definition of $\hat{z}(u)$ we obtain the following theorem.

THEOREM 3.1. *Consider the adjoint system* (3.4). *Then there exists a constant K_{10}, independent of $u \in \mathscr{U}$, such that*

$$|z(u)(x, t)| \leq K_{10}, \tag{3.13}$$

for almost all $(x, t) \in Q$. Furthermore, $z(u)$ is continuous on Q.

Our next aim is to show that z, considered as a mapping from $\mathscr{U}$ into $L_1(Q)$, is uniformly continuous. For this we need the following Lemma.

LEMMA 3.1. *Let*

$$\check{\mathring{W}}_2^{2,1}(Q) \equiv \{\psi \in \mathring{W}_2^{2,1}(Q) : \psi(x, 0) = 0,\ x \in \Omega\}.$$

Then for any $\Phi \in \check{\mathring{W}}_2^{2,1}(Q)$,

$$\iint_Q (L(u)\Phi)z(u)\,dx\,dt = \int_\Omega \Phi(x, T)g(x, \phi(u)(x, T))\,dx, \tag{3.14}$$

for all $u \in \mathscr{U}$.

Proof. Since $z(u)$ is the weak solution of the adjoint problem (3.4) corresponding to $u \in \mathscr{U}$ and $\check{\mathring{W}}_2^{2,1}(Q)$ is contained in

$$\check{\mathring{W}}_2^{1,1}(Q) \equiv \{\psi \in \mathring{W}_2^{1,1}(Q) : \psi(x, 0) = 0,\ x \in \Omega\},$$

it follows from Definition 3.1 that

$$\begin{aligned}\iint_Q \Bigg\{ & z(u)(x, t)\Phi_t(x, t) \\ & + \sum_{i=1}^n \left[\sum_{j=1}^n a_{ij}(x, t)z(u)_{x_j}(x, t) + a_i(x, t, u(\hat{x}, t))z(u)(x, t)\right]\Phi_{x_i}(x, t) \\ & - c(x, t, u(\hat{x}, t))z(u)(x, t)\Phi(x, t)\Bigg\}\,dx\,dt = \int_\Omega \Phi(x, T)g(x, \phi(u)(x, T))\,dx,\end{aligned}$$

for any $\Phi \in \check{W}_2^{2,1}(Q)$.

Performing the integration by parts with respect to x_j and then using the definitions of a_i and $L(u)$, we obtain the conclusion of the lemma. ■

THEOREM 3.2. *The mapping* $z : \mathscr{U} \to L_1(Q)$ *is uniformly continuous.*

Proof. Let $u^1, u^2 \in \mathscr{U}$ be arbitrary, and let $e : Q \to R^1$ be defined by

$$e(x, t) \equiv \begin{cases} 1, & \text{if } z(u^1)(x, t) \geq z(u^2)(x, t), \\ -1, & \text{elsewhere.} \end{cases} \tag{3.15}$$

Clearly, $e \in L_\infty(Q)$.

Consider the following first boundary-value problem:

$$L(u^1)\psi = e, \qquad (x, t) \in Q \tag{3.16a}$$

$$\psi|_{t=0} = 0, \qquad x \in \Omega \tag{3.16b}$$

$$\psi|_\Gamma = 0, \qquad (x, t) \in \Gamma. \tag{3.16c}$$

Then from Theorem II.8.1, it follows that problem (3.16) has a unique almost everywhere solution ψ. Furthermore, again from the same theorem, there exists a constant N_0, independent of $u^1, u^2 \in \mathscr{U}$, such that

$$\|\psi\|_{p,Q}^{(2,1)} \le N_0, \tag{3.17}$$

for all $p \in (\frac{3}{2}, \infty]$. In particular, $\psi \in \mathring{W}_2^{2,1}(Q) \cap \mathring{W}_\infty^{2,1}(Q)$. Thus

$$\begin{aligned}
0 \le \|z(u^1) - z(u^2)\|_{1,Q} &= \iint_Q (L(u^1)\psi)[z(u^1) - z(u^2)]\,dx\,dt \\
&= \iint_Q (L(u^1)\psi)z(u^1)\,dx\,dt - \iint_Q (L(u^2)\psi)z(u^2)\,dx\,dt \\
&\quad - \iint_Q [(L(u^1) - L(u^2))\psi]z(u^2)\,dx\,dt \\
&= \int_\Omega \psi(x,T)[g(x,\phi(u^1)(x,T)) - g(x,\phi(u^2)(x,T))]\,dx \\
&\quad + \iint_Q \sum_{i=1}^n [b_i(u^1) - b_i(u^2)]\psi_{x_i} z(u^2)\,dx\,dt \\
&\quad + \iint_Q [c(u^1) - c(u^2)]\psi z(u^2)\,dx\,dt \\
&\le \int_\Omega |\psi(x,T)|[|g(x,\phi(u^1)(x,T)) \\
&\quad - g(x,\phi(u^2)(x,T))|]\,dx \\
&\quad + \sum_{i=1}^n \|b_i(u^1) - b_i(u^2)\|_{\infty,Q}\|\psi_{x_i}\|_{\infty,Q}\|z(u^2)\|_{1,Q} \\
&\quad + \|c(u^1) - c(u^2)\|_{\infty,Q}\|\psi\|_{\infty,Q}\|z(u^2)\|_{1,Q}.
\end{aligned} \tag{3.18}$$

Using Remark 2.2 and Eqs. (2.3) and (3.11), we can verify that, for any $\varepsilon > 0$, there exists a $\delta_1 > 0$ such that, for any $u^1, u^2 \in \mathscr{U}$,

$$\begin{aligned}
&\sum_{i=1}^n \|b_i(u^1) - b_i(u^2)\|_{\infty,Q}\|\psi_{x_i}\|_{\infty,Q}\|z(u^2)\|_{1,Q} \\
&\qquad + \|c(u^1) - c(u^2)\|_{\infty,Q}\|\psi\|_{\infty,Q}\|z(u^2)\|_{1,Q} \le \varepsilon/2,
\end{aligned} \tag{3.19}$$

whenever $\|u^1 - u^2\|_{\mathscr{U}} < \delta_1$.

It remains to show that

$$\int_\Omega |\psi(x,T)|[|g(x,\phi(u^1)(x,T)) - g(x,\phi(u^2)(x,T))|]\,dx$$

can be made arbitrary small by choosing u^1 and u^2 arbitrary closed to each other in the norm $\|\cdot\|_{\mathscr{U}}$. To begin we note that

$$\mathring{\hat{W}}_2^{2,1}(Q) \subset \mathring{W}_2^{1,1}(Q) \subset \mathring{V}_2^{1,0}(Q).$$

Thus it follows that $\psi(\cdot, T) \in L_2(\Omega)$ and hence $\psi(\cdot, T) \in L_1(\Omega)$, since Ω is bounded. Define

$$g(\phi) = g(\cdot, \phi(\cdot)),$$

for all $\phi \in L_\infty(\Omega)$. Then by (A.5) (iv) and (2.6), we obtain

$$\begin{aligned}\|g(\phi(u^1)) - g(\phi(u^2))\|_{\infty,\Omega} &\leq N_1 \|\phi(u^1)(\cdot, T) - \phi(u^2)(\cdot, T)\|_{\infty,\Omega} \\ &\leq N_1 \|\phi(u^1) - \phi(u^2)\|_{\infty,Q},\end{aligned}$$

where the constant N_1 is independent of $u^1, u^2 \in \mathscr{U}$. On this basis, it follows from Hölder's inequality that

$$\begin{aligned}&\int_\Omega |\psi(x, T)|[|g(x, \phi(u^1)(x, T)) - g(x, \phi(u^2)(x, T))|]\, dx \\ &\qquad \leq N_2 \|\psi(\cdot, T)\|_{2,\Omega} \|\phi(u^1) - \phi(u^2)\|_{\infty,Q},\end{aligned} \tag{3.20}$$

where $N_2 \equiv N_1(|\Omega|)^{1/2}$ is independent of $u^1, u^2 \in \mathscr{U}$, and $|\Omega|$ denotes the Lebesgue measure of Ω.

Using the preceding inequality and Theorem 2.1, we conclude that, for any $\varepsilon > 0$, there exists a $\delta_2 > 0$ such that, for any $u^1, u^2 \in \mathscr{U}$,

$$\int_\Omega |\psi(x, T)|[|g(x, \phi(u^1)(x, T)) - g(x, \phi(u^2)(x, T))|]\, dx < \varepsilon/2, \tag{3.21}$$

whenever $\|u^1 - u^2\|_{\mathscr{U}} < \delta_2$.

Now, let $\varepsilon > 0$ be given and choose $\delta = \min\{\delta_1, \delta_2\}$. Then the conclusion of the theorem follows readily from (3.19) and (3.21). ■

III.4. The Hamiltonian Functions

For each $u \in \mathscr{U}$, let $I(u)\colon \bar{Q} \times U \to R^1$ and $H(u)\colon \hat{Q} \times U \to R^1$ be defined by

$$I(u)[x, t, v] \equiv \sum_{i=1}^{n} b_i(x, t, v)\phi(u)_{x_i}(x, t) + c(x, t, v)\phi(u)(x, t) + f(x, t, v), \tag{4.1}$$

and

$$H(u)[\hat{x}, t, v] \equiv \int_{\Omega_{\hat{\hat{x}}}} I(u)[\hat{x}, \hat{\hat{x}}, t, v] z(u)(\hat{x}, \hat{\hat{x}}, t)\, d\hat{\hat{x}}. \tag{4.2}$$

The function $H(u)$ is called the Hamiltonian function for $u \in \mathscr{U}$.

In the case when $n_1 = n$, $H(u)$ becomes a function on $Q \times U$ (not just $\hat{Q} \times U$) defined by

$$H(u)[x, t, v] = I(u)[x, t, v]z(u)(x, t). \tag{4.2$'$}$$

Our next aim is to show that the variation in the cost functional resulting from the variation in control can be estimated in terms of the integral of the Hamiltonian function together with two additional terms. To begin we introduce the following notation.

Let β and γ be two functionals on $\mathscr{U} \times \mathscr{U}$ defined by

$$\beta(u^1, u^2) \equiv \iint_Q \sum_{i=1}^{n} [b_i(u^1) - b_i(u^2)][\phi(u^1)_{x_i} - \phi(u^2)_{x_i}]z(u^1)\, dx\, dt, \tag{4.3}$$

and

$$\gamma(u^1, u^2) \equiv \iint_{\hat{Q}} [c(u^1) - c(u^2)][\phi(u^1) - \phi(u^2)]z(u^1)\, dx\, dt. \tag{4.4}$$

LEMMA 4.1. *For any $u^1, u^2 \in \mathscr{U}$, let*

$$\psi = \phi(u^1) - \phi(u^2).$$

Then

$$\begin{aligned}\int_\Omega &\psi(x, T)g(x, \phi(u^1)(x, T))\, dx \\ &= \iint_{\hat{Q}} \{H(u^1)[\hat{x}, t, u^1(\hat{x}, t)] - H(u^1)[\hat{x}, t, u^2(\hat{x}, t)]\}\, d\hat{x}\, dt \\ &\quad - \beta(u^1, u^2) - \gamma(u^1, u^2).\end{aligned} \tag{4.5}$$

Proof. From the definition of ψ it is clear that

$$\begin{aligned}L(u^1)\psi &= L(u^1)\phi(u^1) - L(u^2)\phi(u^2) - [L(u^1) - L(u^2)]\phi(u^1) \\ &\quad + [L(u^1) - L(u^2)][\phi(u^1) - \phi(u^2)].\end{aligned} \tag{4.6}$$

Thus by virtue of (2.1) and the definitions of L and I, we obtain

$$\begin{aligned}L(u^1)\psi(x, t) &= I(u^1)[x, t, u^1(\hat{x}, t)] - I(u^1)[x, t, u^2(\hat{x}, t)] \\ &\quad - \sum_{i=1}^{n} [b_i(x, t, u^1(\hat{x}, t)) - b_i(x, t, u^2(\hat{x}, t))][\phi(u^1)_{x_i}(x, t) \\ &\quad - \phi(u^2)_{x_i}(x, t)] - [c(x, t, u^1(\hat{x}, t)) - c(x, t, u^2(\hat{x}, t))] \\ &\quad \times [\phi(u^1)(x, t) - \phi(u^2)(x, t)] \\ &\equiv Y(x, t).\end{aligned} \tag{4.7}$$

Using (2.3) and (A.3) we see that the function Y is bounded and measurable on Q.

Now, we note that $\psi \in \mathring{\hat{W}}_2^{2,1}(Q)$, where $\mathring{\hat{W}}_2^{2,1}(Q)$ is defined in Lemma 3.1. Thus by the same lemma we have

$$\iint_Q (L(u^1)\psi)z(u^1)\,dx\,dt = \int_\Omega \psi(x, T)g(x, \phi(u^1)(x, T))\,dx. \tag{4.8}$$

From (4.7) and the definitions of H, β, and γ, we obtain

$$\begin{aligned}\iint_Q & L(u^1)\psi z(u^1)\,dx\,dt \\ &= \iint_{\hat{Q}} \{H(u^1)[\hat{x}, t, u^1(\hat{x}, t)] - H(u^2)[\hat{x}, t, u^2(\hat{x}, t)]\}\,d\hat{x}\,dt - \beta(u^1, u^2) \\ &\quad - \gamma(u^1, u^2).\end{aligned} \tag{4.9}$$

Combining (4.8) and (4.9) we obtain the conclusion of the lemma. ■

THEOREM 4.1. *Let $J(u)$ be the cost functional given by* (3.1). *Then for any $u^1, u^2 \in \mathscr{U}$,*

$$\begin{aligned}J(u^2) - J(u^1) \le & \iint_{\hat{Q}} \{H(u^1)[\hat{x}, t, u^2(\hat{x}, t)] - H(u^1)[\hat{x}, t, u^1(\hat{x}, t)]\}\,d\hat{x}\,dt \\ & + \beta(u^1, u^2) + \gamma(u^1, u^2).\end{aligned} \tag{4.10}$$

Proof. We have

$$J(u^2) - J(u^1) = \int_\Omega \{\gamma(x, \phi(u^2)(x, T)) - \gamma(x, \phi(u^1)(x, T))\}\,dx.$$

Thus by (A.5) (iii) we obtain

$$J(u^2) - J(u^1) \le -\int_\Omega \psi(x, T)g(x, \phi(u^1)(x, T))\,dx,$$

where

$$\psi \equiv \phi(u^1) - \phi(u^2).$$

Therefore, the conclusion of the theorem follows readily from Lemma 4.1. ■

The main aim of this chapter is to use the strong variational method to produce a computational algorithm for solving the optimal control problem (P). To achieve this goal, we shall encounter the following question: given an admissible control u^1 is there an admissible control u^2 such that

$$H(u^1)[\hat{x}, t, u^2(\hat{x}, t)] \le H(u^1)[\hat{x}, t, v]$$

for all $(\hat{x}, t, v) \in \hat{Q} \times U$?

The answer to this question is positive and is given in the next theorem. First, we need

LEMMA 4.2. *Let $H(u)$ be given by* (4.2). *Then*

(i) *for each $u \in \mathscr{U}$, $H(u)$ is continuous on $\hat{Q} \times U$;*
(ii) *for each $u \in \mathscr{U}$ and $(\hat{x}, t) \in \hat{Q}$ the function*

$$H(u)[\hat{x}, t, \cdot]: U \to R^1$$

has a minimum; and
(iii) *$H(u)$ is bounded almost everywhere on $\hat{Q} \times U$ uniformly with respect to $u \in \mathscr{U}$.*

Proof. From the definition of $I(u)$ we note that it is made up by the sum and product of functions which, either by the hypotheses or by the estimate (2.6), are continuous on $\bar{Q} \times U$. Thus $I(u)$ is also continuous on $\bar{Q} \times U$. Similarly, we can show that $I(u)$ is bounded on $\bar{Q} \times U$ uniformly with respect to $u \in \mathscr{U}$.

Since $I(u)$ is continuous on $\bar{Q} \times U$, $z(u)$ is, by Theorem 3.1, continuous on Q, and Ω (and hence $\Omega_{\hat{x}}$) is bounded, we can easily verify that the function $H(u)$ is continuous on $\hat{Q} \times U$. In particular, for each $(\hat{x}, t) \in \hat{Q}$, the function $H(u)[\hat{x}, t, \cdot]$ is continuous on U. Since U is compact, $H(u)[\hat{x}, t, \cdot]$ attains its minimum on U.

Finally, since $I(u)$ is bounded on $\bar{Q} \times U$ uniformly with respect to $u \in \mathscr{U}$ and Ω (and hence $\Omega_{\hat{x}}$) is bounded, $H(u)$ is bounded almost everywhere on $\hat{Q} \times U$ uniformly with respect to $u \in \mathscr{U}$, using the first part of Theorem 3.1. ■

From the preceding lemma we observe that, for each $u \in \mathscr{U}$, there exist functions from $\hat{Q}$ into U that minimize the Hamiltonian function $H(u)[\hat{x}, t, \cdot]$, for each $(\hat{x}, t) \in \hat{Q}$. However, such functions are not necessarily measurable. In the next theorem we shall show that an admissible control can be obtained from such functions.

THEOREM 4.2. *For any $u \in \mathscr{U}$, there exists an admissible control $V(u)$ such that*

$$H(u)[\hat{x}, t, V(u)(\hat{x}, t)] \leq H(u)[\hat{x}, t, v], \tag{4.11}$$

for all $(\hat{x}, t, v) \in \hat{Q} \times U$.

Proof. Define $r: \hat{Q} \to R^1$ by

$$r(\hat{x}, t) \equiv \min_{v \in U} \{H(u)[\hat{x}, t, v]\}.$$

Then r is measurable and

$$r(\hat{x}, t) \in H(u)[\hat{x}, t, U] \equiv \{H(u)[\hat{x}, t, v]: v \in U\},$$

for each $(\hat{x}, t) \in \hat{Q}$. Thus by Filippov's implicit function lemma (Theorem I.6.1), there exists a measurable function $V(u)$ from $\hat{Q}$ into U such that

$$r(\hat{x}, t) = H(u)[\hat{x}, t, V(u)(\hat{x}, t)].$$

This implies that $V(u) \in \mathscr{U}$ and satisfies condition (4.11). ■

III.5. The Successive Controls

The first-order differential operator θ is a mapping from $\mathscr{U}$ into R^1 defined by

$$\theta(u) \equiv (|\hat{\Omega}|)^{-1} \iint_{\hat{Q}} \{H(u)[\hat{x}, t, V(u)(\hat{x}, t)] - H(u)[\hat{x}, t, u(\hat{x}, t)]\} \, d\hat{x} \, dt, \quad (5.1)$$

where $|\hat{\Omega}|$ denotes the Lebesgue measure of the set $\hat{\Omega}$.

DEFINITION 5.1. *A control $u \in \mathscr{U}$ is said to be an* extremal control *if* $\theta(u) = 0$.

Throughout the rest of this section u will be used to denote a fixed, non-extremal admissible control, that is, $u \in \mathscr{U}$ and $\theta(u) < 0$.

Consider the set

$$\Xi \equiv \Xi(u) \equiv \left\{ \hat{x} \in \hat{\Omega} : \int_0^T \{H(u)[\hat{x}, t, V(u)(\hat{x}, t)] - H(u)[\hat{x}, t, u(\hat{x}, t)]\} \, dt \le \theta(u) \right\}. \quad (5.2)$$

Let $\{\hat{\Omega}_\alpha : \alpha \in [0, |\hat{\Omega}|]\}$ be a family of measurable subsets of $\hat{\Omega}$ such that

$$|\hat{\Omega}_\alpha| = \alpha \quad \text{for all} \quad \alpha \in [0, |\hat{\Omega}|], \quad (5.3a)$$

$$\hat{\Omega}_\alpha \subsetneqq \hat{\Omega}_{\alpha'} \quad \text{for all } \alpha, \alpha' \in [0, |\hat{\Omega}|] \text{ and } \alpha < \alpha', \quad (5.3b)$$

$$\hat{\Omega}_\alpha = \Xi \quad \text{for} \quad \alpha = |\Xi|. \quad (5.3c)$$

Furthermore, for each $\alpha \in [0, |\hat{\Omega}|]$, let

$$\hat{Q}_\alpha \equiv \hat{\Omega}_\alpha \times (0, T), \quad (5.4)$$

and let u^α be a mapping from $\hat{Q}$ into U defined by

$$u^\alpha(\hat{x}, t) \equiv \begin{cases} V(u)(\hat{x}, t), & (\hat{x}, t) \in \hat{Q}_\alpha, \\ u(\hat{x}, t), & (\hat{x}, t) \in \hat{Q} \backslash \hat{Q}_\alpha. \end{cases} \quad (5.5)$$

REMARK 5.1. Note that $\hat{\Omega}_\alpha$, $\hat{Q}_\alpha$, and u^α all depend on u. However, their dependency is suppressed from the notation for the sake of brevity. This abbreviation will be used throughout the rest of this section.

For each $\alpha \in [0, |\hat{\Omega}|]$, set

$$\psi_\alpha \equiv \phi(u) - \phi(u^\alpha), \tag{5.6}$$

where u^α is defined by (5.5). Then it follows that, for almost all $(x, t) \in Q$,

$$\begin{aligned} L(u^\alpha)\psi_\alpha(x, t) &= L(u)\phi(u)(x, t) - L(u^\alpha)\phi(u^\alpha)(x, t) \\ &\quad - (L(u) - L(u^\alpha))\phi(u)(x, t) \\ &= I(u)(x, t, u(\hat{x}, t)) - I(u)(x, t, u^\alpha(\hat{x}, t)) \equiv Y_\alpha(x, t). \end{aligned} \tag{5.7}$$

Moreover, we have

$$\psi_\alpha|_{t=0} = 0, \qquad x \in \Omega \tag{5.8}$$

$$\psi_\alpha|_\Gamma = 0, \qquad (x, t) \in \Gamma. \tag{5.9}$$

Consider the following family of first boundary-value problems

$$L(u^\alpha)\psi(x, t) = Y_\alpha(x, t), \qquad (x, t) \in Q, \tag{5.10a}$$

$$\psi|_{t=0} = 0, \qquad x \in \Omega, \tag{5.10b}$$

$$\psi|_\Gamma = 0, \qquad (x, t) \in \Gamma. \tag{5.10c}$$

Then for each $\alpha \in [0, |\hat{\Omega}|]$, ψ_α is clearly an almost everywhere solution of problem (5.10). To prove the uniqueness we shall use Theorem II.8.1. Thus we need to verify that all the hypotheses of Theorem II.8.1 are satisfied. By comparing the assumptions of this chapter and those of Theorem II.8.1, we observe that only the condition on the forcing term of Eq. (5.10a) is required to be verified. First, we note that the coefficients of the differential operators $L(u)$ and $L(u^\alpha)$ satisfy the corresponding assumptions (A.1)–(A.3). Furthermore, $\phi(u)$ and $\phi(u^\alpha)$ satisfies estimate (2.3). Thus it follows that Y_α is measurable for each $\alpha \in [0, |\hat{\Omega}|]$ and that there exists a constant K_{11}, independent of $u \in \mathscr{U}$ and $\alpha \in [0, |\hat{\Omega}|]$, such that

$$|Y_\alpha(x, t)| \leq K_{11}, \tag{5.11}$$

for all $(x, t) \in Q$. This, in turn, implies that Y_α satisfies the required assumption. Therefore, for each $\alpha \in [0, |\hat{\Omega}|]$, ψ_α is the *unique* almost everywhere solution of problem (5.10). In addition, by estimate (II.8.3), we have

$$\|\psi_\alpha\|_{p,Q}^{(2,1)} \leq K_{12}\{\|Y_\alpha\|_{p,Q}\}, \tag{5.12}$$

for all $p \in (\frac{3}{2}, \infty]$, where the constant K_{12} is independent of $u \in \mathscr{U}$ and $\alpha \in [0, |\hat{\Omega}|]$.

LEMMA 5.1. *Let ψ_α be as given by* (5.6). *Then, there exists a constant K_{13}, independent of $u \in \mathscr{U}$ and $\alpha \in [0, |\hat{\Omega}|]$, such that*

$$\|\psi_\alpha\|_{2,Q}^{(2,1)} \leq K_{13}(|\hat{\Omega}_\alpha|)^{1/2}. \tag{5.13}$$

Proof. Using the definitions of Y_α, u^α, and $I(u)$, estimate (2.5), and assumption (A.3), it is easy to verify from (5.12) with $p = 2$ that the conclusion of the lemma is valid. ■

In the next lemma we shall show that β and γ defined, respectively, by (4.3) and (4.4) are of "higher" order terms.

LEMMA 5.2. *Let β and γ be as defined by* (4.3) *and* (4.4), *respectively. Then there exist constants K_{14} and $s \in (0, 1)$, both independent of $u \in \mathscr{U}$ and $\alpha \in [0, |\hat{\Omega}|]$, such that*

$$\beta(u, u^\alpha) + \gamma(u, u^\alpha) \leq K_{14}(\alpha)^{1+s}. \tag{5.14}$$

Proof. From assumption (A.3) and estimate (3.13), there exists a constant N_0, independent of $u \in \mathscr{U}$, such that

$$\|[b_i(u) - b_i(V(u))]z(u)\|_{\infty,Q} \leq N_0, \tag{5.15}$$

for all $i = 1, \ldots, n$, where $V(u)$ is as defined in Theorem 4.2.

Let p and p' be any pair of real numbers with $p > 2$ and $1/p + 1/p' = 1$. Then there exists a real number $s > 0$ such that $1/p' = \frac{1}{2} + s$.

By using the definition of β it follows from Hölder's inequality that

$$\begin{aligned}
|\beta(u, u^\alpha)| \leq \sum_{i=1}^{n} \int_{\hat{\hat{\Omega}}} \int_0^T \Bigg\{ \int_{\Omega_{\hat{\hat{x}}}} \Big| & [b_i(\hat{x}, \hat{\hat{x}}, t, u(\hat{x}, t)) - b_i(\hat{x}, \hat{\hat{x}}, t, u^\alpha(\hat{x}, t))] \\
& \times [\phi(u)_{x_i}(\hat{x}, \hat{\hat{x}}, t) - \phi(u^\alpha)_{x_i}(\hat{x}, \hat{\hat{x}}, t)] z(u)(\hat{x}, \hat{\hat{x}}, t) \Big| \, d\hat{x} \Bigg\} \, dt \, d\hat{\hat{x}} \\
\leq \sum_{i=1}^{n} \int_{\hat{\hat{\Omega}}} \int_0^T \Bigg\{ \Bigg[\int_{\Omega_{\hat{\hat{x}}}} & |(b_i(\hat{x}, \hat{\hat{x}}, t, u(\hat{x}, t)) \\
& - b_i(\hat{x}, \hat{\hat{x}}, t, u^\alpha(\hat{x}, t)) z(u)(\hat{x}, \hat{\hat{x}}, t)|^{p'} \, d\hat{x} \Bigg]^{1/p'} \\
& \times \left[\int_{\Omega_{\hat{\hat{x}}}} |(\psi_\alpha)_{x_i}(\hat{x}, \hat{\hat{x}}, t)|^p \, d\hat{x} \right]^{1/p} \Bigg\} \, dt \, d\hat{\hat{x}},
\end{aligned} \tag{5.16}$$

where

$$\psi_\alpha \equiv \phi(u) - \phi(u^\alpha).$$

From the definition of u^α and inequality (5.15) we have

$$\left\{\int_{\Omega_{\hat{\hat{x}}}} |[b_i(\hat{x}, \hat{\hat{x}}, t, u(\hat{x}, t)) - b_i(\hat{x}, \hat{\hat{x}}, t, u^\alpha(\hat{x}, t))]z(u)(\hat{x}, \hat{\hat{x}}, t)|^{p'}\, d\hat{x}\right\}^{1/p'}$$

$$= \left\{\int_{\hat{\Omega}_\alpha \cap \Omega_{\hat{\hat{x}}}} |[b_i(\hat{x}, \hat{\hat{x}}, t, u(\hat{x}, t)) - b_i(\hat{x}, \hat{\hat{x}}, t, V(u)(\hat{x}, t))]z(u)(\hat{x}, \hat{\hat{x}}, t)|^{p'}\, d\hat{x}\right\}^{1/p'}$$

$$\leq N_0(\alpha)^{1/p'}, \tag{5.17}$$

for almost all $(\hat{\hat{x}}, t) \in \hat{\hat{\Omega}} \times (0, T) \equiv \hat{\hat{Q}}$.

Substituting (5.17)' into (5.16) we obtain

$$|\beta(u, u^\alpha)| \leq N_0(\alpha)^{1/p'} \left\{\sum_{i=1}^{n} \int_{\hat{\hat{\Omega}}} \int_0^T \left[\int_{\Omega_{\hat{\hat{x}}}} |(\psi_\alpha)_{x_i}(\hat{x}, \hat{\hat{x}}, t)|^p\, d\hat{x}\right]^{1/p} dt\, d\hat{\hat{x}}\right\}. \tag{5.18}$$

Now, by using inequality (I.4.5) we can find a constant N_1, independent of $u \in \mathscr{U}$, $\alpha \in [0, |\hat{\Omega}|]$ and $i = 1, \ldots, n$, such that

$$\int_{\hat{\hat{\Omega}}} \left[\int_{\Omega_{\hat{\hat{x}}}} |(\psi_\alpha)_{x_i}(\hat{x}, \hat{\hat{x}}, t)|^p\, d\hat{x}\right]^{1/p} d\hat{\hat{x}} \leq N_1(|\hat{\hat{\Omega}}|)^{1/p'} \left\{\left[\int_\Omega |(\psi_\alpha)_{x_i}|^2\, dx\right]^{1/2} + \sum_{j=1}^{n} \left[\int_\Omega |(\psi_\alpha)_{x_i x_j}|^2\, dx\right]^{1/2}\right\}. \tag{5.19}$$

Next, for any $q \in L_2(Q)$ it follows from Hölder's inequality that

$$\int_0^T \left[\int_\Omega |q|^2\, dx\right]^{1/2} dt \leq (T)^{1/2} \|q\|_{2,Q}. \tag{5.20}$$

Integrating (5.19) over $(0, T)$, summing i from 1 to n, and then using inequality (5.20), we obtain

$$\sum_{i=1}^{n} \int_0^T \int_{\hat{\hat{\Omega}}} \left[\int_{\Omega_{\hat{\hat{x}}}} |(\psi_\alpha)_{x_i}(\hat{x}, \hat{\hat{x}}, t)|^p\, d\hat{x}\right]^{1/p} d\hat{\hat{x}}\, dt$$

$$\leq N_1(|\hat{\hat{\Omega}}|)^{1/p'}(T)^{1/2}\left[\sum_{i=1}^{n} \|(\psi_\alpha)_{x_i}\|_{2,Q} + \sum_{i,j=1}^{n} \|(\psi_\alpha)_{x_i x_j}\|_{2,Q}\right]$$

$$\leq N_1(|\hat{\hat{\Omega}}|)^{1/p'}(T)^{1/2} \|\psi_\alpha\|_{2,Q}^{(2,1)}. \tag{5.21}$$

Combining (5.18) and (5.21) we have

$$|\beta(u, u^\alpha)| \leq N_2(\alpha)^{1/p'}(|\hat{\hat{\Omega}}|)^{1/p'}(T)^{1/2} \|\psi_\alpha\|_{2,Q}^{(2,1)}, \tag{5.22}$$

where $N_2 \equiv N_0 N_1$.

Since $p' = \frac{1}{2} + s$, it follows from Lemma 5.1 and (5.3a) that the preceding inequality is reduced to

$$|\beta(u, u^\alpha)| \leq N_2(\alpha)^{(1/2)+s}(|\hat{\hat{\Omega}}|)^{1/p'} K_{13}(T)^{1/2}(|\hat{\Omega}_\alpha|)^{1/2} \leq N_3(\alpha)^{1+s}, \tag{5.23}$$

where $N_3 \equiv N_2(|\hat{\hat{\Omega}}|)^{1/p'}(T)^{1/2} K_{13}$ and K_{13} is given in Lemma 5.1.

Similarly, it can be shown that there exists a constant N_4, independent of $u \in \mathscr{U}$ and $\alpha \in [0, |\hat{\Omega}|]$, such that

$$|\gamma(u, u^\alpha)| \leq N_4(\alpha)^{1+s}. \tag{5.24}$$

Thus the conclusion of the lemma follows readily from inequalities (5.23) and (5.24). ■

LEMMA 5.3. *Consider problem (P). Then*

$$\iint_{\hat{Q}} \{H(u)[\hat{x}, t, u^\alpha(\hat{x}, t)] - H(u)[\hat{x}, t, u(\hat{x}, t)]\}\, d\hat{x}\, dt \leq \alpha\theta(u), \tag{5.25}$$

for all $\alpha \in [0, |\hat{\Omega}|]$.

Proof. First, we consider the case when $\alpha \in [0, |\Xi|]$. Then by using the definitions of u^α and Ξ given in (5.5) and (5.2), respectively, we obtain

$$\begin{aligned} &\iint_{\hat{Q}} \{H(u)[\hat{x}, t, u^\alpha(\hat{x}, t)] - H(u)[\hat{x}, t, u(\hat{x}, t)]\}\, d\hat{x}\, dt \\ &= \int_{\hat{\Omega}_\alpha} \left\{ \int_0^T [H(u)(\hat{x}, t, V(u)(\hat{x}, t)) - H(u)(\hat{x}, t, u(\hat{x}, t))]\, dt \right\} d\hat{x} \\ &\leq \int_{\hat{\Omega}_\alpha} \{\theta(u)\}\, d\hat{x} = \alpha\theta(u). \end{aligned} \tag{5.26}$$

We now consider the case when $\alpha \in (|\Xi|, |\hat{\Omega}|]$. Then by the definition of Ξ and because $\hat{\Omega} \backslash \hat{\Omega}_\alpha$ is disjoint from Ξ, we obtain

$$\int_0^T \{H(u)[\hat{x}, t, V(u)(\hat{x}, t)] - H(u)[\hat{x}, t, u(\hat{x}, t)]\}\, dt > \theta(u), \tag{5.27}$$

for all $\hat{x} \in \hat{\Omega} \backslash \hat{\Omega}_\alpha$. Thus from (5.1), (5.5), (5.3), and (5.27), it follows that

$$\begin{aligned} &\iint_{\hat{Q}} \{H(u)[\hat{x}, t, u^\alpha(\hat{x}, t)] - H(u)[\hat{x}, t, u(\hat{x}, t)]\}\, d\hat{x}\, dt \\ &= \iint_{\hat{Q}} \{H(u)[\hat{x}, t, V(u)(\hat{x}, t)] - H(u)[\hat{x}, t, u(\hat{x}, t)]\}\, d\hat{x}\, dt \\ &\quad - \iint_{\hat{Q}} \{H(u)[\hat{x}, t, V(u)(\hat{x}, t)] - H(u)[\hat{x}, t, u^\alpha(\hat{x}, t)]\}\, d\hat{x}\, dt \\ &= |\hat{\Omega}|\theta(u) - \int_{\hat{\Omega}\backslash\hat{\Omega}_\alpha} \left\{ \int_0^T [H(u)(\hat{x}, t, V(u)(\hat{x}, t)) - H(u)(\hat{x}, t, u(\hat{x}, t))]\, dt \right\} d\hat{x} \\ &\leq |\hat{\Omega}|\theta(u) - \int_{\hat{\Omega}\backslash\hat{\Omega}_\alpha} \{\theta(u)\}\, d\hat{x} = |\hat{\Omega}|\theta(u) - (|\hat{\Omega}| - |\hat{\Omega}_\alpha|)\theta(u) = \alpha\theta(u). \end{aligned} \tag{5.28}$$

This completes the proof. ■

From the preceding two lemmas we can obtain bounds for the terms appearing on the right-hand side of Eq. (4.10). These bounds are crucial in the proof of the following theorem.

THEOREM 5.1. *Consider problem (P). Then there exists a constant* K_{15}, *independent of* $u \in \mathcal{U}$ *and* $\alpha \in [0, |\hat{\Omega}|]$, *such that*

$$J(u^\alpha) - J(u) \leq \alpha\theta(u) + K_{15}(\alpha)^{1+s}, \tag{5.29}$$

for all $\alpha \in [0, |\hat{\Omega}|]$, *where s is given in Lemma 5.2. Furthermore,*

$$(-\theta(u)/K_{15})^{1/s} \in [0, |\hat{\Omega}|]. \tag{5.30}$$

Proof. From Lemma 4.2 we can find a constant N_0 such that

$$\|H(u)\|_{\infty,\hat{Q}} \leq N_0,$$

uniformly with respect to $u \in \mathcal{U}$. Thus by the definition of $\theta(u)$, it follows that

$$|\theta(u)| \leq 2N_0 T. \tag{5.31}$$

Let K_{14} be the constant given in Lemma 5.2, and let

$$K_{15} \equiv \max\{K_{14}, 2N_0 T/(|\hat{\Omega}|)^s\}.$$

Then it is clear that

$$K_{15} \geq 2N_0 T/(|\hat{\Omega}|)^s.$$

This, in turn, implies that

$$|\hat{\Omega}| \geq (2N_0 T/K_{15})^{1/s}.$$

However, from (5.31), we have $0 \leq -\theta(u) \leq 2N_0 T$. Thus it follows that

$$|\hat{\Omega}| \geq (-\theta(u)/K_{15})^{1/s} \geq 0.$$

This proves the second part of the theorem.
The first part of the theorem follows easily from the application of Lemmas 5.2 and 5.3 to Theorem 4.1. ■

REMARK 5.2. Note that $\theta(u) < 0$ and $K_{15}(\alpha)^{1+s} \geq 0$. Thus from inequality (5.29), we observe that u^α will be a better control than u only if $\alpha \in [0, |\hat{\Omega}|]$ with $|\alpha\theta(u)| > K_{15}(\alpha)^{1+s}$.

Define

$$\alpha^*(u) \equiv \sup\{\alpha \in [0, |\hat{\Omega}|] : J(u^\alpha) - J(u) \leq \alpha\theta(u)/2\}. \tag{5.32}$$

Then the admissible control $u^{\alpha^*(u)}$, *defined by* (5.5) *with* $\alpha = \alpha^*(u)$, *is called the successive control of the control* $u \in \mathcal{U}$.

Consider the set

$$\Lambda \equiv \{\alpha \in [0, |\hat{\Omega}|] : J(u^\alpha) - J(u) \leq \alpha\theta(u)/2\}. \tag{5.33}$$

Clearly, $0 \in \Lambda$ and $|\hat{\Omega}|$ is an upper bound of Λ. Thus $\alpha^*(u)$ is well defined.

In the next lemma we shall locate $\alpha^*(u)$ in a more precise interval.

LEMMA 5.4. *Consider problem (P). Then there exists a constant* K_{16}, *independent of* $u \in \mathcal{U}$ *and* $s \in (0, 1)$, *such that*

$$\alpha^*(u) \in [K_{16}(|\theta(u)|)^{1/s}, |\hat{\Omega}|]. \tag{5.34}$$

Proof. Let K_{15} be as given in Theorem 5.1., and let

$$\alpha_1 \equiv (|\theta(u)|/(2K_{15}))^{1/s}. \tag{5.35}$$

Then

$$K_{15}(\alpha_1)^s = |\theta(u)|/2 = -\theta(u)/2, \tag{5.36}$$

so

$$\alpha_1\theta(u) + K_{15}(\alpha_1)^{1+s} = \alpha_1\theta(u)/2. \tag{5.37}$$

From (5.30) and (5.35) we see that $\alpha_1 \in [0, |\hat{\Omega}|)$. Thus by (5.29) and (5.37) we have

$$J(u^{\alpha_1}) - J(u) \leq \alpha_1\theta(u)/2. \tag{5.38}$$

Hence, $\alpha_1 \in \Lambda$ so it follows from the definition of $\alpha^*(u)$ that

$$\alpha_1 \leq \alpha^*(u) \leq |\hat{\Omega}|.$$

Therefore, by setting $K_{16} = (2K_{15})^{-1/s}$ we obtain the conclusion of the lemma. ■

Note that $\alpha^*(u)$ is the supremum (not the maximum!) of the set Λ. Thus it is *not* necessarily true that

$$J(u^{\alpha^*(u)}) - J(u) \leq \alpha^*(u)\theta(u)/2.$$

However, a weaker result presented in the following lemma is valid.

LEMMA 5.5. *Consider problem (P). Then*

$$J(u^{\alpha^*(u)}) - J(u) \leq \alpha^*(u)\theta(u)/8. \tag{5.39}$$

Proof. Let $\alpha \in [0, \alpha^*(u)]$. Then setting $u^1 = u^\alpha$ and $u^2 = u^{\alpha^*(u)}$ in inequality (4.10), and using the definitions of β and γ, we obtain

$$\begin{aligned}
&J(u^{\alpha^*(u)}) - J(u^\alpha)\\
&\quad \leq \iint_{\hat{Q}} \{H(u^\alpha)[\hat{x}, t, u^{\alpha^*(u)}(\hat{x}, t)] - H(u^\alpha)[\hat{x}, t, u^\alpha(\hat{x}, t)]\}\, d\hat{x}\, dt\\
&\quad\quad + \iint_Q \sum_{i=1}^{n} [b_i(u^\alpha) - b_i(u^{\alpha^*(u)})][\phi(u^\alpha)_{x_i} - \phi(u^{\alpha^*(u)})_{x_i}]z(u^\alpha)\, dx\, dt\\
&\quad\quad + \iint_Q [c(u^\alpha) - c(u^{\alpha^*(u)})][\phi(u^\alpha) - \phi(u^{\alpha^*(u)})]z(u^\alpha)\, dx\, dt. \qquad (5.40)
\end{aligned}$$

From assumption (A.3), Lemma 4.2, and estimate (2.3), it follows that there exists a constant N_0 such that it is an almost everywhere bound for each of the three integrands appearing on the right-hand side of inequality (5.40). Furthermore, three integrands are equal to zero on $\hat{Q}_{\alpha^*(u)} \backslash \hat{Q}_\alpha$. Thus

$$J(u^{\alpha^*(u)}) - J(u^\alpha) \leq N_1 |\hat{Q}_{\alpha^*(u)} \backslash \hat{Q}_\alpha| = N_1(\alpha^*(u) - \alpha)T, \qquad (5.41)$$

where $N_1 \equiv N_0(1 + 2|\hat{\hat{\Omega}}|)$.

Since u is a nonextremal control we can choose an $\alpha \in [0, \alpha^*(u))$ such that

$$\alpha^*(u)/2 < \alpha < \alpha^*(u); \qquad (5.42)$$

$$J(u^\alpha) - J(u) \leq \alpha\theta(u)/2; \qquad (5.43)$$

and

$$\alpha^*(u) - \alpha \leq -\alpha^*(u)\theta(u)/8N_1T. \qquad (5.44)$$

Note that $\theta(u) < 0$. Thus $\alpha\theta(u) < \alpha^*(u)\theta(u)/2$ and hence

$$\begin{aligned}
J(u^{\alpha^*(u)}) - J(u) &= J(u^{\alpha^*(u)}) - J(u^\alpha) + J(u^\alpha) - J(u)\\
&\leq N_1(\alpha^*(u) - \alpha)T + \alpha\theta(u)/2\\
&\leq -\alpha^*(u)\theta(u)/8 + \alpha^*(u)\theta(u)/4\\
&= \alpha^*(u)\theta(u)/8.
\end{aligned}$$

This completes the proof. ■

THEOREM 5.2. *Consider problem (P). Then there exists a positive constant K_{17}, independent of $u \in \mathscr{U}$ and $s \in (0, 1)$, such that*

$$J(u^{\alpha^*(u)}) - J(u) \leq -K_{17}(|\theta(u)|)^{1+(1/s)}. \qquad (5.45)$$

Proof. Since

$$\alpha^*(u) \in [K_{16}(|\theta(u)|)^{1/s}, |\hat{\Omega}|],$$

and $\theta(u) < 0$, it follows from (5.39) that

$$J(u^{\alpha^*(u)}) - J(u) \leq -K_{16}(|\theta(u)|)^{1+(1/s)}/8.$$

Letting $K_{17} \equiv K_{16}/8$ we obtain the conclusion of the theorem. ∎

III.6. The Algorithm

Consider the optimal control problem (P). If u^0 is a given nonextremal admissible control, then it follows from Theorem 5.2 that the successive control $u^{0,\alpha^*(u^0)} \in \mathscr{U}$ can be constructed. This successive control improves the value of the cost functional by at least $-K_{17}(|\theta(u^0)|)^{1+(1/s)}$. Thus by repeating this process we obtain a sequence of control $\{u^k\} \subset \mathscr{U}$ such that u^{k+1} is the successive control of the control u^k, for $k = 0, 1, 2, \ldots$. *This sequence of controls is called the sequence of successive controls corresponding to* $u^0 \in \mathscr{U}$. The details of the construction are given in the following algorithm:

Algorithm (A)

(1) Let $u^0 \in \mathscr{U}$ and set $k = 0$.
(2) Solve the system (2.1) for $\phi(u^k)$, and then calculate $J(u^k)$ using (3.1).
(3) Solve the adjoint system (3.4) for $z(u^k)$.
(4) Find a function $V(u^k)$ that minimizes the Hamiltonian function $H(u^k)(\hat{x}, t, \cdot)$ on U, for each $(\hat{x}, t) \in \hat{Q}$.
(5) Calculate the number $\theta(u^k)$ given by (5.1), and determine the set $\Xi(u^k)$ defined by (5.2).
(6) By some rule, specify a sequence of sets $\hat{Q}_\alpha$, for $\alpha \in [0, |\hat{\Omega}|]$, given by (5.4).
(7) Find, for each $\alpha \in [0, |\hat{\Omega}|]$, the control $u^{k,\alpha}$ defined by (5.5), and then evaluate $J(u^{k,\alpha})$.
(8) Find $\alpha^*(u^k)$ defined by (5.32).
(9) Set $u^{k+1} = u^{\alpha^*(u^k)}$, $k = k + 1$, and then go to step 2.

For a given nonextremal admissible control u^0, let $\{u^k\}$ be the corresponding sequence of successive controls constructed by algorithm (A). If any control u^k in the sequence is extremal, then its successive control is going to be again u^k, and hence the algorithm is terminated. However, this is only a very special situation. In general, there does not exist a positive finite integer k such that u^k is an extremal control. Thus under this general situation we shall show that any accumulation point of the sequence $\{u^k\}$ in the L_∞ topology, if it exists, is an extremal control.

LEMMA 6.1. *Let G be a mapping from $\mathscr{U} \times \mathscr{U}$ into $L_1(\hat{Q})$ given by*

$$G(u^1)(u^2)(\hat{x}, t) \equiv H(u^1)[\hat{x}, t, u^2(\hat{x}, t)], \tag{6.1}$$

for any $u^1, u^2 \in \mathscr{U}$ and for all $(\hat{x}, t) \in \hat{Q}$. Then G is uniformly continuous.

Proof. Let $(u^1, u^2), (\tilde{u}^1, \tilde{u}^2) \in \mathscr{U} \times \mathscr{U}$ be arbitrary. Then we have

$$\begin{aligned}
&\|G(\tilde{u}^1)(\tilde{u}^2) - G(u^1)(u^2)\|_{1,\hat{Q}} \\
&\quad \leq \|G(\tilde{u}^1)(\tilde{u}^2) - G(\tilde{u}^1)(u^2)\|_{1,\hat{Q}} + \|G(\tilde{u}^1)(u^2) - G(u^1)(u^2)\|_{1,\hat{Q}} \\
&\quad \leq \iint_Q |I(\tilde{u}^1)[x, t, \tilde{u}^2(\hat{x}, t)]z(\tilde{u}^1)(x, t) - I(\tilde{u}^1)[x, t, u^2(\hat{x}, t)]z(\tilde{u}^1)(x, t)|\, dx\, dt \\
&\qquad + \iint_Q |I(\tilde{u}^1)[x, t, u^2(\hat{x}, t)]z(\tilde{u}^1)(x, t) - I(u^1)[x, t, u^2(\hat{x}, t)]z(u^1)(x, t)|\, dx\, dt \\
&\quad \leq \iint_Q \{|I(\tilde{u}^1)[x, t, \tilde{u}^2(\hat{x}, t)] - I(\tilde{u}^1)[x, t, u^2(\hat{x}, t)]|\, |z(\tilde{u}^1)(x, t)|\}\, dx\, dt \\
&\qquad + \iint_Q \{|I(\tilde{u}^1)[x, t, u^2(\hat{x}, t)] - I(u^1)[x, t, u^2(\hat{x}, t)]|\, |z(\tilde{u}^1)(x, t)|\}\, dx\, dt \\
&\qquad + \iint_Q \{|I(u^1)[x, t, u^2(\hat{x}, t)]|\, |z(\tilde{u}^1)(x, t) - z(u^1)(x, t)|\}\, dx\, dt \\
&\quad \leq \|I(\tilde{u}^1)[\cdot, \cdot, \tilde{u}^2(\cdot, \cdot)] - I(\tilde{u}^1)[\cdot, \cdot, u^2(\cdot, \cdot)]\|_{\infty,Q} \|z(\tilde{u}^1)\|_{1,Q} \\
&\qquad + \|I(\tilde{u}^1)[\cdot, \cdot, u^2(\cdot, \cdot)] - I(u^1)[\cdot, \cdot, u^2(\cdot, \cdot)]\|_{\infty,Q} \|z(\tilde{u}^1)\|_{1,Q} \\
&\qquad + \|I(u^1)[\cdot, \cdot, u^2(\cdot, \cdot)]\|_{\infty,Q} \|z(\tilde{u}^1) - z(u^1)\|_{1,Q}.
\end{aligned} \tag{6.2}$$

From the proof of Lemma 4.2 we see that there exists a constant N_0 such that $I(u)$ is bounded by N_0 on $\bar{Q} \times U$ uniformly with respect to $u \in \mathscr{U}$. Furthermore we observe from estimate (3.11) that $\|z(u)\|_{1,Q}$ is bounded by K_8 uniformly with respect to $u \in \mathscr{U}$. Thus (6.2) becomes

$$\begin{aligned}
&\|G(\tilde{u}^1)(\tilde{u}^2) - G(u^1)(u^2)\|_{1,\hat{Q}} \\
&\quad \leq K_8 \|I(\tilde{u}^1)[\cdot, \cdot, \tilde{u}^2(\cdot, \cdot)] - I(\tilde{u}^1)[\cdot, \cdot, u^2(\cdot, \cdot)]\|_{\infty,Q} \\
&\qquad + K_8 \|I(\tilde{u}^1)[\cdot, \cdot, u^2(\cdot, \cdot)] - I(u^1)[\cdot, \cdot, u^2(\cdot, \cdot)]\|_{\infty,Q} \\
&\qquad + N_0 \|z(\tilde{u}^1) - z(u^1)\|_{1,Q}.
\end{aligned} \tag{6.3}$$

By using (4.1) and (A.3) it follows that

$$\|I(\tilde{u}^1)(\cdot,\cdot,u^2(\cdot,\cdot)) - I(u^1)(\cdot,\cdot,u^2(\cdot,\cdot))\|_{\infty,Q}$$
$$\le N_1\left\{\sum_{i=1}^{n}\|\phi(\tilde{u}^1)_{x_i} - \phi(u^1)_{x_i}\|_{\infty,Q} + \|\phi(\tilde{u}^1) - \phi(u^1)\|_{\infty,Q}\right\}, \tag{6.4}$$

where the constant N_1 is determined by assumption (A.3) and is independent of $u \in \mathscr{U}$.

From (4.1) and (2.3) we obtain

$$\|I(\tilde{u}^1)(\cdot,\cdot,\tilde{u}^2(\cdot,\cdot)) - I(\tilde{u}^1)(\cdot,\cdot,u^2(\cdot,\cdot))\|_{\infty,Q}$$
$$\le K_1\left\{\sum_{i=1}^{\infty}\|b_i(\tilde{u}^2) - b_i(u^2)\|_{\infty,Q} + \|c(\tilde{u}^2) - c(u^2)\|_{\infty,Q} + \|f(\tilde{u}^2) - f(u^2)\|_{\infty,Q}\right\}. \tag{6.5}$$

Thus substituting (6.4) and (6.5) into (6.3), and then using Remark 2.2, Theorem 2.1, and Theorem 3.2, we can verify that G is uniformly continuous. ∎

LEMMA 6.2. *The operator $\theta: \mathscr{U} \to R^1$ defined by* (5.1) *is uniformly continuous.*

Proof. For any $u^1, u^2 \in \mathscr{U}$ it follows from (5.1) and (6.1) that

$$|\theta(u^1) - \theta(u^2)|$$
$$\le (|\hat{\Omega}|)^{-1}\|G(u^1)(V(u^1)) - G(u^1)(u^1) - G(u^2)(V(u^2)) + G(u^2)(u^2)\|_{1,\hat{Q}}$$
$$\le (|\hat{\Omega}|)^{-1}\{\|G(u^1)(V(u^1)) - G(u^2)(V(u^2))\|_{1,\hat{Q}} + \|G(u^1)(u^1) - G(u^2)(u^2)\|_{1,\hat{Q}}\}$$
$$\le (|\hat{\Omega}|)^{-1}\left\{\iint_{\hat{Q}}|H(u^1)[\hat{x},t,V(u^1)(\hat{x},t)] - H(u^2)[\hat{x},t,V(u^2)(\hat{x},t)]|\,d\hat{x}\,dt + \|G(u^1)(u^1) - G(u^2)(u^2)\|_{1,\hat{Q}}\right\}. \tag{6.6}$$

Set

$$\hat{\Xi} = \{(\hat{x},t) \in \hat{Q} : H(u^1)[\hat{x},t,V(u^1)(\hat{x},t)] \ge H(u^2)[\hat{x},t,V(u^2)(\hat{x},t)]\}.$$

Then by virtue of (4.11) we obtain

$$\iint_{\hat{\Xi}} |H(u^1)[\hat{x}, t, V(u^1)(\hat{x}, t)] - H(u^2)[\hat{x}, t, V(u^2)(\hat{x}, t)]| \, d\hat{x} \, dt$$

$$= \iint_{\hat{\Xi}} \{H(u^1)[\hat{x}, t, V(u^1)(\hat{x}, t)] - H(u^1)[\hat{x}, t, V(u^2)(\hat{x}, t)]\} \, d\hat{x} \, dt$$

$$+ \iint_{\hat{\Xi}} \{H(u^1)[\hat{x}, t, V(u^2)(\hat{x}, t)] - H(u^2)[\hat{x}, t, V(u^2)(\hat{x}, t]\} \, d\hat{x} \, dt$$

$$\leq \iint_{\hat{\Xi}} \{H(u^1)[\hat{x}, t, V(u^2)(\hat{x}, t)] - H(u^2)[\hat{x}, t, V(u^2)(\hat{x}, t)]\} \, d\hat{x} \, dt$$

$$\leq \|G(u^1)(V(u^2)) - G(u^2)(V(u^2))\|_{1,\hat{Q}}. \tag{6.7}$$

Similarly, we have

$$\iint_{\hat{Q}\setminus\hat{\Xi}} |H(u^1)[\hat{x}, t, V(u^1)(\hat{x}, t)] - H(u^2)[\hat{x}, t, V(u^2)(\hat{x}, t)]| \, d\hat{x} \, dt$$

$$= \iint_{\hat{Q}\setminus\hat{\Xi}} \{H(u^2)[\hat{x}, t, V(u^2)(\hat{x}, t)] - H(u^1)[\hat{x}, t, V(u^1)(\hat{x}, t)]\} \, d\hat{x} \, dt$$

$$= \iint_{\hat{Q}\setminus\hat{\Xi}} \{H(u^2)[\hat{x}, t, V(u^2)(\hat{x}, t)] - H(u^2)[\hat{x}, t, V(u^1)(\hat{x}, t)]\} \, d\hat{x} \, dt$$

$$+ \iint_{\hat{Q}\setminus\hat{\Xi}} \{H(u^2)[\hat{x}, t, V(u^1)(\hat{x}, t)] - H(u^1)[\hat{x}, t, V(u^1)(\hat{x}, t)]\} \, d\hat{x} \, dt$$

$$\leq \|G(u^1)(V(u^1)) - G(u^2)(V(u^1))\|_{1,\hat{Q}}. \tag{6.8}$$

Combining (6.6), (6.7), and (6.8), we obtain

$$\begin{aligned} |\theta(u^1) - \theta(u^2)| \leq (|\hat{\Omega}|)^{-1}\{&\|G(u^1)(V(u^2)) - G(u^2)(V(u^2))\|_{1,\hat{Q}} \\ &+ \|G(u^1)(V(u^1)) - G(u^2)(V(u^1))\|_{1,\hat{Q}} \\ &+ \|G(u^1)(u^1) - G(u^2)(u^2)\|_{1,\hat{Q}}\}. \end{aligned} \tag{6.9}$$

From Lemma 6.1, it follows that each of the terms appearing on the right-hand side of the preceding inequality tends to zero as $\|u^1 - u^2\|_{\mathscr{U}} \to 0$. Hence, θ is uniformly continuous. This completes the proof. ■

The uniform continuity of the operator θ obtained in Lemma 6.2 will be used in conjunction with estimate (5.45) in the proof of the following lemma.

LEMMA 6.3. *Let $u \in \mathscr{U}$ be a nonextremal control. Then there exist an $\varepsilon(u) > 0$ and a $\delta(u) > 0$ such that, for any $u^1 \in \mathscr{U}$,*

$$J(u^2) - J(u^1) \leq -\delta(u) \qquad \text{whenever} \quad \|u^1 - u\|_{\mathscr{U}} < \varepsilon(u), \tag{6.10}$$

where u^2 is the successive control of u^1.

Proof. Since $u \in \mathscr{U}$ is not an extremal control, $\theta(u) < 0$. This, in turn, implies that $-\theta(u)/2 > 0$. Thus by virtue of Lemma 6.2 there exists an $\varepsilon(u) > 0$, such that, for any $u^1 \in \mathscr{U}$,

$$|\theta(u) - \theta(u^1)| < -\theta(u)/2 \qquad \text{whenever} \quad \|u - u^1\|_{\mathscr{U}} < \varepsilon(u). \tag{6.11}$$

Then for such u^1, we have

$$\theta(u^1) < \theta(u)/2 < 0,$$

so by (5.45) we obtain

$$J(u^2) - J(u^1) \leq -K_{17}(|\theta(u^1)|)^{1+(1/s)} \leq -K_{17}(|\theta(u)|/2)^{1+(1/s)},$$

where u^2 is the successive control of u^1. Thus by setting $K_{17}(|\theta(u)|/2)^{1+(1/s)} \equiv \delta(u)$, we see that, for any $u^1 \in \mathscr{U}$,

$$J(u^2) - J(u^1) \leq -\delta(u) \qquad \text{whenever} \quad \|u^1 - u\|_{\mathscr{U}} < \varepsilon(u). \quad \blacksquare$$

The next theorem presents a convergence result for algorithm (A).

THEOREM 6.1. *Consider problem (P), and let $\{u^k\}$ be a sequence of successive controls constructed by algorithm (A). If $u^* \in \mathscr{U}$ is an accumulation point of the sequence $\{u^k\}$ in the topology generated by $\|\cdot\|_{\mathscr{U}}$, then it is an extremal control.*

Proof. First, we consider the case when $\{u^k\}$ is a finite sequence, that is, there exists a finite integer $k_0 \geq 0$ such that u^{k_0} is an extremal control. The conclusion of this case is obvious.

We now consider the case when $\{u^k\}$ is an infinite sequence. We shall prove that the corresponding conclusion is valid by contradiction. To begin we assume that u^* is not an extremal control. Then by virtue of Lemma 6.3 it follows that there exists an $\varepsilon(u^*) > 0$ and a $\delta(u^*) > 0$ such that, for any $u \in \mathscr{U}$,

$$J(\hat{u}) - J(u) \leq -\delta(u^*), \tag{6.12}$$

whenever

$$\|u - u^*\|_{\mathscr{U}} < \varepsilon(u^*), \tag{6.13}$$

where $\hat{u}$ is the successive control of u.

Since u^* is an accumulation point of the sequence $\{u^k\}$, there exists a subsequence $\{u^{k(l)}\}$ of the sequence $\{u^k\}$ such that

$$\|u^{k(l)} - u^*\|_{\mathscr{U}} \to 0, \tag{6.14}$$

as $l \to \infty$. Consequently, there exists an integer $l_0 \geq 0$ such that

$$\|u^{k(l)} - u^*\|_{\mathscr{U}} < \varepsilon(u^*), \tag{6.15}$$

for all integers $l > l_0$. This implies that all such $\{u^{k(l)}\}$ satisfy (6.13). Thus it follows from (6.12) that

$$J(u^{k(l)+1}) - J(u^{k(l)}) \leq -\delta(u^*), \tag{6.16}$$

for all integers $l > l_0$.

Let $j(l) \equiv k(l + 1) - k(l)$. Then we have

$$J(u^{k(l+1)}) - J(u^{k(l)}) = \sum_{i=2}^{j(l)} [J(u^{k(l)+i}) - J(u^{k(l)+i-1})] + [J(u^{k(l)+1}) - J(u^{k(l)})]. \tag{6.17}$$

Since $u^{k(l)+i-1}$ is not an extremal control for any $i = 2, 3, \ldots$, it is clear that

$$J(u^{k(l)+i}) - J(u^{k(l)+i-1}) < 0, \tag{6.18}$$

for all $i = 2, \ldots, j(l)$. Hence

$$J(u^{k(l+1)}) - J(u^{k(l)}) \leq -\delta(u^*), \tag{6.19}$$

for all $l > l_0$. This implies that the sequence $\{J(u^{k(l)})\}$ is decreasing without bound. However, from assumption (A.5) and estimate (2.6), it is easy to verify that J is bounded uniformly with respect to $u \in \mathscr{U}$. This is a contradiction, hence u^* is an extremal control. ∎

III.7. Necessary and Sufficient Conditions for Optimality

In this section our aim is to derive some necessary conditions for optimality, all for problem (P). First, we have the following result that follows immediately from Definition 5.1 and Lemma 5.5.

THEOREM 7.1. *Consider the optimal control problem* (P). *If* $u^* \in \mathscr{U}$ *is an optimal control, then it is an extremal control.*

The preceding theorem implies that extremality is a necessary condition for optimality. Using this result we shall derive, in the next theorem, a necessary condition for optimality in terms of the Hamiltonian function.

THEOREM 7.2. *Consider the optimal control problem (P). If $u^* \in \mathscr{U}$ is an optimal control, then*

$$H(u^*)[\hat{x}, t, u^*(\hat{x}, t)] = \min_{v \in U} H(u^*)[\hat{x}, t, v]. \tag{7.1}$$

for almost all $(\hat{x}, t) \in \hat{Q}$.

Proof. Since $u^* \in \mathscr{U}$ is an optimal control, u^* is an extremal control by Theorem 7.1 and so $\theta(u^*) = 0$.

From (4.11) we have

$$H(u^*)[\hat{x}, t, V(u^*)(\hat{x}, t)] - H(u^*)[\hat{x}, t, u^*(\hat{x}, t)] \leq 0, \tag{7.2}$$

for all $(\hat{x}, t) \in \hat{Q}$. Since $\theta(u^*) = 0$, it follows from (5.1) and (7.2) that

$$H(u^*)[\hat{x}, t, V(u^*)(\hat{x}, t)] = H(u^*)[\hat{x}, t, u^*(\hat{x}, t)], \tag{7.3}$$

for almost all $(\hat{x}, t) \in \hat{Q}$. But

$$H(u^*)[\hat{x}, t, V(u^*)(\hat{x}, t)] = \min_{v \in U} H(u^*)[\hat{x}, t, v], \tag{7.4}$$

for almost all $(\hat{x}, t) \in \hat{Q}$. Consequently,

$$H(u^*)[\hat{x}, t, u^*(\hat{x}, t)] = \min_{v \in U} H(u^*)[\hat{x}, t, v],$$

for almost all $(\hat{x}, t) \in \hat{Q}$. ■

We now consider problem (P) with $n_1 = n$ and recall that g is a function given in assumption (A.5) of Section 3. If the function g is assumed additionally to be nonnegative, then a sufficient condition for optimality can be derived.

THEOREM 7.3. *Consider the optimal control problem (P) with $n_1 = n$, and let the function g be nonnegative on $\overline{\Omega} \times R^1$. If $u^* \in \mathscr{U}$ satisfies the condition*

$$I(u^*)[x, t, u^*(x, t)] = \min_{v \in U} I(u^*)[x, t, v], \tag{7.5}$$

for almost all $(x, t) \in Q$, then u^* is an optimal control.

Proof. For $u \in \mathscr{U}$, define

$$\psi(x, t) \equiv \phi(u^*)(x, t) - \phi(u)(x, t). \tag{7.6}$$

Then for almost all $(x, t) \in Q$,

$$\begin{aligned} L(u)\psi(x, t) &= L(u^*)\phi(u^*)(x, t) - L(u)\phi(u)(x, t) \\ &\quad - [L(u^*) - L(u)]\phi(u^*)(x, t) \\ &= I(u^*)[x, t, u^*(x, t)] - I(u^*)[x, t, u(x, t)]. \end{aligned} \tag{7.7}$$

Clearly, $\psi \in \mathring{W}^{2,1}_{\infty}(Q)$. Then it follows from (4.10), (4.5), (3.14), and (7.7) that

$$J(u^*) - J(u) \leq -\int_{\Omega} \psi(x, T)g(x, \phi(u)(x, T))\, dx$$
$$= -\iint_Q L(u)\psi(x, t)z(u)(x, t)dx\, dt$$
$$= \iint_Q \{I(u^*)[x, t, u^*(x, t)] - I(u^*)[x, t, u(x, t)]\}z(u)(x, t)\, dx\, dt. \tag{7.8}$$

Since g is nonnegative we deduce from Theorem II. 9.2 that $z(u)(x, t) \geq 0$ on Q for all $u \in \mathscr{U}$. Thus by (7.5), the right-hand side of inequality (7.8) is nonpositive, and hence

$$J(u^*) - J(u) \leq 0, \qquad u \in \mathscr{U}.$$

Consequently, u^* is an optimal control. ■

REMARK 7.1. In the proof of Theorem 7.3 we note that $z(u)(x, t) \geq 0$ on Q for all $u \in \mathscr{U}$. If $z(u^*)$ is *strictly* greater than zero on Q, then the sufficient condition (7.5) for u^* to be an optimal control is also a necessary condition for optimality. The proof is a direct consequence of the necessary condition (7.1) and the assumption that $z(u^*)(x, t) > 0$ on Q. Of course, this positivity assumption on $z(u^*)$ is rather artificial. It would be interesting to check its validity from the theory of partial differential equations. This has yet to be investigated.

III.8. Numerical Consideration

In algorithm (A) we assume tacitly that, for each $u \in \mathscr{U}$, $\phi(u)$, and $z(u)$ can be calculated analytically. This is clearly impossible, although we know that they exist. The search for α^* will be even more difficult. For these reasons numerical techniques based on discretizing the optimal control problem (P) will be briefly discussed in this section.

The discretization will be performed only on a restricted class of the optimal control problem (P). These restrictions are

(i) $n = 2$;
(ii) $n_1 = 1$;
(iii) $m = 1$ (and hence $U = [\mu_1, \mu_2]$, where μ_i, $i = 1, 2$, are fixed constants);
(iv) $\Omega = (0, 1) \times (0, 1)$;
(v) $T = 1$;
(vi) $a_{ij}(x, t) = a\delta_{ij}$ for all $(x, t) \in \bar{Q}$, where a is a positive constant, δ_{ij} is the Kronecker delta and $\bar{Q} \equiv [0, 1] \times [0, 1] \times [0, 1]$;

(vii) $\gamma(x, \phi) = \phi z_T(x)$ for all $(x, \phi) \in \Omega \times R^1$, where z_T is a given element in $L_\infty(Q)$.

The aim of choosing these restrictions is to allow the use of simpler notation without destroying the special feature of the problem. It should be stressed that the method of this section is applicable to the general optimal control problem (*P*). However, the notation will become very much involved in the general case.

From assumption (A.5) and restriction (vii) we readily observe that the obvious choice of g in (A.5) is to take g as z_T. Such choice will be used throughout the rest of this section.

The class of admissible controls $\mathscr{U}$ under the restrictions (i)–(v) will be denoted by $\mathscr{U}_1$; and problem (*P*) under restrictions (i)–(vii) may now be stated explicitly as follows:

Problem (P_{r1}) Subject to the following system:

$$\begin{aligned}\phi_t(x_1, x_2, t) = a\{\phi_{x_1 x_1}(x_1, x_2, t) + \phi_{x_2 x_2}(x_1, x_2, t)\}\\ + b_1(x_1, x_2, t, u(x_1, t))\phi_{x_1}(x_1, x_2, t)\\ + b_2(x_1, x_2, t, u(x_1, t))\phi_{x_2}(x_1, x_2, t)\\ + c(x_1, x_2, t, u(x_1, t))\phi(x_1, x_2, t) + f(x_1, x_2, t, u(x_1, t)),\\ (x_1, x_2, t) \in (0, 1) \times (0, 1) \times (0, 1), \qquad (8.1a)\end{aligned}$$

$$\phi(x_1, x_2, 0) = \phi_0(x_1, x_2), \qquad (x_1, x_2) \in (0, 1) \times (0, 1), \qquad (8.1b)$$

$$\phi(x_1, x_2, t) = 0, \qquad (x, x_2, t) \in \Gamma, \qquad (8.1c)$$

find a control $u \in \mathscr{U}_1$ that minimizes the cost functional

$$J(u) = \int_{-1}^{1} \int_{-1}^{1} \phi(u)(x_1, x_2, 1) z_T(x_1, x_2)\, dx_1\, dx_2. \qquad (8.2)$$

Note that the set Γ, in (8.1c), is given by

$$\Gamma \equiv \{[(\{0\} \cup \{1\}) \times [0, 1]] \cup [[0, 1] \cup (\{0\} \cup \{1\})]\} \times [0, 1]. \quad (8.3)$$

Strictly speaking the theory developed in the previous sections of this chapter does not apply to the restricted problem (P_{r1}) because Ω is a square and hence its boundary does not belong to the class C^3. Since the discretization of the problem on a square will lead to the use of the simplest notation, we shall not try to be too rigorous mathematically at this point and shall assume that the theory is applicable to the present problem.

The discretization is performed by placing a rectangular grid on $\bar{Q}$. Let N_x, N_t be positive integers, and define $h_x \equiv 1/N_x$ and $h_t \equiv 1/N_t$.

Let Q_D and $\bar{Q}_D$ denote, respectively, the sets of the rectangular cells of the grid lying within the sets Q and $\bar{Q}$, namely,

$$Q_D = \{(qh_x, rh_x, sh_t) : q, r = 1, \ldots, N_x - 1 \text{ and } s = 1, \ldots, N_t - 1\}$$

and

$$\bar{Q}_D \equiv \{(qh_x, rh_x, sh_t) : q, r = 0, 1, \ldots, N_x \text{ and } s = 0, 1, \ldots, N_t\}.$$

Let $u_{q,s}$, $q = 1, \ldots, N_x - 1$ and $s = 1, \ldots, N_t - 1$ be a set of points in $U = [\mu_1, \mu_2]$. Consider a function $u : \mathscr{U}_1 \to R^1$ be such that

$$u(qh_x, sh_t) \equiv u_{q,s},$$

for $q = 1, \ldots, N_x - 1$ and $s = 1, \ldots, N_t - 1$. Then u restricted to the points (qh_x, sh_t), over all such q, s, is called a discretized control and is again denoted by u. Let $\mathscr{U}_1^D$ denote the class of all such discretized controls.

Let α be a function from $Q \times U \equiv (0, 1) \times (0, 1) \times (0, 1) \times [\mu_1, \mu_2]$ into R^1. Then, for each $v \in U$, we define

$$\alpha_{q,r,s}^v \equiv \alpha(qh_x, rh_x, sh_t, v).$$

Thus for a given $u \in \mathscr{U}_1^D$, we have $\alpha_{q,r,s}^{u_{q,s}}$, where $\{u_{q,s}\}$ is the set of points from U generated by the control u. To keep the notation simple $\alpha_{q,r,s}^{u_{q,s}}$ will, however, be denoted by $\bar{\alpha}(u)_{q,r,s}$.

Note that ϕ_0 is defined only on $\Omega \equiv (0, 1) \times (0, 1)$. Its discretized version is denoted by $\phi_{q,r}^0$.

For a given control u in $\mathscr{U}_1^D$ we can determine a function $\phi(u)_{q,r,s}$, over all q, r, s, that satisfies the following equations:

$$\begin{aligned}(\phi_{q,r,s} - \phi_{q,r,s-1})/h_t &= a(\phi_{q+1,r,s} + \phi_{q-1,r,s} + \phi_{q,r+1,s} + \phi_{q,r-1,s} - 4\phi_{q,r,s})/(h_x)^2 \\ &\quad + \bar{b}_1(u)_{q,r,s}(\phi_{q+1,r,s} - \phi_{q-1,r,s})/2h_x \\ &\quad + \bar{b}_2(u)_{q,r,s}(\phi_{q,r+1,s} - \phi_{q,r-1,s})/2h_x \\ &\quad + \bar{c}(u)_{q,r,s}\phi_{q,r,s} + \bar{f}(u)_{q,r,s}, \quad q, r = 1, \ldots, N_x - 1; \quad s = 1, \ldots, N_t,\end{aligned} \tag{8.4a}$$

$$\phi_{q,r,0} = \phi_{q,r}^0, \qquad q, r = 1, \ldots, N_x - 1, \tag{8.4b}$$

$$\phi_{q,r,s} = 0, \qquad (q, r, s) \in \Gamma_D. \tag{8.4c}$$

Note that the set Γ_D in Eq. (8.4c) is a discretization of the set Γ given by (8.3). More precisely,

$$\begin{aligned}\Gamma_D \equiv \{(q, r, s) : q, r = 0, 1, \ldots, N_x \text{ and either } q \text{ or } r \\ \text{belongs to } \{0\} \cup \{1\}, s = 0, 1, \ldots, N_t\}.\end{aligned} \tag{8.5}$$

Note also that Eqs. (8.4a), (8.4b), and (8.4c) are, respectively, the discretized versions of Eqs. (8.1a), (8.1b), and (8.1c). The values of $\phi(u)_{q,r,s}$ are found by solving a set of $N_t(N_x - 1)^2$ linear equations in the same number of unknowns. In practice these equations are solved by using the successive over relaxation method (SORM), which is an iterative technique.

For the function z_T, its discretization is denoted by $z_{q,r}^T$.

Using the trapezoidal rule the cost functional $J(u)$, defined by (8.2), can be approximated by

$$\bar{J}(u) \equiv (h_x)^2 \left\{ \sum_{q,r=1}^{N_x-1} \phi(u)_{q,r,N_t} z_{q,r}^T \right\}. \tag{8.6}$$

For the corresponding adjoint system, it is discretized as follows:

$$\begin{aligned}(z_{q,r,s} - z_{q,r,s+1})/h_t \\ &= a(z_{q+1,r,s} + z_{q-1,r,s} + z_{q,r+1,s} + z_{q,r-1,s} - 4z_{q,r,s})/(h_x)^2 \\ &\quad + [\bar{b}_1(u)_{q-1,r,s} z_{q-1,r,s} - \bar{b}_1(u)_{q+1,r,s} z_{q+1,r,s}]/2h_x \\ &\quad + [\bar{b}_2(u)_{q,r-1,s} z_{q,r-1,s} - \bar{b}_2(u)_{q,r+1,s} z_{q,r+1,s}]/2h_x \\ &\quad + \bar{c}(u)_{q,r,s} z_{q,r,s}, \qquad q, r = 1, \ldots, N_x - 1; \qquad s = 1, \ldots, N_t,\end{aligned} \tag{8.7a}$$

$$z_{q,r,N_t} = z_{q,r}^T, \qquad q, r = 1, \ldots, N_x - 1, \tag{8.7b}$$

$$z_{q,r,s} = 0, \qquad (q, r, s) \in \Gamma_D, \tag{8.7c}$$

where the set Γ_D in (8.7c) is given by (8.5). For each $u \in \mathscr{U}_1^D$, let $z(u)_{q,r,s}$, over all such q, r, and s, denote the solution of Eqs. (8.7a), (8.7b), and (8.7c).

The discretized version of the corresponding Hamiltonian function is then given by

$$\begin{aligned}\bar{H}(u)_{q,s}(v) \equiv h_x \sum_{r=1}^{Nx-1} \{&\bar{b}_1(v)_{q,r,s}[\phi(u)_{q+1,r,s} - \phi(u)_{q-1,r,s}]/2h_x \\ &+ \bar{b}_2(v)_{q,r,s}[\phi(u)_{q,r+1,s} - \phi(u)_{q,r-1,s}]/2h_x \\ &+ \bar{c}(v)_{q,r,s}\phi(u)_{q,r,s} + \bar{f}(u)_{q,r,s}\} z(u)_{q,r,s},\end{aligned} \tag{8.8}$$

where $u \in \mathscr{U}_1^D$, $v \in U$, $q = 1, \ldots, N_x - 1$ and $s = 1, \ldots, N_t$.

For the examples to be studied in the next section, the concept of searching on decreasing set sizes was tried but found unnecessary. Thus the discretization of the expression for $\Xi(u)$, defined by (5.2), is not required. It should be warned that this omission is not necessarily true in general.

On the basis of all these comments, the following algorithm is posed to search for an approximate optimal solution to problem (P_{r1}).

Algorithm (DA_1)

(1) Guess $u^0 \in \mathscr{U}_1^D$ and set $k = 0$.

(2) Solve Eqs. (8.4a), (8.4b), and (8.4c) for $\phi(u^k)_{q,r,s}$ corresponding to u^k, and then evaluate $\bar{J}(u^k)$ according to formula (8.6).

(3) Solve Eqs. (8.7a), (8.7b), and (8.7c) for $z(u^k)_{q,r,s}$.

(4) For each q, s, find $V_{q,s}^k \in U$ that minimizes $\bar{H}(u^k)_{q,s}(\cdot)$, where $\bar{H}(u^k)_{q,s}(\cdot)$ is defined by (8.8).

(5) Set $u_{q,s}^{k+1} = V_{q,s}^k$ for each q, s, set $k = k + 1$ and go to step 2.

In practice a stopping criterion is required, otherwise the algorithm will not, in general, terminate in a finite number of iterations. We stop the program as soon as one of the following two conditions is satisfied:

(i) $|\bar{J}(u^{k+1}) - \bar{J}(u^k)| < \varepsilon_1$, where ε_1 is a preset tolerance; and
(ii) $\max_{q,s}|u_{q,s}^{k+1} - u_{q,s}^k| < \varepsilon_2$, where ε_2 is another preset tolerance.

For bang–bang controls, the value of $u_{q,s}$ is either on its upper bound or on its lower bound. In this case the second stopping criterion is less important. The important detail is that we may need to stop oscillations of certain points of $u_{q,s}$ between its extremes. A major source of error that can give rise to the oscillations is the use of

$$[\phi(u^k)_{q+1,r,s} - \phi(u^k)_{q-1,r,s}]/2h_x \quad \text{and} \quad [\phi(u^k)_{q,r+1,s} - \phi(u^k)_{q,r-1,s}]/2h_x$$

to approximate $\phi(u^k)_{x_1}$ and $\phi(u^k)_{x_2}$, respectively. For near the turning point of $\phi(u^k)$ in, say, the x_1 direction, $\phi(u^k)_{q+1,r,s}$ is very nearly equal to $\phi(u^k)_{q-1,r,s}$. Thus it is most likely that the sign of this approximate partial derivative is opposite to the true one because of round-off error. In the case of bang–bang controls the value of $V(u^k)_{q,s}$ is determined primarily by the signs of these approximate partial derivatives—hence the oscillation.

Another source of instability in the program is a result of the smallness of the constant a, where a is the second-order coefficient appearing in the partial differential equation (8.1a). For the stability of the program, the constant a must be larger than a certain factor that depends on h_t and h_x. For the values of h_t and h_x used in the examples of the next section, Dr. D. W. Reid [R.1] has found that the value of a less than 0.05 will cause the program for solving that particular example to be unstable.

We now consider the optimal control problem (P) under the following restrictions:

(viii) $n_1 = 2$ (rather than $n_1 = 1$ as in the previous case);
(ix) Restriction (i) and restrictions (iii)–(vii); and
(x) $z_T(x_1, x_2) > 0$ for all $(x_1, x_2) \in (0, 1) \times (0, 1)$, where z_T is a function defined in restriction (vii).

The class of admissible controls $\mathscr{U}$ under restrictions (i), (iii)–(v), and (viii) will be denoted by $\mathscr{U}_2$. Problem (P) under these restrictions may now be stated explicitly as follows:

Problem (P_{r2}) Subject to the system

$$\begin{aligned}\phi_t(x_1, x_2, t) = a\{&\phi_{x_1 x_1}(x_1, x_2, t) + \phi_{x_2 x_2}(x_1, x_2, t)\}\\ &+ b_1(x_1, x_2, t, u(x_1, x_2, t))\phi_{x_1}(x_1, x_2, t)\\ &+ b_2(x_1, x_2, t, u(x_1, x_2, t))\phi_{x_2}(x_1, x_2, t)\\ &+ c(x_1, x_2, t, u(x_1, x_2, t))\phi(x_1, x_2, t)\\ &+ f(x_1, x_2, t, u(x_1, x_2, t)),\end{aligned}$$

$$(x_1, x_2, t) \in (0, 1) \times (0, 1) \times (0, 1), \quad (8.9a)$$

$$\phi(x_1, x_2, 0) = \phi_0(x_1, x_2), \qquad (x_1, x_2) \in (0, 1) \times (0, 1), \quad (8.9b)$$

$$\phi(x_1, x_2, t) = 0, \qquad (x_1, x_2, t) \in \Gamma, \quad (8.9c)$$

find a control $u \in \mathscr{U}_2$ that minimizes the cost functional

$$J(u) = \int_0^1 \int_0^1 \phi(u)(x_1, x_2, 1) z_T(x_1, x_2)\, dx_1\, dx_2. \quad (8.10)$$

Note that the only difference between problem (P_{r1}) and problem (P_{r2}) is their classes of admissible controls. For the first problem, $n_1 = 1$ (and hence admissible controls depend only on x_1 and t); for the second problem, $n_1 = 2$ (and hence admissible controls depend not only on x_1 and t but also on x_2).

The discretized versions of Eqs. (8.9a), (8.9b), (8.9c), and (8.10) are given, respectively, by Eqs. (8.4a), (8.4b), (8.4c), and (8.6). However, the control u is to be understood as taking from $\mathscr{U}_2$ rather than from $\mathscr{U}_1$.

Let $z(u)$ denote the weak solution of the corresponding adjoint problem. Then by virtue of Remark 7.1 we note that if $z(u^*)(x_1, x_2, t) > 0$ on $(0, 1) \times (0, 1) \times (0, 1)$, then $u^* \in \mathscr{U}_2$ is an optimal control if and only if

$$I(u^*)[x_1, x_2, t, u^*(x_1, x_2, t)] \leq I(u^*)[x_1, x_2, t, v], \quad (8.11)$$

for almost all $(x_1, x_2, t) \in (0, 1) \times (0, 1) \times (0, 1)$ and for all $v \in U$, where $I(u)$, in this case, becomes

$$\begin{aligned}I(u)[x_1, x_2, t, v] \equiv &\sum_{i=1}^{n} b_i(x_1, x_2, t, v)\phi_{x_i}(u)(x_1, x_2, t)\\ &+ c(x_1, x_2, t, v)\phi(u)(x_1, x_2, t) + f(x_1, x_2, t, v), \quad (8.12)\end{aligned}$$

for all $u \in \mathscr{U}_2$ and for all $v \in U$.

The discretized version of the function $I(u^k)(x, t, v)$ is

$$I(u^k)_{q,r,s}(v) \equiv \bar{b}_1(v)_{q,r,s}[\phi(u^k)_{q+1,r,s} - \phi(u^k)_{q-1,r,s}]/2h_x$$
$$+ \bar{b}_2(v)_{q,r,s}[\phi(u^k)_{q,r+1,s} - \phi(u^k)_{q,r-1,s}]/2h_x$$
$$+ \bar{c}(v)_{q,r,s}\phi(u^k)_{q,r,s} + \bar{f}(v)_{q,r,s}.$$

The corresponding numerical algorithm is as follows.

Algorithm (DA_2)

(1) Guess $u^0 \in \mathscr{U}_2^D$ (defined as the class of all discretized controls corresponding to $\mathscr{U}_2$), and set $k = 0$.

(2) Solve Eqs. (8.4a), (8.4b), and (8.4c) for $\phi(u^k)_{q,r,s}$ corresponding to u^k.

(3) For each q, r, s, find the $V(u^k)_{q,r,s} \in U$ that minimizes the function $I(u^k)_{q,r,s}(v)$ for all $v \in U$.

(4) Set $u_{q,r,s}^{k+1} = V(u^k)_{q,r,s}$.

(5) If one of the two stopping criteria given for Algorithm DA_1 is satisfied, calculate $\bar{J}(u^{k+1})$ using (8.6) and stop. Otherwise, set $k + 1 = k$ and go to Step 2.

Note that each of these two numerical algorithms, (DA_1) and (DA_2), is applied to a practical example in the next section.

In closing this section we shall refer the reader to [Co.1] and [Sau.1] for techniques that can be used to solve the system (8.1a), (8.1b), and (8.1c) and its adjoint system for cases in which the set Ω is not necessarily a square.

III.9. Examples

In this section our aim is to apply the numerical algorithms (DA_1) and (DA_2) to two simple practical examples. As will be seen subsequently, the solutions so obtained do agree with our intuition.

The examples have been kept simple, but are by no means trivial. Initially, these examples are formulated as stochastic optimal control problems. They are then converted into the corresponding optimal control problems of distributed parameter systems by using the results of Appendix A.1. Throughout this section τ and $t \equiv T - \tau$ are used to denote the actual time and the time-to-go, respectively.

Natural resources such as forests and fisheries are renewable after harvesting. Such resources are often under government control. A common problem is to determine the rate of harvesting under which the maximum return is obtained without causing the extinction of the resource. This area has been substantially studied in [Cl. 1] and [Go. 1]. However, the dynamics of population are formulated as deterministic models, and hence the optimal controls can be and, in fact, are obtained analytically using Pontryagin's Maximum Principle. Since the dynamics of population are not deterministic, stochastic equations would be better descriptions. The aim of this section is to study one such stochastic model.

Given a renewable resource, the rate of growth of its population size is given by the differential equation

$$\dot{\xi}(\tau) = F(\xi(\tau)) - h(\tau), \tag{9.1}$$

where $F(\xi)$ is the natural growth rate if the population is of size ξ and h the rate of harvesting. A simple, but adequate as a first approximation, function for $F(\xi)$ is

$$F(\xi) = K_1\xi(1 - \xi), \tag{9.2}$$

where K_1 is a positive constant determined by the specified problem. In deriving this equation we assume that there is a maximum population that the environment can support, and ξ is the proportion of this maximum population that the environment is maintained. Note that this equation is the simplest one that allows for exponential growth initially when ξ is near to 0, but has ξ converging asymptotically to 1. The rate of harvesting can be controlled. We assume that u is the amount of effort that is put into harvesting the resource. This effort together with the size of the population will determine the rate of harvesting. The simplest model for this harvesting rate is

$$h(\tau) = K_2\xi(\tau)u(\tau). \tag{9.3}$$

Combining (9.1), (9.2), and (9.3) we obtain the Schaefer model for the population dynamic of a renewable resource, namely,

$$\dot{\xi}(\tau) = K_3\xi(\tau)(1 - \xi(\tau)) - K_4\xi(\tau)u(\tau), \tag{9.4}$$

where ξ is the population size of the resource expressed as a proportion of the maximum maintainable population size and u the effort in harvesting expressed as a proportion of the maximum possible effort.

For an industry such as fishing, $u(\tau)$ denotes the proportion of all the available boats that are fishing at time τ. However, it is most unlikely that the same effort in fishing will result in catching the same amount of fish. Disturbances may also appear in the natural growth in fish population because of other causes. Thus there may be appreciable noise in the fish population when compared with a path determined by Eq. (9.4). This noise is assumed to be representable by an additive white noise term in Eq. (9.4). Thus the corresponding stochastic differential equation is

$$d\xi(\tau) = [K_1\xi(\tau)(1 - \xi(\tau)) - K_2\xi(\tau)u(\tau)]\,d\tau + \sigma\,dw(\tau). \tag{9.5}$$

This and the next stochastic models are proposed by Dr. D. W. Reid in his Ph.D. thesis [R.1].

To test algorithm (DA_1) we need to consider the optimal control problem (P) with $1 \leq n_1 < n$. This clearly implies that $n \geq 2$. Thus it is required to generalize the fishing model into the case involving two populations.

To begin, we consider two ecologically independent fish populations that can be caught simultaneously using the same equipment. Let ξ_1 and ξ_2 denote the populations of these two species expressed as proportions of their respective maximum maintainable populations. Let $u(\tau)$ be the amount of boats fishing at time τ expressed as a proportion of the maximum amount of boats available. Let w_1 and w_2 denote two independent standard Wiener processes. Then from (9.5) the population dynamics are

$$d\xi_1(\tau) = [K_3\xi_1(\tau)(1 - \xi_1(\tau)) - K_4\xi_1(\tau)u(\tau)]\,d\tau + \sigma_1\,dw_1(\tau), \tag{9.6}$$

$$d\xi_2(\tau) = [K_5\xi_2(\tau)(1 - \xi_2(\tau)) - K_6\xi_2(\tau)u(\tau)]\,d\tau + \sigma_2\,dw_2(\tau). \tag{9.7}$$

This stochastic fishing model was developed from its deterministic counterpart reported in [Cl.1, Chapter 9, Section 1].

The other important function in the description of the corresponding optimal control problem is the cost functional, which is also known as the performance criterion. Using the performance criterion defined by Eq. (9.2) of [Cl. 1], which is linear in u, the optimal control is of bang–bang type. This means that all available boats are used if the fish population size is large enough for making a profit, and do not fish at all if it is not profitable to do so. To test the algorithm more extensively, a criterion, which is nonlinear in the control u, is introduced. We assume that the prices of these two species are independent of the amount caught. Furthermore, K_7 and K_8 would be the respective incomes from the two species if the fish populations remain at their maximum maintainable levels (that is, $\xi_1 = \xi_2 = 1$) and the harvesting is kept at its maximum level (that is $u = 1$). The actual income derived from fishing over the period from the time 0 to the time τ is

$$\int_0^\tau \{K_7\xi_1(s)u(s) + K_8\xi_2(s)u(s)\}\,ds. \tag{9.8}$$

We assume that the rate of expenditure in fishing depends quadratically on the effort. Thus the total expenditure over the period from 0 to τ is

$$\int_0^\tau \{K_9 + K_{10}u(s) + K_{11}(u(s))^2\}\,ds. \tag{9.9}$$

Since maximizing the profit is equivalent to minimizing the cost, the corresponding cost functional, allowing for discounting the future profit, is

$$\begin{aligned} J(u) = \mathscr{E}\bigg\{\int_0^T & e^{-\delta s}[K_9 + K_{10}u(s) + K_{11}(u(s))^2 \\ & - K_7\xi_1(s)u(s) - K_8\xi_2(s)u(s)]\,ds\bigg\}, \end{aligned} \tag{9.10}$$

where $\mathscr{E}$ stands for the mathematical expectation, δ is a positive constant denoting the discount factor for future profit, and

$$\Upsilon \equiv \inf\{\{t \in [0, T] : \xi_1(t) \notin (0, 1) \quad \text{or} \quad \xi_2(t) \notin (0, 1)\} \cup \{T\}\} \tag{9.11}$$

the random variable Υ is the stopping time.

From (9.11) we see that the process stops when the fish population is fished out or reaches its maximum maintainable level. This assumption is rather unreasonable, but is essential for the simple boundary conditions to be obtained for the distributed parameter system. Despite this the assumption may still be interpreted as follows. If the state does enter the stopping region, something else will happen—wiping out a species of fish would be very unwise, and reaching the maximum maintainable level of a species would put some doubt on the parameters used in the model.

Thus as a first approximation Eq. (9.11) will be accepted as the stopping criterion for our stochastic model.

To complete the specification of the fishing problem, two more concepts are needed. The first one is the initial conditions. Let us assume that initially ξ_1 and ξ_2 are known to be uniformly distributed on $[K_{12}, K_{13}]$ and $[K_{14}, K_{15}]$, respectively. These two random variables and the two Wiener processes are all statistically independent. The second concept is the class of admissible controls. To specify this concept, two fishing problems will be considered. They are distinguished by the two different classes of admissible controls. For the first fishing problem we assume that

$$u(\tau) \equiv \bar{u}(\xi_1(\tau), \tau), \tag{9.12}$$

where $\bar{u} \in \mathscr{U}_1$ and $\mathscr{U}_1$ is defined by

$$\mathscr{U}_1 \equiv \{u : u \text{ is a measurable function from } (0, 1) \times (0, T) \text{ into } [0, 1]\}. \tag{9.13}$$

This fishing problem is a partially observed feedback optimal control problem, because the controls depend only on ξ_1, the first component of the vector $\xi \equiv (\xi_1, \xi_2)$. The second fishing problem assumes that

$$u(\tau) \equiv \bar{u}(\xi_1(\tau), \xi_2(\tau), \tau), \tag{9.14}$$

where $\bar{u} \in \mathscr{U}_2$ and $\mathscr{U}_2$ is defined by

$$\mathscr{U}_2 \equiv \{u : u \text{ is a measurable function from } (0, 1) \times (0, 1) \times (0, T) \text{ into } [0, 1]\}. \tag{9.15}$$

This is a fully observed feedback optimal control problem. Thus it should have a lower minimum cost when compared with the first fishing problem.

Combining all the relating elements together, the first fishing problem may now be stated as follows.

Problem (P_{F1}) Subject to the dynamic equations

$$d\xi_1(\tau) = [K_3\xi_1(\tau)(1 - \xi_1(\tau)) - K_4\xi_1(\tau)\bar{u}(\xi_1(\tau), \tau)]\,d\tau + \sigma_1\,dw_1(\tau), \quad \tau \in [0, T], \tag{9.16a}$$

$$d\xi_2(\tau) = [K_5\xi_2(\tau)(1 - \xi_2(\tau)) - K_6\xi_2(\tau)\bar{u}(\xi_1(\tau), \tau)]\,d\tau + \sigma_2\,dw_2(\tau), \quad \tau \in [0, T], \tag{9.16b}$$

with the initial conditions

$$\xi_1(0) \sim U[K_{12}, K_{13}], \tag{9.16c}$$

(that is, $\xi_1(0)$ is uniformly distributed in $[K_{12}, K_{13}]$) and

$$\xi_2(0) \sim U[K_{14}, K_{15}], \tag{9.16d}$$

find a control $u \in \mathscr{U}_1$ such that the cost functional

$$J(\bar{u}) = \mathscr{E}\left\{\int_0^T e^{-\delta\tau}[K_9 + K_{10}\bar{u}(\xi_1(\tau), \tau) + K_{11}(\bar{u}(\xi_1(\tau), \tau))^2 - K_7\xi_1(\tau)\bar{u}(\xi_1(\tau), \tau) - K_8\xi_2(\tau)\bar{u}(\xi_1(\tau), \tau)]\,d\tau\right\}, \tag{9.17}$$

is minimized.

Applying the results of Appendix A.1, the preceding optimal control problem can be converted into the following optimal control problem.

Problem $(\hat{P}_{F1})$ Subject to the dynamic system

$$\begin{aligned}\phi_t(x_1, x_2, t) = {} & \tfrac{1}{2}(\sigma_1)^2\phi_{x_1x_1}(x_1, x_2, t) + \tfrac{1}{2}(\sigma_2)^2\phi_{x_2x_2}(x_1, x_2, t)\\ & + (K_3x_1(1 - x_1) - K_4x_1u(x_1, t))\phi_{x_1}(x_1, x_2, t)\\ & + (K_5x_2(1 - x_2) - K_6x_2u(x_1, t))\phi_{x_2}(x_1, x_2, t)\\ & + e^{-\delta(T-t)}[K_9 + K_{10}u(x_1, t) + K_{11}(u(x_1, t))^2\\ & \qquad - K_7x_1u(x_1, t) - K_8x_2u(x_1, t)],\\ & \qquad (x_1, x_2, t) \in (0, 1) \times (0, 1) \times (0, T),\end{aligned} \tag{9.18a}$$

$$\phi(x_1, x_2, 0) = 0, \qquad (x_1, x_2) \in (0, 1) \times (0, 1), \tag{9.18b}$$

$$\phi(x_1, x_2, t) = 0, \qquad (x_1, x_2, t) \in \Gamma, \tag{9.18c}$$

find a control $u \in \mathscr{U}_1$ such that the cost functional

$$\hat{J}(u) = \int_{K_{12}}^{K_{13}}\int_{K_{14}}^{K_{15}} \phi(u)(x_1, x_2, T)\,dx_1\,dx_2, \tag{9.19}$$

is minimized, where

$$\Gamma \equiv \{(x_1, x_2, t) \in [0, 1] \times [0, 1] \times [0, T]: \text{ either } x_1 \text{ or } x_2 \text{ belongs to } \{0\} \cup \{1\}\},$$

and $\phi(u)$ is the almost everywhere solution of problem (9.18) corresponding to $u \in \mathscr{U}_1$.

Now, given a control $\bar{u} \in \mathscr{U}_1$, consider the function

$$u(x_1, t) \equiv \bar{u}(x_1, T - t). \tag{9.20}$$

Then it is clear that u belongs also to the class $\mathscr{U}_1$. Furthermore, $\hat{J}(u)$ calculated by (9.19) is equal to $J(\bar{u})$ calculated by (9.17). Thus once the reduced optimal control problem is solved, an optimal control to the first fishing problem can be obtained by calculating the corresponding $\bar{u}$ according to formula (9.20).

Corresponding to the optimal control problem $(\hat{P}_{F1})$ the adjoint system is

$$\begin{aligned} -z_t(x_1, x_2, t) &= \tfrac{1}{2}(\sigma_1)^2 z_{x_1 x_1}(x_1, x_2, t) + \tfrac{1}{2}(\sigma_1)^2 z_{x_2 x_2}(x_1, x_2, t) \\ &\quad - ((K_3 x_1(1 - x_1) - K_4 x_1 u(x_1, t))z(x_1, x_2, t))_{x_1} \\ &\quad - ((K_5 x_2(1 - x_2) - K_6 x_2 u(x_1, t))z(x_1, x_2, t))_{x_2}, \\ &\qquad (x_1, x_2, t) \in (0, 1) \times (0, 1) \times (0, T), \end{aligned} \tag{9.21a}$$

$$z(x_1, x_2, t) = 0, \qquad (x_1, x_2, t) \in \Gamma, \tag{9.21b}$$

$$z(x_1, x_2, T) = \begin{cases} 1, & (x_1, x_2) \in [K_{12}, K_{13}] \times [K_{14}, K_{15}], \\ 0, & \text{otherwise}. \end{cases} \tag{9.21c}$$

For each $u \in \mathscr{U}_1$, let $z(u)$ denote the corresponding weak solution of the problem (9.21).

The corresponding Hamiltonian function is

$$\begin{aligned} H(u)[x_1, t, v] = \int_0^1 & z(u)(x_1, x_2, t)\{-K_4 x_1 v \phi(u)_{x_1}(x_1, x_2, t) \\ & - K_6 x_2 v \phi(u)_{x_2}(x_1, x_2, t) \\ & + [K_{10} v + K_{11}(v)^2 - K_7 x_1 v - K_8 x_2 v] e^{-\delta(T-t)}\}\, dx_2 + \tilde{f}, \end{aligned} \tag{9.22}$$

where $\tilde{f}$ is a function independent of v. The function that minimizes this Hamiltonian function over $v \in R^1$ is $V_0(u)$ defined by

$$\begin{aligned} V_0(u)(x_1, t) = \Big\{ \int_0^1 & z(u)(x_1, x_2, t)[K_4 x_1 \phi(u)_{x_1}(x_1, x_2, t) \\ & + K_6 x_2 \phi(u)_{x_2}(x_1, x_2, t) \\ & + e^{-\delta(T-t)}(K_7 x_1 + K_8 x_2 - K_{10})]\, dx_2 \Big\} \\ \times \Big\{ 2 \int_0^1 & z(u)(x_1, x_2, t) e^{-\delta(T-t)} K_{11}\, dx_2 \Big\}^{-1}. \end{aligned} \tag{9.23}$$

The function $V(u): \hat{Q} \to U$ is given by

$$V(u)(x_1, t) \equiv \begin{cases} V_0(u)(x_1, t), & 0 \leq V_0(u)(x_1, t) \leq 1, \\ 0, & V_0(u)(x_1, t) < 0, \\ 1, & V_0(u)(x_1, t) > 1. \end{cases} \tag{9.24}$$

Algorithm (DA_1) can now be used to solve the optimal control problem $(\hat{P}_{F1})$. The results are recorded in Table 9.1, where the time is the elapsed time τ rather than the time-to-go t. The initial control was chosen so that

$$u^0(x_1, t) = 0,$$

for all $(x_1, t) \in (0, 1) \times (0, T)$.

The parameters of the problem were

$$T = 1, \qquad \sigma_1 = \sigma_2 = \tfrac{1}{2}, \qquad \delta = 0.005,$$

$$K_3 = 2, \qquad K_4 = 1, \qquad K_5 = 1,$$

$$K_6 = 0.9, \qquad K_7 = 2, \qquad K_8 = 1,$$

$$K_9 = K_{10} = K_{11} = 0.5, \qquad K_{12} = 0.4,$$

$$K_{13} = 0.6, \qquad K_{14} = 0.4, \qquad K_{15} = 0.6.$$

From Table 9.1 we observe that if ξ_1 is 0.55 or higher, then the best policy is to fish at full capacity. The computed solution also recommends that some fishing be done even if it is not profitable to offset the fixed cost associated with the performance criterion. However, the lower the value of ξ_1, the lower the effort is recommended. For the given parameters, the computed optimal expected profit is 0.3628080×10^{-3}.

To state the second fishing problem we consider the stochastic system

$$d\xi_1(\tau) = [K_3\xi_1(\tau)(1 - \xi_1(\tau)) - K_4\xi_1(\tau)\bar{u}(\xi_1(\tau), \xi_2(\tau), \tau)]\,d\tau + \sigma_1\,dw_1(\tau), \quad \tau \in [0, T], \tag{9.25a}$$

$$d\xi_2(\tau) = [K_5\xi_2(\tau)(1 - \xi_2(\tau)) - K_6\xi_2(\tau)\bar{u}(\xi_1(\tau), \xi_2(\tau), \tau)]\,d\tau + \sigma_2\,dw_2(\tau), \quad \tau \in [0, T], \tag{9.25b}$$

with the initial conditions

$$\xi_1(0) \sim U[K_{12}, K_{13}], \tag{9.25c}$$

$$\xi_2(0) \sim U[K_{14}, K_{15}]. \tag{9.25d}$$

TABLE 9.1

Computed Optimal Control $u(t, x_1)$ for the First Fishing Problem

	x_1						
t	0.1	0.2	0.3	0.4	0.5	0.6	Higher
0.05	0.1928	0.3846	0.5728	0.7603	0.9493	1.000	...
0.10	0.1932	0.3828	0.5661	0.7478	0.9326	1.000	...
0.15	0.1932	0.3821	0.5636	0.7433	0.9268	1.000	...
0.20	0.1932	0.3817	0.5627	0.7417	0.9249	1.000	...
0.25	0.1931	0.3815	0.5623	0.7412	0.9243	1.000	...
0.30	0.1931	0.3814	0.5622	0.7410	0.9241	1.000	...
0.35	0.1930	0.3814	0.5621	0.7409	0.9241	1.000	...
0.40	0.1930	0.3813	0.5620	0.7409	0.9241	1.000	...
0.45	0.1930	0.3813	0.5620	0.7408	0.9241	1.000	...
0.50	0.1930	0.3813	0.5620	0.7408	0.9241	1.000	...
0.55	0.1930	0.3813	0.5620	0.7408	0.9241	1.000	...
0.60	0.1930	0.3813	0.5620	0.7408	0.9241	1.000	...
0.65	0.1930	0.3812	0.5620	0.7408	0.9241	1.000	...
0.70	0.1930	0.3812	0.5619	0.7408	0.9241	1.000	...
0.75	0.1929	0.3812	0.5619	0.7408	0.9241	1.000	...
0.80	0.1929	0.3812	0.5619	0.7407	0.9240	1.000	...
0.85	0.1929	0.3811	0.5618	0.7406	0.9238	1.000	...
0.90	0.1931	0.3812	0.5617	0.7402	0.9232	1.000	...
0.95	0.1941	0.3821	0.5618	0.7392	0.9209	1.000	...
1.00	0.1973	0.3850	0.5625	0.7353	0.9128	1.000	...

The second fishing problem may now be stated as:

Problem (P_{F2}) Subject to system (9.25), find a control $u \in \mathcal{U}_2$ such that the performance criterion

$$J(\bar{u}) \equiv \mathscr{E}\left\{ \int_0^{\Upsilon} e^{-\delta\tau}[K_9 + K_{10}\bar{u}(\xi_1(\tau), \xi_2(\tau), \tau) + K_{11}(\bar{u}(\xi_1(\tau), \xi_2(\tau), \tau))^2 \right.$$
$$\left. - K_7\xi_1(\tau)\bar{u}(\xi_1(\tau), \xi_2(\tau), \tau) - K_8\xi_2(\tau)\bar{u}(\xi_1(\tau), \xi_2(\tau), \tau)]\, d\tau \right\}, \tag{9.26}$$

is minimized.

In this second fishing problem the control $\bar{u}$ depends on both ξ_1 and ξ_2 rather than just ξ_1. Thus it is known as the fully observed optimal control problem.

Applying the results of Appendix A.1 and letting $t = T - \tau$, the second fishing problem is converted into the following optimal control problem.

Problem $(\hat{P}_{F2})$ Subject to the system

$$\begin{aligned}\phi_t(x_1, x_2, t) = {} & \tfrac{1}{2}(\sigma_1)^2\phi_{x_1x_1}(x_1, x_2, t) + \tfrac{1}{2}(\sigma_2)^2\phi_{x_2x_2}(x_1, x_2, t) \\ & + (K_3x_1(1 - x_1) - K_4x_1u(x_1, x_2, t))\phi_{x_1}(x_1, x_2, t) \\ & + (K_5x_2(1 - x_2) - K_6x_2u(x_1, x_2, t))\phi_{x_2}(x_1, x_2, t) \\ & + e^{-\delta(T-t)}[K_9 + K_{10}u(x_1, x_2, t) + K_{11}(u(x_1, x_2, t))^2 \\ & - (K_7x_1 + K_8x_2)u(x_1, x_2, t)], \\ & \qquad (x_1, x_2, t) \in (0, 1) \times (0, 1) \times (0, T), \end{aligned} \tag{9.27a}$$

$$\phi(x_1, x_2, t) = 0, \qquad (x_1, x_2, t) \in \Gamma, \tag{9.27b}$$

$$\phi(x_1, x_2, 0) = 0, \qquad (x_1, x_2) \in (0, 1) \times (0, 1), \tag{9.27c}$$

find a control $u \in \mathscr{U}_2$ such that the cost functional

$$\hat{J}(u) \equiv \int_{K_{12}}^{K_{13}} \int_{K_{14}}^{K_{15}} \phi(u)(x_1, x_2, T)\, dx_1\, dx_2, \tag{9.28}$$

is minimized.

If $u^* \in \mathscr{U}_2$ is an optimal control for the optimal control problem $(\hat{P}_{F2})$, then $\bar{u}^*$ defined by

$$\bar{u}^*(x_1, x_2, \tau) \equiv u^*(x_1, x_2, T - \tau) \tag{9.29}$$

is an optimal control for the second fishing problem (P_{F2}). Furthermore,

$$J(\bar{u}) = \hat{J}(u), \tag{9.30}$$

if $\bar{u}(x_1, x_2, \tau) \equiv u(x_1, x_2, T - \tau)$ and $u \in \mathscr{U}_2$.

The optimal control problem $(\hat{P}_{F2})$ is a special case of problem (P) with $n = n_1$. Thus Algorithm (DA_2) is applicable. In this algorithm the solution of the corresponding adjoint problem is not needed.

The function $I(u)$ is

$$\begin{aligned} I(u)(x_1, x_2, t, v) = {} & -K_4x_1v\phi_{x_1}(x_1, x_2, t) - K_6x_2v\phi_{x_2}(x_1, x_2, t) \\ & + e^{-\delta(T-t)}[K_{10}v + K_{11}(v)^2 - K_7x_1v - K_8x_2v] + \tilde{f}, \end{aligned} \tag{9.31}$$

where $\tilde{f}$ is a function independent of v. Let $V_0(u)$ be defined by

$$\begin{aligned} V_0(u)(x_1, x_2, t) = {} & [K_4x_1\phi_{x_1}(x_1, x_2, t) + K_6x_2\phi_{x_2}(x_1, x_2, t) \\ & + e^{-\delta(T-t)}(-K_{10} + K_7x_1 + K_8x_2)]/2K_{11}e^{-\delta(T-t)}. \end{aligned} \tag{9.32}$$

TABLE 9.2

Computed Optimal Control $u(t, x_1, x_2)$ for the Second Fishing Problem

	x_1								
x_2	0.1	0.2	0.3	0.4	0.5	0.6	0.7	0.8	0.9
For time-to-go t = 0.1									
0.100	0.000	0.113	0.302	0.485	0.667	0.853	1.00	1.00	1.00
0.200	0.0124	0.208	0.393	0.572	0.751	0.936	1.00	1.00	1.00
0.300	0.109	0.300	0.482	0.659	0.837	1.00	1.00	1.00	1.00
0.400	0.204	0.392	0.571	0.747	0.925	1.00	1.00	1.00	1.00
0.500	0.299	0.484	0.662	0.838	1.00	1.00	1.00	1.00	1.00
0.600	0.393	0.576	0.756	0.937	1.00	1.00	1.00	1.00	1.00
0.700	0.486	0.670	0.857	1.00	1.00	1.00	1.00	1.00	1.00
0.800	0.571	0.761	0.968	1.00	1.00	1.00	1.00	1.00	1.00
0.900	1.00	1.00	1.00	1.00	1.00	1.00	1.00	1.00	1.00
For time-to-go t = 0.2									
0.100	0.000	0.114	0.300	0.481	0.660	0.845	1.00	1.00	1.00
0.200	0.0131	0.207	0.389	0.564	0.740	0.925	1.00	1.00	1.00
0.300	0.109	0.298	0.476	0.648	0.823	1.00	1.00	1.00	1.00
0.400	0.203	0.388	0.563	0.734	0.910	1.00	1.00	1.00	1.00
0.500	0.297	0.480	0.654	0.827	1.00	1.00	1.00	1.00	1.00
0.600	0.392	0.573	0.750	0.929	1.00	1.00	1.00	1.00	1.00
0.700	0.485	0.668	0.855	1.00	1.00	1.00	1.00	1.00	1.00
0.800	0.572	0.763	0.973	1.00	1.00	1.00	1.00	1.00	1.00
0.900	1.00	1.00	1.00	1.00	1.00	1.00	1.00	1.00	1.00
For time-to-go t = 0.9									
0.100	0.000	0.112	0.298	0.478	0.658	0.844	1.00	1.00	1.00
0.200	0.0121	0.205	0.386	0.561	0.737	0.923	1.00	1.00	1.00
0.300	0.107	0.296	0.473	0.645	0.820	1.00	1.00	1.00	1.00
0.400	0.202	0.386	0.560	0.731	0.908	1.00	1.00	1.00	1.00
0.500	0.297	0.478	0.652	0.825	1.00	1.00	1.00	1.00	1.00
0.600	0.392	0.573	0.750	0.930	1.00	1.00	1.00	1.00	1.00
0.700	0.486	0.670	0.858	1.00	1.00	1.00	1.00	1.00	1.00
0.800	0.574	0.767	0.979	1.00	1.00	1.00	1.00	1.00	1.00
0.900	1.00	1.00	1.00	1.00	1.00	1.00	1.00	1.00	1.00
For time-to-go t = 1.0									
0.100	0.000	0.112	0.298	0.478	0.658	0.844	1.00	1.00	1.00
0.200	0.0121	0.205	0.386	0.561	0.737	0.923	1.00	1.00	1.00
0.300	0.107	0.296	0.473	0.645	0.820	1.00	1.00	1.00	1.00
0.400	0.202	0.386	0.560	0.731	0.908	1.00	1.00	1.00	1.00
0.500	0.297	0.478	0.652	0.825	1.00	1.00	1.00	1.00	1.00
0.600	0.392	0.573	0.750	0.930	1.00	1.00	1.00	1.00	1.00
0.700	0.486	0.670	0.858	1.00	1.00	1.00	1.00	1.00	1.00
0.800	0.574	0.767	0.979	1.00	1.00	1.00	1.00	1.00	1.00
0.900	1.00	1.00	1.00	1.00	1.00	1.00	1.00	1.00	1.00

The function $V(u)\colon Q \to U$ is given by

$$V(u)(x_1, x_2, t) \equiv \begin{cases} V_0(u)(x_1, x_2, t), & 0 \le V_0(u)(x_1, x_2, t) \le 1, \\ 1, & V_0(u)(x_1, x_2, t) > 1, \\ 0, & V_0(u)(x_1, x_2, t) < 0. \end{cases} \tag{9.33}$$

Assume that the parameters of this second fishing problem are the same as those of the first fishing problem. The corresponding problem is then solved by using Algorithm (DA_2). The results are recorded in Table 9.2, where the time is to be understood as the time-to-go t. The computed optimal expected profit is 0.147×10^{-2}. This is, as expected, an improvement over that of the first fishing problem.

The main difference between the corresponding solutions of these two fishing problems is that the optimal control for the first fishing problem settles down to a stationary control by $t = 0.5$, whereas the optimal control of the second fishing problem does not.

The numerical solutions correspond to the solutions of discrete problems. A natural question to ask is how accurately do these solutions correspond to those of the original (continuous) problems. This has yet to be investigated.

III.10. Discussion

Optimal control theory of distributed parameters systems is a productive field. There are already four books devoted entirely to this branch of the optimal control theory. These books are [But.1], [Li.1], [Li.5] and [AT.5] of this text.

[But.1] has an engineering flavor. Many physical problems are considered and their mathematical models are constructed. These models are in terms of distributed parameter systems. Necessary and sufficient conditions for optimality are derived for those related optimal control problems. Furthermore, some approximate and computational methods, such as finite difference method, for solving some simple optimal control problems are also discussed. However, general results on this topic are lacking in this reference.

[Li.1] deals with optimal control of systems governed by elliptic, parabolic and hyperbolic partial differential equations. The concepts of distribution theory and Sobolev spaces are used extensively in the study of these classes of optimal control problems. The majority of the systems considered are linear with controls acting through the forcing term and, in some cases, through the initial and the boundary conditions. The emphases are not only on necessary and sufficient conditions for optimality but also on feedback problems and their related integro–differential equations of the Riccati type. Furthermore, questions concerning existence of optimal controls and controllability are also discussed. Finally, various procedures of regularization, approximation, and penalization are also considered in this reference. These procedures may be used in obtaining numerical solutions of optimal control problems. [Li.5] will be discussed in Section IV.10.

[AT.5] was published in 1981. It consists of five chapters with the first two chapters concerning the preparatory ground. The third chapter deals with optimal control problems involving linear second-order parabolic partial differential equations with first boundary condition. The controls are assumed to act on the coefficients and the forcing term of the differential equation. This class of optimal control problems corresponds naturally to a general class of nonlinear stochastic optimal control problems involving Ito stochastic differential equations. (For a detailed discussion on this relationship, see Appendix I.) Questions concerning necessary conditions for optimality and existence of optimal controls for these optimal control problems are discussed in full detail. Such questions have also been investigated in [F1.1], [AT.1], [AT.2], [RT.1], and [Z.1] for similar classes of optimal control problems. Furthermore, in Chapter III of [AT.5] a few results on the computational methods are discussed. However, no convergence results are given. To be more specific, it was shown that a sequence $\{u^k\}$ of controls can be constructed so that $J(u^{k+1}) < J(u^k)$ for all $k = 1, 2, \ldots$, where J is the cost functional. However, no convergence results on $\{u^k\}$ are given. In the construction of these improved controls, any of the two methods can be used. The first one is the strong variational technique, and the second one is the conditional gradient technique. For the strong variational technique, the result was originally reported in [TRB.1].

In [TR.1] a more sophisticated scheme based on the strong variational technique is given. The sequence of subsets on which the control is perturbed varies from that used in [TRB.1]. Instead of being any sequence of rectangles that converges to a point, it is necessary to specify the Lebesgue measures of the subsets as part of the construction. This technique can be considered as being the generalized version of that reported in [MP.1], where the governing system is an ordinary differential equation.

The advantage of this more complicated scheme is that the sequence $\{u^k\}$ of improved controls so generated converges in the sense of Theorem 6.1. This convergence result is introduced to optimal control algorithms for the first time in [MP.1]. Since then, it has become a common type of convergence result in this area.

[TR.1] is the main reference for all but the last three sections of this chapter. The crucial step for the success of this method is the specification of the sequence of sets on which the control is perturbed. [For details, see (5.3).] On this basis estimate (5.45) can be proved. This estimate, in turn, gives rise to the sequence of improved controls (see Section 6). The main convergence result reported in Theorem 6.1 is obtained by using the uniform continuity property of an operator (see Lemma 6.2) in conjunction with estimate (5.45).

The technique of [TR.1] has been extended to an optimal control problem involving a second-order hyperbolic partial differential equation with Darboux boundary condition in [WuT.1]. This class of optimal control problems was first introduced by Yegorov (see [But.1], p. 35), and then studied extensively in [Su.1], [Su.2], and [Su.3] by following the approach proposed in [Ce.3]. The main concerns of these articles are necessary conditions for optimality and existence of optimal controls. They are the main references for Section 4.3 of [AT.5], where a new result on the existence of optimal controls is also included.

In Section 4.3.7 of [AT.5] a computational algorithm based on the strong variational technique is devised. This result is parallel to that for the parabolic partial differential equations considered in Section 3.3.2 of the same reference (and hence to that of [TRB.1]). Similarly, no convergence results are given. The relationship between the results of [WuT.1] and Section 4.3.7 of [AT.5] is similar to that between the results of [TR.1] and Section 3.3.2 of [AT.5] (and hence [TRB.1]).

Note that optimal control problems involving hyperbolic partial differential equations have been extensively studied in [Ah.1], [Az.1], [But.1], [Li.1], [Su.2], [Su.3], [Wa.2], and many others. The problems considered in [Ah.1], [Ru.2], and [Wa.2] arise in studying the optimal control of power flow in electrical networks and of counterflow processes in chemical engineering, vibration, and plasma confinement. Chapter IV of [AT.5] is also devoted to the study of optimal control problems involving hyperbolic partial differential equations. Three classes of problems are discussed separately in three different sections. The class of problems considered in Section 4.3 of [AT.5] has already been discussed previously. We shall briefly discuss the other two classes of problems. In Section 4.1 of [AT.5] a class of first-order hyperbolic partial differential equations is considered. The controls are assumed to act on the boundary conditions. This class of optimal control problems is originally due to Russell [Ru.2]. Further results are obtained in [CTW.1]. More precisely, in [CTW.1], a similar class of optimal control problems with slightly more general cost functional is considered and a computational algorithm that generates minimizing sequences of controls is devised. In Section 4.2 of [AT.5] a class of optimal control problems involving second-order hyperbolic system arising in the study of power flow problem in electrical engineering is considered. This class of problems was originally due to Ahmed [Ah.1]. Similar to the relationship between [CTW.1] and Section 4.1 of [AT.5], results additional to that given in Section 4.2 of [AT.5] can be found in [CTW.2].

The final chapter of [AT.5] deals basically with abstract evolution equations, both linear and nonlinear. A very large class of distributed parameter systems can be modeled as an abstract differential equation on a suitable Banach space or on a suitable manifold therein. The advantage of an abstract formulation lies not ony in its generality but also in the insight about many common unifying properties. Many other related works can also be found in those related articles cited therein.

The notes given in [Li.1] and [AT.5] are very useful. In [Li.1] many significant results dating up to 1968 are discussed. In [AT.5] many results appearing after 1968 are included. Thus we shall not reproduce topics that have already been discussed in those notes.

In Section 8 we use a simple type of discretization scheme to discretize the corresponding algorithm for a special case of the optimal control problem under the discussion of this chapter. Since the discretization scheme is rather elementary, much improvement in this area appears possible. Thus further research in this direction should produce interesting results. In Section 9 two examples are considered. These two examples arise from problems in fishing. The models can be considered as the generalization of the model proposed in [C1.1], by including uncertainty terms in the differential equations that govern the populations of the two different species. The corresponding optimal control problems are stochastic optimal control problems. In the second problem controls depend on the populations of both the species. By contrast, controls depend only on the population of the first species in the first problem. Using the results of Appendix I, both stochastic optimal control problems are converted into the corresponding deterministic optimal control problems involving parabolic partial differential equations. The reduced problems are in the form of the optimal control problem P considered in this chapter. Thus the discretized algorithm reported in Section 8 is applicable. Note that both Sections 8 and 9, including the subsequent numerical results, are from Chapter VI of the Ph.D. thesis of Dr. D. W. Reid [R.1].

In [MP.2] optimal control problems with control and terminal equality constraints are considered, where the system dynamics are governed by ordinary differential equations. An algorithm, together with its convergence properties is obtained for such problems. Both the conceptual and implemental versions of the algorithm are given. The terminal equality constraint

$J_1(u)$ and the cost functional $J_0(u)$ in the original problem are replaced by the functional

$$\gamma_c(u) = \max\{J_0(u)/c + J_1(u), J_0(u)/c - J_1(u)\},$$

subject to control constraint. This new problem P_c is discussed in detail. The nondifferentiability of the new cost functional $\gamma_c(u)$ requires special attention. The control constraint is incorporated into the search direction subproblem. The choice of parameter c is also discussed. Namely, c must be chosen to satisfy some test depending on the current control u. An equivalent problem utilizing an exact penalty function is also described.

This result has not been extended to optimal control problems of distributed parameter systems.

Note that many other interesting contributions in the area of optimal control algorithm can also be found in the literature, such as [CM.1], [GG.1], [K.1], and [Sc.1]. However, the convergence properties of these algorithms are usually not available.

In [Li.4] the applicability of asymptotic methods for solving optimal control problems involving perturbations is discussed. Attention is focused on the following three main cases:

(i) perturbation of state equation;
(ii) perturbation of cost functional; and
(iii) degeneracy of cost functional.

Each of these three cases is discussed with the aid of specific examples in which the state equations are partial differential equations.

In the strong variational algorithm we need to calculate $\alpha^*(u)$ [see (5.32)], which is the supremum of a set. Clearly, it is very expensive to calculate this $\alpha^*(u)$ accurately. Thus the following question arises: is it possible just to calculate $\alpha^*(u)$ approximately without destroying the convergence property of the algorithm? This question remains open.

For the same algorithm one may also ask: will the corresponding algorithm converge if the Hamiltonian function is minimized approximately in each iteration [see (4.11)]. This question is also open.

CHAPTER IV

Optimal Control of First Boundary Problems: Gradient Techniques

IV.1. Introduction

In this chapter we shall consider a similar class of systems as in the previous chapter. However, we shall assume that both parameter vectors and control functions are permitted to appear in the coefficients and in the forcing term of the differential equation. Furthermore, assumptions imposed on the coefficients are also to be slightly different.

Several gradient-type algorithms are to be devised for solving the optimal control problems under discussion.

IV.2. System Description

As in Chapter II, Ω is a bounded domain in R^n with its boundary and closure denoted by $\partial\Omega$ and $\overline{\Omega}$, respectively. *The boundary $\partial\Omega$ is assumed to belong to the class C^3 throughout this chapter.* Let T be a fixed positive constant, $Q \equiv \Omega \times (0, T)$, $\Gamma \equiv \partial\Omega \times [0, T]$, and $\bar{Q} \equiv \bar{\Omega} \times [0, T]$. Let n_1 be an integer with $0 \leq n_1 \leq n$. Then for any $x \equiv (x_1, \ldots, x_n)$ define

$$\hat{x} \equiv (x_1, \ldots, x_{n_1}) \in R^{n_1}, \qquad \hat{\hat{x}} \equiv (x_{n_1+1}, \ldots, x_n) \in R^{n-n_1},$$

and let

$$\hat{\Omega} \equiv \{\hat{x} \in R^{n_1} : x \in \Omega\}, \qquad \Omega_{\hat{x}} \equiv \{\hat{\hat{x}} \in R^{n-n_1} : (\hat{x}, \hat{\hat{x}}) \in \Omega\}, \qquad \hat{Q} \equiv \hat{\Omega} \times (0, T).$$

In Chapter III the integer n_1 must be strictly greater than zero and hence the case involving open loop controls is excluded in that chapter. Here, this restriction is removed; we allow the integer n_1 to be zero.

Let S (resp. U) be a given nonempty compact and convex subset of R^{m_1} (resp. R^{m_2}). A measurable function $u: \hat{Q} \to U$ is called an admissible control. *Let $\mathcal{U}$ denote the class of all such admissible controls.* Define

$$\mathcal{D} \equiv R^{m_1} \times L_\infty(\hat{Q}, R^{m_2}),$$

and

$$\mathcal{D}_p \equiv S \times \mathcal{U}.$$

For convenience, an element in $\mathcal{D}_p$ is to be referred to as a *policy and $\mathcal{D}_p$ is to be called the class of policies.*

Note that $\mathcal{D}$ is a vector space and becomes a Banach space when equipped with the norm $\|\cdot\|_{\mathcal{D}}$ defined by

$$\|(\sigma, u)\|_{\mathcal{D}} \equiv |\sigma| + \|u\|_{\infty, \hat{Q}},$$

for all $\sigma \equiv (\sigma_1, \ldots, \sigma_{m_1}) \in R^{m_1}$ and $u \equiv (u_1, \ldots, u_{m_2}) \in L_\infty(\hat{Q}, R^{m_2})$, where

$$|\sigma| \equiv \left\{\sum_{i=1}^{m_1} |\sigma_i|^2\right\}^{1/2},$$

and

$$\|u\|_{\infty, \hat{Q}} \equiv \operatorname*{ess\ sup}_{(\hat{x}, t) \in \hat{Q}} \left\{\sum_{i=1}^{m_2} |u_i(\hat{x}, t)|^2\right\}^{1/2}.$$

Note also that $\mathcal{D}_p$ becomes a normed space with the relative norm induced by that of $\mathcal{D}$, that is,

$$\|(\sigma, u)\|_{\mathcal{D}_p} \equiv \|(\sigma, u)\|_{\mathcal{D}}, \qquad (\sigma, u) \in \mathcal{D}_p.$$

We consider the following first boundary-value problem:

$$L(\sigma, u)\phi(x, t) = f(x, t, \sigma, u(\hat{x}, t)), \qquad (x, t) \in Q, \tag{2.1a}$$

$$\phi|_{t=0} = \phi_0(x), \qquad x \in \Omega, \tag{2.1b}$$

$$\phi|_\Gamma = 0, \qquad (x, t) \in \Gamma, \tag{2.1c}$$

where $(\sigma, u) \in \mathscr{D}$ and, for each $(\sigma, u) \in \mathscr{D}$, $L(\sigma, u)$ is a linear second-order parabolic partial differential operator in general form defined by

$$L(\sigma, u)\psi \equiv \psi_t - \sum_{i,j=1}^{n} a_{ij}(x, t)\psi_{x_i x_j} - \sum_{i=1}^{n} b_i(x, t, \sigma, u(\hat{x}, t))\psi_{x_i} - c(x, t, \sigma, u(\hat{x}, t))\psi. \tag{2.2}$$

The solution of problem (2.1) is to be understood as in the sense of Definition III.2.1 and hence is to be called the *almost everywhere solution.*

We assume throughout this chapter that the following conditions are satisfied.

(A.1) $a_{ij} \in C(\bar{Q})$, $i, j = 1, \ldots, n$.

(A.2) There exist positive constants α_l, α_u such that

$$\alpha_l |\xi|^2 \leq \sum_{i,j=1}^{n} a_{ij}(x, t)\xi_i \xi_j \leq \alpha_u |\xi|^2,$$

for all $\xi \equiv (\xi_1, \ldots, \xi_n) \in R^n$ and for all $(x, t) \in \bar{Q}$.

(A.3) b_i, $i = 1, \ldots, n$, and f are continuous on $\bar{Q} \times R^{m_1} \times R^{m_2}$.

(A.4) $\phi_0 \in C_0^2(\Omega)$.

REMARK 2.1. Let h denote any function appearing in assumption (A.3). Define

$$h(\sigma, u) \equiv h(\cdot, \cdot, \sigma, u(\cdot, \cdot)),$$

for all $(\sigma, u) \in \mathscr{D}$. Then it is clear that h can be considered as a mapping from $\mathscr{D}$ into $L_\infty(Q)$.

Let $(\sigma, u) \in \mathscr{D}$. Then it is clear from assumption (A.3) that $b_i(\sigma, u)$, $i = 1, \ldots, n$, $c(\sigma, u)$ and $f(\sigma, u)$ are bounded and measurable on Q. Hence, condition (iii) of Theorem II.8.1 is satisfied. The other conditions of this theorem are implied by assumptions (A.1), (A.2), and (A.4). Thus it follows that corresponding to each $(\sigma, u) \in \mathscr{D}$, problem (2.1) admits a unique almost everywhere solution $\phi(\sigma, u)$. Furthermore, $\phi(\sigma, u)$ satisfies the estimate:

$$\|\phi(\sigma, u)\|_{p,Q}^{(2,1)} \leq K_0\{\|f(\sigma, u)\|_{\infty,Q} + \|\phi_0\|_{\infty,\Omega}^{(2)}\}, \tag{2.3}$$

for all $p \in (\frac{3}{2}, \infty]$, where the constant K_0 depends only on n, α_l, T, Ω, and bounds for $b_i(\sigma, u)$, $i = 1, \ldots, n$, and $c(\sigma, u)$.

REMARK 2.2. Consider system (2.1) under the restriction that

$$(\sigma, u) \in \mathscr{D}_p \, (\subset \mathscr{D}).$$

In view of the definition of $\mathscr{D}_p$ we note that S and U are compact.

Thus by virtue of inequality (2.3) and assumption (A.3), there exists a constant K_1, independent of $(\sigma, u) \in \mathscr{D}_p$, such that

$$\|\phi(\sigma, u)\|_{p,Q}^{(2,1)} \leq K_1\{\|f(\sigma, u)\|_{\infty,Q} + \|\phi_0\|_{\infty,\Omega}^{(2)}\}, \tag{2.4}$$

for all $p \in (\frac{3}{2}, \infty]$. Therefore, from assumptions (A.3) and (A.4), we can find a constant K_2, again independent of $(\sigma, u) \in \mathscr{D}_p$, such that

$$\|\phi(\sigma, u)\|_{p,Q}^{(2,1)} \leq K_2, \tag{2.5}$$

for all $p \in (\frac{3}{2}, \infty]$.

From Corollary II.8.1 we recall that

$$|\phi(\sigma, u)|_{Q}^{(1+\mu,(1+\mu)/2)} \leq K_3\|\phi(\sigma, u)\|_{p,Q}^{(2,1)} \tag{2.6}$$

for all $p > n + 2$, where $\mu = 1 - (n + 2)/p$, $|\cdot|_{Q}^{(\lambda,\lambda/2)}$ denotes the norm in the Hölder space $\mathscr{H}^{\lambda,\lambda/2}(\bar{Q})$, and the constant K_3 depends only on Q and p. In particular, when $p = 2(n + 2)$, we have

$$|\phi(\sigma, u)|_{Q}^{(3/2,3/4)} \leq K_3\|\phi(\sigma, u)\|_{2(n+2),Q}^{(2,1)}. \tag{2.7}$$

REMARK 2.3. Consider system (2.1) under the same restriction as in Remark 2.2. Then it follows from (2.5) and (2.7) that

$$|\phi(\sigma, u)|_{Q}^{(3/2,3/4)} \leq K_4, \tag{2.8}$$

where $K_4 \equiv K_2K_3$ is again independent of $(\sigma, u) \in \mathscr{D}_p$.

REMARK 2.4. Let $S_0 \subset R^{m_1}$ and $U_0 \subset R^{m_2}$ be compact. Define

$$\mathscr{D}_0 \equiv \{(\sigma, u) \in \mathscr{D} : \sigma \in S_0 \quad \text{and} \quad u(\hat{x}, t) \in U_0 \quad \text{for almost all } (\hat{x}, t) \in \hat{Q}\}.$$

Then by the same token it can be verified that the corresponding versions of estimates (2.5) and (2.8) are valid, namely,

$$\|\phi(\sigma, u)\|_{p,Q}^{(2,1)} \leq K_2', \tag{2.5$'$}$$

for all $p \in (\frac{3}{2}, \infty]$, and

$$|\phi(\sigma, u)|_{Q}^{(3/2,3/4)} \leq K_4', \tag{2.8$'$}$$

where the constants K_2' and K_4' are independent of $(\sigma, u) \in \mathscr{D}_0$.

In the rest of this chapter $\phi(\sigma, u)$ will denote the almost everywhere solution of problem (2.1) corresponding to $(\sigma, u) \in \mathscr{D}$. *Thus we can clearly consider ϕ as a mapping from $\mathscr{D}$ into $W_\infty^{2,1}(Q)$.*

REMARK 2.5. Let h and $\mathscr{D}_0$ be as defined in Remark 2.1 and Remark 2.4, respectively. Since $\bar{Q} \times S_0 \times U_0$ is compact, it is easy to verify that h is a uniformly continuous mapping from $\mathscr{D}_0$ into $L_\infty(Q)$.

The proof of the next theorem is similar to that given for Theorem III.2.1.

THEOREM 2.1. *Let $\mathscr{D}_0$ be as defined in Remark* 2.4. *Then ϕ is a uniformly continuous mapping from $\mathscr{D}_0$ into $W_\infty^{2,1}(Q)$.*

REMARK 2.6. Since $\mathscr{D}_p$ can be taken as $\mathscr{D}_0$, it follows from Remark 2.5 and Theorem 2.1 that the following two statements are valid:

(i) h is a uniformly continuous mapping from $\mathscr{D}_p$ into $L_\infty(Q)$; and
(ii) ϕ is a uniformly continuous mapping from $\mathscr{D}_p$ into $W_\infty^{2,1}(Q)$.

IV.3. The Optimization Problem

In this chapter we consider a similar class of the dynamic systems as that in Chapter III. However, we allow policies rather than admissible controls to appear in the first- and zeroth-order coefficients and in the forcing term of Eq. (2.1a). Furthermore, the assumptions on these functions are also different from those of Chapter III [for details, compare assumption (A.3) with assumption (III.A.3)].

The class of cost functionals considered in this chapter is

$$J(\sigma, u) = \int_\Omega \phi(\sigma, u)(x, T) z_T(x)\, dx, \tag{3.1}$$

where $\phi(\sigma, u)$ is the almost everywhere solution of problem (2.1) corresponding to $(\sigma, u) \in \mathscr{D}$, and z_T is a given real-valued function defined on Ω.

For the function z_T we need the following condition:

(A.5) $z_T \in L_\infty(\Omega)$.

REMARK 3.1.

(i) The cost functional J is well defined in $\mathscr{D}$.
(ii) In view of inequality (2.8) and assumption (A.5), we can verify that the cost functional J is bounded on $\mathscr{D}_p$.

Our optimization problem may now be specified as follows.

Problem (P) Subject to the dynamic system (2.1), find a policy $(\sigma^*, u^*) \in \mathscr{D}_p$ such that

$$J(\sigma^*, u^*) \leq J(\sigma, u),$$

for all $(\sigma, u) \in \mathscr{D}_p$. This policy (σ^*, u^*) is called an *optimal policy*.

The first algorithm to be devised in this chapter is based on the conditional gradient method. To achieve this goal we need to consider an operator $L^*(\sigma, u)$, the formal adjoint of the operator $L(\sigma, u)$, given by

$$L^*(\sigma, u)\psi \equiv -\psi_t - \sum_{i=1}^{n} \left[\sum_{j=1}^{n} a_{ij}(x, t)\psi_{x_j} + a_i(x, t, \sigma, u(\hat{x}, t))\psi \right]_{x_i} - c(x, t, \sigma, u(\hat{x}, t))\psi, \tag{3.2}$$

where

$$a_i(x, t, \sigma, v) \equiv \sum_{j=1}^{n} \frac{\partial a_{ij}(x, t)}{\partial x_j} - b_i(x, t, \sigma, v). \tag{3.3}$$

As it is done in Section III.3 we shall replace, throughout the rest of this chapter, assumption (A.1) by the following stronger assumption.

(A.1)′ There exists a positive constant K_5 such that

$$\frac{|a_{ij}(x, t) - a_{ij}(x', t')|}{|x - x'| + |t - t'|} \leq K_5,$$

for all $i, j = 1, \ldots, n$, and for all $(x, t), (x', t') \in \bar{Q}$.

Under assumptions (A.1)′ and (A.3), it is clear that, for each $(\sigma, u) \in \mathscr{D}$, the functions $a_i(\sigma, u)$, $i = 1, \ldots, n$, are measurable and bounded on $\bar{Q}$.

We now consider the following adjoint system:

$$L^*(\sigma, u)z = 0, \qquad (x, t) \in Q, \tag{3.4a}$$

$$z|_{t=T} = z_T(x), \qquad x \in \Omega, \tag{3.4b}$$

$$z|_{\Gamma} = 0, \qquad (x, t) \in \Gamma. \tag{3.4c}$$

For adjoint problem (3.4), *its solution is to be understood as in the sense of Definition III.3.1 and so is to be called the weak solution.*

Letting $t = T - t'$ and then setting $\hat{z}(x, t) \equiv z(x, T - t)$, adjoint problem (3.4) is reduced to

$$\hat{L}^*(\sigma, u)\hat{z} = 0 \qquad (x, t) \in Q, \tag{3.5a}$$

$$\hat{z}|_{t=0} = z_T(x), \qquad x \in \Omega, \tag{3.5b}$$

$$\hat{z}|_{\Gamma} = 0, \qquad (x, t) \in \Gamma, \tag{3.5c}$$

where, for each $(\sigma, u) \in \mathscr{D}$, the operator $\hat{L}^*(\sigma, u)$ is defined by

$$\hat{L}^*(\sigma, u) \equiv \psi_t - \sum_{i=1}^{n} \left[\sum_{j=1}^{n} a_{ij}(x, T - t)\psi_{x_j} + a_i(x, T - t, \sigma, u(\hat{x}, T - t))\psi \right]_{x_i} - c(x, T - t, \sigma, u(\hat{x}, T - t))\psi. \tag{3.6}$$

Let $(\sigma, u) \in \mathscr{D}$. Then it can be verified from assumptions (A.1)′ and (A.3) that $a_i(\sigma, u)$, $i = 1, \ldots, n$, and $c(\sigma, u)$ are bounded measurable on Q. Since Q is bounded, assumption (II.A.3) is satisfied. This assumption is one of the hypotheses needed in Theorem II.5.6; the other required hypotheses are implied by assumptions (A.1)′, (A.2), and (A.5). Thus from the same theorem, it follows that, corresponding to each $(\sigma, u) \in \mathscr{D}$, problem (3.5) admits a unique weak solution $\hat{z}(\sigma, u)$ from the space $V_2^{1,0}(Q)$ (in the sense of Definition II.2.1). Furthermore, since Q is bounded, it follows from estimate (II.4.67) that

$$\|\hat{z}(\sigma, u)\|_Q \le K_6\{\|z_T\|_{2,\Omega}\}, \tag{3.7}$$

where $\|\cdot\|_Q$ is the norm in the Banach space $V_2^{1,0}(Q)$ and the constant K_6 depends only on n, α_l, T, Ω, and bounds for the functions $b_i(\sigma, u)$, $i = 1, \ldots, n$, and $c(\sigma, u)$ on $\bar{Q}$.

Let us consider problem (3.5) under the restriction $(\sigma, u) \in \mathscr{D}_p$. Then by virtue of assumptions (A.3) and (A.4), it can be verified from estimate (3.7) that

$$\|\hat{z}(\sigma,u)\|_Q \le K_7, \tag{3.8}$$

where the constant K_7 is independent of $(\sigma, u) \in \mathscr{D}_p$.

From the definition of $\hat{z}$ we obtain the following remark.

Remark 3.2. Adjoint problem (3.4) admits, for each $(\sigma, u) \in \mathscr{D}$, a unique weak solution $z(\sigma, u)$. Furthermore,

$$\|z(\sigma, u)\|_Q \le K_7, \tag{3.9}$$

where K_7 is the same constant as for estimate (3.8).

Since Q is bounded, $V_2^{1,0}(Q)$ is continuously embedded in $L_1(Q)$. Thus for each $(\sigma, u) \in \mathscr{D}$, $z(\sigma, u)$, which is in $V_2^{1,0}(Q)$, is also in $L_1(Q)$. *Hence, z can be considered as a mapping from $\mathscr{D}$ into $L_1(Q)$.*

In the next theorem we shall show that the mapping z when restricted to $\mathscr{D}_p$ is uniformly continuous. First, we need the following lemma. Apart from some obvious modifications, its proof is otherwise the same as that given for Lemma III.3.1.

LEMMA 3.1. *Let $\mathring{\tilde{W}}_2^{2,1}(Q)$ be as defined in Lemma III.3.1. Then for any $\Phi \in \mathring{\tilde{W}}_2^{2,1}(Q)$,*

$$\iint_Q (L(\sigma, u)\Phi)z(\sigma, u)\,dx\,dt = \int_\Omega \Phi(x, T)z_T(x)\,dx, \tag{3.10}$$

for all $(\sigma, u) \in \mathscr{D}$.

THEOREM 3.1 *The mapping $z\colon \mathscr{D}_p \to L_1(Q)$ is uniformly continuous.*

The proof of this theorem is basically the same as that given for Theorem III.3.2, except with Lemma III.3.1 replaced by Lemma 3.1 and some other minor modifications.

IV.4. An Increment Formula

In this section we shall introduce certain notation and derive an increment formula for the cost functional J.

For each $(\sigma^0, u^0) \in \mathscr{D}$, let

$$I(\sigma^0, u^0): \bar{Q} \times R^{m_1} \times R^{m_2} \to R^1$$

be defined by

$$\begin{aligned} &I(\sigma^0, u^0)[x, t, \sigma, v] \\ &\quad \equiv \sum_{i=1}^{n} b_i(x, t, \sigma, v)\phi(\sigma^0, u^0)_{x_i}(x, t) + c(x, t, \sigma, v)\phi(\sigma^0, u^0)(x, t) \\ &\qquad + f(x, t, \sigma, v). \end{aligned} \tag{4.1}$$

In the next theorem we shall derive an increment formula for the cost functional J defined by (3.1).

THEOREM 4.1. *Let $J: \mathscr{D} \to R^1$ be the cost functional defined by* (3.1). *Then for any* $(\sigma^1, u^1), (\sigma^2, u^2) \in \mathscr{D}$,

$$\begin{aligned} &J(\sigma^2, u^2) - J(\sigma^1, u^1) \\ &\quad = \iint_Q \{I(\sigma^2, u^2)[x, t, \sigma^2, u^2(\hat{x}, t)] - I(\sigma^2, u^2)[x, t, \sigma^1, u^1(\hat{x}, t)]\} \\ &\qquad \times z(\sigma^1, u^1)(x, t)\, dx\, dt. \end{aligned} \tag{4.2}$$

Proof. For any $(\sigma^1, u^1), (\sigma^2, u^2) \in \mathscr{D}$, set

$$\psi \equiv \phi(\sigma^2, u^2) - \phi(\sigma^1, u^1). \tag{4.3}$$

Then

$$\begin{aligned} &L(\sigma^1, u^1)\psi(x, t) \\ &\quad = L(\sigma^2, u^2)\phi(\sigma^2, u^2)(x, t) - L(\sigma^1, u^1)\phi(\sigma^1, u^1)(x, t) \\ &\qquad - [L(\sigma^2, u^2) - L(\sigma^1, u^1)]\phi(\sigma^2, u^2)(x, t) \\ &\quad = I(\sigma^2, u^2)[x, t, \sigma^2, u^2(\hat{x}, t)] - I(\sigma^2, u^2)[x, t, \sigma^1, u^1(\hat{x}, t)]. \end{aligned} \tag{4.4}$$

From estimate (2.5) and assumption (A.3), we can verify that the right-hand side of Eq. (4.4) is an element in $L_\infty(Q)$. Furthermore, ψ, given in (4.3), belongs to $\mathring{\tilde{W}}_2^{2,1}(Q)$. Thus it follows from Lemma 3.1 that

$$\iint_Q (L(\sigma^1, u^1)\psi)z(\sigma^1, u^1)\, dx\, dt = \int_\Omega \psi(x, T)z_T(x)\, dx. \tag{4.5}$$

Combining (3.1), (4.3), (4.4), and (4.5), we obtain

$$\begin{aligned} J(\sigma^2, u^2) &- J(\sigma^1, u^1) \\ &= \int_\Omega [\phi(\sigma^2, u^2)(x, T) - \phi(\sigma^1, u^1)(x, T)]z_T(x)\, dx \\ &= \int_\Omega \psi(x, T)z_T(x)\, dx \\ &= \iint_Q (L(\sigma^1, u^1)\psi)z(\sigma^1, u^1)\, dx\, dt \\ &= \iint_Q \{I(\sigma^2, u^2)[x, t, \sigma^2, u^2(\hat{x}, t)] - I(\sigma^2, u^2)[x, t, \sigma^1, u^1(\hat{x}, t)]\} \\ &\quad \times z(\sigma^1, u^1)(x, t)\, dx\, dt. \end{aligned}$$

This completes the proof. ■

IV.5. The Gradient of the Cost Functional

We begin with the following definition.

DEFINITION 5.1. *Let $(\sigma^0, u^0) \in \mathscr{D}$ and J be a functional defined on $\mathscr{D}$. Then J is said to be Fréchet differentiable at (σ^0, u^0) if there is a continuous linear functional $J_{(\sigma^0, u^0)}$ on $\mathscr{D}$ such that*

$$\lim_{\|(\sigma, u) - (\sigma^0, u^0)\|_{\mathscr{D}} \to 0} \frac{|J(\sigma, u) - J(\sigma^0, u^0) - J_{(\sigma^0, u^0)}[(\sigma, u) - (\sigma^0, u^0)]|}{\|(\sigma, u) - (\sigma^0, u^0)\|_{\mathscr{D}}} = 0.$$

The continuous functional $J_{(\sigma^0, u^0)}$ is called the Fréchet derivative (or the gradient) of J at $(\sigma^0, u^0) \in \mathscr{D}$.

On the basis of Theorem 4.1 we shall present a result concerning the derivative of the cost functional J in the next theorem. For this we need to introduce certain notation.

REMARK 5.1. Let h be a continuous function defined on $\bar{Q} \times R^{m_1} \times R^{m_2}$. Furthermore, it is assumed that, for each $(x, t, v) \in \bar{Q} \times R^{m_2}$, $h(x, t, \cdot, v) \in C^1(R^{m_1})$; and that, for each $(x, t, \sigma) \in \bar{Q} \times R^{m_1}$, $h(x, t, \sigma, \cdot) \in C^1(R^{m_2})$. Then for each $(x, t, v) \in \bar{Q} \times R^{m_2}$, the gradient of $h(x, t, \cdot, v)$ at $\sigma^0 \in R^{m_1}$ is denoted by $h_\sigma(x, t, \sigma^0, v)$; and, for each $(x, t, \sigma) \in \bar{Q} \times R^{m_1}$, the gradient of $h(x, t, \sigma, \cdot)$ at $v^0 \in R^{m_2}$ is denoted by $h_v(x, t, \sigma, v^0)$.

To proceed further, certain additional assumptions on the functions b_i, $i = 1, \ldots, n$, c and f are required.

(A.6) Let h denote any of the functions b_i, $i = 1, \ldots, n$, c and f. Then h_σ and h_v are continuous on

$$\bar{Q} \times R^{m_1} \times R^{m_2}.$$

REMARK 5.2. Let h and $\mathscr{D}_0$ be as defined in assumption (A.6) and Remark 2.4, respectively. Since $\bar{Q} \times S_0 \times U_0$ is compact, it can be verified that both h_σ and h_v, when considered as mapping from $\mathscr{D}_0$ into $L_\infty(Q)$, are uniformly continuous.

THEOREM 5.1. *Let $J: \mathscr{D} \to R^1$ be the cost functional defined by* (3.1). *Then J is Fréchet differentiable everywhere on $\mathscr{D}$. Furthermore, the gradient $J_{(\sigma^0, u^0)}$ of J at $(\sigma^0, u^0) \in \mathscr{D}$ is given by*

$$\begin{aligned} &J_{(\sigma^0, u^0)}[(\sigma, u)] \\ &\quad = \iint_Q \langle I(\sigma^0, u^0)_\sigma[x, t, \sigma^0, u^0(\hat{x}, t)], \sigma \rangle z(\sigma^0, u^0)(x, t)\, dx\, dt \\ &\quad\quad + \iint_Q \langle I(\sigma^0, u^0)_v[x, t, \sigma^0, u^0(\hat{x}, t)], u(\hat{x}, t)\rangle \\ &\quad\quad \times z(\sigma^0, u^0)(x, t)\, dx\, dt, \end{aligned} \tag{5.1}$$

where $\langle \cdot, \cdot \rangle$ denotes the usual inner product on a Euclidean space.

Proof. Let $(\sigma^0, u^0), (\sigma, u) \in \mathscr{D}$. Then from Theorem 4.1 we have

$$\begin{aligned} &J(\sigma^0, u^0) - J(\sigma, u) \\ &\quad = \iint_Q \{I(\sigma^0, u^0)[x, t, \sigma^0, u^0(\hat{x}, t)] - I(\sigma^0, u^0)[x, t, \sigma, u(\hat{x}, t)]\} \\ &\quad\quad \times z(\sigma, u)(x, t)\, dx\, dt. \end{aligned}$$

Consequently,

$$J(\sigma^0, u^0) - J(\sigma, u)$$
$$= - \iint_Q \{I(\sigma^0, u^0)[x, t, \sigma, u(\hat{x}, t)] - I(\sigma^0, u^0)[x, t, \sigma^0, u^0(\hat{x}, t)]\}$$
$$\times z(\sigma^0, u^0)(x, t)\, dx\, dt$$
$$+ \iint_Q \{I(\sigma^0, u^0)[x, t, \sigma, u(\hat{x}, t)] - I(\sigma^0, u^0)[x, t, \sigma^0, u^0(\hat{x}, t)]\}$$
$$\times [z(\sigma^0, u^0)(x, t) - z(\sigma, u)(x, t)]\, dx\, dt. \tag{5.2}$$

Let B denote the first integral on the right-hand side of equality (5.2). Then it follows from the definition of the function I defined by (4.1) that

$$[1/\|(\sigma, u) - (\sigma^0, u^0)\|_{\mathscr{D}}]$$
$$\times \Big[B - \iint_Q z(\sigma^0, u^0)(x, t)\{\langle I(\sigma^0, u^0)_{\sigma}[x, t, \sigma^0, u^0(\hat{x}, t)], \sigma - \sigma^0\rangle$$
$$+ \langle I(\sigma^0, u^0)_{v}[x, t, \sigma^0, u^0(\hat{x}, t)], u(\hat{x}, t) - u^0(\hat{x}, t)\rangle\}\, dx\, dt\Big]$$
$$= \iint_Q z(\sigma^0, u^0)(x, t)\{I(\sigma^0, u^0)[x, t, \sigma, u(\hat{x}, t)]$$
$$- I(\sigma^0, u^0)[x, t, \sigma^0, u^0(\hat{x}, t)] - \langle I(\sigma^0, u^0)_{\sigma}[x, t, \sigma^0, u^0(\hat{x}, t)], \sigma - \sigma^0\rangle$$
$$- \langle I(\sigma^0, u^0)_{v}[x, t, \sigma^0, u^0(\hat{x}, t)], u(\hat{x}, t) - u^0(\hat{x}, t)\rangle\}$$
$$\times [1/\|(\sigma, u) - (\sigma^0, u^0)\|_{\mathscr{D}}]\, dx\, dt. \tag{5.3}$$

Define

$$O[(\sigma, u), (\sigma^0, u^0)](x, t)$$
$$\equiv I(\sigma^0, u^0)[x, t, \sigma, u(\hat{x}, t)] - I(\sigma^0, u^0)[x, t, \sigma^0, u^0(\hat{x}, t)]$$
$$- \langle I(\sigma^0, u^0)_{\sigma}[x, t, \sigma^0, u^0(\hat{x}, t)], \sigma - \sigma^0\rangle$$
$$- \langle I(\sigma^0, u^0)_{v}[x, t, \sigma^0, u^0(\hat{x}, t)], u(\hat{x}, t) - u^0(\hat{x}, t)\rangle.$$

Then for almost every $(x, t) \in Q$, we have

$$\lim_{[|\sigma - \sigma^0| + |u(\hat{x}, t) - u^0(\hat{x}, t)|] \to 0} \frac{|O[(\sigma, u), (\sigma^0, u^0)](x, t)|}{|\sigma - \sigma^0| + |u(\hat{x}, t) - u^0(\hat{x}, t)|} = 0.$$

Since $[|\sigma - \sigma^0| + |u(\hat{x}, t) - u^0(\hat{x}, t)|] \le \|(\sigma, u) - (\sigma^0 - u^0)\|_{\mathscr{D}}$ for almost all $(\hat{x}, t) \in \hat{Q}$, it follows that

$$\lim_{\|(\sigma, u) - (\sigma^0, u^0)\|_{\mathscr{D}} \to 0} \frac{O[(\sigma, u), (\sigma^0, u^0)](x, t)}{\|(\sigma, u) - (\sigma^0, u^0)\|_{\mathscr{D}}} = 0,$$

for almost all $(x, t) \in Q$. Therefore, the integrand on the right-hand side of (5.3) tends to zero for almost all $(x, t) \in Q$. To apply the Lebesgue dominated convergence theorem, we need to show that this integrand is bounded on Q uniformly with respect to $(\sigma, u) \in \mathscr{D}_{(\sigma^0, u^0)}(\varepsilon)$, where $\varepsilon > 0$ is arbitrary but fixed and

$$\mathscr{D}_{(\sigma^0, u^0)}(\varepsilon) \equiv \{(\sigma, u) \in \mathscr{D} : \|(\sigma, u) - (\sigma^0, u^0)\|_{\mathscr{D}} \le \varepsilon\}. \tag{5.4}$$

For this, we note from the definition of $\mathscr{D}_{(\sigma^0, u^0)}(\varepsilon)$ that there exists a compact convex subset $\Xi_1 \times \Xi_2$ of $R^{m_1} \times R^{m_2}$ such that for any $(\sigma, u) \in \mathscr{D}_{(\sigma^0, u^0)}(\varepsilon)$, $\sigma \in \Xi_1$ and $u(\hat{x}, t) \in \Xi_2$, for almost all $(\hat{x}, t) \in \hat{Q}$. Thus by virtue of assumption (A.6), Taylor's theorem, and estimate (2.5)′ given in Remark 2.4 with $\mathscr{D}_0$ taken as $\mathscr{D}_{(\sigma^0, u^0)}(\varepsilon)$, we can conclude that the integrand under discussion is, indeed, bounded on Q uniformly with respect to $(\sigma, u) \in \mathscr{D}_{(\sigma^0, u^0)}(\varepsilon)$. Therefore, it follows from the Lebesgue dominated convergence theorem that

$$\lim_{\|(\sigma, u) - (\sigma^0, u^0)\|_{\mathscr{D}} \to 0} \left\{ \frac{1}{\|(\sigma, u) - (\sigma^0, u^0)\|_{\mathscr{D}}} \right.$$
$$\times \left[B - \iint_Q z(\sigma^0, u^0)(x, t) \{ \langle I(\sigma^0, u^0)_\sigma[x, t, \sigma^0, u^0(\hat{x}, t)], \sigma - \sigma^0 \rangle \right.$$
$$\left.\left. + \langle I(\sigma^0, u^0)_v[x, t, \sigma^0, u^0(\hat{x}, t), u(\hat{x}, t)] - u^0(\hat{x}, t) \rangle \} \, dx \, dt \right] \right\} = 0. \tag{5.5}$$

Next, we shall prove that

$$\beta[(\sigma, u), (\sigma^0, u^0)] / \|(\sigma, u) - (\sigma^0, u^0)\|_{\mathscr{D}} \to 0, \tag{5.6}$$

as $\|(\sigma, u) - (\sigma^0, u^0)\|_{\mathscr{D}} \to 0$, where $\beta[(\sigma, u), (\sigma^0, u^0)]$ denotes the second integral on the right-hand side of Eq. (5.2).

First, let $\mathscr{D}_{(\sigma^0, u^0)}(\varepsilon)$ be as defined by (5.4). Then from assumption (A.6) and estimate (2.5)′ given in Remark 2.4 with $\mathscr{D}_0$ taken as $\mathscr{D}_{(\sigma^0, u^0)}(\varepsilon)$, we can verify that $I(\sigma^0, u^0)_\sigma[x, t, \sigma, u(\hat{x}, t)]$ and $I(\sigma^0, u^0)_v[x, t, \sigma, u(\hat{x}, t)]$ are bounded for almost all $(x, t) \in Q$ uniformly with respect to $(\sigma, u) \in \mathscr{D}_{(\sigma^0, u^0)}(\varepsilon)$. Let N be such a bound. Then it follows from Taylor's theorem that

$$\begin{aligned} &|I(\sigma^0, u^0)[x, t, \sigma, u(\hat{x}, t)] - I(\sigma^0, u^0)[x, t, \sigma^0, u^0(\hat{x}, t)]| \\ &\quad \le N |(\sigma - \sigma^0, u(\hat{x}, t) - u^0(\hat{x}, t))| \\ &\quad \le N \|(\sigma, u) - (\sigma^0, u^0)\|_{\mathscr{D}}, \end{aligned}$$

for almost all $(x, t) \in Q$, where N is independent of $(\sigma, u) \in \mathscr{D}_{(\sigma^0, u^0)}(\varepsilon)$.

Consequently,

$$[1/\|(\sigma, u) - (\sigma^0, u^0)\|_{\mathscr{D}}] \iint_Q |\{I(\sigma^0, u^0)[x, t, \sigma, u(\hat{x}, t)]$$

$$- I(\sigma^0, u^0)[x, t, \sigma^0, u^0(\hat{x}, t)]\} [z(\sigma, u)(x, t) - z(\sigma^0, u^0)(x, t)]| \, dx \, dt$$

$$\leq N \|z(\sigma, u) - z(\sigma^0, u^0)\|_{1,Q}.$$

However, from Theorem 3.1, we have

$$\lim_{\|(\sigma, u) - (\sigma^0, u^0)\|_{\mathscr{D}} \to 0} \|z(\sigma, u) - z(\sigma^0, u^0)\|_{1,Q} = 0.$$

Thus relation (5.6) is established.

Combining (5.2), (5.5), and (5.6) we obtain

$$\lim_{\|(\sigma, u) - (\sigma^0, u^0)\|_{\mathscr{D}} \to 0} \frac{1}{\|(\sigma, u) - (\sigma^0, u^0)\|_{\mathscr{D}}}$$

$$\times \Bigg\{ J(\sigma, u) - J(\sigma^0, u^0)$$

$$- \iint_Q z(\sigma^0, u^0)(x, t) \{\langle I(\sigma^0, u^0)_{\sigma}[x, t, \sigma^0, u^0(\hat{x}, t)], \sigma - \sigma^0 \rangle$$

$$+ \langle I(\sigma^0, u^0)_{v}[x, t, \sigma^0, u^0(\hat{x}, t)], u(\hat{x}, t) - u^0(\hat{x}, t) \rangle\} \, dx \, dt \Bigg\} = 0.$$

This relation implies that the cost functional J is differentiable and that its derivative is expressed by (5.1). Thus the proof is complete. ■

In the rest of the section we shall investigate the uniform continuity of the derivative $J_{(\sigma, u)}$. This result will be used in proving the convergence of the algorithm to be presented in the next section. For this we need the following lemma.

LEMMA 5.1. *Let $H_{\sigma}: \mathscr{D}_p \to L_1(Q)$ and $H_{v}: \mathscr{D}_p \to L_1(Q)$ be defined by*

$$H(\sigma, u)_{\sigma} \equiv I(\sigma, u)_{\sigma}[\cdot, \cdot, \sigma, u(\cdot, \cdot)] z(\sigma, u)(\cdot, \cdot),$$

and

$$H(\sigma, u)_{v} \equiv I(\sigma, u)_{v}[\cdot, \cdot, \sigma, u(\cdot, \cdot)] z(\sigma, u)(\cdot, \cdot).$$

Then H_{σ} and H_{v} are uniformly continuous.

Proof. Let $(\sigma^1, u^1), (\sigma^2, u^2) \in \mathscr{U}$. Then

$$\begin{aligned}
&\iint_Q |H(\sigma^1, u^1)_\sigma - H(\sigma^2, u^2)_\sigma| \, dx \, dt \\
&\quad = \iint_Q |I(\sigma^1, u^1)_\sigma[x, t, \sigma^1, u^1(\hat{x}, t)] z(\sigma^1, u^1)(x, t) \\
&\qquad - I(\sigma^2, u^2)_\sigma[x, t, \sigma^2, u^2(\hat{x}, t)] z(\sigma^2, u^2)(x, t)| \, dx \, dt \\
&\quad \leq \int_Q \{|I(\sigma^1, u^1)_\sigma[x, t, \sigma^1, u^1(\hat{x}, t)] \\
&\qquad - I(\sigma^2, u^2)_\sigma[x, t, \sigma^2, u^2(\hat{x}, t)]|\} |z(\sigma^1, u^1)(x, t)| \, dx \, dt \\
&\qquad + \iint_Q |I(\sigma^2, u^2)_\sigma[x, t, \sigma^2, u^2(\hat{x}, t)]| \\
&\qquad \times [|z(\sigma^1, u^1)(x, t) - z(\sigma^2, u^2)(x, t)|] \, dx \, dt \\
&\quad \leq \|z(\sigma^1, u^1)\|_{1,Q} \|I(\sigma^1, u^1)_\sigma[\cdot, \cdot, \sigma^1, u^1(\cdot, \cdot)] \\
&\qquad - I(\sigma^2, u^2)_\sigma[\cdot, \cdot, \sigma^2, u^2(\cdot, \cdot)]\|_{\infty,Q} \\
&\qquad + \|I(\sigma^2, u^2)_\sigma[\cdot, \cdot, \sigma^2, u^2(\cdot, \cdot)]\|_{\infty,Q} \|z(\sigma^1, u^1) - z(\sigma^2, u^2)\|_{1,Q} \\
&\quad \leq \|z(\sigma^1, u^1)\|_{1,Q} \|I(\sigma^1, u^1)_\sigma[\cdot, \cdot, \sigma^1, u^1(\cdot, \cdot)] \\
&\qquad - I(\sigma^1, u^1)_\sigma[\cdot, \cdot, \sigma^2, u^2(\cdot, \cdot)]\|_{\infty,Q} \\
&\qquad + \|z(\sigma^1, u^1)\|_{1,Q} \|I(\sigma^1, u^1)_\sigma[\cdot, \cdot, \sigma^2, u^2(\cdot, \cdot)] \\
&\qquad - I(\sigma^2, u^2)_\sigma[\cdot, \cdot, \sigma^2, u^2(\cdot, \cdot)]\|_{\infty,Q} \\
&\qquad + \|I(\sigma^2, u^2)_\sigma[\cdot, \cdot, \sigma^2, u^2(\cdot, \cdot)]\|_{\infty,Q} \|z(\sigma^1, u^1) - z(\sigma^2, u^2)\|_{1,Q}.
\end{aligned}$$

Thus by (4.1) assumption (A.6), (2.5), (3.9), and the boundedness of the set Q, we obtain

$$\begin{aligned}
&\iint_Q |H(\sigma^1, u^1)_\sigma - H(\sigma^2, u^2)_\sigma| \, dx \, dt \\
&\quad \leq N \Bigg\{ \sum_{i=1}^n \|b_i(\sigma^1, u^1)_\sigma - b_i(\sigma^2, u^2)_\sigma\|_{\infty,Q} + \|c(\sigma^1, u^1)_\sigma - c(\sigma^2, u^2)_\sigma\|_{\infty,Q} \\
&\qquad + \|f(\sigma^1, u^1)_\sigma - f(\sigma^2, u^2)_\sigma\|_{\infty,Q} + \sum_{i=1}^n \|\phi(\sigma^1, u^1)_{x_i} - \phi(\sigma^2, u^2)_{x_i}\|_{\infty,Q} \\
&\qquad + \|\phi(\sigma^1, u^1) - \phi(\sigma^2, u^2)\|_{\infty,Q} \Bigg\} + \|z(\sigma^1, u^1) - z(\sigma^2, u^2)\|_{1,Q},
\end{aligned} \tag{5.7}$$

where N is a constant independent of $(\sigma^1, u^1), (\sigma^2, u^2) \in \mathscr{D}_p$.

By Remark 5.2, Theorem 2.1, and Theorem 3.1, it follows from inequality (5.7) that

$$\iint_Q |H(\sigma^1, u^1)_\sigma[x, t, \sigma^1, u^1(\hat{x}, t)] - H(\sigma^2, u^2)_\sigma[x, t, \sigma^2, u^2(\hat{x}, t)]|\, dx\, dt \to 0,$$

as $\|(\sigma^1, u^1) - (\sigma^2, u^2)\|_{\mathscr{D}} \to 0$. Thus H_σ is a uniformly continuous mapping from $\mathscr{D}_p$ into $L_1(Q)$.

By a similar argument, we can show that H_v is also a uniformly continuous mapping from $\mathscr{D}_p$ into $L_1(Q)$ and hence the proof is complete. ■

With the help of the preceding lemma and Theorem 5.1, we are in a position to prove a continuity theorem concerning the derivative $J_{(\sigma, u)}$.

THEOREM 5.2. *Let $J: \mathscr{D} \to R^1$ be the cost functional given by* (3.1). *Then the derivative $J_{(\sigma, u)}$ of the cost functional J, which is a linear functional from $\mathscr{D}$ $(\equiv R^{m_1} \times L_\infty(Q, R^{m_2}))$ into $[R^{m_1} \times L_\infty(Q, R^{m_2})]^*$, (the dual space of the Banach space $R^{m_1} \times L_\infty(Q, R^{m_2})$), is uniformly continuous on $\mathscr{D}_p$.*

Proof. Let $(\sigma^1, u^1), (\sigma^2, u^2) \in \mathscr{D}_p$. Then for any $(\sigma, u) \in \mathscr{D}$ it follows from (5.1) that

$$\begin{aligned}
&|J_{(\sigma^2, u^2)}[(\sigma, u)] - J_{(\sigma^1, u^1)}[(\sigma, u)]| \\
&\quad \le \iint_Q |\langle H(\sigma^2, u^2)_\sigma[x, t, \sigma^2, u^2(\hat{x}, t)] \\
&\qquad - H(\sigma^1, u^1)_\sigma[x, t, \sigma^1, u^1(\hat{x}, t)], \sigma\rangle|\, dx\, dt \\
&\qquad + \iint_Q |\langle H(\sigma^2, u^2)_v[x, t, \sigma^2, u^2(\hat{x}, t)] \\
&\qquad - H(\sigma^1, u^1)_v[x, t, \sigma^1, u^1(\hat{x}, t)], u(\hat{x}, t)\rangle|\, dx\, dt \\
&\quad \le \left\{\iint_Q |H(\sigma^2, u^2)_\sigma[x, t, \sigma^2, u^2(\hat{x}, t)] \right. \\
&\qquad - H(\sigma^1, u^1)_\sigma[x, t, \sigma^1, u^1(\hat{x}, t)]|\, dx\, dt \\
&\qquad + \iint_Q |H(\sigma^2, u^2)_v[x, t, \sigma^2, u^2(\hat{x}, t)] \\
&\qquad \left. - H(\sigma^1, u^1)_v[x, t, \sigma^1, u^1(\hat{x}, t)]|\, dx\, dt \right\} \|(\sigma, u)\|_{\mathscr{D}}.
\end{aligned}$$

This implies that

$$\begin{aligned}\|J_{(\sigma^2, u^2)} - J_{(\sigma^1, u^1)}\| &\leq \iint_Q |H(\sigma^2, u^2)_\sigma[x, t, \sigma^2, u^2(\hat{x}, t)] \\ &\quad - H(\sigma^1, u^1)_\sigma[x, t, \sigma^1, u^1(\hat{x}, t)]|\, dx\, dt \\ &\quad + \iint_Q |H(\sigma^2, u^2)_v[x, t, \sigma^2, u^2(\hat{x}, t)] \\ &\quad - H(\sigma^1, u^1)_v[x, t, \sigma^1, u^1(\hat{x}, t)]|\, dx\, dt,\end{aligned}$$

where

$$\|J_{(\sigma^2, u^2)} - J_{(\sigma^1, u^1)}\| \equiv \sup_{(\sigma, u) \in \mathscr{D}} \frac{|J_{(\sigma^2, u^2)}[(\sigma, u)] - J_{(\sigma^1, u^1)}[(\sigma, u)]|}{\|(\sigma, u)\|_{\mathscr{D}}}.$$

Thus it follows from Lemma 5.1 that $J_{(\sigma, u)}$ is uniformly continuous on $\mathscr{D}_p$. ■

IV.6. A Conditional Gradient Algorithm

On the basis of the formula for the gradient of the cost functional, we are now able to devise a conditional gradient algorithm to solve problem (P). This algorithm, *which is to be referred to as algorithm* (*A*), is given as follows:

Step 1 Choose constants $\alpha, \beta \in (0, 1)$, and an initial policy $(\sigma^0, u^0) \in \mathscr{D}_p$. Set $k = 0$.

Step 2 Solve system (2.1) for $\phi(\sigma^k, u^k)$, and then calculate $J(\sigma^k, u^k)$ by using formula (5.1).

Step 3 Find a parameter vector $\sigma^{k,*} \in S$ such that

$$\left\langle \iint_Q H(\sigma^k, u^k)_\sigma[x, t, \sigma^k, u^k(\hat{x}, t)]\, dx\, dt. \sigma^{k,*} \right\rangle \leq \left\langle \iint_Q H(\sigma^k, u^k)_\sigma[x, t, \sigma^k, u^k(\hat{x}, t)]\, dx\, dt, \sigma \right\rangle, \tag{6.1}$$

for all $\sigma \in S$.

Step 4 Find a control $u^{k,*} \in \mathscr{U}$ such that

$$\left\langle \int_{\Omega_{\hat{x}}} H(\sigma^k, u^k)_v [\hat{x}, \hat{\hat{x}}, t, \sigma^k, u^k(\hat{x}, t)] \, d\hat{\hat{x}}, u^{k,*}(\hat{x}, t) \right\rangle$$
$$\leq \left\langle \int_{\Omega_{\hat{x}}} H(\sigma^k, u^k)_v [\hat{x}, \hat{\hat{x}}, t, \sigma^k, u^k(\hat{\hat{x}}, t)] \, d\hat{\hat{x}}, v \right\rangle, \tag{6.2}$$

for all $v \in U$ and for almost all $(\hat{x}, t) \in \hat{Q}$.

Step 5 If $J_{(\sigma^k, u^k)}[(\sigma^{k,*}, u^{k,*}) - (\sigma^k, u^k)] = 0$, set $(\sigma^{k+l}, u^{k+l}) = (\sigma^k, u^k)$ for all positive integers l and stop.

Step 6 Choose α^m to be the first elements in the sequence $1, \alpha, \alpha^2, \ldots,$ such that

$$J(\sigma^k + \alpha^m(\sigma^{k,*} - \sigma^k), u^k + \alpha^m(u^{k,*} - u^k)) - J(\sigma^k, u^k)$$
$$\leq \alpha^m \beta J_{(\sigma^k, u^k)}[(\sigma^{k,*}, u^{k,*}) - (\sigma^k, u^k)]. \tag{6.3}$$

(Clearly, m depends on k.)

Step 7 Set $(\sigma^{k+1}, u^{k+1}) = (\sigma^k, u^k) + \alpha^m(\sigma^{k,*} - \sigma^k, u^{k,*} - u^k)$. Go to Step 2 with $k = k + 1$.

Our next aim is to show that this algorithm is well defined. Steps 1 and 2 are admissible. The existence of a $(\sigma^{k,*}, u^{k,*}) \in \mathscr{D}_p$ will be proved in the next lemma and hence Steps 3 and 4 are also well defined. There is no problem with Step 5. For Step 6 we note that S and U are convex. Thus for any $\varepsilon, 0 \leq \varepsilon \leq 1$, $(\sigma^k, u^k) + \varepsilon(\sigma^{k,*} - \sigma^k, u^{k,*} - u^k)$ belongs to $\mathscr{D}_p$ $(\equiv S \times \mathscr{U})$. Consequently,

$$\lim_{\varepsilon \downarrow 0} \frac{J(\sigma^k + \varepsilon(\sigma^{k,*} - \sigma^k), u^k + \varepsilon(u^{k,*} - u^k)) - J(\sigma^k, u^k)}{\varepsilon}$$
$$= J_{(\sigma^k, u^k)}[(\sigma^{k,*} - \sigma^k, u^{k,*} - u^k)]. \tag{6.4}$$

This, in turn, implies that Step 6 does define a number α^m.

Finally, using the convexity of the sets S and U, and the fact that $\alpha^m \in [0, 1]$, we obtain

$$(\sigma^{k+1}, u^{k+1}) \equiv (1 - \alpha^m)(\sigma^k, u^k) + \alpha^m(\sigma^{k,*}, u^{k,*}) \in \mathscr{D}_p. \tag{6.5}$$

Therefore, Step 7 is also well defined.

LEMMA 6.1. *For each* $(\sigma^0, u^0) \in \mathscr{D}_p$, *there exists a policy* $(\sigma^{0,*}, u^{0,*}) \in \mathscr{D}_p$ *such that*

(i) $\sigma^{0,*}$ *minimizes the linear function*

$$\left\langle \iint_Q H(\sigma^0, u^0)_\sigma[x, t, \sigma^0, u^0(\hat{x}, t)]\, dx\, dt, \cdot \right\rangle \tag{6.6}$$

over S; *and*

(ii) *For each* $(\hat{x}, t) \in \hat{Q}$, $u^{0,*}(\hat{x}, t)$ *minimizes the linear function*

$$\left\langle \int_{\Omega_{\hat{x}}} H(\sigma^0, u^0)_v[\hat{x}, \hat{\hat{x}}, t, \sigma^0, u^0(\hat{x}, t)]\, d\hat{\hat{x}}, \cdot \right\rangle \tag{6.7}$$

over U.

Proof. The existence of a $\sigma^{0,*} \in S$ is obvious since the linear function (6.6) is minimized over the compact set S. It remains to show the existence of a control $u^{0,*} \in \mathscr{U}$ such that the linear function (6.7) is minimized over U, for each $(\hat{x}, t) \in \hat{Q}$. For this we define

$$r(\hat{x}, t) \equiv \inf_{v \in U} \left\{ \left\langle \int_{\Omega_{\hat{x}}} H(\sigma^0, u^0)_v[\hat{x}, \hat{\hat{x}}, t, \sigma^0, u^0(\hat{x}, t)]\, d\hat{\hat{x}}, v \right\} \right\rangle.$$

Clearly, r is a measurable function, and, for each $(\hat{x}, t) \in \hat{Q}$,

$$r(\hat{x}, t) \in \left\{ \left\langle \int_{\Omega_{\hat{x}}} H(\sigma^0, u^0)_v[\hat{x}, \hat{\hat{x}}, t, \sigma^0, u^0(\hat{x}, t)]\, d\hat{\hat{x}}, v \right\rangle : v \in U \right\}.$$

Thus it follows from Theorem I.6.1 that there exists a measurable function $u^{0,*}$ defined on $\hat{Q}$ with values in U such that

$$r(\hat{x}, t) = \left\langle \int_{\Omega_{\hat{x}}} H(\sigma^0, u^0)_v[\hat{x}, \hat{\hat{x}}, t, \sigma^0, u^0(\hat{x}, t)]\, d\hat{\hat{x}}, u^{0,*}(\hat{x}, t) \right\rangle.$$

This implies that $u^{0,*} \in \mathscr{U}$ and that, for each $(\hat{x}, t) \in \hat{Q}$, $u^{0,*}(\hat{x}, t)$ minimizes the linear function (6.7). Thus the proof is complete. ■

In what follows we shall present a necessary condition for optimality for problem P in terms of the derivative of the cost functional.

THEOREM 6.1. *If* $(\tilde{\sigma}, \tilde{u}) \in \mathscr{D}_p$ *is an optimal policy, then*

$$J_{(\tilde{\sigma}, \tilde{u})}[(\tilde{\sigma}, \tilde{u})] \leq J_{(\tilde{\sigma}, \tilde{u})}[(\sigma, u)], \tag{6.8}$$

for all $(\sigma, u) \in \mathscr{D}_p$, *or equivalently,*

$$J_{(\tilde{\sigma}, \tilde{u})}[(\tilde{\sigma}^*, \tilde{u}^*) - (\tilde{\sigma}, \tilde{u})] = 0, \tag{6.9}$$

where $(\tilde{\sigma}^*, \tilde{u}^*)$ *belongs to* $\mathscr{D}_p$ *and minimizes* $J_{(\tilde{\sigma}, \tilde{u})}[(\cdot, \cdot)]$ *over* $\mathscr{D}_p$.

Proof. For any $(\sigma, u) \in \mathscr{D}_p$ and ε, $0 < \varepsilon \leq 1$, we have

$$(1 - \varepsilon)(\tilde{\sigma}, \tilde{u}) + \varepsilon(\sigma, u) \in \mathscr{D}_p.$$

Thus

$$J((1 - \varepsilon)(\tilde{\sigma}, \tilde{u}) + \varepsilon(\sigma, u)) \equiv J((1 - \varepsilon)\tilde{\sigma} + \varepsilon\sigma, (1 - \varepsilon)\tilde{u} + \varepsilon u) \geq J(\tilde{\sigma}, \tilde{u}),$$

for all ε, $0 < \varepsilon \leq 1$. This, in turn, implies that

$$[J(\tilde{\sigma} + \varepsilon(\sigma - \tilde{\sigma}), \tilde{u} + \varepsilon(u - \tilde{u})) - J(\tilde{\sigma}, \tilde{u})]/\varepsilon \geq 0.$$

Letting $\varepsilon \downarrow 0$, we obtain

$$J_{(\tilde{\sigma}, \tilde{u})}[(\sigma, u) - (\tilde{\sigma}, \tilde{u})] \geq 0.$$

Therefore, the proof is complete. ■

In the next theorem, we shall present a convergence result for the algorithm.

THEOREM 6.2. *Let $\{(\sigma^k, u^k)\}$ be a sequence of policies generated by the conditional gradient algorithm (A). If $(\bar{\sigma}, \bar{u})$ is an accumulation point of the sequence $\{(\sigma^k, u^k)\}$ in the strong topology of $\mathscr{D}$, then it satisfies the necessary condition* (6.8).

Proof. If there is some (σ^k, u^k) belonging to $\mathscr{D}_p$ and satisfying the necessary condition (6.8), then, by virtue of Step 5 of the algorithm, we have $(\sigma^{k+l}, u^{k+l}) = (\sigma^k, u^k)$, $l = 1, 2, \ldots$. In this case the theorem is trivial. Thus we only need to consider the case when $J_{(\sigma^k, u^k)}[(\sigma^{k,*}, u^{k,*}) - (\sigma^k, u^k)] \neq 0$, for all $k = 1, 2, 3, \ldots$.

Since $(\bar{\sigma}, \bar{u})$ is an accumulation point of the sequence $\{(\sigma^k, u^k)\}$ in the strong topology of $\mathscr{D}$, there is a subsequence of the sequence $\{(\sigma^k, u^k)\}$, again indexed by k, which converges to $(\bar{\sigma}, \bar{u})$ in the norm $\|\cdot\|_{\mathscr{D}}$.

In view of (6.3) we observe that

$$\alpha^m \beta |J_{(\sigma^k, u^k)}[(\sigma^{k,*}, u^{k,*}) - (\sigma^k, u^k)]| \leq |J(\sigma^{k+1}, u^{k+1}) - J(\sigma^k, u^k)|. \quad (6.10)$$

By contrast, it follows from the definition of α^m given in Step 6 of the algorithm that

$$J\left((\sigma^k, u^k) + \frac{\alpha^m}{\alpha}[(\sigma^{k,*}, u^{k,*}) - (\sigma^k, u^k)]\right) - J(\sigma^k, u^k)$$

$$> \frac{\alpha^m}{\alpha} \beta J_{(\sigma^k, u^k)}[(\sigma^{k,*}, u^{k,*}) - (\sigma^k, u^k)], \quad (6.11)$$

whenever $\alpha^m < 1$. By using Taylor's theorem in remainder form this inequality can be written as

$$J_{(\hat{\sigma}^k, u^k)}[(\sigma^{k,*}, u^{k,*}) - (\sigma^k, u^k)] > \beta J_{(\sigma^k, u^k)}[(\sigma^{k,*}, u^{k,*}) - (\sigma^k, u^k)], \quad (6.12)$$

where

$$(\hat{\sigma}^k, \hat{u}^k) \equiv (\sigma^k, u^k) + \frac{\alpha^m}{\alpha}(\theta^k)[(\sigma^{k,*}, u^{k,*}) - (\sigma^k, u^k)], \quad (6.13)$$

for some θ^k, $0 \leq \theta^k \leq 1$, determined by Taylor's theorem in remainder form, and $\alpha^m < 1$.

Adding $-J_{(\sigma^k, u^k)}[(\sigma^{k,*}, u^{k,*}) - (\sigma^k, u^k)]$ to both sides of inequality (6.12), we obtain

$$\begin{aligned} &J_{(\hat{\sigma}^k, \hat{u}^k)}[(\sigma^{k,*}, u^{k,*}) - (\sigma^k, u^k)] - J_{(\sigma^k, u^k)}[(\sigma^{k,*}, u^{k,*}) - (\sigma^k, u^k)] \\ &\quad > (\beta - 1) J_{(\sigma^k, u^k)}[(\sigma^{k,*}, u^{k,*}) - (\sigma^k, u^k)]. \end{aligned} \quad (6.14)$$

Since the right-hand side of the preceding inequality is always positive, it is easy to verify that

$$\begin{aligned} 0 &< J_{(\sigma^k, u^k)}[(\sigma^k, u^k) - (\sigma^{k,*}, u^{k,*})] \\ &< \frac{1}{1-\beta} \,| J_{(\hat{\sigma}^k, \hat{u}^k)}[(\sigma^{k,*}, u^{k,*}) - (\sigma^k, u^k)] \\ &\quad - J_{(\sigma^k, u^k)}[(\sigma^{k,*}, u^{k,*}) - (\sigma^k, u^k)] \,| \\ &\leq \frac{2N}{1-\beta} \| J_{(\hat{\sigma}^k, \hat{u}^k)} - J_{(\sigma^k, u^k)} \|, \end{aligned} \quad (6.15)$$

where $N > 0$ is an upper bound of the set $\{\|(\sigma, u)\|_{\mathscr{D}} : (\sigma, u) \in \mathscr{D}_p\}$.

Since $\{J(\sigma^k, u^k)\}$ is a decreasing sequence and is bounded below on $\mathscr{D}_p$, it is convergent. Thus

$$J(\sigma^{k+1}, u^{k+1}) - J(\sigma^k, u^k) \to 0, \quad (6.16)$$

as $k \to \infty$.

From (6.10) and (6.16) we have

$$\alpha^m \beta J_{(\sigma^k, u^k)}[(\sigma^{k,*}, u^{k,*}) - (\sigma^k, u^k)] \to 0, \quad (6.17)$$

as $k \to \infty$.

To complete the proof we shall show that

$$J_{(\sigma^k, u^k)}[(\sigma^{k,*}, u^{k,*}) - (\sigma^k, u^k)] \to 0 \quad (6.18)$$

as $k \to \infty$.

Suppose it were false. Then there exists a subsequence of the sequence $\{(\sigma^k, u^k)\}$, again indexed by k, and a $\rho_0 > 0$ such that

$$J_{(\sigma^k, u^k)}[(\sigma^{k,*}, u^{k,*}) - (\sigma^k, u^k)] < -\rho_0 < 0, \tag{6.19}$$

for all $k = 1, 2, 3, \ldots$.

Thus from (6.17) we see that $\alpha^m \to 0$, as $k \to \infty$, and hence, by using (6.13)

$$\|(\hat{\sigma}^k, \hat{u}^k) - (\sigma^k, u^k)\|_{\mathscr{D}} \to 0, \tag{6.20}$$

as $k \to \infty$. Since $J_{(\sigma, u)}$ is uniformly continuous on $\mathscr{D}_p$ (Theorem 5.2) we have

$$\|J_{(\hat{\sigma}^k, \hat{u}^k)} - J_{(\sigma^k, u^k)}\| \to 0, \tag{6.21}$$

as $k \to \infty$. Thus it follows from (6.15) that

$$J_{(\sigma^k, u^k)}[(\sigma^k, u^k) - (\sigma^{k,*}, u^{k,*})] \to 0,$$

as $k \to \infty$. (Note that for sufficiently large k, we have $\alpha^m < 1$, and hence inequality (6.11) holds.) This contradicts inequality (6.19). Thus (6.18) holds.

Since

$$\|(\sigma^k, u^k) - (\bar{\sigma}, \bar{u})\|_{\mathscr{D}} \to 0, \tag{6.22}$$

it can be verified from Theorem 5.2 and the definition of $J_{(\sigma, u)}$ given in (5.1) that

$$J_{(\sigma^k, u^k)}[(\sigma^k, u^k)] \to J_{(\bar{\sigma}, \bar{u})}[(\bar{\sigma}, \bar{u})]. \tag{6.23}$$

Therefore, it follows from (6.18) and (6.23) that

$$\lim_{k\to\infty} J_{(\sigma^k, u^k)}[(\sigma^{k,*}, u^{k,*})] = \lim_{k\to\infty} J_{(\sigma^k, u^k)}[(\sigma^k, u^k)] = J_{(\bar{\sigma}, \bar{u})}[(\bar{\sigma}, \bar{u})]. \tag{6.24}$$

Using the definitions of $\sigma^{k,*}$ and $u^{k,*}$ given, respectively, in Steps 3 and 4 of the algorithm, we obtain

$$J_{(\sigma^k, u^k)}[(\sigma^{k,*}, u^{k,*})] \le J_{(\sigma^k, u^k)}[(\sigma, u)],$$

for all $(\sigma, u) \in \mathscr{D}_p$.

Letting $k \to \infty$ in the preceding inequality, it follows from (6.24) and Theorem 5.2 that.

$$J_{(\bar{\sigma}, \bar{u})}[(\bar{\sigma}, \bar{u})] \le J_{(\bar{\sigma}, \bar{u})}[(\sigma, u)],$$

for all $(\sigma, u) \in \mathscr{D}_p$. Thus $(\bar{\sigma}, \bar{u})$ satisfies the necessary condition (6.8). This completes the proof. ∎

IV.7. Numerical Consideration and Examples

Unlike the strong variational method, the conditional gradient method also works for the case when $n_1 = 0$. In other words, it is also applicable to optimal parameter selection problems. Optimal parameter selection problems can arise in many practical situations. For example, problems involving system parameter identification can be turned into optimal parameter selection problems. Furthermore, in many economic planning or industrial management applications, decisions are generally made at regular intervals. That is, the values of the control variables may be set daily, monthly, or quarterly, but may not be changed at intermediate times. This type of economic or industrial decision problems can be formally converted into problems of optimal parameter selection type.

For the parameter selection problems the corresponding class of admissible controls is rather restricted when compared with that of the general optimal control problems. However, the optimal control obtained from this restricted class of admissible controls is normally much simpler to implement.

Although the conditional gradient method is studied for the general class of problems, the application is, however, taken from an optimal parameter selection problem.

The class of optimal control problems considered in this chapter is similar to that of Chapter III. The main difference is that u is replaced by (σ, u) in this chapter.

As in Section III.8 we shall only discuss the discretization of problem P under the following restrictions:

(i) $n = 2$;
(ii) $n_1 = 1$ (note that the conditional gradient method is basically indifferent whether n_1 is equal to 0, 1, or 2);
(iii) $m_1 = 1$ (and hence $S \equiv [\beta_1, \beta_2]$, where β_i, $i = 1, 2$, are fixed given constants);
(iv) $m_2 = 1$ (and hence $U \equiv [\mu_1, \mu_2]$, where μ_i, $i = 1, 2$, are fixed given constants);
(v) $\Omega = (0, 1) \times (0, 1)$;
(vi) $T = 1$; and
(vii) $a_{ij}(x, t) = a\delta_{ij}$, for all $(x, t) \in \bar{Q} \equiv [0, 1] \times [0, 1] \times [0, 1]$, where a is a given positive constant and δ_{ij} is the Kronecker delta.

For convenience, let the corresponding $\mathscr{U}$ be denoted by $\mathscr{U}_1$, and let $\mathscr{D}_{p1} \equiv S \times \mathscr{U}_1$.

To proceed further, problem P under the restrictions (i)–(vii) is stated explicitly as the following problem.

Problem P_r Subject to the system

$$\phi_t(x_1, x_2, t) - \sum_{i=1}^{2} a\phi_{x_i x_i}(x_1, x_2, t)$$
$$- \sum_{i=1}^{2} b_i(x_1, x_2, t, \sigma, u(x_1, t))\phi_{x_i}(x_1, x_2, t)$$
$$- c(x_1, x_2, t, \sigma, u(x_1, t))\phi(x_1, x_2)$$
$$= f(x_1, x_2, t, u(x_1, t)), \qquad (x_1, x_2, t) \in (0, 1) \times (0, 1) \times (0, 1), \tag{7.1a}$$

$$\phi(x_1, x_2, 0) = \phi_0(x_1, x_2), \qquad (x_1, x_2) \in (0, 1) \times (0, 1), \tag{7.1b}$$

$$\phi(x_1, x_2, t) = 0, \qquad (x_1, x_2, t) \in \Gamma, \tag{7.1c}$$

find a policy $(\sigma, u) \in \mathscr{D}_{p1}$ that minimizes the cost functional

$$J(\sigma, u) = \int_0^1 \int_0^1 \phi(\sigma, u)(x_1, x_2, 1) z_T(x_1, x_2)\, dx_1\, dx_2 \tag{7.2}$$

over $\mathscr{D}_{p1}$, where the set Γ in (7.1c) is defined by (III.8.3) and $\phi(\sigma, u)$ denotes the almost everywhere solution of system (7.1) corresponding to $(\sigma, u) \in \mathscr{D}_{p1}$.

Let N_x, N_t, h_x, h_t, q, r, and s be as defined in Section III.8.

Let α be a function from $Q \times S \times U \equiv (0, 1) \times (0, 1) \times (0,1) \times [\beta_1, \beta_2] \times [\mu_1, \mu_2]$ into R^1. Then, for each $(\sigma, u) \in \mathscr{D}_{p1}$, we define

$$(\alpha^{\sigma, u})_{q,r,s} \equiv \alpha(qh_x, rh_x, sh_t, \sigma, u(qh_x, sh_t)).$$

Furthermore, as in Section III.8, $\phi^0_{q,r}$ is used to denote the discretized version of the function ϕ^0.

For a given policy $(\sigma, u) \in \mathscr{D}_{p1}$, the discretized version of system (7.1) is

$$(\phi_{q,r,s} - \phi_{q,r,s-1})/h_t$$
$$= a(\phi_{q+1,r,s} + \phi_{q-1,r,s} + \phi_{q,r+1,s} + \phi_{q,r-1,s} - 4\phi_{q,r,s})/(h_x)^2$$
$$+ (b_1^{\sigma,u})_{q,r,s}(\phi_{q+1,r,s} - \phi_{q-1,r,s})/2h_x$$
$$+ (b_2^{\sigma,u})_{q,r,s}(\phi_{q,r+1,s} - \phi_{q,r-1,s})/2h_x$$
$$+ (c^{\sigma,u})_{q,r,s}\phi_{q,r,s} + (f^{\sigma,u})_{q,r,s}, \qquad q, r = 1, \ldots, N_x - 1, \quad s = 1, \ldots, N_t, \tag{7.3a}$$

$$\phi_{q,r,0} = \phi^0_{q,r}, \qquad q, r = 1, \ldots, N_x - 1, \tag{7.3b}$$

$$\phi_{q,r,s} = 0, \qquad (q, r, s) \in \Gamma_D, \tag{7.3c}$$

where the set Γ_D in (7.3c) is defined by (III.8.5).

Corresponding to each $(\sigma, u) \in \mathscr{D}_{p1}$, let $(\phi^{\sigma,u})_{q,r,s}$ denote the solution of Eqs. (7.3a), (7.3b), and (7.3c), where the values of $(\phi^{\sigma,u})_{q,r,s}$, over all such q, r, and s, can be found by solving these $N_t(N_x - 1)^2$ linear equations. In practice, these equations can be solved by using the successive over relaxation method.

Let $z_{q,r}^T$ denote the discretized version of the function z_T. Then by using the trapezoidal rule the cost functional $J(\sigma, u)$, defined by (7.2), can be approximated by

$$\bar{J}(\sigma, u) \equiv (h_x)^2 \left\{ \sum_{q,r=1}^{N_x-1} (\phi^{\sigma,u})_{q,r,N_t} z_{q,r}^T \right\}. \tag{7.4}$$

For the corresponding adjoint system it is discretized as follows:

$$(z_{q,r,s} - z_{q,r,s+1})/h_t$$
$$= a(z_{q+1,r,s} + z_{q-1,r,s} + z_{q,r+1,s} + z_{q,r-1,s} - 4z_{q,r,s})/(h_x)^2$$
$$+ [(b_1^{\sigma,u})_{q-1,r,s} z_{q-1,r,s} - (b_1^{\sigma,u})_{q+1,r,s} z_{q+1,r,s}]/2h_x$$
$$+ [(b_2^{\sigma,u})_{q,r-1,s} z_{q,r-1,s} - (b_2^{\sigma,u})_{q,r+1,s} z_{q,r+1,s}]/2h_x$$
$$+ (c^{\sigma,u})_{q,r,s} z_{q,r,s}, \qquad q,r = 1,\ldots, N_x - 1, \qquad s = 1,\ldots, N_t, \tag{7.5a}$$

$$z_{q,r,N_t} = z_{q,r}^T, \qquad\qquad q,r = 1,\ldots, N_x - 1, \tag{7.5b}$$

$$z_{q,r,s} = 0, \qquad\qquad (q,r,s) \in \Gamma_D, \tag{7.5c}$$

where the set Γ_D in (7.5c) is defined by (III.8.5). For each $(\sigma, u) \in \mathscr{D}_{p1}$, let $(z^{\sigma,u})_{q,r,s}$, over all such q, r, and s, denote the solution of Eqs. (7.5a), (7.5b), and (7.5c).

For each $(\sigma, u) \in \mathscr{D}_{p1}$, let

$$[(\alpha^{\sigma,u})_{\sigma}]_{q,r,s} \equiv \alpha_{\sigma}(qh_x, rh_x, sh_t, \sigma, u(qh_x, sh_t)),$$

and

$$[(\alpha^{\sigma,u})_{v}]_{q,r,s} \equiv \alpha_{v}(qh_x, rh_x, sh_t, \sigma, u(qh_x, sh_t)),$$

where α_{σ} and α_{v} are as defined in Remark 5.1.

We now consider the vectors

$$A^{\sigma,u} \equiv \sum_{s=1}^{N_t} \sum_{q,r=1}^{N_x-1} (z^{\sigma,u})_{q,r,s} \{ [(b_1^{\sigma,u})_{\sigma}]_{q,r,s} [(\phi^{\sigma,u})_{q+1,r,s} - (\phi^{\sigma,u})_{q-1,r,s}]/2h_x$$
$$+ [(b_2^{\sigma,u})_{\sigma}]_{q,r,s} [(\phi^{\sigma,u})_{q,r+1,s} - (\phi^{\sigma,u})_{q,r-1,s}]/2h_x$$
$$+ [(c^{\sigma,u})_{\sigma}]_{q,r,s} (\phi^{\sigma,u})_{q,r,s} + [(f^{\sigma,u})_{\sigma}]_{q,r,s} \}, \tag{7.6}$$

and

$$(B^{\sigma,u})_{q,s}$$
$$\equiv \sum_{r=1}^{N_x-1} (z^{\sigma,u})_{q,r,s} \{ [(b_1^{\sigma,u})_{v}]_{q,r,s} [(\phi^{\sigma,u})_{q+1,r,s} - (\phi^{\sigma,u})_{q-1,r,s}]/2h_x$$
$$+ [(b_2^{\sigma,u})_{v}]_{q,r,s} [(\phi^{\sigma,u})_{q,r+1,s} - (\phi^{\sigma,u})_{q,r-1,s}]/2h_x$$
$$+ [(c^{\sigma,u})_{v}]_{q,r,s} (\phi^{\sigma,u})_{q,r,s} + [(f^{\sigma,u})_{v}]_{q,r,s} \}. \tag{7.7}$$

Then the discretized versions of functions (6.6) and (6.7) are given, respectively, by

$$\langle A^{\sigma,u}, \cdot \rangle, \tag{7.8}$$

and

$$\langle (B^{\sigma,u})_{q,s}, \cdot \rangle. \tag{7.9}$$

On the basis of these preparations, the following algorithm is posed to search for an approximate optimal solution of problem P_r.

Algorithm (DA)

(1) Specify $\sigma^0 \in S_1$ and $u^0 \in \mathscr{U}_1$. Set $k = 0$.

(2) Solve Eqs. (7.3a), (7.3b), and (7.3c) for $(\phi^{\sigma k, uk})_{q,r,s}$, and then evaluate $\bar{J}(\sigma^k, u^k)$ according to formula (7.4).

(3) Solve Eqs. (7.5a), (7.5b), and (7.5c) for $(z^{\sigma k, uk})_{q,r,s}$.

(4) Find $\sigma^{k,*} \in S_1$ such that

$$\langle A^{\sigma k, uk}, \sigma^{k,*} - \sigma^k \rangle \le \langle A^{\sigma k, uk}, \sigma - \sigma^k \rangle,$$

for all $\sigma \in S$.

(5) For each q, s find $V_{q,s}^{k,*} \in U$ such that

$$\langle (B^{\sigma k, uk})_{q,s}, V_{q,s}^{k,*} - u_{q,s}^k \rangle \le \langle (B^{\sigma k, uk})_{q,s}, v - u_{q,s}^k \rangle,$$

for all $v \in U$.

(6) Use a quadratic fit search technique to find a $\alpha^k \in [0, 1]$ such that

$$\begin{aligned} &\bar{J}(\sigma^k + \alpha^k(\sigma^{k,*} - \sigma^k), u^k + \alpha^*(V^{k,*} - u^k)) - \bar{J}(\sigma^k, u^k) \\ &\quad \le \bar{J}(\sigma^k + \alpha^k(\sigma^{k,*} - \sigma^k), u^k + \alpha^k(V^{k,*} - u^k)) - \bar{J}(\sigma^k, u^k) \end{aligned}$$

for all $\alpha \in [0, 1]$.

(7) Let

$$\sigma^{k+1} \equiv \sigma^k + \alpha^k(\sigma^{k,*} - \sigma^k), \; u_{q,s}^{k+1} \equiv u_{q,s}^k + \alpha^k(V_{q,s}^{k,*} - u_{q,s}^k),$$

set $k = k + 1$, and go to Step 2.

Comparing algorithm (A) and algorithm (DA) it is easy to observe that Step 6 of the second algorithm is not the discretized version of Step 6 of the first algorithm. At first sight it appears that we have done more than required in the second algorithm. This impression is not true, in general, because the quadratic fit technique (or any practical line search technique) does not necessarily find a global minimum. Thus α^k obtained in Step 6 of the second algorithm is only known to be a local rather than global minimizer. In this situation the convergence result reported in Theorem 6.2 may not be guaranteed. However, from the practical experience the modified algorithm works very well for many problems, such as the example to be discussed later in this section.

Again as in Section III.8, a stopping criterion is required in any practical application. More precisely, we stop the program as soon as one of the following two conditions is satisfied:

(i) $|\bar{J}(\sigma^{k+1}, u^{k+1}) - \bar{J}(\sigma^k, u^k)| < \varepsilon_1$, where ε_1 is a preset tolerance; and

(ii) $\alpha^k < \varepsilon_2$, where α^k is given in Step 6 of algorithm (DA) and ε_2 is another preset tolerance.

In what follows we shall apply the algorithm (DA) to a simple practical example arising in the study of choosing optimal level of advertising.

Consider a firm that produces a single product and sells it in a market that can absorb no more than M dollars of the product per unit time. It is assumed that, if the firm does no advertising, its rate of sales at any point in time will decrease at a rate proportional to the rate of sales at that time. If the firm advertises, the rate of sales will increase at a rate proportional to the rate of advertising, but this increase affects only that share of the market that is not already purchasing the product.

Let

$$y(t) \equiv S(t)/M = (\text{rate of sales/saturation rate}) \text{ at time } t,$$

$$A(t) = \text{rate of advertising at time } t,$$

$$K_1 = \text{constant} \qquad (K_1 > 0),$$

and

$$v(t) = A(t)/M.$$

Then

$$1 - y(t) = \text{the part of the market affected by advertising at time } t.$$

Under these assumptions and a suitable scale for the time variable, the change in (rate of sales/saturation rate) is given by

$$dy(t)/dt = -y(t) + K_1 v(t)[1 - y(t)]. \tag{7.10}$$

This is the well known Vidale–Wolfe model (see [VW.1)].

In this section we shall study a stochastic version of the Vidale–Wolfe model, namely,

$$d\xi(t) = \{-\xi(t) + K_1 v(t)[1 - \xi(t)]\}\, dt + K_2\, dw(t), \tag{7.11}$$

where K_2 is a positive constant and $w(t)$ is a standard Wiener process. It is assumed that the process stops at the time

$$\tau \equiv \inf\{\{t \in [0, 1] : \xi(t) \notin (0, 1)\} \cup \{1\}\}, \tag{7.12}$$

and that the initial state $\xi(0)$ is distributed with a density

$$q^0(x) = \begin{cases} 6x(1-x), & x \in (0, 1), \\ 0, & \text{otherwise.} \end{cases} \tag{7.13}$$

Given a control $v(t)$, the expected profit is

$$P(v) = \mathscr{E}\left\{ \int_0^\tau [K_3 \xi(t) - K_4 v(t)]\, dt \right\}, \tag{7.14}$$

where $\mathscr{E}$ denotes the mathematical expectation and K_3, K_4 are positive constants. K_3 is the gross income if maximum sales was achieved for the whole period; K_4 is the total cost of a full advertising campaign over the whole period.

It is assumed that only piecewise constant open loop controls with switching at predetermined times $0 = t_1 < t_2 < \cdots < t_r < 1$ are admissible controls. Let

$$\sigma \equiv (\sigma_1, \ldots, \sigma_r)$$

be the levels of advertising on each of the time intervals. Then the admissible controls are those of the form

$$v(t) = \sum_{l=1}^{r} \sigma_l \chi_{[t_l, t_{l+1})}(t), \tag{7.15}$$

where $t_{r+1} = 1$ and χ_Z denotes the indicator function of the set Z. Clearly, $v(t) \in [0, 1]$, for all $t \in [0, 1]$, if $\sigma_l \in [0, 1]$, for $l = 1, \ldots, r$.

The advertising problem is to find a $\sigma \in \sum \equiv [0, 1]^r$ (r copies of [0, 1]) that maximizes (7.14) subject to system (7.11) with initial distribution (7.13), where $v(t)$ is taken as in the form of (7.15) and τ is defined by (7.12).

This stochastic optimal control problem can be converted, using the results in Appendix A.1, to the following distributed optimal control problem.

Subject to the system

$$\begin{aligned} \phi_t(x, t) = {} & \tfrac{1}{2}(K_2)^2 \phi_{xx}(x, t) \\ & + \left\{ \left[K_1 \left(\sum_{l=1}^{r} \sigma_l \chi_{[t_l, t_{l+1})}(1-t) \right)(1-x) \right] - x \right\} \phi_x(x, t) \\ & + K_4 \left[\sum_{l=1}^{r} \sigma_l \chi_{[t_l, t_{l+1})}(1-t) \right] - K_3 x, \end{aligned}$$

$$(x, t) \in (0, 1) \times (0,1), \tag{7.16a}$$

$$\phi(x, t) = 0, \qquad (x, t) \in (\{0, 1\} \times [0, 1]) \cup ((0, 1) \times \{0\}) \tag{7.16b}$$

find a parameter vector $\sigma \in [0, 1]^r$ such that the cost functional

$$J(\sigma) = 6 \int_0^1 \phi(\sigma)(x, 1)x(1 - x)\, dx \tag{7.17}$$

is minimized, where $\phi(\sigma)$ denotes the almost everywhere solution of system (7.16) corresponding to $\sigma \in [0, 1]^r$.

The corresponding adjoint system is

$$-z_t(x, t) = \tfrac{1}{2}(K_2)^2 z_{xx}(x, t) - \frac{\partial}{\partial x}\left\{\left[K_1\left(\sum_{l=1}^{r} \sigma_l \chi_{[t_l, t_{l+1})}(1 - t)\right)(1 - x) - x\right] z(x, t)\right\}, \quad (x, t) \in (0, 1) \times (0, 1), \tag{7.18a}$$

$$z(x, t) = 6x(1 - x), \qquad x \in (0, 1), \tag{7.18b}$$

$$z(x, t) = 0, \qquad (x, t) \in \{0, 1\} \times [0, 1]. \tag{7.18c}$$

Since the coefficient appearing under the x differential is differentiable with respect to x, adjoint system (7.18), which is in divergence form, can be written in general form, i.e.,

$$-z_t(x, t) = \tfrac{1}{2}(K_2)^2 z_{xx}(x, t) - \left[K_1\left(\sum_{l=1}^{r} \sigma_l \chi_{[t_l, t_{l+1})}(1 - t)\right)(1 - x) - x\right] z_x(x, t) + \left[K_1\left(\sum_{l=1}^{r} \sigma_l \chi_{[t_l, t_{l+1})}(1 - t)\right) + 1\right] z(x, t), \quad (x, t) \in (0, 1) \times (0, 1), \tag{7.19a}$$

$$z(x, t) = 6x(1 - x), \qquad x \in (0, 1), \tag{7.19b}$$

$$z(x, t) = 0, \qquad (x, t) \in [0, 1] \times \{0, 1\}. \tag{7.19c}$$

Thus it admits, for each $\sigma \in [0, 1]^r$, a unit weak solution $z(\sigma)$ that is also the almost everywhere solution.

From Eq. (5.1), we see that, for this distributed optimal control problem, the ith component of the gradient of J at $\sigma \in [0, 1]^r$ is

$$\begin{aligned} &\int_0^1 \int_0^1 \{K_1 \chi_{[t_l, t_{l+1})}(1 - t)(1 - x)\phi(\sigma)_x(x, t) \\ &\qquad + K_4 \chi_{[t_l, t_{l+1})}(1 - t)\} z(\sigma)(x, t)\, dx\, dt \\ &= \int_{1-t_l}^{1-t_{l+1}} \int_0^1 \{K_1(1 - x)\phi(\sigma)_x(x, t) + K_4\} z(\sigma)(x, t)\, dx\, dt. \end{aligned} \tag{7.20}$$

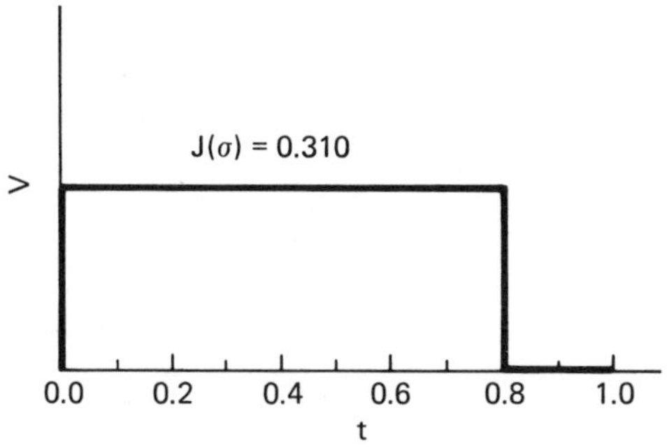

Fig. 1. Optimal piecewise constant control calculated by the optimal parameter selection technique. Reprinted by permission of D. W. Reid and K. L. Teo, Optimal Parameter Selection of Parabolic Systems, Mathematics of Operations Research, Volume 5, November 3, August 1980, copyright 1980. The Institute of Management Sciences.

The calculations were performed with the constants taking the following values:

$$K_2 = \tfrac{1}{2}, \qquad K_1 = K_3 = 1, \qquad K_4 = \tfrac{1}{10},$$

$$t_l = (l - 1)/10, \qquad l = 1, 2, \ldots, 10.$$

Using algorithm (DA) an optimal set of parameters is obtained; the calculated values are 1 for $\sigma_1, \ldots, \sigma_8$ and 0 for σ_9 and σ_{10}. The calculated performance criteria is the negative of the profit using the control constructed from the parameter vector. In Fig. 1 the control found by substituting the calculated values of σ_l, $l = 1, \ldots, 10$, into (7.15) has been plotted. The expected profit, if this control is used, is 0.310. For the same coefficients the optimal feedback control has already been calculated for the stochastic optimal control problem in [Boy.1]. This optimal feedback control is reproduced in Fig. 2. Both controls are of the bang–bang type. However, parametrized control switches only once at a predetermined time, whereas feedback control requires that the process be continually monitored and switching occurs when the state crosses the switching curve. In the present case the decrease in performance is only 2.5% of the optimal feedback solution. Because there is far less effort required to use the parametrized control, this decrease may well be tolerable. However, it should be noted that the decrease in performance is *not* always necessarily small between parametrized control and feedback control in a given optimal control problem.

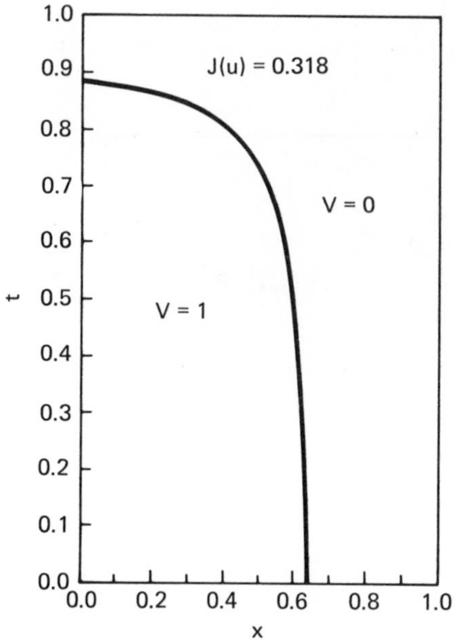

Fig. 2. $V(t, x)$ for the optimal feedback control problem.

IV.8. Optimal Control Problems with Terminal Inequality Constraints

In this section we shall consider a class of optimal control problems involving control and terminal inequality constraints. To simplify the presentation, the class of dynamical systems involved is, however, confined to a special case of that introduced in Section 2. More precisely, in this section, only controls with $n_1 = n$, rather than policies, are allowed to appear in the first- and zeroth-order coefficients, and in the forcing term of the system. However, it should be noted that parallel results are also valid for the general case.

We now consider the first boundary-value problem:

$$L(u)\phi(x, t) = f(x, t, u(x, t)), \qquad (x, t) \in Q, \tag{8.1a}$$

$$\phi|_{t=0} = \phi_0(x), \qquad x \in \Omega, \tag{8.1b}$$

$$\phi|_{\Gamma} = 0, \qquad (x, t) \in \Gamma, \tag{8.1c}$$

where $u \in L_\infty(Q, R^m)$ and, for each $u \in L_\infty(Q, R^m)$, $L(u)$ is a linear second-order parabolic partial differential operator defined by

$$L(u)\psi \equiv \psi_t - \sum_{i,j=1}^{n} a_{ij}(x, t)\psi_{x_i x_j} - \sum_{i=1}^{n} b_i(x, t, u(x, t))\psi_{x_i}$$
$$-c(x, t, u(x, t))\psi. \tag{8.2}$$

Let U be a fixed compact and convex subset of R^m. A measurable function $u: Q \to U$ is called an admissible control. Let $\mathscr{U}$ be the class of all such admissible controls. Let the functions $h^j: R^1 \to R^1, j = 0, 1, \ldots, l$, be continuously differentiable and let

$$g(u) \equiv \int_\Omega \phi(u)(x, T)z_T(x)\, dx, \tag{8.3}$$

where $\phi(u)$ is the almost everywhere solution (in the sense of Definition III.2.1) of system (8.1) corresponding to $u \in L_\infty(Q, R^m)$, and $z_T \in L_\infty(\Omega)$ is the weight function as defined in Section 3.

The optimal control problem may now be stated as follows.

Subject to system (8.1) and the terminal inequality constraints

$$J^j(u) \equiv h^j(g(u)) \leq 0, \qquad j = 1, \ldots, l, \tag{8.4}$$

find a control $u \in \mathscr{U}$ that minimizes the cost functional

$$J^0(u) \equiv h^0(g(u)). \tag{8.5}$$

For convenience, this optimal control problem will be referred to as Problem (PT).

An admissible control is said to be feasible if it satisfies constraints (8.4). *Let* $\mathscr{F}$ *denote the class of all such feasible controls*, i.e.,

$$\mathscr{F} \equiv \{u \in \mathscr{U} : J^j(u) \equiv h^j(g(u)) \leq 0, \qquad j = 1, 2, \ldots, l\}.$$

On this basis, problem (PT) can also be stated as follows: subject to system (8.1), find a feasible control $u \in \mathscr{F}$ that minimizes cost functional (8.5) over $\mathscr{F}$.

The assumptions to be imposed in this section are similar to those for problem (P). Only minor changes are needed. More precisely, we assume that assumptions (A.1)′, (A.2), (A.4), and (A.5) are satisfied. For assumptions (A.3) and (A.6), they are replaced, respectively, by

(A.3)′ $b_i, i = 1, \ldots, n, c$, and f are continuous on $\bar{Q} \times R^m$; and

(A.6)′ Let h denote any of the functions b_i, $i = 1, \ldots, n$, c, and f. Then h_v, which is as defined in Remark 5.1, is continuous on $\bar{Q} \times R^m$.

The adjoint system to problem (PT) is

$$L^*(u)z = 0, \qquad (x, t) \in Q, \tag{8.6a}$$

$$z|_{t=T} = z_T(x), \qquad x \in \Omega, \tag{8.6b}$$

$$z|_\Gamma = 0, \qquad (x, t) \in \Gamma, \tag{8.6c}$$

where the operator L^*, which is the formal adjoint of the operator L, is given by

$$L^*(u)\psi \equiv -\psi_t - \sum_{i=1}^{n} \left\{ \sum_{j=1}^{n} a_{ij}(x, t)\psi_{x_j} + a_i(x, t, u(x, t))\psi \right\}_{x_i} - c(x, t, u(x, t))\psi \tag{8.7}$$

with

$$a_i(x, t, u(x, t)) \equiv \sum_{j=1}^{n} \frac{\partial a_{ij}(x, t)}{\partial x_j} - b_i(x, t, u(x, t)).$$

Under the assumptions of this section, adjoint system (8.6) admits, for each $u \in \mathscr{U}$, a weak solution $z(u)$ in the sense of Definition III.3.1.

In the next theorem the formulas for the gradients of the functionals $J^j(u)$, $j = 0, 1, \ldots, l$, will be presented.

THEOREM 8.1. *Let $J^j\colon L_\infty(Q, R^m) \to R^1$, $j = 0, 1, \ldots, l$, be the functionals defined in* (8.4) *and* (8.5). *Then, for each $j = 0, 1, \ldots, l$, J^j is Frechet differentiable everywhere on $L_\infty(Q, R^m)$ and the gradient $J^j_{u^0}$ of J^j at $u^0 \in L_\infty(Q, R^m)$ is given by*

$$J^j_{u^0}[u] = \iint_Q \langle I(u^0)_v[x, t, u^0(x, t)], u(x, t)\rangle z(u^0)(x, t) h^j_g(g(u^0))\, dx\, dt, \tag{8.8}$$

where

$$h^j_g(g) \equiv dh^j(g)/dg \tag{8.9}$$

for any $g \in R^1$. Furthermore, the gradient $J^j_u\colon \mathscr{U} \to L_\infty(Q, R^m)^*$ is uniformly continuous on $\mathscr{U}$.

Proof. The proof follows readily from Theorem 5.1 and Theorem 5.2. ∎

In the computational algorithm to be presented for solving optimal control problem (PT), a search direction is needed in each iteration. Each of these search directions corresponds to a subproblem that is itself an optimal control problem and can be solved by a standard convex program (Meyer–Polak Proximity Algorithm, see Appendix A. VI).

For any $\varepsilon > 0$ and $u \in \mathscr{F}$, let $q_\varepsilon(u)$ denote the ε active index set, i.e.,

$$q_\varepsilon(u) \equiv \{0\} \cup \{j \in \hat{q} : J^j(u) \geq -\varepsilon\}, \tag{8.10}$$

where

$$\hat{q} \equiv \{1, \ldots, l\}. \tag{8.11}$$

For any subset q of the set $\{0\} \cup \hat{q}$, let $\psi_q \colon \mathscr{F} \to R^1$ be defined by

$$\psi_q(u) \equiv \min_{s \in \mathscr{U} - u} \max_{j \in q} \{J_u^j[s]\}. \tag{8.12}$$

LEMMA 8.1. *Let q be any subset of the index set $\{0\} \cup \hat{q}$. Then, for any $u \in \mathscr{F}$, there exists a $s_q^u \in \mathscr{U} - u \equiv \{v - u : v \in \mathscr{U}\}$ such that*

$$\psi_q(u) = \max_{j \in q} \{J_u^j[s_q^u]\}. \tag{8.13}$$

Proof. Since U is a compact and convex subset of R^m, it follows that $\mathscr{U}$ is sequentially compact in the weak * topology (of $L_\infty(Q, R^m)$), and hence so is $\mathscr{U} - u$. Therefore, $\max_{j \in q}\{J_u^j[\cdot]\}$ attains its minimum on $\mathscr{U} - u$, because $\max_{j \in q}\{J_u^i[\cdot]\}$ is continuous on $\mathscr{U} - u$ with respect to the weak* topology. This implies that there exists a $s_q^u \in \mathscr{U} - u$ such that

$$\min_{s \in \mathscr{U} - u} \max_{j \in q} \{J_u^j[s]\} = \max_{j \in q} \{J_u^j[s_q^u]\}.$$

The proof is complete. ■

The subproblem can now be stated as follows.

Problem (PTS) For each $u \in \mathscr{F}$ and $\varepsilon > 0$, find a search direction $s_\varepsilon^u \in \mathscr{U} - u$ that minimizes

$$\max_{j \in q_\varepsilon(u)} \{J_u^j[s]\},$$

that is,

$$\begin{aligned} \psi_{q_\varepsilon(u)}(u) &\equiv \min_{s \in \mathscr{U} - u} \max_{j \in q_\varepsilon(u)} \{J_u^j[s]\} \\ &= \max_{j \in q_\varepsilon(u)} \{J_u^j[s_\varepsilon^u]\}. \end{aligned} \tag{8.14}$$

To present an algorithm for solving this problem we need some preparation.

Let n_ε^u denote the cardinality of the set $q_\varepsilon(u)$ and let

$$C_\varepsilon^u \equiv \{\xi \in R^{n_\varepsilon^u} : \xi_j = J_u^j[s], j \in q_\varepsilon(u), s \in \mathscr{U} - u\}. \tag{8.15}$$

From (8.8) it follows that C_ε^u is a compact and convex subset of $R^{n_\varepsilon^u}$. Let $h_g(g(\cdot))$ be an n_ε^u dimensional vector valued function on $\mathscr{U}$ such that its components are $(h_g(g(\cdot)))_j$ arranged in the natural order of $j \in q_\varepsilon(u)$.

LEMMA 8.2. *Let λ be a constant vector in $R^{n_\varepsilon^u}$. Then, for each $u \in \mathscr{F}$, there exists a $s_{\varepsilon,\lambda}^u \in \mathscr{U} - u$ such that*

$$\min_{v \in U - u(x,t)} \{\langle I(u)_v[x, t, u(x, t)], v\rangle z(u)(x, t)\lambda^{\mathrm{T}} g_g(g(u))\}$$

$$= \langle I(u)_v[x, t, u(x, t)], s_{\varepsilon,\lambda}^u(x, t)\rangle z(u)(x, t)\lambda^{\mathrm{T}} h_g(g(u)), \qquad (8.16)$$

for all $(x, t) \in Q$, where the superscript T *denotes the transpose; and*

$$\langle \lambda, \xi_{\varepsilon,\lambda}^u\rangle \leq \langle \lambda, \xi\rangle, \qquad (8.17)$$

for all $\xi \in C_\varepsilon^u$, where the components $(\xi_{\varepsilon,\lambda}^u)_j$ of the vector $\xi_{\varepsilon,\lambda}^u$ are $J_u^j[s_{\varepsilon,\lambda}^u]$ arranged in the natural order of $j \in q_\varepsilon(u)$.

Proof. For each $(x, t) \in Q$, let

$$\hat{r}(x, t) \equiv \min_{v \in U} r(x, t, v),$$

where

$$r(x, t, v) \equiv \langle I(u)_v[x, t, u(x, t)], v - u(x, t)\rangle z(u)(x, t)\lambda^{\mathrm{T}} h_g(g(u)).$$

Clearly, $\hat{r}(x, t)$ is measurable in Q. Since U is compact, the linear function $r(x, t, \cdot)$ attains its minimum on U. Thus, for each $(x, t) \in Q$,

$$\hat{r}(x, t) \in r(x, t, U).$$

At this stage, it follows readily from Theorem I.6.1 that there exists a measurable function $\bar{s}(x, t) \in U$ such that

$$\hat{r}(x, t) = r(x, t, \bar{s}(x, t)).$$

Let $s_{\varepsilon,\lambda}^u \equiv \bar{s} - u$. Then it is clear that $s_{\varepsilon,\lambda}^u$ is in $\mathscr{U} - u$ and satisfies (8.16). It remains to prove the second part of the lemma. For any

$$\xi \equiv (\xi_1, \ldots, \xi_{n_\varepsilon^u}) \in C_\varepsilon^u,$$

there exists an $s \in \mathscr{U} - u$ such that

$$\xi_j = J_u^j[s], \qquad j \in q_\varepsilon(u).$$

Therefore, it follows from (8.8) that

$$\langle \lambda, \xi\rangle = \iint_Q \langle I(u)_v[x, t, u(x, t)], s(x, t)\rangle z(u)(x, t)\lambda^{\mathrm{T}} h_g(g(u))\, dx\, dt$$

and

$$\langle \lambda, \xi_{\varepsilon,\lambda}^u\rangle = \iint_Q \langle I(u)_v[x, t, u(x, t)], s_{\varepsilon,\lambda}^u(x, t)\rangle z(u)(x, t)\lambda^{\mathrm{T}} h_g(g(u))\, dx\, dt.$$

Hence, (8.17) follows readily from (8.16). This completes the proof. ■

Now, let

$$D^u_{\varepsilon,a} \equiv \{\eta \equiv (\eta_1, \ldots, \eta_{n^u_\varepsilon}) \in R^{n^u_\varepsilon} : \eta_j \in [b(u, \varepsilon)_j, a], j = 1, \ldots, n^u_\varepsilon\},$$

where $b(u, \varepsilon) \equiv (b(u, \varepsilon)_1, \ldots, b(u, \varepsilon)_{n^u_\varepsilon}) \in R^{n^u_\varepsilon}$

$$b(u, \varepsilon)_j \equiv (\xi^u_{\varepsilon, e^j})_j, j = 1, \ldots, n^u_\varepsilon,$$

and for each $i = 1, \ldots, n^u_\varepsilon$, e^i denotes the ith unit vector in $R^{n^u_\varepsilon}$.

In the following text ξ will denote a point in C^u_ε and η a point in $D^u_{\varepsilon,a}$. Then the Meyer–Polak Proximity Algorithm can be used to determine the least value of a such that $C^u_\varepsilon \cap D^u_{\varepsilon,a} \neq \emptyset$ and to determine a point in the intersection. Let $\hat{\xi}^u_\varepsilon$ be such a point in the intersection. Then

$$\psi_{q_\varepsilon(u)} = \max\{(\hat{\xi}^u_\varepsilon)_j : j = 1, \ldots, n^u_\varepsilon\}$$

We can now present the Meyer–Polak Proximity Algorithm for determining $\psi_{q_\varepsilon(u)}(u)$.

Algorithm 8.1

Data $u \in \mathscr{F}$, $\varepsilon > 0$, and $q_\varepsilon(u)$.

Step 0 Set $\xi^0 = 0$. Set $s^0 = 0$. Compute $b = b(u, \varepsilon)$. Set $\eta^0 = b$. Set $a_0 = \max\{b_j : j = 1, 2, \ldots, n^u_\varepsilon\}$. Set $i = 0$.

Step 1 Set $\sigma^i = \eta^i - \xi^i$. Compute $s^u_{\varepsilon,\sigma^i}$ and $\xi^u_{\varepsilon,\sigma^i}$. Set $\overline{s^i} = s^u_{\varepsilon,\sigma^i}$, $\overline{\xi^i} = \xi^u_{\varepsilon,\sigma^i}$.

Step 2 If $\langle \sigma^i, \overline{\xi^i}\rangle \geq \langle \sigma^i, \eta^i\rangle$, set $a_{i+1} = a_i$, $\overline{\eta^i} = \eta^i$. Else set $a_{i+1} = \min\{a : D^u_{\varepsilon,a} \cap H \neq \emptyset, a \geq a_i\}$, where $H = \{y \in R^{n^u_\varepsilon} : \langle y, \sigma^i\rangle = \langle \overline{\xi^i}, \sigma^i\rangle\}$. Compute any $\overline{\eta^i} \in D^\varepsilon_{u,a_{i+1}} \cap H$.

Step 3 Compute $\xi^{i+1} \in [\xi^i, \overline{\xi^i}]$, $\eta^{i+1} \in [\eta^i, \overline{\eta^i}]$ such that $|\xi^{i+1} - \eta^{i+1}| = \min\{|\xi - \eta| : \xi \in [\xi^i, \overline{\xi^i}], \eta \in [\eta^i, \overline{\eta^i}]\}$. If $|\xi^{i+1} - \eta^{i+1}| = 0$, stop. Else set $s^{i+1} = s^i + (\overline{s^i} - s^i)|\xi^i - \xi^{i+1}|/|\xi^i - \overline{\xi^i}|$. Set $i = i + 1$, go to Step 1.

REMARK 8.1. For each i, ξ^i, which is a point in C^u_ε, is generated by

$$s^i \in \mathscr{U} \text{ i.e., } (\xi^i)_j = J^j_u[s^i], j \in q_\varepsilon(u).$$

REMARK 8.2. From Appendix A.V1 we note that either $\{(\xi^i, \eta^i)\}$ is finite and its last element (ξ^k, η^k) satisfies $\xi^k = \eta^k$, or it is infinite and its every accumulation point $(\bar{\xi}, \bar{\eta})$ satisfies $\bar{\xi} = \bar{\eta}$.

REMARK 8.3. For each i, it is clear that

$$\max_j\{(\eta^i)_j\} \leq \psi_{q_\varepsilon(u)}(u) \leq \max_j\{(\xi^i)_j\}.$$

REMARK 8.4. Since $|\xi^i - \eta^i|$ is decreasing, it follows from Remark 8.2 that $|\xi^i - \eta^i| \to 0$. Hence, $\max_j [(\xi^i)_j - (\eta^i)_j] \to 0$, as $i \to \infty$. Therefore, there exists an integer $i_0 > 0$ such that

$$\max_j\{(\xi^{i_0})_j\} - \max_j\{(\eta^{i_0})_j\} \leq \varepsilon/2.$$

REMARK 8.5. Let $\bar{\psi}_\varepsilon(u)$, $\underline{\psi}_\varepsilon(u)$ and $\bar{s}^u_\varepsilon$ denote $\max_j \{(\xi^{i_0})_j\}$, $\max_j \{(\eta^{i_0})_j\}$ and s_{i_0}, respectively. Then $\bar{\psi}_\varepsilon(u)$, $\underline{\psi}_\varepsilon(u)$, and $\bar{s}^u_\varepsilon$, which can be computed in finite number of iterations, satisfy

$$\psi_{q_\varepsilon(u)}(u) \in [\underline{\psi}_\varepsilon(u), \bar{\psi}_\varepsilon(u)],$$

$$\bar{\psi}_\varepsilon(u) - \underline{\psi}_\varepsilon(u) \le \varepsilon/2,$$

and

$$\bar{\psi}_\varepsilon(u) = \max_{j \in q_\varepsilon(u)} \{J^j_u[\bar{s}^u_\varepsilon]\}.$$

In what follows we wish to present a feasible directions algorithm, called Algorithm 8.2, for solving problem (PT) and to study its convergence properties.

Algorithm 8.2

Data $\alpha, \beta \in (0, 1)$, and $\varepsilon' > 0$.

Step 0 Select a $u^0 \in \mathscr{F}$; set $i = 0$.

Step 1 Set $\varepsilon_0 = \varepsilon'$; set $j = 0$.

Step 2 Compute, using Algorithm 8.1, a search direction $\bar{s}^{u^i}_{\varepsilon_j}$, together with $\bar{\psi}_{\varepsilon_j}(u^i)$ and $\underline{\psi}_{\varepsilon_j}(u^i)$.

Step 3 If $\bar{\psi}_{\varepsilon_j}(u^i) > -\varepsilon_j/2$, set $\varepsilon_{j+1} = \beta\varepsilon_j$, set $j = j + 1$, and go to Step 2. If $\bar{\psi}_{\varepsilon_j}(u^i) \le -\varepsilon_j/2$, proceed.

Step 4 Compute the smallest integer k such that

$$J^0(u^i + (\beta)^k \bar{s}^{u^i}_{\varepsilon_j}) - J^0(u^i) \le \alpha(\beta)^k \bar{\psi}_{\varepsilon_j}(u^i), \tag{8.18}$$

$$J^r(u^i + (\beta)^k \bar{s}^{u^i}_{\varepsilon_j}) \le 0, \qquad r = 1, 2, \ldots, \ell. \tag{8.19}$$

Step 5 Set $u^{i+1} = u^i + (\beta)^k \bar{s}^{u^i}_{\varepsilon_j}$, set $i = i + 1$, go to Step 1.

Let

$$\mathscr{D} \equiv \{u \in \mathscr{F} : \psi_{q_0(u)}(u) = 0\}.$$

For any feasible control $u \notin \mathscr{D}$, let

$$\varepsilon_a(u) \equiv \max\{\varepsilon : \bar{\psi}_\varepsilon(u) \le -\varepsilon/2, \varepsilon = (\beta)^k \varepsilon', \qquad k = 0, 1, 2, \ldots\}, \tag{8.20}$$

and let $k(u)$ be the smallest nonnegative integer satisfying (8.18) and (8.19).

LEMMA 8.3. *For any subset q of the index set $\{0\} \cup \hat{q}$, $\psi_q(\cdot)$, defined by* (8.12), *is upper semicontinuous with respect to the L_∞ topology.*

Proof. From Theorem 8.1 it follows that, for each $s \in \mathscr{U} - u$, $\max_{j \in q} \{J^j_u[s]\}$ considered as a function of u is continuous with respect to the strong topology of L_∞. Furthermore, it is well known that the infimum of a class of continuous mappings is upper semicontinuous. Thus

$$\min_{s \in \mathscr{U} - u} \max_{j \in q}\{J_u^j[s]\}$$

is upper semicontinuous. This completes the proof. ∎

LEMMA 8.4. *Let $\{u^i\}$ be an infinite sequence in $\mathscr{F}$ converging to $\bar{u} \notin \mathscr{D}$ in the strong topology of L_∞. Then there exists an $\hat{\varepsilon} > 0$ and an integer i_0 such that*

$$\varepsilon_a(u^i) \geq \hat{\varepsilon} > 0,$$

for all $i > i_0$.

Proof. Let

$$\varepsilon(u) \equiv \max\{\varepsilon : \psi_{q_{\varepsilon(u)}}(u) \leq -\varepsilon,\ \varepsilon = (\beta)^k \varepsilon',\ k = 0, 1, 2, \ldots\}.$$

Then by construction

$$\begin{aligned} \bar{\psi}_{\varepsilon(u)}(u) &\leq \psi_{q_{\varepsilon(u)}(u)}(u) + \varepsilon(u)/2 \\ &\leq -\varepsilon(u) + \varepsilon(u)/2 \\ &= -\varepsilon(u)/2, \end{aligned}$$

and hence,

$$\varepsilon_a(u) \geq \varepsilon(u).$$

Thus to achieve the conclusion of the lemma, all we have to do is to prove that there exists an $\hat{\varepsilon} > 0$ and an integer i_0 such that

$$\varepsilon(u^i) \geq \hat{\varepsilon} > 0,$$

for all $i > i_0$.

Since $\bar{u} \notin \mathscr{D}$, there exists a

$$\delta \in E_\beta \equiv \{(\beta)^k \varepsilon' : k = 0, 1, \ldots\},$$

such that

$$\psi_{q_0(\bar{u})}(\bar{u}) \leq -\delta.$$

Hence, there exists an $\bar{\varepsilon} \in E_\beta$ such that

$$\psi_{q_\varepsilon(\bar{u})}(\bar{u}) \leq -\delta,$$

for all $\varepsilon \in [0, \bar{\varepsilon}]$. Let $\bar{\bar{\varepsilon}} \equiv \min\{\bar{\varepsilon}, \delta\}$. Then it is clear that

$$\psi_{q_{\bar{\bar{\varepsilon}}}(\bar{u})}(\bar{u}) \leq -\bar{\bar{\varepsilon}},$$

and

$$\bar{\bar{\varepsilon}} \in E_\beta.$$

Hence,

$$\varepsilon(\bar{u}) \geq \bar{\bar{\varepsilon}} > 0. \tag{8.21}$$

Since $J^j(u)$, $j = 1, \ldots, l$, are continuous in u with respect to the strong topology of L_∞, it follows that there exists an integer i_1 such that

$$q_{\varepsilon(\bar{u})}(u^i) \subset q_{\varepsilon(\bar{u})}(\bar{u}) \equiv \bar{q},$$

for all $i \geq i_1$.

Thus, for all $i \geq i_1$,

$$\psi_{q_{\varepsilon(\bar{u})}(u^i)}(u^i) \leq \psi_{\bar{q}}(u^i). \tag{8.22}$$

Since $\psi_{\bar{q}}(\cdot)$ is upper semicontinuous, there exists an integer $i_0 \geq i_1$ such that

$$\psi_{\bar{q}}(u^i) \leq \beta\psi_{\bar{q}}(\bar{u}) \leq -\beta\varepsilon(\bar{u}), \tag{8.23}$$

for all $i \geq i_0$, where the second inequality of (8.23) follows from the definition of $\varepsilon(u)$.

Combining (8.22) and (8.23), we have

$$\psi_{q_{\beta\varepsilon(\bar{u})}(u^i)}(u^i) \leq \psi_{q_{\varepsilon(\bar{u})}(u^i)}(u^i) \leq -\beta\varepsilon(\bar{u}),$$

for all $i \geq i_0$, and consequently,

$$\varepsilon(u^i) \geq \beta\varepsilon(\bar{u}) \equiv \hat{\varepsilon} > 0,$$

for all $i \geq i_0$. This completes the proof. ■

LEMMA 8.5. *Let $\{u^i\}$ be an infinite sequence in $\mathscr{F}$ converging to $\bar{u} \notin \mathscr{D}$ in the strong topology of L_∞. Then there exists a $\delta > 0$ and positive integers $\hat{k}$ and i_0 such that, for all $i \geq i_0$,*

$$k(u^i) \leq \hat{k}, \tag{8.24}$$

$$J^0(u^{i,\prime}) - J^0(u^i) \leq -\delta, \tag{8.25}$$

$$J^j(u^{i,\prime}) \leq 0, \qquad j = 1, 2, \ldots, l, \tag{8.26}$$

where

$$u^{i,\prime} \equiv u^i + (\beta)^{k(u^i)}\bar{s}(u^i),$$
$$\bar{s}(u^i) \equiv \bar{s}^{u^i}_{\varepsilon_a(u^i)},$$

and $\bar{s}^{u^i}_{\varepsilon_a(u^i)}$ is as defined in Remark 8.5.

Proof. Since $u \notin \mathscr{D}$ and $u^i \to \bar{u}$ in the strong topology of L_∞, it follows from Lemma 8.4 that there exist a positive integer i_0 and an $\hat{\varepsilon} > 0$ such that, for all $i \geq i_0$,

$$\bar{\psi}_{\varepsilon_a(u^i)}(u^i) \leq -\varepsilon_a(u^i) \leq -\hat{\varepsilon}. \tag{8.27}$$

By the mean-value theorem, we have

$$J^0[u^i + \omega\bar{s}(u^i)] - J^0(u^i) = \int_0^1 J^0_{[u^i+\tau\omega\bar{s}(u^i)]}[\omega\bar{s}(u^i)]\,d\tau. \tag{8.28}$$

From (8.28), Remark 8.5, and (8.27), it follows that

$$\begin{aligned}
&J^0(u^i + \omega\bar{s}(u^i)) - J^0(u^i) - \omega\alpha\bar{\psi}_{\varepsilon_a(u^i)}(u^i)\\
&= \omega J^0_{u^i}[s(u^i)] - \omega\alpha\bar{\psi}_{\varepsilon_a(u^i)}(u^i)\\
&\quad + \omega\int_0^1 \{J^0_{[u^i+\tau\omega\bar{s}(u^i)]}[\bar{s}(u^i)] - J^0_{u^i}[\bar{s}(u^i)]\}\,d\tau\\
&\le \omega\left[(1-\alpha)\bar{\psi}_{\varepsilon_a(u^i)}(u) + \int_0^1 \|J^0_{[u^i+\sigma\omega\bar{s}(u^i)]} - J^0_{u^i}\|\,\|\bar{s}(u^i)\|_\infty\,d\tau\right]\\
&\le \omega\left[-(1-\alpha)\hat{\varepsilon} + \int_0^1 \|J^0_{[u^i+\tau\omega\bar{s}(u^i)]} - J^0_{u^i}\|\,\|\bar{s}(u^i)\|_\infty\,d\tau\right].
\end{aligned} \tag{8.29}$$

Let

$$\bar{c} \equiv \sup\{|u - v| : u, v \in U\}.$$

Then it is clear that

$$\|\bar{s}(u^i)\|_\infty \le \bar{c},$$

for all i.

From Theorem 8.1 we recall that J^0_u is uniformly continuous on $\mathscr{U}$. Thus there exists an integer $\hat{k}_0$ such that, for all $\omega \in [0, (\beta)^{\hat{k}_0}]$ and for all $\tau \in [0, 1]$,

$$\bar{c}\|J^0_{[u^i+\tau\omega\bar{s}(u^i)]} - J^0_{u^i}\| \le (1-\alpha)\hat{\varepsilon}.$$

Hence, for all $i \ge i_0$ and for all $\omega \in [0, (\beta)^{\hat{k}_0}]$,

$$J^0(u^i + \omega\bar{s}(u^i)) - J^0(u^i) \le \omega\alpha\bar{\psi}_{\varepsilon_a(u^i)}(u^i) \le -\omega\alpha\hat{\varepsilon}.$$

By similar arguments we can conclude that there exist positive integers $\hat{k}_j$, $j = 1, \ldots, l$, such that, for each $j = 1, \ldots, l$,

$$J^j(u^i + \omega\bar{s}(u^i)) - J^j(u^i) \le 0,$$

for all $i \ge i_0$ and for all $\omega \in [0, (\beta)^{\hat{k}_j}]$. Setting $\hat{k} \equiv \max\{\hat{k}_0, \hat{k}_1, \ldots, \hat{k}_l\}$ and $\delta \equiv (\beta)^{\hat{k}}\alpha\hat{\varepsilon}$, we obtain the conclusion of the lemma. ■

The next two corollaries follow from Lemma 8.4 and Lemma 8.5.

COROLLARY 8.1. *For any $u^i \in \mathscr{F}\backslash\mathscr{D}$, the computations of $\varepsilon_a(u^i)$ and $k(u^i)$ in Algorithm 8.2 require only a finite number of iterations.*

COROLLARY 8.2. *Suppose u^* is an optimal control, then $u^* \in \mathscr{D}$.*

Proof. Suppose $u^* \notin \mathscr{D}$. Then by a similar argument as that given for Lemma 8.5, it can be shown that there exists a $\delta > 0$ and a $u^{*,\prime} \in \mathscr{F}$ such that

$$J^0(u^{*,\prime}) - J^0(u^*) \le -\delta.$$

This contradicts the optimality of u^* and hence the proof is complete. ∎

We are now in a position to present the convergence theorem.

THEOREM 8.2. *Let $\{u^i\}$ be a sequence of feasible controls generated by Algorithm 8.2. Then either the sequence is finite, in which case the algorithm jams in the inner loop of Steps 2 and 3 and the last element of the sequence is in $\mathscr{D}$, or the sequence is infinite and each L_∞ accumulation point is in $\mathscr{D}$.*

Proof. From Corollary 8.1 we note that the algorithm can jam only if the last u^i is in $\mathscr{D}$. Therefore, it remains to prove the second part of the theorem. Suppose $\{u^i\}$ is infinite and u^* is an L_∞ accumulation point of $\{u^i\}$. Then there exists a subsequence $\{u^{i(k)}\}$ of the sequence $\{u^i\}$ such that $u^{i(k)} \to u^*$ in the strong topology of L_∞, as $k \to \infty$. Since $\{J^0(u^i)\}$ is monotonically decreasing, it follows that

$$J^0(u^{i(k+1)}) - J^0(u^{i(k)}) \le J^0(u^{i(k)+1}) - J^0(u^{i(k)}). \tag{8.30}$$

Suppose u^* is not in $\mathscr{D}$. Then for sufficiently large k, we have, by inequality (8.30) and Lemma 8.5,

$$J^0(u^{i(k+1)}) - J^0(u^{i(k)}) \le -\delta, \tag{8.31}$$

where $\delta > 0$ is a constant independent of integers $i(k)$, $k = 1, 2, \ldots$.

We now note that J^0 is continuous in u with respect to the strong topology of L_∞. Thus by taking the limit in (8.31), we obtain

$$0 \le -\delta.$$

This is a contradiction and hence the proof is complete. ∎

IV.9. The Finite Element Method†

In view of the algorithms developed in Section III.6 and Sections 6 and 8, we see that certain discretization schemes of these algorithms are needed in practice. In this section we shall adopt a different approach in the sense that

† This section was written on the basis of an unpublished work by K. L. Teo, H. Tao, and D. J. Clements under the support of the Australian Research Grants Committee. The first author wishes to acknowledge Mr. Tao and Dr. Clements for their contribution and the Australian Grants Committee for the financial support.

a distributed optimal control problem is discretized first and then a computational algorithm is devised for the discretized problem. The main tool for the discretization is the well-known finite element Galerkin's scheme. The key features are as follows.

(i) The spatial domain is divided into finite elements, usually of the same shape.

(ii) On each element, the state and distributed control are represented by polynomials in such a way that the collections of the interpolation polynomials over the whole domain provide piecewise approximations to state and distributed control. These piecewise approximate polynomials are continuous and possess a certain order of differentiability at the inner-element boundary.

(iii) Using Galerkin's method, the given distributed optimal control problem is approximated by an optimal control problem involving a lumped parameter system, in which the state and distributed control are represented by piecewise polynomials. The objective functional is expressed in terms of state and control variables of the lumped parameter problem.

To simplify the discussion, this technique is illustrated for a specific problem arising in the study of advertising.

In [TC.1] the Vidale–Wolfe model (for details, see Section 7) is modified to a second-order model by making the rate of change of sales rate depends explicitly on a weighted sum of the entire past history of advertising expenditures. However, this modified model simplifies the Vidale–Wolfe model by eliminating a term that allows for the reduced effect of advertising as the sales rate approaches the full market potential. This restriction is removed in [Boy.1]. The new model is

$$\frac{dy(t)}{dt} = -y(t) + K_1[1 - y(t)] \int_{-\infty}^{t} v(\tau)e^{-K_2(t-\tau)}\, d\tau, \qquad t \in (0, T), \quad (9.1)$$

where K_1 and K_2 are positive constants, $T = 1$, and y is as defined for Eq. (7.10).

Clearly, Eq. (9.1) can be readily written as

$$dy(t)/dt = -y(t) + [1 - y(t)]x(t), \qquad t \in (0, 1), \quad (9.2a)$$

$$dx(t)/dt = -K_2 x(t) + K_1 v(t), \qquad t \in (0, 1), \quad (9.2b)$$

where

$$x(t) \equiv K_1 \int_{-\infty}^{t} v(\tau)e^{-K_2(t-\tau)}\, d\tau \quad (9.3)$$

is the accumulated advertising effectiveness.

In this section we shall study a stochastic version of this model.

Let us now assume that the rate of change of the sales rate includes a white noise component. In addition, we introduce a white noise component in the rate of change of the accumulated advertising effectiveness. Both these noises are assumed to be statistically independent. Since the accumulated advertising effectiveness cannot be measured, we assume that the controller is of the form $v(t, y(t))$. Now, to be consistent in notation with Section 7, the sales rates y and the accumulated advertising effectiveness x are to be written as ξ_1 and ξ_2, respectively. At this stage we are in a position to write down the corresponding stochastic model:

$$d\xi_1(t) = [-\xi_1(t) + (1 - \xi_1(t))\xi_2(t)]\,dt + K_3\,dW_1(t), \qquad t \in (0, 1), \tag{9.4a}$$

$$d\xi_2(t) = [-K_2\xi_2(t) + K_1 v(t, \xi_1(t))]\,dt + K_4\,dW_2(t), \qquad t \in (0, 1), \tag{9.4b}$$

$$\xi_1(0) = \xi_1^0, \tag{9.4c}$$

$$\xi_2(0) = \xi_2^0, \tag{9.4d}$$

where K_3 and K_4 are positive constants, W_1 and W_2 standard Wiener processes that are statistically independent, and the initial state (ξ_1^0, ξ_2^0) a random variable with known probability density q^0 and is statistically independent of the Wiener processes W_1 and W_2.

In this stochastic model we assume that the system stops if the sales rate fall to zero because this corresponds roughly to bankruptcy. The system also stops if the sales rate encompasses the entire potential market because this corresponds to an almost impossible situation. The system will also stop if the accumulated advertising effectiveness falls to zero because the firm is then likely not to be a viable ongoing concern in the future. To ensure that the state space is bounded, an upper limit of 1 is placed on $\xi_2(t)$. We could again postulate that the upper limit corresponds to an almost impossible situation.

On the basis of the discussion given in the preceding paragraph, we can define the corresponding stopping time for system (9.4) as follows:

$$\tau \equiv \inf\{\{t \in [0, 1] : \xi_1 \notin (0, 1) \quad \text{or} \quad \xi_2 \notin (0, 1)\} \cup \{1\}\}. \tag{9.5}$$

We now assume that the class $\hat{\mathscr{U}}$ of admissible controls consists only of those measurable functions from $(0, 1) \times (0, 1)$ into $[0, 1]$.

Corresponding to system (9.4), our aim is to find an admissible control v^* that maximizes the profit functional

$$J(v) = \mathscr{E}\left\{\int_0^\tau [K_5\xi_1(t) - K_6 v(t, \xi_1(t))]\,dt\right\}, \tag{9.6}$$

over $\hat{\mathscr{U}}$, where $\mathscr{E}$ denotes the standard mathematical expectation, and K_5 and K_6 are positive constants.

This stochastic optimal control problem can be converted, using the results in Appendix A.1, to the deterministic optimal control problem P to be defined later.

Consider the parabolic partial differential operator $L(u)$ defined by

$$L(u)\psi \equiv \psi_t - [\tfrac{1}{2}(K_3)^2\psi_{x_1}]_{x_1} - [\tfrac{1}{2}(K_4)^2\psi_{x_2}]_{x_2} + [x_1 - (1 - x_1)x_2]\psi_{x_1} + [K_2 x_2 - K_1 u(x_1, t)]\psi_{x_2}. \quad (9.7)$$

Let

$$\partial\Omega \equiv \{(x_1, x_2) \in [0, 1] \times [0, 1] : \text{either} \quad x_1 = 0 \text{ or } 1, \text{ or } x_2 = 0 \text{ or } 1\}, \quad (9.8)$$

and let $\mathscr{U}$ be the class of all those functions u such that

$$u(x_1, t) = v(1 - t. x_1)$$

with $v \in \hat{\mathscr{U}}$.

The distributed optimal control problem P may now be specified as follows.

Subject to the dynamical system

$$L(u)\phi(x_1, x_2, t) = K_5 x_1 - K_6 u(x_1, t), \quad (x_1, x_2, t) \in (0, 1) \times (0, 1) \times (0.1), \quad (9.9a)$$

$$\phi(x_1, x_2, 0) = 0, \qquad (x_1, x_2) \in (0, 1) \times (0, 1), \quad (9.9b)$$

$$\phi(x_1, x_2, t) = 0, \qquad (x_1, x_2, t) \in \partial\Omega \times [0, 1], \quad (9.9c)$$

find a control $u^* \in \mathscr{U}$ such that the objective functional

$$J(u) = \int_0^1 \int_0^1 \phi(x_1, x_2, 1) q^0(x_1, x_2)\, dx_1\, dx_2 \quad (9.9d)$$

is minimized over $\mathscr{U}$.

Clearly, problem P is an infinite dimensional optimal control problem. Using the finite-element Galerkin approach, this infinite dimensional problem can be approximated into a finite dimensional one. For this, let Ω ($\equiv (0, 1) \times (0,1)$) be subdivided into $N_1 N_2$ rectangles (called finite elements) as shown in Fig. 3. Let $S_1(x)$ denote the first-order spline function:

$$S_1(x) = \begin{cases} 1 + x, & x \in [-1, 0], \\ 1 - x, & x \in [0, 1], \\ 0, & \text{elsewhere.} \end{cases} \quad (9.10)$$

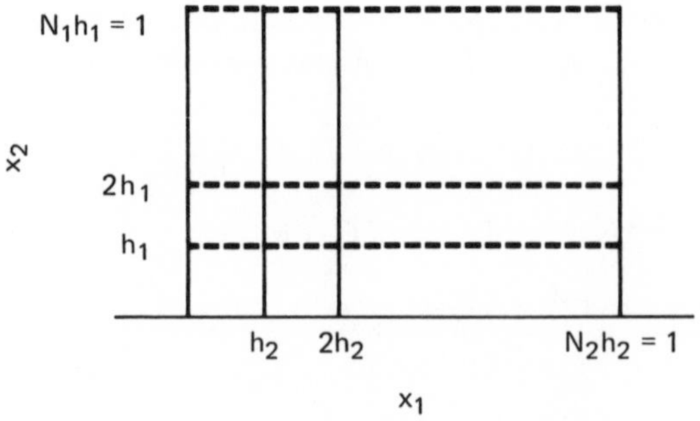

Fig. 3. Partition of the domain Ω.

Define

$$\Phi_i(x_1, x_2) = \Phi_{i_1}(x_1)\Phi_{i_2}(x_2), \tag{9.11}$$

where

$$\Phi_{i_1}(x_1) \equiv S_1\left(\frac{x_1}{h_1} - i_1\right), \tag{9.12a}$$

$$\Phi_{i_2}(x_2) \equiv S_1\left(\frac{x_2}{h_2} - i_2\right), \tag{9.12b}$$

$i \equiv (i_1, i_2)$, $i_1 = 0, 1, \ldots, N_1$, and $i_2 = 0, 1, \ldots, N_2$.

Using a finite-element scheme, we approximate, respectively, state and distributed control with the relations

$$\phi^N(x_1, x_2, t) = \sum_{i\in I} \Psi_i(t)\Phi_{i_1}(x_1)\Phi_{i_2}(x_2), \tag{9.13}$$

and

$$u^N(x_1, t) = \sum_{k_1=0}^{N_1} V_{k_1}(t)\Phi_{k_1}(x_1), \tag{9.14}$$

where $\Psi_i(t)$ and $V_{k_1}(t)$ represents the nodal values of state and distributed control variables; and

$$I \equiv \{(i_1, i_2) : i_1 = 0, 1, \ldots, N_1; i_2 = 0, 1, \ldots, N_2\}. \tag{9.15}$$

In view of the definition of $\mathscr{U}$ we note that

$$0 \le V_{k_1}(t) \le 1, \qquad k_1 = 0, 1, \ldots, N_1, \tag{9.16}$$

for all $t \in [0, 1]$.

Let $\mathscr{X}$ denote the class of all measurable functions $V \equiv (V_0, V_1, \ldots, V_{N_1})$ defined on $[0, 1]$ such that V_{k_1}, $k_1 = 0, 1, \ldots, N_1$, satisfy constraints (9.16).

Substituting Φ^N and u^N for ϕ and u, respectively, in Eq. (9.9a), we obtain

$$R_d = L(u^N)\phi^N(x_1, x_2, t) - K_5 x_1 + K_6 u^N(x, t). \tag{9.17}$$

The finite-element Galerkin equations are

$$\iint_\Omega \Phi_j L(u^N)\phi^N(x_1, x_2, t)\, dx_1\, dx_2 = \iint_\Omega \Phi_j[K_5 x_1 - K_6 u^N(x_1, t)]\, dx_1\, dx_2,$$

$$j \equiv (j_1, j_2) \in I. \tag{9.18}$$

Integrating the second-order terms by parts and using the boundary conditions, we obtain

$$\begin{aligned}
&\sum_{i\in I} \frac{d\Psi_i(t)}{dt} \iint_\Omega \Phi_j \Phi_i\, dx_1\, dx_2 \\
&\quad + \sum_{i\in I} \Psi_i(t) \iint_\Omega \left[\tfrac{1}{2}(K_3)^2 \frac{\partial \Phi_j}{\partial x_1}\frac{\partial \Phi_i}{\partial x_1} + \tfrac{1}{2}(K_4)^2 \frac{\partial \Phi_j}{\partial x_2}\frac{\partial \Phi_i}{\partial x_2} \right.\\
&\qquad\qquad \left. + \Phi_j \gamma \frac{\partial \Phi_i}{\partial x_1} + K_2 x_2 \Phi_j \frac{\partial \Phi_i}{\partial x_2}\right] dx_1\, dx_2 \\
&\quad - \sum_{i\in I} \Psi_i(t) \sum_{k_1=0}^{N_1} V_{k_1}(t) \iint_\Omega K_1 \Phi_j(x_1, x_2)\Phi_{k_1}(x_1) \frac{\partial \Phi_i}{\partial x_2}\, dx_1\, dx_2 \\
&= K_5 \iint_\Omega x_1 \Phi_j(x_1, x_2)\, dx_1\, dx_2 \\
&\quad - K_6 \sum_{k_1=0}^{N_1} V_{k_1}(t) \iint_\Omega \Phi_j(x_1, x_2)\Phi_{k_1}(x_1)\, dx_1\, dx_2,
\end{aligned} \tag{9.19}$$

where $j \in I$ and

$$\gamma(x_1, x_2) \equiv x_1 - (1 - x_1)x_2. \tag{9.20}$$

Since ϕ^N, defined by (9.13), must satisfy initial condition (9.9b) and boundary condition (9.9c), it follows that

$$\Psi_{(j_1, N_2)}(t) = 0, \qquad j_1 = 0, 1, \ldots, N_1, \tag{9.21a}$$

$$\Psi_{(N_1, j_2)}(t) = 0, \qquad j_2 = 0, 1, \ldots, N_2, \tag{9.21b}$$

$$\Psi_{(j_1, 0)}(t) = 0, \qquad j_1 = 0, 1, \ldots, N_1, \tag{9.21c}$$

$$\Psi_{(0, j_2)}(t) = 0, \qquad j_2 = 0, 1, \ldots, N_2, \tag{9.21d}$$

$$\Psi_{(j_1, j_2)}(0) = 0, \qquad j \equiv (j_1, j_2) \in I, \tag{9.21e}$$

Thus Eqs. (9.19) need only to be considered when $j_1 = 1, \ldots, N_1 - 1$ and $j_2 = 1, \ldots, N_2 - 1$. This set of equations is now written in a matrix form as

$$A\frac{d\Psi(t)}{dt} + [B - D(V(t))]\Psi(t) = E - FV(t), \tag{9.22}$$

where

$$\begin{aligned}
\Psi(t) &\equiv (\Psi_{(1,1)}(t), \Psi_{(2,1)}(t), \ldots, \Psi_{(N_1-1,N_2-1)}(t)),\\
A &\equiv (a_{ij}), \qquad B \equiv (b_{ij}),\\
V(t) &\equiv (V_0(t), V_1(t), \ldots, V_{N_1}(t)),\\
D(V(t)) &\equiv (D(V)_{ij}(t)),\\
D(V)_{ij}(t) &\equiv \sum_{k_1=0}^{N_1} D_{ijk_1}V_{k_1}(t),\\
E &\equiv (E_j),\\
F &\equiv (f_{ik_1}).
\end{aligned}$$

The elements of all these matrices can be calculated explicitly according to the following formulas:

$$a_{ij} \equiv \iint_\Omega \Phi_{j_1}(x_1)\Phi_{j_2}(x_2)\Phi_{i_1}(x_1)\Phi_{i_2}(x_2)\,dx_1\,dx_2, \tag{9.23a}$$

$$\begin{aligned}
b_{ij} \equiv {} & \iint_\Omega \left\{\tfrac{1}{2}(K_3)^2 \frac{d\Phi_{j_1}(x_1)}{dx_1}\frac{d\Phi_{i_1}(x_1)}{dx_1}\Phi_{j_2}(x_2)\Phi_{i_2}(x_2)\right.\\
& \left. + \tfrac{1}{2}(K_4)^2\Phi_{j_1}(x_1)\Phi_{i_1}(x_1)\frac{d\Phi_{j_2}(x_2)}{dx_2}\frac{d\Phi_{i_2}(x_2)}{dx_2}\right\}dx_1\,dx_2\\
& + \iint_\Omega \gamma(x_1, x_2)\Phi_{j_1}(x_1)\frac{d\Phi_{i_1}(x_1)}{dx_1}\Phi_{j_2}(x_2)\Phi_{i_2}(x_2)\,dx_1\,dx_2\\
& + \iint_\Omega K_2 x_2 \Phi_{j_1}(x_1)\Phi_{i_1}(x_1)\Phi_{j_2}(x_2)\frac{d\Phi_{i_2}(x_2)}{dx_2}\,dx_1\,dx_2,
\end{aligned} \tag{9.23b}$$

$$D_{ijk_1} \equiv \iint_\Omega K_1\Phi_{j_1}(x_1)\Phi_{j_2}(x_2)\Phi_{i_1}(x_1)\frac{d\Phi_{i_2}(x_2)}{dx_2}\Phi_{k_1}(x_1)\,dx_1\,dx_2, \tag{9.23c}$$

$$E_j \equiv K_5 \iint_\Omega x_1 \Phi_{j_1}(x_1)\Phi_{j_2}(x_2)\,dx_1\,dx_2, \tag{9.23d}$$

$$f_{jk_1} \equiv K_6 \iint_\Omega \Phi_{j_1}(x_1)\Phi_{k_1}(x_1)\Phi_{j_2}(x_2)\,dx_1\,dx_2. \tag{9.23e}$$

To go a step further we define

$$(x_1/h_1) - j_1 = \zeta_1, \qquad (x_2/h_2) - j_2 = \zeta_2.$$

Then it follows from (9.12) that

$$\begin{aligned} a_{ij} &= h_1 h_2 \int_{-j_1}^{N_1 - j_1} S_1(\zeta_1)S_1(\zeta_1 + j_1 - i_1)\,d\zeta_1 \int_{-j_2}^{N_2 - j_2} S_1(\zeta_2)S_1(\zeta_2 + j_2 - i_2)\,d\zeta_2 \\ &= h_1 h_2 \int_{-1}^{1} S_1(\zeta_1)S_1(\zeta_1 + j_1 - i_1)\,d\zeta_1 \int_{-1}^{1} S_1(\zeta_2)S_1(\zeta_2 + j_2 - i_2)\,d\zeta_2, \end{aligned} \tag{9.24a}$$

where $i \equiv (i_1, i_2)$, $j \equiv (j_1, j_2) \in I$;

$$\begin{aligned} b_{ij} &= \tfrac{1}{2}(K_3)^2(h_2/h_1) \int_{-j_1}^{N_1 - j_1} S_1'(\zeta_1)S_1'(\zeta_1 + j_1 - i_1)\,d\zeta_1 \\ &\quad \times \int_{-j_2}^{N_2 - j_2} S_1(\zeta_2)S_1(\zeta_2 + j_2 - i_2)\,d\zeta_2 \\ &\quad + \tfrac{1}{2}(K_4)^2(h_1/h_2) \int_{-j_1}^{N_1 - j_1} S_1(\zeta_1)S_1(\zeta_1 + j_1 - i_1)\,d\zeta_1 \\ &\quad \times \int_{-j_2}^{N_2 - j_2} S_1'(\zeta_2)S_1'(\zeta_2 + j_2 - i_2)\,d\zeta_2 \\ &\quad + \int_{-j_1}^{N_2 - j_1} \left\{ \int_{-j_2}^{N_2 - j_2} \gamma((\zeta_1 + j_1)h_1, (\zeta_2 + j_2)h_2)S_1(\zeta_1)S_1'(\zeta_1 + j_1 - i_1)\,d\zeta_1 \right\} \\ &\quad \times S_1(\zeta_2)S_1(\zeta_2 + j_2 - i_2)\,d\zeta \\ &\quad + K_2 \int_{-j_1}^{N_1 - j_1} S_1(\zeta_1)S_1(\zeta_1 + j_1 - i_1)\,d\zeta_1 \\ &\quad \times \int_{-j_2}^{N_2 - j_2} (\zeta_2 h_2 + j_2 h_2)S_1(\zeta_2)S_1'(\zeta_2 + j_2 - i_2)\,d\zeta_2 \end{aligned} \tag{9.24b}$$

[*continued*]

$$= \tfrac{1}{2}(K_3)^2(h_2/h_1) \int_{-1}^{1} S_1'(\zeta_1)S_1'(\zeta_1 + j_1 - i_1)\, d\zeta_1$$

$$\times \int_{-1}^{1} S_1(\zeta_2)S_1(\zeta_2 + j_2 - i_2)\, d\zeta_2$$

$$+ \tfrac{1}{2}(K_4)^2(h_1/h_2) \int_{-1}^{1} S_1(\zeta_1)S_1(\zeta_1 + j_1 - i_1)\, d\zeta_1$$

$$\times \int_{-1}^{1} S_1'(\zeta_2)S_1'(\zeta_2 + j_2 - i_2)\, d\zeta_2$$

$$+ h_2 \int_{-1}^{1} \left\{ \int_{-1}^{1} \gamma((\zeta_1 + j_1)h_1, (\zeta_2 + j_2)h_2)S_1(\zeta_1)S_1'(\zeta_1 + j_1 - i_1)\, d\zeta_1 \right\}$$

$$\times S_1(\zeta_2)S_1(\zeta_2 + j_2 - i_2)\, d\zeta_2$$

$$+ K_2 h_1 h_2 \int_{-1}^{1} S_1(\zeta_1)S_1(\zeta_1 + j_1 - i_1)\, d\zeta_1$$

$$\times \int_{-1}^{1} (\zeta_2 + j_2)S_1(\zeta_2)S_1'(\zeta_2 + j_2 - i_2)\, d\zeta_2,$$

where $i, j \in I$;

$$D_{ijk_1} = h_1 K_1 \int_{-j_1}^{N_1 - j} S_1(\zeta_1)S_1(\zeta_1 + j_1 - i_1)S_1(\zeta_1 + j_1 - k_1)\, d\zeta_1$$

$$\times \int_{-j_2}^{N_2 - j_2} S_1(\zeta_2)S_1'(\zeta_2 + j_2 - i_2)\, d\zeta_2$$

$$= h_1 K_1 \int_{-1}^{1} S_1(\zeta_1)S_1(\zeta_1 + j_1 - i_1)S_1(\zeta_1 + j_1 - k_1)\, d\zeta_1$$

$$\times \int_{-1}^{1} S_1(\zeta_2)S_1'(\zeta_2 + j_2 - i_2)\, d\zeta_2, \tag{9.24c}$$

where $i, j \in I$ and $k_1 = 0, 1, \ldots, N_1$;

$$E_j = K_5(h_1)^2 h_2 \int_{-j_1}^{N_1 - j_1} (\zeta_1 + j_1)S_1(\zeta_1)\, d\zeta_1 \int_{-j_2}^{N_2 - j_2} S_1(\zeta_2)\, d\zeta_2$$

$$= K_5(h_1)^2 h_2 \int_{-1}^{1} (\zeta_1 + j_1)S_1(\zeta_1)\, d\zeta_1, \tag{9.24d}$$

where $j \in I$; and

$$f_{jk_1} = K_6 h_1 h_2 \int_{-j_1}^{N_1 - j_1} S_1(\zeta_1) S_1(\zeta_1 + j_1 - k_1)\, d\zeta_1 \int_{-j_2}^{N_2 - j_2} S_1(\zeta_2)\, d\zeta_2$$

$$= K_6 h_1 h_2 \int_{-1}^{1} S_1(\zeta_1) S_1(\zeta_1 + j_1 - k_1)\, d\zeta_1, \tag{9.24e}$$

where $j \in I$ and $k_1 = 0, 1, \ldots, N_1$.

Assuming $q^0(x_1, x_2) = 1$, the objective functional defined by (9.9d) is approximated by

$$J^N(V) = \iint_\Omega \sum_{i \in I} \Psi_i(1) \Phi_{i_1}(x_1) \Phi_{i_2}(x_2)\, dx_1\, dx_2$$

$$= h_1 h_2 \sum_{i \in I} \Psi_i(1) \int_{-i_1}^{N_1 - i_1} S_1(\zeta_1)\, d\zeta_1 \int_{-i_2}^{N_2 - i_2} S_1(\zeta_2)\, d\zeta_2$$

$$= h_1 h_2 \sum_{i \in I} \Psi_i(1) \equiv G^{\mathrm{T}} \Psi(1), \tag{9.25}$$

where G is an $(N_1 - 1)(N_2 - 1)$ dimensional column vector defined by

$$G \equiv (h_1 h_2, \ldots, h_1 h_2),$$

and the superscript T denotes the transpose.

The approximate problem to the optimal control problem P may now be stated as follows.

Subject to the dynamical system

$$d\Psi(t)/dt = A^{-1}[-B + D(V(t))]\Psi(t) - A^{-1}FV(t) + A^{-1}E, \tag{9.26a}$$

$$\Psi(0) = 0, \tag{9.26b}$$

find a control $V^* \in \mathscr{X}$ so that the objective functional

$$J^N(V) = G^{\mathrm{T}} \Psi(1) \tag{9.27}$$

is maximized over $\mathscr{X}$.

For convenience this approximate optimal control problem is to be referred to as P^N.

The Hamiltonian function for the optimal control problem P^N is

$$H \equiv [-A^{-1}B\Psi + A^{-1}E]^T Z + [A^{-1}D(V)\Psi - A^{-1}FV]^{\mathrm{T}} Z, \tag{9.28}$$

and the costate system is

$$\frac{dZ(t)}{dt} = -\frac{\partial H}{\partial \Psi} = [A^{-1}B - A^{-1}D(V(t))]^{\mathrm{T}} Z, \tag{9.29a}$$

$$Z(1) = G. \tag{9.29b}$$

TABLE 1

Values of $\sigma^{k_1, l}$ with $N = (4, 4)$

	k_1				
l	0	1	2	3	4
1	0.49997	0.49986	0.49979	0.49981	0.49996
2	0.49885	0.49927	0.49885	0.49897	0.49979
3	0.49917	0.49608	0.49385	0.49440	0.49886
4	0.49567	0.48021	0.46902	0.47121	0.49413
5	0.47947	0.41129	0.36180	0.36758	0.47271
6	0.41864	0.16842	0.00000	0.00000	0.39462
7	0.24157	0.00000	0.00000	0.00000	0.16586
8	0.00000	0.00000	0.00000	0.00000	0.00000
9	0.00000	0.00000	0.00000	0.00000	0.00000
10	0.00000	0.00000	0.00000	0.00000	0.00000

TABLE 2

Values of $\sigma^{k_1, l}$ with $N = (6, 6)$

	k_1						
l	0	1	2	3	4	5	6
1	0.48455	0.47090	0.54582	0.42525	0.58088	0.42112	0.47120
2	0.51641	0.52908	0.45601	0.57106	0.41868	0.57961	0.52905
3	0.49428	0.48914	0.50875	0.47411	0.51862	0.47072	0.49013
4	0.50288	0.49951	0.47534	0.49535	0.45723	0.50198	0.50373
5	0.49531	0.47142	0.43382	0.42055	0.39489	0.43223	0.48810
6	0.45794	0.36566	0.32832	0.15389	0.25682	0.15950	0.41916
7	0.46068	0.26636	0.00000	0.00000	0.00000	0.00000	0.40303
8	0.38059	0.00000	0.00000	0.00000	0.00000	00.0000	0.24006
9	0.26793	0.00000	0.00000	0.00000	0.00000	0.00000	0.00000
10	0.00000	0.00000	0.00000	0.00000	0.00000	0.00000	0.00000

Now, for each given $N \equiv (N_1, N_2)$, problem P^N can be solved by using the control parametrization method reported in Appendix A.V. To use this method, we partition the time interval [0, 1] into p equal subintervals for the control function V. Then with $K_1 = 10$, $K_2 = 1$, $K_3 = 1$, $K_4 = 1$, $K_5 = 1$, $K_6 = 10$, and $p = 10$, the problem P^N is solved with $N \equiv (N_1, N_2) = (4, 4)$, and $(6, 6)$. The suboptimal values of the objective functionals

$J^{(4,4)}$ and $J^{(6,6)}$ are 0.03644 and 0.031567, respectively. The corresponding suboptimal controls are given by

$$u^{N_1}(x_1, t) = \sum_{k_1=0}^{N_1} \left\{ \sum_{l=1}^{10} \sigma^{k_1,l} \chi_{[t_{l-1}, t_l)}(t) \right\} \Phi_{k_1}(x_1),$$

where $N = (4, 4)$ and $(6, 6)$, χ_Z denotes the indicator function of the set Z, $\Phi_{k_1}(x_1)$, $k_1 = 0, 1, \ldots, N_1$, are as defined by (9.12a), and $\sigma^{k_1,1}$, $k_1 = 0, 1, \ldots, N_1$; $l = 1, \ldots, 10$ are given in Tables 1 and 2.

IV.10. Discussion

The gradient method was first suggested to optimal control problems of lumped parameter systems in 1962 by Kelly [K.1].

In [Le.1] a general convergence theorem (similar to, but not identical with, that of Theorem 6.2) for gradient algorithms in normed spaces is given and applied to unconstrained optimal control problems of lumped parameter systems.

In [Le.2] it is shown that in the standard control problem of a lumped parameter system, the trajectory is, in general, a continuously Fréchet differentiable function of the control, with the space of admissible controls being given the supremum norm. A formula is given for the Fréchet derivative. From this formula it follows that a general cost functional on the system is a Fréchet differentiable functional of the control. It is further shown in [Le.2] that similar results are also true for neutral time-lag systems.

If the control region is a compact subset of a Euclidean Space, then the gradient algorithms of [Le.1] and [Le.2] are not directly applicable.

Intuitively, control constraints can be handled by algorithms of the penalty function type. However, these algorithms are sometimes computationally very expensive. Thus there is a need for other more suitable algorithms, such as the gradient projection algorithm discussed in [LP.1]. The gradient algorithm of [Le.1] can also be modified to produce a suitable algorithm. This is done along the line of the conditional gradient method found in the constrained optimization theory of finite dimensional space. We refer the interested reader to [PD.1] for a well-written discussion on this latter topic.

The modification of the gradient algorithm of [Le.1] is carried out for optimal distributed parameter system of a parabolic type with piecewise continuous controls in Chapter V of [R.1] under the name of projected gradient method, where the convergence result is in the form of Theorem 6.2. In [WuT.3] a similar approach is applied to an optimal control problem involving a class of hyperbolic partial differential equations with Darboux boundary conditions, where the class of admissible controls consists, however, of bounded measurable controls. Furthermore, the algorithm is now called the conditional gradient algorithm.

Up to and including Section 7 of this Chapter, the optimization problem under discussion is the one considered in Chapter V of [R.1] but with piecewise continuous controls replaced by bounded measurable controls. The proofs of Theorem 5.1 and Lemma 6.1 are in line with the corresponding parts of [WuT.3]; and the other results are adapted from those reported in Chapter V and Chapter VI of [R.1]. The uniform continuity of the Fréchet derivative of the cost functional (see Theorem 5.2) is a crucial property needed in the proof of the convergence result of Theorem 6.2.

Consider optimization problem P, but with $\mathscr{D}_p$ replaced by $\mathscr{D}$. This modified problem is to be referred to as $\hat{\mathrm{P}}$. We can devise a conjugate gradient algorithm for solving problem $\hat{\mathrm{P}}$. For this we first reduce from formula (5.1) that the gradient $J_{(\sigma^0, u^0)}$ of the cost functional J at $(\sigma^0, u^0) \in \mathscr{D}$ is given by

$$J_{(\sigma^0, u^0)} \equiv \Big(\iint_Q I(\sigma^0, u^0)_\sigma[x, t, \sigma^0, u^0(\hat{x}, t)] z(\sigma^0, u^0)\, dx\, dt,$$

$$\int_{\Omega_{\hat{x}}} I(\sigma^0, u^0)_v[\cdot, \hat{\hat{x}}, \cdot, \sigma^0, u^0(\cdot, \cdot)] z(\sigma^0, u^0)(\cdot, \hat{\hat{x}}, \cdot)\, d\hat{\hat{x}} \Big).$$

The details of this conjugate gradient algorithm may now be stated as follows.

Step 0 Select a policy $(\sigma^0, u^0) \in \mathscr{D}$. If $J_{(\sigma^0, u^0)}[(\sigma^0, u^0)] = 0$, stop; else go to Step 1.

Step 1 Set $k = 0$ and set $(\delta^0, w^0) = (\rho^0, \Delta^0) = J_{(\sigma^0, u^0)}$.

Step 2 Compute $\lambda_k > 0$ such that

$$J(\sigma^k + \lambda_k \delta^k, u^k + \lambda_k w^k) = \min\{J(\sigma^k + \lambda \delta^k, u^k + \lambda w^k) : \lambda > 0\}.$$

Step 3 Set $(\sigma^{k+1}, u^{k+1}) = (\sigma^k, u^k) + \lambda_k(\delta^k, w^k)$.

Step 4 Compute $J_{(\sigma^{k+1}, u^{k+1})}$

Step 5 If $J_{(\sigma^{k+1}, u^{k+1})}[(\sigma^{k+1}, u^{k+1})] = 0$, stop; else, set $(\delta^{k+1}, w^{k+1}) = J_{(\sigma^{k+1}, u^{k+1})}$, and $(\rho^{k+1}, \Delta^{k+1}) = (\delta^{k+1}, w^{k+1}) + \gamma_k(\rho^k, \Delta^k)$ with

$$\gamma_k = \frac{\langle (\delta^{k+1}, w^{k+1}) - (\delta^k, w^k), (\delta^{k+1}, w^{k+1}) \rangle}{\langle (\delta^k, w^k), (\delta^k, w^k) \rangle}$$

Set $k = k + 1$ and go to Step 2.

Note that this version of the conjugate gradient algorithm is known as the Polak–Ribiére algorithm. It differs from the Fletcher–Reeves algorithm only in the formula for γ_k. For details see [P.1, p. 54].

A research monograph that contains a treatment of selected mathematical theory and applications of computational methods for optimal control problems can be found in [GS.1]. The techniques included can be viewed as extensions of nonlinear programming methods for the control of dynamic systems described by ordinary and partial differential equations.

The first chapter (of [GS.1]) contains introductory materials, including some motivational examples. In Chapter 2 inexact step length rules and their relationship to the Zontendijk condition are discussed. The emphasis of the subsequent three chapters is on quasi-Newton methods. The conjugate gradient method, as derived from quasi-Newton methods, is discussed in Chapter 6. The subject matters of Chapters 7 and 8 are the conditional gradient and projected gradient methods for constrained optimal controls problems, respectively. Chapter 9 deals with approximation-type methods. In the subsequent three chapters the focus is on the control of linear and nonlinear systems described by partial differential equations. However, the emphasis of these three chapters is different from ours. For example, no mathematical convergence results, such as Theorem 6.2, are included in [GS.1], and the types of distributed parameter systems considered in these three chapters also lack generality. Besides, the approaches are also different. The last four chapters of [GS.1] are devoted to the selection of some applications.

In [PM.2] an optimal control problem with bounded control region and terminal inequality constraints (on the state variable) is considered. However, the dynamical system involves only ordinary differential equations. Given a control u, let $S(u)$ be the set of all permissible control perturbations about u. A control perturbation that belongs to $S(u)$, and also decreases the linear approximation of the cost and ε active terminal constraints, is determined by solving an appropriate subproblem. The control perturbation is then used as a search direction. This in conjunction with a standard step length rule and a procedure for reducing ε form a complete algorithm, where ε is the parameter for determining the ε active constraints. The search direction subproblem is itself an optimal control problem for a system linear in state and control.

Two algorithms are then devised. In the first algorithm the exact solution of the search direction subproblem is needed in each iteration. Thus it is only a conceptual algorithm because the subproblem itself requires an infinite number of iterations. In the second algorithm only an approximate solution to the subproblem, with a specified degree of accuracy, is needed. Since the subproblem is convex, its approximate solution can be computed by the

Meyer–Polak proximity algorithm (see Appendix VI) in a finite number of iterations. Furthermore, the accuracy is automatically increased in such a way that the convergence in the form of Theorem 8.2 is ensured. This second algorithm is thus called an implementable algorithm.

From Remark 5.1 of [WuT.5] we note that the implementable algorithm of [MP.2] is valid *only if* the initial control is a feasible control (i.e., it must be such that the terminal inequality constraints are satisfied). Thus regarding the implementable algorithm of [PM.2], only those results related to Phase II of the algorithm are valid. In [TWC.2] these results are extended to an optimal control problem, in which the governing system is an ordinary differential equation with discrete time delayed arguments. In this reference it also contains a method that can produce a feasible control in a finite number of iterations. This method, which is obtained by using the control parametrization technique (see Appendix V) and the algorithm of [MPH.1], works like Phase I of a linear programming problem.

The results related to Phase II of the implementable algorithm of [MP.2] have also been extended to an optimal problem involving distributed parameter systems of parabolic type in [WuT.5]. This, in turn, is the main reference for Section 8.

The success of all these implementable algorithms lies heavily on the fact that the corresponding direction search subproblem is *convex*, and hence its approximate solution, up to any given degree of accuracy, can be computed by the Meyer–Polak proximity algorithm in a finite number of iterations.

Note that the gradient projection algorithms [LP.1] have not been extended to cope with optimal control problems with the terminal inequality constraints just discussed.

In [S.1] an algorithm is devised for solving optimal control problems of lumped parameter systems with state-dependent control constraints. Under certain additional assumptions, it is also shown (see Theorem 3 of [S.1]) that the sequence of controls generated by the algorithm converges locally to the optimal control. Note that the algorithm is based on the minimum principle reported in [He.1]. Note also that this algorithm has not been extended to cope with optimal control problems involving distributed parameter systems, such as those considered in this text.

The sequential gradient-restoration algorithms have been developed by A. Miele and his associates in a series of papers (see [MPD.1], [MDCT.1], [GoM.1], [MCMW.1], [ML.1] and the references cited therein).

In [MPD.1] the problem is to minimize the functional

$$J = \int_0^1 f(x, u, \pi, t)\, dt + [g(x, t, \pi)]_1$$

with respect to the functions x, u, and the parameter π, subject to the condition

$$\dot{x} - \phi(x, u, \pi, t) = 0,$$

a certain initial condition on $[x]_0$, and the final condition $[\psi(x, \pi)]_1 = 0$ (initial time $t = 0$, final time $t = 1$, $x(t)$ an n vector and π a p vector). For this Bolza problem a sequential algorithm that consists of an alternate succession of gradient and restoration phases is developed. This algorithm is devised in such a way that the differential equations and boundary conditions are satisfied at the end of each iteration. In the gradient phase nominal functions $x(t)$, $u(t)$, and parameter π satisfying all the differential equations and boundary conditions are assumed. Variations $\Delta x(t)$, $\Delta u(t)$, $\Delta\pi$ leading to varied functions $\tilde{x}(t)$, $\tilde{u}(t)$, and parameter $\tilde{\pi}$ are determined so that the value of the cost functional is decreased. A restoration phase is, in general, necessary because the constraints are only satisfied to first order during the gradient phase. In this algorithm both phases involve linear dynamics and quadratic cost functionals, leading to linear boundary-value problems.

In [MDCT.1] the work of [MPD.1] is extended to the case in which the state and control vectors satisfy algebraic relations for each instant t. The linear boundary-value problems for the two phases now involve linearized algebraic coupling relations that make their solutions more complicated. In both papers numerical results are used to demonstrate the feasibility and convergence of the respective algorithms.

In [GoM.1] two classes of optimal control problems, P_1 and P_2, are considered.

Problem P_1 is to minimize the cost functional

$$J = \int_0^1 f(x, u, \pi, t)\, dt + [h(z, \pi_0)]_0 + [g(x, \pi)]_1$$

with respect to the functions $x(t)$, $u(t)$, and the parameter π, subject to the differential constraints

$$\dot{x} - \phi(x, u, \pi, t) = 0, \qquad 0 \le t \le 1,$$

and the boundary conditions

$$y(0) = y_0,\ [w(z, \pi)]_0 = 0, \qquad \text{and} \qquad [\psi(x, \pi)]_1 = 0.$$

Here, the vector y consists of those components of the state x that are described at the initial point, and the vector z of those that are not.

Problem P_2 is a more general problem. It consists of the problem P_1 together with a nondifferentiable constraint:

$$S(x, u, \pi, t) = 0.$$

The algorithms obtained for Problems P_1 and P_2 are of the sequential gradient-restoration type. Each algorithm includes a sequence of two-phase cycles composed of a gradient phase and a restoration phase. The gradient phase is started only when $G < \varepsilon_1$, where G is the constraint error and ε_1 is a small, preassigned number. The gradient phase is characterized by a descent property on the augmented functional

$$\hat{J} = J + L,$$

where

$$L \equiv \int_0^1 \{\lambda^T(\dot{x} - \phi) + \rho^T s\}\, dt + [\sigma^T w]_0 + [\mu\psi]_1,$$

and the superscript T denotes the transpose. The descent property on the augmented functional $\hat{J}$ implies a descent property on the functional J, and the constraints are satisfied to first order. It involves one iteration. The restoration phase is started only when $G > \varepsilon_1$. It involves one or more iterations, each designed to decrease the constraint error G, and the norm squared of the variations of the control $u(t)$, the parameter π, and the missing components $z(0)$ of the initial state is minimized. The step lengths in both phases are chosen such that the restoration phase preserves the descent property of the gradient phase. In other words, they are chosen so that the value of the cost functional J at the end of each cycle is smaller than that at the beginning of the same cycle. The gradient step length is determined by a one-dimensional search on $\hat{J}$; and the restoration step length is obtained by a one-dimensional search on G. The algorithms terminated when both $G < \varepsilon_1$ and $Q < \varepsilon_2$, where Q is the error in the optimality conditions and ε_2 is a small, preassigned number. Unlike the algorithms obtained in [MPD.1] and [MDCT.1], these new algorithms do not require that the state vector be given at the initial point, and they allow for very general initial conditions. The feasibility and convergence properties of the new algorithms are indicated by many examples.

The minimization problem considered in [MCMW.1] is similar to Problem P_2 of [GoM.1], except with the initial condition being simplified to

$$x(0) = x_0,$$

where x_0 is a given n vector. The algorithm developed in [MCMW.1] is also similar to that of [GoM.1]. The main differences are (i) the ordinary gradient phase is now replaced by the conjugate gradient phase in each cycle; and (ii) since the whole state vector is now given at the initial time, there are no missing components in the initial state.

From the numerical experience found in [MCMW.1], the conjugate gradient-restoration algorithm is superior to the ordinary gradient-restoration algorithm in the situation when both algorithms are applicable.

In [ML.1] it is shown that the Lagrange multipliers associated with the gradient phase are the optimal solution to an unconstrained problem whose cost functional involves the Hamiltonian gradient with respect to controls and whose dynamic is the adjoint equation.

For other members in the family of gradient-restoration algorithms, we refer the reader to the references cited in [MPD.1], [MDCT.1], [MCMW.1], [GoM.1], and [ML.1].

In practice, algorithms developed in Sections III.6, 6, and 8 need certain discretization schemes. This approach is called "the discretized-at-the-end approach." In Section 9, a different approach is used. More precisely, both the state and distributed control are approximated in terms of first-order spline functions. (In fact, they could also be approximated in terms of higher-order spline functions.) The approximate cost functional is expressed in terms of the approximate state and control. Thus the optimal control problem of the distribution parameter system is approximated into an optimal control problem of a lumped parameter system. (This approach is called "the discretized-in-the-beginning approach".) The accuracy of the approximation depends on the dimensionality of the approximate problem. However, the exact relationship has yet to be investigated. For the approximate problem it can be solved by any algorithm for lumped parameter systems, such as those reported in [MP.1], [WP.1], [War.2] (for nonlinear systems without terminal inequality constraints), [Barn.1], [Barn.2] (for linear systems and convex cost functionals, but without terminal inequality constraints), and Appendix V (for linear systems with or without terminal inequality constraints). From our experience it appears that those algorithms based on control parametrization approach, such as those reported in [HR.1], [Si.1], [Sc.1], and Appendix V should be very efficient for most problems, and hence are recommended.

In [VW.1] Vidale and Wolfe present a simple deterministic model that describes the interaction of advertising and sales based on controlled experiments performed on a large number of products and several advertising media.

An optimal control problem involving a stochastic version of this Vidale–Wolfe model with fully observed controls is considered in [Boy.1]. A similar stochastic optimal control problem is also considered in [RT.1]. The only difference is that admissible controls are now open loop and piecewise constant with possible discontinuities at the preassigned switching points. Each stochastic optimal control problem is reduced to a deterministic problem in the form of problem P posed in Section 3; the first one is with σ deleted and the second one is with u deleted. The main tool is the appropriate result in Appendix I; and the structure of admissible controls is also used in the reduction of the second problem. Both the reduced problems are solved numerically in [Boy.1] and [RT.1], respectively.

Note that [Boy.1] and [RT.1] are the main references for those results regarding the example considered in Section 7.

In the Vidale–Wolfe model no time delay is included in the sales rate generated by advertising. In [CT.1] the model is generalized to second order by making the rate of change of sales rate explicitly depend on a weighted sum of the entire past history of advertising expenditure. This effectively includes the time delay referred to previously. However, they simplify the original model by eliminating the term that corresponds to the reduced effect of advertising as sales approach the full market potential.

This restriction is removed in Chapter 5 of [Boy.1], where stochastic elements are also introduced. The resultant model is the one considered in Section 9. The corresponding stochastic optimal control problem is reduced to a deterministic problem of the form of problem P posed in Section 3 with σ deleted by using the appropriate result in Appendix I. Following the discretized-at-the-beginning approach, the reduced problem is approximated by a sequence of optimal control problems of lumped parameter systems via first-order spline functions. Each element in the sequence corresponds to the dimension of a particular lumped parameter system. The latter, in turn, determines the "accuracy" of the approximation. For each approximate problem it is solved by the control parametrization algorithm reported in Appendix V. In the discretized-in-the-beginning approach the computation time will become less if the distributed controls depend on fewer variables. This point is not supported by the discretized-at-the-end approach. Note that [RT.1] and [Boy.1] are the main references of Section 9.

We refer the interested reader to [RPM.1] for other linear distributed optimal control problems and [RPM.2] for nonlinear distributed optimal control problems. In these two articles and Section 9, no results on the convergence of the approximate optimal solutions to the true optimal solution are available. This appears to be an interesting and important area of future research.

In 1981, [Li.5] was published. This book is well written, motivated, and contains many new ideas. Its main aim is on the methods that can be used to solve some problems connected with the analysis and with the control of distributed parameter systems. These methods include:

(a) the averaging principle in calculus of variations;

(b) the various asymptotic expansions;

(c) the method of transposition for the definitions of weak solutions of linear partial differential equations;

(d) the method of artificial domain;

(e) the systematic use of duality theory in convex analysis;

(f) the method of new function spaces;

(g) the method for the study of asymptotic optimal control; and

(h) the methods for dealing with optimal control of nonwell-posed systems.

CHAPTER V

Relaxed Controls and the Convergence of Optimal Control Algorithms

V.1. Introduction

The aim of this chapter is to improve the convergence results for the algorithms of Chapters III and IV.

V.2. The Strong Variational Algorithm

In this section we consider optimal control problem (P) posed in Section III.3. For convenience this optimal control problem is to be referred to as problem (III.3.P). Furthermore, all the conditions imposed in Sections III.2 and III.3 are assumed to hold throughout the rest of this section.

For any given initial control u^0, the strong variational algorithm of Chapter III can generate a sequence of controls $\{u^k\}$ such that $J(u^{k+1}) < J(u^k)$ for $k = 0, 1, 2, \ldots$, where J is the cost functional defined by (III.3.1). Furthermore, any accumulation point, if it exists, of the sequence $\{u^k\}$ in the L_∞

topology satisfies condition (III.7.1), which is a necessary condition for optimality for optimal control problem (III.3.P). This result is not satisfactory in the sense that there is no guarantee of the existence of such an accumulation point. The purpose of this section is to present and illustrate a more natural convergence theory for the strong variational algorithm of Chapter III. The theory is based on a topology arising in the study of relaxed controls and ensures that accumulation points for the sequence $\{u^k\}$ always exist. However, it can only be shown that any such accumulation point satisfies a certain necessary condition for optimality for the corresponding optimal relaxed control problem [rather than necessary condition (III.7.1) for the original problem].

V.2.1. RELAXED CONTROLS

In Chapter III we see that the set $\mathscr{U}$ of all admissible controls is just $L_\infty(\hat{Q}, U)$. Unfortunately, $L_\infty(\hat{Q}, U)$ is not sequentially compact, and so accumulation points of sequences of admissible controls do not necessarily exist. This weakness can be overcome by the result of Section I.5. Let us briefly recall this matter.

Consider the set $\mathscr{N}$ of all functions $v: \hat{Q} \to fm(U)$ that are measurable and satisfy

$$\operatorname*{ess\,sup}_{(\hat{x}, t) \in \hat{Q}} |v(\hat{x}, t)|(U) < \infty. \tag{2.1}$$

The topology of $\mathscr{N}$ is induced by the weak * topology of $L_1(\hat{Q}, C(U))^*$, where $L_1(\hat{Q}, C(U))^*$ is the topological dual of $L_1(\hat{Q}, C(U))$. A *(measurable) relaxed control* is defined to be an element of $\mathscr{N}$ for which $v(\hat{x}, t) \in pm(U)$ almost everywhere on $\hat{Q}$. *Let $\mathscr{V}$ be the set of all such relaxed controls.*

Clearly, the set $\mathscr{U}$ of all admissible controls can be embedded in $\mathscr{V}$ by identifying each element $u \in \mathscr{U}$ with the Dirac measure $\delta_u \in \mathscr{V}$. *This identification is to remain in force throughout the rest of this section.*

For any $v \in \mathscr{V}$ and for any $q \in L_1(Q, C(U))$, $q[v]$ is a real-valued function on Q defined by

$$q[v](x, t) \equiv \int_U q(x, t, w)v(\hat{x}, t)(dw). \tag{2.2}$$

DEFINITION 2.1. *Let $\{v^k\}$ be a sequence of relaxed controls in $\mathscr{V}$ and $v \in \mathscr{V}$. Then $\{v^k\}$ is said to converge to v in the sense of control measure* (iscm), *if*

$$\iint_Q q[v^k](x, t)\, dx\, dt \to \iint_Q q[v](x, t)\, dx\, dt, \tag{2.3}$$

for all $q \in L_1(Q, C(U))$.

For brevity we shall write $v^k \xrightarrow{\text{iscm}} v$ if v^k converges to v in the sense of control measure.

REMARK 2.1. From Theorem I.5.1 we observe that the set $\mathscr{V}$ of all relaxed controls is sequentially compact. More precisely, for any sequence $\{v^k\}$ of relaxed controls in $\mathscr{V}$, there exists a subsequence $\{v^{k(l)}\}$ of the sequence $\{v^k\}$ and an element $\bar{v} \in \mathscr{V}$ such that

$$v^{k(l)} \xrightarrow{\text{iscm}} \bar{v},$$

as $l \to \infty$.

V.2.2. THE RELAXED PROBLEM

Consider system (III.2.1) for each $v \in \mathscr{V}$ rather than $u \in \mathscr{U}$:

$$L[v]\phi(x, t) = f[v](x, t), \qquad (x, t) \in Q, \tag{2.4a}$$

$$\phi|_{t=0} = \phi_0, \qquad x \in \Omega, \tag{2.4b}$$

$$\phi|_{\Gamma} = 0, \qquad (x, t) \in \Gamma, \tag{2.4c}$$

where, for each $v \in \mathscr{V}$, $L[v]$ is defined by

$$L[v]\psi \equiv \psi_t - \sum_{i,j=1}^{n} a_{ij}(x, t)\psi_{x_i x_j} - \sum_{i=1}^{n} b_i[v](x, t)\psi_{x_i} - c[v](x, t)\psi. \tag{2.5}$$

Furthermore, $f[v]$, $b_i[v]$, $i = 1, \ldots, n$, and $c[v]$ are defined as in (2.2).

REMARK 2.2.

(i) From assumption (III.A.3), it follows that there exists a constant M_1, independent of $v \in \mathscr{V}$, such that

$$\|b_i[v]\|_{\infty,Q} \le M_1, \qquad i = 1, \ldots, n;$$

$$\|c[v]\|_{\infty,Q} \le M_1;$$

and

$$\|f[v]\|_{\infty,Q} \le M_1.$$

(ii) On the basis of Remark 2.1, it follows readily from assumption (III.A.3) that if $v^{k(l)} \xrightarrow{\text{iscm}} \bar{v}$, as $l \to \infty$, then

$$b_i[v^{k(l)}] \xrightarrow{w^*} b_i[\bar{v}], \qquad i = 1, \ldots, n,$$

$$c[v^{k(l)}] \xrightarrow{w^*} c[\bar{v}],$$

and

$$f[v^{k(l)}] \xrightarrow{w^*} f[\bar{v}],$$

in (the weak* topology of) $L_\infty(Q)$, as $l \to \infty$.

The following theorem follows immediately from Theorem II.8.1 and Remark 2.2(i).

THEOREM 2.1. *For each $v \in \mathscr{V}$, relaxed system (2.4) has a unique almost everywhere solution $\phi(v)$ (in the sense of Definition III.2.1). Furthermore, $\phi(v)$ satisfies the estimate*

$$\|\phi(v)\|_{p,Q}^{(2,1)} \leq M_2\{\|f[v]\|_{\infty,Q} + \|\phi_0\|_{\infty,\Omega}^{(2)}\}, \tag{2.6}$$

for all $p \in (\frac{3}{2}, \infty]$, where M_2 is a constant independent of $v \in \mathscr{V}$.

From Remark 2.2(i) and assumptions (III.A.3) and (III.A.4), we can find a constant M_3, independent of $v \in \mathscr{V}$, such that estimate (2.6) is reduced to

$$\|\phi(v)\|_{p,Q}^{(2,1)} \leq M_3, \tag{2.7}$$

for all $p \in (\frac{3}{2}, \infty]$.

On this basis, it follows from the same argument as that given for estimate (III.2.6) that

$$|\phi(v)|_{\bar{Q}}^{(3/2,3/4)} \leq M_4, \tag{2.8}$$

where M_4 is a constant, again independent of $v \in \mathscr{V}$.

In the rest of this section let $\phi(v)$ denote the almost everywhere solution of relaxed system (2.4) corresponding to each $v \in \mathscr{V}$.

THEOREM 2.2. *Consider relaxed system (2.4). Let $\{v^k\}$ be a sequence in $\mathscr{V}$. Then there exists a subsequence $\{v^{k(l)}\}$ of the sequence $\{v^k\}$ and an element $\bar{v} \in \mathscr{V}$ such that, as $l \to \infty$,*

$$v^{k(l)} \xrightarrow{\text{iscm}} \bar{v};$$

and

$$\phi(v^{k(l)}) \xrightarrow{u} \phi(\bar{v});$$
$$\phi(v^{k(l)})_{x_i} \xrightarrow{u} \phi(\bar{v})_{x_1}, \qquad i = 1, \ldots, n;$$

on $\bar{Q}$.

Proof. By Remark 2.1 and Remark 2.2(ii), we see that there exists a subsequence of the sequence $\{v^k\}$, again denoted by $\{v^k\}$, and an element $\bar{v} \in \mathscr{V}$ such that, as $k \to \infty$,

$$v^k \xrightarrow{\text{iscm}} \bar{v};$$
$$b_i[v^k] \xrightarrow{w^*} b_i[\bar{v}], \qquad i = 1, \ldots, n;$$
$$c[v^k] \xrightarrow{w^*} c[\bar{v}];$$

and

$$f[v^k] \xrightarrow{w^*} f[\bar{v}];$$

in $L_\infty(Q)$.

Let $\zeta(v^k)$ denote any of the functions $\phi(v^k)$ and $\phi(v^k)_{x_i}$, $i = 1, \ldots, n$. Then it follows from estimate (2.8) that

$$|\zeta(v^k)| + \frac{|\zeta(v^k)(x', t') - \zeta(v^k)(x, t)|}{\{|x' - x|^2 + |t' - t|\}^{1/4}} \le M_4, \tag{2.9}$$

for all $(x, t), (x', t') \in \bar{Q}$, where the constant M_4 is independent of k. Thus from the Ascoli–Arzela theorem, it can be shown that there exists a system of subsequences

$$\{\phi(v^{k(l)}), \phi(v^{k(l)})_{x_i}, i = 1, \ldots, n\},$$

and a system of functions

$$\{\phi, \phi^i, i = 1, \ldots, n\},$$

such that, as $l \to \infty$,

$$\phi(v^{k(l)}) \xrightarrow{u} \phi;$$

$$\phi(v^{k(l)})_{x_i} \xrightarrow{u} \phi^i, \qquad i = 1, \ldots, n,$$

(uniformly) on $\bar{Q}$. Clearly, the limit functions ϕ, ϕ^i, $i = 1, \ldots, n$, satisfy estimate (2.9).

Since $\phi(v^{k(l)})$ is a subsequence of the sequence $\phi(v^k)$, it follows from estimate (2.7) that there exists a common system of subsequences

$$\{\phi(v^{k(l(s))}), \phi(v^{k(l(s))})_t, \phi(v^{k(l(s))})_{x_i}, i = 1, \ldots, n, \phi(v^{k(l(s))})_{x_i x_j}, i, j = 1, \ldots, n\},$$

and a system of functions

$$\{\phi, \psi, \phi^i, i = 1, \ldots, n, \phi^{ij}, i, j = 1, \ldots, n\},$$

such that, as $s \to \infty$,

$$\phi(v^{k(l(s))}) \xrightarrow{w(w^*)} \phi;$$

$$\phi(v^{k(l(s))})_t \xrightarrow{w(w^*)} \psi;$$

$$\phi(v^{k(l(s))})_{x_i} \xrightarrow{w(w^*)} \phi^i, \qquad i = 1, \ldots, n; \tag{2.10}$$

and

$$\phi(v^{k(l(s))})_{x_i x_j} \xrightarrow{w(w^*)} \phi^{ij}, \qquad i, j = 1, \ldots, n;$$

in $L_p(Q)$ for $p \in (\frac{3}{2}, \infty)$ (in $L_\infty(Q)$ for $p = \infty$).

Clearly, the limit functions satisfy the estimate

$$\|\phi\|_{p,Q} + \|\psi\|_{p,Q} + \sum_{i=1}^{n} \|\phi^i\|_{p,Q} + \sum_{i,j=1}^{n} \|\phi^{ij}\|_{p,Q} \leq M_3, \tag{2.11}$$

for all $p > \frac{3}{2}$.

Next, for any $Z \in C_0^1(Q)$, it follows from integration by parts that

$$\iint_Q \phi(v^{k(l(s))})_{x_i} Z\, dx\, dt = -\iint_Q \phi(v^{k(l(s))}) Z_{x_i}\, dx\, dt, \qquad i = 1, \ldots, n;$$

$$\iint_Q \phi(v^{k(l(s))})_t Z\, dx\, dt = -\iint_Q \phi(v^{k(l(s))}) Z_t\, dx\, dt;$$

$$\iint_Q \phi(v^{k(l(s))})_{x_i x_j} Z\, dx\, dt = -\iint_Q \phi(v^{k(l(s))})_{x_i} Z_{x_j}\, dx\, dt, \qquad i, j = 1, \ldots, n.$$

Thus, by letting $s \to \infty$, we have

$$\iint_Q \phi^i Z\, dx\, dt = -\iint_Q \phi Z_{x_i}\, dx\, dt, \qquad i = 1, \ldots, n;$$

$$\iint_Q \psi Z\, dx\, dt = -\iint_Q \phi Z_t\, dx\, dt;$$

$$\iint_Q \phi^{ij} Z\, dx\, dt = -\iint_Q \phi^i Z_{x_j}\, dx\, dt, \qquad i, j = 1, \ldots, n.$$

This implies that the functions ϕ^i, ψ, and ϕ^{ij} are, respectively, the generalized derivatives of ϕ with respect to x_i, ϕ with respect to t, and ϕ^i with respect to x_j. Hence, they can be written as ϕ_{x_i}, ϕ_t, and $\phi_{x_i x_j}$, respectively. Thus from (2.11) it follows that $\phi \in W_p^{2,1}(Q)$, $p \in (\frac{3}{2}, \infty]$.

At this stage we have, as $s \to \infty$,

$$\phi(v^{k(l(s))}) \xrightarrow{u} \phi, \; \phi(v^{k(l(s))})_{x_i} \xrightarrow{u} \phi_{x_i}, \qquad i = 1, \ldots, n; \tag{2.12}$$

on $\bar{Q}$, and

$$\phi(v^{k(l(s))})_t \xrightarrow{w(w^*)} \phi_t, \; \phi(v^{k(l(s))})_{x_i x_j} \xrightarrow{w(w^*)} \phi_{x_i x_j}, \qquad i, j = 1, \ldots, n; \tag{2.13}$$

in $L_p(Q)$ for $p \in (\frac{3}{2}, \infty)$(in $L_\infty(Q)$ for $p = \infty$).

We shall now show that the function ϕ satisfies Eq. (2.4a) with $v = \bar{v}$ almost everywhere on Q. First, we note that, for each positive integer s, $\phi(v^{k(l(s))})$

satisfies such an equation with $v = v^{k(l(s))}$ almost everywhere on Q. Thus for almost all $(x, t) \in Q$

$$\begin{aligned}
&\phi_t(x, t) - \sum_{i,j=1}^{n} a_{ij}(x, t)\phi_{x_i x_j}(x, t) \\
&\qquad - \sum_{i=1}^{n} b_i[\bar{v}](x, t)\phi_{x_i}(x, t) - c[\bar{v}](x, t)\phi(x, t) - f[\bar{v}](x, t) \\
&\quad = \{\phi_t(x, t) - \phi(v^{k(l(s))})_t(x, t)\} \\
&\qquad - \sum_{i,j=1}^{n} a_{ij}(x, t)\{\phi_{x_i x_j}(x, t) - \phi(v^{k(l(s))})_{x_i x_j}(x, t)\} \\
&\qquad - \sum_{i=1}^{n} \{b_i[\bar{v}](x, t)\phi_{x_i}(x, t) - b_i[v^{k(l(s))}](x, t)\phi(v^{k(l(s))})_{x_i}(x, t)\} \\
&\qquad - \{c[\bar{v}](x, t)\phi(x, t) - c[v^{k(l(s))}](x, t)\phi(v^{k(l(s))})(x, t)\} \\
&\qquad - \{f[\bar{v}](x, t) - f[v^{k(l(s))}](x, t)\}.
\end{aligned}$$

From estimates (2.11) and (2.6) and Remark 2.2(i), it is easily verified that all the terms involved in the preceding relation are elements of $L_\infty(Q)$. Consequently,

$$\begin{aligned}
&\iint_Q \left\{\phi_t - \sum_{i,j=1}^{n} a_{ij}\phi_{x_i x_j} - \sum_{i=1}^{n} b_i[\bar{v}]\phi_{x_i} - c[\bar{v}]\phi - f[\bar{v}]\right\} Z \, dx \, dt \\
&\quad = \iint_Q \Bigg\{\{\phi_t - \phi(v^{k(l(s))})_t\}Z - \sum_{i,j=1}^{n} a_{ij}\{\phi_{x_i x_j} - \phi(v^{k(l(s))})_{x_i x_j}\} Z \\
&\qquad - \sum_{i=1}^{n} \{b_i[\bar{v}]\phi_{x_i} - b_i[v^{k(l(s))}]\phi(v^{k(l(s))})_{x_i}\}Z \\
&\qquad - \{c[\bar{v}]\phi - c[v^{k(l(s))}]\phi(v^{k(l(s))})\}Z - \{f[\bar{v}] - f[v^{k(l(s))}]\}Z\Bigg\} \, dx \, dt,
\end{aligned} \tag{2.14}$$

for any $Z \in L_1(Q)$.

By taking the limit in (2.14), it follows that

$$\iint_Q \left\{\phi_t - \sum_{i,j=1}^{n} a_{ij}\phi_{x_i x_j} - \sum_{i=1}^{n} b_i[\bar{v}]\phi_{x_i} - c[\bar{v}]\phi - f[\bar{v}]\right\}Z \, dx \, dt = 0,$$

for any $Z \in L_1(Q)$. Hence

$$\phi_t - \sum_{i,j=1}^{n} a_{ij}\phi_{x_i x_j} - \sum_{i=1}^{n} b_i[\bar{v}]\phi_{x_i} - c[\bar{v}]\phi = f[\bar{v}],$$

for almost all $(x, t) \in Q$. This shows that ϕ satisfies (2.4a) with $v = \bar{v}$ almost everywhere in Q.

To show that ϕ is an almost everywhere solution of relaxed system (2.4) with $v = \bar{v}$, it remains to show that ϕ satisfies the boundary and initial conditions of system (2.4). For this we recall that

(i) $\phi(v^{k(l(s))}) \xrightarrow{u} \phi$ on $\bar{Q}$ as $l \to \infty$,
(ii) $\phi(v^{k(l(s))})(x, t) = 0$ on Γ for all integers s,

and

(iii) $\phi(v^{k(l(s))})(x, 0) = \phi_0(x)$ on Ω.

Thus we have $\phi(x, t) = 0$ on Γ and $\phi(x, 0) = \phi_0(x)$ on Ω. Therefore, we conclude that $\phi \in W_\infty^{2,1}(Q)$ and is an almost everywhere solution of relaxed system (2.4) with $v = \bar{v}$ and hence is written as $\phi(\bar{v})$. The uniqueness of the almost everywhere solution $\phi(\bar{v})$ follows from Theorem 2.1, and the conclusions of the theorem follow from (2.12). This completes the proof. ■

V.2.3. OPTIMAL RELAXED CONTROL PROBLEM

Consider the following cost functional

$$\hat{J}(v) = \int_\Omega \gamma(x, \phi(v)(x, T))\, dx, \tag{2.15}$$

where γ is as defined in (III.3.1) and satisfies assumption (III.A.5), and $\phi(v)$ is the almost everywhere solution of relaxed system (2.4) corresponding to the relaxed control $v \in \mathscr{V}$. We note that the cost functional $\hat{J}(v)$ is well defined by Theorem 2.1. Thus we may now pose the following optimal relaxed control problem, *which is to be referred to as problem* (*RP*).

Subject to relaxed system (2.4), find a $v^* \in \mathscr{V}$ such that

$$\hat{J}(v^*) \leq \hat{J}(v),$$

for all $v \in \mathscr{V}$. v^* is called an optimal relaxed control.

As in Chapter III we need some preparations. First, we introduce the adjoint system for relaxed problem (*RP*) as follows:

$$L^*[v]z = 0, \qquad (x, t) \in Q, \tag{2.16a}$$

$$z|_{t=T} = g(x, \phi(v)(x, T)), \qquad x \in \Omega, \tag{2.16b}$$

$$z|_\Gamma = 0, \qquad (x, t) \in \Omega, \tag{2.16c}$$

where g is the function given in assumption (III.A.5), and for each $v \in \mathscr{V}$, $L^*[v]$ is defined by

$$L^*[v]\psi \equiv -\psi_t - \sum_{i=1}^{n} \left(\sum_{j=1}^{n} a_{ij}(x, t)\psi_{x_j} + a_i[v](x, t)\psi \right)_{x_i} - c[v](x, t)\psi,$$

where

$$a_i[v](x, t) \equiv \sum_{j=1}^{n} \frac{\partial a_{ij}(x, t)}{\partial x_j} - b_i[v](x, t), \qquad i = 1, \ldots, n.$$

For the adjoint system, the solution is to be understood as in the sense of Definition III.3.1.

Following arguments similar to those appeared in Section III.3, we have the following remark.

REMARK 2.3.

(i) For each $v \in \mathscr{V}$, adjoint system (2.16) admits a unique weak solution $z(v)$ (in the sense of Definition III.3.1) that satisfies the following estimate

$$\|z(v)\|_Q \leq M_5, \tag{2.17}$$

where M_5 is a constant independent of $v \in \mathscr{V}$.

(ii) There exists a constant M_6, independent of $v \in \mathscr{V}$, such that

$$\|z(v)\|_{1,Q} \leq M_6. \tag{2.18}$$

(iii) There exists a constant M_7, independent of $v \in \mathscr{V}$, such that

$$|z(v)(x, t)| \leq M_7, \tag{2.19}$$

for almost all $(x, t) \in Q$. Furthermore, for each $v \in \mathscr{V}$, $z(v)$ is continuous on Q.

From Remark 2.3(ii), z can be considered as a mapping from $\mathscr{V}$ into $L_1(Q)$. The next theorem shows the continuity of this mapping.

THEOREM 2.3. *Let $\{v^k\}$ be a sequence in $\mathscr{V}$ and $\bar{v}$ be an element in $\mathscr{V}$. If $v^k \xrightarrow{\text{iscm}} \bar{v}$ then $z(v^k) \xrightarrow{s} z(\bar{v})$ in $L_1(Q)$, as $k \to \infty$.*

Proof. Let $e^k: Q \to R^1$ be defined by

$$e^k(x, t) = \begin{cases} 1, & \text{if } \; z(v^k)(x, t) \geq z(\bar{v})(x, t), \\ -1, & \text{otherwise.} \end{cases} \tag{2.20}$$

Clearly, for each integer $k \geq 1$, $e^k \in L_\infty(Q)$.

Consider the following first boundary value problem:

$$L[v^k]\psi = e^k, \qquad (x, t) \in Q, \tag{2.21a}$$

$$\psi|_{t=0} = 0, \qquad x \in \Omega, \tag{2.21b}$$

$$\psi|_\Gamma = 0, \qquad (x, t) \in \Gamma, \tag{2.21c}$$

where $L[v^k]$ is given by (2.5) with $v = v^k$.

Then from Theorem II.8.1, it follows that, for each $k \geq 1$, problem (2.21) has a unique almost everywhere solution ψ^k (in the sense of Definition II.8.1) and that there exists a constant N_0, independent of k, such that

$$\|\psi^k\|_{p,Q}^{(2,1)} \leq N_0, \tag{2.22}$$

for all $p \in (\frac{3}{2}, \infty]$. In particular, we have

$$\psi^k \in \mathring{\tilde{W}}_{\infty}^{2,1}(Q).$$

Next, by the same argument as that used to obtain estimate (III.2.6) from estimate (III.2.3), we deduce from estimate (2.22) that

$$|\psi^k|_{\bar{Q}}^{(3/2,3/4)} \leq N_1, \tag{2.23}$$

where N_1 is a constant, again independent of k.

In view of (2.20) we note that $\|e^k\|_{\infty,Q} \leq 1$. Thus there exists a subsequence of the sequence $\{e^k\}$, again denoted by the original sequence, and an element $\bar{e} \in L_{\infty}(Q)$ such that $e^k \overset{w^*}{\to} \bar{e}$ in $L_{\infty}(Q)$, as $k \to \infty$. Now, by using an argument similar to that given for Theorem 2.2, we obtain, as $k \to \infty$,

$$(\psi^k)_{x_i} \overset{u}{\to} \bar{\psi}_{x_i}, \qquad i = 1, \ldots, n; \tag{2.24a}$$

$$\psi^k \overset{u}{\to} \bar{\psi}; \tag{2.24b}$$

on $\bar{Q}$, where $\bar{\psi}$ is the almost everywhere solution of system (2.21) with $v^k = \bar{v}$ and $e^k = \bar{e}$.

From the properties of ψ^k, Eq. (A.II.9)†, and the definition of $L[v]$, it follows that

$$\begin{aligned}
0 \leq \|z(v^k) - z(\bar{v})\|_{1,Q} &= \iint_Q (L[v^k]\psi^k)(z(v^k) - z(\bar{v}))\, dx\, dt \\
&= \iint_Q (L[v^k]\psi^k) z(v^k)\, dx\, dt - \iint_Q (L[\bar{v}]\psi^k) z(\bar{v})\, dx\, dt \\
&\quad - \iint_Q ((L[v^k] - L[\bar{v}])\psi^k) z(\bar{v})\, dx\, dt = \int_\Omega \psi^k(x, T)\{g(x, \phi(v^k)(x, T)) \\
&\quad - g(x, \phi(\bar{v})(x, T))\}\, dx + \iint_Q \sum_{i=1}^n \{b_i[v^k] - b_i[\bar{v}]\}(\psi^k)_{x_i} z(\bar{v})\, dx\, dt \\
&\quad + \iint_Q \{c[v^k] - c[\bar{v}]\}\psi^k z(\bar{v})\, dx\, dt \\
&\leq \int_\Omega |\psi^k(x, T)|\{|g(x, \phi(v^k)(x, T)) - g(x, \phi(\bar{v})(x, T))|\}\, dx \\
&\quad + \iint_Q \sum_{i=1}^n \{b_i[v^k] - b_i[\bar{v}]\}(\psi^k)_{x_i} z(\bar{v})\, dx\, dt \\
&\quad + \iint_Q \{c[v^k] - c[\bar{v}]\}\psi^k z(\bar{v})\, dx\, dt.
\end{aligned} \tag{2.25}$$

† Within the same Appendix, equation number 7 is called Eq. (7), but outside that Appendix, equation number 7 in Appendix III is referred to as Eq. (A.III.7).

From Remark 2.2 and (2.18) and (2.23), it is easy to verify that the second and the third terms on the right-hand side of inequality (2.25) converge to zero as $k \to \infty$. To complete the proof, it remains to show that the first term also converges to zero as $k \to \infty$.

Using an argument similar to that given for inequality (III.3.20), we obtain

$$\int_{\Omega} |\psi^k(x, T)| \{ |g(x, \phi(v^k)(x, T)) - g(x, \phi(\bar{v})(x, T))| \} \, dx$$
$$\leq N \|\psi^k(\cdot, T)\|_{2,\Omega} \|\phi(v^k) - \phi(\bar{v})\|_{\infty, Q},$$

where N is a constant independent of k and $\bar{v}$.

Using the preceding inequality, inequality (2.23), and Theorem 2.2 the desired conclusion follows. This completes the proof. ■

V.2.4. *THE HAMILTONIAN FUNCTIONS*

For each $v \in \mathscr{V}$, let $I(v): \bar{Q} \times U \to R^1$ and $H(v): \hat{Q} \times U \to R^1$ be defined, respectively, by

$$I(v)(x, t, v) \equiv \sum_{i=1}^{n} b_i(x, t, v)\phi(v)_{x_i}(x, t) + c(x, t, v)\phi(v)(x, t) + f(x, t, v), \tag{2.26}$$

and

$$H(v)(\hat{x}, t, v) \equiv \int_{\hat{\Omega}_{\hat{x}}} I(v)(\hat{x}, \hat{\hat{x}}, t, v) z(v)(\hat{x}, \hat{\hat{x}}, t) \, d\hat{\hat{x}}. \tag{2.27}$$

The function $H(v)$ is called the *Hamiltonian function* for $v \in \mathscr{V}$.

For the case when $n_1 = n$, $H(v)$ becomes a function on $Q \times U$ (rather than just on $\hat{Q} \times U$) defined by

$$H(v)(x, t, v) \equiv I(v)(x, t, v) z(v)(x, t). \tag{2.28}$$

Similar to the approach used for the original optimal control problem (III.3.P), we shall show that the variation in the cost functional due to the variation in control can be estimated in terms of the integral of the Hamiltonian function together with β and γ, where β and γ are two functionals on $\mathscr{V} \times \mathscr{V}$ defined by

$$\beta(v^1, v^2) \equiv \iint_Q \sum_{i=1}^{n} \{b_i[v^1] - b_i[v^2]\}\{\phi(v^1)_{x_i} - \phi(v^2)_{x_i}\} z(v^1) \, dx \, dt, \tag{2.29}$$

and

$$\gamma(v^1, v^2) \equiv \iint_Q \{c[v^1] - c[v^2]\}\{\phi(v^1) - \phi(v^2)\} z(v^1) \, dx \, dt. \tag{2.30}$$

Now, for $v^1 \in \mathscr{V}$, let

$$H(v^1)[v](\hat{x}, t) \equiv \int_U H(v^1)(\hat{x}, t, w)v(\hat{x}, t)(dw), \tag{2.31}$$

for all $v \in \mathscr{V}$.

LEMMA 2.1. *For any $v^1, v^2 \in \mathscr{V}$, let $\psi = \phi(v^1) - \phi(v^2)$. Then*

$$\int_\Omega \psi(x, T)g(x, \phi(v^1)(x, T))\,dx$$

$$= \iint_{\hat{Q}} \{H(v^1)[v^1] - H(v^1)[v^2]\}\,d\hat{x}\,dt - \beta(v^1, v^2) - \gamma(v^1, v^2). \tag{2.32}$$

Proof. The proof is similar to that given for Lemma III.4.1. The main differences are to replace u^1, u^2, and $L(u^1)$ by v^1, v^2, and $L[v^1]$, and change the subsequent arguments appropriately. ■

The proof of the following theorem is similar to that given for Theorem III.4.1, except with Lemma III.4.1 replaced by Lemma 2.1.

THEOREM 2.4. *Let $\hat{J}(v)$ be the cost functional given by* (2.15). *Then for any $v^1, v^2 \in \mathscr{V}$*

$$\hat{J}(v^1) - \hat{J}(v^2) = \iint_Q \{H(v^1)[v^2] - H(v^1)[v^1]\}\,dx\,dt + \beta(v^1, v^2) + \gamma(v^1, v^2). \tag{2.33}$$

Following arguments similar to those given for Lemma III.4.2(i), (ii), and Theorem III.4.2, we obtain the corresponding results for our present situation. These results are given in the following remark for the convenience of references.

REMARK 2.4.

(i) For each $v \in \mathscr{V}$, $H(v)$ is continuous on $\hat{Q} \times U$.

(ii) $H(v)$ is bounded almost everywhere on $\bar{\hat{Q}} \times U$ uniformly with respect to $v \in \mathscr{V}$.

(iii) For any $v \in \mathscr{V}$, there exists an admissible control $V(v) \in \mathscr{U}$ such that

$$H(v)(\hat{x}, t, V(v)(\hat{x}, t)) \leq H(v)(\hat{x}, t, v),$$

for all $(\hat{x}, t, v) \in \hat{Q} \times U$.

V.2.5. THE SUCCESSIVE RELAXED CONTROLS

The first-order differential operator θ is extended to the class of all relaxed controls (rather than just the class of all admissible controls). More precisely, θ is now a mapping from $\mathscr{V}$ (rather than just $\mathscr{U}$) into R^1 defined by

$$\theta(v) \equiv (|\hat{\Omega}|)^{-1}\left\{\iint_{\hat{Q}} \{H(v)(\hat{x}, t, V(v)(\hat{x}, t)) - H(v)[v](\hat{x}, t)\}\, d\hat{x}\, dt\right\}, \tag{2.34}$$

where $|\hat{\Omega}|$ denotes the Lebesgue measure of the set $\hat{\Omega}$.

DEFINITION 2.2. *A relaxed control $v \in \mathscr{V}$ is said to be extremal if* $\theta(v) = 0$.

Similar to Section III.5, we shall denote by v a fixed, nonextremal relaxed control throughout the rest of this subsection. Clearly, $\theta(v) < 0$.

Consider the set

$$\Xi \equiv \Xi(v)$$

$$\equiv \left\{\hat{x} \in \hat{\Omega} : \int_0^T \{H(v)(\hat{x}, t, V(v)(\hat{x}, t)) - H(v)[v](\hat{x}, t)\}\, dt \leq \theta(v)\right\}. \tag{2.35}$$

Let $\{\hat{\Omega}_\alpha : \alpha \in [0, |\hat{\Omega}|]\}$ be a family of measurable subsets of $\hat{\Omega}$ such that

$$|\hat{\Omega}_\alpha| = \alpha, \qquad \text{for all } \alpha \in [0, |\hat{\Omega}|], \tag{2.36a}$$

$$\hat{\Omega}_\alpha \subsetneqq \hat{\Omega}_{\alpha'}, \qquad \text{for all } \alpha, \alpha' \in [0, |\hat{\Omega}|], \text{ and } \alpha < \alpha', \tag{2.36b}$$

$$\hat{\Omega}_\alpha = \Xi, \qquad \text{for } \alpha = |\Xi|. \tag{2.36c}$$

Furthermore, for each $\alpha \in [0, |\hat{\Omega}|]$, let

$$\hat{\theta}_\alpha = \hat{\Omega}_\alpha \times (0, T). \tag{2.37}$$

For each $v \in \mathscr{V}$ and for each $\alpha \in [0, |\hat{\Omega}|]$, we can now define another relaxed control v^α as follows:

$$v^\alpha(\hat{x}, t) = \begin{cases} \delta_{V(v)(\hat{x}, t)}, & (\hat{x}, t) \in \hat{\theta}_\alpha, \\ v(\hat{x}, t), & \text{otherwise}, \end{cases} \tag{2.38}$$

where $\delta_{V(v)(\hat{x},t)}$ is a Dirac measure in $pm(U)$.

REMARK 2.5. Note that $\hat{\Omega}_\alpha$, $\hat{\theta}_\alpha$, and v^α are all depending on v. However, their dependency is suppressed from the notation for the sake of brevity. This abbreviation will be used throughout the rest of this section.

Let

$$\alpha^* \equiv \alpha^*(v) \equiv \sup\{\alpha : 0 \leq \alpha \leq |\hat{\Omega}| \text{ and } \hat{J}(v^\alpha) - \hat{J}(v) \leq \alpha\theta(v)/2\}. \quad (2.39)$$

Clearly, α^* is well defined since $\alpha = 0$ is always a candidate.

THEOREM 2.5 *Consider Problem (RP). Then there exists a positive constant M_8, independent of $v \in \mathscr{V}$ and $s \in (0, 1)$, such that*

$$\hat{J}(v^{\alpha^*}) - \hat{J}(v) \leq -M_8 |\theta(v)|^{1+(1/s)}. \quad (2.40)$$

Proof. The proof is similar to that given for Theorem III.5.2. ∎

From Theorem 2.5, it follows immediately that the next theorem is valid.

THEOREM 2.6. *Consider Problem (RP). If $v^* \in \mathscr{V}$ is optimal, then $\theta(v^*) = 0$.*

V.2.6. CONVERGENCE OF THE ALGORITHM

Consider optimal control problem (III.3.P) If u^0 is a nonextremal *admissible* control, then, by algorithm (III.A), a sequence $\{u^k\}$ of admissible controls can be generated such that $J(u^{k+1}) < J(u^k)$, for all $k \geq 0$, where J is defined by (III.3.1). Furthermore, if $\{u^k\}$ has an accumulation point u^* in the strong topology of L_∞, then, by Theorem III.6.1, u^* is an extremal control in the sense of Definition III.5.1. However, such accumulation controls need not exist.

The purpose of this subsection is to present and illustrate a more natural convergence theory for algorithm (III.A). More precisely, this theory ensures that accumulation points for the sequence $\{u^k\}$ of admissible controls always exist. It is then shown (Theorem 2.7) that any such accumulation point is extremal for the relaxed control problem (see Definition 2.2). For this purpose we need some preparation.

LEMMA 2.2. *Let G be a mapping from $\mathscr{V} \times \mathscr{V}$ into $L_1(\hat{Q})$ given by*

$$G(v^1)[v^2](\hat{x}, t) \equiv H(v^1)[v^2](\hat{x}, t), \quad (2.41)$$

for any $v^1, v^2 \in \mathscr{V}$, and for all $(\hat{x}, t) \in \hat{Q}$. Then

(i) *There exists a constant $M_9 > 0$ such that*

$$\|G(v^1)[v^2]\|_{1,\hat{Q}} \leq M_9,$$

for all $(v^1, v^2) \in \mathscr{V} \times \mathscr{V}$.

(ii)

$$\iint_{\hat{Q}} \{G(v^{1,k})[v^{2,k}] - G(v^1)[v^2]\}\, d\hat{x}\, dt \to 0,$$

whenever $\{(v^{1,k}, v^{2,k})\} \subset \mathscr{V} \times \mathscr{V}$ *and* $(v^1, v^2) \in \mathscr{V} \times \mathscr{V}$ *such that* $v^{1,k} \xrightarrow{\text{iscm}} v^1$ *and* $v^{2,k} \xrightarrow{\text{iscm}} v^2$.

Proof. In view of (2.41), (2.31), (2.27), and (2.2) we have

$$\iint_{\hat{Q}} \{G(v^1)[v^2] - G(v^{1,k})[v^{2,k}]\}\, d\hat{x}\, dt$$

$$= \iint_{\hat{Q}} \{G(v^1)[v^2] - G(v^1)[v^{2,k}]\}\, d\hat{x}\, dt$$

$$+ \iint_{\hat{Q}} \{G(v^1)[v^{2,k}] - G(v^{1,k})[v^{2,k}]\}\, d\hat{x}\, dt$$

$$= \iint_{Q} \{I(v^1)[v^2]z(v^1) - I(v^1)[v^{2,k}]z(v^1)\}\, dx\, dt$$

$$+ \iint_{Q} \{I(v^1)[v^{2,k}]z(v^1) - I(v^{1,k})[v^{2,k}]z(v^{1,k})\}\, dx\, dt$$

$$= \iint_{Q} \left\{\sum_{i=1}^{n} \{b_i[v^2]\phi(v^1)_{x_i}z(v^1) - b_i[v^{2,k}]\phi(v^1)_{x_i}z(v^1)\}\right\} dx\, dt$$

$$+ \iint_{Q} \{c[v^2]\phi(v^1)z(v^1) - c[v^{2,k}]\phi(v^1)z(v^1)\}\, dx\, dt$$

$$+ \iint_{Q} \{f[v^2]z(v^1) - f[v^{2,k}]z(v^1)\}\, dx\, dt$$

$$+ \iint_{Q} \left\{\sum_{i=1}^{n} \{b_i[v^{2,k}]\phi(v^1)_{x_i}z(v^1) - b_i[v^{2,k}]\phi(v^{1,k})_{x_i}z(v^{1,k})\}\right\} dx\, dt$$

$$+ \iint_{Q} \{c[v^{2,k}]\phi(v^1)z(v^1) - c[v^{2,k}]\phi(v^{1,k})z(v^{1,k})\}\, dx\, dt$$

$$+ \iint_{Q} \{f[v^{2,k}]z(v^1) - f[v^{2,k}]z(v^{1,k})\}\, dx\, dt.$$

The conclusion of the lemma follows from the application of Remarks 2.2 and 2.3 and Theorems 2.1–2.3. ■

LEMMA 2.3. *Let* $\{v^k\}$ *be a sequence in* $\mathscr{V}$. *Then there exists a subsequence* $\{v^{k(l)}\}$ *of the sequence* $\{v^k\}$ *and an element* $\bar{v} \in \mathscr{V}$ *such that* $v^{k(l)} \xrightarrow{\text{iscm}} \bar{v}$ *and* $\theta(v^{k(l)}) \to \theta(\bar{v})$, *as* $l \to \infty$, *where* θ *is the operator defined by* (2.34).

Proof. From Theorem 2.2 and 2.3, it is easy to verify that there exists a subsequence $\{v^{k(l)}\}$ of the sequence $\{v^k\}$ and an element $\bar{v} \in \mathscr{V}$ such that

$$\phi(v^{k(l)})_{x_i} z(v^{k(l)}) \xrightarrow{s} \phi(\bar{v})_{x_i} z(\bar{v}), \qquad i = 1, \dots, n; \tag{2.42}$$

and

$$\phi(v^{k(l)}) z(v^{k(l)}) \xrightarrow{s} \phi(\bar{v}) z(\bar{v}); \tag{2.43}$$

in $L_1(Q)$.

Next, from the definition of θ, we have

$$\begin{aligned} |\theta(v^{k(l)}) - \theta(\bar{v})| &\le (|\hat{\Omega}|)^{-1} \Bigg\{ \Bigg| \iint_{\hat{Q}} \{H(v^{k(l)})(\hat{x}, t, V(v^{k(l)})(\hat{x}, t)) \\ &\qquad - H(\bar{v})(\hat{x}, t, V(\bar{v})(\hat{x}, t))\} \, d\hat{x}\, dt \Bigg| \\ &\qquad + \Bigg| \iint_{\hat{Q}} \{H(v^{k(l)})[v^{k(l)}](\hat{x}, t) - H(\bar{v})[\bar{v}](\hat{x}, t)\} \, d\hat{x}\, dt \Bigg| \Bigg\}. \end{aligned} \tag{2.44}$$

In view of (2.31), (2.27), and (2.26) it follows that

$$\begin{aligned} &\Bigg| \iint_{\hat{Q}} \{H(v^{k(l)})[v^{k(l)}](\hat{x}, t) - H(\bar{v})[\bar{v}](\hat{x}, t)\} \, d\hat{x}\, dt \Bigg| \\ &\quad \le \Bigg| \iint_{Q} \Bigg\{ \sum_{i=1}^{n} \{b_i[v^{k(l)}] \phi(v^{k(l)})_{x_i} z(v^{k(l)}) - b_i[\bar{v}] \phi(\bar{v})_{x_i} z(\bar{v})\} \Bigg\} \, dx\, dt \Bigg| \\ &\quad\quad + \Bigg| \iint_{Q} \{c[v^{k(l)}] \phi(v^{k(l)}) z(v^{k(l)}) - c[\bar{v}] \phi(\bar{v}) z(\bar{v})\} \, dx\, dt \Bigg| \\ &\quad\quad + \Bigg| \iint_{Q} \{f[v^{k(l)}] z(v^{k(l)}) - f[\bar{v}] z(\bar{v})\} \, dx\, dt \Bigg|. \end{aligned} \tag{2.45}$$

From (2.42) and (2.43), it can be easily shown that

$$b_i(x, t, u) \phi(v^{k(l)})_{x_i}(x, t) z(v^{k(l)})(x, t) \to b_i(x, t, u) \phi(\bar{v})_{x_i}(x, t) z(\bar{v})(x, t),$$

$$c(x, t, u) \phi(v^{k(l)})(x, t) z(v^{k(l)})(x, t) \to c(x, t, u) \phi(\bar{v})(x, t) z(\bar{v})(x, t),$$

and

$$f(x, t, u) z(v^{k(l)})(x, t) \to f(x, t, u) z(\bar{v})(x, t),$$

all strongly in $L_1(Q, C(U))$, as $l \to \infty$. Thus it follows from Theorem I.5.3 that the right-hand side of (2.45) tends to zero as $l \to \infty$. Hence, the second term of the right-hand side of (2.44) tends to zero as $l \to \infty$.

We shall now show that

$$\left|\iint_{\hat{Q}} \{H(v^{k(l)})(\hat{x}, t, V(v^{k(l)})(\hat{x}, t)) - H(\bar{v})(\hat{x}, t, V(\bar{v})(\hat{x}, t))\}\, d\hat{x}\, dt\right| \to 0, \quad (2.46)$$

as $l \to \infty$.

From (2.26), (2.27), and the definition of $V(v)$, we note that

$$H(v)(\hat{x}, t, V(v)(\hat{x}, t)) = \min_{v \in U} H(v)(\hat{x}, t, v),$$

for all $v \in \mathscr{V}$ and for almost all $(\hat{x}, t) \in \hat{Q}$. Thus it follows that

$$\begin{aligned}
&\iint_{\hat{Q}} \{H(\bar{v})(\hat{x}, t, V(\bar{v})(\hat{x}, t)) - H(v^{k(l)})(\hat{x}, t, V(\bar{v})(\hat{x}, t))\}\, d\hat{x}\, dt \\
&\quad \leq \iint_{\hat{Q}} \{H(\bar{v})(\hat{x}, t, V(\bar{v})(\hat{x}, t)) - H(v^{k(l)})(\hat{x}, t, V(v^{k(l)})(\hat{x}, t))\}\, d\hat{x}\, dt \\
&\quad \leq \iint_{\hat{Q}} \{H(\bar{v})(\hat{x}, t, V(v^{k(l)})(\hat{x}, t)) - H(v^{k(l)})(\hat{x}, t, V(v^{k(l)})(\hat{x}, t))\}\, d\hat{x}\, dt.
\end{aligned} \quad (2.47)$$

We shall prove the validity of (2.46) by showing the convergence to zero of both the lower bounding sequence and the upper bounding sequence in (2.47), as $l \to \infty$.

The proof of the convergence to zero of the lower bounding sequence in (2.47) is identical to the proof of the convergence to zero of (2.45) since $V(\bar{v})$ can be thought of as a trivially convergent sequence. Therefore, it remains to show the convergence to zero of the upper bounding sequence of (2.47). For this we write

$$\begin{aligned}
&\iint_{\hat{Q}} \{H(\bar{v})(\hat{x}, t, V(v^{k(l)})(\hat{x}, t)) - H(v^{k(l)})(\hat{x}, t, V(v^{k(l)})(\hat{x}, t))\}\, dx\, dt \\
&= \iint_{Q} \sum_{i=1}^{n} b_i(x, t, V(v^{k(l)})(\hat{x}, t))\{\phi(\bar{v})_{x_i}(x, t) z(\bar{v})(x, t) \\
&\qquad\qquad - \phi(v^{k(l)})_{x_i}(x, t) z(v^{k(l)})(x, t)\}\, dx\, dt \\
&\quad + \iint_{Q} c(x, t, V(v^{k(l)})(\hat{x}, t))\{\phi(\bar{v})(x, t) z(\bar{v})(x, t) \\
&\qquad\qquad - \phi(v^{k(l)})(x, t) z(v^{k(l)})(x, t)\}\, dx\, dt \\
&\quad + \iint_{Q} f(x, t, V(v^{k(l)})(\hat{x}, t))\{z(\bar{v})(x, t) - z(v^{k(l)})(x, t)\}\, dx\, dt.
\end{aligned} \quad (2.48)$$

In each of the terms on the right-hand side of (2.48), the term in the curly brackets converges to zero strongly in $L_1(Q)$, by (2.42), (2.43), and Theorem 2.3; and the remaining part of the integrand is uniformly (with respect to $v^{k(l)}$) bounded in the L_∞ norm. Hence, each term on the right-hand side of (2.48) converges to zero, as $l \to \infty$. Consequently, we have shown the validity of (2.46). This completes the proof. ∎

For any $u^0 \in \mathscr{U}$, algorithm (III.A) constructs a sequence $\{u^k\}$ of admissible controls in $\mathscr{U}$. However, in proving convergence, we must use relaxed controls. Therefore, with each *admissible* control u, we associate a *relaxed* control $v \in \mathscr{V}$ that is the Dirac measure δ_u. On this basis, it can be considered that, for each $u^0 \in \mathscr{U}$, algorithm (III.A) generates a sequence of relaxed controls $\{v^k\} \subset \mathscr{V}$.

THEOREM 2.7. *Let $\{u^k\}$ be a sequence of admissible controls in $\mathscr{U}$ constructed by algorithm (III.A). Then*

(i) *If the sequence $\{u^k\}$ is finite, then the last element of the sequence is extremal.*

(ii) *If the sequence $\{u^k\}$ is infinite, then there exists a subsequence $\{u^{k(l)}\}$ of the sequence $\{u^k\}$ and an element $\bar{v} \in \mathscr{V}$ such that $\delta_{u^{k(l)}} \xrightarrow{\text{iscm}} \bar{v}$ and $\bar{v}$ is extremal.*

Proof. If the sequence is finite, then the proof is trivial. So suppose that the sequence is infinite and let $\{v^k\} \equiv \{\delta_{u^k}\}$ be the sequence of the corresponding relaxed controls in $\mathscr{V}$.

It follows from Lemma 2.3 that there exists a subsequence $\{v^{k(l)}\}$ of the sequence $\{v^k\}$ and an element $\bar{v} \in \mathscr{V}$ such that $v^{k(l)} \xrightarrow{\text{iscm}} \bar{v}$ and $\theta(v^{k(l)}) \to \theta(\bar{v})$, as $l \to \infty$.

From assumption (III.A.5) and estimate (2.8), we see that $\hat{J}(v)$ is bounded uniformly with respect to $v \in \mathscr{V}$. Thus $\{\hat{J}(v^{k(l)})\}$ is bounded below. Therefore,

$$|\hat{J}(v^{k(l+1)}) - \hat{J}(v^{k(l)})| \to 0, \qquad \text{as} \quad l \to \infty.$$

Since $\{\hat{J}(v^k)\}$ is monotonically decreasing, it follows that

$$|\hat{J}(v^{k(l+1)}) - \hat{J}(v^{k(l)})| \geq |\hat{J}(v^{k(l)+1}) - \hat{J}(v^{k(l)})|.$$

Hence,

$$|\hat{J}(v^{k(l)+1}) - \hat{J}(v^{k(l)})| \to 0, \qquad \text{as} \quad l \to \infty. \tag{2.49}$$

For each $k(l)$, $l = 1, 2, \ldots$, we deduce from (2.40) that

$$\hat{J}(v^{k(l)+1}) - \hat{J}(v^{k(l)}) \leq -M_8 |\theta(v^{k(l)})|^{1+(1/s)}, \tag{2.50}$$

where the constant M_8 is independent of $\{v^{k(l)}\}$ and $s \in (0, 1)$. By taking limits it follows from (2.49) that

$$\theta(\bar{v}) = 0.$$

This completes the proof. ■

REMARK 2.6. The proof of Theorem 2.7 can be argued in the same manner as that given for Theorem III.6.1, and vice versa. However, by examining these two proofs, it appears that the present one is simpler.

V.3. The Conditional Gradient Algorithm

In this section we consider optimal policy problem (P) posed in Section IV.3. For convenience this optimization problem is to be referred to as problem (IV.3.P). Furthermore, all the conditions imposed in Sections IV.2, IV.3 and IV.5 are assumed to hold throughout the rest of this section.

Similar to Theorem III.6.1, the weakness of the convergence results of Theorem IV.6.2 is that a sequence $\{(\sigma^k, u^k)\}$ of policies in $\mathscr{D}_p$ constructed by algorithm (IV.A) does not necessarily possess accumulation points in the strong topology of $R^{m_1} \times L_\infty(\hat{Q}, U)$. The aim of this section is to overcome this weakness. For this we need to define a topology on the space of relaxed policies. This topology is weak enough that, for any sequence of ordinary policies generated by algorithm (IV.A), its associated sequence of relaxed policies has accumulation points. However, the topology is strong enough to ensure that such accumulation points satisfy a meaningful necessary condition for optimality.

V.3.1. RELAXED POLICIES

Let S (resp. U) be a given nonempty compact and convex subset of R^{m_1} (resp. R^{m_2}). As in Chapter IV, the set $\mathscr{U}$ of all admissible controls is just $L_\infty(\hat{Q}, U)$ and the class $\mathscr{D}_p$ of policies is defined by

$$\mathscr{D}_p \equiv S \times \mathscr{U}.$$

The set $\mathscr{V}$ of relaxed controls is as defined in Section V.2.1. Let

$$\mathscr{R}_p \equiv S \times \mathscr{V},$$

and $\mathscr{R}_p$ *is called the class of relaxed policies.*

REMARK 3.1. The set $\mathscr{D}_p$ of all policies can be embedded in $\mathscr{R}_p$ by identifying each element $(\sigma, u) \in \mathscr{D}_p$ with the element $(\sigma, \delta_u) \in \mathscr{R}_p$, where δ_u is the

Dirac measure. This identification is to remain in force throughout the rest of the section.

For each $v \in \mathscr{V}$ and for any $q \in L_1(Q, C(S \times U))$, $q[v]$ is a real-valued function on $Q \times S$, defined by

$$q[v](x, t, \sigma) = \int_U q(x, t, \sigma, w)v(\hat{x}, t)(dw). \tag{3.1}$$

DEFINITION 3.1. *Let* $\{(\sigma^k, v^k)\}$ *be a sequence of relaxed policies in* $\mathscr{R}_p$ *and* $(\bar{\sigma}, \bar{v}) \in \mathscr{R}_p$. *Then* (σ^k, v^k) *is said to converge to* $(\bar{\sigma}, \bar{v})$ *in the sense of policy measure* (ispm) *if*

$$\sigma^k \to \bar{\sigma} \quad \text{in} \quad R^{m_1}, \tag{3.2a}$$

and

$$v^k \rightharpoonup v \quad \text{in} \quad \mathscr{V}. \tag{3.2b}$$

For brevity we write

$$(\sigma^k, v^k) \xrightarrow{\text{ispm}} (\bar{\sigma}, \bar{v}), \tag{3.3}$$

if $\{(\sigma^k, v^k)\}$ *converges to* $(\bar{\sigma}, \bar{v})$ *in the sense of policy measure.*

REMARK 3.2. If $(\sigma^k, v^k) \xrightarrow{\text{ispm}} (\bar{\sigma}, \bar{v})$, then it follows that, for any $q \in L_1(Q, C(S \times U))$,

$$\iint_Q q[v^k](x, t, \sigma^k)\, dx\, dt \to \iint_Q q[\bar{v}](x, t, \bar{\sigma})\, dx\, dt, \tag{3.4}$$

as $k \to \infty$.

REMARK 3.3. Recall that S is compact in R^{m_1}, and recall from Remark 2.1 that $\mathscr{V}$ is sequentially compact in $\mathscr{N}$. Thus it is clear that the set $\mathscr{R}_p$ is sequentially compact in $R^{m_1} \times \mathscr{N}$. In other words, for any sequence $\{(\sigma^k, v^k)\}$ of relaxed policies in $\mathscr{R}_p$, there exists a subsequence $\{(\sigma^{k(l)}, v^{k(l)})\}$ and an element $(\bar{\sigma}, \bar{v}) \in \mathscr{R}_p$ such that

$$(\sigma^{k(l)}, v^{k(l)}) \xrightarrow{\text{ispm}} (\bar{\sigma}, \bar{v}),$$

as $l \to \infty$.

V.3.2. THE RELAXED PROBLEM

Consider system (IV.2.1) for each $(\sigma, v) \in \mathscr{R}_p$ rather than for each $(\sigma, u) \in \mathscr{D}_p$:

$$L[\sigma, v]\phi(x, t) = f[v](x, t, \sigma), \qquad (x, t) \in Q, \tag{3.5a}$$

$$\phi|_{t=0} = \phi_0(x), \qquad x \in \Omega, \tag{3.5b}$$

$$\phi|_\Gamma = 0, \qquad (x, t) \in \Gamma, \tag{3.5c}$$

where, for each $(\sigma, v) \in \mathscr{R}_p$, $L[\sigma, v]$ is defined by

$$L[\sigma, v]\psi \equiv \psi_t - \sum_{i,j=1}^{n} a_{ij}(x, t)\psi_{x_i x_j} - \sum_{i=1}^{n} b_i[v](x, t, \sigma)\psi_{x_i} - c[v](x, t, \sigma)\psi. \tag{3.6}$$

Moreover, $b_i[v](\cdot, \cdot, \sigma)$, $i = 1, \ldots, n$, $c[v](\cdot, \cdot, \sigma)$, and $f[v](\cdot, \cdot, \sigma)$ are as defined in (3.1).

Let h denote any of the functions b_i, $i = 1, \ldots, n$, c, and f. Define

$$h[\sigma, v] \equiv h[v](\cdot, \cdot, \sigma), \tag{3.7}$$

for all $(\sigma, v) \in \mathscr{R}_p$. For brevity, this notation is to be used throughout the rest of this section.

REMARK 3.4. From assumption (IV.A.3), it follows that there exists a constant M_1, independent of $(\sigma, v) \in \mathscr{R}_p$, such that

$$\|b_i[\sigma, v]\|_{\infty,Q} \leq M_1, \qquad i = 1, \ldots, n,$$

$$\|c[\sigma, v]\|_{\infty,Q} \leq M_1,$$

and

$$\|f[\sigma, v]\|_{\infty,Q} \leq M_1.$$

REMARK 3.5. Consider a sequence $\{(\sigma^k, v^k)\}$ of relaxed policies in $\mathscr{R}_p$ converging ispm to $(\bar{\sigma}, \bar{v}) \in \mathscr{R}_p$. Then it follows readily from Remarks 3.3 and 3.4 that

$$b_i[\sigma^k, v^k] \overset{w^*}{\to} b_i[\bar{\sigma}, \bar{v}], \qquad i = 1, \ldots, n,$$

$$c[\sigma^k, v^k] \overset{w^*}{\to} c[\bar{\sigma}, \bar{v}],$$

and

$$f[\sigma^k, v^k] \overset{w^*}{\to} f[\bar{\sigma}, \bar{v}],$$

in $L_\infty(Q)$, as $k \to \infty$.

The next theorem follows immediately from Theorem II.8.1 and Remark 3.4.

THEOREM 3.1. *For each $(\sigma, v) \in \mathscr{R}_p$, relaxed system* (3.5) *has a unique almost everywhere solution $\phi(\sigma, v)$ (in the sense of Definition III.2.1). Furthermore, $\phi(\sigma, v)$ satisfies the estimate*

$$\|\phi(\sigma, v)\|_{p,Q}^{(2,1)} \leq M_2\{\|f[\sigma, v]\|_{\infty,Q} + \|\phi_0\|_{\infty,\Omega}^{(2)}\}, \tag{3.8}$$

for all $p \in (\frac{3}{2}, \infty]$, where M_2 is a constant independent of $(\sigma, v) \in \mathscr{R}_p$.

From Remark 3.4 and assumption (IV.A.4), we can find a constant M_3, independent of $(\sigma, v) \in \mathscr{R}_p$, such that estimate (3.8) reduces to

$$\|\phi(\sigma, v)\|_{p,Q}^{(1,2)} \leq M_3, \tag{3.9}$$

for all $p \in (\frac{3}{2}, \infty]$.

On this basis, it follows from the same argument as that given for estimate (IV.2.8) that

$$|\phi(\sigma, v)|_{\bar{Q}}^{(3/2,3/4)} \leq M_4, \tag{3.10}$$

where M_4 is a constant, again independent of $(\sigma, v) \in \mathscr{R}_p$.

In the rest of this section, let $\phi(\sigma, v)$ denote the almost everywhere solution of relaxed system (3.5) corresponding to each $(\sigma, v) \in \mathscr{R}_p$.

LEMMA 3.1. *Consider relaxed system* (3.5). *Suppose* $\{(\sigma^k, v^k)\}$ *is a sequence of relaxed policies in* $\mathscr{R}_p$ *converging* ispm *to* $(\bar{\sigma}, \bar{v}) \in \mathscr{R}_p$. *Then, as* $k \to \infty$,

$$\phi(\sigma^k, v^k) \xrightarrow{u} \phi(\bar{\sigma}, \bar{v}),$$

$$\phi(\sigma^k, v^k)_{x_i} \xrightarrow{u} \phi(\bar{\sigma}, \bar{v})_{x_i}, \qquad i = 1, \ldots, n,$$

on $\bar{Q}$.

Proof. Following an argument similar to that given for Theorem 2.2, we can find a subsequence $\{(\sigma^{k(l)}, v^{k(l)})\}$ of the sequence $\{(\sigma^k, v^k)\}$ such that, as $l \to \infty$,

$$\phi(\sigma^{k(l)}, v^{k(l)}) \xrightarrow{u} \phi(\bar{\sigma}, \bar{v})$$

$$\phi(\sigma^{k(l)}, v^{k(l)})_{x_i} \xrightarrow{u} \phi(\bar{\sigma}, \bar{v})_{x_i}, \qquad i = 1, \ldots, n,$$

on $\bar{Q}$. However, $\phi(\bar{\sigma}, \bar{v})$ is unique. Thus the preceding convergence results are valid for the whole sequence and hence the proof is complete. ∎

V.3.3. OPTIMAL RELAXED POLICY PROBLEM

Consider the following cost functional

$$\hat{J}(\sigma, v) = \int_{\Omega} \phi(\sigma, v)(x, T) z_T(x)\, dx, \tag{3.11}$$

where $\phi(\sigma, v)$ is the almost everywhere solution of relaxed system (3.5) corresponding to the relaxed policy $(\sigma, v) \in \mathscr{R}_p$, and z_T is a given real-valued function defined on Ω and satisfies assumption (IV.A.5). In view of inequality (3.10) and assumption (IV.A.5), we can easily verify that the cost functional

$\hat{J}$ is bounded on $\mathscr{R}_p$. We may now pose the following optimal relaxed policy problem, *which is to be referred to as problem* (RP').

Subject to relaxed system (3.5), find a $(\sigma^*, v^*) \in \mathscr{R}_p$ such that

$$\hat{J}(\sigma^*, v^*) \leq \hat{J}(\sigma, v),$$

for all $(\sigma, v) \in \mathscr{R}_p$. This relaxed policy, (σ^*, v^*), is called an *optimal relaxed policy*.

As in Chapter IV, we need some preparations. First, we introduce the adjoint system for relaxed problem (RP') as follows:

$$L^*[\sigma, v]z = 0, \qquad (x, t) \in Q, \tag{3.12a}$$

$$z|_{t=T} = z_T(x), \qquad x \in \Omega, \tag{3.12b}$$

$$z|_{\Gamma} = 0, \qquad (x, t) \in \Gamma, \tag{3.12c}$$

where, for each $(\sigma, v) \in \mathscr{R}_p$, $L^*[\sigma, v]$ is defined by

$$L^*[\sigma, v]\psi \equiv -\psi_t - \sum_{i=1}^{n} \left(\sum_{j=1}^{n} a_{ij}(x, t)\psi_{x_j} + a_j[\sigma, v](x, t)\psi \right)_{x_i} - c[\sigma, v](x, t)\psi,$$

and

$$a_i[\sigma, v](x, t) = \sum_{j=1}^{n} \frac{\partial a_{ij}(x, t)}{\partial x_j} - b_i[\sigma, v](x, t), \qquad i = 1, \ldots, n.$$

For the adjoint system, the solution is to be understood as in the sense of Definition III.3.1.

Following arguments similar to those appearing in Section IV.3, we obtain this remark.

REMARK 3.6.

(i) For each $(\sigma, v) \in \mathscr{R}_p$, adjoint system (3.12) admits a unique weak solution $z(\sigma, v)$ that satisfies the estimate

$$\|z(\sigma, v)\|_Q \leq M_5, \tag{3.13}$$

where M_5 is a constant independent of $(\sigma, v) \in \mathscr{R}_p$.

(ii) There exists a constant M_6, independent of $(\sigma, v) \in \mathscr{R}_p$, such that

$$\|z(\sigma, v)\|_{1,Q} \leq M_6. \tag{3.14}$$

(iii) There exists a constant M_7, independent of $(\sigma, v) \in \mathscr{R}_p$, such that

$$|z(\sigma, v)(x, t)| \leq M_7, \tag{3.15}$$

for almost all $(x, t) \in Q$. Furthermore, for each $(\sigma, v) \in \mathscr{R}_p$, $z(\sigma, v)$ is continuous on Q.

From Remark 3.6(ii), z can be considered as a mapping from $\mathscr{R}_p$ into $L_1(Q)$. The next lemma shows the continuity of this mapping.

LEMMA 3.2. *Let* $\{(\sigma^k, v^k)\}$ *be a sequence in* $\mathscr{R}_p$ *and* $(\bar{\sigma}, \bar{v})$ *an element in* $\mathscr{R}_p$. *If* $(\sigma^k, v^k) \xrightarrow{\text{ispm}} (\bar{\sigma}, \bar{v})$, *then* $z(\sigma^k, v^k) \overset{s}{\to} z(\sigma, v)$ *in* $L_1(Q)$, *as* $k \to \infty$.

Proof. The proof is similar to that given for Theorem 2.3. ■

Now, for each $(\sigma^0, v^0) \in \mathscr{R}_p$, let

$$I(\sigma^0, v^0): \bar{Q} \times S \times U \to R^1$$

be defined by

$$\begin{aligned} I(\sigma^0, v^0)(x, t, \sigma, v) &\equiv \sum_{i=1}^{n} b_i(x, t, \sigma, v)\phi(\sigma^0, v^0)_{x_i}(x, t) \\ &\quad + c(x, t, \sigma, v)\phi(\sigma^0, v^0)(x, t) + f(x, t, \sigma, v). \end{aligned} \tag{3.16}$$

In view of (3.1), it follows that, for any $(\sigma^1, v^1) \in \mathscr{R}_p$,

$$\begin{aligned} I(\sigma^0, v^0)[\sigma^1, v^1](x, t) &= \sum_{i=1}^{n} b_i[\sigma^1, v^1](x, t)\phi(\sigma^0, v^0)_{x_i}(x, t) \\ &\quad + c[\sigma^1, v^1](x, t)\phi(\sigma^0, v^0)(x, t) + f[\sigma^1, v^1](x, t). \end{aligned} \tag{3.17}$$

To proceed further, let us introduce some more notation.

For each $(\sigma^0, v^0) \in \mathscr{R}_p$, let

$$H(\sigma^0, v^0)(x, t, \sigma, v) \equiv I(\sigma^0, v^0)(x, t, \sigma, v)z(\sigma^0, v^0)(x, t), \tag{3.18}$$

for all $(x, t, \sigma, v) \in \bar{Q} \times S \times U$; and, for each $(\sigma^0, v^0) \in \mathscr{R}_p$, let

$$H(\sigma^0, v^0)_\sigma[\sigma, v](x, t) \equiv \int_U H(\sigma^0, v^0)_\sigma(x, t, \sigma, w)v(\hat{x}, t)(dw), \tag{3.19}$$

and

$$H(\sigma^0, v^0)_v[\sigma, v](x, t) \equiv \int_U H(\sigma^0, v^0)_v(x, t, \sigma, w)v(\hat{x}, t)(dw), \tag{3.20}$$

for all $v \in \mathscr{V}$ and for all $(x, t, \sigma) \in \bar{Q} \times S$, where $H(\sigma, v)_\sigma$ and $H(\sigma, v)_v$ are as defined in Remark IV.5.1.

LEMMA 3.3. *Consider optimal relaxed policy problem (RP′). Then for any* $(\sigma^0, v^0) \in \mathscr{R}_p$, *there exists a* $(\sigma^*, u^*) \in \mathscr{D}_p$ *such that*

$$\left\langle \iint_Q H(\sigma^0, v^0)_\sigma[\sigma^0, v^0]\, dx\, dt, \sigma^* \right\rangle \le \left\langle \iint_Q H(\sigma^0, v^0)_\sigma[\sigma^0, v^0]\, dx\, dt, \sigma \right\rangle, \tag{3.21}$$

for all $\sigma \in S$; *and*

$$\left\langle \int_{\hat{\Omega}_{\hat{x}}} H(\sigma^0, v^0)_v[\sigma^0, v^0](\hat{x}, \hat{\hat{x}}, t)\, d\hat{\hat{x}}, u^*(\hat{x}, t) \right\rangle \leq \left\langle \int_{\hat{\Omega}_{\hat{x}}} H(\sigma^0, v^0)_v[\sigma^0, v^0](\hat{x}, \hat{\hat{x}}, t)\, d\hat{\hat{x}}, v \right\rangle, \tag{3.22}$$

for all $v \in U$ *and for almost all* $(\hat{x}, t) \in \hat{Q}$, *where* $\langle \cdot, \cdot \rangle$ *denotes the usual inner product in a Euclidean space.*

Proof. The proof is similar to that given for Lemma IV.6.1. ■

For each $(\sigma^0, v^0) \in \mathscr{R}_p$, define

$$\bar{\theta}(\sigma^0, v^0) \equiv \left\langle \iint_Q H(\sigma^0, v^0)_\sigma[\sigma^0, v^0]\, dx\, dt, \sigma^* - \sigma^0 \right\rangle + \iint_Q \left\{ \int_U \langle H(\sigma^0, v^0)_v(x, t, \sigma^0, w), u^*(\hat{x}, t) - w \rangle v^0(\hat{x}, t)(dw) \right\} dx\, dt, \tag{3.23}$$

where σ^* and u^* are as defined in Lemma 3.3.

Clearly, if $v^0 = \delta_{u^0}$ with $u^0 \in \mathscr{U}$, then

$$\begin{aligned} \bar{\theta}(\sigma^0, \delta_{u^0}) &= \left\langle \iint_Q H(\sigma^0, u^0)_\sigma[x, t, \sigma^0, u^0(\hat{x}, t)]\, dx\, dt, \sigma^* - \sigma^0 \right\rangle \\ &\quad + \iint_Q \langle H(\sigma^0, u^0)_v[x, t, \sigma^0, u^0(\hat{x}, t)], u^*(\hat{x}, t) - u^0(\hat{x}, t) \rangle\, dx\, dt \\ &= J_{(\sigma^0, u^0)}[(\sigma^*, u^*) - (\sigma^0, u^0)], \end{aligned} \tag{3.24}$$

where $J_{(\sigma^0, u^0)}$ is as defined in (IV.5.1).

DEFINITION 3.2. *A relaxed policy* $(\sigma, v) \in \mathscr{R}_p$ *is said to be extremal if*

$$\bar{\theta}(\sigma, v) = 0. \tag{3.25}$$

LEMMA 3.4. *Consider relaxed optimal policy problem (RP′). Let* $(\sigma, v) \in \mathscr{R}_p$ *be nonextremal, and* $\alpha, \beta \in (0, 1)$. *Then there exists a sequence* $\{(\sigma^m, v^m)\}$ *of relaxed policies in* $\mathscr{R}_p$ *and a positive integer* $\hat{m} > 0$ *such that*

$$\hat{J}(\sigma^m, v^m) - \hat{J}(\sigma, v) \leq (\alpha)^m \beta \bar{\theta}(\sigma, v), \tag{3.26}$$

for all integers $m \geq \hat{m}$, *where*

$$\sigma^m \equiv \sigma + (\alpha)^m(\sigma^* - \sigma). \tag{3.27}$$

Furthermore, if $v = \delta_u$ *with* $u \in \mathscr{U}$, *then*

$$v^m = \delta_{u + (\alpha)^m(u^* - u)}.$$

Proof. Let h denote any of the functions b_i, $i = 1, \ldots, n$, c, and f appearing in the Eq. (IV.2.1a). For each positive integer m, let

$$h_m(x, t) \equiv \int_U h(x, t, \sigma^m, w + (\alpha)^m(u^*(\hat{x}, t) - w))v(\hat{x}, t)(dw), \qquad (3.29)$$

where σ^m is defined by (3.27).

Since U is convex, it follows from Theorem I.3.1 that there exists, for each positive integer m, a relaxed control $v^m \in \mathscr{V}$ such that

$$h_m(x, t) = \int_U h(x, t, \sigma^m, w)v^m(x, t)(dw) \equiv h[\sigma^m, v^m](x, t). \qquad (3.30)$$

Note that the sets $\bar{Q}$, S, and U are compact. Thus by using assumption (IV.A.6) and Taylor's Theorem, we obtain

$$\begin{aligned} h(x, t, \sigma^m, w &+ (\alpha)^m(u^*(\hat{x}, t) - w)) \\ &= h(x, t, \sigma, w) + (\alpha)^m\langle h_\sigma(x, t, \sigma, w), \sigma^* - \sigma\rangle \\ &\quad + (\alpha)^m\langle h_v(x, t, \sigma, w), u^*(\hat{x}, t) - w\rangle + o((\alpha)^m), \end{aligned} \qquad (3.31)$$

where $o((\alpha)^m)/(\alpha)^m \to 0$, as $m \to \infty$, uniformly with respect to $(x, t, \sigma, w) \in \bar{Q} \times S \times U$.

From this equation, it follows that, for each positive integer m,

$$\begin{aligned} &\int_U h(x, t, \sigma^m, w + (\alpha)^m(u^*(\hat{x}, t) - w))v(\hat{x}, t)(dw) \\ &\quad = h[\sigma, v](x, t) + (\alpha)^m\langle h_\sigma[\sigma, v](x, t), \sigma^* - \sigma\rangle \\ &\quad\quad + (\alpha)^m \int_U \langle h_v(x, t, \sigma, w), u^*(\hat{x}, t) - w\rangle v(\hat{x}, t)(dw) + o((\alpha)^m), \end{aligned} \qquad (3.32)$$

and hence

$$\int_U h(x, t, \sigma^m, w + (\alpha)^m(u^*(\hat{x}, t) - w))v(\hat{x}, t)(dw) - h[\sigma, v](x, t) = O((\alpha)^m), \qquad (3.33)$$

where $|O((\alpha)^m)/(\alpha)^m| \leq N$ for all positive integers m, and the constant N is independent of $(x, t, \sigma, v) \in \bar{Q} \times \mathscr{R}_p$.

Consider the following sequence of the first boundary-value problems:

$$L[\sigma^m, v^m]\phi(x, t) = f[\sigma^m, v^m](x, t), \qquad (x, t) \in Q, \qquad (3.34a)$$

$$\phi|_{t=0} = \phi_0, \qquad x \in \Omega, \qquad (3.34b)$$

$$\phi|_\Gamma = 0, \qquad (x, t) \in \Gamma, \qquad (3.34c)$$

where σ^m and v^m are defined in (3.27) and (3.30), respectively.

For each positive integer m, let $\phi(\sigma^m, v^m)$ denote the almost everywhere solution of problem (3.34).

Now, in view of (3.11), we have

$$\hat{J}(\sigma^m, v^m) - \hat{J}(\sigma, v) = -\int_\Omega \psi^m(x, T)z_T(x)\,dx, \tag{3.35}$$

where

$$\psi^m \equiv \phi(\sigma, v) - \phi(\sigma^m, v^m). \tag{3.36}$$

Thus by following a similar argument as that given for Lemma III.4.1, we obtain

$$\begin{aligned}
&\int_\Omega \psi^m(x, T)z_T(x)\,dx \\
&\quad = \iint_Q \left\{\int_U \{H(\sigma, v)(x, t, \sigma, w)\right. \\
&\qquad \left. - H(\sigma, v)(x, t, \sigma^m, w + (\alpha)^m(u^*(\hat{x}, t) - w))\}v(\hat{x}, t)(dw)\right\} dx\,dt \\
&\qquad - \beta^m - \gamma^m,
\end{aligned} \tag{3.37}$$

where

$$\beta^m \equiv \iint_Q \sum_{i=1}^n (b_i[\sigma, v] - b_i[\sigma^m, v^m])(\phi(\sigma, v)_{x_i} - \phi(\sigma^m, v^m)_{x_i})z(\sigma, v)\,dx\,dt, \tag{3.38}$$

and

$$\gamma^m \equiv \iint_Q (c[\sigma, v] - c[\sigma^m, v^m])(\phi(\sigma, v) - \phi(\sigma^m, v^m))z(\sigma, v)\,dx\,dt. \tag{3.39}$$

Since $(\sigma^m, v^m) \xrightarrow{\text{ispm}} (\sigma, v)$, it is clear from Lemma 3.1 that

$$\phi(\sigma^m, v^m) \xrightarrow{u} \phi(\sigma, v), \tag{3.40a}$$

and

$$\phi(\sigma^m, v^m)_{x_i} \xrightarrow{u} \phi(\sigma, v)_{x_i}, \qquad i = 1, \ldots, n, \tag{3.40b}$$

on $\bar{Q}$, as $m \to \infty$.

Now, by noting that Q is bounded and using (3.30), (3.33), and (3.40), it follows from (3.38) and (3.39) that

$$\beta^m = o((\alpha)^m), \tag{3.41}$$

and

$$\gamma^m = o((\alpha)^m). \tag{3.42}$$

Combining (3.35), (3.37), (3.41), and (3.42), we have

$$\begin{aligned}\hat{J}(\sigma^m, v^m) - \hat{J}(\sigma, v) &= \iint_Q \left\{ \int_U \{H(\sigma, v)(x, t, \sigma^m, w + (\alpha)^m(u^*(\hat{x}, t) - w)) \right. \\ &\quad \left. - H(\sigma, v)(x, t, \sigma, w)\} v(\hat{x}, t)(dw) \right\} dx\, dt \\ &\quad + o((\alpha)^m). \end{aligned} \tag{3.43}$$

From the definition of $H(\sigma, v)$ and Eq. (3.32), we readily deduce from (3.43), (3.19), (3.20), and (3.23) that

$$\begin{aligned}\hat{J}(\sigma^m, v^m) - \hat{J}(\sigma, v) &= (\alpha)^m \left\langle \iint_Q H(\sigma, v)_\sigma[\sigma, v](x, t)\, dx\, dt, \sigma^* - \sigma \right\rangle \\ &\quad + (\alpha)^m \iint_Q \left\{ \int_U \langle H(\sigma, v)_v(x, t, \sigma, w), u^*(\hat{x}, t) - w \rangle v(\hat{x}, t)(dw) \right\} dx\, dt \\ &\quad + o((\alpha)^m) = (\alpha)^m \bar{\theta}(\sigma, v) + o((\alpha)^m). \end{aligned} \tag{3.44}$$

Since $\beta \in (0, 1)$, it follows from (3.44) that there exists a positive integer $\hat{m}$ such that

$$\hat{J}(\sigma^m, v^m) - \hat{J}(\sigma, v) \leq (\alpha)^m \beta \bar{\theta}(\sigma, v), \tag{3.45}$$

for all integers $m \geq \hat{m}$.

It remains to prove the last part of the lemma. For this we note that if $v = \delta_u$ with $u \in \mathscr{U}$, then Eq. (3.30) becomes

$$\begin{aligned} h[\sigma^m, v^m](x, t) &= \int_U h(x, t, \sigma^m, w + (\alpha)^m(u^*(\hat{x}, t) - w)) v(\hat{x}, t)(dw) \\ &= h(x, t, \sigma^m, u(\hat{x}, t) + (\alpha)^m(u^*(\hat{x}, t) - u(\hat{x}, t))) \\ &= \int_U h(x, t, \sigma^m, w) \delta_{u(\hat{x}, t) + (\alpha)^m(u^*(\hat{x}, t) - u(\hat{x}, t))}(dw). \end{aligned}$$

This simply implies that $v^m = \delta_{u + (\alpha)^m(u^* - u)}$. Thus the proof is complete. ■

The next theorem presents a necessary condition for optimality for relaxed policy problem (RP′).

THEOREM 3.2. *Consider relaxed policy problem (RP′). If $(\bar{\sigma}, \bar{v}) \in \mathscr{R}_p$ is optimal, then it is extremal. That is to say, $(\bar{\sigma}, \bar{v}) \in D$, where*

$$D \equiv \{(\sigma, v) \in \mathscr{R}_p : \bar{\theta}(\sigma, v) = 0\}.$$

Proof. The proof follows immediately from Lemma 3.4. ■

V.3.4. CONVERGENCE OF THE ALGORITHM

Consider optimal policy problem (IV.3.P). Let $\{(\sigma^k, u^k)\}$ be a sequence of ordinary policies constructed by algorithm (IV.A). In Theorem IV.6.2 we have shown that its accumulation points in the strong topology of $R^{m_1} \times L_\infty(\hat{Q}, U)$ satisfy optimality condition (IV.6.9). Since such accumulation points may not exist, the concept of convergence in the sense of policy measure is employed in Section 3.3. In the present section, the primary aim is to show that accumulation points in this sense (which are guaranteed to exist by Remark 3.3) satisfy condition (3.25), which is a necessary condition for optimality for the corresponding optimal relaxed policy problem (RP′).

To begin, we need to show that the function $\bar{\theta}$ is upper semicontinuous. More precisely, we need the following lemma.

LEMMA 3.5. *Let $\{(\sigma^k, v^k)\}$ be a sequence in $\mathscr{R}_p$. Then there exists a subsequence $\{(\sigma^{k(l)}, v^{k(l)})\}$ of the sequence $\{(\sigma^k, v^k)\}$ and an element $(\bar{\sigma}, \bar{v}) \in \mathscr{R}_p$ such that*

$$(\sigma^{k(l)}, v^{k(l)}) \xrightarrow{\text{ispm}} (\bar{\sigma}, \bar{v}),$$

as $l \to \infty$. Furthermore, for any $\varepsilon > 0$, there exists a positive integer $\hat{l}$ such that

$$\bar{\theta}(\sigma^{k(l)}, v^{k(l)}) \leq \bar{\theta}(\bar{\sigma}, \bar{v}) + \varepsilon, \tag{3.46}$$

for all $l \geq \hat{l}$ (i.e., $\bar{\theta}$ is upper semicontinuous).

Proof. The first part of the lemma follows readily from Remark 3.3.

To prove the second part of the lemma, let $\sigma^{k(l),*}$ and $u^{k(l),*}$ be as defined in (3.21) and (3.22), respectively. Similarly, $\bar{\sigma}^*$ and $\bar{u}^*$ are also as defined in (3.21) and (3.22), respectively. Then it is clear that, for all $\tau \in [0, 1]$,

$$\left\langle \iint_Q H(\sigma^{k(l)}, v^{k(l)})_\sigma[\sigma^{k(l)}, v^{k(l)}]\, dx\, dt, \sigma^{k(l),*} \right\rangle$$
$$\leq \left\langle \iint_Q H(\sigma^{k(l)}, \sigma^{k(l)})_\sigma[\sigma^{k(l)}, \sigma^{k(l)}]\, dx\, dt, \bar{\sigma}^* + \tau(\sigma^{k(l),*} - \bar{\sigma}^*) \right\rangle \tag{3.47}$$

and

$$\iint_Q \langle H(\sigma^{k(l)}, v^{k(l)})_v[\sigma^{k(l)}, v^{k(l)}](x, t), u^{k(l),*}(\hat{x}, t)\rangle\, dx\, dt$$
$$\leq \iint_Q \langle H(\sigma^{k(l)}, v^{k(l)})_v[\sigma^{k(l)}, v^{k(l)}](x, t),$$
$$\bar{u}^*(\hat{x}, t) + \tau(u^{k(l),*}(\hat{x}, t) - \bar{u}^*(\hat{x}, t))\rangle\, dx\, dt. \tag{3.48}$$

Using Lemmas 3.1 and 3.2, (3.9), (3.14), assumption (IV.A.6), the first part of Lemma 3.5, Remarks 3.2 and 3.4, and the compactness of sets S and U, it can be verified that, for any $\varepsilon > 0$, there exists a $\tau_0 \in (0, 1]$ and a positive integer l_0 such that

$$\left| \iint_Q \langle H(\sigma^{k(l)}, v^{k(l)})_v[\sigma^{k(l)}, v^{k(l)}](x, t), \bar{u}^*(\hat{x}, t) + \tau(u^{k(l),*}(\hat{x}, t) - \bar{u}^*(\hat{x}, t))\rangle \, dx \, dt \right.$$

$$\left. - \iint_Q \langle H(\bar{\sigma}, \bar{v})_v[\bar{\sigma}, \bar{v}](x, t), \bar{u}^*(\hat{x}, t)\rangle \, dx \, dt \right|$$

$$\leq \left| \iint_Q \langle H(\sigma^{k(l)}, v^{k(l)})_v[\sigma^{k(l)}, v^{k(l)}](x, t), \right.$$

$$\bar{u}^*(\hat{x}, t) + \tau(u^{k(l),*}(\hat{x}, t) - \bar{u}^*(\hat{x}, t))\rangle \, dx \, dt$$

$$- \iint_Q \langle H(\bar{\sigma}, \bar{v})_v[\sigma^{k(l)}, v^{k(l)}](x, t),$$

$$\left. \bar{u}^*(\hat{x}, t) + \tau(u^{k(l),*}(\hat{x}, t) - \bar{u}^*(\hat{x}, t))\rangle \, dx \, dt \right|$$

$$+ \left| \iint_Q \langle H(\bar{\sigma}, \bar{v})_v[\sigma^{k(l)}, v^{k(l)}](x, t), \right.$$

$$\bar{u}^*(\hat{x}, t) + \tau(u^{k(l),*}(\hat{x}, t) - \bar{u}^*(\hat{x}, t))\rangle \, dx \, dt$$

$$\left. - \iint_Q \langle H(\bar{\sigma}, \bar{v})_v[\sigma^{k(l)}, v^{k(l)}](x, t), \bar{u}^*(\hat{x}, t)\rangle \, dx \, dt \right|$$

$$+ \left| \iint_Q \langle H(\bar{\sigma}, \bar{v})_v[\sigma^{k(l)}, v^{k(l)}](x, t), \bar{u}^*(\hat{x}, t)\rangle \, dx \, dt \right.$$

$$\left. - \iint_Q \langle H(\bar{\sigma}, \bar{v})_v[\bar{\sigma}, v^{k(l)}](x, t), \bar{u}^*(\hat{x}, t)\rangle \, dx \, dt \right|$$

$$+ \left| \iint_Q \langle H(\bar{\sigma}, \bar{v})_v[\bar{\sigma}, v^{k(l)}](x, t), \bar{u}^*(\hat{x}, t)\rangle \, dx \, dt \right.$$

$$\left. - \iint_Q \langle H(\bar{\sigma}, \bar{v})_v[\bar{\sigma}, \bar{v}](x, t), \bar{u}^*(\hat{x}, t)\rangle \, dx \, dt \right|$$

$$< \varepsilon/4, \tag{3.49}$$

for all $\tau \in [0, \tau_0]$ and for all integers $l \geq l_0$.

Similarly, there exists a $\tau_1 \in (0, 1]$ and a positive integer l_1 such that

$$\left|\left\langle \iint_Q H(\sigma^{k(l)}, v^{k(l)})_\sigma[\sigma^{k(l)}, v^{k(l)}]\, dx\, dt, \bar{\sigma}^* + \tau(\sigma^{k(l),*} - \bar{\sigma}^*)\right\rangle - \left\langle \iint_Q H(\bar{\sigma}, \bar{v})_\sigma[\bar{\sigma}, \bar{v}]\, dx\, dt, \bar{\sigma}^*\right\rangle\right| < \varepsilon/4, \tag{3.50}$$

for all $\tau \in [0, \tau_1]$ and for all integers $l \geq l_1$.

Again, by a similar token we can show that there exists a positive integer l_2 such that, for all integers $l \geq l_2$,

$$\left|\left\langle \iint_Q H(\sigma^{k(l)}, v^{k(l)})_\sigma[\sigma^{k(l)}, v^{k(l)}]\, dx\, dt, \sigma^{k(l)}\right\rangle - \left\langle \iint_Q H(\bar{\sigma}, \bar{v})_\sigma[\bar{\sigma}, \bar{v}]\, dx\, dt, \bar{\sigma}^*\right\rangle\right| < \varepsilon/4, \tag{3.51}$$

and

$$\left|\iint_Q \left\{\int_U \langle H(\sigma^{k(l)}, v^{k(l)})_v(x, t, \sigma^{k(l)}, w), w\rangle\, v^{k(l)}(\hat{x}, t)(dw)\right\} dx\, dt - \iint_Q \left\{\int_U \langle H(\bar{\sigma}, \bar{v})_v(x, t, \bar{\sigma}, w), w\rangle \bar{v}(\hat{x}, t)(dw)\right\} dx\, dt\right| < \varepsilon/4. \tag{3.52}$$

On the basis of (3.23), it can be verified that inequality (3.46) follows from inequalities (3.47)–(3.52), by setting $\hat{\tau} \equiv \min\{\tau_0, \tau_1\}$ and $\hat{l} \equiv \max\{l_0, l_1, l_2\}$. This completes the proof. ■

LEMMA 3.6. *Consider a sequence $\{(\sigma^k, u^k)\}$ of ordinary policies in $\mathscr{D}_p$, together with the associated sequence $\{(\sigma^k, \delta_{u^k})\} \equiv \{(\sigma^k, v^k)\}$ of relaxed policies in $\mathscr{R}_p$. Let $\alpha \in (0, 1)$, and let*

$$\sigma^{k,m} \equiv \sigma^k + (\alpha)^m(\sigma^{k,*} - \sigma^k), \tag{3.53}$$

and

$$v^{k,m} \equiv \delta_{u^k + (\alpha)^m(u^{k,*} - u^k)}, \tag{3.54}$$

where $\sigma^{k,*}$ and $u^{k,*}$ are as defined in (3.21) and (3.22), respectively. Then for any $\varepsilon > 0$, there exists a positive integer $\hat{m}$ such that, for all integers $m \geq \hat{m}$,

$$\|\phi(\sigma^{k,m}, v^{k,m}) - \phi(\sigma^k, v^k)\|_{\infty,Q}^{(2,1)} < \varepsilon \tag{3.55}$$

uniformly with respect to integers $k \geq 0$.

Proof. From Remark 3.4 and Theorem A.II.1 (of Appendix II), and the definitions of $\sigma^{k,m}$ and $v^{k,m}$, we obtain

$$\|\phi(\sigma^{k,m}, v^{k,m}) - \phi(\sigma^k, v^k)\|_{\infty,Q}^{(2,1)}$$

$$\leq N\Big\{\sum_{i=1}^{n} \|b_i[\sigma^{k,m}, v^{k,m}] - b_i[\sigma^k, v^k]\|_{\infty,Q}$$

$$+ \|c[\sigma^{k,m}, v^{k,m}] - c[\sigma^k, v^k]\|_{\infty,Q} + \|f[\sigma^{k,m}, v^{k,m}] - f[\sigma^k, v^k]\|_{\infty,Q}\Big\}$$

$$= N\Big\{\sum_{i=1}^{n} \|b_i(\sigma^{k,m}, u^{k,m}) - b_i(\sigma^k, u^k)\|_{\infty,Q}$$

$$+ \|c(\sigma^{k,m}, u^{k,m}) - c(\sigma^k, u^k)\|_{\infty,Q} + \|f(\sigma^{k,m}, u^{k,m}) - f(\sigma^k, u^k)\|_{\infty,Q}\Big\},$$

where

$$u^{k,m} \equiv u^k + (\alpha)^m(u^{k,*} - u^k),$$

and the constant N is independent of integers k, $m \geq 0$. Thus by virtue of the compactness of sets S and U, the conclusion of the lemma follows readily from Remark IV.2.6(i). ■

To prove the desired convergence result for algorithm (IV.A), we need the next lemma.

LEMMA 3.7. *Consider a sequence of ordinary policies* $\{(\sigma^k, u^k)\}$ *in* $\mathscr{D}_p$ *such that the associated sequence* $\{(\sigma^k, \delta_{u^k})\} \equiv \{(\sigma^k, v^k)\}$ *of relaxed policies in* $\mathscr{R}_p$ *converges ispm to* $(\bar{\sigma}, \bar{v}) \in \mathscr{R}_p \backslash D$, *where* D *is defined in Theorem 3.2. Let* $\sigma^{k,m}$ *and* $v^{k,m}$ *be defined by (3.53) and (3.54), respectively,* $\alpha, \beta \in (0, 1)$, *and* $m_k \equiv m(\sigma^k, v^k)$ *be the smallest positive integer* m *such that*

$$\hat{J}(\sigma^{k,m}, v^{k,m}) - \hat{J}(\sigma^k, v^k) \leq (\alpha)^m \beta \bar{\theta}(\sigma^k, v^k). \tag{3.56}$$

Then there exist a constant $\hat{\rho} > 0$ *and positive integers* $\hat{m}$ *and* $\hat{k}$ *such that, for all* $k \geq \hat{k}$,

$$m_k \leq \hat{m}, \tag{3.57}$$

and

$$\hat{J}(\hat{\sigma}^k, \hat{v}^k) - \hat{J}(\sigma^k, v^k) \leq -\hat{\rho}, \tag{3.58}$$

where $\hat{\sigma}^k \equiv \sigma^{k,m_k}$ *and* $\hat{v}^k \equiv v^{k,m_k}$.

REMARK 3.7. Under the situation of Lemma 3.7, it is easy to observe that

$$\hat{J}(\sigma^{k,m}, v^{k,m}) - \hat{J}(\sigma^k, v^k) = J(\sigma^k + (\alpha)^m(\sigma^{k,*} - \sigma^k), u^k + (\alpha)^m(u^{k,*} - u^*)) - J(\sigma^k, u^k), \tag{3.59}$$

and

$$\bar{\theta}(\sigma^k, v^k) = J_{(\sigma^k, u^k)}[(\sigma^{k,*}, u^{k,*}) - (\sigma^k, u^k)], \tag{3.60}$$

where $J_{(\sigma^k, u^k)}$ is as defined by (IV.5.1.).

We now return to prove Lemma 3.7.

Proof of Lemma 3.7. Following the proof of equality (3.44) with (σ, v), (σ^m, v^m), and the corresponding versions of relations (3.40) replaced, respectively, by (σ^k, v^k), $(\sigma^{k,m}, v^{k,m})$, and inequality (3.55), we can easily show that

$$\begin{aligned}\hat{J}(\sigma^{k,m}, v^{k,m}) - \hat{J}(\sigma^k, v^k) &\leq (\alpha)^m\bar{\theta}(\sigma^k, v^k) + o((\alpha)^m)\\ &= (\alpha)^m\beta\bar{\theta}(\sigma^k, v^k) + (\alpha)^m(1 - \beta)\bar{\theta}(\sigma^k, v^k) + o((\alpha)^m),\end{aligned} \tag{3.61}$$

for all integers $m \geq 0$, where $o((\alpha)^m)$ is uniform with respect to integers $k \geq 0$.

Since $\beta \in (0, 1)$ and $\bar{\theta}(\bar{\sigma}, \bar{v}) < 0$, we have

$$\bar{\theta}(\bar{\sigma}, \bar{v}) < \beta\bar{\theta}(\bar{\sigma}, \bar{v}). \tag{3.62}$$

Furthermore, there exists a positive integer m_0 such that

$$\bar{\theta}(\bar{\sigma}, \bar{v}) \leq -(\alpha)^{m_0} \equiv -\rho. \tag{3.63}$$

Using Lemma 3.5 and inequality (3.62), we can find a positive integer k_0 such that

$$\bar{\theta}(\sigma^k, v^k) < \beta\bar{\theta}(\bar{\sigma}, \bar{v}), \tag{3.64}$$

for all $k \geq k_0$. Thus it is clear that

$$(\alpha)^m(1 - \beta)\bar{\theta}(\sigma^k, v^k) + o((\alpha)^m) \leq (\alpha)^m(1 - \beta)\beta\bar{\theta}(\bar{\sigma}, \bar{v}) + o((\alpha)^m), \tag{3.65}$$

for all $k \geq k_0$.

Since $(1 - \beta)\beta\bar{\theta}(\bar{\sigma}, \bar{v}) < 0$, there exists, by using the definition of $o((\alpha)^m)$, a positive integer $\hat{m}_0$ such that

$$(\alpha)^m(1 - \beta)\beta\bar{\theta}(\bar{\sigma}, \bar{v}) + o((\alpha)^m) < 0, \tag{3.66}$$

for all $m \geq \hat{m}_0$.

Combining (3.61), (3.65), and (3.66), and then setting $\hat{m} = \max\{m_0, \hat{m}_0\}$, we obtain

$$\hat{J}(\sigma^{k,m}, v^{k,m}) - \hat{J}(\sigma^k, v^k) \leq (\alpha)^m\beta\bar{\theta}(\sigma^k, v^k), \tag{3.67}$$

for all $k \geq k_0$ and $m \geq \hat{m}$. However, from the definition of m_k, we see that m_k is the smallest positive integer m such that condition (3.67) is satisfied. Thus we have

$$m_k \leq \hat{m}, \tag{3.68}$$

for all $k \geq k_0$.

To show the validity of condition (3.58), we use the definition of m_k, (3.64), (3.63), and (3.68) to obtain

$$\hat{J}(\sigma^{k,m_k}, v^{k,m_k}) - \hat{J}(\sigma^k, v^k) \leq -(\alpha)^{m_k}(\beta)^2\rho \leq -(\alpha)^{\hat{m}}(\beta)^2\rho.$$

Now, by setting $\hat{\rho} \equiv (\alpha)^{\hat{m}}(\beta)^2\rho$ in the preceding inequality, we obtain condition (3.58) and hence the proof is complete. ■

The next theorem presents a convergence result for algorithm (IV.A).

THEOREM 3.3. *Let $\{(\sigma^k, u^k)\}$ be a sequence of ordinary policies in $\mathscr{D}_p$ constructed by algorithm* (IV.A). *Then there exists a subsequence $\{(\sigma^{k(l)}, u^{k(l)})\}$ of the sequence $\{(\sigma^k, u^k)\}$ and the element $(\bar{\sigma}, \bar{v}) \in \mathscr{R}_p$ such that*

$$(\sigma^{k(l)}, v^{k(l)}) \xrightarrow{\text{ispm}} (\bar{\sigma}, \bar{v}),$$

as $l \to \infty$, where $v^{k(l)} \equiv \delta_{u^{k(l)}}$. Furthermore,

$$\bar{\theta}(\bar{\sigma}, \bar{v}) = 0.$$

Proof. The first part of the theorem follows readily from Remark 3.3. For the second part of the theorem, we assume the contrary:

$$\bar{\theta}(\bar{\sigma}, \bar{v}) \neq 0.$$

Then from Lemma 3.7 there exist a positive constant $\hat{\rho}$ and a positive integer l_0 such that, for all $l \geq l_0$,

$$\hat{J}(\sigma^{k(l)+1}, \sigma^{k(l)-1}) - \hat{J}(\sigma^{k(l)}, v^{k(l)}) \leq -\hat{\rho}.$$

Thus

$$\hat{J}(\sigma^{k(l)}, v^{k(l)}) \to -\infty,$$

as $l \to \infty$. This contradicts the boundedness of the set

$$\{\hat{J}(\sigma, v) : (\sigma, v) \in \mathscr{R}_p\}.$$

Therefore, we conclude that

$$\bar{\theta}(\bar{\sigma}, \bar{v}) = 0.$$

This completes the proof. ■

V.4. The Feasible Directions Algorithm

Similar to previous sections, the aim of this section is to improve the convergence result of the feasible directions algorithm presented in Section IV.8 for solving the optimal control problem with terminal inequality constraints. All the assumptions imposed in Section IV.8 are assumed to hold throughout the rest of this section.

V.4.1. RELAXED OPTIMAL CONTROL PROBLEM

Consider the relaxed version of system (IV.8.1) for each $v \in \mathscr{V}$:

$$L[v]\phi(x,t) = f[v](x,t), \qquad (x,t) \in Q, \tag{4.1a}$$

$$\phi|_{t=0} = \phi_0(x), \qquad x \in \Omega, \tag{4.1b}$$

$$\phi|_{\Gamma} = 0, \qquad (x,t) \in \Gamma, \tag{4.1c}$$

where

$$L[v]\psi \equiv \psi_t - \sum_{i,j=1}^{n} a_{ij}(x,t)\psi_{x_i x_j} - \sum_{i=1}^{n} b_i[v](x,t)\psi_{x_i} - c[v](x,t)\psi, \tag{4.2}$$

and $b_i[v]$, $i = 1, 2, \ldots, n$, $c[v]$, and $f[v]$ are as defined in (2.2).

Let

$$g(v) \equiv \int_{\Omega} \phi(v)(x,T) z_T(x)\, dx, \tag{4.3}$$

where $\phi(v)$ is the almost everywhere solution (in the sense of Definition III.2.1) of system (4.1) corresponding to the $v \in \mathscr{V}$, and $z_T \in L_\infty(\Omega)$ is the weight function as defined in Section IV.8.

The class $\hat{\mathscr{F}}$ of feasible relaxed controls is defined as

$$\hat{\mathscr{F}} \equiv \{v \in \mathscr{V} : \hat{J}^j(v) \equiv h^j(g(v)) \le 0, j = 1, 2, \ldots, l\}, \tag{4.4}$$

where h^j, $j = 1, \ldots, l$, are as given in Section IV.8.

The optimal relaxed control problem, hereafter referred to as problem (RPT), can then be stated as follows.

Subject to system (4.1), find a feasible relaxed control $v \in \hat{\mathscr{F}}$ that minimizes the cost functional

$$\hat{J}^0(v) \equiv h^0(g(v)), \tag{4.5}$$

where h^0 is as given in Section IV.8.

REMARK 4.1. Let $\{v^k\}$ be a sequence of relaxed controls in $\mathscr{V}$ converging iscm to $\bar{v} \in \mathscr{V}$. Then it follows from assumption (A.3)′ in Section IV.8 that

$$b_i[v^k] \overset{w^*}{\to} b_i[\bar{v}], \qquad i = 1, 2, \ldots, n,$$

$$c[v^k] \overset{w^*}{\to} c[\bar{v}],$$

and

$$f[v^k] \overset{w^*}{\to} f[\bar{v}],$$

in $L_\infty(Q)$, as $k \to \infty$.

REMARK 4.2. Suppose $\{v^k\}$ is a sequence of relaxed controls in $\mathscr{V}$ converging iscm to $\bar{v} \in \mathscr{V}$. Then by virtue of Lemma 3.1 we see that, as $k \to \infty$,

$$\phi(v^k) \overset{u}{\to} \phi(\bar{v})$$

$$\phi(v^k)_{x_i} \overset{u}{\to} \phi(\bar{v})_{x_i}, \qquad i = 1, 2, \ldots, n,$$

on $\bar{Q}$.

The adjoint system to the relaxed control problem (RPT) is

$$L^*[v]z = 0, \qquad (x, t) \in Q, \tag{4.6a}$$

$$z|_{t=T} = z_T(x), \qquad x \in \Omega, \tag{4.6b}$$

$$z|_\Gamma = 0, \qquad (x, t) \in \Gamma, \tag{4.6c}$$

where the operator L^* is given by

$$L^*[v]\psi \equiv -\psi_t - \sum_{i=1}^{n} \left\{ \sum_{j=1}^{n} a_{ij}(x, t)\psi_{x_j} + a_i[v](x, t)\psi \right\}_{x_i} - c[v](x, t)\psi \tag{4.7}$$

with

$$a_i[v](x, t) \equiv \sum_{j=1}^{n} \frac{\partial a_{ij}(x, t)}{\partial x_j} - b_i[v](x, t). \tag{4.8}$$

For the adjoint system, the solution is to be understood as in the sense of Definition III.3.1.

REMARK 4.3. In view of Remark 3.6(ii), it follows that there exists a constant M, independent of $v \in \mathscr{V}$, such that

$$\|z(v)\|_{1,Q} \leq M.$$

REMARK 4.4. Let $\{v^k\}$ be a sequence in $\mathscr{V}$ converging iscm to $\bar{v} \in \mathscr{V}$. Then it is clear from Lemma 3.2 that

$$z(v^k) \xrightarrow{s} z(\bar{v}),$$

in $L_1(Q)$, as $k \to \infty$.

For a given $u \in \mathscr{U}$ and $v \in \mathscr{V}$, let

$$I(v)(x, t, u) \equiv \sum_{i=1}^{n} b_i(x, t, u)\phi(v)_{x_i}(x, t) + c(x, t, u)\phi(v)(x, t) + f(x, t, u),$$

and define

$$H(v)(x, t, u) \equiv I(v)(x, t, u)z(v)(x, t). \tag{4.9}$$

For each $\omega \in \mathscr{U}$ and $v \in \mathscr{V}$ we let

$$\theta^j(\omega \mid v) \equiv \iint_Q \left\{ \int_U \langle H(v)_v(x, t, w), \omega(x, t) - w \rangle v(x, t)(dw) \right\} h_g^j(g(v))\, dx\, dt, \tag{4.10}$$

where

$$h_g^j(g) \equiv \frac{dh^j(g)}{dg}.$$

If $v = \delta_u$ with $u \in \mathscr{U}$, then

$$\theta^j(\omega \mid \delta_u) = \iint_Q \langle H(\delta_u)_v(x, t, u(x, t)), \omega(x, t) - u(x, t) \rangle\, h_g^j(g(\delta_u))\, dx\, dt.$$

Thus from Theorem IV.8.1 we have

$$\theta^j(\omega \mid \delta_u) = J_u^j[\omega - u]. \tag{4.11}$$

Hence, $\theta^j(\omega \mid \delta_u)$ denotes the gradient of the functional J^j at the ordinary control u in the direction of $\omega - u$.

REMARK 4.5. Since h^j, $j = 0, 1, 2, \ldots, l$, are continuously differentiable, it follows from (4.3), Remark 4.2, and Remark 4.3 that

$$h_g^j(g(v^k)) \to h_g^j(g(\bar{v})),$$

as $v^k \xrightarrow{\text{iscm}} \bar{v}$.

Let $\hat{q} \equiv \{1, 2, \ldots, l\}$, $q_1 \equiv \{0\} \cup \hat{q}$, and q be an arbitrary subset of q_1. Define

$$\psi_q(v) \equiv \min_{\omega \in \mathscr{U}} \max_{j \in q} \{\theta^j(\omega \mid v)\}.$$

Furthermore, let $u_q^v \in \mathscr{U}$ be the ordinary control realizing this minimum, i.e.,

$$\psi_q(v) = \max_{j \in q} \{\theta^j(u_q^v \mid v)\}. \tag{4.12}$$

In particular, when $v = \delta_u$ with $u \in \mathscr{U}$, it follows from (4.11) that $\psi_q(\delta_u)$ is just the one defined in (IV.8.12).

REMARK 4.6. Note that $\psi_q(v) \leq 0$, for any $v \in \mathscr{V}$.

For reasons similar to that given in Section IV.8, we need to define the ε active constraints, i.e., for given $\varepsilon > 0$ and $v \in \mathscr{V}$, let

$$q_\varepsilon(v) \equiv \{0\} \cup \{j \in \hat{q} : \hat{J}^j(v) \geq -\varepsilon\}. \tag{4.13}$$

DEFINITION 4.1. *A relaxed control $v \in \mathscr{V}$ is said to be extremal if $v \in D$, where $D \equiv \{v \in \hat{\mathscr{F}} : \psi_{q_0(v)}(v) = 0\}$.*

V.4.2. CONVERGENCE ANALYSIS

In this subsection let $\{u^i\}$ be a sequence of feasible controls generated by the algorithm. From Lemma 2.3 the sequence $\{v^i\} \equiv \{\delta_{u^i}\}$ of the corresponding relaxed controls in $\hat{\mathscr{F}}$ has an accumulation point $\bar{v} \in \mathscr{V}$. Our aim is to show that $\bar{v} \in D$.

LEMMA 4.1. *Suppose $v^i \xrightarrow{\text{iscm}} \bar{v}$. Then for a given $\varepsilon > 0$, there exists an $i_0 > 0$ such that*

$$\psi_q(v^i) \leq \psi_q(\bar{v}) + \varepsilon, \tag{4.14}$$

for all $i \geq i_0$.

Proof. Let $\tau \in (0, 1)$, and let u_q^i and $\bar{u}_q$ be, respectively, the ordinary controls realizing the minimum in $\psi_q(v^i)$ and $\psi_q(\bar{v})$ [for the definition, see (4.12)]. Then

$$\psi_q(v^i) \leq \max_{j \in q} \iint_Q \left\{ \int_U \langle H[v^i]_v(x, t, w), \right.$$
$$\left. \bar{u}_q + \tau(u_q^i - \bar{u}_q) - w \rangle v^i(x, t)(dw) \right\} h_g^j(g(v^i))\, dx\, dt.$$

Now

$$\begin{aligned}
&\Bigg|\max_{j\in q}\iint_Q\left\{\int_U \langle H[v^i]_v(x,t,w),\bar{u}_q+\tau(u_q^j-\bar{u}_q)-w\rangle\right.\\
&\qquad\left.\times\, v^i(x,t)(dw)\right\}h_g^j(g(v^i))\,dx\,dt\\
&\qquad-\max_{j\in q}\iint_Q\left\{\int_U \langle H[v]_v(x,t,w),\bar{u}_q-w\rangle\bar{v}(x,t)(dw)\right\}h_g^j(g(\bar{v}))\,dx\,dt\Bigg|\\
&\le\max_{j\in q}\Bigg|\iint_Q\left\{\int_U \langle H[v^i]_v(x,t,w),\bar{u}_q+\tau(u_q^i-\bar{u}_q)-w\rangle\right.\\
&\qquad\left.\times\, v^i(x,t)(dw)\right\}h_g^j(g(v^i))\,dx\,dt\\
&\qquad-\iint_Q\left\{\int_U \langle H[\bar{v}]_v(x,t,w),\bar{u}_q+\tau(u_q^i-\bar{u}_q)-w\rangle\right.\\
&\qquad\left.\times\, v^i(x,t)(dw)\right\}h_g^j(g(v^i))\,dx\,dt\Bigg|\\
&\qquad+\max_{j\in q}\Bigg|\iint_Q\left\{\int_U \langle H[\bar{v}]_v(x,t,w),\bar{u}_q+\tau(u_q^i-\bar{u}_q)-w\rangle\right.\\
&\qquad\left.\times\, v^i(x,t)(dw)\right\}h_g^j(g(v^i))\,dx\,dt\\
&\qquad-\iint_Q\left\{\int_U \langle H[\bar{v}]_v(x,t,w),\bar{u}_q-w\rangle v^i(x,t)(dw)\right\}h_g^j(g(v^i))\,dx\,dt\Bigg|\\
&\qquad+\max_{j\in q}\Bigg|\iint_Q\left\{\int_U \langle H[\bar{v}]_v(x,t,w),\bar{u}_q-w\rangle v^i(x,t)(dw)\right\}h_g^j(g(v^i))\,dx\,dt\\
&\qquad-\iint_Q\left\{\int_U \langle H[\bar{v}]_v(x,t,w),\bar{u}_q-w\rangle v^i(x,t)(dw)\right\}h_g^j(g(\bar{v}))\,dx\,dt\Bigg|\\
&\qquad+\max_{j\in q}\Bigg|\iint_Q\left\{\int_U \langle H[\bar{v}]_v(x,t,w),\bar{u}_q-w\rangle v^i(x,t)(dw)\right\}h_g^j(g(\bar{v}))\,dx\,dt\\
&\qquad-\iint_Q\left\{\int_U \langle H[v]_v(x,t,w),\bar{u}_q-w\rangle\bar{v}(x,t)(dw)\right\}h_g^j(g(\bar{v}))\,dx\,dt\Bigg|.
\end{aligned}$$

The result then follows from Remarks 4.1–4.5, assumption (A.3)′ in Section IV.8, and that the set U is compact (and hence bounded) and $\tau \in (0, 1)$. can be chosen arbitrarily small. ■

Let $\varepsilon_a(u^i)$ be defined in (IV.8.20), i.e., the smallest value of ε_k at the exit of Step 3 in algorithm IV.8.2. Furthermore, let $k(u^i)$ be the smallest integer k at the exit of Step 4 in the same algorithm.

LEMMA 4.2. *Given $\bar{v} \in \hat{\mathscr{F}} \setminus D$, let $\{v^i\} \equiv \{\delta_{ui}\}$ be any infinite sequence of relaxed controls converging iscm to $\bar{v}$. Then*

(i) *there exist $\hat{\varepsilon} > 0$ and $i_0 > 0$ such that*

$$\varepsilon_a(u^i) \geq \hat{\varepsilon} > 0,$$

for all $i \geq i_0$;

(ii) *there exist $\delta > 0$, positive integers $\hat{k} > 0$, and $i_0 > 0$ such that, for all $i \geq i_0$,*

$$k(u^i) \leq \hat{k},$$

$$J^0(u'^i) - J^0(u^i) \leq -\delta,$$

$$J^j(u'^i) \leq 0, \qquad j \in \hat{q},$$

where

$$u'^i \equiv u^i + \beta^{k(u^i)}\bar{s}(u^i),$$

with

$$\bar{s}(u^i) \equiv \bar{s}^{u^i}_{\varepsilon_a(u^i)}$$

as defined in Remark IV.8.5.

Proof. The proof of (i) is similar to that of Lemma IV.8.4. The only difference is that (IV.8.23) is now obtained by Lemma 4.1 rather than the upper semicontinuity of $\psi(\cdot)$ in $\mathscr{U}$. The conclusion of (ii) follows directly from Lemma IV.8.5. ■

THEOREM 4.1. *Let $\{\bar{u}^i\}$ be a sequence of feasible controls generated by algorithm* (IV.8.2).*Then either the sequence is finite, in which case the algorithm jams in the inner loop of Step* 2 *and Step* 3, *and the last element of the sequence is in D, or the sequence is infinite and each accumulation point is in $\mathscr{D}$.*

Proof. The result follows from Lemma 4.2, by using a similar argument as that given for Theorem IV.8.2. ■

To close this section, we wish to show that $\psi_{q_0(v^*)}(v^*) = 0$ is a necessary condition for optimality for the optimal relaxed control problem (RPT).

THEOREM 4.2. *Suppose $v^* \in \hat{\mathscr{F}}$ is optimal for the relaxed control problem* (RPT). *Then*

$$\psi_{q_0(v^*)}(v^*) = 0.$$

Proof. From Remark 4.6, we recall that $\psi_{q_0(v^*)}(v^*) \le 0$. Thus to obtain a contradiction, we assume that $\psi_{q_0(v^*)}(v^*) < 0$.

Let $u^* \in \mathscr{U}$ be such that

$$\psi_{q_0(v^*)}(v^*) = \max_{j \in q_0(v^*)} \{\theta^j(u^* | v^*)\},$$

that is,

$$u^* \equiv u^{v^*}_{q_0(v^*)}.$$

Using a similar argument as that given for (3.45), we can show that there exists a sequence $\{v^m\}$ of relaxed controls in $\mathscr{V}$ and an integer $\hat{m}_0$ such that

$$[g(v^m) - g(v^*)]h^0_g(g(v^*))$$
$$= \left\{\int_\Omega [\phi(v^m)(x, T) - \phi(v^*)(x, T)]z_T(x)\,dx\right\}h^0_g(g(v^*)) \le (\alpha)^m \beta\theta^0(u^* | v^*), \tag{4.15}$$

for all integers $m > \hat{m}_0$, where $\alpha, \beta \in (0, 1)$.

From (4.13) and (4.12) we have

$$\theta^0(u^* | v^*) \le \max_{j \in q_0(v^*)} \theta^j(u^* | v^*) = \psi_{q_0(v^*)}(v^*). \tag{4.16}$$

On this basis, it follows from (4.15) that

$$[g(v^m) - g(v^*)]h^0_g(g(v^*)) \le (\alpha)^m \beta\psi_{q_0(v^*)}(v^*), \tag{4.17a}$$

for all $m > \hat{m}_0$.

From a similar argument as given for (3.44), we can show that

$$[g(v^m) - g(v^*)] = (\alpha)^m \bar{\theta}(v^*) + o((\alpha)^m), \tag{4.17b}$$

where

$$\bar{\theta}(v^*) \equiv \iint_Q \left\{\int_U \langle H(v^*)_v(x, t, w), u^*(x, t) - w\rangle v(x, t)(dw)\right\} dx\,dt.$$

By Taylor's theorem in remainder form, we obtain

$$\begin{aligned} h^0(g(v^m)) &- h^0(g(v^*)) \\ &= h^0_g(g(v^*))[g(v^m) - g(v^*)] \\ &\quad + \tfrac{1}{2}h^0_{gg}(g(v^*) + \tau(g(v^m) - g(v^*)))[g(v^m) - g(v^*)]^2 \end{aligned} \tag{4.18}$$

for some $\tau \in (0, 1)$.

From (4.3), (2.8) and because $z_T \in L_\infty(\Omega)$, we can find a constant N_0 such that

$$|g(v)| \le N_0,$$

for all $v \in \mathscr{V}$.

Since $h^0 \in C^2(R^1)$, it follows from the preceding inequality that

$$\tfrac{1}{2}|h^0_{gg}(\tau g(v^1) + (1 - \tau)g(v^2))| \leq N_1, \tag{4.19}$$

where the constant N_1 is independent of $v^1, v^2 \in \mathscr{V}$, and $\tau \in [0, 1]$.

By virtue of (4.18), (4.17), and (4.19), we obtain

$$h^0(g(v^m)) - h^0(g(v^*)) \leq (\alpha)^m \beta \psi_{q_0(v^*)}(v^*) + N_1[(\alpha)^m \bar{\theta}(v^*) + o((\alpha)^m)]^2, \tag{4.20}$$

for all $m > \hat{m}_0$.

Similarly, for all $j \in q_0(v^*)\backslash\{0\}$ there exists an integer $\hat{m}_1$ such that

$$h^j(g(v^m)) \leq (\alpha)^m \beta \psi_{q_0(v^*)}(v^*) + N_2[(\alpha)^m \bar{\theta}(v^*) + o((\alpha)^m)]^2, \tag{4.21}$$

for all $m > \hat{m}_1$, where the constant N_2 is such that

$$\tfrac{1}{2}|h^j_{gg}(\tau g(v^1) + (1 - \tau)g(v^2))| \leq N_2, \qquad j \in q_0(v^*)\backslash\{0\}, \qquad \tau \in [0, 1],$$

and $v^1, v^2 \in \mathscr{V}$.

For all other $j \in \hat{q}\backslash q_0(v^*)$, we can also find an integer $\hat{m}_2$ such that

$$h^j(g(v^m)) < 0, \tag{4.22}$$

for all $m > \hat{m}_2$.

Recall that $\theta_{q_0(v^*)}(v^*) < 0$ and that $\alpha \in (0, 1)$. Thus by virtue of (4.20), (4.21), and (4.22) there exists an integer $\bar{m} \geq \max\{\hat{m}_0, \hat{m}_1, \hat{m}_2\}$ such that

$$h_0(g(v^m)) - h^0(g(v^*)) < 0,$$

and

$$h^j(g(v^m)) \leq 0, \qquad j \in \hat{q},$$

for all $m > \bar{m}$. But this contradicts the optimality of v^* and hence the proof is complete. ■

V.5. Discussion

From the convergence result presented in Theorem III.6.1, we note that it is not satisfactory in the sense that a sequence $\{u^k\}$ of controls generated by algorithm III.A does not necessarily possess L_∞ accumulation points. In fact, since the class $\mathscr{U}$ of admissible controls is just $L_\infty(\hat{Q}, U)$, it is clear that the most natural type of convergence result should be in terms of the weak* topology of L_∞. However, unless the system dynamic is *linear* in u, the validity of this convergence result is *not* known even for lumped parameter systems.

Similar comments apply also to the convergence result reported in Theorem IV.6.2.

It is well known that the techniques used in the derivation of necessary conditions for optimality and the proof of the existence of optimal controls are completely different.

In the study of computational algorithms, it is interesting to observe that the techniques used to obtain improved controls are developed from or closely related to those for necessary conditions. By contrast, the tools used to analyze the convergence properties of sequences of controls so generated are often similar to those for existence theorems. Thus it appears that the topic of computational algorithms is a bridge connecting that of necessary conditions and that of existence theorems. Much research is needed in this area before the connection and relationship can be visualized in full.

The aim of this chapter is to improve the convergence results of Theorem III.6.2 and Theorem IV.6.2. The technique used is well known in the area of existence theorems. This technique uses a topology arising in the study of relaxed controls. Although the algorithm generates a sequence of ordinary controls (resp. policies), it is possible to associate with each ordinary control (resp. policy) an equivalent relaxed control (resp. policy). The topology on the space of relaxed controls (resp. policies) is weak enough to ensure that any infinite sequence of L_∞ bounded relaxed controls (resp. $R^{m_1} \times L_\infty$ bounded relaxed policies) has accumulation points, yet it is strong enough to ensure that its accumulation points satisfy a necessary condition for optimality for the corresponding relaxed optimal control (resp. policy) problem. This type of convergence result was introduced to the study of convergence of algorithms for optimal control problems for the first time in [WP.1]. It has been generalized to the case involving terminal inequality constraints in [MP.2]. Other related articles are [SV.1] and [War.2]. However, all these references involve only ordinary differential equations.

The concept of relaxed controls was introduced to the study of convergence of a strong variational algorithm for an optimal control problem involving a second-order hyperbolic partial differential equation with a Darboux boundary condition in [TCWC.1]. Note that the definition of relaxed control used in [WP.1] and [MP.2] is from the book by Young [Y.1]. In contrast, the definition introduced by Warga [War.1] appears to be more appropriate for the problem considered in [TCWC.1]. On the basis of this definition and other related results available in [War.1], some new results in this area are also obtained in [TCWC.1].

By introducing the topology on the space of relaxed controls (resp. policies), we obtain the corresponding relaxed optimal control (resp. policy) problem. Furthermore, any sequence $\{u^k\}$ (resp. $\{(\sigma^k, u^k)\}$) of L_∞ bounded relaxed controls (resp. $R^{m_1} \times L_\infty$ bounded relaxed policies) always has an accumulation point u^* (resp. (σ^*, u^*)). This sequential compactness result is a result of Warga [War.1] and is quoted in Remark 2.1 (resp. Remark 3.3). On this basis, the continuity properties needed in the proof of convergence of relaxed controls (resp. policies) can be established. Many of the techniques used are similar to those used for the existence theorems. For example, the proof of Theorem 2.2 (resp. Lemma 3.1) follows exactly the same approach for Theorem 3.1.5 of [AT.5], where the main concern is on existence theorems.

The technique of [TCWC.1] has been extended to optimal control problems involving different types of distributed parameter systems in [T.5] (strong variational algorithms for first boundary-value problems of a parabolic type) and [T.4] (conditional gradient algorithms for first boundary-value problems of a parabolic type). These two articles are, respectively, the main references of Sections 2 and 3 of this chapter.

The result of [T.4] has been extended to the case involving terminal inequality constraints in [WiT.1], which is, in turn, the main reference of Section 4 of Chapter V.

Part II of [MP.2] is devoted to showing that the sequences constructed by the algorithm in Part I of [MP.2] always have accumulation points that satisfy the necessary condition for optimality for the corresponding optimal relaxed control problems.

CHAPTER VI

Optimal Control Problems Involving Second Boundary-Value Problems

VI.1. Introduction

In Sections VI.2–VI.6 of this chapter three classes of optimal control problems involving second boundary-value problems of a parabolic type are considered. The controls are assumed to act on the forcing terms, and the initial and boundary conditions.

A sufficient condition for optimality is derived for the first optimal control problem. For the second problem a necessary and sufficient condition for optimality is derived and a method for constructing an optimal control is given. For the third problem a necessary and sufficient condition for optimality is derived, a result on the existence of optimal controls is proved, an iterative method for solving this optimal control problem is devised, and, finally, the convergence property of this iterative method is established.

In Section VI.7, an example arising naturally in the problem of optimally heating a slab of metal in a furnace is considered. Using the technique suggested in Section IV.9, the spline functions are used to approximate the problem with a sequence of optimal control problems of lumped parameter systems. Each of the approximate problems is in the form solvable by the algorithm of Appendix V.

VI.2. The General Problem Statement

As in Section II.2, Ω is a bounded domain in R^n with its boundary and closure denoted by $\partial\Omega$ and $\bar{\Omega}$, respectively. It is assumed throughout this chapter that *the boundary* $\partial\Omega$ *of the domain* Ω *is of the class* C^3. Let T be a fixed positive real number, $Q \equiv \Omega \times (0, T)$, $\bar{Q} \equiv \bar{\Omega} \times [0, T]$, and $\Gamma \equiv \partial\Omega \times [0, T]$.

Consider the parabolic partial differential operator L defined by

$$L\psi \equiv \psi_t - \sum_{i=1}^{n} \left[\sum_{j=1}^{n} a_{ij}(x, t)\psi_{x_j} + a_i(x, t)\psi \right]_{x_i} - \sum_{i=1}^{n} b_i(x, t)\psi_{x_i} - c(x, t)\psi, \tag{2.1}$$

where a_{ij}, $i, j = 1, \ldots, n$, a_i, $i = 1, \ldots, n$, b_i, $i = 1, \ldots, n$, and c are measurable functions from Q into R^1.

Let U_1, U_2, and U_3 be fixed compact and convex subsets of R^{m_1}, R^{m_2}, and R^{m_3}, respectively. Let u_1, u_2, and u_3 be measurable functions from Q, Ω, and Γ into U_1, U_2, and U_3, respectively. Then $u \equiv (u_1, u_2, u_3)$ is called an *admissible control*. We denote by $\mathscr{U} \equiv (\mathscr{U}_1, \mathscr{U}_2, \mathscr{U}_3)$ the class *of all such admissible controls*.

Let $F_i\colon Q \times U_1 \to R^1$, $i = 1, \ldots, n$, $f\colon Q \times U_1 \to R^1$, $\phi_0\colon \Omega \times U_2 \to R^1$, and $\Psi\colon \Gamma \times U_3 \to R^1$ be measurable functions.

We now consider the second boundary-value problem:

$$L\phi(x, t) = \sum_{i=1}^{n} [F_i(x, t, u_1(x, t))]_{x_i} - f(x, t, u_1(x, t)), \qquad (x, t) \in Q, \tag{2.2a}$$

$$\phi|_{t=0} = \phi_0(x, u_2(x)), \qquad x \in \Omega, \tag{2.2b}$$

$$\left[\frac{\partial\phi}{\partial\mathscr{N}} + \sigma(s, t)\phi \right]\Bigg|_{\Gamma} = \Psi(s, t, u_3(s, t)), \qquad (s, t) \in \Gamma, \tag{2.2c}$$

where

$$\frac{\partial\phi}{\partial\mathscr{N}} \equiv \sum_{i=1}^{n} \left[\sum_{j=1}^{n} a_{ij}(s, t)\phi_{x_j} + a_i(s, t)\phi \right] \cos\alpha_i, \qquad (s, t) \in \Gamma,$$

α_i is the angle formed by the outward normal to $\partial\Omega$ with the x_i axis, and $\sigma\colon \Gamma \to R^1$ a measurable function.

Since problem (2.2) is in the form of the second boundary-value problems introduced in Section II.2, it admits only weak solutions. To recall the notion of weak solutions, we need the following notation for the sake of brevity. Let

$$\mathscr{L}_1(\phi, \eta)(t) \equiv \int_\Omega \left\{ \sum_{i=1}^n \left(\sum_{j=1}^n a_{ij}(x, t)\phi_{x_j}(x, t) + a_i(x, t)\phi(x, t) \right) \eta_{x_i}(x, t) - \sum_{i=1}^n b_i(x, t)\phi_{x_i}(x, t)\eta(x, t) - c(x, t)\phi(x, t)\eta(x, t) \right\} dx, \tag{2.3}$$

$$\mathscr{L}_2(u_3)(\phi, \eta)(t) \equiv \int_{\partial\Omega} \{\sigma(s, t)\phi(s, t) - \Psi(s, t, u_3(s, t))\eta(s, t)\}\, ds, \tag{2.4}$$

and

$$\mathscr{L}_3(\hat{f}(u_1), \eta)(t) \equiv \int_\Omega \left\{ \sum_{i=1}^n F_i(x, t, u_1(x, t))\eta_{x_i}(x, t) + f(x, t, u_1(x, t))\eta(x, t) \right\} dx\, dt. \tag{2.5}$$

DEFINITION 2.1. *For each $u \in \mathscr{U}$, a function $\phi(u)$ is said to be a weak solution of the second boundary-value problem* (2.2) *if*

(i) $\phi(u) \in V_2^{1,0}(Q)$,
(ii) $\phi(u)$ *satisfies the integral identity*:

$$-\iint_Q \phi(u)(x, t)\eta_t(x, t)\, dx\, dt + \int_0^T \{\mathscr{L}_1(\phi(u), \eta)(t) + \mathscr{L}_2(u_3)(\phi(u), \eta)(t) + \mathscr{L}_3(\hat{f}(u_1), \eta)(t)\}\, dt = \int_\Omega \phi_0(x, u_2(x))\eta(x, 0)\, dx, \tag{2.6}$$

for any $\eta \in \tilde{W}_2^{1,1}(Q)$, where $\tilde{W}_2^{1,1}(Q)$ is defined in Section II.2.

Throughout this chapter, the following conditions are assumed.

(A.1) Assumption (II.A.1).

(A.2) Assumption (II.A.2).

(A.3) Assumption (II.A.3).

(A.4) $F_i(u_1) \equiv F_i(\cdot, \cdot, u_1(\cdot, \cdot)) \in L_2(Q)$, $i = 1, \ldots, n$, for each $u_1 \in \mathscr{U}_1$.

(A.5) $f(u_1) \equiv f(\cdot, \cdot, u_1(\cdot, \cdot)) \in L_{q_2, r_2}(Q)$, for any $u_1 \in \mathscr{U}_1$, where q_2 and r_2 are defined in assumption (II.A.5).

(A.6) Assumption (II.A.7).

(A.7) $\phi_0(u_2) \equiv \phi_0(\cdot, u_2(\cdot)) \in L_2(\Omega)$, for any $u_2 \in \mathscr{U}_2$.

(A.8) $\Psi(u_3) \equiv \Psi(\cdot, \cdot, u_3(\cdot, \cdot)) \in L_{q_4, r_4}(\Gamma)$ for any $u_3 \in \mathscr{U}_3$, where q_4 and r_4 are defined in assumption (II.A.8).

From Theorem II.5.5 and Theorem II.4.1, it follows that, for each $u \in \mathscr{U}$, problem (2.2) has a unique weak solution $\phi(u)$. Furthermore, $\phi(u)$ satisfies the following estimate:

$$\|\phi(u)\|_Q \leq K_1\{\|F(u_1)\|_{2,Q} + \|f(u_1)\|_{q_2,r_2,Q} + \|\phi_0(u_2)\|_{2,\Omega} + \|\Psi(u_3)\|_{q_4,r_4,\Gamma}\}, \tag{2.7}$$

where

$$\|F(u_1)\|_{2,Q} \equiv \left\{\iint_Q \sum_{i=1}^n [F_i(x, t, u_1(x, t))]^2 \, dx \, dt\right\}^{1/2}, \tag{2.8}$$

and the constant K_1 depends only on n, α_l, M_1, and the quantities q_2, r_2, q_4, and r_4.

Throughout the rest of this chapter, let $\phi(u)$ denote the weak solution of problem (2.2) corresponding to the control $u \equiv (u_1, u_2, u_3) \in \mathscr{U}$.

To specify our optimal control problem, we need to introduce a cost functional. For this, let $G_1: Q \times R^1 \to R^1$, $G_2: \Omega \times R^1 \to R^1$, $G_3: \Gamma \times R^1 \to R^1$, $H_1: Q \times U_1 \to R^1$, $H_2: \Omega \times U_2 \to R^1$ and $H_3: \Gamma \times U_3 \to R^1$ be measurable functions. Furthermore, we assume throughout that $G_1(x, t, \cdot)$, $G_2(x, \cdot)$, $G_3(s, t, \cdot)$, $H_1(x, t, \cdot)$, $H_2(x, \cdot)$ and $H_3(s, t, \cdot)$ are differentiable and convex functions on their respective domains of definition.

Our optimal control problem may now be stated as follows.

Subject to system (2.2), find a control $u \in \mathscr{U}$ that minimizes the cost functional

$$\begin{aligned} J(u) = & \iint_Q \{G_1(x, t, \phi(u)(x, t)) + H_1(x, t, u_1(x, t))\} \, dx \, dt \\ & + \int_\Omega \{G_2(x, \phi(u)(x, T)) + H_2(x, u_2(x))\} \, dx \\ & + \iint_\Gamma \{G_3(s, t, \phi(u)(s, t)) + H_3(s, t, u_3(s, t))\} \, ds \, dt. \end{aligned} \tag{2.9}$$

For convenience this optimal control problem will be referred to as problem (P).

VI.3. Preparatory Results

In this section we shall establish certain results that will be needed later. To begin, define

$$\nabla G_1(x, t, \hat{\phi}) \equiv \left.\frac{\partial G_1(x, t, \phi)}{\partial \phi}\right|_{\phi=\hat{\phi}},$$

$$\nabla G_2(x, \hat{\phi}) \equiv \left.\frac{\partial G_2(x, \phi)}{\partial \phi}\right|_{\phi=\hat{\phi}},$$

and

$$\nabla G_3(s, t, \hat{\phi}) \equiv \left.\frac{\partial G_3(s, t, \phi)}{\partial \phi}\right|_{\phi=\hat{\phi}},$$

where G_i, $i = 1, 2, 3$ are given in the definition of the cost functional J.

The following system is called the adjoint system.

$$L^*z(x, t) = \nabla G_1(x, t, \phi(u)(x, t)), \qquad (x, t) \in Q, \tag{3.1a}$$

$$z(x, t)|_{t=T} = \nabla G_2(x, \phi(u)(x, T)), \qquad x \in \Omega, \tag{3.1b}$$

$$\left.\left[\frac{\partial z}{\partial \mathcal{N}^*} + \sigma z\right]\right|_{\Gamma} = \nabla G_3(s, t, \phi(u)(s, t)), \qquad (s, t) \in \Gamma, \tag{3.1c}$$

where the operator L^* is defined by

$$L^*\psi \equiv -\frac{\partial \psi}{\partial t} - \sum_{i=1}^{n} \frac{\partial}{\partial x_i}\left(\sum_{j=1}^{n} a_{ij}(x, t)\psi_{x_j} - b_i(x, t)\psi\right)$$
$$+ \sum_{i=1}^{n} a_i(x, t)\psi_{x_i} - c(x, t)\psi, \tag{3.2}$$

and

$$\frac{\partial z}{\partial \mathcal{N}^*} \equiv \sum_{i=1}^{n}\left[\sum_{j=1}^{n} a_{ij}(s, t)z_{x_j} - b_i(s, t)z\right]\cos \alpha_i, \tag{3.3}$$

with α_i as defined for system (2.2).

For the adjoint system we introduce the following definition.

DEFINITION 3.1. *For each $u \in \mathscr{U}$, a function $z(u)$ is said to be a weak solution of the adjoint problem* (3.1) *if*

(i) $z(u) \in V_2^{1,0}(Q)$;

and

(ii) *$z(u)$ satisfies the integral identity:*

$$\iint_Q z(u)(x,t)\eta_t(x,t)\,dx\,dt$$

$$+\int_0^T \{\mathscr{L}_1^*(z(u),\eta)(t)+\mathscr{L}_2^*(u)(z(u),\eta)(t)+\mathscr{L}_3^*(\nabla G_1(u),\eta)(t)\}\,dt$$

$$=\int_\Omega \nabla G_2(x,\phi(u)(x,T))\eta(x,T)\,dx, \tag{3.4}$$

for any $\eta\in \tilde{W}_2^{1,1}(Q)\equiv\{\eta\in W_2^{1,1}(Q):\eta(x,0)=0\quad for\quad x\in\Omega\}$, where

$$\mathscr{L}_1^*(z,\eta)(t)\equiv\int_\Omega\left\{\sum_{i=1}^n\left[\sum_{j=1}^n a_{ij}(x,t)z_{x_j}(x,t)-b_i(x,t)z(x,t)\right]\eta_{x_i}(x,t)\right.$$
$$\left.+\sum_{i=1}^n a_i(x,t)z_{x_i}(x,t)\eta(x,t)-c(x,t)z(x,t)\eta(x,t)\right\}dx, \tag{3.5}$$

$$\mathscr{L}_2^*(u)(z,\eta)(t)\equiv\int_{\partial\Omega}\{[\sigma(s,t)z(s,t)-\nabla G_3(s,t,\phi(u)(s,t))]\eta(s,t)\}\,ds, \tag{3.6}$$

and

$$\mathscr{L}_3^*(\nabla G_1(u),\eta)(t)=-\int_\Omega \nabla G_1(x,t,\phi(u)(x,t))\eta(x,t)\,dx. \tag{3.7}$$

To proceed further, the following additional conditions on the functions G_i, $i=1,2,3$ are assumed throughout.

(A.9)

(i) For each $u\in\mathscr{U}$, $\nabla G_1(u)\equiv\nabla G_1(\cdot,\cdot,\phi(u)(\cdot,\cdot))\in L_{q_2,r_2}(Q)$, where q_2 and r_2 are defined in assumption (II.A.5);

(ii) for each $u\in\mathscr{U}$, $\nabla G_2(u)\equiv\nabla G_2(\cdot,\phi(u)(\cdot,T))\in L_2(\Omega)$; and

(iii) for each $u\in\mathscr{U}$, $\nabla G_3(u)\equiv\nabla G_3(\cdot,\cdot,\phi(u)(\cdot,\cdot))\in L_{q_4,r_4}(\Gamma)$, were q_4 and r_4 are defined in assumption (II.A.8).

Letting $t'=T-t$ and then setting $z(u)(x,T-t')\equiv\hat{z}(u)(x,t')$, adjoint system (3.1) can be reduced to the one involving the function $\hat{z}(u)$. This reduced system is in the form of system (2.2), for which all the hypotheses of Theorem II.4.5 and Theorem II.3.1 are satisfied. Thus from the same theorems and the definitions of $\hat{z}(u)(x,t')$, it follows that, for each $u\in\mathscr{U}$, adjoint system (3.1) has a unique weak solution $z(u)$ that satisfies the estimate

$$\|z(u)\|_Q\le K_2\{\|\nabla G_1(u)\|_{q_2,r_2,Q}+\|\nabla G_2(u)\|_{2,\Omega}+\|\nabla G_3(u)\|_{q_4,r_4,\Gamma}\}, \tag{3.8}$$

where the constant K_2 depends only on n, α_l, and M_1 and the quantities q_2, r_2, q_4, and r_4.

In our later analysis we need to smooth the coefficients and data of adjoint system (3.1) so that it admits classical solutions. For this we shall adopt the following convention:

$$a_{ii}(x, t) \equiv 1, \qquad i = 1, 2, \ldots, n,$$

$$a_{ij}(x, t) \equiv 0, \qquad i \neq j, \quad i, j = 1, 2, \ldots, n,$$

$$a_i(x, t) \equiv b_i(x, t) \equiv 0, \qquad i = 1, 2, \ldots, n,$$

for all $(x, t) \in R^{n+1} \backslash Q$;

$$\nabla G_1(u)(x, t) \equiv 0,$$

for all $u \in \mathscr{U}$ and for all $(x, t) \in R^{n+1} \backslash Q$; and

$$\nabla G_2(u)(x) \equiv 0,$$

for all $u \in \mathscr{U}$ and for all $x \in R^n \backslash \Omega$.

REMARK 3.1. Let α denote any of the functions a_{ij}, $i, j = 1, \ldots, n$, $a_i, i = 1, \ldots, n, b_i, i = 1, \ldots, n$, and c. Then let α^k be the integral average of α. Furthermore, let $\nabla G_1^k(u)$ and $\nabla G_2^k(u)$ be the integral averages of $\nabla G_1(u)$ and $\nabla G_2(u)$, respectively.

REMARK 3.2. From Theorem I.4.1(iii) we note that a_{ij}^k, $i, j = 1, \ldots, n$, $a_i^k, i = 1, \ldots, n, b_i^k, i = 1, \ldots, n, c^k, \nabla G_1^k(u)$, and $\nabla G_2^k(u)$ converge, respectively, to a_{ij}, $i, j = 1, \ldots, n$, a_i, $i = 1, \ldots, n$, b_i, $i = 1, \ldots, n$, c, $\nabla G_1(u)$, and $\nabla G_2(u)$ in the norms of the spaces to which they belong.

REMARK 3.3. Since $\partial\Omega$ is of the class C^3 and hence is obviously of the class C^2, it follows that there exist two sequences of functions, denoted by $\{\nabla G_3^k(u)\}$ and $\{\sigma^k\}$, in $C^{2,1}(\Gamma)$ such that , as $k \to \infty$, $\nabla G_3^k(u) \xrightarrow{s} \nabla G_3(u)$ in $L_{q_4, r_4}(\Gamma)$ and $\sigma^k \xrightarrow{s} \sigma$ in $L_{q_4, r_4}(\Gamma)$. Furthermore, since $\mathscr{H}^{l+1, (l+1)/2}(\Gamma) \supset C^{2,1}(\Gamma)$ for each $l \in (0, 1)$, we note that both the sequences $\{\nabla G_3^k(u)\}$ and $\{\sigma^k\}$ are also in $\mathscr{H}^{l+1, (l+1)/2}(\Gamma)$.

Let $\{\Omega^k\}$ be a sequence of open connected sets with sufficiently smooth boundaries such that $\overline{\Omega^k} \subset \Omega^{k+1} \subset \overline{\Omega^{k+1}} \subset \Omega$ for all integers $k \geq 1$ and $\lim_{k \to \infty} \Omega^k = \Omega$. For each $k \geq 1$, let d_k be an element in $C_0^\infty(\overline{\Omega})$ so that $d_k(x) = 1$ on Ω^k and $0 \leq d_k(x) \leq 1$ on $\overline{\Omega} \backslash \Omega^k$. Again, let $\{I^k\}$ be a sequence of open intervals such that $\overline{I^k} \subset I^{k+1} \subset \overline{I^{k+1}} \subset (0, T)$, for all integers $k \geq 1$ and $\lim_{k \to \infty} I^k = (0, T)$. For each $k \geq 1$, let $\tilde{d}_k$ be an element in $C_0^\infty([0, T])$ so that $\tilde{d}_k(t) = 1$ on I^k and $0 \leq \tilde{d}_k(t) \leq 1$ on $[0, T] \backslash I^k$.

We now consider the following sequence of second boundary-value problems:

$$L^{*,k}z(x,t) = \nabla G_1^k(u)(x,t), \qquad (x,t)\in Q, \tag{3.9a}$$

$$z(x,t)|_{t=T} = \nabla G_2^k(u)(x)d_k(x), \qquad x\in\Omega, \tag{3.9b}$$

$$\left[\frac{\partial}{\partial\mathcal{N}^{*,k}}z + \sigma^k(s,t)z\right]\bigg|_\Gamma = \nabla G_3^k(u)(s,t)\tilde{d}_k(t), \qquad (s,t)\in\Gamma, \tag{3.9c}$$

where, for each k, the operators $L^{*,k}$ and $\partial/\partial\mathcal{N}^{*,k}$ are as defined by L^* and $\partial/\partial\mathcal{N}^*$, in (3.2) and (3.3), with a_{ij}, a_i, b_i, and c replaced, respectively, by the corresponding integral averages.

It is clear that system (3.9) satisfies all the hypotheses required in Theorem II.8.4. Thus it follows that the system admits, for each k, a unique classical solution $z^k(u)$.

REMARK 3.4. Note that, for each $u\in\mathscr{U}$ and for each k, the classical solution $z^k(u)$ of system (3.9) is also the weak solution of the same system.

Recall that system (3.1) can be reduced to the one involving the function $\hat{z}(u)$, by letting $t' = T - t$ and then setting $z(u)(x, T-t') \equiv \hat{z}(u)(x,t')$. Similarly, system (3.9) can also be so reduced. Thus by virtue of Remarks 3.2 and 3.3, the definitions of the functions d_k and $\tilde{d}_k$, and Remark 3.4, it follows from Theorem II.5.1 that, for each $u\in\mathscr{U}$,

$$\hat{z}^k(u) \xrightarrow{s} \hat{z}(u)$$

in $V_2^{1,0}(Q)$, as $k\to\infty$. On this basis, it is clear from the definitions of $\hat{z}^k(u)$ and $\hat{z}(u)$ that

$$z^k(u) \xrightarrow{s} z(u) \tag{3.10}$$

in $V_2^{1,0}(Q)$, as $k\to\infty$.

Next, we need to consider another sequence of second boundary-value problems:

$$L^k\phi(x,t) = \sum_{i=1}^n (F_i(x,t,u_1(x,t)))_{x_i} - f(x,t,u_1(x,t)),$$
$$(x,t)\in Q, \tag{3.11a}$$

$$\phi(x,t)|_{t=0} = \phi_0(x,u_2(x)), \qquad x\in\Omega, \tag{3.11b}$$

$$\left[\frac{\partial\phi}{\partial\mathcal{N}^k} + \sigma^k(s,t)\phi\right]\bigg|_\Gamma = \Psi(s,t,u_3(s,t)), \qquad (s,t)\in\Gamma, \tag{3.11c}$$

where, for each k, the operators L^k and $\partial/\partial\mathcal{N}^k$ are as defined, respectively, by L and $\partial/\partial\mathcal{N}$, in system (2.2), with the coefficients a_{ij}, a_i, b_i, and c replaced by the corresponding integral averages.

From Theorem II.4.1, we note that, for each $u\in\mathscr{U}$ and for each positive integer k, problem (3.11) has a unique weak solution $\phi^k(u)$ (in the sense of

Definition 2.1). Thus by virtue of Remarks 3.2 and 3.3 and Theorem II.6.1, it follows that, for each $u \in \mathscr{U}$,

$$\phi^k(u) \xrightarrow{s} \phi(u) \tag{3.12}$$

in $V_2^{1,0}(Q)$, as $k \to \infty$.

VI.4. A Basic Inequality

In this section we shall derive a basic inequality that will then be used to derive a sufficient condition for optimality for problem (P).

To begin, we assume, unless otherwise stated, that the following additional conditions on the functions G_i, $i = 1, 2, 3$, and H_i, $i = 1, 2, 3$ are satisfied throughout.

(A.10) For each $u \equiv (u_1, u_2, u_3) \in \mathscr{U}$, $G_1(u) \equiv G_1(\cdot, \cdot, \phi(u)(\cdot, \cdot)) \in L_1(Q)$, and $H_1(u_1) \equiv H_1(\cdot, \cdot, u_1(\cdot, \cdot)) \in L_1(Q)$.

(A.11) For each $u \equiv (u_1, u_2, u_3) \in \mathscr{U}$, $G_2(u) \equiv G_2(\cdot, \phi(u)(\cdot, T)) \in L_1(\Omega)$, and $H_2(u_2) \equiv H_2(\cdot, u_2(\cdot)) \in L_1(\Omega)$.

(A.12) For each $u \equiv (u_1, u_2, u_3) \in \mathscr{U}$, $G_3(u) \equiv G_3(\cdot, \cdot, \phi(u)(\cdot, \cdot)) \in L_1(\Gamma)$, and $H_3(u_3) \equiv H_3(\cdot, \cdot, u_3(\cdot, \cdot)) \in L_1(\Gamma)$.

THEOREM 4.1. *Consider problem (P). Let $u^0 \equiv (u_1^0, u_2^0, u_3^0) \in \mathscr{U}$ be an admissible control, and let $z(u^0)$ be the weak solution of adjoint system* (3.1) *corresponding to the control u^0. Then*

$$\begin{aligned} J(u) - J(u^0) & \\ \geq \iint_Q \Bigg\{ & -\sum_{i=1}^{n} (F_i(x, t, u_1(x, t)) - F_i(x, t, u_1^0(x, t)))z(u^0)_{x_i}(x, t) \\ & - (f(x, t, u_1(x, t)) - f(x, t, u_1^0(x, t)))z(u^0)(x, t) \\ & + (H_1(x, t, u_1(x, t)) - H_1(x, t, u_1^0(x, t)))\Bigg\}\, dx\, dt \\ + \int_\Omega & \{(\phi_0(x, u_2(x)) - \phi_0(x, u_2^0(x)))z(u^0)(x, 0) \\ & + (H_2(x, u_2(x)) - H_2(x, u_2^0(x)))\}\, dx \\ + \iint_\Gamma & \{(\Psi(s, t, u_3(s, t)) - \Psi(s, t, u_3^0(s, t)))z(u^0)(s, t) \\ & + (H_3(s, t, u_3(s, t)) - H_3(s, t, u_3^0(s, t)))\}\, ds\, dt \end{aligned} \tag{4.1}$$

for all $u \in \mathscr{U}$.

Proof. Let

$$\Delta H(u, u^0) \equiv \iint_Q [H_1(x, t, u_1(x, t)) - H_1(x, t, u_1^0(x, t))]\, dx\, dt$$
$$+ \int_\Omega [H_2(x, u_2(x)) - H_2(x, u_2^0(x))]\, dx$$
$$+ \iint_\Gamma [H_3(s, t, u_3(s, t)) - H_3(s, t, u_3^0(s, t))]\, ds\, dt. \quad (4.2)$$

By the convexity properties of the functions G_i, $i = 1, 2, 3$ we obtain

$$J(u) - J(u^0)$$
$$\geq \iint_Q \nabla G_1(u^0)(x, t)(\phi(u)(x, t) - \phi(u^0)(x, t))\, dx\, dt$$
$$+ \int_\Omega \nabla G_2(u^0)(x)(\phi(u)(x, T) - \phi(u^0)(x, T))\, dx$$
$$+ \iint_\Gamma \nabla G_3(u^0)(s, t)(\phi(u)(s, t) - \phi(u^0)(s, t))\, ds\, dt + \Delta H(u, u^0).$$
$$(4.3)$$

From Remarks 3.2 and 3.3 we recall that $\nabla G_i^k(u^0)$, $i = 1, 2, 3$ converge, respectively, to $\nabla G_i(u^0)$, $i = 1, 2, 3$ in the norm of the spaces to which they belong. Thus by virtue of (3.12) it follows from inequality (4.3) that

$$J(u) - J(u^0)$$
$$\geq \lim_{k\to\infty} \left\{ \iint_Q \nabla G_1^k(u^0)(x, t)(\phi^k(u)(x, t) - \phi^k(u^0)(x, t))\, dx\, dt \right.$$
$$+ \int_\Omega \nabla G_2^k(u^0)(x) d_k(x)(\phi^k(u)(x, T) - \phi^k(u^0)(x, T))\, dx$$
$$\left. + \iint_\Gamma \nabla G_3^k(u^0)(s, t)\tilde{d}_k(t)(\phi^k(u)(s, t) - \phi^k(u^0)(s, t))\, ds\, dt \right\}$$
$$+ \Delta H(u, u^0). \quad (4.4)$$

In view of (3.9), the preceding inequality can be written as

$$J(u) - J(u^0) \geq \lim_{k\to\infty}\left\{\iint_Q L^{*,k}z^k(u^0)(x, t)(\phi^k(u)(x, t) - \phi^k(u^0)(x, t))\,dx\,dt\right.$$
$$+ \int_\Omega z^k(u^0)(x, T)(\phi^k(u)(x, T) - \phi^k(u^0)(x, T))\,dx$$
$$+ \iint_\Gamma \left[\frac{\partial}{\partial \mathcal{N}^{*,k}}\, z^k(u^0)(s, t) + \sigma^k(s, t)z^k(u^0)(s, t)\right]$$
$$\left.\times\,(\phi^k(u)(s, t) - \phi^k(u^0)(s, t))\,ds\,dt\right\} + \Delta H(u, u^0). \quad (4.5)$$

Since $z^k(u^0) \in W_2^{1,1}(Q)$ and $\phi^k(u)$ are the weak solution of system (3.11) corresponding to $u \in \mathcal{U}$, it follows from Lemma II.3.3 that

$$\int_\Omega \phi^k(u)(x, T)z^k(u^0)(x, T)\,dx - \iint_Q \phi^k(u)(x, t)z^k(u^0)_t(x, t)\,dx\,dt$$
$$+ \int_0^T \{\mathcal{L}_1^k(\phi^k(u), z^k(u^0))(t) + \mathcal{L}_2^k(u_3)(\phi^k(u), z^k(u^0))(t)$$
$$+ \mathcal{L}_3(\hat{f}(u_1), z^k(u^0))(t)\}\,dt$$
$$= \int_\Omega \phi_0(x, u_2(x))z^k(u^0)(x, 0)\,dx, \quad (4.6)$$

where

$$\mathcal{L}_1^k(\phi^k(u), z^k(u^0))(t)$$

[resp. $\mathcal{L}_2^k(u_3)(\phi^k(u), z^k(u^0))(t)$ and $\mathcal{L}_3(\hat{f}(u_1), z^k(u^0))(t)$] is defined by (2.3) [resp. (2.4) and (2.5)], with a_{ij}, a_i, b_i, c, σ, ϕ, and η replaced, respectively, by a_{ij}^k, a_i^k, b_i^k, c^k, σ^k, $\phi^k(u)$, and $z^k(u^0)$.

However, as a result of integration by parts with respect to x_i in those appropriate terms, we have

$$\int_0^T \mathcal{L}_1^k(\phi^k(u), z^k(u^0))(t)\,dt$$
$$= \iint_Q \left\{-\sum_{i=1}^n \frac{\partial}{\partial x_i}\left[\sum_{j=1}^n a_{ij}^k z^k(u^0)_{x_j} - b_i^k z^k(u^0)\right]\right.$$
$$\left. + \sum_{i=1}^n a_i^k z^k(u^0)_{x_i} - c^k z^k(u^0)\right\}\phi^k(u)\,dx\,dt$$
$$+ \int_0^T \left\{\int_{\partial\Omega}\left[\sum_{i=1}^n \left(\sum_{j=1}^n a_{ij}^k z^k(u^0)_{x_j} - b_i^k z^k(u^0)\right)\cos\alpha_i\right]\phi^k(u)(s, t)\,ds\right\}dt$$
$$= \iint_Q [L^{*,k}z^k(u^0) + z^k(u^0)_t]\phi^k(u)\,dx\,dt$$
$$+ \iint_\Gamma \left[\frac{\partial}{\partial \mathcal{N}^{*,k}}\, z^k(u^0)\right]\phi^k(u)\,ds\,dt. \quad (4.7)$$

By virtue of (4.7), equality (4.6) can be reduced to

$$\int_\Omega \phi^k(u)(x, T)z^k(u^0)(x, T)\,dx + \iint_Q (L^{*,k}z^k(u^0))\phi^k(u)\,dx\,dt$$
$$+ \iint_\Gamma \left(\frac{\partial}{\partial \mathcal{N}^{*,k}} z^k(u^0) + \sigma^k z^k(u^0)\right)\phi^k(u)\,ds\,dt$$
$$= \iint_Q \left\{- \sum_{i=1}^n F_i(x, t, u_1(x, t))z^k(u^0)_{x_i}(x, t)\right.$$
$$\left. - f(x, t, u_1(x, t))z^k(u^0)(x, t)\right\} dx\,dt$$
$$+ \int_\Omega \phi_0(x, u_2(x))z^k(u^0)(x, 0)\,dx$$
$$+ \iint_\Gamma \Psi(s, t, u_3(s, t))z^k(u^0)(s, t)\,ds\,dt. \tag{4.8}$$

Using (4.8), it follows from (4.5) that

$$J(u) - J(u^0)$$
$$\geq \lim_{k\to\infty} \left\{\iint_Q \left[- \sum_{i=1}^n (F_i(x, t, u_1(x, t)) - F_i(x, t, u_1^0(x, t)))z^k(u^0)_{x_i}(x, t)\right.\right.$$
$$\left. - (f(x, t, u_1(x, t)) - f(x, t, u_1^0(x, t)))z^k(u^0)(x, t)\right] dx\,dt$$
$$+ \int_\Omega (\phi_0(x, u_2(x)) - \phi_0(x, u_2^0(x)))z^k(u^0)(x, 0)\,dx$$
$$\left. + \iint_\Gamma (\Psi(s, t, u_3(s, t)) - \Psi(s, t, u_3^0(s, t)))z^k(u^0)(s, t)\,ds\,dt\right\}$$
$$+ \Delta H(u, u^0). \tag{4.9}$$

By Cauchy's inequality, we have

$$\left| \iint_Q \left\{\sum_{i=1}^n [F_i(x, t, u_1(x, t)) - F_i(x, t, u_1^0(x, t)]\right.\right.$$
$$\left.\left. \times (z^k(u^0)_{x_i}(x, t) - z(u^0)_{x_i}(x, t))\right\} dx\,dt\right|$$
$$\leq \sum_{i=1}^n \|F_i(u_1) - F_i(u_1^0)\|_{2,Q}\|z^k(u^0)_{x_i} - z(u^0)_{x_i}\|_{2,Q}$$
$$\leq \sum_{i=1}^n \|F_i(u_1) - F_i(u_1^0)\|_{2,Q}\|z^k(u^0) - z(u^0)\|_Q. \tag{4.10}$$

Again from Cauchy's inequality, it follows that

$$\left| \int_\Omega [\phi_0(x, u_2(x)) - \phi_0(x, u_2^0(x))] \right.$$

$$\left. \times [z^k(u^0)(x, 0) - z(u^0)(x, 0)]\, dx \right|$$

$$\leq \|\phi_0(u_2) - \phi_0(u_2^0)\|_{2,\Omega} \|z^k(u^0)(\cdot, 0) - z(u^0)(\cdot, 0)\|_{2,\Omega}$$

$$\leq \|\phi_0(u_2) - \phi_0(u_2^0)\|_{2,\Omega} \|z^k(u^0) - z(u^0)\|_Q. \tag{4.11}$$

By Hölder's inequality and Theorem I.4.5(ii), we obtain

$$\left| \iint_Q (f(x, t, u_1(x, t)) - f(x, t, u_1^0(x, t))) \right.$$

$$\left. \times (z^k(u^0)(x, t) - z(u^0)(x, t))\, dx\, dt \right|$$

$$\leq \|f(u_1) - f(u_1^0)\|_{q_2, r_2, Q} \|z^k(u^0) - z(u^0)\|_{\bar{q}_2, \bar{r}_2, Q}$$

$$\leq \|f(u_1) - f(u_1^0)\|_{q_2, r_2, Q} [\beta_2 \|z^k(u^0) - z(u^0)\|_Q], \tag{4.12}$$

where $\bar{q}_2 \equiv q_2/(q_2 - 1)$, $\bar{r}_3 \equiv r_3/(r_3 - 1)$, and the constant β_2 is as defined in Theorem I.4.5.

Again, by Hölder's inequality and Theorem I.4.8, we have

$$\left| \iint_\Gamma [\Psi(s, t, u_3(s, t)) - \Psi(s, t, u_3^0(s, t)] \right.$$

$$\left. \times [z^k(u^0)(s, t) - z(u^0)(s, t)]\, ds\, dt \right|$$

$$\leq \|\Psi(u_3) - \Psi(u_3^0)\|_{q_4, r_4, \Gamma} \|z^k(u^0) - z(u^0)\|_{\bar{q}_4, \bar{r}_4, \Gamma}$$

$$\leq \|\Psi(u_3) - \Psi(u_3^0)\|_{q_4, r_4, \Gamma} [\beta_3 \|z^k(u^0) - z(u^0)\|_Q], \tag{4.13}$$

where $\bar{q}_4 \equiv q_4/(q_4 - 1)$, $\bar{r}_4 \equiv r_4/(r_4 - 1)$, and the constant β_3 is as defined in Theorem I.4.8.

Combining (4.10)–(4.13), and then using (3.10), we see that the limit of the right-hand side of inequality (4.9) exists and is equal to the right-hand side of inequality (4.1). This completes the proof. ■

REMARK 4.1. We have shown, in deriving relationships (4.3)–(4.8), that

$$\iint_Q \nabla G_1(u^0)(x, t)(\phi(u)(x, t) - \phi(u^0)(x, t))\, dx\, dt$$
$$+ \int_\Omega \nabla G_2(u^0)(x)[\phi(u)(x, T) - \phi(u^0)(x, T)]\, dx$$
$$+ \iint_\Gamma \nabla G_3(u^0)(s, t)[\phi(u)(s, t) - \phi(u^0)(s, t)]\, ds\, dt$$
$$= \iint_Q \Big\{ - \sum_{i=1}^{n} [F_i(x, t, u_1(x, t)) - F_i(x, t, u_1^0(x, t))] z(u^0)_{x_i}(x, t)$$
$$- [f(x, t, u_1(x, t)) - f(x, t, u_1^0(x, t))] z(u^0)(x, t) \Big\}\, dx\, dt$$
$$+ \int_\Omega [\phi_0(x, u_2(x)) - \phi_0(x, u_2^0(x))] z(u^0)(x, 0)\, dx$$
$$+ \iint_\Gamma [\Psi(s, t, u_3(s, t)) - \Psi(s, t, u_3^0(s, t))] z(u^0)(s, t)\, ds\, dt. \quad (4.14)$$

In closing this section we present a sufficient condition for optimality for problem (P) in the following theorem.

THEOREM 4.2. *Consider problem (P). Then* $u^* \equiv (u_1^*, u_2^*, u_3^*) \in \mathscr{U}$ *is an optimal control if the following conditions are satisfied:*

$$- \sum_{i=1}^{n} F_i(x, t, u_1^*(x, t)) z(u^*)_{x_i}(x, t) - f(x, t, u_1^*(x, t)) z(u^*)(x, t)$$
$$+ H_1(x, t, u_1^*(x, t))$$
$$\leq - \sum_{i=1}^{n} F_i(x, t, v_1) z(u^*)_{x_i}(x, t) - f(x, t, v_1) z(u^*)(x, t)$$
$$+ H_1(x, t, v_1), \quad (4.15)$$

for all $v_1 \in U_1$ *and for almost all* $(x, t) \in Q$;

$$\phi_0(x, u_2^*(x)) z(u^*)(x, 0) + H_2(x, u_2^*(x))$$
$$\leq \phi_0(x, v_2) z(u^*)(x, 0) + H_2(x, v_2), \quad (4.16)$$

for all $v_2 \in U_2$ *and for almost all* $x \in \Omega$; *and*

$$\Psi(s, t, u_3^*(s, t)) z(u^*)(s, t) + H_3(s, t, u_3^*(s, t))$$
$$\leq \Psi(s, t, v_3) z(u^*)(s, t) + H_3(s, t, v_3), \quad (4.17)$$

for all $v_3 \in U_3$ *and for almost all* $(s, t) \in \Gamma$.

Proof. For any $u \in \mathscr{U}$, it follows from Theorem 4.1 and conditions (4.15)–(4.17) that

$$J(u) - J(u^*) \geq 0.$$

Therefore, u^* is an optimal control for problem (P). ■

REMARK 4.2. In the proofs of Theorems 4.1 and 4.2 we note that the convexity property of H_1, H_2, and H_3 in u is not used. This property is required only in proving the necessary condition for optimality and the existence of optimal controls.

VI.5. An Optimal Control Problem with a Linear Cost Functional

In this section we shall consider problem (P) under certain linearity assumptions. More precisely, we shall assume that the cost functional J takes the following special form:

$$\begin{aligned} J_1(u) = & \iint_Q \{\bar{G}_1(x, t)\phi(u)(x, t) + H_1(x, t, u_1(x, t))\}\, dx\, dt \\ & + \int_\Omega \{\bar{G}_2(x)\phi(u)(x, T) + H_2(x, u_2(x))\}\, dx \\ & + \iint_\Gamma \{\bar{G}_3(s, t)\phi(u)(s, t) + H_3(s, t, u_3(s, t))\}\, ds\, dt. \qquad (5.1) \end{aligned}$$

The functions $\bar{G}_i$, $i = 1, 2, 3$, are assumed throughout this section to satisfy the following conditions:

(A.13) $\bar{G}_1 \in L_{q_2, r_2}(Q)$, where q_2 and r_2 are defined in assumption (II.A.5).

(A.14) $\bar{G}_2 \in L_2(\Omega)$.

(A.15) $\bar{G}_3 \in L_{q_4, r_4}(\Gamma)$, where q_4 and r_4 are defined in assumption (II.A.8).

REMARK 5.1. Using the same arguments as those used to obtain inequalities (4.11)–(4.13), we can show that all the integrals involving the functions $\bar{G}_1$, $\bar{G}_2$, and $\bar{G}_3$ in the definition of the cost functional J_1 are finite under assumptions (A.13)–(A.15). Furthermore, assumption (A.9) is also guaranteed by these three assumptions.

For convenience, problem (P) with the cost functional J replaced by the cost functional J_1 will be referred as problem (P1).

The adjoint system for problem (P1) takes the following form:

$$L^*z(x,t) = \bar{G}_1(x,t), \qquad (x,t)\in\Omega, \tag{5.2a}$$

$$z(x,t)|_{t=T} = \bar{G}_2(x), \qquad x\in\Omega, \tag{5.2b}$$

$$\left[\frac{\partial z}{\partial \mathcal{N}^*} + \sigma(s,t)z\right]\Bigg|_{\Gamma} = \bar{G}_3(s,t), \qquad (s,t)\in\Gamma, \tag{5.2c}$$

where L^* and $\partial/\partial\mathcal{N}^*$ are as defined, respectively, in (3.9) and (3.10).

Note that adjoint system (5.2) is independent of the control $u\in\mathcal{U}$. Hence, the weak solution of the adjoint system, which is denoted by z, is also independent of $u\in\mathcal{U}$.

LEMMA 5.1. *Consider problem (P1). Then*

$$\begin{aligned} J_1(u) - J_1(u^0) &= \iint_Q \Bigg\{-\sum_{i=1}^n [F_i(x,t,u_1(x,t)) - F_i(x,t,u_1^0(x,t))]z_{x_i}(x,t) \\ &\qquad - [f(x,t,u_1(x,t)) - f(x,t,u_1^0(x,t))]z(x,t) \\ &\qquad + [H_1(x,t,u_1(x,t)) - H_1(x,t,u_1^0(x,t))]\Bigg\}\,dx\,dt \\ &\quad + \int_\Omega \{[\phi_0(x,u_2(x)) - \phi_0(x,u_2^0(x))]z(x,0) \\ &\qquad + [H_2(x,u_2(x)) - H_2(x,u_2^0(x))]\}\,dx \\ &\quad + \iint_\Gamma \{[\Psi(s,t,u_3(s,t)) - \Psi(s,t,u_3^0(s,t))]z(s,t) \\ &\quad + [H_3(s,t,u_3(s,t)) - H_3(s,t,u_3^0(s,t))]\}\,ds\,dt, \end{aligned} \tag{5.3}$$

for any $u\equiv(u_1,u_2,u_3)$ *and* $u^0\equiv(u_1^0,u_2^0,u_3^0)\in\mathcal{U}$.

Proof. The proof is similar to that given for Theorem 4.1, except with the cost functional J and adjoint system (3.1) being replaced, respectively, by the cost functional J_1 and adjoint system (5.2). Furthermore, inequality (4.3) becomes, in the present case, an equality. ■

THEOREM 5.1. *A necessary and sufficient condition for an admissible control* $u^*\equiv(u_1^*,u_2^*,u_3^*)$ *to be an optimal control is that*

$$\begin{aligned} &-\sum_{i=1}^n F_i(x,t,u_1^*(x,t))z_{x_i}(x,t) - f(x,t,u_1^*(x,t))z(x,t) + H_1(x,t,u_1^*(x,t)) \\ &\qquad \le -\sum_{i=1}^n F_i(x,t,v_1)z_{x_i}(x,t) - f(x,t,v_1)z(x,t) + H_1(x,t,v_1), \end{aligned} \tag{5.4}$$

for all $v_1 \in U_1$ *and for almost all* $(x, t) \in Q$;

$$\phi_0(x, u_2^*(x))z(x, 0) + H_2(x, u_2^*(x)) \le \phi_0(x, v_2)z(x, 0) + H_2(x, v_2), \tag{5.5}$$

for all $v_2 \in U_2$ *and for almost all* $x \in \Omega$; *and*

$$\Psi(s, t, u^*(s, t))z(s, t) + H_3(s, t, u^*(s, t)) \le \Psi(s, t, v_3)z(s, t) + H_3(s, t, v_3), \tag{5.6}$$

for all $v_3 \in U_3$ *and for almost all* $(s, t) \in \Gamma$.

Proof. The sufficiency of the condition follows as a special case from Theorem 4.2. It remains to prove that the condition is necessary. For this let $u^* \in \mathscr{U}$ be an optimal control. Let $v_1 \in U_1$ and (x_0, t_0) be an interior point of Q such that it is also a regular point for all those functions appearing on both sides of inequality (5.4). Let $\{S_n\} \subset Q$ be a sequence of balls with (x_0, t_0) as their center such that $|S_n| \to 0$ as $n \to \infty$ (where $|S_n|$ denotes the Lebesgue measure of S_n). Furthermore, let

$$u_1^n(x, t) = \begin{cases} v_1, & \text{if } (x, t) \in S_n, \\ u_1^*(x, t), & \text{if } (x, t) \notin S_n, \end{cases}$$

and define

$$u^n \equiv (u_1^n, u_2^*, u_3^*).$$

Then it follows from Lemma 5.1 and the optimality of u^* that

$$\begin{aligned} &J_1(u^n) - J_1(u^*) \\ &\quad = \iint_{S_n} \Big\{ -\sum_{i=1}^{n} (F_i(x, t, v_1) - F_i(x, t, u_1^*(x, t)))z_{x_i}(x, t) \\ &\quad\quad - (f(x, t, v_1) - f(x, t, u_1^*(x, t)))z(x, t) \\ &\quad\quad + (H_1(x, t, v_1) - H_1(x, t, u_1^*(x, t)))\Big\}\, dx\, dt \ge 0. \end{aligned}$$

Thus we have

$$\begin{aligned} &\lim_{n\to\infty} \Big\{ \frac{1}{|S_n|} \iint_{S_n} \Big[-\sum_{i=1}^{n} (F_i(x, t, v_1) - F_i(x, t, u_1^*(x, t)))z_{x_i}(x, t) \\ &\qquad - (f(x, t, v_1) - f(x, t, u_1^*(x, t)))z(x, t) \\ &\qquad + (H_1(x, t, v_1) - H_1(x, t, u_1^*(x, t)))\Big]\, dx\, dt \Big\} \\ &\quad = -\sum_{i=1}^{n} (F_i(x_0, t_0, v_1) - F_i(x_0, t_0, u_1^*(x_0, t_0)))z_{x_i}(x_0, t_0) \\ &\qquad - (f(x_0, t_0, v_1) - f(x_0, t_0, u_1^*(x_0, t_0)))z(x_0, t_0) \\ &\qquad + (H_1(x_0, t_0, v_1) - H_1(x_0, t_0, u_1^*(x_0, t_0))) \ge 0. \end{aligned} \tag{5.7}$$

Note that, for each $v_1 \in U_1$, almost all $(x, t) \in Q$ are regular points, that U_1 has countably dense subsets, and that all functions appearing in inequality (5.4) are continuous with respect to v_1. Thus we conclude from (5.7) that inequality (5.4) holds for every $v_1 \in U_1$ and for almost all $(x, t) \in Q$.

Inequalities (5.5) and (5.6) can also be derived similarly. This completes the proof. ■

The next theorem deals with the existence of optimal controls for problem (P1).

THEOREM 5.2. *Consider problem* (*P*1). *Then there exists an admissible control* $u^* \equiv (u_1^*, u_2^*, u_3^*) \in \mathcal{U}$ *such that*

$$-\sum_{i=1}^{n} F_i(x, t, u_1^*(x, t))z_{x_i}(x, t) - f(x, t, u_1^*(x, t))z(x, t) + H_1(x, t, u_1^*(x, t))$$
$$= \inf_{v_1 \in U_1} \left\{ -\sum_{i=1}^{n} F_i(x, t, v_1)z_{x_i}(x, t) - f(x, t, v_1)z(x, t) + H_1(x, t, v_1) \right\}, \tag{5.8}$$

for all $(x, t) \in Q$;

$$\phi_0(x, u_2^*(x))z(x, 0) + H_2(x, u_2^*(x)) = \inf_{v_2 \in U_2} \{\phi_0(x, v_2)z(x, 0) + H_2(x, v_2)\}, \tag{5.9}$$

for all $x \in \Omega$; *and*

$$\Psi(s, t, u_3^*(s, t))z(s, t) + H_3(s, t, u_3^*(s, t))$$
$$= \inf_{v_3 \in U_3} \{\Psi(s, t, v_3)z(s, t) + H_3(s, t, v_3)\}, \tag{5.10}$$

for all $(s, t) \in \Gamma$. *Furthermore,* u^* *is an optimal control.*

Proof. Let

$$B(x, t) = \inf_{v_1 \in U_1} \left\{ -\sum_{i=1}^{n} F_i(x, t, v_1)z_{x_i}(x, t) - f(x, t, v_1)z(x, t) + H_1(x, t, v_1) \right\}.$$

Since all the functions in the right-hand side of the preceding expression are continuous in $v_1 \in U_1$ and measurable in $(x, t) \in Q$, B is measurable in Q. Furthermore, since U_1 is compact, we have

$$B(x, t) \in \left\{ -\sum_{i=1}^{n} F_i(x, t, U_1)z_{x_i}(x, t) - f(x, t, U_1)z(x, t) + H_1(x, t, U_1) \right\}.$$

Thus it readily follows from Theorem I.6.1 that there exists a measurable function $u_1^*: Q \to U_1$ such that

$$B(x, t) = -\sum_{i=1}^{n} F_i(x, t, u_1^*(x, t))z_{x_i}(x, t) - f(x, t, u_1^*(x, t))z(x, t)$$
$$+ H_1(x, t, u_1^*(x, t)).$$

This means that $u_1^* \in \mathscr{U}_1$ and satisfies (5.8). Similarly, it can also be shown that there exist measurable functions $u_2^* \in \mathscr{U}_2$ and $u_3^* \in \mathscr{U}_3$ such that they satisfy (5.9) and (5.10), respectively.

Finally, since $u^* \equiv (u_1^*, u_2^*, u_3^*)$ belongs to $\mathscr{U}$ and satisfies the sufficient conditions (5.4)–(5.6), it is an optimal control. Thus the proof is complete. ∎

On the basis of the preceding theorem, an algorithm for constructing an optimal control for problem (P1) can be described as follows:

(1) Solve system (5.2) to find the function $z(x, t)$ and its derivatives $z_{x_i}(x, t)$.

(2) Find an admissible control $u^* \equiv (u_1^*, u_2^*, u_3^*)$ (whose existence is ensured by the first part of Theorem 5.2) such that Eqs. (5.8)–(5.10) hold. Then by virtue of the second part of Theorem 5.2, u^* is an optimal control for problem (P1).

VI.6. An Optimal Control Problem with a Linear System

In this section we shall consider problem (P) under certain linearity assumptions on the forcing terms and the initial and boundary data. More precisely, system (2.2) will take the following special form:

$$L\phi(x, t) = \sum_{i=1}^{n} \frac{\partial}{\partial x_i} [\bar{F}_i(x, t) \cdot u_1(x, t)] - \bar{f}(x, t) \cdot u_1(x, t), \qquad (x, t) \in Q, \tag{6.1a}$$

$$\phi|_{t=0} = \bar{\phi}_0(x) \cdot u_2(x), \qquad x \in \Omega, \tag{6.1b}$$

$$\left[\frac{\partial \phi}{\partial \mathscr{N}} + \sigma(s, t)\phi\right]\Bigg|_{\Gamma} = \bar{\Psi}(s, t) \cdot u_3(s, t), \qquad (s, t) \in \Gamma, \tag{6.1c}$$

where $\cdot$ denotes the usual inner product in any Euclidean space.

The vector values functions $\bar{F}_i$, $i = 1, \ldots, n$, $\bar{f}$, $\bar{\phi}_0$, and $\bar{\Psi}$ are assumed, throughout this section, to satisfy the following conditions.

(A.16) $\bar{F}_i \in L_2(Q, R^{m_1})$ for $i = 1, \ldots, n$.

(A.17) $\bar{f} \in L_{q_2, r_2}(Q, R^{m_1})$, where q_2 and r_2 are defined in assumption (II.A.5).

(A.18) $\bar{\phi}_0 \in L_2(\Omega, R^{m_2})$.

(A.19) $\bar{\Psi} \in L_{q_4, r_4}(\Gamma, R^{m_3})$, where q_4 and r_4 are defined in assumption (II.A.8).

For convenience, problem (P) with system (2.2) replaced by system (6.1) will be referred to as problem (P2).

REMARK 6.1. Consider problem (P2). Then the corresponding version of inequality (4.1) may be written as

$$\begin{aligned}
J(u) &- J(u^0) \\
&\geq \iint_Q \Big\{ -\sum_{i=1}^n (\bar{F}_i(x,t)\cdot(u_1(x,t) - u_1^0(x,t)))z(u^0)_{x_i}(x,t) \\
&\qquad - (\bar{f}(x,t)\cdot(u_1(x,t) - u_1^0(x,t)))z(u^0)(x,t) \\
&\qquad + (H_1(x,t,u_1(x,t)) - H_1(x,t,u_1^0(x,t)))\Big\}\,dx\,dt \\
&\quad + \int_\Omega \{(\bar{\phi}_0(x)\cdot(u_2(x) - u_2^0(x)))z(u^0)(x,0) \\
&\qquad + (H_2(x,u_2(x)) - H_2(x,u_2^0(x)))\}\,dx \\
&\quad + \iint_\Gamma \{(\bar{\Psi}(s,t)\cdot(u_3(s,t) - u_3^0(s,t)))z(u^0)(s,t) \\
&\qquad + (H_3(s,t,u_3(s,t)) - H_3(s,t,u_3^0(s,t)))\}\,ds\,dt, \qquad (6.2)
\end{aligned}$$

where $u \equiv (u_1, u_2, u_3)$, $u^0 \equiv (u_1^0, u_2^0, u_3^0) \in \mathscr{U}$, and $z(u^0)$ is the weak solution of adjoint system (3.1) corresponding to the control u^0.

In the rest of this section let $\nabla H_1(u_1)(x,t)$ denote the gradient of $H_1(x,t,\cdot)$ evaluated at $u_1(x,t)$. Furthermore, $\nabla H_2(u_2)(x)$ and $\nabla H_3(u_3)(s,t)$ are defined similarly.

THEOREM 6.1. *The control problem (P2) has a solution.*

Proof. In view of inequality (6.2) and the assumptions of those functions appearing on the right-hand side of (6.2), we note that the cost functional J subject to system (6.1) is bounded below on $\mathscr{U}$, that is,

$$\inf_{u\in\mathscr{U}} J(u) = \rho > -\infty. \qquad (6.3)$$

Let $\{u^k\} \subset \mathscr{U}$ be a sequence such that

$$\lim_{k\to\infty} J(u^k) = \rho. \qquad (6.4)$$

This sequence is known as a minimizing sequence. Define

$$\begin{aligned}
\bar{\mathscr{U}} \equiv \{u \equiv (u_1,u_2,u_3) : u_1(x,t) \in U_1 &\quad \text{for almost all} \quad (x,t)\in Q, \\
u_2(x) \in U_2 &\quad \text{for almost all} \quad x \in \Omega, \quad \text{and} \\
u_3(s,t) \in U_3 &\quad \text{for almost all} \quad (s,t)\in\Gamma\}.
\end{aligned}$$

Since U_1, U_2, and U_3 are compact and convex subsets of R^{m_1}, R^{m_2}, and R^{m_3}, respectively, $\tilde{\mathscr{U}}$ is sequentially compact in the weak* topology of $L_\infty(Q, R^{m_1}) \times L_\infty(\Omega, R^{m_2}) \times L_\infty(\Gamma, R^{m_3})$. Thus there exists a function $\tilde{u}^* \in \tilde{\mathscr{U}}$ and a subsequence of the sequence $\{u^k\}$, again indexed by k, such that $u^k \to \tilde{u}^*$, as $k \to \infty$, in the weak* topology just mentioned.

Let

$$u^*(x, t) = \begin{cases} \tilde{u}^*(x, t), & \text{if} \quad \tilde{u}^*(x, t) \in U, \\ v^*, & \text{if} \quad \tilde{u}^*(x, t) \notin U, \end{cases}$$

where $v^* \equiv (v_1^*, v_2^*, v_3^*)$ is any fixed vector in $U \equiv U_1 \times U_2 \times U_3$. Then $u^* \in \mathscr{U}$ and, furthermore, the sequence $\{u^k\}$ also converges to u^* in the same topology, as $k \to \infty$. We shall show that u^* is an optimal control.

In view of Remark 6.1 and the convexity of functions H_i, $i = 1, 2, 3$, we observe that

$$\begin{aligned} J(u^k) &- J(u^*) \\ \geq \iint_Q \Big\{ &- \sum_{i=1}^n [\bar{F}_i(x, t) \cdot (u_1^k(x, t) - u_1^*(x, t))] z(u^*)_{x_i}(x, t) \\ &- [\bar{f}(x, t) \cdot (u_1^k(x, t) - u_1^*(x, t))] z(u^*)(x, t) \\ &+ \nabla H_1(u_1^*)(x, t) \cdot (u_1^k(x, t) - u_1^*(x, t)) \Big\}\, dx\, dt \\ + \int_\Omega &\{[\bar{\phi}_0(x) \cdot (u_2^k(x) - u_2^*(x))] z(u^*)(x, 0) \\ &+ \nabla H_2(u_2^*)(x) \cdot (u_2^k(x) - u_2^*(x))\}\, dx \\ + \iint_\Gamma &\{[\bar{\Psi}(s, t) \cdot (u_3^k(s, t) - u_3^*(s, t))] z(u^*)(s, t) \\ &+ \nabla H_3(u_3^*)(s, t) \cdot (u_3^k(s, t) - u_3^*(s, t))\}\, ds\, dt. \end{aligned}$$

Since $\{u^k\}$ converges to u^* in the weak* topology, the right-hand side of the preceding inequality converges to zero, as $k \to \infty$. Thus

$$\lim_{k \to \infty} [J(u^k) - J(u^*)] \geq 0,$$

and hence from (6.3) and (6.4), we obtain

$$\inf_{u \in \mathscr{U}} J(u) \geq J(u^*).$$

This implies that u^* is an optimal control. Thus the proof is complete. ∎

REMARK 6.2. By examining the arguments given for Theorem 6.1, we note that

(i) $\mathscr{U}$ is sequentially compact in the weak* topology.
(ii) If a minimizing sequence converges to $u^* \in \mathscr{U}$ in the weak* topology, then u^* is an optimal control.

We now present a necessary and sufficient condition for optimality for problem (P2) in the next theorem.

THEOREM 6.2 *Consider problem (P2). A necessary and sufficient condition for $u^* \equiv (u_1^*, u_2^*, u_3^*) \in \mathscr{U}$ to be an optimal control is that*

$$-\sum_{i=1}^{n} (\bar{F}_i(x,t) \cdot u_1^*(x,t)) z(u^*)_{x_i}(x,t) - (\bar{f}(x,t) \cdot u_1^*(x,t)) z(u^*)(x,t) + H_1(x,t,u_1^*(x,t)) \equiv \min_{v_1 \in U_1} \left\{ -\sum_{i=1}^{n} (\bar{F}_i(x,t) \cdot v_1) z(u^*)_{x_i}(x,t) - (\bar{f}(x,t) \cdot v_1) z(u^*)(x,t) + H_1(x,t,v_1) \right\}, \tag{6.5}$$

for almost all $(x,t) \in Q$;

$$(\bar{\phi}_0(x) \cdot u_2^*(x)) z(u^*)(x,0) + H_2(x, u_2^*(x)) = \min_{v_2 \in U_2} \{(\bar{\phi}_0(x) \cdot v_2) z(u^*)(x,0) + H_2(x, v_2)\}, \tag{6.6}$$

for almost all $x \in \Omega$; and

$$(\bar{\Psi}(s,t) \cdot u_3^*(s,t)) z(u^*)(s,t) + H_3(s,t,u_3^*(s,t)) = \min_{v_3 \in U_3} \{(\bar{\Psi}(s,t) \cdot v_3) z(u^*)(s,t) + H_3(s,t,v_3)\}, \tag{6.7}$$

for almost all $(s,t) \in \Gamma$.

Proof. The sufficiency of the condition follows readily from inequality (6.2).

To prove that the condition is also necessary, let $u^* \in \mathscr{U}$ be an optimal control. Then for any $u \in \mathscr{U}$ and $0 < \varepsilon \leq 1$, we have

$$(J(u^* + \varepsilon(u - u^*)) - J(u^*))/\varepsilon \geq 0,$$

and hence

$$\lim_{\varepsilon \to 0} (J(u^* + \varepsilon(u - u^*)) - J(u^*))/\varepsilon = J_{u^*}(u) - J_{u^*}(u^*) \geq 0, \tag{6.8}$$

where

$$J_{u^*}(u) \equiv \iint_Q \{\nabla G_1(u^*)(x, t)\phi(u)(x, t) + \nabla H_1(u_1^*)(x, t) \cdot u_1(x, t)\}\, dx\, dt$$
$$+ \int_\Omega \{\nabla G_2(u^*)(x)\phi(u)(x, T) + \nabla H_2(u_2^*)(x, t) \cdot u_2(x)\}\, dx$$
$$+ \iint_\Gamma \{\nabla G_3(u^*)(s, t)\phi(u)(s, t) + \nabla H_3(u_3^*)(s, t) \cdot u_3(s, t)\}\, ds\, dt. \quad (6.9)$$

By virtue of (4.14) and the convexity of the functions H_i, $i = 1, 2, 3$, we have

$$\iint_Q \Bigg\{ - \sum_{i=1}^{n} (\bar{F}_i(x, t) \cdot (u_1(x, t) - u_1^*(x, t)))z(u^*)_{x_i}(x, t)$$
$$- (\bar{f}(x, t) \cdot (u_1(x, t) - u_1^*(x, t)))z(u^*)(x, t)$$
$$+ (H_1(x, t, u_1(x, t)) - H_1(x, t, u_1^*(x, t)))\Bigg\}\, dx\, dt$$
$$+ \int_\Omega \{(\bar{\phi}_0(x) \cdot (u_2(x) - u_2^*(x)))z(u^*)(x, 0)$$
$$+ (H_2(x, u_2(x)) - H_2(x, u_2^*(x)))\}\, dx$$
$$+ \iint_\Gamma \{(\bar{\Psi}(s, t) \cdot (u_3(s, t) - u_3^*(s, t)))z(u^*)(s, t)$$
$$+ (H_3(s, t, u_3(s, t)) - H_3(s, t, u_3^*(s, t)))\}\, ds\, dt$$
$$\geq J_{u^*}(u) - J_{u^*}(u^*) \geq 0. \quad (6.10)$$

Using the same approach as that used in the proof of the necessity of the condition in Theorem 5.1, conditions (6.5)–(6.7) follow easily from inequality (6.10). Thus the proof is complete. ■

In what follows we shall devise an algorithm for solving problem (P2). This algorithm is an iterative method and can be used to construct a minimizing sequence of controls $\{u^k\} \subset \mathscr{U}$ corresponding to any given initial control $u^1 \in \mathscr{U}$. Its detailed statement is now given as follows.

Step 1 Choose an initial control $u^1 \equiv (u_1^1, u_2^1, u_3^1) \in \mathscr{U}$ and set $k = 1$.

Step 2 Choose $\tilde{u}^k \in \mathscr{U}$ by the requirement that

$$- \sum_{i=1}^{n} [\bar{F}_i(x, t) \cdot \tilde{u}_1^k(x, t)]z(u^k)_{x_i}(x, t) - [\bar{f}(x, t) \cdot \tilde{u}_1^k(x, t)]z(u^k)(x, t)$$
$$+ \nabla H_1(u_1^k)(x, t) \cdot \tilde{u}_1^k(x, t)$$
$$= \min_{v_1 \in U_1} \Bigg\{ - \sum_{i=1}^{n} (\bar{F}_i(x, t) \cdot v_1)z(u^k)_{x_i}(x, t) - (\bar{f}(x, t) \cdot v_1)z(u^k)(x, t)$$
$$+ \nabla H_1(u_1^k)(x, t) \cdot v_1 \Bigg\}, \quad (6.11)$$

for almost all $(x, t) \in Q$;

$$(\bar{\phi}_0(x) \cdot \tilde{u}_2^k(x)) z(u^k)(x, 0) + \nabla H_2(u_2^k)(x) \cdot \tilde{u}_2^k(x) = \min_{v_2 \in U_2} \{(\bar{\phi}_0(x) \cdot v_2) z(u^k)(x, 0) + \nabla H_2(u_2^k)(x) \cdot v_2\}, \qquad (6.12)$$

for almost all $x \in \Omega$; and

$$(\bar{\Psi}(s, t) \cdot \tilde{u}_3^k(s, t)) z(u^k)(s, t) + \nabla H_3(u_3^k)(s, t) \cdot \tilde{u}_3^k(s, t) = \min_{v_3 \in U_3} \{(\bar{\Psi}(s, t) \cdot v_3) z(u^k)(s, t) + \nabla H_3(u_3^k)(s, t) \cdot v_3\}, \qquad (6.13)$$

for almost all $(s, t) \in \Gamma$, where $z(u^k)$ is the solution of adjoint system (3.1) corresponding to the control u^k.

Step 3 Let $u^{k+1} = u^k + \alpha_k(\tilde{u}^k - u^k)$, where α_k is such that

$$J(u^k + \alpha_k(\tilde{u}^k - u^k)) = \inf_{0 \le \alpha \le 1} J(u^k + \alpha(\tilde{u}^k - u^k)).$$

Step 4 Go to Step 2 with k replaced by $k + 1$.

For convenience, this algorithm will be referred to as algorithm (A).

REMARK 6.3. Consider an optimal control problem that consists of system (6.1) and the following cost functional:

$$\begin{aligned} J_{u^k}(u) \equiv & \iint_Q \{\nabla G_1(u^k)(x, t) \phi(u)(x, t) + \nabla H_1(u_1^k)(x, t) \cdot u_1(x, t)\} \, dx \, dt \\ & + \int_\Omega \{\nabla G_2(u^k)(x) \phi(u)(x, T) + \nabla H_2(u_2^k)(x) \cdot u_2(x)\} \, dx \\ & + \iint_\Gamma \{\nabla G_3(u^k)(s, t) \phi(u)(s, t) + \nabla H_3(u_3^k)(s, t) \cdot u_3(s, t)\} \, ds \, dt. \qquad (6.14) \end{aligned}$$

By applying Theorem 5.1 to the present case, it is easy to verify that $\tilde{u}^k$ [determined by Step 2 of algorithm (A)] minimizes the cost functional $J_{u^k}(u)$.

For the convergence of the algorithm, we need the following additional assumptions:

(A.20) $G_1(x, t, y)$, $G_2(x, y)$, and $G_3(x, t, y)$ are twice differentiable with respect to y such that

$$\|\nabla^2 G_1(\cdot, \cdot, \phi(u)(\cdot, \cdot))\|_{2,Q} \le M_3,$$

$$\|\nabla^2 G_2(\cdot, \phi(u)(\cdot, T))\|_{2,\Omega} \le M_3,$$

$$\|\nabla^2 G_3(\cdot, \cdot, \phi(u)(\cdot, \cdot))\|_{2,\Gamma} \le M_3,$$

for all $u \in \mathscr{U}$, where M_3 is a constant independent of $u \in \mathscr{U}$, and $\nabla^2 G_i$, $i = 1, 2, 3$, denote the Hessians of G_i, $i = 1, 2, 3$, with respect to y.

(A.21) $H_1(x, t, u_1)$, $H_2(x, u_2)$, and $H_3(x, t, u_3)$ are twice differentiable with respect to u_1, u_2, and u_3, respectively, such that

$$\|\nabla^2 H_1(\cdot, \cdot, u_1(\cdot, \cdot))\|_{1,Q} \leq M_4,$$
$$\|\nabla^2 H_2(\cdot, u_2(\cdot))\|_{1,\Omega} \leq M_4,$$
$$\|\nabla^2 H_3(\cdot, \cdot, u_3(\cdot, \cdot))\|_{1,\Gamma} \leq M_4,$$

for all $u \equiv (u_1, u_2, u_3) \in \mathscr{U}$, where M_4 is a constant independent of $u \in \mathscr{U}$, and $\nabla^2 H_i$, $i = 1, 2, 3$, denote the Hessians of H_i, $i = 1, 2, 3$, with respect to u_i, $i = 1, 2, 3$, respectively.

THEOREM 6.3. *The sequence $\{u^k\}$ generated by algorithm (A) is a minimizing sequence. That is to say*

$$\lim_{k\to\infty} J(u^k) = J(u^*),$$

where u^* is an optimal control.

Proof. Let

$$C_k(\varepsilon) \equiv J(u^k + \varepsilon(\tilde{u}^k - u^k)),$$

where $\varepsilon \in [0, 1]$ and $\tilde{u}^k$ is obtained from u^k as stated in Step 2 of algorithm (A). Then by Taylor's Theorem in remainder form, it follows that

$$C_k(\varepsilon) = C_k(0) + \varepsilon C_k'(0) + \tfrac{1}{2}(\varepsilon)^2 C_k''(\theta\varepsilon), \tag{6.15}$$

for some $\theta \in (0, 1)$.

Clearly,

$$C_k(0) = J(u^k), \tag{6.16}$$
$$C_k'(0) = J_{u^k}(\tilde{u}^k) - J_{u^k}(u^k), \tag{6.17}$$

where $J_{u^k}(u)$ is as defined by (6.14) and

$$\begin{aligned} C_k''(\theta\varepsilon) = &\iint_Q \{\nabla^2 G_1(x, t, \phi(\xi)(x, t))(\phi(\tilde{u}^k) - \phi(u^k))^2 \\ &+ (\nabla^2 H_1(x, t, \xi_1(x, t))(\tilde{u}_1^k(x, t) - u_1^k(x, t)))\cdot(\tilde{u}_1^k(x, t) - u_1^k(x, t))\}\,dx\,dt \\ &+ \int_\Omega \{\nabla^2 G_2(x, \phi(\xi)(x, T))(\phi(\tilde{u}^k)(x, T) - \phi(u^k)(x, T))^2 \\ &+ (\nabla^2 H_2(x, \xi_2(x))(\tilde{u}_2^k(x) - u_2^k(x)))\cdot(\tilde{u}_2^k(x) - u_2^k(x))\}\,dx \\ &+ \iint_\Gamma \{\nabla^2 G_3(s, t, \phi(\xi)(s, t))(\phi(\tilde{u}^k)(s, t) - \phi(u^k)(s, t))^2 \\ &+ (\nabla^2 H_3(s, t, \xi_3(s, t))(\tilde{u}_3^k(s, t) - u_3^k(s, t)))\cdot(\tilde{u}_3^k(s, t) - u_3^k(s, t))\}\,ds\,dt \end{aligned} \tag{6.18}$$

where $\xi \equiv (\xi_1, \xi_2, \xi_3) = u^k + \theta\varepsilon(\tilde{u}^k - u^k)$.

By virtue of assumptions (A.20) and (A.21) and estimate (2.7), it follows from (6.18) that there exists a positive constant M_5 such that

$$|C_k''(\theta\varepsilon)| \leq M_5 \tag{6.19}$$

where M_5 is independent of k and ε.

Then it follows from (6.15)–(6.19) that

$$J(u^k + \varepsilon(\tilde{u}^k \quad u^k)) \leq J(u^k) + \varepsilon(J_{u^k}(\tilde{u}^k) - J_{u^k}(u^k)) + \tfrac{1}{2}(\varepsilon)^2 M_5. \tag{6.20}$$

Let u^* be an optimal control. Then by Remark 6.3 we have

$$J_{u^k}(\tilde{u}^k) \leq J_{u^k}(u^*). \tag{6.21}$$

Thus it follows from (6.20) and (6.21) that

$$\begin{aligned} J(u^k + \varepsilon(\tilde{u}^k - u^k)) - J(u^*) \leq J(u^k) - J(u^*) &+ \tfrac{1}{2}\varepsilon(J_{u^k}(\tilde{u}^k) - J_{u^k}(u^k)) \\ &+ \tfrac{1}{2}\varepsilon(J_{u^k}(u^*) - J_{u^k}(u^k)) + \tfrac{1}{2}(\varepsilon)^2 M_5. \end{aligned} \tag{6.22}$$

Let

$$\varepsilon = \varepsilon^* \equiv \min\left\{\frac{1}{M_5}(J_{u^k}(u^k) - J_{u^k}(\tilde{u}^k)), 1\right\}. \tag{6.23}$$

Then it is clear that $\varepsilon^* \in [0, 1]$ and that inequality (6.22) reduces to

$$J(v^*) - J(u^*) \leq J(u^k) - J(u^*) + \tfrac{1}{2}\varepsilon^*(J_{u^k}(u^*) - J_{u^k}(u^k)), \tag{6.24}$$

where $v^* = u^k + \varepsilon^*(\tilde{u}^k - u^k)$.

By virtue of the convexity of the functions G_i and H_i, $i = 1, 2, 3$, we have

$$J(u^*) - J(u^k) \geq J_{u^k}(u^*) - J_{u^k}(u^k). \tag{6.25}$$

In view of Step 3 of algorithm (A), we note that

$$J(u^{k+1}) \leq J(v^*). \tag{6.26}$$

Thus from (6.24) and (6.26), it follows that

$$J(u^{k+1}) - J(u^*) \leq (1 - \tfrac{1}{2}\varepsilon^*)(J(u^k) - J(u^*)). \tag{6.27}$$

From (6.23), (6.21), and (6.25), we have

$$\begin{aligned} 1 - \tfrac{1}{2}\varepsilon^* &= \max\left\{1 - \frac{1}{2M_5}(J_{u^k}(u^k) - J_{u^k}(\tilde{u}^k)), \tfrac{1}{2}\right\} \\ &\leq \max\left\{1 - \frac{1}{2M_5}(J_{u^k}(u^k) - J_{u^k}(u^*)), \tfrac{1}{2}\right\} \\ &\leq \max\left\{1 - \frac{1}{2M_5}(J(u^k) - J(u^*)), \tfrac{1}{2}\right\}. \end{aligned} \tag{6.28}$$

Let $a^k \equiv (1/2M_5)(J(u^k) - J(u^*))$. Then it follows from (6.28) that

$$1 - \tfrac{1}{2}\varepsilon^* \leq \max\{1 - a^k, \tfrac{1}{2}\}. \tag{6.29}$$

Combining (6.27) and (6.29), we obtain

$$a^{k+1} \leq a^k \max\{1 - a^k, \tfrac{1}{2}\}. \tag{6.30}$$

This inequality shows that the nonnegative sequence $\{a^k\}$ is monotonically decreasing. Thus it follows that $a^* = \lim_{k\to\infty} a^k$ exists and, by (6.30),

$$a^* \leq a^* \max\{1 - a^*, \tfrac{1}{2}\}. \tag{6.31}$$

This, in turn, implies that $a^* = 0$, and hence we have

$$\lim_{k\to\infty} J(u^k) = J(u^*).$$

Thus the proof is complete. ■

Next, we shall present some results concerning the convergence of the sequence of controls $\{u^k\}$ generated by algorithm (A).

THEOREM 6.4. *The sequence $\{u^k\}$, generated by algorithm (A), has a subsequence that converges to an optimal control in the weak* topology of $L_\infty(Q, R^{m_1}) \times L_\infty(\Omega, R^{m_2}) \times L_\infty(\Gamma, R^{m_3})$. Furthermore, if $u^* \in \mathscr{U}$ is an accumulation point of the sequence $\{u^k\}$ (with respect to the weak* topology), then it is an optimal control.*

Proof. The proof follows readily from Theorem 6.3 and Remark 6.2. ■

THEOREM 6.5. *Suppose that $H_1(x, t, \cdot)$, $H_2(x, \cdot)$, and $H_3(s, t, \cdot)$ are, respectively, strictly convex in u_1, u_2, and u_3 for almost all $(x, t) \in Q$, $x \in \Omega$ and $(s, t) \in \Gamma$. Then the sequence $\{u^k\}$, generated by algorithm (A), converges to the optimal control in the weak* topology.*

Proof. Since H_i, $i = 1, 2, 3$, are strictly convex and system (6.1) is linear, it is easy to verify that the functional $J(u)$ is also strictly convex on $\mathscr{U}$ (here, we identify all the elements of $\mathscr{U}$ that are equal almost everywhere).

Thus $J(u)$ has a unique minimum on $\mathscr{U}$, and hence problem (P2) has a unique optimal control. Let the optimal control be denoted by u^*. Then by virtue of Remark 6.2(i), it follows that every subsequence of the sequence $\{u^k\}$ has a further subsequence that converges to the unique optimal control u^* in the weak* topology. Thus the whole sequence $\{u^k\}$ converges to u^* in the same topology. The proof is complete. ■

Under the same assumption of Theorem 6.5, we can also show that the sequence $\{u^k\}$ converges to the optimal control in the almost everywhere topology. This is a stronger result than that obtained in Theorem 6.5 because, for the class of admissible controls considered in this chapter, almost everywhere convergence implies weak* convergence.

THEOREM 6.6. *Under the assumptions of Theorem 6.5, the sequence $\{u^k\}$, generated by algorithm (A), converges almost everywhere to the optimal control u^*.*

Proof. By Remark 6.1, we have

$$
\begin{aligned}
J(u^k) - J(u^*) &\\
\geq \iint_Q \Big\{ &- \sum_{i=1}^{n} (\bar{F}_i(x,t)\cdot(u_1^k(x,t) - u_1^*(x,t)))z(u^*)_{x_i}(x,t) \\
&- (\bar{f}(x,t)\cdot(u_1^k(x,t) - u_1^*(x,t)))z(u^*)(x,t) \\
&+ (H_1(x,t,u_1^k(x,t)) - H_1(x,t,u_1^*(x,t)))\Big\}\, dx\, dt \\
&+ \int_\Omega \{(\bar{\phi}_0(x)\cdot(u_2^k(x) - u_2^*(x)))z(u^*)(x,0) \\
&\quad + (H_2(x,u_2^k(x)) - H_2(x,u_2^*(x)))\}\, dx \\
&+ \iint_\Gamma \{(\bar{\Psi}(s,t)\cdot(u_3^k(s,t) - u_3^*(s,t)))z(u^*)(s,t) \\
&\quad + (H_3(s,t,u_3^k(s,t)) - H_3(s,t,u_3^*(s,t)))\}\, ds\, dt. \qquad (6.32)
\end{aligned}
$$

According to Theorem 6.2, those integrands on the right-hand side of (6.32) are nonnegative almost everywhere in their domains of definition. Since the left-hand side of (6.32) tends to zero as $k \to \infty$, it follows that

$$
\begin{aligned}
&- \sum_{i=1}^{n} (\bar{F}_i(x,t)\cdot u_1^k(x,t))z(u^*)_{x_i}(x,t) - (\bar{f}(x,t)\cdot u_1^k(x,t))z(u^*)(x,t) \\
&\quad + H_1(x,t,u_1^k(x,t)) \\
&\quad \to - \sum_{i=1}^{n} (\bar{F}_i(x,t)\cdot u_1^*(x,t))z(u^*)_{x_i}(x,t) - (\bar{f}(x,t)\cdot u_1^*(x,t))z(u^*)(x,t) \\
&\quad + H_1(x,t,u_1^*(x,t)) \qquad (6.33)
\end{aligned}
$$

for almost all $(x,t) \in Q$;

$$
\begin{aligned}
&(\bar{\phi}_0(x)\cdot u_2^k(x))z(u^*)(x,0) + H_2(x,u_2^k(x)) \\
&\quad \to (\bar{\phi}_0(x)\cdot u_2^*(x))z(u^*)(x,0) + H_2(x,u_2^*(x)), \qquad (6.34)
\end{aligned}
$$

for almost all $x \in \Omega$; and

$$(\overline{\Psi}(s, t) \cdot u_3^k(s, t))z(u^*)(s, t) + H_3(s, t, u_3^k(s, t)) \to (\overline{\Psi}(s, t) \cdot u_3^*(s, t))z(u^*)(s, t) + H_3(s, t, u_3^*(s, t)), \tag{6.35}$$

for almost all $(s, t) \in \Gamma$.

We are now going to prove that $u_1^k(x, t) \to u_1^*(x, t)$, as $k \to \infty$, for almost all $(x, t) \in Q$.

Note that the strict convexity assumption on $H_1(x, t, \cdot)$ ensures that the minimum in (6.5) is attained at a unique point $u_1^*(x, \hat{t})$, for almost all $(x, t) \in Q$. Let $(\hat{x}, \hat{t})$ be a point in Q at which (6.33) and the unique minimum condition (6.5) hold. Then we shall show that $u_1^k(\hat{x}, \hat{t}) \to u_1^*(\hat{x}, \hat{t})$. If this were false, we could choose a subsequence $\{u_1^{k_i}(\hat{x}, \hat{t})\}$ of the sequence $\{u_1^k(\hat{x}. \hat{t})\}$ and a point $\hat{u}_1 \neq u_1^*(\hat{x}, \hat{t})$ such that

$$\lim_{i \to \infty} u_1^{k_i}(\hat{x}, \hat{t}) = \hat{u}_1. \tag{6.36}$$

Thus it follows from relation (6.33) and the continuity of $H_1(\hat{x}, \hat{t}, \cdot)$ that

$$\begin{aligned} &- \sum_{i=1}^{n} (\overline{F}_i(\hat{x}, \hat{t}) \cdot \hat{u}_1)z(u^*)_{x_i}(x, t) - (\bar{f}(\hat{x}, \hat{t}) \cdot \hat{u}_1)z(u^*)(x, t) + H_1(\hat{x}, \hat{t}, \hat{u}_1) \\ &= - \sum_{i=1}^{n} (\overline{F}_i(\hat{x}, \hat{t}) \cdot u_1^*(\hat{x}, \hat{t}))z(u^*)_{x_i}(\hat{x}, \hat{t}) \\ &\quad - (\bar{f}(\hat{x}, \hat{t}) \cdot u_1^*(\hat{x}, \hat{t}))z(u^*)(\hat{x}, \hat{t}) + H_1(\hat{x}, \hat{t}, u_1^*(\hat{x}, \hat{t})). \end{aligned}$$

Clearly, this contradicts the unique minimum condition at $(\hat{x}, \hat{t})$. Thus $u_1^k(\hat{x}, \hat{t}) \to u_1^*(\hat{x}, \hat{t})$. Since almost all points in Q can be chosen as $(\hat{x}, \hat{t})$, $u_1^k \to u_1^*$ almost everywhere on Q.

Similarly, we can prove that $u_2^k \to u_2^*$ and $u_3^k \to u_3^*$ almost everywhere in their respective domains of definition. This completes the proof. ■

VI.7. The Finite Element Method

In this section we consider a distributed optimal control problem arising in the study of optimal one-sided heating of a metal slab in a furnace by a gas medium, where the fuel flow rate is taken as the control variable. As in Section IV.9, the finite-element Galerkin's scheme is to be used to approximate the distributed optimal control problem by an optimal control problem involving lumped parameter system. For the approximate problem, it can be solved by using the efficient algorithm reported in Appendix V. Before going into detail, we note that the finite-element Galerkin's scheme is a common scheme used for solving partial differential equations (for details, see [MW.1] and [SF.1]) and that the technique in this section is applicable to many distributed optimal control problems, not just the one under discussion, which is adapted from [Barn.1] and [RPM.1].

Consider a model that describes the one-sided heating of a metal slab in a furnace by a gas medium, where the fuel flow rate is taken as the control variable. Let $\phi(x, t)$, $(x, t) \in [0, 1] \times [0, T]$, denote the temperature of the slab at point x and at time t. Then the corresponding dynamical system is described by the linear second-order parabolic partial differential equation

$$L\phi(x, t) \equiv \phi_t(x, t) - \phi_{xx}(x, t) = 0, \qquad (x, t) \in (0, 1) \times (0, T), \tag{7.1a}$$

together with the initial condition

$$\phi(x, 0) = 0, \qquad x \in (0, 1), \tag{7.1b}$$

and the boundary conditions

$$\phi_x|_{x=0} = \gamma[\phi(0, t) - g(t)], \qquad t \in [0, T], \tag{7.1c}$$

$$\phi_x|_{x=1} = 0, \qquad t \in [0, T]. \tag{7.1d}$$

Here, γ is a constant and g is the temperature of the gas medium heating the slab. The furnace dynamic is modeled by

$$\tau\dot{g}(t) + g(t) = u(t), \tag{7.2a}$$

with the initial condition

$$g(0) = 0, \tag{7.2b}$$

where τ denotes the furnace time constant and u, which denotes the fuel flow rate, is taken as the control variable. We assume that u is subject to the constraints:

$$0 \leq u(t) \leq 1, \qquad t \in [0, T]. \tag{7.3}$$

Any measurable function satisfying such constraints is called an admissible control. Let $\mathscr{U}$ be the class of all admissible controls.

To continue the specification of the optimal control problem, we denote by ϕ_d the desired temperature distribution at the terminal time T.

In [RPM.1] the objective functional

$$\hat{J}(u) = \int_0^1 [\phi(x, T) - \phi_{\mathrm{d}}(x)]^2 \, dx \tag{7.4}$$

is used in an attempt to achieve the desired temperature distribution at T. Here, we are interested in a more realistic problem—we wish to minimize the amount of fuel used to bring the final temperature distribution to within 1% of the desired temperature distribution ϕ_d. Mathematically, this is equivalent to an attempt of minimizing the objective functional

$$J(u) = \int_0^T u(t)\,dt \tag{7.5}$$

subject to dynamical system (7.1), furnace model (7.2), control constraints (7.3), and the terminal inequality constraints

$$0.99\phi_d(x) \le \phi(x, T) \le 1.01\phi_d(x), \qquad x \in [0, 1]. \tag{7.6}$$

This is called problem P for the convenience of future references.

To obtain the approximate problem to problem P, we let η be an arbitrary function in $C^1((0, 1))$. Then by multiplying (7.1a) by η, integrating the second-order term of the resultant equation by parts, and using the boundary conditions, it gives rise to

$$\begin{aligned}\int_0^1 \eta(x)\phi_t(x, t) &= \int_0^1 \eta(x)\phi_{xx}(x, t)\,dx\\ &= \eta(1)\phi_x(1, t) - \eta(0)\phi_x(0, t) - \int_0^1 \eta_x(x)\phi_x(x, t)\,dx\\ &= -\eta(0)\gamma[\phi(0, t) - g(t)] - \int_0^1 \eta_x(x)\phi_x(x, t)\,dx.\end{aligned} \tag{7.7}$$

Let the spatial domain [0, 1] be divided into N equal subintervals, and B_i^k, $i = 0, 1, \ldots, N$, be the corresponding B splines of order k. [For $k = 1$, $B_i^k = S_1(Nx - i)$, $i = 0, 1, \ldots, N$, where S_1 is defined by (IV.9.10).]

Define

$$\phi^N(x, t) \equiv \sum_{i=0}^{N} X_i(t)B_i^k(x). \tag{7.8}$$

Substituting ϕ^N and B_j^k for ϕ and η, respectively, in Eq. (7.7), we obtain

$$\begin{aligned}\sum_{i=0}^{N} \dot{X}_i(t) \int_0^1 B_i^k(x)B_j^k(x)\,dx &= -\gamma B_j^k(0)\left[\sum_{i=0}^{N} X_i(t)B_i^k(0) - g(t)\right]\\ &\quad - \sum_{i=0}^{N} X_i(t) \int_0^1 \dot{B}_i^k(x)\dot{B}_j^k(x)\,dx.\end{aligned} \tag{7.9}$$

Define

$$A_{ij} \equiv \int_0^1 B_i^k(x) B_j^k(x)\,dx, \qquad i, j = 0, 1, \ldots, N, \tag{7.10a}$$

$$\tilde{A}_{ij} \equiv \int_0^1 \dot{B}_i^k(x) \dot{B}_j^k(x)\,dx, \qquad i, j = 0, 1, \ldots, N, \tag{7.10b}$$

$$D_{ij} \equiv B_i^k(0) B_j^k(0), \qquad i, j = 0, 1, \ldots, N, \tag{7.10c}$$

and

$$E_i \equiv B_i^k(0), \qquad i = 0, 1, \ldots, N. \tag{7.10d}$$

Here, A_{ij}, $\tilde{A}_{ij}$, D_{ij}, and E_i are all dependent on k. However, their dependency is suppressed from the notation for the sake of brevity.

Let

$$X(t) \equiv (X_0(t), X_1(t), \ldots, X_N(t)). \tag{7.11}$$

Then, Eq. (7.9) can be written in matrix form

$$A\dot{X}(t) = -\gamma D X(t) - \tilde{A} X(t) + \gamma g(t) E, \tag{7.12}$$

where $A \equiv (A_{ij})$, $\tilde{A} \equiv (\tilde{A}_{ij})$, $D \equiv (D_{ij})$, and $E \equiv (E_0, E_1, \ldots, E_N)$.

For terminal inequality constraints (7.6), we substitute ϕ^N for ϕ to obtain

$$0.99\phi_d(x) \le \sum_{i=0}^{N} X_i(T) B_i(x) \le 1.01\phi_d(x), \qquad x \in [0, 1]. \tag{7.13}$$

These, in turn, imply

$$0.99\phi_d(x_i) \le X_i(T) \le 1.01\phi_d(x_i), \qquad i = 0, 1, \ldots, N, \tag{7.14}$$

where the x_i, $i = 0, 1, \ldots, N$, denote the nodal coordinate values. Similarly, for initial condition (7.1b), we have

$$X_i(0) = 0, \qquad i = 0, 1, \ldots, N.$$

Let

$$Y(t) \equiv (X_0(t), X_1(t), \ldots, X_N(t), g(t)). \tag{7.15}$$

Then it follows from (7.2) and (7.12) that

$$\dot{Y}(t) = VY(t) + Wu(t), \qquad t \in (0, T] \tag{7.16a}$$

$$Y(0) = 0, \tag{7.16b}$$

where

$$V \equiv \begin{bmatrix} -A^{-1}(\tilde{A} + \gamma D) & \gamma A^{-1} E \\ 0^T & -\tau^{-1} \end{bmatrix}, \tag{7.16c}$$

and

$$W \equiv \begin{bmatrix} 0 \\ \tau^{-1} \end{bmatrix}. \tag{7.16d}$$

For each $u \in \mathscr{U}$, let $Y(u)$ be the corresponding solution of system (7.16). Then terminal inequality constraints (7.14) can be written as

$$0.99\hat{\phi}_d \le FY(u)(T) \le 1.01\hat{\phi}_d, \tag{7.17}$$

where

$$\hat{\phi}_d \equiv (\phi_d(x_0), \phi_d(x_1), \ldots, \phi_d(x_N)), \tag{7.18a}$$

and

$$F \equiv \begin{bmatrix} 1 & 0 & \cdots & 0 & 0 \\ 0 & 1 & \cdots & 0 & 0 \\ & 0 & & & \\ \vdots & \vdots & & \vdots & \vdots \\ 0 & 0 & \cdots & 1 & 0 \end{bmatrix}. \tag{7.18b}$$

Clearly, not all $u \in \mathscr{U}$ will satisfy constraints (7.17). Let $\mathscr{F}$ be a subset of $\mathscr{U}$ such that constraints (7.17) are satisfied for each $u \in \mathscr{F}$. Elements of $\mathscr{F}$ are called feasible controls, and $\mathscr{F}$ itself is called the class of feasible controls.

The approximate problem to problem P may now be specified as follows.

Find a control $u \in \mathscr{F}$ such that objective functional (7.5) is minimized over $\mathscr{F}$. For convenience, this approximate problem is to be referred to as problem P^N. Use linear B splines (order $k = 1$) with a spatial domain of [0, 1] being divided into N equal subintervals. In this case, the matrices A and $\tilde{A}$ are given by

$$\begin{aligned}
A_{00} &= A_{NN} = \frac{1}{3N}; & \tilde{A}_{00} &= \tilde{A}_{NN} = N; & & \\
A_{ii} &= \frac{2}{3N}; & \tilde{A}_{ii} &= 2N, & i &= 1, 2, \ldots, N-1; \\
A_{i,i+1} &= \frac{1}{6N}; & \tilde{A}_{i,i+1} &= -N, & i &= 0, 1, \ldots, N-1; \\
A_{i,i-1} &= \frac{1}{6N}; & \tilde{A}_{i,i-1} &= -N, & i &= 1, 2, \ldots, N; \\
A_{ij} &= 0; & \tilde{A}_{ij} &= 0, & & \text{otherwise.}
\end{aligned}$$

The matrix D and the vector E are given by $D_{00} = 1$, $D_{ij} = 0$ otherwise and $E_0 = 1$, $E_i = 0$ otherwise, respectively.

We can also use higher-order B splines (in particular, cubic B splines of order $k = 3$) if the matrices A and $\tilde{A}$ defined, respectively, by (7.10a) and (7.10b) are evaluated accordingly.

TABLE 7.1

The Heat Conduction Problem for $k = 1$, $N = 6$, $M = 10$, and $T = 0.2$

Problem	Solution
P	No feasible solutions
Q	$\hat{u}^{10,*}(t) = \sum_{i=1}^{10} \hat{\sigma}_i^* \chi_{[t_{i-1}, t_i)}(t)$, where $\sigma^* \equiv (1, 1, 1, 1, 1, 0.129, 0, 0, 0, 0.181)$, χ_I denotes the characteristic function of I, and $t_i = 0.02i$, $i = 0, 1, \ldots, 10$, and $\hat{J}(\hat{u}^{10,*}) = 0.0023$.

Following [RPM.1], the values of the parameters are taken as $\gamma = 10$, $\tau = 0.04$, and $\phi_d(x) = 0.2$, with two time intervals $T = 0.2$ and $T = 0.4$.

The terminal time $T = 0.2$ is less than the minimum time needed to bring the final state to the feasible region [i.e., the region described by the terminal inequality constraints (7.17)]. Thus there is no solution to the approximate problem P^N and hence the original problem P.

Replacing the objective functional of problem P by objective functional (7.4), and dropping terminal inequality constraints (7.6), we have the problem considered in [RPM.1], which is to be referred to as problem Q. With $k = 1$ and $N = 6$, the corresponding approximate problem to problem Q is solved by using the control parametrization algorithm reported in Appendix V, where M (the number of equal subintervals of $[0, T]$ for the control variable u) is taken as 10. The results are given in Table 7.1, where $\hat{u}^{10,*}$ is the suboptimal control of problem Q produced by the control parametrization algorithm.

In Table 7.1 we note that the results obtained for problem Q are in close agreement with those of [RPM.1].

With $T = 0.4$ the feasible region is reachable and the results are summarized in Table 7.2, where $u^{10,*}$ and $\hat{u}^{10,*}$ are, respectively, the suboptimal controls of problem P and problem Q produced by the control parametrization algorithm.

Note that the purpose of constraints (7.6) is to ensure that the final temperature distribution is within 1 % of the desired one. These constraints can be easily altered whenever a higher accuracy is needed. For example, if the allowable percentage is 0.1 %, then the corresponding versions of the constraints are

$$0.99\phi_d(x) \leq \phi(x, T) \leq 1.001\phi_d(x), \qquad x \in [0, 1].$$

TABLE 7.2

The Heat Conduction Problem for $k = 1$, $N = 6$, $M = 10$, and $T = 0.4$

Problem	Solution
P	$u^{10,*}(t) = \sum_{i=1}^{10} \sigma_i^* \chi_{[t_{i-1}, t_i)}(t)$, where $\sigma^* = (0, 0.072, 1, 1, 1, 0.321, 0, 0, 0.234, 0.200)$ and $t_i = 0.04i$, $i = 0, 1, \ldots, 10$; $J(u^{10,*}) = 0.154$; and $X(u^{10,*})(0.4) = (0.198, 0.198, 0.201, 0.202, 0.200, 0.198, 0.200)$
Q	$\hat{u}^{10,*}(t) = \sum_{i=1}^{10} \hat{\sigma}_i^* \chi_{[t_{i-1}, t_i)}(t)$, where $\hat{\sigma}^* \equiv (0.367, 1, 1, 1, 0.056, 0, 0, 0.303, 0.194, 0.200)$ and $t_i = 0.04i$, $i = 0, 1, \ldots, 10$; $\hat{J}(\hat{u}^{10,*}) = 0.3 \times 10^{-8}$.

The approximate problem of this "new" optimal control problem is also solved by using the control parametrization algorithm of Appendix V, where the values of all the parameters concerned are taken to be the same as before. With $u^{10,*}$ denoting the suboptimal control produced by the control parametrization algorithm, results are listed as follows:

$$u^{10,*}(t) = \sum_{i=1}^{10} \sigma_i^* \chi_{[t_{i-1}, t_i)}(t),$$

where

$$\sigma^* \equiv (0, 0.368, 1, 1, 1, 0.048, 0, 0, 0.306, 0.191),$$

and

$$t_i \equiv 0.04i, \qquad i = 0, 1, \ldots, 10,$$

$$J(u^{10,*}) = 0.156,$$

$$X(u^{10,*})(0.4) = (0.1998, 0.1999, 0.1998, 0.2002, 0.2001, 0.1998, 0.1990).$$

Note that all the preceding problems were also solved using cubic B splines ($k = 3$) with very little difference in the values of $J(u^{10,*})$, $\hat{J}(\hat{u}^{10,*})$, $X(u^{10,*})(T)$, and $X(\hat{u}^{10,*})(T)$, but with some variation in $u^{10,*}$ and $\hat{u}^{10,*}$.

VI.8. Discussion

This chapter contains the results reported in [WuT.4]. It considers three classes of optimal control problems involving second boundary-value problems of a parabolic type with controls appearing in the forcing terms and on the boundary and initial conditions. The first problem is the most general case, in which a convex cost functional is considered. A sufficient condition for optimality (see Theorem 4.2) is derived for this general optimal control problem. In the second problem, the cost functional is assumed to be linear with respect to the solution of the second boundary-value problem. The third problem, which overlaps the second one, involves the convex cost functional and a special case of the second boundary-value problem. More precisely, the forcing terms and the initial and boundary conditions of this special second boundary-value problem are linear with respect to the control variable.

For the second and third problems, answers to four major questions found in the study of optimal control theory are provided. These four questions are

(i) necessary conditions for optimality,
(ii) sufficient conditions for optimality,
(iii) existence of optimal controls,
(iv) a method for constructing an optimal control.

For the second problem, an optimal control can be computed in only one iteration. This is not possible for the third problem. However, the method proposed, which is an iterative method, always produces sequences of controls with the following properties.

(i) The sequence of controls so constructed is a minimizing sequence. This result was established in optimal control problems for the first time in [Barn.1], where the system dynamic is governed by an ordinary differential equation. Since then it has also been shown to be valid for optimal control problems of time-lag systems in [TWuC.1] and of different types of distributed parameter systems in [CTW.1] (for first-order hyperbolic system with boundary control), [CTW.2] (for second-order hyperbolic system with boundary control), [WuT.2] (for second-order hyperbolic system with Darboux boundary condition), and Section 6 of [WuT.4] (for second boundary-value problem of a parabolic type).

(ii) The sequence converges in the weak* topology of L_∞ to the optimal control. This convergence result, which is introduced to optimal control algorithms for the first time in [WuT.2], is also a common result in [TWuC.1], [CTW.1], [CTW.2] and Section 6 of [WuT.4].

(iii) The sequence converges in the almost everywhere topology to the optimal control. This result is introduced to optimal control algorithms for the first time in [Barn.1], where the dynamical system involves only ordinary differential equations. It has also been shown to be valid for different types of optimal control problems in [TWuC.1], [WuT.2], and Section 6 of [WuT.4].

Unfortunately, this approach, which is basically the conditional gradient method with exact line search (see Step 3 of Algorithm VI.A), works only for optimal control problems involving convex cost functional and linear system dynamic.

For many optimal control problems involving *linear* cost functional and *linear* dynamical systems, it is interesting to note that complete answers to the previously mentioned four major questions are possible. These points are not only true for lumped parameter systems (see [Barn.1] and [TWuC.1]) but also true for many distributed parameter systems (see Chapter III of [Wu.1], [WuT.2], [CTW.2] and Section 5 of [WuT.4]). In fact, solving these kinds of problems is the most crucial step in the investigation of all those optimal control problems involving convex cost functionals and linear dynamical systems just discussed. For details, see how the second optimal control problem is used in Section 6 for the third problem.

A precursor of the conditional gradient method appears in a paper by Frank and Wolfe [FW.1] on quadratic programming problems in finite dimensional spaces.

The optimal control algorithms reported in [G.1] and [Barn.1] can be considered as generalized versions of the Frank–Wolfe algorithm. All of these algorithms are used in lumped parameter systems and involve a linearization of the given problem at each iteration. In [Barn.2], a modification of these algorithms is offered. This modification does not require the problem to be completely linearized at each iteration. The result is that a geometrically convergent algorithm is obtained. It is known that the Frank–Wolfe algorithm cannot converge geometrically fast unless it is under some additional restrictions on the cost functional and the constraint set (for details, see the note in [LP.1], p. 26).

In [DR.1] a general iterative process is given for minimizing a smooth convex functional f over a bounded set Ω in a Banach space. At each stage in this process, the original minimization problem is replaced by a (presumably) simpler problem in which the local linear approximation to f, specified by f's derivative at the current point x^n in Ω, is minimized over Ω. Every solution y^n of the latter problem yields a descent direction vector $p^n = y^n - x^n$, and the next point x^{n+1} is then computed by moving a certain distance from x^n in the direction p^n, according to one of the two basic types of step length rule. The first rule is a classical line minimization scheme in which x^{n+1} is obtained by minimizing the functional f over a line segment of the descent direction p^n, with the starting point at x^n. If f is quadratic, there is a simple formula for x^{n+1}. However, it is, in general, required to approximate x^{n+1} with an inner iterative line search loop that may entail numerous and possibly costly evaluation of f. More critically, any line minimization scheme is only a "locally" optimal strategy. Thus in a certain iteration the "solution" obtained may be very far from the true optimal. It could also happen over *many* iterations. This is clearly seen in the behavior of the gradient method when the level sets of f resemble highly elongated ellipsoids (see [Be.1, p.1]; and [Lu.1]). The second step length rule proposed in [DR.1] avoids this difficulty by minimizing a certain upper bound on the one-dimensional section of f, in place of f itself. The bounding function is a simple quadratic expression in the step length parameter. Thus it is an easy matter to solve for x^{n+1}. Moreover, it has been shown in [DR.1] that if f is convex, the derivative f' of f is Lipschitz continuous, and the constraint set Ω is convex and weakly compact, then this simple step length rule always produces minimizing sequence with $O(1/n)$ convergence at least, and geometric convergence under certain additional conditions of the uniform convexity type on Ω. However, this rule requires explicit knowledge of a Lipschitz constant for f', i.e., a constant L satisfying

$$L \geq L_0 = \sup_{x,\, y;\, x \neq y} \frac{\|f'(x) - f'(y)\|}{\|x - y\|}.$$

Computing a bound on L_0 can be a formidable problem in its own right. Moreover, if the rule is used with a constant $L < L_0$, then the resulting step length parameter may never become small enough to ensure that $\{x^n\}$ is a minimizing sequence for f.

Ideally, one would like to have a conditional gradient algorithm, in which the step length rule does not require line search and inaccessible "nonlocal" parameters of Lipschitz type, and yet manages to match the performance of other known rules. The simplest one is the open-loop step length rule devised in [DH.1]. More precisely, let $\{\alpha_n\} \subset (0, 1)$ be the sequence of step lengths with the following properties:

$$\sum_{n=0}^{\infty} (\alpha_n)^2 < \infty$$

$$\sum_{n=0}^{\infty} a_n = \infty.$$

If f' is Lipschitz continuous, then the sequence $\{x^n\}$ of points generated by the conditional gradient algorithm with such step lengths is a minimizing sequence. The convergence rate is $0(1/n)$, which is quite a remarkable conclusion in view of the fact that $0(1/n)$ convergence rate is the best one can expect of the conditional gradient algorithm with standard closed-loop step lengths, such as the one in [DR.1], for certain f and Ω included in the formulation of [DH.1].

In [Du.1] an analytical device employed in [DR.1] is modified to produce the one parameter family of simple closed-loop step length rules. These rules are similar to those of [DR.1], but require no Lipschitz constants.

Under the same conditions invoked in [DR.1] on f and Ω, any member of the family generates minimizing sequences with asymptotic properties comparable to sequences obtained in [DR.1]. In fact, for certain values of the parameter, the a priori error estimates obtained in [Du.1] are actually better than the corresponding estimates obtained in [DR.1]. Furthermore, convergence rate estimates are similar in both the algorithms of [DR.1] and [Du.1]. They depend critically on the way the function

$$a(\sigma) = \inf\{\rho = \langle f'(\xi), y - \xi \rangle : y \in \Omega, \|y - \xi\| \geq \sigma\}$$

grows with increasing σ. It has been shown in [Du.1] that if f is convex and f' is Lipschitz continuous, then both the algorithms converge like $0(1/n)$, geometrically, or in finite many steps according to whether $a(\sigma) > 0$ for $\sigma > 0$, or $a(\sigma) \geq A\sigma^2$ with $A > 0$, or $a(\sigma) \geq A$ with $A > 0$. These three abstract conditions are closely related to established notions of nonsingularity for an important class of optimal control problems with bounded control inputs.

To our best knowledge, it appears that the algorithms developed in [DR.1], [DH.1], [Du.1], and [Du.2] have not been applied to general optimal control problems, especially to distributed parameter systems. The investigation in this area will certainly produce interesting results.

Optimal control problems involving second boundary-value problems of a parabolic type have also been treated in [Barn.1], [Bar.2], [But.1], Volume II of [LiM.1], [M.2] and many others.

In [Barn.1] and [But.1] only very special cases of the third optimal control problem of this chapter is considered.

Volume II of [LiM.1] deals with the case involving a quadratic cost functional and a linear parabolic system with constant coefficients. Furthermore, only a necessary condition for optimality is derived for this case.

In [M.2] an abstract convex optimal control problem is considered. A method of estimating the rate of convergence of approximation to this problem is proposed, and a necessary condition for optimality involving projections on the set of admissible controls is derived. These general abstract results are then applied to a class of optimal control problems involving second boundary-value problems.

In [Bar.1] a class of boundary-distributed linear control systems in Banach space is considered. A necessary condition for optimality is then derived for a convex optimal control problem involving such systems. A duality result is also obtained. These results are applicable to convex optimal control problems involving first or second boundary-value problems of a parabolic type.

In both [Bar.1] and [M.2] the second boundary-value problems concerned are only special cases of that of the third optimal control problem considered in this chapter in the sense that the coefficients of their differential equations are all independent of the time variable.

For the first and second optimal control problems considered in this chapter, we note that the controls enter the data for the linear equation in a nonlinear way (in distinction to truly nonlinear problems, where the governing equation is itself nonlinear). The problem of optimal control of induction heating discussed in [But.1, p. 19] is an example for such problems.

Note that the heavily worked time optimal control problem does not fit the framework of this chapter. For references on some of such time optimal control problems, see [But.1], [Kn.1], [Kn.2], [Sc.1], [F.1], Chapter 5 of [AT.5], and the relevant articles cited therein.

In Section 7 an example arising naturally in the problem of optimal heating a slab of metal in a furnace is considered. This example is adapted from those of [Barn.1] and [RPM.1]. Using the technique suggested in Section IV.9, the spline functions are used to approximate the problem with a sequence of optimal control problems of lumped parameter systems. Each of the approximate problems can be solved by using the algorithm of Appendix V.

The question concerning the convergence properties of optimal controls of the approximate problems to the true optimal control remains open. This is an interesting problem yet to be solved.

APPENDIX I

Stochastic Optimal Control Problems†

It is well known that the behavior of natural phenomena is subject to random disturbances and hence does not follow strict deterministic laws. Thus every known deterministic mathematical model can be considered as a simplification of a certain stochastic model. However, the simplification is acceptable only if the noise is of little consequence. Otherwise it must be taken into consideration. In fact, it has been shown in [D.1] that a feedback control based on the deterministic formulation can be a poor approximation to the optimal feedback control computed from a stochastic formulation.

In the study of stochastic optimal control theory, the two most commonly used models are the Ito stochastic differential equation and the Ito stochastic functional differential equations, both with Poisson random measure omitted. The optimal control problems considered in Chapters III and IV are related to a class of nonlinear feedback optimal control problems involving the first model. Thus our aim in this Appendix is to provide a brief review on certain results for this class of stochastic optimal control problems.

† Within the same Appendix, equation number 7 is called Eq. (7), but outside that Appendix, equation number 7 in Appendix III is referred to as Eq. (A.III.7).

For more information on stochastic models and their related optimal control problems, we refer the interested reader to [Ah.5], [AT.1], [AT.2], [AW.1], [Bh.1], [D.1], [Fl.1], [Fl.2], [FR.1], [Kus.1], [R.1], [RT.1], [T.1], [TA.1], and the references cited therein.

Let T be a positive constant, let Ω be a region in R^n, and let S and U be compact subsets of R^{m_1} and R^{m_2}, respectively.

We consider the following stochastic differential system.

$$d\xi(t) = f(t, \xi(t), \sigma, y(t))\, dt + G(t, \xi(t))\, dw(t), \; t \in (0, T], \tag{1a}$$

$$\xi(0) = \xi_0 \qquad (\pi_0 \text{ initial probability measure}), \tag{1b}$$

where $\xi(t)$ denotes the state of the system at time t, σ a parameter vector in R^{m_1}, $y(t)$ a control used at time t, $f\colon (0, T) \times \Omega \times S \times U \to R^n$ and $G\colon (0, T) \times \Omega \to R^{nn}$ continuous functions, w the standard n dimensional Wiener process, and ξ_0 a given random variable that is statistically independent of $w(t)$.

Let σ be a parameter vector in S and y a measurable function from $(0, T)$ into U. Then it follows from [SV.1] that system (1) admits a unique weak solution ξ that is a Markov process.

Given system (1), the stochastic optimization problem is to find a pair (σ, u) from some admissible class $\mathscr{D}_p$, to be defined later, such that the cost functional

$$J(u) = \mathscr{E}\left\{\int_0^\tau f_0(t, \xi(t), \sigma, y(t))\, dt\right\} \tag{2}$$

is minimized over $\mathscr{D}_p$, where $\mathscr{E}$ denotes the mathematical expectation of the random variable enclosed by the brackets, τ the stopping time to be specified later, and $f_0 : (0, T) \times \Omega \times S \times U \to R^1$ a continuous function.

If $\Omega = R^n$ and $\tau = T$, then the corresponding stochastic optimal control problem is called the stochastic optimal control problem with fixed end time.

To describe the second type of stochastic optimal control problems, let the region Ω be bounded, and define

$$\tau \equiv \inf\{\{t \in [0, T] : \xi(t) \notin \Omega\} \cup \{T\}\} \tag{3}$$

to be the first exit time of process $(t, \xi(t))$ from the cylinder $(0, T) \times \Omega$. Then the corresponding stochastic optimal control problem is called the stochastic control problem with Markov end time.

The optimal control problems considered in Chapters III and IV are related to the stochastic optimal control problem with Markov end time.

Stochastic optimal control problems have more classes of admissible controls than their deterministic counterparts. Open-loop controls set $y(t)$

a priori. Feedback controls make use of the observed values of state $\xi(t)$. If the control uses the current value of $\xi(t)$, then the control is said to be fully observed. However, if the control uses only the current value of $n_1 < n$ components of $\xi(t)$, then the control is said to be partially observed.

Consider the optimal control problem, which consists of system (1) and cost functional (2), with $\tau = T$, $U = R^{m_1}$, and the parameter vector deleted from all the functions involved. Suppose the drift term f is linear and the cost integrand is quadratic, both with respect to the state and control variables. Then the solution in closed form is available in [D.1].

For general stochastic optimal control problems with fully observed controls, dynamic programming can be used to derive a set of necessary conditions for optimality. Let a function $u: (0, T) \times \Omega \to U$ be a fully observed control satisfying some regularity conditions, such as Lipschitzian, so that $y(t) = u(t, \xi(t))$ is the control used.

If u^* is an optimal fully observed control, then it is known from [Fl.2] that $u^*(t, x)$ minimizes

$$f_0(t, x, \cdot) + \sum_{i=1}^{n} \phi_{x_i}(t, x) f_i(t, x, \cdot) \tag{4}$$

over U, for almost all $(t, x) \in (0, T) \times \Omega$, where ϕ is the solution of the system involving quasi-linear parabolic partial differential equation:

$$\phi_t(t, x) + \sum_{i, j=1}^{n} \tfrac{1}{2}(GG^{\mathrm{T}})_{ij}(t, x)\phi_{x_i x_j}(t, x)$$

$$+ \min_{v \in U} \left[f_0(t, x, v) + \sum_{i=1}^{n} f_i(t, x, v)\phi_{x_i}(t, x) \right] = 0, \quad (t, x) \in (0, T) \times \Omega, \tag{5a}$$

$$\phi|_{t=T} = 0, \qquad x \in \Omega, \tag{5b}$$

$$\phi|_{[0, T] \times \partial\Omega} = 0, \qquad (t, x) \in [0, T] \times \partial\Omega. \tag{5c}$$

Here the superscript T denotes the transpose, and $\partial\Omega$ the boundary of the region Ω.

For the case involving partially observed controls two approaches have been used. The probabilistic approach using the Martingale theory is applicable to the case involving nonanticipative feedback controls. In this case u is a function of *all* the information that has been observed up to and including the current time, rather than just the information at the current time. Define

$$\xi_t(s) = \begin{cases} \xi(s), & \text{if } s \le t, \\ \xi(t), & \text{if } s > t. \end{cases}$$

Then $y(t) \equiv u(t, \xi_t)$ is a nonanticipative feedback control. Necessary conditions for optimality for such problems can be found in [Va.1] and others.

If the control depends only on the current value of the observed components of $\xi(t)$, the resultant optimal control is suboptimal when compared with nonanticipative optimal control. However, such an optimal control problem can be converted into a deterministic optimization problem involving a first boundary-value problem of a parabolic type as considered in Chapter IV. To be more specific, let n_1 be an integer with $0 \leq n_1 \leq n$. Then, for any $\xi \equiv (\xi_1, \ldots, \xi_n)$ and any $x \equiv (x_1, \ldots, x_n)$, define

$$\hat{\xi} \equiv (\xi_1, \ldots, \xi_{n_1}) \in R^{n_1},$$

and

$$\hat{x} \equiv (x_1, \ldots, x_{n_1}) \in R^{n_1}.$$

Let

$$\hat{\Omega} \equiv \{\hat{x} \in R^{n_1} : x \in \Omega\},$$

and let a partially observed control be a function $u: (0, T) \times \hat{\Omega} \to U$ such that $y(t) \equiv u(t, \hat{\xi}(t))$ can be used as an admissible control. Let $\mathscr{U}$ be the class of all such functions u. Furthermore, as in Chapter IV, elements of the set $\mathscr{S} \times \mathscr{U} \equiv \mathscr{D}_p$ will be referred to as policies.

Consider the stochastic optimization problem (P). Subject to system (1), find a policy $(\sigma, u) \in \mathscr{D}_p$ such that cost functional (2) is minimized over $\mathscr{D}_p$, where the stopping time τ, which appears in the cost functional, is taken as Markov end time [i.e., τ is defined by (3)].

To describe the deterministic optimization problem just mentioned, let us consider the following first boundary-value problems:

$$L(\sigma, u)\phi(t, x) = f_0(T - t, x, \sigma, u(T - t, \hat{x})), \qquad (t, x) \in (0, T) \times \Omega, \tag{7a}$$

$$\phi|_{t=0} = 0, \qquad x \in \Omega, \tag{7b}$$

$$\phi|_{[0, T] \times \partial\Omega} = 0, \qquad (t, x) \in [0, T] \times \partial\Omega, \tag{7c}$$

where $(\sigma, u) \in \mathscr{D}_p$ and, for each $(\sigma, u) \in \mathscr{D}_p$, $L(\sigma, u)$ is a linear second-order parabolic partial differential operator defined by

$$L(\sigma, u)\psi \equiv \psi_t - \sum_{i,j=1}^{n} a_{ij}(T - t, x)\psi_{x_i x_j} - \sum_{i=1}^{n} f_i(T - t, x, \sigma, u(T - t, \hat{x}))\psi_{x_i}, \tag{8}$$

and where $a_{ij}(t, x) \equiv \frac{1}{2}(GG^{\mathrm{T}})_{ij}$, $i, j = 1, \ldots, n$.

From Theorem II.8.1, it follows that, for each $(\sigma, u) \in \mathscr{D}_p$, system (7) admits a unique almost everywhere solution $\phi(\sigma, u)$.

Now, under certain sufficient conditions on the functions f_0, f, G, and u, stochastic optimization problem (P) can be converted (see [TA.1] and [Fl.1]) into the deterministic optimization problem (P′).

Subject to system (8), find a policy $(\sigma, u) \in \mathscr{D}_p$ such that the cost functional

$$J(\sigma, u) = \int_{\Omega} \phi(\sigma, u)(0, x)\pi_0(dx) \tag{9}$$

is minimized over $\mathscr{D}_p$, where π_0 is the initial probability measure defined in (1b).

The main tool used in the proof of the conversion is Ito's lemma, and hence all the conditions required by Ito's lemma are obviously also needed for this result to be valid. However, the reduced problem may still be considered as an approximation to the stochastic problem, even in the case when not all the required conditions are satisfied. In this situation, intuition should, of course, play a more important role in accepting the results so obtained.

For the reduced problem and its related versions, questions concerning necessary and sufficient conditions for optimality, and existence of optimal controls have been extensively studied in the literature. Some results on computational algorithms, which are the subject matters of Chapters III, IV, V, and VI, are also available in the literature. The relevant references may be found in the bibliography section of [AT.5].

APPENDIX II

Certain Results on Partial Differential Equations Needed in Chapters III, IV, and V

With reference to the following two sets of coefficients:

$$\{a_{ij}, i, j = 1, \ldots, n; b_i^1, i = 1, \ldots, n; c^1\}, \tag{1}$$

and

$$\{a_{ij}, i, j = 1, \ldots, n; b_i^2, i = 1, \ldots, n; c^2\}, \tag{2}$$

we consider the operators

$$L_1\phi \equiv \phi_t - \sum_{i,j=1}^{n} a_{ij}(x, t)\phi_{x_i x_j} - \sum_{i=1}^{n} b_i^1(x, t)\phi_{x_i} - c^1(x, t)\phi, \tag{3}$$

and

$$L_2\phi \equiv \phi_t - \sum_{i,j=1}^{n} a_{ij}(x, t)\phi_{x_i x_j} - \sum_{i=1}^{n} b_i^2(x, t)\phi_{x_i} - c^2(x, t)\phi. \tag{4}$$

Throughout Appendix II we assume that the coefficients of the operators L_1 and L_2 satisfy assumptions (III.A.1)′–(III.A.4) with u deleted. Furthermore, it is also assumed that the boundary $\partial\Omega$ belongs to the class C^3.

Clearly, the formal adjoints of the operators L_1 and L_2 are given, respectively, by

$$L_1^*\psi \equiv -\psi_t - \sum_{i=1}^{n}\left(\sum_{j=1}^{n} a_{ij}(x,t)\psi_{x_j} + a_i^1(x,t)\psi\right)_{x_i} - c^1(x,t)\psi, \tag{5}$$

and

$$L_2^*\psi \equiv -\psi_t - \sum_{i=1}^{n}\left(\sum_{j=1}^{n} a_{ij}(x,t)\psi_{x_j} + a_i^2(x,t)\psi\right)_{x_i} - c^2(x,t)\psi, \tag{6}$$

where

$$a_i^l(x,t) \equiv \sum_{j=1}^{n} \frac{\partial a_{ij}(x,t)}{\partial x_j} - b_i^l(x,t), \qquad l = 1, 2. \tag{7}$$

For each $l \in \{1, 2\}$, let z^l be the weak solution from the space $V_2^{1,0}(Q)$ (see Definition III.3.1) of the problem

$$L_l^* z = 0, \qquad (x,t) \in Q, \tag{8a}$$

$$z|_{t=T} = z_T, \qquad x \in \Omega, \tag{8b}$$

$$z|_{\Gamma} = 0, \qquad (x,t) \in \Gamma. \tag{8c}$$

The function z_T is assumed to be an element in $L_2(\Omega)$.

Let $\eta \in \overset{\circ}{W}{}_{\infty}^{2,1}(Q)$. Then integrating by parts those terms involving second-order coefficients, we obtain

$$\begin{aligned}
&\iint_Q (L_1\eta)z^1\,dx\,dt \\
&= \iint_Q \left\{ z^1\eta_t + \sum_{i=1}^{n}\left[\sum_{j=1}^{n} a_{ij} z^1_{x_j}\eta_{x_i} \right.\right. \\
&\qquad\qquad \left.\left. + \sum_{j=1}^{n} \frac{\partial a_{ij}}{\partial x_j} z^1\eta_{x_i} - b_i^1 z^1 \eta_{x_i}\right] - c^1 z^1 \eta \right\} dx\,dt \\
&= \iint_Q \left\{ z^1\eta_t + \sum_{i=1}^{n}\left[\sum_{j=1}^{n} a_{ij} z^1_{x_j}\eta_{x_i} + a_i^1 z^1 \eta_{x_i}\right] - c^1 z^1 \eta \right\} dx\,dt.
\end{aligned}$$

However, z^1 is the weak solution of problem (8) with $l = 1$. Thus it follows from Definition III.3.1 that

$$\iint_Q (L_1\eta)z^1\,dx\,dt = \int_\Omega \eta(x,T)z_T(x,T)\,dx. \tag{9}$$

Similarly, we have

$$\iint_Q (L_2\eta)z^2\,dx\,dt = \int_\Omega \eta(x,T)z_T(x,T)\,dx. \tag{10}$$

THEOREM 1. *Consider the problems*

$$L_1\phi = f^1, \qquad (x,t)\in Q, \tag{11a}$$

$$\phi|_{t=0} = \phi_0, \qquad x\in\Omega, \tag{11b}$$

$$\phi|_\Gamma = 0, \qquad (x,t)\in\Gamma, \tag{11c}$$

and

$$L_2\phi = f^2, \qquad (x,t)\in Q, \tag{12a}$$

$$\phi|_{t=0} = \phi_0, \qquad x\in\Omega, \tag{12b}$$

$$\phi|_\Gamma = 0, \qquad (x,t)\in\Gamma. \tag{12c}$$

Let ϕ^1 and ϕ^2 be the respective almost everywhere solutions (see Definition III.2.1) *of the preceding problems. Define*

$$\psi \equiv \phi^1 - \phi^2. \tag{13}$$

Furthermore, the second-order coefficients a_{ij}, $i, j = 1, \ldots, n$, and the domain Q together with its boundary $\partial\Omega$ are assumed, additionally, to be fixed. Then ψ satisfies

$$\|\psi\|_{p,Q}^{(2,1)} \le K\left\{\sum_{i=1}^n \|b_i^1 - b_i^2\|_{\infty,Q} + \|c^1 - c^2\|_{\infty,Q} + \|f^1 - f^2\|_{\infty,Q}\right\}, \tag{14}$$

for all $p\in(\frac{3}{2},\infty]$, where the constant K depends only on T and bounds for $b_i^1, b_i^2, i = 1,\ldots,n, c^1$ and c^2 on $\overline{Q}$.

Proof. From (13), we have

$$\begin{aligned} L_1\psi &= L_1\phi^1 - L_2\phi^2 - (L_1 - L_2)\phi^2 \\ &= \sum_{i=1}^n [b_i^1(x,t) - b_i^2(x,t)]\phi_{x_i}^2 + [c^1(x,t) - c^2(x,t)]\phi^2 \\ &\quad + [f^1(x,t) - f^2(x,t)], \end{aligned} \tag{15a}$$

for almost all $(x,t)\in Q$. Furthermore, since ϕ^1 and ϕ^2 are almost everywhere solutions of problems (11) and (12), respectively, it is clear that

$$\psi|_\Gamma = 0 \tag{15b}$$

in Γ, and

$$\psi|_{t=0} = 0 \tag{15c}$$

in Ω. Thus by the statement made in the paragraph following Remark III.2.1, we note that ψ is the unique almost everywhere solution of problem (15) and satisfies estimate (14). Thus the proof is complete. ■

APPENDIX III

An Algorithm of Quadratic Programming

In Appendix III we shall briefly describe an algorithm for solving quadratic programming problems. The details can be found in [Fle.1]. Our problem is to minimize a quadratic function

$$q(X) = \tfrac{1}{2}X^{\mathrm{T}}GX + g^{\mathrm{T}}X, \tag{1a}$$

subject to

$$a_i^{\mathrm{T}}X = b_i, \qquad i \in E, \tag{1b}$$

$$a_i^{\mathrm{T}}X \geq b_i, \qquad i \in I, \tag{1c}$$

where X represents a point in R^n, G a symmetric $n \times n$ matrix, g an n vector, $E \cup I = \{1, 2, \ldots, m\}$ with $m \leq n$, and a_i, $i \in I \cup E$, n vectors.

We first present a method to deal with the case in which only equality constraints are involved, i.e.,

$$\text{minimize} \qquad q(X) = \tfrac{1}{2}X^{\mathrm{T}}GX + g^{\mathrm{T}}X, \tag{2a}$$

$$\text{subject to} \qquad A^{\mathrm{T}}X = b, \tag{2b}$$

where $m \leq n$, b is an m vector, and A, which is an $n \times m$ matrix, has rank m.

Let S and Z be, respectively, $n \times m$ and $n \times (n - m)$ matrices such that $A^TS = I$ and $A^TZ = 0$. A general scheme for computing suitable S and Z matrices is given below. Choose any $n \times (n - m)$ matrix V such that $[A \vdots V]$ is nonsingular. Let the inverse of matrix $[A \vdots V]$ be expressed in the partitioned form

$$[A \vdots V]^{-1} = \begin{bmatrix} S^T \\ Z^T \end{bmatrix},$$

where S and Z are $n \times m$ and $n \times (n - m)$ matrices, respectively. Then it follows that $S^TA = I$ and $Z^TA = 0$. Thus any feasible point X [i.e., any X such that constraints (2b) are satisfied] can be written as

$$X = Sb + ZY, \tag{3}$$

where $Y \equiv (y_1, y_2, \ldots, y_{n-m}) \in R^{n-m}$.

Substituting (3) into $q(X)$ defined in (2a), we obtain the reduced quadratic function

$$\psi(Y) = \tfrac{1}{2}Y^TZ^TGZY + (g + GSb)^TZY + \tfrac{1}{2}(g + GSb)^TSb. \tag{4}$$

Setting $\nabla\psi(Y) = 0$, it follows that

$$(Z^TGZ)Y = -Z^T(g + GSb). \tag{5}$$

If Z^TGZ is positive definite, then linear system (5) has a unique solution Y^* that is also the unique minimizer to the function ψ. In this situation, solution X^* to problem (1) can be easily obtained by substituting Y^* into (3):

$$X^* = Sb - Z(Z^TGZ)^{-1}Z^T(g + GSb). \tag{6}$$

The Lagrange multipliers λ^* of problem (2) are given by

$$\lambda^* = S^Tg^*, \tag{7}$$

where $g^* \equiv \nabla q(X^*) = g + GX^*$. Clearly, (7) can be written as

$$\lambda^* = S^T(g + GX^*). \tag{8}$$

We are now able to give an algorithm to solve general problem (1) by means of an active set method.

ALGORITHM

Step 1 Choose a feasible point $X^{(0)}$ [i.e., choose a point $X^{(0)}$ such that constraints (1b) and (1c) are satisfied]. Identify the corresponding active set $\mathscr{A}^{(0)}$ (i.e., identify a subset $\mathscr{A}^{(0)}$ of $E \cup I$ such that $a_i^TX^{(0)} = b_i$ for all $i \in \mathscr{A}^{(0)}$). Set $k = 0$.

Step 2 Consider a problem with equality constraints

$$\underset{\delta}{\text{minimize}} \quad \tfrac{1}{2}\delta^{\mathrm{T}}G\delta + \delta^{\mathrm{T}}(g + GX^{(k)}), \tag{9a}$$

$$\text{subject to} \quad a_i^{\mathrm{T}}\delta = 0, \qquad i \in \mathscr{A}^{(k)}. \tag{9b}$$

If $\delta = 0$ does not solve problem (9), go to Step 4.

Step 3 Since $\delta = 0$ solves problem (9), $X^{(k)}$ solves the problem

$$\underset{X}{\text{minimize}} \quad \tfrac{1}{2}X^{\mathrm{T}}GX + g^{\mathrm{T}}X \tag{10a}$$

$$\text{subject to} \quad a_i^{\mathrm{T}}X = b_i, \qquad i \in \mathscr{A}^{(k)}. \tag{10b}$$

Compute the Lagrange multipliers $\lambda^{(k)} \equiv (\lambda_i^{(k)})_{i \in \mathscr{A}^{(k)}}$ according to the corresponding version of (8). Select ρ such that $\lambda_\rho^{(k)} = \min_{i \in \mathscr{A}^{(k)} \cap I} \lambda_i^{(k)}$. If $\lambda_\rho^{(k)} \geq 0$ terminate with $X^* = X^{(k)}$; otherwise set $\mathscr{A}^{(k+1)} = \mathscr{A}^{(k)} \backslash \{\rho\}$, and set $k = k + 1$.

Step 4 Solve problem (9). Let $s^{(k)}$ be the solution of this problem.

Step 5 Compute $\alpha^{(k)}$ according to

$$\alpha^{(k)} = \min\left[1, \min_{\substack{i \in \{E \cup I\} \backslash \mathscr{A}^{(k)} \\ a_i^{\mathrm{T}} s^{(k)} < 0}} \frac{b_i - a_i^{\mathrm{T}}X^{(k)}}{a_i^{\mathrm{T}}s^{(k)}}\right] \tag{11}$$

and set $X^{(k+1)} = X^{(k)} + \alpha^{(k)}s^{(k)}$.

Step 6 If $\alpha^{(k)} < 1$, set $\mathscr{A}^{(k+1)} = \mathscr{A}^{(k)} \cup \{p\}$, where $p \in \{E \cup I\} \backslash \mathscr{A}^{(k)}$ achieves the minimum in (11).

Step 7 Set $k = k + 1$ and go to Step 2.

APPENDIX IV

A Quasi-Newton Method for Nonlinear Function Minimization with Linear Constraints

In Appendix IV we shall briefly describe a constraint Quasi-Newton method for solving a general linearly constrained finite-dimensional optimization problem. Dr. R. Womersley has already written software for this algorithm that is available through the School of Mathematics at the University of New South Wales, Australia.

Consider the following linearly constrained optimization problem (LCOP):

$$\min_{y \in R^r} f(y), \tag{1}$$

subject to

$$C_i(y) = D_i^T y - d_i \geq 0, \qquad i = 1, \ldots, m_1, \tag{2a}$$

$$\bar{C}_i(y) = \bar{D}_i^T y - \bar{d}_i = 0, \qquad i = 1, \ldots, m_2, \tag{2b}$$

where $f(y)$ is a general nonlinear function with gradient $g \equiv g(y)$ and Hessian $G \equiv G(y)$; D_i, $\bar{D}_i$ r vectors; and d_i, $\bar{d}_i$ real numbers.

Since all the constraints are linear, ∇C_i, $i = 1, \ldots, m_1$, and $\nabla \bar{C}_i$, $i = 1, \ldots, m_2$, are constants. The set Γ of all feasible points of LCOP consists of those vectors $y \in R^r$ such that inequalities (2) are satisfied, i.e.,

$$\Gamma \equiv \{y \in R^r : C_i(y) \geq 0, i = 1, \ldots, m_1, \quad \text{and} \quad \bar{C}_i(y) = 0, i = 1, \ldots, m_2\}.$$

The initial point y^0 of the problem is chosen to be in Γ. The point y^{k+1} can be found from the point y^k by solving a quadratic programming subprogram. A quadratic model $q_k(s)$ is made by using the Taylor series expansion about the point y^k, truncated after the second-order terms. That is,

$$f(y^k + s) \approx q_k(s) = f(y^k) + s^{\mathrm{T}}g(y^k) + \tfrac{1}{2}s^{\mathrm{T}}G(y^k)s.$$

To make $y^k + s$ feasible, we need

$$C_i(y^k + s) = D_i^{\mathrm{T}}(y^k + s) - d_i = D_i^{\mathrm{T}}s + C_i(y^k) \geq 0, \qquad i = 1, \ldots, m_1,$$

$$\bar{C}_i(y^k + s) = \bar{D}_i^{\mathrm{T}}(y^k + s) - \bar{d}_i = \bar{D}_i^{\mathrm{T}}s + \bar{C}_i(y^k) = 0, \qquad i = 1, \ldots, m_2.$$

Thus the point $y^{k+1} = y^k + s$ is generated from the point y^k by solving the following quadratic programming subproblem $(\mathrm{QP})_k$

$$\min_{s \in R^r}\{\tfrac{1}{2}s^{\mathrm{T}}G(y^k)s + s^{\mathrm{T}}g(y^k)\},$$

subject to

$$D_i^{\mathrm{T}}s + C_i(y^k) \geq 0, \qquad i = 1, \ldots, m_1,$$

$$\bar{D}_i^{\mathrm{T}}s + \bar{C}_i(y^k) = 0, \qquad i = 1, \ldots, m_2.$$

Problem $(\mathrm{QP})_k$ is solved by the method described in Appendix III. The current model of the objective function at the point y^k requires the evaluation of the Hessian $G(y^k)$, which is approximated by a positive definite symmetric matrix B^k by the Broyden–Fletcher–Goldfard–Shanno (BFGS) formula

$$B^{k+1} = B^k + \frac{\gamma^k(\gamma^k)^{\mathrm{T}}}{(\delta^k)^{\mathrm{T}}\gamma^k} + \frac{B^k\delta^k(\delta^k)^{\mathrm{T}}B^k}{(\delta^k)^{\mathrm{T}}B^k\delta^k}, \tag{3}$$

where $\delta^k \equiv y^{k+1} - y^k$ and $\gamma^k \equiv g(y^{k+1}) - g(y^k)$. It is well known that if B^0 is a symmetric positive definite matrix, then so are all successive matrices B^k. The algorithm for solving LCOP can now be stated as follows:

(1) Choose a point $y^0 \in R^r$ such that y^0 is a feasible point of LCOP. (This can be achieved by the phase I of a linear programming problem.) Approximate $G(y^0)$ by a positive definite symmetric matrix B^0. Choose an $\varepsilon > 0$, set $k = 0$.

(2) If $k \neq 0$, update B^k according to BFGS formula (3).

(3) Solve the quadratic programming subprogram $(\mathrm{QP})_k$ with the term $G(y^k)$ replaced by B^k.

(4) Choose α_k as the approximate minimizer of $f(y^k + \alpha s^k)$ subject to $\alpha_k \leq 1$ by doing a line search, where s^k is the solution of problem $(\mathrm{QP})_k$.

(5) If $\|s^k\| < \varepsilon$, set $y^{k+j} = y^k$, for all j, and stop. Otherwise set $y^{k+1} = y^k + \alpha_k s^k$ and set $k = k + 1$; go to Step 2.

REMARK. In Step 4 of the preceding algorithm, the point $y^k + \alpha_k s^k$ is a feasible point provided that the point y^k is a feasible point. Thus the preceding algorithm generates a sequence of feasible points $\{y^k\}$, if the initial point y^0 is chosen to be so in Step 1.

APPENDIX V

An Algorithm for Optimal Control Problems of Linear Lumped Parameter Systems

In Appendix V our aim is to report an efficient computational algorithm based on control parametrization technique for a class of optimal control problems involving linear lumped parameter systems.

Consider the following linear differential equation defined on a fixed time interval $(0, T]$:

$$\frac{dx(t)}{dt} = A(t)x(t) + B(t)u(t), \tag{1a}$$

where $x \equiv (x_1, \ldots, x_n)$ and $u \equiv (u_1, \ldots, u_r)$ are, respectively, the state and control vectors, and A and B are, respectively, real continuous $n \times n$ and $n \times r$ matrices defined on $[0, T]$.

The initial condition for the differential equation (1a) is

$$x(0) = x^0, \tag{1b}$$

where x^0 is a given vector in R^n.

Let

$$U \equiv \{v \equiv (v_1, \ldots, v_r) \in R^r : (C^i)^T v \le b_i, i = 1, \ldots, q\},$$

where C^i, $i = 1, \ldots, q$, are r vectors, b_i, $i = 1, \ldots, q$, real numbers, and the superscript T denotes the transpose.

A bounded measurable function from $[0, T]$ into U is called an *admissible control. Let $\mathscr{U}$ be the class of all such admissible controls.*

For each $u \in \mathscr{U}$, let $x(u)$ denote the corresponding solution of system (1). It is well known that $x(u)$ can be expressed in terms of the fundamental matrix of differential equation (1a). More precisely,

$$x(u)(t) = N(t, 0)x^0 + \int_0^t N(t, s)B(s)u(s)\, ds, \tag{2}$$

where $N(t, \tau)$ [the fundamental matrix of the differential equation (1a)] is the real continuous $n \times n$ matrix defined on $0 \le \tau \le t \le T$, and satisfies the following system:

$$\frac{dN(t, \tau)}{dt} = A(t)N(t, \tau), \qquad 0 \le \tau \le t \le T, \tag{3a}$$

$$N(\tau, \tau) = I \qquad \text{(identity matrix)}. \tag{3b}$$

Now, let us specify the terminal inequality constraints as follows:

$$(D^i)^T x(u)(T) \le d_i, \qquad i = 1, \ldots, m, \tag{4}$$

where D^i, $i = 1, \ldots, m$, are n vectors, and d_i, $i = 1, \ldots, m$, real numbers.

Clearly, not all controls from $\mathscr{U}$ will satisfy constraints (4). Let $\mathscr{F}$ denote the class of all those controls from $\mathscr{U}$ such that constraints (4) are satisfied. *Elements from $\mathscr{F}$ are called feasible controls, and $\mathscr{F}$ is called the class of feasible controls*. Here, we assume that $\mathscr{F}$ is nonempty.

Our optimal control problem, denoted by P, may now be formally stated. Find a control $u \in \mathscr{F}$ such that the cost functional

$$J(u) = h(x(u)(T)) + \int_0^T \{f(t, x(u)(t)) + g(t, u(t))\}\, dt \tag{5}$$

is minimized over $\mathscr{F}$.

For the functions h, f, and g, we assume throughout that they are continuous on R^n, $[0, T] \times R^n$ and $[0, T] \times R^r$, respectively. Furthermore, $h(\cdot)$, $f(t, \cdot)$, and $g(t, \cdot)$ are continuously differentiable in their respective domains of definition.

Next, we wish to use problem P to construct a sequence of problems P_p such that the solution of each of these approximate problems is a suboptimal solution to problem P, and, as p tends to infinity, these suboptimal solutions "converge" to the optimal solution of problem P.

To avoid notational problems, we simply describe the procedure to generate subproblems $\{P_p\}$. First, let $\{I^p\}$ be a sequence of partitions of the interval $[0, T]$ such that I^p has n_p elements, I^{p+1} is a refinement of I^p and $|I^p| \to 0$ as $p \to \infty$, where $|I^p|$ denotes the length of the largest interval in the partition I^p.

Let $\mathscr{D}_p$ be the class of all those piecewise constant functions that are consistent with partition I^p. Let σ^p be the vector of values that uniquely describes a function u in $\mathscr{D}_p$, and Σ_p be the class of all such vectors.

To restrict the controls to $\mathscr{U} \cap \mathscr{D}_p$, the corresponding control constraints are reduced to

$$(C^i)^{\mathrm{T}}\sigma^{p,k} \leq d_i, \qquad k = 1, \ldots, n_p; \qquad i = 1, \ldots, q, \tag{6}$$

where $\sigma^p \equiv (\sigma^{p,1}, \ldots, \sigma^{p,n_p}) \in \Sigma_p$.

Observe that system (1) and terminal inequality constraints (4) are all linear. We shall show that when the controls are restricted to $\mathscr{F} \cap \mathscr{D}_p$, the reduced versions of constraints (4) can be expressed explicitly in terms of σ^p. To find these expressions, we consider system (1) with $u \in \mathscr{D}_p$; namely,

$$\frac{dx(t)}{dt} = A(t)x(t) + B(t) \sum_{k=1}^{n_p} \sigma^{p,k}\chi_{I_k^p}(t), \qquad t \in (0, T], \tag{7a}$$

$$x(0) = x^0, \tag{7b}$$

where I_k^p is the kth subinterval of partition I^p, and χ_I the indicator function of the set I.

For each $i = 1, \ldots, m$, let us consider the following "optimal parameter selection problem $P_{p,i}$."

Subject to system (7), find a parameter vector $\sigma^p \in \Sigma_p$ such that the "objective functional"

$$\tilde{J}^i(\sigma^p) = (D^i)^{\mathrm{T}}x(\sigma^p)(T) \tag{8}$$

is minimized over Σ_p, where $x(\sigma^p)$ denotes the solution of system (7) corresponding to the vector $\sigma^p \in \Sigma_p$.

Note that the "objective functional" $\tilde{J}^i$ is just the left-hand side of the ith term of constraints (4).

For the problem $P_{p,i}$, it is well known that the Fréchet differential $\delta\tilde{J}^i$ of $\tilde{J}^i$ at the vector σ^p is

$$\delta\tilde{J}^i(\sigma^p) = \int_0^T G^p(t)\psi^i(t)\, dt \equiv \tilde{G}_p^i, \tag{9}$$

where $G^p(t) \equiv \nabla_\sigma \tilde{B}(t, \sigma^p)$ (the gradient of the function $\tilde{B}(t, \sigma^p)$), $\tilde{B}(t, \sigma^p) \equiv B(t) \sum_{k=1}^{n_p} \sigma^{p,k} \chi_{I_k^p}(t)$, and $\psi^i: [0, T] \to R^n$ is the solution of the "adjoint system"

$$\frac{d\psi^i(t)}{dt} = -(A(t))^{\mathrm{T}} \psi^i(t), \qquad t \in [0, T), \tag{10a}$$

$$\psi^i(T) = -D^i. \tag{10b}$$

Clearly, G^p and ψ^i are all independent of $\sigma^p \in \Sigma_p$, and hence so is $\tilde{G}_p^i$. Since $(D^i)^{\mathrm{T}} x(\sigma^p)(T) - (D^i)^{\mathrm{T}} x(0)(T) = (\tilde{G}_p^i)^{\mathrm{T}}(\sigma^p)$, the terminal inequality constraints (4) with controls restricted to $\mathscr{U} \cap \mathscr{D}_p$ become

$$(\tilde{G}_p^i)^{\mathrm{T}} \sigma^p \leq \tilde{d}_i, \qquad i = 1, \ldots, m, \tag{11}$$

where $\tilde{d}_i \equiv d_i - (D^i)^{\mathrm{T}} x(0)(T)$.

Let $\mathscr{F}_p \equiv \mathscr{F} \cap \mathscr{D}_p$, and let Ξ_p be the class of all those vectors in Σ_p such that each of them describes uniquely a control in $\mathscr{F}_p$ and vice versa. Equivalently, Ξ_p is the set that consists of all those vectors in Σ_p such that constraints (6) and (11) are satisfied.

We are now in a position to describe the subproblems $\{P_p\}_{p=1}^{\infty}$ as follows. Subject to system (7), find a parameter $\sigma^p \in \Xi_p$ such that the cost functional

$$\tilde{J}(\sigma^p) \equiv \tilde{h}(\sigma^p) + \int_0^T \{\tilde{f}(t, \sigma^p) + \tilde{g}(t, \sigma^p)\}\, dt \tag{5'}$$

is minimized over Ξ_p, where $\tilde{h}$, $\tilde{f}$, and $\tilde{g}$ are derived from h, f, and g, respectively, in an obvious manner.

For each σ^p, let the absolutely continuous function $\psi(\sigma^p): [0, T] \to R^n$ be the solution of the adjoint system:

$$\frac{d\psi(t)}{dt} = -(A(t))^{\mathrm{T}} \psi - \nabla_x f(t, x(\sigma^p)(t)), \qquad t \in [0, T), \tag{12a}$$

$$\psi(T) = -\nabla_x h(x(\sigma^p)(T)). \tag{12b}$$

Then it is well known that the Fréchet differential $\delta \tilde{J}$ of the cost functional $\tilde{J}$ is

$$\delta \tilde{J} = \int_0^T \{\nabla_\sigma \tilde{g}(t, \sigma^p) + (\nabla_\sigma \tilde{B}(t, \sigma^p))\psi(\sigma^p)(t)\}\, dt, \tag{13}$$

where $\tilde{B}(t, \sigma^p) \equiv B(t) \sum_{k=1}^{n_p} \sigma^{p,k} \chi_{I_k^p}(t)$. Thus to solve optimal control problem P, we suggest that one solves the finite dimensional optimization problem P_p successively for $p = p_0, 2p_0, 4p_0, \ldots$ until the cost decreases by a negligible value, (say 1 % of the preceding value).

Since, for each p, the problem P_p is a finite dimensional optimization problem with linear constraints, it can be solved by using the constrained Quasi-Newton algorithm reported in Appendix IV.

Dr. E. J. Moore has already written software for a corresponding algorithm for solving the problem P_p. This software is available at the School of Mathematics, the University of New South Wales, Australia.

In what follows we shall investigate certain convergence properties of the sequence of approximate optimal controls to the optimal control. For this, we need to assume, additionally, that the class of feasible controls $\mathscr{F}$ contains nonempty interior [i.e., there exists a $u \in \mathscr{U}$ such that $(D^i)^T x(u)(T) < d_i$, $i = 1, \ldots, m$]. Furthermore, the sequence $\{I^p\}_{p=0}^{\infty}$ of the partitions of the interval $[0, T]$ needs to be specified explicitly as follows.

Let the n_p elements of the partition I^p be denoted by $\{I_j^p\}_{j=1}^{n_p}$ and defined by

$$I_j^p = [t_{j-1}^p, t_j^p), \qquad j = 1, \ldots, n_p - 1, \quad \text{and} \quad I_{n_p}^p = [t_{n_p-1}^p, T] \tag{14}$$

where $0 = t_0^p < t_1^p < \cdots < t_{n_p}^p = T$.

As before, I^{p+1} denotes a refinement of I^p such that

$$|I^p| \equiv \max_{1 \le j \le n_p} |t_j^p - t_{j-1}^p| \to 0, \qquad \text{as} \quad p \to \infty. \tag{15}$$

For each $u \in \mathscr{U}$ and each p, define

$$u^p(t) = \sum_{j=1}^{n_p} V(u)^j \chi_{I_j^p}(t), \qquad t \in [0, T], \tag{16}$$

where

$$V(u)^j = \frac{1}{|I_j^p|} \int_{I_j^p} u(s)\, ds, \qquad j = 1, \ldots, n_p,$$

and $|I_j^p| = |t_j^p - t_{j-1}^p|$. Since U is closed and convex, it is clear that $V(u)^j \in U$. Hence, $u^p \in \mathscr{U} \cap \mathscr{D}_p$. However, u^p does not necessarily belong to $\mathscr{F}_p$ for all $u \in \mathscr{U}$.

For each $u \in \mathscr{F}_p$, let $x(u)$ be the corresponding solution of system (1). Define

$$\|u\|_\infty = \operatorname*{ess\,sup}_{t \in [0, T]} \left[\sum_{i=1}^{r} (u_i(t))^2 \right]^{1/2},$$

and

$$\|x(u)\|_\infty = \operatorname*{ess\,sup}_{t \in [0, T]} \left[\sum_{i=1}^{n} (x_i(u)(t))^2 \right]^{1/2}.$$

We assume, additionally, that the following hold.

(A.i) If $\{u^i\}_{i=1}^{\infty}$ is a sequence of functions in $\mathscr{F}$ such that $\|u^i\|_\infty \to \infty$ as $i \to \infty$, then $J(u^i) \to \infty$.

(A.ii) The functions $h(\cdot)$, $f(t, \cdot)$, and $g(t, \cdot)$ are convex on R^n, R^n, and R^r, respectively.

LEMMA 1. *Suppose that $u^0 \in \mathscr{U}$ and that $u^{0,p}$ is defined by* (16) *for u^0. Then*

$$\lim_{p\to\infty} \int_0^T |u^{0,p}(t) - u^0(t)|\, dt = 0.$$

Proof. Let t_1 be a regular point of u^0. Clearly, there exists a sequence of intervals $\{I_{j_p}^p\}_{p=0}^{\infty}$ such that $t_1 \in I_{j_{p+1}}^{p+1} \subset I_{j_p}^p$, for all p, and $|I_{j_p}^p| \to 0$ as $p \to \infty$, where $|I_{j_p}^p|$ denotes the length of the interval $I_{j_p}^p$. From Theorem I.4.16 and (16), we have

$$u^0(t_1) = \lim_{p\to\infty} \frac{1}{|I_{j_p}^p|} \int_{I_{j_p}^p} u^0(\tau)\, d\tau = \lim_{p\to\infty} u^{0,p}(t_1).$$

Note that almost all points in $[0, T]$ are regular points for u^0. Thus we conclude that $u^{0,p} \to u^0$ almost everywhere on $[0, T]$. However, u^0 is a bounded measurable function on $[0, T]$. It is clear from the construction of $u^{0,p}$ that $\{u^{0,p}\}_{p=0}^{\infty}$ are uniformly bounded. Thus the result follows from the Lebesgue dominated convergence theorem. ■

LEMMA 2. *Let $u^0 \in \mathscr{F}$. Then there exists a constant K, independent of p, such that*

$$\|x(u^{0,p})\|_\infty \le K.$$

Furthermore,

$$\lim_{p\to\infty} \int_0^T |x(u^{0,p})(t) - x(u^0)(t)|\, dt = 0.$$

Proof. The first part of the lemma follows from (2), the continuity properties of the functions $N(t, \tau)$ on $0 \le \tau \le t \le T$ and $B(t)$ on $0 \le t \le T$, and the uniform boundedness of the sequence $\|u^{0,p}\|_\infty$. The proof of the second part of the lemma requires (2), the continuity properties of the functions $N(t, \tau)$ on $0 \le \tau \le t \le T$ and $B(t)$ on $0 \le t \le T$, and Lemma 1. ■

LEMMA 3. *Suppose u^0 is in the interior $\mathscr{F}^0$ of the class $\mathscr{F}$ of feasible controls. Then there exists an integer $\hat{p}$ such that $u^{0,p} \in \mathscr{F}$, for all $p \ge \hat{p}$.*

Proof. Since $u^0 \in \mathscr{F}^0$, there exists an $\varepsilon > 0$ such that

$$(D^i)^T\left\{N(T, 0)x^0 + \int_0^T N(T, \tau)B(\tau)u^0(\tau)\, d\tau\right\} \leq d_i - \varepsilon, \qquad i = 1, \ldots, m.$$

By the continuity properties of the functions $N(T, \cdot)$ and $B(\cdot)$ on $[0, T]$, we deduce from Lemma 1 that, for any $\varepsilon > 0$, there exists an integer $\hat{p} > 0$ such that, for all $p \geq \hat{p}$,

$$\left|\int_0^T N(T, s)B(s)|u^{0,p}(s) - u^0(s)|\, d\tau\right| < \varepsilon/2.$$

Thus it readily follows that $u^{0,p} \in \mathscr{F}$, for all $p \geq \hat{p}$. This completes the proof. ■

LEMMA 4. *Let $u^* \in \mathscr{F}$ be an optimal control. Then, for any $\varepsilon > 0$, there exists a control $\hat{u} \in \mathscr{F}^\circ$ such that*

$$\lim_{p\to\infty} J(\hat{u}^p) < J(u^*) + \varepsilon.$$

Proof. Note that $\mathscr{F}^0$ is nonempty. Thus there exists a control $\tilde{u} \in \mathscr{F}^0$. Since $\mathscr{F}$ is convex, it is clear that $u^\alpha \equiv \alpha\tilde{u} + (1 - \alpha)u^* \in \mathscr{F}$ for all $\alpha \in [0, 1]$. Thus, for any $\varepsilon_0 > 0$, there exists an $\alpha_0 \in (0, 1]$ such that

$$\|u^\alpha - u^*\|_\infty < \varepsilon_0, \tag{17}$$

for all $\alpha \in [0, \alpha_0)$. Furthermore, $u^\alpha \in \mathscr{F}^0$ whenever $\alpha > 0$.

By expression (2), the continuity properties of the functions $N(t, \tau)$ on $0 \leq \tau \leq t \leq T$ and $B(t)$ on $0 \leq t \leq T$, and (17), it is easy to verify that, for any $\varepsilon_1 > 0$, there exists an $\alpha_1 \in (0, 1]$ such that

$$\sup_{t\in[0,T]} |x(u^\alpha)(t) - x(u^*)(t)| < \varepsilon_1, \tag{18}$$

for all $\alpha \in [0, \alpha_1)$.

Define $B_1 \equiv \{y \in R^n : |y| \leq K\}$ and $B_2 \equiv \{y \in R^r : |y| \leq \hat{K}\}$, where K is defined in Lemma 2, and $\hat{K} \equiv \{\|u^*\|_\infty, \|\tilde{u}\|_\infty\}$. Then h, f, and g are uniformly continuous on the compact sets B_1, $[0, T] \times B_1$ and $[0, T] \times B_2$, respectively. Thus, from (17) and (18), it follows that for any $\varepsilon > 0$ there exists an $\hat{\alpha} \in (0, 1]$ such that

$$|J(u^\alpha) - J(u^*)| < \varepsilon \tag{19}$$

for all $\alpha \in [0, \hat{\alpha})$. Set $\bar{\alpha} \equiv \hat{\alpha}/2$ and note that u^* is an optimal control. Thus we deduce from (19) that

$$J(u^{\bar{\alpha}}) < J(u^*) + \varepsilon.$$

To complete the proof, it remains to show that

$$\lim_{p\to\infty} J(u^{\bar{\alpha}, p}) = J(u^{\bar{\alpha}}). \tag{20}$$

For this we recall that h, f, and g are uniformly continuous on the compact sets B_1, $[0, T] \times B_1$ and $[0, T] \times B_2$, respectively. Thus by an application of the Lebesgue dominated convergence theorem to each of the integrals of the cost functional J, we obtain (20) and hence the proof of the lemma is complete. ■

THEOREM 1. *The sequence $\{\bar{u}^p\}_{p=0}^{\infty}$ of optimal controls of the approximate problems $\{\mathrm{P}_p\}_{p=0}^{\infty}$ has a subsequence converging, in the weak* topology of L_∞, to an optimal control $\bar{u}^*$ of problem* P.

Proof. Since $\{J(\bar{u}^p)\}_{p=0}^{\infty}$ is monotonically nonincreasing sequence of finite numbers, we know from (A.i) that there exists a subsequence of the sequence $\{\bar{u}^p\}_{p=0}^{\infty}$, again denoted by $\{\bar{u}^p\}_{p=0}^{\infty}$, that is uniformly bounded in L_∞. Let the bound be denoted by β. Then the sequence $\{\bar{u}^p\}_{p=0}^{\infty}$ of controls is contained in the set $\mathscr{U}(U_\beta)$ of measurable functions from $[0, T]$ into the compact, convex set $U_\beta \equiv U \cap B_\beta$, where B_β is a closed ball with radius β. From Theorem I.6.2, it is known that $\mathscr{U}(U_\beta)$ is sequentially compact in the weak* topology of L_∞. Thus it follows that there exists a subsequence, again denoted by $\{\bar{u}^p\}_{p=0}^{\infty}$, converging to $\bar{u}^* \in \mathscr{U}(U_\beta)$ in the weak* topology of L_∞. Next, we need to show that $\bar{u}^* \in \mathscr{F}$. For this we note from (2) and (4) that constraints (4) depend linearly on the control u. Thus by the continuity properties of the functions $N(T, \cdot)$ and $B(\cdot)$ on $[0, T]$, and the convergence of the sequence $\{\bar{u}^p\}_{p=0}^{\infty}$ to $\bar{u}^*$ in the weak* topology, we deduce that $\bar{u}^* \in \mathscr{F}$.

To complete the proof, it remains to show that $\bar{u}^*$ is an optimal control of problem P. From (2) it is easy to see that

$$\lim_{p\to\infty} x(\bar{u}^p)(t) = x(\bar{u}^*)(t),$$

for each $t \in [0, T]$. Consequently, since g is continuous on R^n, it follows that

$$\lim_{p\to\infty} g(x(\bar{u}^p)(T)) = g(x(\bar{u}^*)(T)).$$

Since U_β is compact, it is easy to deduce from (2) that $\{x(\bar{u}^p)\}_{p=0}^{\infty}$ is uniformly bounded. Thus we can show that, as $p \to \infty$,

$$x(\bar{u}^p) \overset{w^*}{\to} x(\bar{u}^*),$$

in L_∞. From this together with the continuity property of the function $f(t, \cdot)$ on R^n, it follows from Theorem I.4.15 that

$$\varliminf_{p\to\infty} \int_0^T f(t, x(\bar{u}^p)(t))\, dt \geq \int_0^T f(t, x(\bar{u}^*)(t))\, dt.$$

Recall that $h(t, \cdot)$ is continuous on R^r. Thus, again by Theorem I.4.15, we have

$$\varliminf_{p\to\infty} \int_0^T h(t, \bar{u}^p(t))\,dt \geq \int_0^T h(t, \bar{u}^*(t))\,dt.$$

Therefore, it is clear from (5) that

$$J(\bar{u}^*) \leq \varliminf_{p\to\infty} J(\bar{u}^p). \tag{21}$$

For any given $\varepsilon > 0$, it follows from Lemma 4 that there exists a control $\hat{u} \in \mathscr{F}^0$ such that

$$\lim_{p\to\infty} J(\hat{u}^p) < J(u^*) + \varepsilon, \tag{22}$$

where u^* is an optimal control.

However, from the definition of $\bar{u}^p$, we observe from Lemma 3 that

$$\varliminf_{p\to\infty} J(\bar{u}^p) \leq \varliminf_{p\to\infty} J(\hat{u}^p). \tag{23}$$

Combining (21), (22), and (23), we have

$$J(\bar{u}^*) < J(u^*) + \varepsilon.$$

Since $\varepsilon > 0$ is arbitrary, we see that $\bar{u}^*$ is also an optimal control of problem P. This completes the proof. ■

The main reference of this appendix is [TW.1]. Since these results can be extended easily to the case involving linear time-lag systems, they can be considered as improved versions of those reported in [TWC.1], where the convergence results are obtained without the presence of terminal inequality constraints (4).

From [WTC.1] we see that the control parametrization technique is also applicable to the case involving nonlinear time-lag systems. However, the convergence results are much weaker in the sense that only the following is available.

For each $p = 0, 1, 2, \ldots$, let $\bar{u}^p$ be the optimal control to the approximate problem. If $\bar{u}^*$ is an accumulation point of the sequence $\{\bar{u}^p\}$ in the strong topology of L_∞, then $\bar{u}^*$ is an optimal control.

APPENDIX VI

Meyer–Polak Proximity Algorithm

In Appendix VI we briefly describe the Meyer–Polak proximity algorithm, which is needed in Chapter IV. For full detail of this algorithm, see [P.1, pp. 234–238].

Let $\mathscr{C} \subset R^n$ be a convex compact set, and $\mathscr{R}(\alpha)$, $\alpha \in [\alpha_0, \infty)$ be a family of compact convex sets in R^n such that

(i) $\mathscr{R}(\alpha') \subset \mathscr{R}(\alpha'')$ if $\alpha' < \alpha''$,

(ii) for any $\alpha \geq \alpha_0$ and for any open set $G \supset \mathscr{R}(\alpha)$, there exists an $\varepsilon > 0$ such that for all $\alpha' \in [\alpha_0, \infty)$ satisfying $|\alpha' - \alpha| < \varepsilon$, $\mathscr{R}(\alpha') \subset G$.

We now define a geometric problem (GP) as follows: find an $\hat{\alpha} \in [\alpha_0, \infty)$ and an $\hat{x} \in \mathscr{C}$ such that

$$\hat{\alpha} = \min \{\alpha : \mathscr{R}(\alpha) \cap \mathscr{C} \neq \varnothing, \alpha \in [\alpha_0, \infty)\}, \text{ and}$$
$$\hat{x} \in \mathscr{R}(\hat{\alpha}) \cap \mathscr{C}$$

It is known that if there exists an $\bar{\alpha} \in [\alpha_0, \infty)$ such that $\mathscr{R}(\bar{\alpha}) \cap \mathscr{C} \neq \varnothing$, then problem (GP) has a solution.

To present the Meyer–Polak proximity algorithm to solve problem (GP), we need to introduce the following notation.

For any nonzero $s \in R^n$, let

$$V(s) \equiv \{v \in \mathscr{C} : \langle x - v, s \rangle \leq 0 \quad \text{for all } x \in \mathscr{C}\},$$

where $\langle \cdot, \cdot \rangle$ is the inner product in R^n, and

$$P(s) \equiv \{x \in R^n : \langle x - v, s \rangle = 0, v \in V(s)\}.$$

Next, let $\mathscr{A} = [\alpha_0, \bar{\alpha}]$. Then for any nonzero $s \in R^n$ such that $P(s) \cap \mathscr{R}(\bar{\alpha}) \neq \varnothing$, let

$$\tilde{d}(s) \equiv \begin{cases} \alpha_0, & \text{if } \langle x - v, s \rangle \leq 0 \text{ for some } x \in \mathscr{R}(\alpha_0), v \in V(s), \\ \min\{\alpha : P(s) \cap \mathscr{R}(\alpha) \neq \varnothing, \alpha \in \mathscr{A}\}, & \text{otherwise.} \end{cases}$$

Finally, for any nonzero $s \in R^n$ such that $P(s) \cap \mathscr{R}(\bar{\alpha}) \neq \varnothing$, let

$$W(s) \equiv \{w \in \mathscr{R}(\tilde{d}(s)) : \langle w - v, s \rangle \leq 0, v \in V(s)\}.$$

Meyer–Polak proximity algorithm

Step 0 Compute an $x^0 \in \mathscr{C}$ and a $y^0 \in \mathscr{R}(\alpha_0)$; set $i = 0$.

Step 1 Set $x^i = x$, $y^i = y$.

Step 2 If $y \in \mathscr{C}$, set $x^{i+1} = y$, $y^{i+1} = y$, and stop; else, set $s = y - x$ and go to Step 3.

Step 3 Compute a $v \in V(s)$.

Step 4 Compute $\tilde{d}(s)$.

Step 5 Compute a $w \in W(s)$.

Step 6 Compute a $y' \in [y, w]$ and an $x' \in [x, v]$ such that

$$\|y' - x'\| = \min\{\|y'' - x''\| : y'' \in [y, w], x'' \in [x, v]\},$$

where $[y, w]$ (resp. $[x, v]$) denotes the line segment joining y (resp. x) and w (resp. v).

Step 7 Set $x^{i+1} = x'$, $y^{i+1} = y'$; set $i = i + 1$ and go to Step 1.

It was reported in [P.1, Theorem 27, p. 238] that if $\{(x^i, y^i)\}$ is a sequence constructed by the Meyer–Polak algorithm, then either this sequence is finite and its last element (x^k, y^k) satisfies $x^k = y^k$ or else it is infinite and every accumulation point (x, y) of this sequence satisfies $x = y$. Furthermore,

$$\sup_i \tilde{d}(y^i - x^i) = \hat{\alpha},$$

and either $x^k = y^k$ or $x = y$ is chosen as $\hat{x}$.

References

[A.1] ADAMS, R. A., "*Sobolev Spaces.*" Academic Press, New York, 1975.

[Ah.1] AHMED, N. U., Optimal control of generating policies in a power system governed by a second order hyperbolic partial differential equation, *SIAM J. Control Optim.* **15**: 1016–1033 (1977).

[Ah.2] AHMED, N. U., Optimal control of a class of strongly nonlinear parabolic systems, *J. Math. Anal. Appl.* **16**: 188–207 (1977).

[Ah.3] AHMED, N. U., Optimal control of stochastic systems, *in* "*Probabilistic Analysis and Related Topics*" (edited by A. T. Bharucha-Reid), Vol. 2, pp. 1–68. Academic Press, New York, 1979.

[Ah.4] AHMED, N. U., Some comments on optimal control of a class of strongly nonlinear parabolic systems, *J. Math. Anal. Appl.* **68**: 595–598 (1979).

[Ah.5] AHMED, N. U., Necessary conditions of optimality for a class of second-order hyperbolic systems with spatially dependent controls in the coefficients, *J. Optim. Theory Appl.* **38**: 423–446 (1982).

[Ah.6] AHMED, N. U., Stochastic control on Hilbert space for linear evolution equations with random operator-valued coefficients, *SIAM J. Control Optim.* **19**: 401–430 (1981).

[Ah.7] AHMED, N. U., Sufficient conditions for controllability of a class of distributed parameter systems, *Systems & Control Letters*, **2**: 237–247 (1982).

[Ah.8] AHMED, N. U., A note on the maximum principle for time optimal controls for a class of distributed-boundary control problems, *J. Optim. Theory Appl.*, in press.

[AT.1] AHMED, N. U., AND TEO, K. L., An existence theorem on optimal control of partially observable diffusions, *SAIM J. Control* **12**:351–355 (1974).

[AT.2] AHMED, N. U., AND TEO, K. L., Optimal control of stochastic Ito differential systems with fixed terminal time, *Adv. Appl. Prob.* **17**:154–178 (1975).

[AT.3] AHMED, N. U., AND TEO, K. L., Necessary conditions for optimality of a Cauchy problem for parabolic partial differential systems, *SIAM J. Control* **13**:981–993 (1975).

[AT.4] AHMED, N. U., AND TEO, K. L., Optimal control of systems governed by a class of nonlinear evolution equations in a reflexive Banach space, *J. Optim. Theory Appl.* **25**:57–81 (1978).

[AT.5] AHMED, N. U., AND TEO, K. L., "Optimal Control of Distributed Parameter Systems." North Holland, New York, 1981.

[AW.1] AHMED, N. U., AND WONG, H. W., A minimum principle for systems governed by Ito differential equations with Markov jump parameters, *in* "*Differential Games and Control Theory II*" (edited by E. O. Roxin, P. T. Liu, and R. L. Sternberg), Lecture Notes in Pure and Applied Mathematics, No. 30. Dekker, New York, 1973.

[Am.1] AMES, W. F., "*Numerical Methods for Partial Differential Equations.*" Nelson, London, 1969.

[Ar.1] ARMIJO, L., Minimization of functions having continuous partial derivatives, *Pac. J. Math.* **16**:1–3 (1966).

[Aro.1] ARONSON, D. G., Non-negative solution of linear parabolic equations, *Annali Scuola Normale Superiore Pisa* **22**:607–694 (1968).

[AS.1] ARONSON, D. G., AND SERRIN, J., Local behaviour of solutions of quasilinear parabolic equations, *Arch. Ration. Mech. Anal.* **25**:81–122 (1967).

[Az.1] AZIZ, A. K., "*Control Theory of Systems Governed by Partial Differential Equations.*" Academic Press, New York, 1977.

[B.1] BALAKRISHNAN, A. V., "*Applied Functional Analysis.*" Springer-Verlag, Berlin, 1976.

[Ba.1] BANKS, H. T., Approximation methods for optimal control problems with delay-differential systems, *Séminaires IRIA: Analyse et Contrôle de Systèmes*, 1976.

[Ba.2] BANKS, H. T., Approximation of nonlinear functional differential equation control systems, *J. Optim. Theory Appl.* **29**:383–408 (1979).

[BB.1] BANKS, H. T., AND BURNS, J. A., Hereditary control problems: Numerical methods based on averaging approximations, *SIAM J. Control Optim.* **16**:169–208 (1978).

[Bar.1] BARBU, V., Convex control problems of Bolza in Hilbert space, *SIAM J. Control Optim.* **13**:754–771 (1976).

[Bar.2] BARBU, V., Boundary control problems with convex criterion, *SIAM J. Control Optim.* **18**:227–243 (1980).

[BP.1] BARBU, V., AND PRECUPANU, T., "Convexity and Optimization in Banach Spaces." Sijthoff and Noordhoff, *The Netherlands*, 1978.

[Barn.1] BARNES, E. R., An extension of Gilbert's algorithm for computing optimal controls, *J. Optim. Theory Appl.* **7**:420–443 (1971).

[Barn.2] BARNES, E. R., A geometrically convergent algorithm for solving optimal control problems, *SIAM J. Control* **10**:434–443 (1972).

[Barr.1] BARRON, E. N., Control problems for parabolic equations on control domains, *J. Math. Anal. Appl.* **66**:632–650 (1978).

[Barro.1] BARROS-NETO, J., "*An Introduction to The Theory of Distributions.*" Dekker, New York, 1973.

[Be.1] BELTRAMI, E., "*An Algorithm Approach to Nonlinear Analysis and Optimization.*" Academic Press, New York, 1970.

[BLP.1] BENSOUSSAN, A., LIONS, J. L., AND PAPANICOLAOU, G., "*Asymptotic Analysis for Periodic Structures.*" (Second edition), North-Holland Publ. Amsterdam, 1981.

[BHN.1] BENSOUSSAN, A., HURST, E., AND NASLUND, B., "*Management Applications of Modern Control Theory.*" North-Holland, New York, 1974.

[Ber.1] BERKOVITZ, L. D., "*Optimal Control Theory.*" Springer-Verlag, New York, 1974.

[Bh.1] BHARUCHA-REID, A. T., "*Random Integral Equations.*" Academic Press, New York, 1972.

[BJ.1] BOSARGE, W. E., JR., AND JOHNSON, O. G., Direct method approximation to the state regulator control problem using a Ritz-Trefftz suboptimal control, *IEEE Trans. Autom. Control AC*-**15**:627–631, 1970.

[BJMT.1] BOSARGE, W. E., JR., JOHNSON, O. G., MCKNIGHT, R. S., AND TIMLAKE, W. P., The Ritz-Galerkin procedure for nonlinear control problems, *SIAM J. Numer. Anal.* **10**:74–111 (1973).

[Boy.1] BOYD, I. E., "Optimal Control of a Production Firm Model," M.Sc. Thesis, University of New South Wales, 1977.

[But.1] BUTKOVSHIY, A. G., "*Distribution Control Systems.*" Elsevier, New York, 1969.

[CC.1] CANON, M. D., AND CULLUM, C. D., A tight upper bound on the rate of convergence of the Frank-Wolfe algorithm, *SIAM J. Control* **6**:509–516 (1968).

[C.1] CEA, J., "*Lectures on Optimization-Theory and Algorithms.*" Springer-Verlag, Berlin, 1978.

[Ce.1] CESARI, L., Existence theorems for weak and usual optimal solution in Lagrange problems with unilateral constraints, I & II, *Trans. Amer. Math. Soc.* **124**:369–412 (1966).

[Ce.2] CESARI, L., Existence theorems for multidimensional Lagrange problems, *J. Optim. Theory Appl.* **1**:87–112 (1967).

[Ce.3] CESARI, L., Optimization with partial differential equations in Dieudonne-Rashevshy form and conjugate problems, *Arch. Ration. Mech. Anal.* **33**:339–357 (1969).

[Ce.4] CESARI, L., Geometric and analytic views in existence theorems for optimal control in Banach Spaces, I, distributed controls, *J. Optim. Theory Appl.* **14**:505–520 (1974).

[Ce.5] CESARI, L., Geometric and analytic views in existence theorems for optimal control in Banach Spaces, III, weak solution, *J. Optim. Theory Appl.* **19**:185–214 (1976). **15**:467–497 (1975).

[Ce.6] CESARI, L., Geometric and analytic views in existence theorems for optimal control in Banach Spaces, III, weak solution, *J. Optim. Theory Appl.* **19**:185–214 (1976).

[Ce.7] CESARI, L., "*Optimization—Theory and Applications.*" Springer-Verlag, New York, 1983.

[Ch.1] CHRYSSOVERGHI, I., Approximate methods for optimal pointwise control of parabolic systems, *Systems & Control Letters*, **1**:216–219, (1981).

[CTW.1] CHOO, K. G., TEO, K. L., AND WU, Z. S., On an optimal control problem involving first order hyperbolic systems with boundary controls, *Numer. Funct. Anal. Optim.* **4**:171–190 (1981–1982).

[CTW.2] CHOO, K. G., TEO, K. L., AND WU, Z. S., On an optimal control problem involving second order hyperbolic systems with boundary controls, *Bull. Aust. Math. Soc.* **27**:139–148 (1983).

[Cho.1] CHOQUET, G., "*Lectures on Analysis,*" Vols. I–III. Benjamin, New York, 1969.

[Cl.1] CLARK, C. W., "*Mathematical Bioeconomics: The Optimal Management of Renewable Resources.*" Wiley and Sons, New York, 1976.

[ClTW.1] CLEMENTS, D. J., TEO, K. L., AND WU, Z. S., An implementable algorithm for linear time optimal control problems, *Int. J. Syst. Sci.* **13**: 1223–1232 (1982).

[Co.1] COLLATZ, L., "*The Numerical Treatment of Differential Equations.*" Springer-Verlag, Berlin, 1960.

[CT.1] CONNORS, M. N., AND TEICHROEW, D., "*Optimal Control of Dynamic Operations Research Models.*" International Textbook Company, Scranton, 1967.

[Con.1] CONTI, R., On some aspects of linear control theory, *in* "*Mathematical Theory of Control*" (edited by A. V. Balakrishnan and L. W. Neustadt). Academic Press, New York, 1967.

[CM.1] CORNICK, D. E., AND MICHEL, A. N., Numerical optimization of linear distributed-parameter systems, *J. Optim. Theory Appl.* **14**: 73–98 (1974).

[Cr.1] CRAVEN, B. D., "*Mathematical Programming and Control Theory.*" Chapman and Hall, London 1978.

[CP.1] CURTAIN, R. F., AND PRITCHARD, A. J., An abstract theory for unbounded control action for distributed parameter systems, *SIAM J. Control Optim.* **15**: 566–611 (1977).

[CP.2] CURTAIN, R. F., AND PRITCHARD, A. J., "*Infinite Dimensional Linear Systems Theory.*" Springer-Verlag, Berlin, 1979.

[DR.1] DEMYANOV, V. F., AND RUBINOV, A. M., "*Approximate Methods in Optimization Problems.*" American Elsevier, New York, 1970.

[DG.1] DI PILLO, G., AND GRIPPO, L., The multiplier method for optimal control problems of parabolic system, *Appl. Math. Optim.* **5**: 253–269 (1979).

[D.1] DREYFUS, S. E., Introduction to stochastic optimization and control, *in* "*Stochastic Optimization and Control*" (edited by H. F. Karreman), pp. 3–23. Wiley, New York, 1968.

[DS.1] DUNFORD, N., AND SCHWARTZ, J. T., "*Linear Operators,*" Part I. Wiley, New York, 1958.

[Du.1] DUNN, J. C., Rates of convergence for conditional gradient algorithms near singular and nonsingular extremals, *SIAM J. Control Optim.* **17**: 187–211 (1979).

[Du.2] DUNN, J. C., Global and asymptotic convergence rate estimates for a class of projected gradient processes, *SIAM J. Control Optim.* **19**: 368–400 (1981).

[DH.1] DUNN, J. C., AND HARSHBARGER, S., Conditional gradient algorithms with open loop step size rules, *J. Math. Anal. Appl.* **6**: 432–444 (1978).

[F.1] FATTORINI, H. O., The time-optimal control for boundary control of the heat equation, *in* "*Calculus of Variations and Control Theory*" (edited by A. V. Balakrishnan). Academic Press, New York, 1976.

[F.2] FATTORINI, H. O., "The Time-Optimal Problems for Distributed Control of Systems Described by the Wave Equation, Proceedings of Conference on Control Theory of Systems Governed by Partial Differential Equations," Naval Surface Weapons Centre, Baltimore, pp. 151–176. Academic Press, New York, 1976.

[Fl.1] FLEMING, W. H., Optimal control of partial observable diffusions, *SIAM J. Control* **6**: 194–213 (1968).

[Fl.2] FLEMING, W. H., Optimal continuous-parameter stochastic control, *SIAM Rev.* **11**: 470–509 (1969).

[FR.1] FLEMING, W. H., AND RISHEL, R. W., "*Deterministics and Stochastic Optimal Control.*" Springer-Verlag, Berlin, 1975.

[Fle.1] FLETCHER, R., "*Practical Methods of Optimizations,*" Vol. 2. Wiley, Chichester, 1981.

[FW.1] FRANK, M., AND WOLFE, P., An algorithm for quadratic programming, *Nav. Res. Logist Quart.* **3**:95–110 (1956).

[Fr.1] FRIEDMAN, A., "*Partial Differential Equations of Parabolic Type.*" Prentice-Hall, Englewood Cliffs, 1964.

[Fr.2] FRIEDMAN, A., Optimal control for parabolic equations, *J. Math. Anal. Appl.* **18**:479–491 (1967).

[Fr.3] FRIEDMAN, A., "*Partial Differential Equations.*" Holt, New York, 1969.

[G.1] GILBERT, E. G., An iterative procedure for computing the minimum of a quadratic form on a convex set, *SIAM J. Control* **4**:61–79 (1966).

[GM.1] GILL, P. E., AND MURRAY, W., "*Numerical Methods for Constrained Optimization.*" Academic Press, New York, 1974.

[GG.1] GLASHOFF, K., AND GUSTAFSON, S. A., Numerical treatment of a parabolic boundary-value control problem, *J. Optim. Theory Appl.* **19**:645–663 (1976).

[Go.1] GOH, B. S., "*Management and Analysis of Biological Populations.*" Elsevier, Amsterdam, 1980.

[Gol.1] GOLDSTEIN, A. A., On steepest descent, *SIAM J. Control* **3**:147–151 (1965).

[GoM.1] GONZALEZ, S., AND MIELE, A., Sequential gradient-restoration algorithms for optimal control problems with general boundary conditions, *J. Optim. Theory Appl.* **26**:395–425 (1978).

[GS.1] GRUVER, W. E., AND SACHS, E., "*Algorithmic Methods in Optimal Control,*" Research Notes in Mathematics, 47. Pitman (Advance Publishing Program), London, 1981.

[H.1] HALMOS, P. R., "*Measure Theory.*" Van Nostrand, New Jersey, 1950.

[Ha.1] HAN, S. P., A globally convergent method for nonlinear programming, *J. Optim. Theory Appl.* **22**:297–309 (1977).

[HL.1] HERMES, H., AND LASALLE, J. P., "*Functional Analysis and Time Optimal Control.*" Academic Press, New York, 1969.

[He.1] HESTENES, M. R., "*Calculus of Variations and Optimal Control Theory.*" Wiley, New York, 1966.

[He.2] HESTENES, M. R., "*Conjugate Direction Methods in Optimization.*" Springer-Verlag, New York, 1980.

[HR.1] HICKS, G. A., AND RAY, W. H., Approximation methods for optimal control systems, *Can. J. Chem. Eng.* **49**:522–228 (1971).

[HP.1] HILL, E., AND PHILLIPS, R. S., "Functional Analysis and Semigroups," Vol. XXXI. *American Mathematical Society Colloquium Publications*, 1957.

[HJV.1] HIMMELBERG, C. J., JACOBS, M. Q., AND VAN VLECK, F. S., Measureable multifunctions, selectors and Filippov's implicit functions lemma, *J. Math. Anal. Appl.* **25**:276–284 (1969).

[HB.1] HO, Y. C., AND BRENTANI, P. B., On computing optimal control with inequality constraints, *SIAM J. Control Ser. A* **1**:319–348 (1964).

[Hu.1] HULLETT, W., Optimal estuary aeration: An application of distributed parameter control theory, *Appl. Math. Optim.* **1**:20–63 (1974).

[IKO.1] IL'IN, A. M., KALASHNIKOV, A. S., AND OLEINIK, O. A., Linear equations of the second order of parabolic type, *Russ. Math. Sur.* **17**:1–143 (1962).

[Io.1] IOFFE, A. D., Survey of measureable selection theorems: Russian literature supplement, *SIAM J. Control Optim.* **16**:728–732 (1978).

[K.1] KELLY, H. J., Methods of gradients, *in* "*Optimization Techniques with Applications*" (edited by G. Leitmann), pp. 206–254. Academic Press, New York, 1962.

[Ki.1] KIM, M., Successive approximation method in optimum distribution-parameter systems, *J. Optim. Theory Appl.* **4**:40–43 (1969).

[KE.1] KIM, M., AND ERZBERZER, H., On the design of optimum distributed parameter systems with boundary functions, *IEEE Trans. Autom. Control* **AC-12**: 22–28 (1967).

[KG.1] KIM, M., AND GAJWANI, S. H., A variational approach to optimum distributed parameter systems, *IEEE Trans. Autom. Control* **AC-13**: 191–193 (1968).

[Kn.1] KNOWLES, G., Time-optimal control of parabolic systems with boundary conditions involving time delays, *J. Optim. Theory Appl.* **25**: 563–574 (1978).

[Kn.2] KNOWLES, G., Some problems in the control of distributed systems, and their numerical solution, *SIAM J. Control Optim.* **17**: 5–22 (1979).

[Kn.3] KNOWLES, G., Finite element approximation of parabolic time optimal control problems, *SIAM J. Control Optim.* **20**: 414–427 (1982).

[Kr.1] KRASNOSEL'SKII, M. A., "*Topological Methods in the Theory of Nonlinear Integral Equations.*" Macmillan, New York, 1964.

[KJF.1] KUFNER, A., JOHN, O., AND FUČIK, S., "*Function Spaces.*" Noordhoft International Publishing, Leyden, 1977.

[Ku.1] KUNISCH, K., Approximation schemes for nonlinear optimal control systems, *J. Math. Anal. Appl.* **82**: 112–143 (1981).

[Kus.1] KUSHNER, H. J., "*Probability Methods for Approximations in Stochastic Control and for Elliptic Equations.*" Academic Press, New York, 1977.

[LSU.1] LADYŽHENSKAJA, O. A., SOLONIKOV, V. A., AND URAL'CEVA, N. N., "*Linear and Quasilinear Equations of Parabolic Type*" (Eng. Transl.). American Mathematical Society, Providence, R.I., 1968.

[LU.1] LADYŽHENSKAYA, O. A., AND URAL'TSEVA, N. N., "*Linear and Quasilinear Elliptic Equations.*" Academic Press, New York, 1968.

[L.1] LARSEN, R., "*Functional Analysis.*" Dekker, New York, 1973.

[LM.1] LASIECKA, I., AND MALANOWSKI, K., On discrete-time Ritz-Galerkin approximation of control constrained optimal control problems for parabolic systems, *Control Cybernetics* **7**: 21–36 (1978).

[LeM.1] LEE, E. B., AND MARKUS, L., "*Foundations of Optimal Control Theory.*" Wiley, New York, 1967.

[Le.1] LEESE, S. J., Convergence of gradient methods for optimal control problems, *J. Optim. Theory Appl.* **21**: 329–337 (1977).

[Le.2] LEESE, S. J., Fréchet differentiability and optimal control, *Int. J. Control* **28**: 809–820 (1978).

[Lei.1] LEIGH, J. R., "*Functional Analysis and Linear Control Theory.*" Academic Press, New York, 1980.

[Leit.1] LEITMANN, G., "*The Calculus of Variations and Optimal Control*—An Introduction." Plenum, New York, 1981.

[LP.1] LEVITIN, E. S., AND POLYAK, B. T., Constrained minimization problems, *USSR Comput. Math. Math. Phys.* **6**: 1–50 (1966).

[LQ.1] LI, Y. S., AND QI, D. X., "*Spline Functions Methods,*" (in Chinese). Science Press, Beijing, China, 1974.

[Li.1] LIONS, J. L., "*Optimal Control of Systems Governed by Partial Differential Equations.*" Springer-Verlag, Berlin, 1971.

[Li.2] LIONS, J. L., "Some Aspects of the Optimal Control of Distributed Parameter Systems," Regional Conference Series in Applied Mathematics. SIAM, 1972.

[Li.3] LIONS, J. L., Various topics in the theory of optimal control of distributed systems, in "*Economics and Mathematical Systems*" (edited by B. J. Kirby). *Springer Lecture Notes* **105**: 166–308 (1976).

[Li.4] LIONS, J. L., Asymptotic methods in the optimal control of distributed systems, *Automatica* **14**: 199–211 (1978).

[Li.5] LIONS, J. L., "*Some Methods in the Mathematical Analysis of Systems and Their Control.*" Science Press, Beijng, China, 1981.

[LiM.1] LIONS, J. L., AND MAGENES, E., "*Non-Homogeneous Boundary Value Problems and Applications*," Vols. I–III. Springer-Verlag, Berlin, 1972.

[Lu.1] LUENBERGER, D. G., "*Optimization by Vector Space Methods.*" Academic Press, New York, 1962.

[LR.1] LUKES, D. L., AND RUSSELL, D. L., The quadratic criterion for distributed systems, *SIAM J. Control* **7**: 101–121 (1969).

[MB.1] MCKNIGHT, R. S., AND BOSARGE, W. E., JR., The Ritz–Galerkin procedure for parabolic control problems, *SIAM J. Control* **11**: 510–524 (1973).

[M.1] MALANOWSKI, K., Convergence of approximations to quadratic optimal control problems with amplitude constrained control, *Control Cybernetics* **9**: 203–218 (1980).

[M.2] MALANOWSKI, K., Convergence of approximations *vs.* regularity of solutions for convex, control- constrained optimal-control problems, *Appl. Math. Optim.* **8**: 69–95 (1981).

[MP.1] MAYNE, D. Q., AND POLAK, E., First-order strong variation algorithms for optimal control, *J. Optim. Theory Appl.* **16**:277–301 (1975).

[MP.2] MAYNE, D. Q., AND POLAK, E., An exact penalty function algorithm for optimal control problems with control and terminal equality constraints, I, II, *J. Optim. Theory Appl.* **32**: 211–246, 345–364 (1980).

[MPH.1] MAYNE, D. Q., POLAK, E., AND HEUNIS, A. J., Solving nonlinear inequalities in a finite number of iterations, *J. Optim. Theory Appl.* **33**: 207–221 (1981).

[MD.1] MEHRA, R. K., AND DAVIES, R. E., A generalized gradient method for optimal control problems with inequality constraints and singular arcs, *IEEE Trans. Autom. Control,* **AC-17**: 69–79 (1972).

[Me.1] MEYER, G. G. L., Convergence conditions for a type of algorithm model, *SIAM J. Control Optim.* **15**: 510–524 (1977).

[Mi.1] MICHEL, P., Necessary conditions for optimality of elliptic systems with positivity constraints on the state, *SIAM J. Control Optim.* **18**: 91–97 (1980).

[MCMW.1] MIELE, A., CLOUTIER, J. R., MOHANTY, B. P., AND WU, A. K., Sequential conjugate gradient-restoration algorithm for optimal control problems with nondifferential constraints, I, II, *Int. J. Control* **29**: 189–211, 213–234 (1979).

[MDCT.1] MIELE, A., DAMOULAKIS, J. N., CLOUTIER, J. R., AND TIETZE, J. L., Sequential gradient-restoration algorithm for optimal control problems with nondifferentiable constraints, *J. Optim. Theory Appl.* **13**: 218–255 (1974).

[ML.1] MIELE, A., AND LIU, C. T., Supplementary optimality properties of gradient-restoration algorithms for optimal control problems, *J. Optim. Theory Appl.* **32**: 577–593 (1980).

[MPD.1] MIELE, A., PRITCHARD, R. E., AND DAMOULAKIS, J. N., Sequential gradient-restoration algorithm for optimal control problems, *J. Optim. Theory Appl.* **5**: 235–282 (1970).

[MWL.1] MIELE, A., WU, A. K., AND LIU, C. T., A transformation technique for optimal control with partially linear state inequality constraints, *J. Optim. Theory Appl.* **28**: 185–212 (1979).

[Mik.1] MIKHAILOV, V. P., "*Partial Differential Equations.*" MIR Publishers, Moscow, 1979.

[MW.1] MITCHELL, A. R., AND WAIT, R., "*The Finite Element Method in Partial Differential Equations.*" Wiley, New York, 1971.

[Mu.1] MURAT, F., Contre-examples pour divers problems ou le controle intervient dan les coefficients, *Annali Matematica Pura Applicata* **112**:49–68 (1977).

[MT.1] MURRAY, J. M., AND TEO, K. L., On a computational algorithm for a class of optimal control problems involving discrete time delayed arguments, *J. Aust. Math. Soc. Ser. B* **20**:315–343 (1978).

[N.1] NABABAN, S., "On the Optimal Control of Delay Differential Systems." Ph.D. Thesis, School of Mathematics, University of New South Wales, Australia, 1978.

[NT.1] NABABAN, S., AND TEO, K. L., On the system governed by parabolic partial delay-differential equations with first boundary conditions, *Annali Matematica Pura Applicata* **119**:39–57 (1979).

[NT.2] NABABAN, S., AND TEO, K. L., On the existence of optimal controls of the first boundary value problems for parabolic delay-differential equations in divergence form, *J. Math. Soc. Jpn.* **32**:343–362 (1980).

[NT.3] NABABAN, S., AND TEO, K. L., Necessary conditions for optimality of Cauchy problems for parabolic partial delay-differential equations, *J. Optim. Theory Appl.* **34**:117–155 (1981).

[NT.4] NABABAN, S., AND TEO, K. L., Necessary conditions for optimal controls for systems governed by parabolic partial delay-differential equations in divergence form with first boundary conditions, *J. Optim. Theory Appl.* **36**:561–613 (1982).

[Ne.1] NEDELJKOVIC, N. B., New algorithms for unconstrained nonlinear optimal control problems, *IEEE Trans. Autom. Control* **AC-26**:868–884 (1981).

[Neu.1] NEUSTADT, L. W., "*Optimization: Theory of Necessary Conditions.*" Princeton University Press, Princeton, 1976.

[NNT.1] NOUSSAIR, E. S., NABABAN, S., AND TEO, K. L., On the existence of optimal controls for quasi linear parabolic partial differential equations, *J. Optim. Theory Appl.* **34**:99–115 (1981).

[O.1] OGUZTÖRELI, M. N., "*Time Lag Control Systems.*" Academic Press, New York, 1966.

[O.2] OGUZTÖRELI, M. N., On sufficient conditions for the existence of optimal policies in distributed parameter control systems, "*Accademia Nazionale dei lincei, Rendiconti della classe di Scienze Fisiche, Matematiche e Naturali,*" Vol. XLVI:693–697 (1969).

[O.3] OGUZTÖRELI, M. N., On the optimal controls in the distributed parameter systems, *Rend. Matematica* **3**:171–180 (1970).

[O.4] OGUZTÖRELI, M. N., Optimal controls in distributed parameter control systems, *Rend. Matematica* **4**:55–74 (1971).

[OK.1] OUTRATA, J. V., AND KŘIZ, O. F., An application of conjugate duality for numerical solution of continuous convex optimal control problems, *Kybernetita* **16**:477–497 (1980).

[PP.1] PIRONNEAU, O., AND POLAK, E., A dual method for optimal control problems with initial and final boundary constraints, *SAIM J. Control* **11**:534–549 (1973).

[P.1] POLAK, E., "*Computational Methods in Optimization.*" Academic Press, New York, 1971.

[P.2] POLAK, E., An historical survey of computational methods in optimal control, *SIAM Rev.* **15**:553–584 (1973).

[PM.1] POLAK, E., AND MAYNE, D. Q., First-order strong variation algorithms for optimal control problems with terminal inequality constraints, *J. Optim. Theory Appl.* **16**:303–325 (1975).

[PM.2] POLAK, E., AND MAYNE, D. Q., A feasible directions algorithm for optimal control problems with control and terminal inequality constraints, *IEEE Trans. Autom. Control* **AC-22**: 741–751 (1977).

[PMW.1] POLAK, E., MAYNE, D. Q., AND WARDI, Y., On the existence of constrained optimization algorithm from differentiable to non-differentiable problems, *SIAM J. Control Optim.* **21**: 179–203 (1983).

[PBGM.1] PONTRYAGIN, L. S., BOLTYANSKII, V. G., GAMKRELIDZE, R. V., AND MISHCHENKO, E. F., "*The Mathematical Theory of Optimal Processes.*" Wiley (Interscience), New York, 1962.

[Ps.1] PSHENICHNYI, B. N., "*Necessary Conditions for an Extremum.*" Dekker, New York, 1971.

[PD.1] PSHENICHNY, B. N., AND DANILIN, Y. M., "*Numerical Methods in Extermal Problems.*" MIR Publishers, Moscow, 1978.

[RPM.1] RAO, K. C., PRABHU, S. S., AND MEHTA, S. C., Optimal control of linear distributed parameter systems by finite-element Galerkin's technique, *Opt. Control Appl. Methods* **3**: 66–77 (1982).

[RPM.2] RAO, K. C., PRABHU, S. S., AND MEHTA, S. C., Optimal control of non-linear distributed parameter systems by a finite-element collocation technique, *Opt. Control Appl. Methods* **3**: 79–90 (1982).

[R.1] REID, D. W., "On the Computational Methods for Optimal Control Problems of Distributed Parameter Systems." Ph.D. Thesis, School of Mathematics, University of New South Wales, Australia, 1980.

[RT.1] REID, D. W., AND TEO, K. L., Optimal parameter selection of parabolic systems, *Math. Oper. Res.* **5**: 467–474 (1980).

[RT.2] REID, D. W., AND TEO, K. L., On the existence of optimal control for systems governed by parabolic partial differential equations with Cauchy boundary conditions, *Annali metematica Pura Applicata* **124**: 13–38 (1980).

[Ro.1] ROBINSON, A. C., A survey of optimal control of distributed parameter systems, *Automatica* **7**: 371–388 (1971).

[Ru.1] RUSSELL, D. L., Optimal regulation of linear symmetric hyperbolic systems with finite dimensional controls, *SIAM J. Control* **4**: 276–294 (1966).

[Ru.2] RUSSELL, D. L., Quadratic performance criteria in boundary control of linear symmetric hyperbolic systems, *SIAM J. Control* **11**: 475–509 (1973).

[Ru.3] RUSSELL, D. L., "*Mathematics of Finite-Dimensional Control Systems—Theory and Design.*" Dekker, New York, 1979.

[S.1] SAKAWA, Y., On local convergence of an algorithm for optimal control, *Numer. Funct. Anal. Optim.* **3**: 301–319 (1981).

[Sa.1] SALUKVADZE, M. E., "*Vector-Valued Optimization Problems in Control Theory.*" Academic Press, New York, 1979.

[Sau.1] SAUL'YEV, V. K., "*Integration of Equations of Parabolic Type by the Method of Nets,*" (Eng. Transl.). Pergamon Press, Oxford, 1964 (Fizmatgiz, Moscow, 1960).

[Sc.1] SCHITTKOWSKI, K., Numerical solution of a time-optimal parabolic boundary-value control problem, *J. Optim. Theory Appl.* **27**: 271–290 (1979).

[Si.1] SIRISENA, H. R., Computation of optimal controls using a piecewise polynomial parameterization, *IEEE Trans. Autom. Control* **AC-18**: 409–411 (1973).

[SC.1] SIRISENA, H. R., AND CHOU, F. S., An efficient algorithm for solving optimal control problems with linear terminal constraints, *IEEE Trans. Autom. Control* **AC-21**: 275–277 (1976).

[SC.2] SIRISENA, H. R., AND CHOU, F. S., Convergence of the control parameterization Ritz method for nonlinear optimal control problems, *J. Optim. Theory Appl.* **29**: 369–382 (1979).

[SC.3] SIRISENA, H. R., AND CHOU, F. S., State parameterization approach to the solution of optimal control problems, *Opt. Control Appl. Methods* **2**:289–298 (1981).

[ST.1] SIRISENA, H. R., AND TAN, K. S., Computation of constrained optimal controls using parameterization techniques, *IEEE Trans. Autom. Control* **AC-19**:431–433 (1974).

[So.1] SOBOLEV, S. L., "Applications of Functional Analysis in Mathematical Physics." *American Mathematical Society*, Providence, 1963.

[SV.1] STASSINOPOULOS, G. I., AND VINTER, R. B., Conditions for convergence of solutions in the computation of optimal controls, *J. Inst. Math. Appl.* **22**:1–14 (1970).

[St.1] STAVROULAKIS, P., State constraints in distributed parameter control systems, *Ric. Autom.* **11**:73–94 (1980).

[SF.1] STRANGE, G., AND FIX, G., "*An Analysis of Finite-Element Method.*" Prentice-Hall, Englewood-Hall, 1973.

[SV.1] STROOCK, D. W., AND VARADHAN, S. R. S., Diffusion processes with continuous coefficients, I. *Commun. Pure Appl. Math.* **22**:345–400 (1969).

[Su.1] SURYANARAYANA, M. B., Necessary conditions for optimization problems with hyperbolic partial differential equations, *SIAM J. Control* **11**:130–147 (1973).

[Su.2] SURYANARAYANA, M. B., Existence theorems for optimization problems concerning hyperbolic partial differential equations, *J. Optim. Theory Appl.* **15**:361–392 (1975).

[Su.3] SURYANARAYANA, M. B., Existence theorems for optimization problems concerning linear, hyperbolic partial differential equations without convexity conditions, *J. Optim. Theory Appl.* **19**:47–61 (1976).

[T.1] TEO, K. L., "Optimal Control of Systems Governed by Ito Stochastic Differential Equations," Ph.D. Thesis, Department of Electrical Engineering, University of Ottawa, Canada, 1974.

[T.2] TEO, K. L., Optimal control of systems governed by time delayed second order linear parabolic partial differential equations with a first boundary condition, *J. Optim. Theory Appl.* **29**:437–481 (1979).

[T.3] TEO, K. L., Existence of optimal controls for systems governed by second order linear parabolic partial delay-differential equations with first boundary conditions, *J. Aust. Math. Soc. Ser. B* **21**:21–36 (1979).

[T.4] TEO, K. L., Convergence of a conditional gradient algorithm for relaxed controls involving first boundary value problems of parabolic type, *Numer. Funct. Anal. Optim.*, in press.

[T.5] TEO, K. L., "Convergence of a Strong Variational Algorithm for Relaxed Controls Involving First Boundary Value Problems of Parabolic Type, Department of Mathematics" (Research Report No. 100). University of Singapore, May, 1983.

[TA.1] TEO, K. L., AND AHMED, N. U., Optimal feedback control for a class of stochastic systems, *Int. J. Syst. Sci.* **5**:357–365 (1974).

[TA.2] TEO, K. L., AND AHMED, N. U., On the optimal control of systems governed by quasilinear intergro-partial differential equation of parabolic type, *J. Math. Anal. Appl.* **59**:33–59 (1977).

[TA.3] TEO, K. L., AND AHMED, N. U., On the optimal controls of a class of systems governed by second order parabolic partial delay-differential equations with first boundary conditions, *Annali Mathematica Pura Applicata*, **122**:61–82 (1979).

[TC.1] TEO, K. L., AND CRAVEN, B. D., On a computational algorithm for time-lag optimal control problems with restricted phase co-ordinates, *J. Aust. Math. Soc. Ser. B* **21**:385–397 (1980).

[TR.1] TEO, K. L., AND REID, D. W., First-order strong variation algorithm for a class of distributed optimal control problems, *Numer. Funct. Anal. Optim.* **5**:141–171 (1982).

[TW.1] TEO, K. L., AND WOMERSLEY, R. A control parametrization algorithm for optimal control problems involving linear systems and linear terminal inequality constraints, *Numer. Funct. Anal. Optim*, in press.

[TAW.1] TEO, K. L., AHMED, N. U., AND WONG, H. W., On optimal parameter selection for parabolic differential systems, *IEEE Trans. Autom. Control* **AC-19**:286–287 (1974).

[TRB.1] TEO, K. L., REID, D. W., AND BOYD, I. E., Stochastic optimal control théory and its computational methods, *Int. J. Syst. Sci.* **11**:77–95 (1980).

[TWuC.1] TEO, K. L., WU, Z. S., AND CLEMENTS, D. J., A computational method for convex optimal control problems involving linear hereditary systems, *Int. J. Syst. Sci.* **12**:1045–1060 (1981).

[TCWC.1] TEO, K. L., CLEMENTS, D. J., WU, Z. S., AND CHOO, K. G., Convergence of a strong variational algorithm for relaxed controls involving a class of hyperbolic systems, *J. Optim. Theory Appl.*, Vol. **42**, No. 3, 1984.

[TWC.1] TEO, K. L., WONG, K. H., AND CLEMENTS, D. J., Optimal control computation for linear time-lag systems with linear terminal constraints, *J. Optim. Theory Appl.*, in press.

[TWC.2] TEO, K. L., WONG, K. H., AND CLEMENTS, D. J., "A feasible directions algorithm for time-lag optimal control problems with control and terminal inequality constraints." *J. Optim. Theory Appl.*, in press.

[V.1] VAINBERG, M. M., "*Variational Methods for the Study of Nonlinear Operators*," (Eng. Transl.), Holden-Day, San Francisco, 1964. (Moscow, 1956.)

[Va.1] VARAIYA, P., Optimal control of a partially observed systems, *in* "*Stochastic Differential Equations*," Vol. VI, pp. 173–208. SIAM-AMS Proc., 1972.

[Var.1] VARIOUS AUTHORS, "Control Theory and Topics in Functional Analysis," Vol. I–III. Lectures presented at an International Seminar Course, Trieste, 11 September–29 November, 1974, International Atomic Energy Agency, Vienna, 1976.

[Vi.1] VICHNEVETSKY, R., "*Computer Methods for Partial Differential Equations*," Vol. I. Prentice-Hall, Englewood Cliffs, 1981.

[VW.1] VIDALE, M. L., AND WOLFE, H. B., An operations research study of sales response to advertizing. *Oper. Res.* **5**:370–381 (1957).

[W.1] WAGNER, D., Survey of measurability of set valued maps, *SIAM J. Control Optim.* **15**:857–903 (1977).

[Wa.1] WANG, P. K. C., Control of distributed parameter systems, *in* "*Advances in Control Systems, Theory and Applications*" (edited by C. T. Leondes), Vol. I, pp. 75–172. Academic Press, New York, 1964.

[Wa.2] WANG, P. K. C., Optimal control of a class of linear symmetric hyperbolic systems with applications to plasma confinement, *J. Math. Anal. Appl.* **28**:594–608 (1969).

[Wa.3] WANG, P. K. C., Optimal control of parabolic systems with boundary conditions involving time delays, *SIAM J. Control* **13**:274–293 (1975).

[War.1] WARGA, J., "*Optimal Control of Differential and Functional Equations.*" Academic Press, New York, 1972.

[War.2] WARGA, J., Steepest descent with relaxed controls, *SIAM J. Control Optim.* **15**:674–682 (1977).

[WP.1] WILLIAMSON, L. J., AND POLAK, E., Relaxed controls and the convergence of algorithms, *SIAM J. Control Optim.* **14**:737–756 (1976).

[WiT.1] WILSON, S. J., AND TEO, K. L., Convergence of a feasible directions algorithm for a distributed optimal control problem of parabolic type with terminal inequality constraints, Department of Mathematics (Research Report No. 95). University of Singapore, April, 1983.

[Wo.1] WONG, H. W., "Optimal Control of Stochastic Differential Systems with Applications." Ph.D. Thesis, Department of Electrical Engineering, University of Ottawa, 1980.

[WTC.1] WONG, K. H., TEO, K. L., AND CLEMENTS, D. J., Optimal control computation for nonlinear time-lag systems, *J. Optim. Theory Appl.*, in press.

[WT.1] WONG, K. H., AND TEO, K. L., A conditional gradient method for a class of time-lag optimal control problems, *J. Aust. Math. Soc. Ser.* **25**:518–537 (1984).

[Wu.1] WU, Z. S., "On the Optimal Control of a Class of Hyperbolic Systems." Ph.D. Thesis, School of Mathematics, University of New South Wales, Australia, 1981.

[WuT.1] WU, Z. S., AND TEO, K. L., First-order strong variation algorithm for optimal control problem involving hyperbolic systems, *J. Optim. Theory Appl.* **39**:561–587 (1983).

[WuT.2] WU, Z. S., AND TEO, K. L., A convex optimal control problem involving a class of linear hyperbolic systems, *J. Optim. Theory Appl.* **39**:541–560 (1983).

[WuT.3] WU, Z. S., AND TEO, K. L., A conditional gradient method for an optimal control problem involving a class of nonlinear second-order hyperbolic partial differential equations, *J. Math. Anal. Appl.* **91**:376–393 (1983).

[WuT.4] WU, Z. S., AND TEO, K. L., Optimal control problems involving second boundary value problems of parabolic type, *SIAM J. Control Optim.* **21**:729–757 (1983).

[WuT.5] WU, Z. S., AND TEO, K. L., A computational algorithm for a distributed optimal control problem of parabolic type with terminal inequality constraints, *J. Optim. Theory Appl.* **43**:457–476 (1984).

[Y.1] YOUNG, L. C., "*Lectures on the Calculus of Variations and Optimal Control Theory.*" Saunders, Philadelphia, 1969.

[Z.1] ZOLEZZI, T., Necessary conditions for optimal control of elliptic or parabolic problems, *SIAM J. Control* **10**:594–607 (1972).

List of Notation

Index